ALCOHOL-RELATED VIOLENCE

Prevention and Treatment

Edited by

Mary McMurran
University of Nottingham, UK

WILEY-BLACKWELL
A John Wiley & Sons, Ltd., Publication

This edition first published 2013
© 2013 John Wiley & Sons, Ltd.

Wiley-Blackwell is an imprint of John Wiley & Sons, formed by the merger of Wiley's global
Scientific, Technical and Medical business with Blackwell Publishing.

Registered Office
John Wiley & Sons Ltd, The Atrium, Southern Gate, Chichester, West Sussex, PO19 8SQ, UK

Editorial Offices
350 Main Street, Malden, MA 02148-5020, USA
9600 Garsington Road, Oxford, OX4 2DQ, UK
The Atrium, Southern Gate, Chichester, West Sussex, PO19 8SQ, UK

For details of our global editorial offices, for customer services, and for information about how to
apply for permission to reuse the copyright material in this book please see our website at www.
wiley.com/wiley-blackwell.

Library of Congress Cataloging-in-Publication Data

Alcohol-related violence: prevention and treatment / Edited by Mary McMurran.
    pages cm
  Includes bibliographical references and index.
    ISBN 978-1-119-95274-9 (cloth) – ISBN 978-1-119-95273-2 (pbk.)   1. Alcoholism and
crime.   2. Violence.   3. Crime.   4. Alcoholism–Prevention.   I. McMurran, Mary.
  HV5053.A463 2013
  364.2'4–dc23
                                    2012029598

A catalogue record for this book is available from the British Library.

Cover image: Bottles background © John_Woodcock/iStockphoto
Cover design by Nicki Averill Design

Set in 10/12 Pt Palatino by Toppan Best-set Premedia Limited

Printed in Malaysia by Ho Printing (M) Sdn Bhd

1   2013

CONTENTS

ABOUT THE EDITOR

Mary McMurran, BSc, MSc, PhD, CPsychol, FBPsS, is Professor in the Institute of Mental Health, University of Nottingham, UK. She worked for 10 years as a prison psychologist in HM Young Offenders' Centre Glen Parva. After qualifying as a clinical psychologist, she worked in Rampton Hospital, a maximum secure psychiatric facility, and then at the East Midlands Centre for Forensic Mental Health, which consisted of a medium secure psychiatric facility and a community forensic mental health service. In 1999, she was awarded a 5-year Senior Baxter Research Fellowship by the National Health Service's (NHS) National Programme on Forensic Mental Health Research and Development and has been an academic ever since. Her research interests are (1) social problem-solving theories and therapies for understanding and treating people with personality disorders, (2) the assessment and treatment of alcohol-related aggression and violence, and (3) understanding and enhancing readiness to engage in treatment. She has written over 150 academic articles and book chapters. She is a Fellow of the British Psychological Society and a former Chair of the Society's Division of Forensic Psychology. She was founding co-editor of the British Psychological Society journal *Legal and Criminological Psychology* and is currently co-editor of *Criminal Behaviour and Mental Health*. In 2005, she was recipient of the Division of Forensic Psychology's Award for a Significant Lifetime Contribution to Forensic Psychology.

CONTRIBUTORS

Danilo Antonio Baltieri, MD, PhD   Department of Psychiatry and Ambulatory for the Treatment of Sexual Disorders (ABSex), ABC Medical School, Santo André, São Paulo, Brazil; Interdisciplinary Group of Studies on Alcohol and Drugs of the Psychiatric Institute of the Clinical Hospital of the University of São Paulo, São Paulo, Brazil

Thomas G. Brown, PhD   Director and Principal Investigator, Addiction Research Program, Research Centre, Douglas Mental Health University Institute, Montreal, Quebec, Canada; Assistant Professor, Department of Psychiatry, McGill University, Montreal, Quebec, Canada; Head of Research, Foster Addiction Rehabilitation Centre, Montreal, Quebec, Canada

Elin K. Bye, PhD   Researcher, SIRUS, the Norwegian Institute for Alcohol and Drug Research, Oslo, Norway

Fernanda Cestaro Prado Cortez, MD, MSc   Department of Psychiatry and Ambulatory for the Treatment of Sexual Disorders (ABSex), ABC Medical School, Santo André, São Paulo, Brazil

Amy Cohn, PhD   Center on Co-Occurring Disorders, Justice, and Multidisciplinary Research and Assistant Professor, Department of Mental Health Law and Policy/Department of Criminology, University of South Florida, Tampa, Florida, USA

Gavin Dingwall, LLB, MPhil   Professor of Criminal Justice Policy, De Montfort University, Leicester, England

Russil Durrant, PhD   Lecturer, Institute of Criminology, School of Social and Cultural Studies, Victoria University of Wellington, Wellington, New Zealand

Caroline J. Easton, PhD   Associate Professor of Psychiatry, Department of Psychiatry, Yale School of Medicine, New Haven, Connecticut, USA

Medhat Emara, MB, ChB   Consultant Psychiatrist, Castlebeck, Darlington, England

Mark Farmer, MSocSci, MSt, CQSW Head of the West of Midlands Regional Sex Offender Unit, Staffordshire and West Midlands Probation Trust, Birmingham, England

Donald Forrester, CQSW, PhD Professor of Social Work Research, Director of Tilda Goldberg Centre for Social Work and Social Care Research, University of Bedfordshire, Luton, England

Alasdair J.M. Forsyth, PhD Senior Research Fellow, Scottish Centre for Crime and Justice Research, and the Institute for Society and Social Justice Research, Glasgow Caledonian University, Glasgow, Scotland

Peter R. Giancola, PhD Professor and Director of the Violence and Alcohol-Related Violence Laboratory, Department of Psychology, University of Kentucky, Lexington, Kentucky, USA

Georgia Glynn, MSc Research Fellow, Institute of Applied Social Research, University of Bedfordshire, Luton, England

Rick Howard, PhD Associate Professor and Reader in Personality Disorders, Institute of Mental Health, University of Nottingham, Nottingham, England

William R. Lindsay, PhD Clinical Director (Scotland), Castlebeck, Darlington, England; Professor of Forensic Psychology, University of Abertay, Dundee, Scotland; Honorary Professor, Bangor University, Bangor, Wales, and Deakin University, Melbourne, Australia

Ruth E. Mann, PhD Head of Evidence and Offence Specialism Commissioning Strategies Group, National Offender Management Service, London, England

Katie McCracken, MSc Director, OpCit Research (opcitresearch.com), London, England

Mary McMurran, PhD Professor of Personality Disorder Research, Institute of Mental Health, University of Nottingham, Nottingham, England

Kim T. Mueser, PhD Professor, Department of Occupational Therapy, and Executive Director, Center for Psychiatric Rehabilitation, Boston University, Boston, Massachusetts, USA

Marie Claude Ouimet, PhD Assistant Professor, Faculty of Medicine and Health Sciences, University of Sherbrooke, Longueuil, Quebec, Canada

Ingeborg Rossow, PhD Senior Researcher, SIRUS, the Norwegian Institute for Alcohol and Drug Research, Oslo, Norway

Franco Sassi, PhD Senior Health Economist, Organisation for Economic Cooperation and Development (OECD), Paris, France (Note: FS was affiliated with the London School of Economics and Political Science when this project started. The project is not part of OECD institutional work.)

Samantha Tinsley, BSc Assistant Psychologist, Castlebeck, Darlington, England

FOREWORD

I first met Mary McMurran in 2003 in Perth, Scotland, where we were part of a workshop on alcohol and violence. In her presentation, she described a new program that she had developed for counseling violent offenders whose offenses were linked to their drinking. I was very impressed with her work. Although the relationship between alcohol and violence has been recognized for millennia, hers is one of the few offender programs to incorporate knowledge about the dynamics of the alcohol–violence relationship. This book expands her thoughtful approach to combining theoretical and applied research to addressing alcohol-related violence.

The relationship between alcohol and violence is a fascinating area of research because this relationship often involves a complex interaction of biological, psychological, social, and cultural factors. For alcohol researchers, it is important to recognize that individual, social, and cultural factors not only determine the drinking pattern of the individual but also affect whether he or she will become aggressive when drinking. From a violence research perspective, because the link with alcohol is pervasive across time and cultures, examining alcohol's role in violence can help increase the understanding of violence generally.

The fact that violence often results from complex interactions of factors means that there are many points of entry into prevention and treatment. Specifically, one can focus on (1) the effects of alcohol, (2) personality/attitudes of the violent person, (3) the situational context, and/or (4) the sociocultural environment. Sometimes, changing only one of these contributors may be sufficient to prevent some instances of violence. Changing several might be expected to have an even bigger impact.

For example, O'Farrell and colleagues (O'Farrell *et al.*, 2004) found that behavioral couples therapy for married and cohabiting male alcoholic patients significantly reduced partner violence with this association partly mediated by reduced problem drinking. This finding does not mean that eliminating alcohol would eliminate all IPV, which is clearly not the case. However, it does mean that for some perpetrators of IPV, alcohol is a key component in the mix leading to their violence, and addressing this one factor can have an impact on reducing their violence.

Thus, the more we know about the complex interactions of factors involved in the process leading to alcohol-related violence, the better our ability to identify the levers most likely to short-circuit this process. For example, for some especially violent individuals, the key factor in the person's aggression may be their personality and attitudes, with alcohol, context, and culture having relatively small influences other than as possible precipitators and potential deterrents. Individually targeted interventions would be essential for this kind of violence. However, for other persons who are not generally violent but engage in occasional violence in particular contexts such as bars, addressing the context may be the most effective strategy for prevention (e.g., the Safer Bars program; Graham *et al.*, 2004).

The broad scope of this book nicely addresses the complexity of the alcohol–violence relationship. The first part of the book contains a wealth of insights for helping to sort out the various factors influencing different types of alcohol-related violence and points to new directions for addressing such violence. For example, Rossow and Bye make the important point that interventions need to address both heavy and non-heavy drinkers because, although alcohol-related violence is more common among heavy drinkers, violence by non-heavy drinkers may be the larger problem due to their greater numbers. They also suggest that alcohol policy is an important strategy for reducing alcohol-related violence because such policy can affect both the amount of alcohol consumed *and* the context in which alcohol is consumed.

In his chapter, Durrant reframes the problem of alcohol-related violence using an evolutionary perspective. Evolutionary theory has been increasingly prominent in violence research but has not yet had an impact on our understanding of the alcohol-related violence. His discussion of implications provides examples of how known approaches to preventing alcohol-related violence can be enhanced by taking into consideration possible evolutionary factors. Thus, this reframing can help to stimulate new and innovative approaches to prevention and treatment.

Durrant's and other chapters highlight the importance of masculinity identity concerns and how these are related to alcohol-related violence (see Wells, Graham, and Tremblay, 2007). Across a range of different cultures, alcohol-related aggression is much more likely to involve men (Graham *et al.*, 2011), primarily young men, as is violence generally. Thus, while alcohol can influence the aggressive behavior of women as well as of men, the role of gender and age is a key element in addressing alcohol-related violence.

The second part of the book focuses on prevention and treatment. As with the preceding chapters, these help to reinforce the multifactorial nature of alcohol-related violence and the various avenues for addressing this problem, including policing and legal issues, addressing the drinking context, and various interventions focused on individuals and their families.

Although these chapters are not always able to point to effective solutions, they provide a useful way of conceptualizing how to address the complex interaction of factors linking alcohol and violence. For example, the findings reported by McCracken and Sassi describing an experimental alcohol intervention with offenders suggest that focusing only on alcohol use may not be enough for these individuals; however, a subsequent chapter by McMurran explores ways to enhance this individual approach by taking into consideration *how* alcohol affects the drinker, the expectations that link alcohol to violence and the role of provocation in the drinking context. Similarly, the chapter by Mann and Farmer describes the multifaceted linkages between alcohol and sexual violence that need to be taken into consideration in order to individualize treatment for sexual offenders and to maximize treatment effectiveness.

In sum, this excellent book provides a valuable resource for researchers, clinicians, and policy specialists working in the area of alcohol-related violence.

Kathryn Graham, PhD
Senior Scientist and Head, Social and Community Interventions and
Policy Research, Centre for Addiction and Mental Health
Adjunct Research Professor, Department of Psychology, University of
Western Ontario, London, Ontario, Canada
Associate Professor, Dalla Lana School of Public Health,
University of Toronto, Canada
Professor (Adjunct), National Drug Research Institute, Curtin University of
Technology, Perth, Western Australia

REFERENCES

Graham, K., Bernards, S., Knibbe, R. *et al.* (2011) Alcohol-related negative consequences among drinkers around the world. *Addiction*, **106**, 1391–1405.

Graham, K., Osgood, D.W., Zibrowski, E. *et al.* (2004) The effect of the *Safer Bars* programme on physical aggression in bars: Results of a randomized controlled trial. *Drug and Alcohol Review*, **23**, 31–41.

O'Farrell, T.J., Murphy, C.M., Stephan, S.H. *et al.* (2004) Partner violence before and after couples-based alcoholism treatment for male alcoholic patients: The role of treatment involvement and abstinence. *Journal of Consulting and Clinical Psychology*, **72**, 202–217.

Wells, S., Graham, K., and Tremblay, P. (2007) Beliefs, attitudes, and male-to-male bar-room aggression: Development of a theoretical predictive model. *Addiction Research and Theory*, **15**, 575–586.

SERIES EDITORS' PREFACE

ALL THINGS MUST PASS

This is the 19th and final book in our *Forensic Clinical Psychology Series*. The first book in the Series was published in 1999 (William L. Marshall, Dana Anderson and Yolanda Fernandez, *Cognitive Behavioural Treatment of Sexual Offenders*), so we have been going at better than a book a year for over a decade. The impetus for the Series came at a time when there was renewed enthusiasm for applying psychological theory and research to working with offenders in order to reduce crime. In the years that span the first text appearing and the present day, there are good grounds for thinking that the treatment and rehabilitation of offenders is now mainstream business within the criminal justice systems of many countries. Indeed, a recent American text has strongly argued for a reassertion of social science in order to inform crime reduction policies (Dvoskin *et al.*, 2012). In a country with a prison population of over two million people, an alternative to punishment is clearly an attractive option.

The starting point for the Series was, of course, the research that gave rise to the *What Works?* literature and the defining characteristics of effective treatments in terms of crime reduction (Andrews and Bonta, 1994; McGuire, 1995). The subsequent development and influence of the risk–need–responsivity (RNR) model and its emphasis on evidence-based practice is evident throughout the Series. Indeed, the robustness of this model and need for evidence is a cornerstone of effective practice. It is the case that other models of practice may come and go, but the RNR remains at the forefront of practice (Andrews, Bonta, and Wormith, 2011).

We were clear from the outset that our aim in developing this Series was to produce texts that both reviewed research and drew on clinical expertise to advance effective work with offenders. Further, we were clear that the books published in the Series would not be practice manuals or 'cookbooks'; rather, we wanted to encourage authors and editors to produce texts that would offer readers authoritative and critical information to enable practice and research into practice to develop.

The full list of titles below reflects the range and diversity of forensic clinical psychology. The range is reflected in the highly specialised nature of some books, the emphasis of clinical practice in others, while some are concerned with systems and organisation of service delivery. The diversity is evident in the range of topics, from sex offenders, mentally disordered offenders, violent offenders, and so on.

So we come to the end of the Series. We have worked together on this Series and several other projects for more years than either of us would care to count. We should mention the role of the publishers in the development of the Series. We worked with several publishing editors and they were always responsive to our ideas, thorough in their approach and constructive in their comments. The quality of the published books is excellent and, as is the way of things, the cover design for the Series, lined up on the shelf, has gone through several rather natty incarnations.

There will be many more books written about forensic clinical psychology, but we feel, after some angst, that this Series has made its contribution. In the words of the late, great George Harrison, all things must pass, and now it is our turn.

ABOUT THIS BOOK

Our earliest venture into book publishing together was on alcohol-related crime – Mary McMurran and Clive R. Hollin (1993), *Young Offenders and Alcohol-Related Crime: A Practitioner's Guidebook*, Chichester: Wiley. Our final book in the Series is on alcohol-related violence. Over the years, concern about alcohol-related crime, violence and disorder has not abated; if anything, it has increased. Yet, our experience has been that all along the line in criminal justice, the treatment of alcohol problems has been a poor relation to the treatment of drug problems. This is despite the truth that alcohol problems and alcohol-related crimes are more prevalent than drug problems and drug crimes, and just as damaging to individuals and to society – perhaps even more damaging.

It is our desire that the prevention and treatment of alcohol-related crime, particularly violent crime, should receive the attention it deserves from commissioners, researchers and practitioners. To this end, matters to do with alcohol need to be distinct from those subsumed under the generic term 'substance misuse'. Alcohol is distinguished not least by the fact that its use is not illegal in many countries. This leads to commercial, licensing, policing, social and contextual factors that need to be addressed when tackling associated problems.

There are a number of eminent researchers and clinicians who have focused their work specifically on aspects of alcohol-related violence for many years. There are others who have specialised in the study of particular crimes, for whom alcohol is but one important contributory factor to be taken into account. We are grateful to these researchers and clinicians for their exceptional contributions to this volume. By writing such outstanding chapters on this perennial and important topic, they have allowed us to finish the Series in a blaze of glory!

Clive Hollin
Mary McMurran
March 2012

REFERENCES

Andrews, D.A. and Bonta, J. (1994) *The Psychology of Criminal Conduct*. Cincinnati, OH: Anderson Publishing.

Andrews, D.A., Bonta, J., and Wormith, J.S. (2011) The risk-need-responsivity (RNR) model: Does adding the good lives model contribute to effective crime prevention? *Criminal Justice and Behavior*, **38**, 735–755.

Dvoskin, J.A., Skeem, J.L., Novaco, R.W., and Douglas, K.S. (2012) *Using Social Science to Reduce Violent Offending*. Oxford: Oxford University Press.

McGuire, J. (ed.) (1995) *What Works: Reducing Reoffending*. Chichester, Sussex: John Wiley & Sons.

WILEY SERIES IN FORENSIC CLINICAL PSYCHOLOGY: THE COMPLETE LIST

1999. William L. Marshall, Dana Anderson, and Yolanda Fernandez, *Cognitive Behavioural Treatment of Sexual Offenders*.

2000. Sheilagh Hodgins and Rüdiger Müller-Isberner (eds), *Violence, Crime and Mentally Disordered Offenders: Concepts and Methods for Effective Treatment and Prevention*.

2001. Gary A. Bernfeld, David P. Farrington, and Alan W. Leschied (eds), *Offender Rehabilitation in Practice: Implementing and Evaluating Effective Programs*.

2002. James McGuire (ed.), *Offender Rehabilitation and Treatment: Effective Programmes and Policies to Reduce Re-offending*.

2002. Arnold P. Goldstein, *The Psychology of Group Aggression*.

2002. Arnold P. Goldstein, Rune Nensén, Bengdt Daleford, and Mikael Kalt (eds), *New Perspectives on Aggression Replacement Training: Practice, Research, and Application*.

2002. Mary McMurran (ed.), *Motivating Offenders to Change: A guide to Enhancing Engagement in Therapy*.

2004. William R. Lindsay, John L. Taylor, and Peter Sturmey (eds), *Offenders with Developmental Disabilities*.

2005. Mary McMurran and James McGuire (eds), *Social Problem Solving and Offending: Evidence, Evaluation and Evolution*.

2006. William L. Marshall, Yolanda M. Fernandez, Liam E. Marshall, and Gerris A. Serran (eds), *Sexual Offender Treatment: Controversial Issues*.

2006. Tony Ward, Devon L.L. Polaschek, and Anthony R. Beech, *Theories of Sexual Offending*.

2006. Kelly Blanchette and Shelley Lynn Brown, *Assessment and Treatment of Women Offenders: An Integrative Perspective*.

2006. Clive R. Hollin and Emma J. Palmer (eds), *Offending Behaviour Programmes: Development, Application, and Controversies*.

2007. Theresa A. Gannon, Tony Ward, Anthony R. Beech, and Dawn Fisher, *Aggressive Offenders' Cognition: Theory, Research and Practice*.

2009. Mary McMurran and Richard Howard (eds), *Personality, Personality Disorder and Violence*.

2009. David Thornton and D. Richard Laws (eds), *Cognitive Approaches to the Assessment of Sexual Interest in Sexual Offenders*.

2010. Michael Daffern, Lawrence Jones, and John Shine (eds), *Offence Paralleling Behaviour: A Case Formulation Approach to Offender Assessment and Intervention*.

2011. Peter Sturmey and Mary McMurran (eds), *Forensic case formulation*.

2012. Mary McMurran (ed.), *Alcohol-Related Violence: Prevention and Treatment*.

PART I

THE EXTENT OF THE PROBLEM

Chapter 1

THE PROBLEM OF ALCOHOL-RELATED VIOLENCE: AN EPIDEMIOLOGICAL AND PUBLIC HEALTH PERSPECTIVE

INGEBORG ROSSOW AND ELIN K. BYE

SIRUS, the Norwegian Institute for Alcohol and Drug Research, Oslo, Norway

INTRODUCTION

An Epidemiological and Public Health Perspective

Violence constitutes a significant health problem globally (Krug *et al.*, 2002). It is widely recognized that alcohol consumption is a significant risk factor for violent perpetration and violence victimization (Abbey, 2011; Chermack and Giancola, 1997; Leonard, 2008; Lipsey *et al.*, 1997; Roizen, 1997). We will in this chapter present an overview of research evidence on how and to what extent alcohol consumption is related to violence within an epidemiological and public health perspective. More specifically, we will show that alcohol use is a common ingredient in violent acts, that the risk of being involved in a violent act is higher among those who consume alcohol frequently and in large quantities, that the amount of violent acts in a society varies systematically with the overall alcohol consumption in that population and with the drinking pattern in that population.

Defining the Problem

What do we mean by 'violence'? While self-inflicted injuries and collective violence (e.g., riots or acts of war) are often included in the term violence (Krug *et al.*, 2002), we have limited the focus here to that of interpersonal violence. According to the World Health Organization, interpersonal violence can be divided into the following subcategories: family and intimate partner violence

Alcohol-Related Violence: Prevention and Treatment, First Edition. Edited by Mary McMurran.
© 2013 John Wiley & Sons, Ltd. Published 2013 by John Wiley & Sons, Ltd.

(between family members and intimate partners, usually taking place in the home) and community violence (between individuals who are unrelated and who may or may not know each other, generally taking place outside the home) (Krug *et al.*, 2002). These subcategories are again divided by the nature of violent acts: physical, sexual, psychological and involving deprivation or neglect. We will in this review address only the former two (physical and sexual violence) in relation to alcohol use.

This leads us to the question of what we mean by alcohol use in relation violence. The term 'alcohol use' covers a wide range of behaviours and is assessed by different types of measures across studies. Examples of the latter are presence of alcohol at the time of the event as measured by breathalyzer or blood sample analysis; self-report in surveys or clinical interviews; assessment of alcohol intoxication by health personnel, police officers and so on; and aggregate measures of alcohol consumption such as sales figures. The various types of behaviour comprise, for instance, any drinking in the few hours prior to the violent event; annual alcohol consumption; frequency of intoxication; and indicators of alcohol dependence or abuse.

Alcohol-related violence is not only a problem for those who suffer violent injuries in terms of health and economic costs, but it has also a wide range of consequences at the societal level, for instance, in terms of its burden on health services, police forces and economic costs to society, and by generating fear and insecurity in the family, neighbourhood and community. While these consequences of alcohol-related violence are indeed part of the problem, a societal analysis is beyond the scope of this review.

THE EVIDENCE OF AN ASSOCIATION BETWEEN ALCOHOL CONSUMPTION AND INTERPERSONAL VIOLENCE

The scientific literature on the alcohol–violence association is overwhelming. A quick search in various literature databases reveals thousands of publications that – based on the title only – address this topic. We will therefore provide a review partly drawing on previous, preferably recent, review studies but also refer to primary studies, when no fairly recent reviews are available or when primary studies add to previous reviews. Given the epidemiological and public health perspective, the literature review mainly covers studies that refer to the general population and that are of relevance to public health strategies.

Numerous studies have demonstrated some kind of statistical association between alcohol consumption and interpersonal violence. These studies have addressed the association between alcohol consumption and interpersonal violence in various ways by examining different aspects of the association and by applying different types of research designs and methods and different types of data. For instance, Roizen (1997) distinguished between event-based research, that is, samples of people to whom a serious event has occurred, and studies of the general population. We have in the following sections briefly summarized broad categories of studies that have demonstrated some kind of association between alcohol consumption and violence.

Those Involved in Violence Have Often Been Drinking

There is a large research literature from event-based research which has demonstrated that alcohol often has been consumed by one or more of those involved in a violent act. Studies of perpetrators of violent crimes (suspected, arrested or convicted) have revealed that these offenders had often consumed alcohol shortly before the violent act (Chermack and Giancola, 1997; Graham *et al.*, 1998; Pernanen, 1991; Roizen, 1997). Yet, it should be noted that the proportion of offenders with alcohol present at the time of the event varies significantly across studies, from around 15% to some 60–85% of offenders (see Roizen, 1997 for a review). Correspondingly, studies of victims of violence have also shown that these had often been drinking prior to the violent act and, yet again, that the proportion of victims that had been drinking varies across studies, ranging from 5% to 85% (Roizen, 1997). The research literature that addresses domestic violence and intimate partner violence specifically has shown that partner-violent men are often heavy drinkers and heavy drinking often accompanies the violence (Leonard, 2001, 2005; Lipsey *et al.*, 1997). Correspondingly, reviews of the literature on alcohol consumption and sexual violence also show that in about half of all sexual assaults, alcohol had been consumed by the victim, the perpetrator or both (Abbey, 2011; Abbey *et al.*, 2004).

A significant part of the event-based research comprises studies of patients admitted to emergency rooms after injuries from violent acts. These have shown that these patients often have a blood alcohol concentration (BAC) above 0.05%, 0.08% or 0.10% (as measured in blood or breath) and/or they often report that they consumed alcohol within 6 hours prior to the injury (Cherpitel, 1997, 2007). Again, the prevalence of alcohol involvement in violent injuries varies significantly across studies, ranging between 22% and 84% in Cherpitel's recent review (2007). It is also evident from these studies that alcohol involvement occurs more frequently among patients with violence-related injury compared with other injured patients in the emergency room (Cherpitel, 2007).

Whether alcohol involvement varies by type and severity of the violent act has been addressed in some studies. Felson, Burchfield, and Teasdale (2007) noted that, as most research on alcohol and violence focuses on specific types of violence or examines violence generally, there is little evidence on whether alcohol intoxication is a greater risk factor for some types of violence than for others. In their study from a general population survey, perpetrators of physical assaults were just as likely as those of sexual assaults to have been intoxicated (Felson *et al.*, 2007). Correspondingly, in a large population-based survey in New Zealand, self-reported events of physical assaults and sexual assaults were compared with respect to the role of alcohol, and for both types of assaults, a little more than half of the victims reported that the perpetrator was affected by alcohol (Connor, You, and Casswell, 2009).

Several studies have, in various ways, addressed whether alcohol involvement varies with the severity of aggressive behaviour. In his classic study, Pernanen (1991) found no increase in the severity of violence when the assailants had been drinking. However, Leonard and colleagues found that a higher level of alcohol consumption was associated with more severe aggression among males (Leonard, Collins, and Quigley, 2003), and similarly, Graham and co-workers found that greater intoxication of those involved in aggressive incidents was related to greater severity of aggression (Graham *et al.*, 2006). In a recent study, Wells and co-workers also found that drinking at the time may contribute to severity of aggression (Wells *et al.*, 2011).

Whereas alcohol involvement in the perpetrator and/or the victim is extensively studied, there are also a few studies that have addressed the role of alcohol in the drinking environment and among bystanders. These studies suggest that the overall level of intoxication of patrons in drinking establishments independently contributes to the frequency and severity of aggression by patrons (Graham and Homel, 2008).

Violence Is More Likely at Times and Places with Heavy Drinking

The distribution of violent events over days of the week and hours of the day tends to display a similar pattern to that of drinking occasions, and, in particular, heavy drinking occasions. Thus, violent events are more likely to occur at nighttime on weekends (Borges, Cherpitel, and Rosovsky, 1998; Briscoe and Donnell, 2003; Engeland and Kopjar, 2000; Pridemore, 2004) as are heavy drinking occasions (Demers, 1997; Mäkelä, Martikainen, and Nihtilä, 2005; Pridemore, 2004). In a similar vein, it is also shown that bars, pubs and clubs, which are often attended by heavy drinkers, are 'hot spots' for violent events (Graham and Homel, 2008).

Those Who Drink Heavily Are at Higher Risk of Being Involved in Violence

Another type of study is surveys of general population samples in which respondents have been asked about their behaviour (for instance, in the past 12 months) and whether they have been involved in violent behaviour. These studies have generally shown that those who report a relatively high alcohol intake and/or frequent heavy drinking occasions are more likely to have been involved in violent acts (Rossow, 1996, 2000; Wells and Graham, 2003; Wells *et al.*, 2005), and it seems that it is, in particular, heavy drinking occasions that account for this association (Bye and Rossow, 2010; Dawson, 1997; Hope and Mongan, 2011; Leonard, 2008; Room and Rossow, 2001; Rossow, 1996; Rossow, Pape, and Wichstrøm, 1999). Thus, with increasing alcohol consumption, and particularly with increasing frequency of heavy drinking occasions, the risk of committing a violent act increases as does the risk of being a victim of violent assault. This has been shown with respect to physical violence, irrespective of subcategory (Room and Rossow, 2001), and with respect to domestic violence and intimate partner violence (Foran and O'Leary, 2008; Leonard, 2001). In a longitudinal cohort study, Boden and co-workers found that young adults with alcohol abuse/dependence symptoms had 4–12 times higher risk than others to be involved in violence, whether as offender or as victim (Boden, Fergusson, and Horwood, 2012). Also, studies of clinical population samples have shown that the prevalence of violence perpetration and victimization is elevated among heavy drinkers (Leonard, 2008).

Heaviest Drinkers Account for a Minor Fraction of Alcohol-Related Violence

Although the risk of violence involvement is highest among those with high consumption and heavy drinking frequency, it should also be noted that these drinkers constitute a relatively small fraction of all drinkers at risk. Thus, the heaviest drinkers in a population contribute to a disproportionately larger fraction of the overall amount of violence. Yet, studies have demonstrated that their share of all violent incidents is less than half and – more or less – it is the moderate drinkers, who constitute the vast majority of all drinkers, who also contribute to the majority of all alcohol-related violence (Poikolainen, Paljärvi, and Mäkelä, 2007; Rossow and Romelsjö, 2006). More specifically, Rossow and Romelsjö (2006) found that, of all self-reported events of alcohol-related quarrels and fights, less than half could be attributed to the 10% of the drinkers who drank the most. Moreover, of all hospital admissions for violent injuries (whether alcohol-related or not), 14% could be attributed to the upper 10% of the drinkers. Correspondingly, Poikolainen and co-workers (2007) found that 25% of all self-reported events of quarrels and arguments and 31% of all scuffles and fights could be ascribed to the upper 10% of the drinkers.

This implies that, from a public health perspective, preventive strategies directed at all drinkers (i.e., population strategies) may be more effective in reducing the overall amount of violent events in a population rather than strategies aimed at the small fraction of heavy drinkers (high-risk strategies). This is what is often referred to as the prevention paradox (Kreitman, 1986; Rossow and Romelsjö, 2006; Skog, 1999).

ACTORS, CONTEXT AND CULTURE

While it is clear that a significant proportion of violent events are precipitated by alcohol consumption by one or several parties involved, it is only a tiny fraction of drinking occasions that are accompanied by aggressive behaviour. For example, among teenagers, the numbers of self-reported fights per 1,000 drinking occasions were in the range of 2–10 (Bye and Rossow, 2010). Thus, the relationship between alcohol consumption and violence is conditional: it is drinking *in combination with other factors* that is implicated (Room and Rossow, 2001). These other factors, which we know of so far, are many and include personal factors (e.g., temperament), contextual factors (e.g., provocation) and cultural factors (e.g., drinking pattern) (Chermack and Giancola, 1997; Graham and Homel, 2008; Graham *et al.*, 1998; Pernanen, 1991). Thus, the alcohol–violence association is highly complex and reflects an interaction of the effects of alcohol and these various other factors. The magnitude of the problem, therefore, varies with these factors, such as the characteristics of the person, the context and the culture. We will briefly address this in the following section with some examples.

Alcohol-Related Violence Occurs More Frequently in Certain Persons

Men are generally heavier drinkers than women and they drink more frequently to intoxication (Babor *et al.*, 2010), and, compared to women, they also account for a larger proportion of alcohol-related violent incidents (Pernanen, 1991). Furthermore, it seems that alcohol consumption increases the likelihood of aggressive behaviour more for men than for women. In experimental studies, alcohol has been shown to increase aggressive behaviour more among men than among women (Giancola *et al.*, 2002), although this is not consistently found (Hoaken and Pihl, 2000). However, in community-based surveys, it is found that alcohol-related violence is more frequently reported by men than by women, even when alcohol consumption and subjective feeling of intoxication is the same (Rossow, 1996). The latter study also demonstrated that, compared to middle-aged and elderly people, young people are at higher risk of being involved in alcohol-related violence, whether as perpetrator or victim, and this was also the case when drinking behaviour was taken into account (Rossow, 1996).

The association between alcohol consumption and violence seems also to be contingent on personality traits. In experimental studies, it has been demonstrated that people with high dispositional aggressivity are more likely to react aggressively under the influence of alcohol as compared with those with low dispositional aggressivity (Giancola, 2002). Using self-report data from a longitudinal cohort study, Norström and Pape (2010) have taken the importance of an aggressive predisposition in the alcohol–violence association further by demonstrating that the effect of alcohol consumption on violent behaviour appears to be confined to those with medium or high levels of suppressed anger (Norström and Pape, 2010).

Alcohol-Related Violence Occurs More Frequently in Certain Drinking Contexts

In most countries (with available statistics), only a minor fraction of all alcohol is consumed in licensed drinking venues, like restaurants, taverns, bars, pubs or other drinking establishments (Babor *et al.*, 2010). Nevertheless, a fairly high proportion of violent incidents occur in such venues, and public drinking places like bars, pubs and clubs are often considered as hot spots for alcohol-related violence (Graham and Homel, 2008). In line with this, there are also indications that alcohol that is consumed in public drinking venues is more strongly associated with violence as compared with that consumed in private settings (Norström, 1998b).

The occurrence of violence differs significantly between various types of drinking venues. In two recent excellent reviews (Graham and Homel, 2008; Hughes *et al.*, 2011), a number of contextual factors in the drinking venues are identified that are particularly important in contributing to alcohol-related aggression. These comprise physical factors, such as crowdedness, noise and low lighting; social factors, such as drunk customers and permissive environment; and staff factors, such as poor staff control (see also Forsyth, Chapter 7).

Alcohol-Related Violence Occurs More Frequently in Certain Drinking Cultures

As noted previously, the proportion of violent perpetrators who have been drinking varies significantly across studies, and it seems likely that much of this variation can be attributed to differences in drinking cultures, that is, differences in drinking patterns and in norms and expectancies about behaviour while drinking (Room and Rossow, 2001). Based on survey data among adolescents in 13 European countries, Bye and Rossow (2010) found that the prevalence of alcohol-related violence varied significantly between countries and was highest in countries where drinking often leads to intoxication. Moreover, there was a clear gradient in the magnitude of the alcohol–violence association; the strongest association was observed for the Nordic countries where drinking often leads to intoxication, whereas the least strong association was observed in the South European countries where intoxication is far less prevalent (Bye and Rossow, 2010).

HOW MUCH VIOLENCE CAN BE ATTRIBUTED TO ALCOHOL?

As we have seen above, it is very clear that there is an *association* between alcohol consumption and violence in the sense that violence is more likely to occur in the event of drinking, at times and places in which heavy drinking occurs, and in persons who drink heavily. However, it is also likely that some of the alcohol-related violent events (i.e., in which alcohol has been consumed by one or several actors) would have occurred also in the absence of any alcohol. Many scholars in the field differ in their views as to whether – or to what extent – alcohol causes violence, yet these differences seem primarily to reflect varying definitions of causation (Room and Rossow, 2001).

From a prevention point of view, a key question is how much of the violence could possibly be prevented by interventions affecting alcohol-related violence. Consequently, assessment of what share of violence that is attributable to drinking is important.

Within the epidemiological literature, we often see that the attributable fraction (the proportion of a problem that can be attributed to one specific risk factor) is estimated from individual-level data by a simple formula comprising an estimate of the relative risk and the fraction of the population exposed to the risk factor (Lilienfeldt and Lilienfeldt, 1980). However, when it comes to alcohol and violence, there are several reasons why the association is not well represented by the traditional attributable fraction estimation. Most importantly, there are three parties or actors for whom alcohol exposure is of importance: the perpetrator(s), the victim(s) and the bystanders, and it seems extremely difficult, if at all possible, to obtain and model data that would capture this complexity at the individual level.

An alternative approach is therefore to use aggregate-level data, where the complexity of underlying mechanisms and selection effects may constitute less of a problem (Norström and Skog, 2001; Room and Rossow, 2001). Next, we will review aggregate-level studies in some more detail and further address estimates of the alcohol attributable fraction derived from aggregate-level analyses.

The Alcohol–Violence Association in a Public Health Perspective

Over the past two decades, we have witnessed a significant growth in studies addressing the alcohol–violence relationship by applying data at the aggregate level. Such data comprise violence rates – either homicide rates or rates of non-fatal violent assaults – and alcohol consumption per adult inhabitant per year, assessed as recorded alcohol sales. In particular, analyses of time series data applying statistical modeling techniques to minimize spurious effects are of relevance here and will be reviewed. These studies have generally demonstrated that an increase in alcohol consumption is followed by an increase in rates of fatal and non-fatal violence and vice versa (Norström, 2011; Rossow, 2000). In Western European countries, analyses of longer time series of violent crime rates have found significant effects of population drinking (Bye, 2007; Lenke, 1990; Norström, 1998a; Skog and Bjørk, 1988). In the same vein, studies of natural experiments, such as sudden and large changes in alcohol consumption due to rationing or strikes, have also demonstrated a significant impact of alcohol consumption on violent crime rates (Lenke, 1990; Rossow, 2002). There are also several studies from the United States that have shown an association between alcohol consumption and homicide rates in studies based on cross-sectional data, time series data and a combination of the two (Parker, 1995, 1998; Parker and Cartmill, 1998; Parker and Rebhun, 1995). Several studies from the former Soviet Republics have also demonstrated a positive and significant association between alcohol consumption (or alcohol-related mortality data as proxy) and homicide (Pridemore and Chamlin, 2006; Razvodovsky, 2003, 2007, 2010).

As we have noted previously, the drinking pattern, particularly in terms of drinking to intoxication, plays an important role in the alcohol–violence association. This is also demonstrated by comparisons of associations estimated by the same modeling technique applying time series data on population drinking (annual per capita volume) and homicide rates. Table 1.1 summarizes the findings from seven studies that have analyzed data from altogether 20 countries (Bye, 2008; Landberg and Norström, 2011; Norström, 2011; Ramstedt, 2011; Rossow, 2001, 2004). The level of hazardous drinking pattern is presented in the fourth column and based on two sources of information. One is that of Rehm and co-workers' (2003) assessment of country-specific hazardous drinking scores. These are on a four-point scale that reflects the degree of hazardous drinking, ranging from 1 (least harmful) to 4 (most harmful). The other source of information is on regional variation in drinking patterns within countries (Norström, 2011; Rossow, 2004).

Table 1.1 Estimates of association between alcohol consumption and homicide rates, hazardous drinking pattern score and estimated fraction of homicides attributable to alcohol consumption.

Author(s)	Country/Area, Period	Parameter Estimate (SE)	Level of Hazardous Drinking Pattern	Attributable Fraction (AF)
Rossow (2001)	North Europe, 1950–1995	0.124 (0.038)	High	0.50
Rossow (2001)	Central Europe, 1950–1995	0.085 (0.023)	Medium	0.55
Rossow (2001)	South Europe, 1950–1995	0.055 (0.017)	Low	0.61
Rossow (2004)	Canada, Ontario, 1950–1995	0.093 (0.040)	Medium	0.58
Rossow (2004)	Canada, Quebec, 1950–1995	−0.030 (0.077)[ns]	Low	na
Bye (2008)	Belarus and Russia, 1959–2004	0.072 (0.016)	Very high	0.57
Bye (2008)	Former Czechoslovakia, 1953–1989	0.117 (0.067)	Medium	0.73
Landberg and Norström (2011)	United States, 1950–2002	0.094 (0.044)	Medium	0.57
Landberg and Norström (2011)	Russia, 1959–1998	0.081 (0.015)	Very high	0.73
Norström (2011)	United States, 1950–2002, 'dry'	0.035 (0.047)[ns]	Low	na
Norström (2011)	United States, 1950–2002, 'moderate'	0.071 (0.037)	Medium	0.51
Norström (2011)	United States, 1950–2002, 'wet'	0.174 (0.045)	High	0.80
Ramstedt (2011)	Australia, 1950–2003	0.075 (0.028)	Medium	0.56

ns, not significant; na, not applicable.

In Table 1.1, we see that all estimates of the association are positive (i.e., an increase in population drinking is associated with an increase in homicide rates) and most are also statistically significant. The magnitude of the estimate varies considerably, however. This variation reflects at least two significant factors: the variation in hazardous drinking patterns between countries or regions and the variation in the level of homicide rates. Thus, as a rule of thumb, it seems that the association between population drinking and homicide is stronger in populations or cultures with a high level of hazardous drinking pattern as compared to those with a low level. The parameter estimates can roughly be interpreted in the following way: a 1 liter increase in per capita consumption is accompanied by a relative increase in homicide rates corresponding (closely) to the estimate. For instance, the estimate of 0.124 for the Northern European countries corresponds to an increase in violence rates of (slightly more than) 12.4% with a 1 liter increase in per capita consumption. Finally, Table 1.1 provides estimates of the fraction of homicide rates attributable to alcohol consumption. As can be seen, these fractions are considerable and higher than what is mostly assumed from individual-level data estimates (Room and Rossow, 2001).

IMPLICATIONS FOR POLICY AND RESEARCH

Can Violence Rates Be Affected by Changes in Alcohol Policy?

As noted previously, the level of violence (in particular homicide rates) in a society tends to vary systematically with variations in alcohol consumption in that society; that is, when consumption goes up, so does the violence rate and vice versa. This would suggest that policies that are effective in reducing the total consumption of alcohol in a population may also be successful in curbing violence rates in that population. So far, there is some evidence to support this, and we will address this in some more detail in the following.

Alcohol policy strategies that are shown to be the most effective in reducing overall consumption in a population are those that limit the economic and physical availability of alcohol, mainly taxation, limitations of the number of outlet, limitations of days and hours of sales, and minimum legal age for purchase of alcohol (Babor *et al.*, 2010). More specifically, a large number of studies have demonstrated a significant association between alcohol prices and alcohol consumption; when prices go up, consumption goes down and vice versa (Wagenaar, Salois, and Komro, 2009). There is also an extensive literature on the association between alcohol outlet density and consumption (Babor *et al.*, 2010; Campbell *et al.*, 2009) and between hours and days of sales and consumption (Hahn *et al.*, 2010; Middleton *et al.*, 2010; Popova *et al.*, 2009), which demonstrates that limiting availability by restricting outlet density and days and hours of sales tends to reduce alcohol consumption. Some studies have further demonstrated the potential impact of these strategies on violence.

There are two fairly recent reviews on the impact of alcohol prices on consumption and related consequences, both of which refer to several studies that suggest that increased alcohol prices are associated with a reduction in violence rates (Chaloupka, Grossman, and Saffer, 2002; Wagenaar *et al.*, 2009). Yet, a recent study from Denmark has found no significant effect on violent injuries after a price decrease, mainly due to a large reduction in spirit taxes (Bloomfield, Rossow, and Norström, 2009).

Bars and pubs tend to be hot spots for alcohol-related violence, and much of the literature on restrictions of the physical availability of alcohol and violence relates to strategies concerning on-premise licences. Several studies have shown a positive association between density of on-premise licences and violence rates, both as spatial correlations (Lipton and Gruenewald, 2002; Livingston, 2008) and in time series analyses (Norström, 2000). Three recent literature reviews (Hahn *et al.*, 2010; Popova *et al.*, 2009; Stockwell and Chikritzhs, 2009) that have addressed a possible impact of restricting sales hours for on-premise licences on violence rates have found that an extension of sales hours was followed by an increase in violence rates, and vice versa, at least when the change in sales hours exceeded 2 hours (Hahn *et al.*, 2010). A couple of examples to illustrate this stem from Iceland and Brazil. In Reykjavik, Iceland, an extension in trading hours for on-premise sales from 2 a.m. to no limits was accompanied by an increase in violent injuries by 34% (Ragnarsdottir, Kjartansdottir, and Davidsdottir, 2002). In Diadema, Brazil, on-premise trading hours were restricted from no limits to 11 p.m., and this restriction led to a decrease in homicide rates by 44% (Duailibi *et al.*, 2007).

Even more recently, a few studies have found that smaller changes in sales hours for bars and pubs had an impact on violence rates. Kypri and co-workers found that restricting on-premise sales hours by 1.5 hours and a lock-out policy reduced violence rates in Newcastle, Australia, by 37% (Kypri *et al.*, 2011), and a recent study from 18 Norwegian cities found that violence rates decreased with restrictions in sales hours and vice versa; on average, a 1-hour restriction in sales hours was accompanied by 16% reduction in violent crimes at nighttime on weekends (Rossow and Norström, 2012).

There are also some examples that various coordinated alcohol policy strategies, in terms of a community prevention project or a national campaign, may have a significant impact on violence rates. Holder and co-workers evaluated a community prevention project in California (Holder *et al.*, 2000). The intervention comprised five components: community mobilization (formation of community coalitions and media advocacy), responsible beverage service (RBS), limiting access of alcohol to the underaged, local enforcement of drinking and driving laws, and closing problem outlets. The authors reported favourable effects of the project in several respects. They found that assault injuries in emergency departments decreased by 46%, whereas a smaller effect (i.e., a 2% decline per month) was observed for assault cases admitted to hospital (Holder *et al.*, 2000). In Stockholm, Sweden, a community project [Stockholm Prevents Alcohol and Drug Problems ('STAD')] aimed at reducing violence and injuries related to alcohol consumption in on-premise licences. The main elements in this prevention project were community mobilization and cooperation between the hospitality industry, the local government and the police; mandatory RBS training; and increased law enforcement and police controls of licensed premises (Wallin, Norström, and Andreasson, 2003). The intervention was implemented in one area in Stockholm and, compared to the control site, police reported violence at nighttime decreased by 29% in the intervention area (Wallin *et al.*, 2003).

A giant natural experiment was that of the anti-alcohol campaign in the Soviet Union from 1985 to 1987. The campaign comprised several elements, including banning drinking at all work places, restriction of sales hours and sales outlets, and increased prices (McKee, 1999). While the campaign resulted in a decline in recorded alcohol sales by 63%, there was also a massive growth in home distilling, and it has been estimated that decline in actual consumption was about 25% (Nemtsov, 2005). Numerous studies have addressed the impact of this campaign on health and mortality in the Soviet Union, and it is clear that mortality rates decreased significantly in the wake of the campaign, and especially so with respect to alcohol-related mortality (Leon *et al.*, 1997; Shkolnikov and Nemtsov,

1997). In line with this, male homicide rates decreased by 40% from 1984 to 1987 (Shkolnikov and Nemtsov, 1997).

Thus, there is ample evidence that implementation of alcohol policies that are effective in reducing alcohol consumption may also have significant effects on violence rates in a society. The observed effects of such policies are highly important in several respects. First, the extent of effectiveness is often impressive and it seems unlikely that individual-level strategies may have such an impact on the population level. Moreover, the observed effectiveness of population strategies is well in line with the prevention paradox (Rose, 2001).

However, these effective strategies, particularly those entailing high prices and limited availability, are rarely popular in the general population, whereas ineffective strategies such as school programs and other education/information strategies are widely supported (Greenfield, Johnson, and Giesbrecht, 2004). This is one reason why effective policies may be politically difficult or even impossible to implement and maintain (Room, 2003). Herein lies a significant challenge in the policy-making arena.

Suggestions for Further Research

A large scientific literature has provided good evidence that alcohol is a significant contributor to violence and an increasingly better understanding of how this may be explained. There is also a growing literature on the effectiveness of various types of interventions to curb alcohol-related violence. The potential of alcohol control policies to prevent alcohol-related violence certainly calls for further studies on the effectiveness and feasibility of such policies. Such studies would evaluate various types of 'natural experiments' as well as designed intervention projects.

However, within the epidemiological and public health perspective, the largest gap in the scientific literature in this area is probably the scarcity of studies from low- and middle-income (LAMI) countries. This is also generally the case in the broader epidemiological and social science research on alcohol consumption and related harms (Babor *et al.*, 2010). An exception to this are the many and excellent studies on alcohol and violence from the former Soviet Republics and eastern European countries. Yet, given the importance of culture for the alcohol–violence association, a culturally and geographically broader empirical basis is needed in order to better obtain a global picture of the problem of alcohol-related violence.

CONCLUSION

In conclusion, a large scientific literature shows that alcohol use is a common ingredient in violent acts, that those who drink heavily are at an increased risk of being involved in violence and that the amount of violence in a society varies systematically with population drinking. In line with the latter, there is significant promise for effective alcohol control policies in the prevention of violence.

REFERENCES

Abbey, A. (2011) Alcohol's role in sexual violence perpetration: Theoretical explanations, existing evidence and future directions. *Drug and Alcohol Review*, 30(5), 481–489.

Abbey, A., Zawacki, T., Buck, P.O. *et al.* (2004) Sexual assault and alcohol consumption: What do we know about their relationship and what types of research are still needed? *Aggression and Violent Behavior*, 9(3), 271–303.

Babor, T., Caetano, R., Casswell, S. *et al.* (2010) *Alcohol: No Ordinary Commodity. Research and Public Policy* (2nd edn). Oxford: Oxford University Press.

Bloomfield, K., Rossow, I., and Norström, T. (2009) Changes in alcohol-related harm after alcohol policy changes in Denmark. *European Addiction Research*, 18(4), 224–231.

Boden, J.M., Fergusson, D.M., and Horwood, L.J. (2012) Alcohol misuse and violent behavior: Findings from a 30-year longitudinal study. *Drug and Alcohol Dependence*, 122, 135–141.

Borges, G., Cherpitel, C.J., and Rosovsky, H. (1998) Male drinking and violence-related injury in the emergency room. *Addiction*, 93(1), 103–112.

Briscoe, S. and Donnell, N. (2003) Problematic licensed premises for assault in inner Sydney, Newcastle and Wollongong. *Australian & New Zealand Journal of Criminology*, 36(1), 18–33.

Bye, E.K. (2007) Alcohol and violence: Use of possible confounders in a time-series analysis. *Addiction*, 102(3), 369–376.

Bye, E.K. (2008) Alcohol and homicide in Eastern Europe. *Homicide Studies*, 12(1), 7–27.

Bye, E.K. and Rossow, I. (2010) The impact of drinking pattern on alcohol related violence among adolescents: An international comparative analysis. *Drug and Alcohol Review*, 29(2), 131–137.

Campbell, C.A., Hahn, R.A., Elder, R. *et al.* (2009) The effectiveness of limiting alcohol outlet density as a means of reducing excessive alcohol consumption and alcohol-related harms. *American Journal of Preventive Medicine*, 37(6), 556–569.

Chaloupka, F.J., Grossman, M., and Saffer, H. (2002) The effects of price on alcohol consumption and alcohol-related problems. *Alcohol Research & Health*, 26, 22–34.

Chermack, S.T. and Giancola, P.R. (1997) The relation between alcohol and aggression: An integrated biopsychosocial conceptualization. *Clinical Psychology Review*, 17(6), 621–649.

Cherpitel, C.J. (1997) Alcohol and violence-related injuries in the emergency room. In M. Galanter (ed.), *Alcohol and Violence* (pp. 105–118). New York: Plenum Press.

Cherpitel, C.J. (2007) Alcohol and injuries: A review of international emergency room studies since 1995. *Drug and Alcohol Review*, 26, 201–214.

Connor, J., You, R., and Casswell, S. (2009) Alcohol-related harm to others: A survey of physical adn sexual assault in New Zealand. *The New Zealand Medical Journal*, 122(1303), 10–20.

Dawson, D.A. (1997) Alcohol, drugs, fighting and suicide attempt/ideation. *Addiction Research & Theory*, 5(6), 451–472.

Demers, A. (1997) When at risk? Drinking contexts and heavy drinking in the Montreal adult population. *Contemporary Drug Problems*, 24, 449–471.

Duailibi, S., Ponicki, W., Grube, J. *et al.* (2007) The effect of restricting opening hours on alcohol-related violence. *American Journal of Public Health*, 97(12), 2276–2280.

Engeland, A. and Kopjar, B. (2000) Injuries connected to violence – An analysis of data from the injury registry. *Tidsskrift for den Norske laegeforening: tidsskrift for praktisk medicin, ny raekke*, 120(6), 714–717.

Felson, R.B., Burchfield, K.B., and Teasdale, B. (2007) The impact of alcohol on different types of violent incidents. *Criminal Justice and Behavior*, 34(8), 1057–1068.

Foran, H.M. and O'Leary, K.D. (2008) Alcohol and intimate partner violence: A meta-analytic review. *Clinical Psychology Review*, 28(7), 1222–1234.

Giancola, P.R. (2002) Alcohol-related aggression in men and women: The influence of dispositional aggressivity. *Journal of Studies on Alcohol*, 63(6), 696–708.

Giancola, P.R., Helton, E.L., Osborn, A.B. *et al.* (2002) The effects of alcohol and provocation on aggressive behavior in men and women. *Journal of Studies on Alcohol*, **63**(1), 64–73.

Graham, K. and Homel, R. (2008) *Raising the Bar. Preventing Aggression in and Around bars, Pubs and Clubs*. Portland, OR: Willan Publishing.

Graham, K., Leonard, K.E., Room, R. *et al.* (1998) Current directions in research on understanding and preventing intoxicated aggression. *Addiction*, **93**(5), 659–676.

Graham, K., Osgood, D.W., Wells, S., and Stockwell, T. (2006) To what extent is intoxication associated with aggression in bars? A multilevel analysis. *Journal of Studies on Alcohol*, **67**(3), 382–390.

Greenfield, T.K., Johnson, S.P., and Giesbrecht, N. (2004) Public opinion on alcohol policy: A review of U.S. research. *Contemporary Drug Problems*, **31**(4), 759–790.

Hahn, R.A., Kuzara, J.L., Elder, R. *et al.* (2010) Effectiveness of policies restricting hours of alcohol sales in preventing excessive alcohol consumption and related harms. *American Journal of Preventive Medicine*, **39**(6), 590–604.

Hoaken, P.N.S. and Pihl, R.O. (2000) The effects of alcohol intoxication on aggressive responses in men and women. *Alcohol and Alcoholism*, **35**(5), 471–477.

Holder, H.D., Gruenewald, P.J., Ponicki, W.R. *et al.* (2000) Effect of community-based interventions on high-risk drinking and alcohol-related injuries. *JAMA: The Journal of the American Medical Association*, **284**(18), 2341–2347.

Hope, A. and Mongan, D. (2011) A profile of self-reported alcohol-related violence in Ireland. *Contemporary Drug Problems*, **38**(2), 237–258.

Hughes, K., Quigg, Z., Eckley, L. *et al.* (2011) Environmental factors in drinking venues and alcohol-related harm: The evidence base for European intervention. *Addiction*, **106**, 37–46.

Kreitman, N. (1986) Alcohol consumption and the preventive paradox. *British Journal of Addiction*, **81**(3), 353–363.

Krug, E., Dahlberg, L., Mercy, J.A. *et al.* (2002) *World Report on Violence and Health*. Geneva: World Health Organization.

Kypri, K., Jones, C., McElduff, P., and Barker, D. (2011) Effects of restricting pub closing times on night-time assaults in an Australian city. *Addiction*, **106**(2), 303–310.

Landberg, J. and Norström, T. (2011) Alcohol and homicide in Russia and the United States: A comparative analysis. *Journal of Studies on Alcohol and Drugs*, **72**, 723–730.

Lenke, L. (1990) *Alcohol and Criminal Violence: Time Series Analysis in a Comparative Perspective*. Stockholm: Almqvist and Wiksell International.

Leon, D.A., Chenet, L., Shkolnikov, V.M. *et al.* (1997) Huge variation in Russian mortality rates 1984â€"94: Artefact, alcohol, or what? *The Lancet*, **350**(9075), 383–388.

Leonard, K. (2001) Domestic violence and alcohol: What is known and what do we need to know to encourage environmental interventions? *Journal of Substance Use*, **6**, 235–247.

Leonard, K.E. (2005) Alcohol and intimate partner violence: When can we say that heavy drinking is a contributing cause of violence? *Addiction*, **100**(4), 422–425.

Leonard, K.E. (2008) The role of drinking patterns and acute intoxication in violent interpersonal behaviors. In I.C.F.A. Policies (ed.), *Alcohol and Violence: Exploring Patterns and Responses*. International Center for Alcohol Policies.

Leonard, K.E., Collins, R.L., and Quigley, B.M. (2003) Alcohol consumption and the occurrence and severity of aggression: An event-based analysis of male to male barroom violence. *Aggressive Behavior*, **29**(4), 346–365.

Lilienfeldt, A.M. and Lilienfeldt, D.E. (1980) *Foundations of Epidemiology* (2nd edn). New York: Oxford University Press.

Lipsey, M.W., Wilson, D.B., Cohen, M.A., and Derzon, J.H. (1997) Is there a causal relationship between alcohol use and violence? A synthesis of evidence. In M. Galanter (ed.), *Alcohol and Violence* (pp. 245–282). New York: Plenum Press.

Lipton, R. and Gruenewald, P. (2002) The spatial dynamics of violence and alcohol outlets. *Journal of Studies on Alcohol*, **63**(2), 187–195.

Livingston, M. (2008) Alcohol outlet density and assault: A spatial analysis. *Addiction*, **103**(4), 619–628.

Mäkelä, P., Martikainen, P., and Nihtilä, E. (2005) Temporal variation in deaths related to alcohol intoxication and drinking. *International Journal of Epidemiology*, **34**(4), 765–771.

McKee, M (1999) Alcohol in Russia. *Alcohol and Alcoholism*, **34**(6), 824–829.

Middleton, J.C., Hahn, R.A., Kuzara, J.L. *et al.* (2010) Effectiveness of policies maintaining or restricting days of alcohol sales on excessive alcohol consumption and related harms. *American Journal of Preventive Medicine*, **39**(6), 575–589.

Nemtsov, A. (2005) Russia: Alcohol yesterday and today. *Addiction*, **100**(2), 146–149.

Norström, T. (1998a) Effects on criminal violence of different beverage types and private and public drinking. *Addiction*, **93**, 689–699.

Norström, T. (1998b) Effects on criminal violence of different beverage types and private and public drinking. *Addiction*, **93**(5), 689–699.

Norström, T. (2000) Outlet density and criminal violence in Norway, 1960–1995. [Article]. *Journal of Studies on Alcohol*, **61**(6), 907–911.

Norström, T. (2011) Alcohol and homicide in the United States: Is the link dependent on wetness? *Drug and Alcohol Review*, **30**(5), 458–465.

Norström, T. and Pape, H. (2010) Alcohol, suppressed anger and violence. *Addiction*, **105**(9), 1580–1586.

Norström, T. and Skog, O.-J. (2001) Alcohol and mortality: Methodological and analytical issues in aggregate analyses. *Addiction*, **96**(Suppl), S5–S17.

Parker, R.N. (1995) Bringing "booze" back in: The relationship between alcohol and homicide. *Journal of Research in Crime and Delinquency*, **32**, 3–38.

Parker, R.N. (1998) Alcohol, homicide, and the cultural context: A cross-national analysis of gender specific homicide victimization. *Homicide Studies*, **2**, 6–30.

Parker, R.N. and Cartmill, R.S. (1998) Alcohol and homicide in the US: Or one reason why US rates of violence may be going down. *Journal of Criminal Law and Criminology*, **88**, 1369–1398.

Parker, R.N. and Rebhun, L.A. (1995) *Alcohol and Homicide: A Deadly Combination of Two American Traditions*. Albany, NY: State University of New York Press.

Pernanen, K. (1991) *Alcohol in Human Violence*. New York: The Guilford Press.

Poikolainen, K., Paljärvi, T., and Mäkelä, P. (2007) Alcohol and the preventive paradox: Serious harms and drinking patterns. *Addiction*, **102**(4), 571–578.

Popova, S., Giesbrecht, N., Bekmuradov, D., and Patra, J. (2009) Hours and days of sale and density of alcohol outlets: Impacts on alcohol consumption and damage: A systematic review. *Alcohol and Alcoholism*, **44**(5), 500–516.

Pridemore, W.A. (2004) Weekend effects on binge drinking and homicide: The social connection between alcohol and violence in Russia. *Addiction*, **99**(8), 1034–1041.

Pridemore, W.A. and Chamlin, M.B. (2006) A time series analysis of the impact of heavy drinking on homicide and and suicide mortality in Russia, 1956–2002. *Addiction*, **101**, 1719–1729.

Ragnarsdottir, T., Kjartansdottir, A., and Davidsdottir, S. (2002) Effects of extended alcohol serving-hours in Reykjavik. In R. Room (ed.), *The Effects of Nordic Alcohol Policies. What Happens to Drinking and Harm When Alcohol Controls Change?* (pp. 145–154). Helsinki: Nordic Council for Alcohol and Drug Research.

Ramstedt, M. (2011) Population drinking and homicide in Australia: A time series analysis of the period 1950–2003. *Drug and Alcohol Review*, **30**(5), 466–472.

Razvodovsky, Y.E. (2003) Association between distilled spirits consumption and violent mortality rate. *Drugs: Education, Prevention and Policy*, **10**, 235–250.

Razvodovsky, Y.E. (2007) Homicide and alcohol intoxication in Russia, 1956–2005. *Alcoholism*, **43**, 36–50.

Razvodovsky, Y.E. (2010) Beverage-specific alcohol sales and violent crime mortality in Russia. *Addicciones*, **22**, 311–315.

Rehm, J., Rehn, N., Room, R. *et al.* (2003) The global distribution of average volume of alcohol consumption and patterns of drinking. *European Addiction Research*, **9**(4), 147–156.

Roizen, J. (1997) Epidemiological issues in alcohol-related violence. In M. Galanter (ed.), *Alcohol and Violence* (pp. 7–40). New York: Plenum Press.

Room, R. (2003) Preventing alcohol problems: Popular approaches are ineffective, effective approaches are politically impossible. Paper presented at the 13th Alcohol Policy Conference.

Room, R. and Rossow, I. (2001) Share of violence attributable to drinking. *Journal of Substance Use*, **6**, 218–228.

Rose, G. (2001) Sick individuals and sick populations. *International Journal of Epidemiology*, **30**(3), 427–432.

Rossow, I. (1996) Alcohol-related violence: The impact of drinking pattern and drinking context. *Addiction*, **91**(11), 1651–1661.

Rossow, I. (2000) Suicide, violence and child abuse: Review of the impact of alcohol consumption on social problems. *Contemporary Drug Problems*, **27**, 397–433.

Rossow, I. (2001) Alcohol and homicide: A cross-cultural comparison of the relationship in 14 European countries. *Addiction*, **96**, 77–92.

Rossow, I. (2002) The strike hits. The 1982 wine and liquor monopoly strike in Norway and its impact on various harm indicators. In R. Room (ed.), *The Effects of Nordic Alcohol Policies: What Happens to Drinking and Harm When Alcohol Controls Change?* Vol. 42 (pp. 133–144). Helsinki: Nordic Council for Alcohol and Drug Research.

Rossow, I. (2004) Alcohol consumption and homicides in Canada, 1950–1999. *Contemporary Drug Problems*, **31**, 541–559.

Rossow, I. and Norström, T. (2012) The impact of small changes in bar closing hours on violence. The Norwegian experience from 18 cities. *Addiction*, **107**, 530–537.

Rossow, I., Pape, H., and Wichstrøm, L. (1999) Young, wet & wild? Associations between alcohol intoxication and violent behaviour in adolescence. *Addiction*, **94**(7), 1017–1031.

Rossow, I. and Romelsjö, A. (2006) The extent of the "prevention paradox" in alcohol problems as a function of population drinking patterns. *Addiction*, **101**, 84–90.

Shkolnikov, V.M. and Nemtsov, A. (1997) The anti-alcohol campaign and variations in Russian mortality. In J.L. Bobadilla, C.A. Costello, and F. Mitchell (eds), *Premature Death in the Nrew Independent States*. Washington, DC: National Academy Press.

Skog, O.-J. (1999) The prevention paradox revisited. *Addiction*, **94**(5), 751–757.

Skog, O.-J. and Bjørk, E. (1988) Alkohol og voldskriminalitet. En analyse av utviklingen i Norge 1931–1982 (Alcohol and violent crime. An analysis of the 1931–1982 trend in Norway). *Nordisk Tidsskrift for Kriminalvidenskab*, **88**, 1–23.

Stockwell, T. and Chikritzhs, T. (2009) Do relaxed trading hours for bars and clubs mean more relaxed drinking? A review of international research on the impacts of changes to permitted hours of drinking. *Crime Prevention and Community Safety*, **11**, 153–170.

Wagenaar, A.C., Salois, M.J., and Komro, K.A. (2009) Effects of beverage alcohol price and tax levels on drinking: A meta-analysis of 1003 estimates from 112 studies. *Addiction*, **104**(2), 179–190.

Wallin, E., Norström, T., and Andreasson, S. (2003) Alcohol prevention targeting licensed premises: A study of effects on violence. *Journal of Studies on Alcohol*, **64**(2), 270–277.

Wells, S., Giesbrecht, N., Ialomiteanu, A., and Graham, K. (2011) The association of drinking pattern with aggression involving alcohol and with verbal versus physical aggression. *Contemporary Drug Problems*, **38**(2), 259–279.

Wells, S. and Graham, K. (2003) Aggression involving alcohol: Relationship to drinking patterns and social context. *Addiction*, **98**(1), 33–42.

Wells, S., Graham, K., Speechley, M., and Koval, J. (2005) Drinking patterns, drinking contexts and alcohol-related aggression among late adolescent and young adult drinkers. *Addiction*, **100**(7), 933–944.

Chapter 2

ALCOHOL-RELATED VIOLENCE: AN INTERNATIONAL PERSPECTIVE

FERNANDA CESTARO PRADO CORTEZ

Department of Psychiatry and Ambulatory for the Treatment of Sexual Disorders (ABSex), ABC Medical School, São Paulo, Brazil

DANILO ANTONIO BALTIERI

Department of Psychiatry and Ambulatory for the Treatment of Sexual Disorders (ABSex), ABC Medical School; and Interdisciplinary Group of Studies on Alcohol and Drugs of the Psychiatric Institute of the Clinical Hospital of the University of São Paulo, São Paulo, Brazil

INTRODUCTION

Alcohol misuse and violence, in conjunction or separately, are recognized as serious health, social, and political problems worldwide (Anderson, Hughes, and Bellis, 2007; Babor *et al.*, 2003; Chermack *et al.*, 2008). Alcohol misuse is associated with about 60 types of diseases and injuries (Rehm *et al.*, 2003), some of which result from violent behavior and accidents (World Health Organization [WHO], 2009). In the Americas, 4.8% of all deaths in 2000 can be attributed to alcohol consumption (Babor and Caetano, 2005). Alcohol is one of the leading causes of death among individuals aged between 12 and 20 years, mainly due to unintentional injuries, homicide, and suicide (Hughes *et al.*, 2011; Innamorati *et al.*, 2010; Saitz and Naimi, 2010). Also, in Europe, one in five police calls for violence stems from bars or clubs frequented by young people (Blay *et al.*, 2010).

In Brazil and in other countries around the world, the penal system does not punish individuals who, at the moment of their crime, did not have the capacity to understand the unlawfulness of their actions or to behave in accordance with this understanding (*mens rea*). But voluntary or culpable drunkenness does not confer impunity, except in cases in which drunkenness is accidental, for example, caused by a *force majeure* or a fortuitous cause. Nevertheless, psychiatrists and psychologists can be called into court to give testimony and to offer opinions on

Alcohol-Related Violence: Prevention and Treatment, First Edition. Edited by Mary McMurran.
© 2013 John Wiley & Sons, Ltd. Published 2013 by John Wiley & Sons, Ltd.

the mental state of criminals who have committed crimes under the influence of alcohol. It is imperative that expert witnesses possess ample knowledge both of penal codes and the detrimental effects of alcohol abuse if they are to provide the judicial authority with valid evidence and good prognostic indicators on which the judge can make sentencing or treatment decisions. Besides knowledge of the laws and penal codes, an integrated understanding of the multiplicity of crime-related risk factors is necessary.

In this chapter, we will discuss the following issues: (1) prevalence data for alcohol-related violence in Brazil and in other parts of the world, (2) the relationship between alcohol and violence, (3) aspects of Brazilian laws regarding alcohol-related violence, and (4) treatments offered to alcohol-dependent offenders in Brazil.

EPIDEMIOLOGY

Alcohol consumption is a worldwide phenomenon and goes beyond national, cultural, social, political, and economic boundaries. The WHO estimates that each year, nearly two billion people in the world consume alcoholic beverages, which corresponds to approximately 40% of the population above 15 years (two out of five people) (WHO, 2008).

As shown in Figure 2.1, based on WHO statistics for the year 2003, the darker-colored countries, including Russia, Ukraine, Hungary, and the Republic of Moldova, presented the highest rates of alcohol consumption *per capita* by people over 15 years old (averaging over 15 L of alcohol per person per year). At the other extreme, we find countries like Afghanistan, Libya, Mauritania, and Pakistan with very low alcohol consumption (0–3 L per capita). Intermediate levels of consump-

Figure 2.1 World estimate for the consumption of pure alcohol per capita (official and unrecorded consumption) for the population over 15 years for each country, in 2003. Map from http://en.wikipedia.org/wiki/File:Alcohol_consumption_per_capita_world_map.PNG#globalusage.

Source: World Health Organization (2008).

tion are found in countries like the United States and Brazil, with a per capita consumption of 9–12 L (WHO, 2008). Nonetheless, in the Americas, the consumption of alcohol is 50% higher than the global average (WHO, 2008).

Data from a large epidemiological study in the United States show that the prevalence rates of alcohol abuse and dependence for 2001–2002 were 4.65% and 3.81%, respectively (Grant *et al.*, 2004). In total, 8.5% of the population aged between 18 and 65 can be considered to have alcohol problems, which equates to approximately 17.6 million people (Grant *et al.*, 2004). Alcohol abuse and dependence are more common among Whites, males, and younger people. Additionally, 25% of young adults between 18 and 24 years drink heavily, defined as more than five drinks per occasion at least 12 times in a year (Grant *et al.*, 2004).

Europe has been pointed out as the continent with the highest production of alcoholic beverages (Rehn, Room, and Edwards, 2001). However, there seems to be a wide variance in the number of people that show alcohol dependence; for instance, approximately 11.5% of the population in Finland shows alcohol dependence, as against 4% in Switzerland (Rehn *et al.*, 2001). In 2004, The European Study of the Epidemiology of Mental Disorders examined the 12-month and lifetime prevalence rates of alcohol disorders and other mental diseases in Belgium, France, Germany, Italy, the Netherlands, and Spain, reporting a lifetime prevalence of 5.2% for any alcohol disorder, with a higher prevalence in males (Innamorati *et al.*, 2010).

In general, the consumption of alcohol is involved in 50% of all homicide cases and in 30% of all suicide cases and suicide attempts, and is involved in the majority of fatal traffic accidents (Minayo and Deslandes, 1998). In a study that included 12,000 injured patients in 16 countries, 21% of them reported recent use of alcohol (Borges *et al.*, 2006). The research also showed that the association between alcohol and increased risk of injury is stronger in some countries (e.g., South Africa) than in others (e.g., Canada) (Borges *et al.*, 2006). In Cali, Colombia, alcohol consumption has been associated with increasing rates of homicides, mainly during weekends and holidays (Sanchéz *et al.*, 2011). In order to change this, local and federal policies have implemented rules to restrict the sales as well as the use of alcoholic beverages in public places after certain hours.

Religion

It is noteworthy that in Islamic countries, alcohol consumption is extremely low because the population respects religious rules requiring abstinence from alcohol and other intoxicants. More generally, there is an influence of religion on alcohol consumption. For example, research on a US national sample showed that conservative Protestants were less likely to consume alcohol than those with no religion, Catholics, liberal Protestants, Lutherans, and Jews (Bock, Cochran, and Beeghley, 1987). In a study carried out in Lebanon involving college students with different religious affiliations, compared with Muslims, Christians were more likely to try alcohol, start drinking at an earlier age, and later proceed to abuse alcohol or become dependent. Nonetheless, when the authors analyzed only students who had already drunk alcohol, the chance of lifetime alcohol use disorders was similar for both religious groups (Ghandour, Karam, and Maalouf, 2009). Thus, a more proscriptive religion may minimize alcohol availability and opportunities to initiate alcohol use, but, once the "barrier is crossed" or alcohol is tried, belonging to these religious groups seems not to protect against alcohol use disorders (Chen *et al.*, 2004). Belief in God and church attendance have been correlated significantly with a less tolerant attitude toward alcohol use; in a review of well-conducted studies, higher levels of religiosity have been shown to be associated with less drug and alcohol abuse and/or dependence (Moreira-Almeida, Neto, and Koenig, 2006).

Brazil

Although Brazilian alcohol consumption per capita is not as high as that of other countries, it is important to note that the annual per capita consumption of alcohol increased from 2 to 5.5 L in a 40-year period (1961–2001), reaching 8.6 L of pure alcohol, well above the world average of 6.2 L (Rehm *et al.*, 2009). A national study carried out by the Brazilian Center on Drug Abuse of the Federal University of São Paulo (CEBRID/UNIFESP) on the use of psychotropic drugs in 108 cities with populations of over 200,000 inhabitants, focused on people between 12 and 65 years old, showed that 74.6% of that sample consumed alcohol. There are an estimated 21 million people in Brazil who are dependent on alcohol (12.3% of the population) and around 19.2% of youth aged 18–24 years may be considered alcoholics (Carlini *et al.*, 2005).

In Brazil, the morbidity and mortality related to alcohol is very significant. In 2004, the percentage of disability-adjusted life years (DALYs) attributable to alcohol consumption among men (17.7%) was the second highest among 10 countries around the world, among them China (12.9%), the United States (12.1%), South Africa (7.8%), Japan (6.7%), India (4.9%), and Nigeria (2.4%), and behind only Russia (28.1%) (Rehm *et al.*, 2009). A Brazilian multicenter study on victims and perpetrators of violence at emergency units showed that the use of alcohol was involved in about 40% of all cases, mainly among patients between 20 and 39 years old (Mascarenhas *et al.*, 2009). This study reported that the majority of the patients came directly from bars (78.2%). Alcohol was involved in 25.4% (20.1% women and 32.4% men) of admissions for suicide attempts. Complementing these data, a study by Castro, Cunha, and Souza (2011) indicates a high prevalence of violence among Brazilian adolescents aged 12–19 years, especially among alcohol and/or drug users. This shows the importance of the impact of alcohol consumption on morbidity and mortality in the Brazilian population and places it as one of the most serious public health problems in Brazil (Meloni and Laranjeira, 2004; Rehm *et al.*, 2009).

ALCOHOL USE AND VIOLENCE

Studies on alcohol abuse point out the close relationship between consumption and crime (Chalub and Telles, 2006; Dawkins, 1997; Hernandez-Avila *et al.*, 2000).

The consumption of alcohol has also been associated with a greater risk of criminal recidivism (Widom and Hiller-Sturmhöfel, 2001). This is not a new phenomenon, and many eminent criminologists of the past have described the association between alcohol abuse and violent crime. For example, in 1899, Lombroso (1912, English translation) wrote that three-quarters of all crimes committed in Britain were related to alcohol consumption. In 1918, the American author George Elliott Howard wrote on this subject and affirmed that alcohol "impaired judgment, disrupted reasoning and weakened will power and, at the same time, excited the senses, inflamed passions, and liberated the most primitive urges that are contained and restricted by society" (Howard, 1918).

While substance abuse can have different roles in diverse types of crimes, violent crimes are more strongly associated with alcohol abuse than with other substances. Among diverse drinking behaviors, heavy episodic or "binge" drinking is the most strongly linked to aggression and violence (Chermack et al., 2010). The harmful consumption of alcohol beverages, especially in episodes of inebriation, represents a risk for the perpetration of acts of violence, which can result in homicides, sexual crimes, and domestic violence (Baltieri and Andrade, 2008; Pelissier, 2004; Schuckit and Russell, 1984). While aggressors and victims of violent crimes frequently report using alcohol before criminal acts, studies on the relationship between crime and alcohol consumption often fail to differentiate harmful use, dependence, and intoxication. According to Sinha and Easton (1999), one of the most common myths in the legal field is that criminals, due to the fact that they usually disregard social rules, also abuse alcohol and drugs. In medical fields, though, the predominant point of view is that most aggressors get involved in illicit activities because of their abuse of and dependence on alcohol and drugs.

While it is true that there are crimes specifically related to alcohol consumption, for example, driving under the influence of alcohol, alcohol use is not a single causal factor that can explain violent crimes. Several theorists have argued that alcohol's effects, such as disruptions in cognitive processing, play a central role in postdrinking violent behavior (see, i.e., Giancola, Chapter 3). Despite this, the association between alcohol use and violence is not as simple as one might suppose. Alcohol may be one of the direct causes of crime in that the use of this substance may lead to loss of control and cognitive impairment. However, it is also important to consider that both alcohol and violent activities may be linked through shared complicating factors, such as personality disorder or social disadvantage. For example, Moffitt et al. (2002) pointed out that the highest consumption of alcohol and marijuana occurs among adolescents of lower social economic classes. Also, a strong association has been observed between early exposure to violence in childhood and substance misuse in adulthood, indicating that experience of violence may be a cause of both substance use and perpetration of violence (Madruga et al., 2011). Although many studies show the close relationship between alcohol and criminal behavior, crime would nonetheless exist without alcohol because other forces would stimulate violent and criminal behavior. These same forces may as well stimulate or even favor alcohol misuse. In addition, criminal activities may lead to drinking, though this association may also be due to other factors.

ALCOHOL: LEGAL ASPECTS IN BRAZIL

Laws with regard to alcohol use have been observed from as early as the Babylonian Hammurabi's Code (promulgated in the years from 1825 to 1787 BC). This is one of the oldest laws of humanity, and it is interesting to note its concerns about the use of alcoholic beverages. Section 110 states that "If a nadïtum or ugbabtum preacher that lives in a convent, opens a tavern or ever enters a tavern to drink some beer, this woman will be burned." This is the only article of the 282 codes contained in Hammurabi's Code that deals with alcohol use and with a severe punishment (death by fire) for women from the upper classes of the Babylonian clergy (Bouzon, 2003). It is important to note that this punishment was not applied to men of any social class or to women of the lower classes of society.

The canonical code is used by members of the Roman Catholic Church. Since the Brazilian population is predominantly affiliated with Catholicism, we cannot disregard the influence of this religion on our conduct and official rules. Although there is no formal religious prohibition against consuming alcoholic beverages, excessive alcohol use and its negative consequences can be considered crimes. The current canonical code, promulgated by Pope John Paul II on January 25, 1983, deals with crimes committed under the influence of alcohol. The punishments imposed in this code are excommunication, expiatory punishments (dismissal from clerical office, prohibition of living in a determinant territory, and impingement of rights, office, and duty), and imprisonment (Conferência Nacional dos Bispos do Brasil [CNBB], 2001). However, there is also concern about the mental health of the offender, and the canon law tries to protect from punishment those that do not possess the means to make proper judgments and do not posses enough self-determination to avoid crime, viz., "Whenever the offender had only an imperfect use of reason, or committed the offence out of fear or necessity or in the heat of passion or with a mind disturbed by drunkenness or a similar cause, the judge can refrain from inflicting any punishment if he considers that the person's reform may be better accomplished in some other way" (Can. 1.345).

According to Article 28 of the Brazilian Penal Code, any person who became intoxicated with or without self-deliberation, and under the influence of intoxication status committed a crime, can receive a punishment (Jesus, 2002). Pedroso (2000) stated that the word "drunkenness" in legal terms means an acute state of intoxication that is transitory in the human body and is caused by ingestion of mind-altering substances (alcohol, ether, chloroform, barbiturates, or hallucinogenic drugs), which would compromise the physiological, physical, and mental functions of the individual. In Brazilian Penal Code, drunkenness is classified as

- *Accidental*: the sort of drunkenness that is caused by accident or by forces beyond the control of the drinker (fortuitous drunkenness and drunkenness by force majeure);
- *Culpable*: due to imprudence or negligence while heavily under the influence of alcohol, or ignorance of the effects of it;
- *Intentional (or* Dolose): when the person wishes to get drunk, but does not intend to commit a crime. The subject knows that, in a drunken state, he might commit a crime but assumes the risk of drinking alcoholic beverages anyway;

- *Preordained*: a state of drunkenness in which the person gets drunk on purpose, with the idea of committing a crime;
- *Habitual*: the person is an alcohol dependent;
- *Pathological*: a result of the ingestion of small amounts of alcohol that result in aggressive, violent, and disproportionate manifestations (Sznick, 2002).

According to the Brazilian law, complete inebriation is not reason enough to avoid culpability. It is necessary that the consequence of drunkenness be due to causes that were of an accidental nature and the person was entirely incapable of understanding the illegality of the acts or was unable to determine his or her own actions (absence of intellectual capacity or volition). It is not necessary, however, that both incapacities be present. In the Brazilian Penal Code, the consumption of alcohol with the goal of committing a crime under its influence adds to the punishment for a crime.

Thus, the law adopts the principle that a person is responsible for his actions from the moment he begins to drink and not just at the instant that he commits a crime under the influence of alcohol. In this case, the Brazilian Penal Code deals with drunkenness from the point of view of legal responsibility as *actio libera in causa*, which involves defendants who create the conditions of their own defense. According to this doctrine, when defendants have created the conditions that produced the lack of voluntariness, they are held liable for their actions. So, voluntary intoxication does not excuse behavior, although accidental intoxication does.

Sznick (1987) described five phases in the development of *actio libera in causa*. They are (1) free will: the subject wants to drink and does so of his own free will; (2) willful state of unconsciousness: the alcohol use was voluntary and the consequent intoxication must be enough to cause impairment of judgment; (3) conduct: the conduct of the person in any given circumstance was provoked by momentary incapacity; (4) prevision and volition of the act: the person that committed the act had the possibility to foresee its consequences at the moment he became incapable; and (5) causal nexus: it is required that, between volition and commitment of the act, there is an objective and subjective nexus that makes the person responsible for his actions.

Criminal responsibility is aggravated in law if the criminal agent drank alcohol with the intention of facilitating the commitment of a violation (Article 61, II, I of the Brazilian Penal Code – Preordained Drunkenness). The same article affirms that, if the criminal agent, by complete drunkenness, was entirely incapable of understanding the illegal act either by force majeure or fortuitous cause, the individual cannot be accused of committing a crime. As well, if the criminal agent, by drunkenness, was partially capable of understanding the illegal character of his actions or was unable to avoid them by force majeure or by fortuitous cause, he can still be accused of a crime and be convicted, but must receive a lighter sentence.

According to França (2001), drunkenness by force majeure and fortuitous drunkenness are defined as follows. *Drunkenness by force majeure* is when an individual is incapable of resisting or preventing the drunkenness. One example is when an individual is forced to drink or even coerced into drinking; another example is when an individual is in a place where he is exposed to alcoholic vapor. In cases of celebrations, such as Carnival, when many people drink, it is common for people to consume alcohol lest they be discordant with the social circumstances. Carnival in Brazil is a national celebration in which the "social" control over the use of alcohol beverages is weaker. In other words, it is presumed that all participants of this party will drink, and nondrinkers may be out of sympathy with the occasion. However, "drinking during Carnival" would not be considered a force majeure because free will is not affected. The Brazilian law, which follows the doctrine of *actio libera in causa*, considers the free action as being that at the time that the aggressor puts himself in a drunken state, not his condition when the aggression occurs. If a person puts himself in a drunken state intentionally or negligently and, as a result, committed a crime, he shall be punished for that crime. By contrast, *fortuitous drunkenness* is a rare occasional state of inebriation that originates from a comprehensible error and not from a predetermined or imprudent action. For example, a person takes a drink without knowing its alcohol content, or an individual takes medicine without knowing that it contains alcohol. According to Bittencourt and Conde (2000), in drunkenness by force majeure, the facts can be foreseen but not avoided, whereas in fortuitous drunkenness, the facts could be avoided but never foreseen.

Formal classification systems distinguish alcohol abuse and alcohol dependence (American Psychiatric Association, 2000). Alcohol abuse is associated with health and social problems but not with tolerance or withdrawal. Dependent drinkers, by contrast, show loss of control over their drinking. Many authors believe that continual drunkenness, as in the case of alcohol dependence, does not exclude or diminish responsibility. However, an alcoholic or a dependent individual should arguably merit a different penal treatment. In some jurisdictions of the United States, an insanity defense may be possible if chronic alcohol use has caused irreversible brain damage, resulting in mental illness or cognitive impairment (Rosner, 2003).

The Brazilian Penal Code advises that is necessary to perform a detailed physical and psychiatric examination of the accused to determine his capacity to discern right from wrong at the time when the crime was committed. This suggests that heavy users do not know right from wrong at the moment they commit a crime, while lighter users do, and, therefore, are held responsible for their actions. The law gives more importance to the degree of intoxication and less to the effects of intoxication on the consciousness and free will of the person at the time the crime was committed (Führer, 2000).

Penal Law Article 45 specifies that "The accused, in case of dependency or under the effects of drugs by accident or force majeure at the time of action or omission, whatever the criminal violation committed, who was proven to be entirely incapable of understanding the illicit character of its acts or omissions or was unable by free will to act in accordance, is exempt from punishment." The sentence may be reduced by as much as one-third to two-thirds if, by force of circumstances foreseen in Article 45 of this law, the accused did not possess at the time of his actions or omissions the full capacity to discern right from wrong or was unable to act in accordance with his own free will (Perias, 2002). Additionally, the law states that "When the accused is absolved of guilt or responsibility at the time of the fact, through clinical expert examination, following the conditions set forth in this article, the judge may determine, in the sentencing, his referral to appropriate medical treatment" (Article 45, only paragraph).

Article 26 states that "Any accused that **is mentally ill, or has incomplete or delayed mental development** at the time of action or omission, whatever the criminal violation committed and was proven to be **entirely incapable** of understanding the illicit character of its actions or omissions or is unable by free will to act in accordance, is exempt from punishment" (Article 26 of Brazilian Penal Code). Our bold type has the function of emphasizing the existence of the legal term "mentally ill." According to Jesus (2002), and according to Brazilian jurisprudence, only those recognized as mentally ill by psychiatrists are exempt from punishment. Of course, alcohol (and drug) dependence is also an illness, with features well established for its diagnosis, a fact that some legislators seem to be unaware of.

The current Penal Code directs the treatment of alcohol and drug dependents so that they can be rehabilitated and can return to society. Once the accused is considered "not responsible" by the conjunction of dependency and full incapacity of understanding and exertion of will (Article 45 of Law n. 11.343/2006 and Article 26 of the Brazilian Penal Code), the judge may determine that the accused be directed to medical treatment since a sentence is inappropriate. Compulsory treatment can occur in a hospital or in outpatient settings. The duration of treatment should be adequate for the offender's recovery. If the duration is not stipulated prior to sentencing, it is reasonable to fix a time frame of 1 year before the first evaluation. This is in accordance with the duration fixed in the Brazilian Penal Code in similar situations (Führer, 2000).

TREATMENT

Treatment for inmates who are dependent on alcohol can be done in prison while they serve their sentence (Taylor, 1995). Swartz and Lurigio (1999) have suggested that there are advantages to treating dependency in prisons, namely, that detention leads to good treatment attendance and that treatment costs are lower in prison than in rehabilitation clinics. However, treatment within the prison system has its drawbacks, particularly the nontherapeutic context, overpopulation, violence, drug trafficking, and the lack of qualified professionals to treat these inmates in prisons. Psychosocial treatments that prisoners receive while in prison can also be limited in that lack of social assistance in the realms of family, social, and work relationships can undermine their full recovery. Therapeutic interventions outside the prison, in the form of alternatives to custody and conditional sentencing, where the prisoner is allowed to serve his sentence in open conditions, may be preferable. These models should have a higher success rate because of the opportunities to reinforce the positive conduct of the prisoner in open society (Gomes and De Molina, 2000).

Despite all the limitations, prisons are nevertheless important centers for alcohol rehabilitation, and proper treatment of alcohol dependency in prison could contribute to avoiding criminal recidivism. Even so, Brazil does not provide appropriate treatment for inmates who suffer from alcohol disorders. There are few doctors available in our penitentiary system, and only a few psychiatrists and specialists. Psychological and social support is still scarce and there is no incentive for inmates to accept treatment. For those admitted to penitentiary hospitals, treatment is available; however, it is rarely carried out by professionals who specialize in the treatment of alcohol dependence. To make matters worse, the measures designed to prevent the entry of alcohol and drugs into Brazilian penitentiary units are still insufficient, with a high frequency of use of illegal substances by prisoners.

On leaving the prison system, ex-prisoners can avail themselves of specialized health care offered free by the state. The Ministry of Health of Brazil supports voluntary treatment for users of alcohol and/or drug, with outpatient treatment provided at specialized centers, where there is psychiatric, psychological, and social support for alcohol and/or drug users and their families. Admissions to psychiatric wards within general hospitals are possible, when necessary. In addition, there are self-help groups, such as Alcoholics Anonymous (AA) and Narcotics Anonymous (NA). These treatment centers are mainly located in large cities, so there is a lack of availability across the country as a whole, which hampers access to treatment for many people and hinders an ideal treatment of alcohol use and of its clinical and social comorbidities.

CONCLUSION

The overconsumption of alcohol and other psychoactive substances represents an important medical and social problem throughout the world. The legal and social repercussions of this consumption have been researched with the highest scientific rigor in the past decades, and this has produced a better comprehension of the relationship between alcohol and crime. In view of the high frequency of alcohol and drug abuse and consequent violence that assails Brazil and other countries around the world, knowledge of laws about, risk factors for, and responses to the consumption of alcohol and drugs and their connection with criminal activity becomes more and more necessary in the world scenario. Science can make a valuable contribution to the improvement of laws, policies, and treatment of drinking, drug use, and violence by clarifying the risk factors and evaluating legal and therapeutic responses.

REFERENCES

American Psychiatric Association (2000) *Diagnostic and Statistical Manual of Mental Disorders, Fourth Edition, Text Revision*. Washington, DC: American Psychiatric Association.

Anderson, Z., Hughes, K., and Bellis, M.A. (2007) *Exploration of Young People's Experience and Perceptions of Violence in Liverpool's Nightlife*. Liverpool: Liverpool John Moores University.

Babor, T.F. and Caetano, R. (2005) Evidence-based alcohol policy in the Americas: Strengths, weaknesses, and future challenges. *Revista Panamericana de Salud Publica*, **18**(4–5), 327–337.

Babor, T.F., Caetano, R., Casswell, S. *et al.* (2003) *Alcohol: No Ordinary Commodity.* Oxford: Oxford University Press.

Baltieri, D.A. and Andrade, A.G. (2008) Alcohol and drug consumption among sexual offenders. *Forensic Science International,* **175**(1), 31–35.

Barrett, E.L., Mills, K.L., and Teesson, M. (2011) Hurt people who hurt people: Violence amongst individuals with comorbid substance use disorder and post traumatic stress disorder. *Addictive Behaviors,* **36**(7), 721–728.

Bittencourt, C.R. and Conde, F.M. (2000) *Teoria geral do delito.* São Paulo: Saraiva.

Blay, N., Calaf, A., Juan, M. *et al.* (2010) Violencia en contextos recreativos nocturnos: su relación con el consumo de alcohol y drogas entre jóvenes españoles. *Psicothema,* **22**(3), 396–402.

Bock, E.W., Cochran, J.C., and Beeghley, L. (1987) Moral messages: The relative influence of denomination on the religiosity–alcohol relationship. *The Sociological Quarterly,* **28**, 86–105.

Borges, G., Cherpitel, C.J., Orozco, R. *et al.* (2006) Acute alcohol use and the risk of non-fatal injury in sixteen countries. *Addiction,* **101**, 993–1002.

Bouzon, E. (2003) *O código de hammurabi.* Petrópolis: Vozes.

Carlini, E.A., Galduroz, J.C.F., Silva, A.A.B. *et al.* (2005) *II Levantamento domiciliar sobre o uso de drogas psicotrópicas no Brasil: estudo envolvendo as 108 maiores cidades do país.* São Paulo: CEBRID/UNIFESP.

Castro, M.L., Cunha, S.S., and Souza, D.P.O. (2011) Violence behavior and factors associated among students of Central-West Brazil. *Revista de Saúde Pública,* **45**(6), 1054–1061.

Chalub, M. and Telles, L.E.B. (2006) Alcohol, drugs and crime. *Revista Brasileira de Psiquiatria,* **28**(SII), S69–S73.

Chen, C.Y., Dormitzer, C.M., Bejarano, J., and Anthony, J.C. (2004) Religiosity and the earliest stages of adolescent drug involvement in seven countries of Latin America. *American Journal of Epidemiology,* **159**, 1180–1188.

Chermack, S.T., Grogan-Kaylorc, A., Perron, B.E. *et al.* (2010) Violence among men and women in substance use disorder treatment: A multi-level event-based analysis. *Drug and Alcohol Dependence,* **112**, 194–200.

Chermack, S.T., Murray, R.L., Walton, M.A. *et al.* (2008) Partner aggression among men and women in substance use disorder treatment: Correlates of psychological and physical aggression and injury. *Drug and Alcohol Dependence,* **98**, 35–44.

Conferência Nacional dos Bispos do Brasil (CNBB) (2001) *Código de direito canônico.* São Paulo: Loyola.

Cruz, J.M. (1999) La victimización por violencia urbana: niveles y factores asociados en ciudades de América Latina y España. *Revista Panamericana de Salud Publica,* **5**(4–5), 259–267.

Dawkins, M.P. (1997) Drug use and violent crime among adolescents. *Adolescence,* **32**(126), 395–405.

Duailibi, S., Ponicki, W., Grube, J. *et al.* (2007) The effect of restricting opening hours on alcohol-related violence. *American Journal of Public Health,* **97**(12), 2276–2280.

Fagan, J. (1993) Interactions among drugs, alcohol and violence. *Health Affairs,* **12**(4), 65–79.

França, G. (2001) *Medicina Legal.* Rio de Janeiro: Guanabara Koogan.

Führer, M.R.E. (2000) *Tratado da inimputabilidade no direito penal.* São Paulo: Malheiros.

Ghandour, L.A., Karam, E.G., and Maalouf, W.E. (2009) Lifetime alcohol use, abuse and dependence among university students in Lebanon: Exploring the role of religiosity in different religious faiths. *Addiction,* **104**, 940–948.

Giancola, P.R. (2002) Alcohol-related aggression in men and women: The influence of dispositional aggressivity. *Journal of Studies on Alcohol,* **63**, 696–708.

Goldstein, P.J. (1985) The drugs/violence nexus: A tripartite conceptual framework. *Journal of Drug Issues,* **15**, 493–506.

Goldstein, P.J. (1998) Drugs, violence, and federal funding: A research odyssey. *Substance Use and Misuse,* **35**(9), 1915–1936.

Gomes, L.F. and De Molina, A.G.P. (2000) *Criminologia*. São Paulo: Editora Revista dos Tribunais.

Grant, B.G., Dawson, D.A., Stinson, F.S. *et al.* (2004) The 12-month prevalence and trends in DSM-IV alcohol abuse and dependence United States, 1991–1992 and 2001–2002. *Drug and Alcohol Dependence*, **74**(3), 223–234.

Hernandez-Avila, C.A., Burleson, J.A., Poling, J. *et al.* (2000) Personality and substance use disorders as predictors of criminality. *Comprehensive Psychiatry*, **41**(4), 276–283.

Howard, G.E. (1918) Alcohol and crime: A study in social causation. *American Journal of Sociology*, **24**, 61–80.

Hughes, K., Bellis, M.A., Calafat, A. *et al.* (2011) Substance use, violence, and unintentional injury in young holidaymakers visiting Mediterranean destinations. *Journal of Travel Medicine*, **18**(2), 80–89.

Innamorati, M., Lester, D., Amore, M. *et al.* (2010) Alcohol consumption predicts the EU suicide rates in young women aged 15–29 years but not in men: Analysis of trends and differences among early and new EU countries since 2004. *Alcohol*, **44**(5), 463–469.

Jesus, D.E. (2002) *Código penal anotado*. São Paulo: Saraiva.

Lombroso, C. (1912) *Crime: Its Causes and Remedies*. Montclair, NJ: Patterson Smith.

Madruga, C.S., Laranjeira, R., Caetano, R. *et al.* (2011) Early life exposure to violence and substance misuse in adulthood – The first Brazilian national survey. *Addictive Behaviors*, **36**, 251–255.

Mascarenhas, M.D.M., Malta, D.C., Silva, M.M.A. *et al.* (2009) Alcohol-related injuries in emergency departments in Brazil, 2006–2007. *Ciência & Saúde Coletiva*, **14**(5), 1789–1796.

Mason, W.A., Hitch, J.E., Kosterman, R. *et al.* (2010) Growth in adolescent delinquency and alcohol use in relation to young adult crime, alcohol use disorders, and risky sex: A comparison of youth from low- versus middle-income backgrounds. *Journal of Child Psychology and Psychiatry*, **51**(12), 1377–1385.

Meloni, J.N. and Laranjeira, R. (2004) The social and health burden of alcohol abuse. *Revista Brasileira de Psiquiatria*, **26**(S1), S7–10.

Minayo, M.C.S. and Deslandes, S.F. (1998) A complexidade das relações entre drogas, álcool e violência. *Cadernos de Saúde Pública*, **14**(1), 35–42.

Moffitt, T.E., Caspi, A., Harrington, H., and Milne, B.J. (2002) Males on the life-course-persistent and adolescence-limited antisocial pathways: Follow-up at age 26 years. *Development and Psychopathology*, **14**, 179–207.

Moreira-Almeida, A., Neto, F.L., and Koenig, H.G. (2006) Religiousness and mental health: A review. *Revista Brasileira de Psiquiatria*, **28**, 242–250.

Pedroso, F.A. (2000) *Direito Penal*. São Paulo: Livraria e Editora Universitária de Direito (Leud).

Pelissier, B. (2004) Gender differences in substance use treatment entry and retention among prisoners with substance use histories. *American Journal of Public Health*, **94**(8), 1418–1424.

Perias, G.R. (2002) *Leis antitóxicos comentadas. Leis ns.10.409/02 e 6.368/76. Doutrina, legislação, jurisprudência e prática. Portaria n. 344 do Ministério da Saúde*. Santa Cruz da Conceição: Vale do Mogi.

Poldrugo, F. (1998) Alcohol and criminal behaviour. *Alcohol and Alcoholism*, **33**(1), 12–15.

Rehm, J., Mathers, C., Popova, S. *et al.* (2009) Global burden of disease and injury and economic cost attributable to alcohol use and alcohol-use disorders. *Lancet*, **373**(9682), 2223–2233.

Rehm, J., Rehn, N., Room, R. *et al.* (2003) The global distribution of average volume of alcohol consumption and patterns of drinking. *European Addiction Research*, **9**(4), 147–156.

Rehn, N., Room, R., and Edwards, G. (2001) *Alcohol in the European Region: Consumption, Harm and Policies*. Copenhagen: Eurocare – World Health Organization Regional Office for Europe.

Reichenheim, M.E., Souza, E.R., Moraes, C.L. *et al.* (2011) Violence and injuries in Brazil: The effect, progress made, and challenges ahead. *Lancet*, **377**, 1962–1975.

Resko, S.M., Walton, M.A., Bingham, C.R. *et al.* (2010) Alcohol availability and violence among inner-city adolescents: A multi-level analysis of the role of alcohol outlet density. *American Journal of Community Psychology*, **46**, 253–262.

Rosner, R. (2003) *Principles and Practice of Forensic Psychiatry* (2nd edn). New York: Hodder Arnold.

Saitz, R. and Naimi, T.S. (2010) Adolescent alcohol use and violence: Are brief interventions the answer? *Journal of the American Medical Association*, **304**(5), 575–577.

Sanchéz, A.I., Villaveces, A., Krafty, R. *et al.* (2011) Policies for alcohol restriction and their association with interpersonal violence: A time-series analysis of homicides in Cali, Colombia. *International Journal of Epidemiology*, **40**(4), 1037–1046.

Schuckit, M.A. and Russell, J.W. (1984) An evaluation of primary alcoholics with histories of violence. *Journal of Clinical Psychiatry*, **45**(1), 3–6.

Scott, K.D., Schafer, J., and Greenfield, T.K. (1999) The role of alcohol in physical assault perpetration and victimization. *Journal of Studies on Alcohol*, **60**(1), 528–536.

Shaw, J., Hunt, I.M., Flynn, S. *et al.* (2006) The role of alcohol and drugs in homicides in England and Wales. *Addiction*, **101**(8), 1071–1072.

Sinha, R. and Easton, C. (1999) Substance abuse and criminality. *Journal of American Academy of Psychiatry and the Law*, **27**(4), 513–526.

Swartz, J.A. and Lurigio, A.J. (1999) Final thoughts on IMPACT: A federally funded, jail-based, drug-user-treatment program. *Substance Use and Misuse*, **34**(6), 887–906.

Sznick, V.A. (1987) *Responsabilidade penal na embriaguez*. São Paulo: Livraria e Editora Universitária de Direito (Leud).

Sznick, V.A. (2002) *Manual de direito penal*. São Paulo: Livraria e Editora Universitária de Direito (Leud).

Taylor, P.J. (1995) Addictions and dependencies: Their association with offending. In J. Gunn and P.J. Taylor (eds), *Forensic Psychiatry: Clinical, Legal and Ethical Issues* (pp. 435–489). London: Butterworth-Heinemann.

Widom, C.S. and Hiller-Sturmhöfel, S. (2001) Alcohol abuse as risk for and consequence of child abuse. *Alcohol Research and Health*, **25**(1), 52–57.

Wiesner, M., Kim, H.K., and Capaldi, D.M. (2005) Developmental trajectories of offending: Validation and prediction to young adult alcohol use, drug use and depressive symptoms. *Development and Psychopathology*, **17**(1), 251–270.

World Health Organization (WHO) (2008) *The Global Burden of Disease: 2004 Update*. Geneva: World Health Organization.

World Health Organization (WHO) (2009) *Global Health Risks: Mortality and Burden of Disease Attributable to Select Major Risks*. Geneva: World Health Organization.

PART II

UNDERSTANDING THE PROBLEM

Chapter 3

ALCOHOL AND AGGRESSION: THEORIES AND MECHANISMS

PETER R. GIANCOLA

Department of Psychology, University of Kentucky, Lexington, Kentucky, USA

For a substance that persists in being so easy to obtain and so heavily marketed, it is nothing short of a worldwide tragedy that alcohol intoxication is involved in a disproportionate number of violent interpersonal acts. The National Crime Victimization Survey reported that alcohol was present, during the time of the transgression, in 63% of intimate partner violence incidents, 39–45% of murders, 32–40% of sexual assaults, and 45–46% of physical assaults in the United States (Greenfeld and Henneberg, 2001). A review of 26 studies carried out in 11 countries corroborated these data by demonstrating that 63% of violent criminals committed their offenses while under the influence of alcohol (Murdoch, Pihl, and Ross, 1990). Moreover, the economic costs associated with alcohol-related crime have been estimated to exceed $205 billion in the United States alone, with 85% of these costs attributable to violent crime and with alcohol being responsible for more than double the costs of all other drugs combined (Miller *et al.*, 2006).

The central purpose of this chapter is to focus on the etiology, or underlying mechanisms, of alcohol-related violence. Hence, its main thrust is to review past theories of alcohol-related violence and to put forth a revised version (i.e., Giancola *et al.*, 2010) of an influential existing theory, the *alcohol myopia model* (*AMM*; Steele and Josephs, 1990). We do not claim the other theories reviewed are incorrect; in fact, much of what is in the AMM overlaps with some of the premises of these other theories; and in other cases, the theories complement one another very well so as to advance the literature on the topic.

Although the association between alcohol intoxication and behavioral disinhibition seems obvious, so, too, is the fact that alcohol does not cause inappropriate decontrolled behavior in all persons. We are all aware of alcohol's *Jekyll and Hyde* effect, in which people who are typically well-tempered when sober sometimes transform into violent barbarians when intoxicated. Alternatively, we are also

Alcohol-Related Violence: Prevention and Treatment, First Edition. Edited by Mary McMurran.
© 2013 John Wiley & Sons, Ltd. Published 2013 by John Wiley & Sons, Ltd.

aware of people who simply become more talkative, friendly, and flirtatious when equally intoxicated. These conflicting popular accounts help explain why meta-analytic studies have found only a medium effect size (d = .47–.61) for the alcohol–aggression relation (Bushman, 1993; Bushman and Cooper, 1990; Ito, Miller, and Pollock, 1996); that is, by not taking into account key moderating factors, this effect size conceals alcohol's true effect on aggressive behavior.

Accordingly, given the range of reactions people experience when intoxicated, it has been hypothesized that alcohol only facilitates aggression for those who are already at risk for such behavior (Collins, 1988; Fishbein, 2003). Specifically, individual difference variables that have been shown to heighten the risk for alcohol-related aggression include dispositional aggressivity (Smucker-Barnwell, Borders, and Earleywine, 2006), irritability (Giancola, 2002), trait anger (Parrott and Zeichner, 2002), hostile rumination (Borders and Giancola, 2011; Borders, Smucker-Barnwell, and Earleywine, 2007), hostility, permissive beliefs about aggression (Leonard and Senchak, 1993), deviant attitudes (Zhang, Wieczorek, and Welte, 1997), sensation seeking (Cheong and Nagoshi, 1999), a desired image of power (Quigley, Corbett, and Tedeschi, 2002), as well as low levels of anger control (Parrott and Giancola, 2004), self-awareness (Bailey *et al.*, 1983), socialization, self-control (Boyatzis, 1975), dispositional empathy (Giancola, 2003), intelligence (Welte and Wieczorek, 1999), and executive cognitive functioning (Giancola, 2004a). Moreover, alcohol has been found to potentiate aggression for persons who have a difficult temperament (Giancola, 2004b), hold beliefs that alcohol causes aggression (Dermen and George, 1989; Smucker-Barnwell *et al.*, 2006), as well as those experiencing high marital conflict (Quigley and Leonard, 1999) and dissatisfaction (Leonard and Senchak, 1993).

Identifying *who* is most at risk for alcohol-related violence is clearly important. However, equally important is understanding *why* alcohol intoxication leads to violence in these at-risk persons. Unfortunately, prevention efforts aimed against intoxicated aggression are hindered by a lack of understanding of these two pieces of the puzzle: who and why. This chapter is significant because it proposes to examine and discuss these key questions.

THEORIES OF ALCOHOL-RELATED AGGRESSION

Prior to reviewing some specific models of alcohol-related aggression, it will be useful to briefly cover some more general theories. The *disinhibition* model is considered to be a very general explanation of the alcohol–aggression relationship. It contends that alcohol has a direct effect on aggression by pharmacologically disinhibiting brain centers important in maintaining inhibitory control over behavior (Collins, 1988; Graham, 1980). This model has limited empirical support because not all persons become aggressive when they drink.

In direct opposition is the *expectancy* model, which stipulates that it is not the pharmacological properties of alcohol that facilitate aggression but, instead, the mere belief that one has consumed alcohol (reviewed in Quigley and Leonard, 2006). This line of thinking rests on the assumption that people have a priori beliefs that alcohol will lead to aggression. However, a wealth of research shows that the belief that one has consumed alcohol has a negligible effect on persons receiving a placebo beverage versus those who knowingly drank a nonalcoholic beverage. Six meta-analytic investigations which reviewed a large body of evidence found that, whereas alcohol groups display significantly greater levels of aggression compared with placebo and sober control groups, placebo and sober controls do not tend to differ significantly from one another (Bushman, 1993, 1997; Bushman and Cooper, 1990; Hull and Bond, 1986; Ito *et al.*, 1996; Steele and Southwick, 1985). These data suggest that the pharmacological effects of alcohol, especially at higher doses, are more important than the effects of believing that alcohol has been consumed (see Duke *et al.*, 2011).

These data are typically used to fuel the argument that alcohol expectancies do not affect aggression. However, this is an erroneous argument because placebo manipulations do not take into account individual differences in beliefs that alcohol will increase aggression; that is, it may be that placebo manipulations are indeed effective in increasing aggression but only in persons who believe that alcohol will increase aggression. The few studies that have been conducted that have taken into account individual differences in alcohol expectancies for aggression have shown modest to good support that expectancies interact with acute alcohol intoxication to increase aggression (i.e., Chermack and Taylor, 1995; Dermen and George, 1989; Leonard and Senchak, 1993). However, only two studies have recently tested, and positively demonstrated, that one's aggressive dispositional character is more influential, or important, compared with one's alcohol expectancies about aggression. Both studies showed that, regardless of one's beliefs about alcohol's effects on aggression, the consumption of the drug along with a higher blood alcohol concentration is paramount in increasing aggression (Giancola, 2006; Giancola, Godlaski, and Parrott, 2005).

Finally, the *indirect-cause* model is a more refined version of the disinhibition model (Graham, 1980). It contends that alcohol detrimentally affects certain psychological and/or physiological processes that can then lead to the expression of aggression. Some of the most prominent contemporary theories of alcohol-related aggression rest upon the indirect-cause model. Specifically, most of them are cognitive models, which suggest that alcohol disrupts a specific type of mentation that then increases the probability of aggression. Presented below, in chronological order of publication, is a review of five important cognitive models of intoxicated aggression.

Cognitive Models of Alcohol-Related Aggression

Pernanen (1976) hypothesized that alcohol consumption increases the probability of aggression reaction by reducing the number of available psychological coping mechanisms that rely on conceptual or abstract reasoning. According to this model, alcohol creates a "narrowing of the perceptual field" (p. 415), which reduces the ability to detect both internal and external cues that may provide crucial information about another person's intentions in a precarious situation. Consequently, a reduction in the perception of these cues will result in a random or an arbitrary interpretation of the other person's intentions. Accordingly, when intoxicated, it is this tendency to interpret incoming information as random or arbitrary (especially if the incoming information is aggressive in nature) that will increase the probability of a violent response. In addition, Pernanen also stated that, due to alcohol's effect of reducing available psychological coping mechanisms, the responses that will be most readily elicited in a precarious situation will be those that are extreme, unstable, and "determined by the immediate situation" (p. 413). Although not explicitly stated by Pernanen, when faced with a potentially violent situation, the "immediate situation" will typically emit cues that are highly provocative and instigatory in nature. Focusing on such cues typically has the effect of increasing the likelihood of an aggressive response. No empirical studies have been conducted to directly test Pernanen's model. The main strength of his model is that it implicates an easily testable cognitive mechanism (i.e., conceptual and abstract reasoning).

Taylor and Leonard (1983) postulated that aggressive behavior is determined by the relative balance of a combination of both instigative (e.g., threats and insults) and inhibitory (e.g., anxiety and norms of reciprocity) cues present in hostile interpersonal situations. Instigative cues increase the probability of an aggressive encounter, whereas inhibitory cues decrease such a probability. These theorists reasoned that the cognitive disruption produced by alcohol reduces the number of information sources (i.e., cues) one can attend to in any given situation. Contrary to Pernanen (1976), who suggested that intoxicated persons respond to situational information in a random or arbitrary fashion, Taylor and Leonard argued that such responses can be accurately predicted. They conjectured that, due to the fact that alcohol reduces the amount of information or cues that can be attended to, the inebriate will respond only to the most salient or dominant cues in a situation. Therefore, violence is most likely to occur in a context where instigatory cues are paramount, as opposed to a situation dominated by inhibitory cues. Nevertheless, Pernanen's model does share a commonality with Taylor and Leonard's model in its suggestion that the responses that will be most readily available in a precarious situation are those that are determined by the immediate context.

Steele and Josephs (1990) proposed an attention-allocation model (AAM) in which alcohol interferes with information processing in such a manner as to disrupt the ability to effectively allocate attention to multiple aspects of a situation. Accordingly, alcohol creates a "myopic" or narrowing effect on attention that results in attention being allocated to only the most salient aspects of a particular situation and not to other less salient cues. Alcohol will therefore decrease the ability to extricate important meaning from less salient, possibly inhibitory, cues. It is thus maintained that in a conflict or in a provocative situation, alcohol's myopic effect on attention may facilitate aggression by forcing attention onto the most salient (i.e., provocative) aspects of that situation and not to other less salient (i.e., inhibitory) cues.

As can be seen quite clearly, Taylor and Leonard's (1983) and Steele and Josephs's (1990) models are very similar (i.e., both maintain that alcohol impairs the ability to attend to inhibitory cues). The main difference between the two models is that Steele and Josephs explicitly posited the hypothetical mechanism of *inhibition conflict* as a determinant of when alcohol will, and will not, facilitate aggression. Inhibition conflict refers to the magnitude of conflict between two opposing response tendencies (Steele and Southwick, 1985). According to Steele and colleagues, a considerable degree of inhibition conflict must be present if alcohol is to facilitate aggression. Their model predicts that an intoxicated person is likely to attack another person in the presence of both inhibitory and instigatory cues because attention will be focused on the most salient cues (i.e., provocative and instigatory). However, in the absence of any inhibitory cues, the model predicts that the effects of alcohol will be irrelevant; that is, without inhibitory cues, an attacker will be just as likely to emit an aggressive response in either an intoxicated or sober state due to the lack of any proscriptions against aggression. Of course, that is a purely theoretical statement made in order to create a clean and tight model. However, we are all aware that alcohol intoxication does indeed increase aggression when all other variables are held constant (Bushman and Cooper, 1990). However, the main point that is trying to be made here is that when there are no internal or external proscriptions against aggression, one is much more likely to emit a violent response than if inhibitory cues are present, but the presence of alcohol will always increase the chances of such behavior. Similarly, from a purely theoretical stance, if no provocative cues are present, a person should not react aggressively whether drunk or sober. However, again, the mere presence of alcohol will increase the probability of aggression. Parenthetically, the mechanism of inhibition conflict is implicit in Taylor and Leonard's model.

Pihl, Peterson, and Lau (1993) posited a biosocial model of intoxicated aggression in which cognitive functioning is but a single aspect of a multidimensional mechanism. According to these theorists, acute alcohol consumption disrupts the functioning of the prefrontal cortex (the primary neural substrate believed to subserve executive cognitive functioning, i.e., the ability to cognitively self-regulate goal-directed behavior) and its subcortical connections, especially the hippocampus, which, according to Pihl et al., "is involved in the recognition of threat" (p. 134). Thus, by disrupting these neural regions and circuits, alcohol eliminates signals of punishment through its anxiolytic effects (i.e., reduces fear reactions), thus resulting in decreased inhibitory control over behavior. Pihl et al. also posited that aggressive responses are enhanced through alcohol's psychomotor stimulant properties and an increased sensitivity to cues of physical pain.

No empirical studies have been conducted to test this model in its entirety. However, two studies have assessed the relation between executive cognitive functioning, alcohol consumption, and aggression (Giancola, 2004a; Lau, Pihl, and Peterson, 1995). In the Lau et al. study, both alcohol administration and low cognitive capacity had independent effects on aggression; however, an interaction between cognitive capacity and alcohol consumption was not observed. Conclusions from this study should be taken with caution because only two neuropsychological tests were used to index prefrontal integrity, thus not capturing the entire executive functioning spectrum (in fact, only tests of working memory were administered), and, as the authors themselves noted, statistical power was also likely too low to detect a significant interaction between cognitive functioning and alcohol consumption. However, the Giancola study utilized an appropriate number of participants ($n = 310$) and a very comprehensive neuropsychological battery. Confirmatory factor analysis revealed that a one-factor solution best fits the data. Thus, unlike Lau *et al.*, Giancola's results indicated that alcohol was significantly more likely to increase aggression in persons with low executive function compared with intoxicated persons with higher executive functioning.

In 2010, Giancola and colleagues revised, and significantly expanded, the attention-allocation model and renamed it the AMM. Much like its predecessor, the AMM postulates that intoxication impairs controlled effortful cognitive processing dependent on intact attentional capacity. This impairment creates a myopic effect on attention that restricts the range of internal and external cues that can be perceived and processed. As a result, remaining attentional resources are allocated to the most salient and easy-to-process cues. In hostile situations, alcohol facilitates aggression by narrowing attention on provocative cues because, given their alarming/threatening nature, they are generally more salient than nonprovocative or inhibitory cues (i.e., the consequences of retaliation). As a result of this alcohol myopia, the impact of the nonprovocative or inhibitory cues is not fully processed, or possibly not even perceived, thus increasing the probability of a violent reaction.

The AMM has been tested on many alcohol-related behaviors and many of these investigations have focused on threat and/or the distraction of threat. One way in which to do this is by examining how the model affects stress and anxiety. For example, after an anxiety induction, alcohol decreased anxiety (*even below levels exhibited by sober subjects*) in persons who were distracted from stressful thoughts by performing a cognitive task (i.e., rating art slides). In persons who were not distracted, alcohol actually *increased* anxiety (Josephs and Steele, 1990; Steele and Josephs, 1988). Similarly, alcohol decreased intentions to engage in risky sex (*again, even below levels seen in sober subjects*) in the presence of salient sexually inhibitory cues; however, it increased such intentions in the presence of sexually permissive cues (MacDonald *et al.*, 2000a,b).

Additionally, via the effects of distraction, the AMM has been used to explain disinhibited eating (Mann and Ward, 2004; Ward and Mann, 2000), smoking (Westling, Mann, and Ward, 2006), drinking and driving (MacDonald, Zanna, and Fong, 1995), and the anxiolytic effects of cigarette smoking (Kassel and Shiffman, 1997; Kassel and Unrod, 2000). Although the AMM is not specific to explaining aggression, theorists have nonetheless repeatedly invoked the model to explain intoxicated aggression (Abbey, 2002; Chermack and Taylor, 1995; George and Norris, 1991; Leonard, 2002; Murphy *et al.*, 2005; Sayette, 1999; Testa, Livingston, and Collins, 2000). However, the model has not been used to programmatically test the alcohol–aggression relation other than in four recent studies from the same laboratory (Giancola and Corman, 2007 – two studies; Giancola, Duke, and Ritz, 2011; Phillips and Giancola, 2008). However, it is noteworthy that two alcohol studies, not designed to formally test the AMM, provide incidental support for how the model pertains to aggression (Leonard, 1989; Zeichner *et al.*, 1982). All of these studies are described fully in the next section.

In accordance with this previous work, the AMM has been hypothesized to *decrease* aggression when attention is distracted away from provocative cues.

Specifically, in a hostile situation, where nonprovocative/inhibitory cues are most salient, the alcohol myopia effect will focus the inebriate's reduced attentional capacity toward those nonaggressive cues, thus leaving limited processing space in working memory to allocate toward less "attention-grabbing" provocative cues that will then lower the probability of an aggressive reaction. As such, the AMM makes the *counterintuitive* prediction that by distracting the inebriate away from provocative cues, alcohol can paradoxically decrease aggression, *even below levels seen in sober individuals*. Because attention is unimpaired in sober persons, they can simultaneously allocate their cognitive resources to both provocative and nonprovocative cues, therefore leading to "moderate" levels of aggression. As intoxicated persons have fewer attentional resources than their sober equivalents, when those resources are distracted away from provocative cues, the result will be *less* aggression than that seen in their sober counterparts.

In summary, alcohol intoxication can exacerbate negative behaviors or, ironically, it can improve prudent ones as well. So, until now, the "take-home" message of this chapter and the AMM is simply that alcohol will direct behavior in accordance with the most salient immediate cues in one's environment whether they are aggressive (Steele and Southwick, 1985) or altruistic in nature (Steele, Critchlow, and Liu, 1985). In other words, when the horse is intoxicated, what it sees (i.e., environmental cues), and it already knows from experience (i.e., internal cues), will cause the cart to easily follow (i.e., behavior).

THE AMM AND AGGRESSION

Alcohol and Aggression

As noted above, although many researchers have invoked the AMM, in one form or another, to explain alcohol-related aggression (Abbey, 2002; Aviles *et al.*, 2005; Chermack and Taylor, 1995; George and Norris, 1991; Leonard, 2002; Murphy *et al.*, 2005; Pernanen, 1976; Pihl and Peterson, 1995; Sayette, 1999; Taylor and Leonard, 1983; Testa *et al.*, 2000), *programmatic efforts aimed at testing the model directly are actually quite rare*.

Interestingly, as also noted, two studies, outside of our laboratory, provide incidental support for the AMM–aggression link (Leonard, 1989; Zeichner *et al.*, 1982). However, as also noted, they do not appear to have been designed as a priori tests of the model. The first of these studies measured aggression using a task in which subjects administered and received mild electric shocks to/ from a fictitious opponent under the guise of a competitive reaction-time task. Aggression was operationalized as the intensity and duration of the shock subjects delivered to their fictitious opponent. Subjects were given an alcohol or placebo beverage and were randomly assigned to one of three experimental conditions. Those in the *distraction* group were required to solve arithmetic problems during the aggression task; those in the *forced attention* group had to focus their attention on the level of pain they expected their opponent to experience as well as the shock level they received; and those in the *control* group simply competed on the aggression task. The results indicated that alcohol produced the greatest levels of aggression in the forced attention group, the lowest levels (similar to the placebo groups) in the distraction group, and intermediate levels in the control group (Zeichner et al., 1982).

The next study used a similar task to assess the effects of explicit aggressive and nonaggressive cues on intoxicated aggression. Subjects were primed to behave aggressively or nonaggressively by overhearing their opponent state explicitly that he was going to administer the highest or lowest shock level allowed. In reality, subjects in both conditions always received the lowest shock level. Alcohol increased aggression when subjects overheard their opponent's explicit intention to behave aggressively, despite the fact that both cues were *always* followed by the most mild shock responses. These data suggest that alcohol consumption narrowed subjects' attention onto the initial aggressive verbal cues and away from subsequent nonaggressive behavioral cues. Subjects in the sober condition suppressed their aggression after presumably noticing that their opponent was delivering only the lowest-intensity shocks (Leonard, 1989).

The findings from these investigations are clearly consistent with the AMM. However, as noted above, a programmatic effort aimed directly at testing the AMM as it relates to alcohol-related aggression has just begun. So, one of the aims of this chapter is to review data from four recent experiments from our laboratory that represent the beginning of a systematic research effort aimed at testing the consequences of AMM for alcohol-related aggression (Giancola and Corman, 2007 – two studies; Giancola et al., 2011; Phillips and Giancola, 2008).

Our investigations assessed aggression in a laboratory setting using a task similar to the one described above in the study by Zeichner et al. (1982). We tested the AMM by determining whether distraction from the provocative cues of the aggression task (i.e., receiving electric shocks) would decrease aggression, namely, the intensity and duration of the electric shock delivered to the opponent. More specifically, while engaged in the aggression task on one computer screen, subjects in the distraction condition were simultaneously engaged in a computerized task that taxed working memory resources on an adjacent computer screen.

For the distraction task, subjects were asked to attend very carefully to a 3×3 matrix of $2 \times 2\,cm$ black squares on a white computer screen. A particular number of these squares were illuminated in a different random sequential order for a given block of trials. Immediately after the trial block terminated, subjects had to use a computer mouse to click on the squares in the order in which they had been illuminated. The trial blocks were presented continuously and the subjects were engaged in this task for the duration of the aggression task. They were not given performance feedback during the task to avoid generating emotional reactions.

Giancola and Corman's (2007) first study revealed that alcohol suppressed aggression (even below levels exhibited by a placebo group) when subjects were distracted from the provocative cues of the aggression task by having to remember a four-light illumination sequence (see Figure 3.1). Their second study was designed to ascertain the magnitude of task difficulty (i.e., cognitive work load) that resulted in the most suppression of aggression. Subjects were assigned to an alcohol or a placebo condition, and within each of these conditions, they were placed into one of five distraction groups that differed in difficulty. Difficulty of

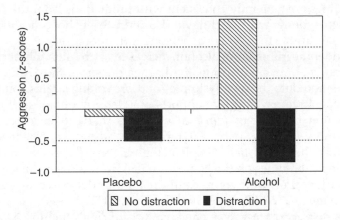

Figure 3.1 The effects of alcohol and distraction on aggression.

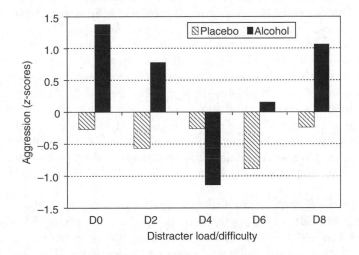

Figure 3.2 The effects of alcohol and variations in cognitive load on aggression.

the distraction task was operationalized by varying the number of illuminated squares in the sequence: no illuminations (i.e., no distraction [D0]), two illuminations (D2), four illuminations (D4, as in study 1), six illuminations (D6), and eight illuminations (D8). As can be seen in Figure 3.2, subjects who received alcohol demonstrated a V-shaped aggression pattern in which groups D0 and D8 exhibited the highest levels of aggression, groups D2 and D6 demonstrated intermediate levels, and group D4 showed the least amount of aggression (*even lower than all five placebo groups*). The placebo groups were not affected by the distraction manipulation (see Figures 3.1 and 3.2).

These findings are generally consistent with predictions from the AMM. However, one might wonder why the difficult (D6 and D8) alcohol conditions increased aggression. We argue that when a person's attentional capacity is overtaxed, especially under the influence of alcohol, increased aggression might cause unnecessary frustration, or even attentionally disengaging from the distracter task and focusing attention onto the more "simple" and provoking aggression task. Recent research in cognitive psychology supports our data by demonstrating that four is the maximum capacity of *unrelated* elements that can be correctly held in working memory (Cowan, 1999, 2000). Finally, adding even greater support to the notion that the AMM helps explain the alcohol–aggression relation is our finding that reaction times on the aggression task were slower during the distraction task and that they were significantly related to decreased aggression when subjects were intoxicated (Giancola and Corman, 2007). In essence, our data indicate that the distraction task was effective in directing attention away from the aggression task and, in turn, had an effect on suppressing aggression in intoxicated subjects.

We then conducted a follow-up study in which an emotional distracter (an anxiety induction) was used in place of a cognitive distracter (Phillips and Giancola, 2008). Before drinks were consumed, subjects in the anxiety induction group were informed that, upon completion of the aggression task, they would be videotaped while giving a short speech on what they disliked about their bodies. During a 6-minute waiting period, anxiety induction subjects were given time to mentally prepare for their speech. Subjects then completed the aggression task after consuming either an alcohol or a placebo beverage. Finally, the anxiety induction subjects were told that the video session would not take place due to supposed "equipment failure." The results of the study were consistent with the AMM – the anxiety induction manipulation eliminated alcohol's effect on aggression. Presumably, the worry elicited by the anxiety induction distracted subjects from the provocative cues of the aggression task, which subsequently attenuated aggression.

To date, the final study of the four provided a preliminary test of whether the AMM would provide a guiding framework for the prevention of alcohol-related violence. The model contends that alcohol has a myopic effect on attentional capacity that presumably facilitates violence by focusing attention onto more salient provocative, rather than less salient inhibitory, cues in hostile situations. Participants were 16 intoxicated male social drinkers who completed a laboratory task in which electric shocks were received from, and administered to, a fictitious opponent under the guise of a competitive reaction-time task while they were exposed to either violence-promoting ($n = 8$) or violence-inhibiting ($n = 8$) cues. Aggression was operationalized as the intensity and duration of shocks administered by the participant to his "opponent." Despite being *equally intoxicated*, participants exposed to violence-inhibiting cues were dramatically less aggressive ($d = 1.65$) than those exposed to the violence-promoting cues (see Figure 3.3). Our data suggest that the AMM holds a great deal of promise to help develop effective prevention interventions for alcohol-related violence.

The violence-inhibiting and violence-promoting stimuli were presented throughout the duration of the aggression task. In accordance with the AMM, to

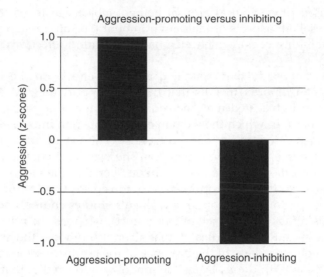

Figure 3.3   Aggression levels in the violence-promoting and violence-inhibiting groups.

be effective, these messages had to be attentionally salient and easy to process. Thus, the violence-inhibiting group watched a video depicting peaceful images (e.g., serene nature scenes, smiling babies, and families spending time together). Peaceful and soothing music was also played during the video. The room in which they watched the video was decorated with posters portraying similar scenes inconsistent with violence (e.g., sad-looking baby seals, smiling children, and cute animals). In contrast, the violence-promoting sounding music was played during their video. The room was decorated with posters depicting violence (e.g., Al Pacino firing a machine gun in the movie *Scarface* and Muhammad Ali snarling over Sonny Liston after knocking him out). Half of the participants were exposed to the violence-inhibiting cues ($n = 8$) and the other half were exposed to the violence-promoting cues ($n = 8$). Our violence-inhibiting and violence-promoting manipulation was a more elaborate version than the one used by Ward *et al.* (2008) in a study that did not use alcohol.

Although alcohol was not administered, it is important to review the findings of a recent study which demonstrated that, just like alcohol or increased cognitive demand, physiological arousal can also create a myopic effect on attention (Ward *et al.*, 2008). Subjects were assigned to a low or a high physiological arousal condition that was achieved via physical exercise. Aggression was then assessed using a laboratory task similar to the one used by Giancola and Corman (2007). However, during the aggression task, subjects were exposed to either aggression-promoting or aggression-inhibiting cues. The highest levels of aggression were observed in persons in the high arousal group who were exposed to aggression-promoting cues, whereas the lowest levels were observed in the high arousal group who were exposed to the aggression-inhibiting cues. Persons in the low arousal groups evinced levels of aggression that were intermediate to these two extremes. In other words, increased physiological arousal helped subjects to focus their attention onto the most salient aspects of their environment (i.e., aggression-promoting or aggression-inhibiting cues), which then had a profound effect on directing their behavior.

Finally, a recent study that examined alcohol's effects on the acceptance of sexual aggression reported results that did not support the AMM (Noel *et al.*, 2009). Sober and intoxicated men viewed a videotape of a young heterosexual couple in a scenario in which the woman enticed the man into a sexual situation whereby the man acted on her cues to have sex; however, upon his attempt to engage in intercourse, she made it clear that she was not interested in going any further (at which time the video ended). In one version, the video had cues built into it that conveyed the inappropriateness of forced sex (e.g., feminist posters on the wall of her apartment, a book for a women's studies course, and the emblem of a rape crisis center on the back of her T-shirt), whereas the other version did not have these cues. Results indicated that alcohol promoted the acceptability of sexual aggression regardless of the presence of the antiforce sex cues. These data are not in keeping with the AMM as the model would predict that the presence of antiforce sex cues would have suppressed the acceptability of the use of forced sex, particularly in the alcohol condition. Given that the preponderance of data supports the AMM, these contradictory findings are curious. For instance, relative to the aforementioned studies that included highly salient aggression-promoting cues (e.g., a provocateur verbally communicating an intent to harm the subject), the antiforced sex cues used by Noel and colleagues (2009) may not have been sufficiently salient to capture the subjects' attention (i.e., a women's studies book might not have been a highly salient enough antiforced sex cue; the emblem of the rape crisis center on the back of her T-shirt might have gone unnoticed; or men might simply not have recognize these as antiforced sex cues, especially feminist posters and books on women's studies). Nevertheless, further research is required to improve our understanding of the underlying mechanisms and viability of the AMM as an explanatory framework for alcohol-related aggression, both sexual and nonsexual.

HYPOTHETICAL ACCOUNTS BY WHICH DISTRACTION REDUCES AGGRESSION: STATE MECHANISMS

How Does Distraction Reduce Aggression?

As just noted, if an intoxicated person's attention is distracted away from a provocative stimulus, the result is a reduction in aggression. However, a question not addressed by the AMM is *exactly how does distraction decrease aggression?* Thus, five state mechanisms by which distraction might have this effect are proposed. These variables were chosen on the basis of sound theoretical and empirical research to support their role as potential mechanisms. They can also be easily and quickly measured immediately following the aggression task, which allows for empirical investigation.

Reducing the Negative Affect

Briefly stated, Berkowitz's (1990, 1993) cognitive neoassociationistic theory of aggression asserts that aversive events such as provocation produce negative affects that, in turn, lead to aggressive inclinations by activating an associative network of aggression-related thoughts, feelings, memories, expressive motor reactions, and physiological responses. As such, distraction might reduce aggression by diverting attention away from one's negative affect.

Reducing Anger

A more specific hypothesis based on the above negative affect prediction is that distraction reduces aggression by diverting attention away from the anger-provoking, "emotionally hot" aspects of the aggression task onto "cooler" non-provocative cerebral matters (i.e., the cognitive distracter task). Thus, distraction might reduce aggression by diverting attention away from an angry affect.

Reducing Cognitive Rumination

Research has shown that ruminating about a prior provocation increases anger and aggression (Aviles *et al.*, 2005; Bushman, 2002; Bushman *et al.*, 2005). As such, distraction can reduce aggression by decreasing the extent to which subjects ruminate about the provocation they have just endured from their fictitious opponent.

Self-Awareness

Increased self-awareness has an attenuating effect on aggression (Carver, 1975; Scheier, Fenigstein, and Buss, 1974). Self-awareness refers to a state in which individuals focus on their thoughts, feelings, attitudes, and values – or, more generally, on their conception of themselves (Carver and Scheier, 1981; Duval and Wicklund, 1972). According to theory, self-awareness increases and reduces aggression because one's inclination to aggress is compared to personal norms and standards as to what action is desirable under the given circumstances, and aggression is often judged to be "wrong" or otherwise undesirable (Carver and Scheier, 1981; Hull, 1981). Therefore, distraction from provocation will reduce aggression by allowing one's "freed-up" attention to be focused upon preexisting self-relevant thoughts about appropriate social behavior.

Empathy

By virtue of its inherent components such as compassion, sympathy, and caring for the well-being of others, empathy has been shown to be inversely related to aggression (reviewed in Bjorkqvist, Osterman, and Kaukiainen, 2000; Miller and Eisenberg, 1988). As with self-awareness, distraction from provocation will reduce aggression by allowing subjects' freed-up attention to be focused upon preexisting empathic thoughts and feelings for their opponent. In fact, Denson *et al.* (2008) hypothesized that alcohol might increase aggression within the context of the AMM via a reduction in the ability to empathize with a provocateur (p. 26).

With regard to self-awareness and empathy, mere distraction will not "increase" or "activate" these processes. There are obviously preexisting individual differences in these traits. It is our hypothesis that provocative cues from the aggression task will direct attention away from considering and acting upon the cognitions/affects brought about by self-awareness and empathy in persons who already possess these traits. Thus, distraction from provocation will give these persons the capability to focus their freed-up attention onto their possibly preexisting traits and perhaps allow them to consider and act upon them to reduce aggression.

PRACTICAL IMPLICATIONS FOR HOW TO REDUCE ALCOHOL-RELATED AGGRESSION

In order to reduce aggression, the AMM requires distraction techniques that will break the link between provocative cues and aggressive reactions. Although this may sound simple, it is more difficult than it sounds. Accordingly, the model calls for highly salient, frequent, and easy-to-process antiviolence cues that will redirect the inebriate's attention away from hostile provocative cues onto more salient nonprovocative, or even inhibitory, cues in situations in which violence often accompanies alcohol intoxication (e.g., bars, sports venues, and college campus parties). Steele and Josephs (1990) proposed that distraction from provocation reduces aggression. However, they did not indicate how distraction is instrumental in suppressing aggression. Thus, I proposed five mechanisms through which distraction may, in part, have its mitigating effect on aggression (i.e., reducing negative affect, anger, and hostile rumination, as well as increasing self-awareness and empathy among those high in self-awareness and empathy).

There are a variety of settings that might lend themselves to AMM-inspired interventions for alcohol-related aggression. In some cases, these would include public venues where alcohol-related violence often occurs. In cases of domestic violence, the home might be more suitable. For those persons willing to attend, or are mandated to attend, psychotherapy sessions, a clinical setting might prove most appropriate. Given the nature of the AMM and its proposed underlying mechanisms, many of these intervention strategies will share some overlap; however, given the setting, they will be presented in different ways.

Public Health Interventions

A successful public health initiative against alcohol-related aggression should target settings where alcohol and violence most readily mix. A recent analysis of three US National Alcohol Surveys found that bars are consistently a preferred drinking context, and people who drink at bars are more likely to engage in arguments and fighting than those who drink the equivalent amount of alcohol at home (Nyaronga, Greenfield, and McDaniel, 2009). Consider a bar fight that is about to erupt; staff members, friends, or other trained personnel might intervene by escorting an intoxicated provoked person outside or to a specially designated "cool-down" room where she/he can be distracted through any number of means (e.g., massage chair, soft music playing in the background, and someone to guide the inebriate in deep-breathing exercises). Interestingly, a study of licensed drinking venues in two Australian cities found the "comfort level" of the establishment to be inversely related to nonphysical aggression (Homel *et al.*, 2004). Alternatively, a cool-down room could contain popular games/activities that are engaging but are not aggressive or arousing in content. Incentives to perform well on the games such as the possibility of winning a no-cover charge voucher could be given to help distract the provoked individual.

Angered patrons might also be distracted from the provocative incident through the use of simple exercises designed to increase their level of mindfulness, which refers to intentionally attending to current experiences in a nonjudgmental and accepting manner (Kabat-Zinn, 2003). Mindfulness practices have a long history in a variety of world religions and were originally intended to reduce suffering and to improve awareness, insight, as well as compassion and empathy for others. If implemented correctly, mindfulness allows intoxicated individuals to refocus attention away from provocative cues toward more salient cues that encourage reflection upon personal standards (i.e., self-awareness) and empathetic feelings toward others. Although such techniques might seem complicated and effective only if administered by a mental health professional, there are many mindfulness techniques that are quite simple. For example, Heppner *et al.* (2008) employed an effective technique of reducing aggression by distracting individuals from provocation by focusing them on the very simple details of eating a raisin!

The interventions described above are designed to distract one's attention away from provocative cues. If effective, they would do so by reducing negative affect, anger, and hostile rumination toward their provocateur. In some individuals, spare attentional space that was previously occupied by hostile thoughts and affect might be replaced by empathetic thoughts and feelings. However, as noted earlier, increased self-awareness has been found to be significantly involved in the attenuation of aggressive behavior. With this in mind, trained bar/nightclub staff can add to their catalog of distraction techniques the ability to initiate conversations with provoked intoxicated patrons that are aimed at increasing their self-awareness and self-monitoring skills. Specifically, Hull *et al.* (1983) suggested that inappropriate alcohol-related behaviors, including aggression, can be lowered by providing ". . . the individual with a cognitive repertoire of self-relevant encoding schemes to employ when he or she has been drinking" (e.g., "what is my behavior saying about the kind of person I am?" or "how would I react if someone were behaving this way toward me?") (p. 471).

Particularly with intoxicated and belligerent patrons, self-awareness can be further enhanced by scattering mirrors around the drinking establishment painted with prison-like vertical bars suggesting not so subtly the consequences of alcohol and aggression. Above these mirrors could be a slogan that reads: *Drink; Fight; See Yourself behind Bars*. This particularly salient intervention (i.e., jail bars and slogan) can exploit the patron's alcohol myopia, and hopefully focus his/her attention onto the possible negative consequences of aggression. These salient "jail mirrors" can also be placed in key locations throughout bars with the same Drink; Fight; See Yourself behind Bars slogan printed above them along with obvious video cameras mounted even further above (and out of reach) to draw intoxicated persons' limited attentional resources toward these objects so that the alcohol myopia effect can be used to make patrons even more self-aware of themselves as well as of proper standards of behavior.

The rationale behind the use of such mirrors comes from laboratory studies that have found that a momentary manipulation designed to increase self-awareness by virtue of adding mirrors and video cameras to a room was effective in suppressing aggression toward others (Bailey *et al.*, 1983) and toward one's self (Berman *et al.*, 2009). The implication is that boosting self-awareness distracts the inebriate from the provocative situation because the person is forced to compare his or her initial impulse to aggress with personal and social norms that admonish such inappropriate behavior. Bolstering this research are other empirical findings showing that an effective means of increasing self-awareness is to place people in front of a mirror (Carver and Scheier, 1978; Silvia, 2002; Wicklund and Duval, 1971). Therefore, mounting mirrors and video cameras in bars and nightclubs, especially those establishments where alcohol-related aggression is most prevalent, would be an easy and effective means of providing patrons with a salient reminder of their self-concept.

Antiviolence messages designed to increase self-awareness in bars could be presented through a number of different mediums such as televisions (most bars and taverns have several televisions; some even have them above male urinals). Brief 15- to 30-second public service announcement broadcasts could be designed to depict the negative consequences of drinking and fighting. However, care should be taken to make such announcements both captivating and unambiguous in content to maximize the amount of cognitive resources people divert away from provocative stimuli. Messages without sound in a noisy environment might be optimal to increase ease of comprehension.

Antiviolence messages in bars and nightclubs need not be restricted to television broadcasts. In most bars, there is ample room for signs, posters, and so on, upon which to place slogans. One such slogan could be a simple five-word phrase – such as *Drink; Fight; Go to Jail* – that might be flashed on a screen at periodic intervals, echoing the state of Texas's highly successful anti-drunk-driving billboard campaign featuring the liberal use of large billboards with the words *Drink; Drive; Go to Jail*. Even coasters, menus, server apparel, and drinking glasses could display such messages. On this latter point, large, graphic warnings could be placed on glasses that contain alcoholic beverages with content that includes the consequences of violent behavior while intoxicated. These manipulations might also be particularly effective in increasing self-awareness by highlighting the potential negative consequences of engaging in violent behavior.

A less subtle method to highlight self-awareness would be to implement a "fight alarm" in drinking establishments when a physical altercation erupts. This intervention could be as simple as turning on all the lights, stopping the music, and calling out over a loud speaker that a fight has broken out followed by a loud announcement that the police will now be called. In theory, these dramatic events, especially the police announcement, might distract the combatants, thus decreasing the chances of further violence by increasing self-awareness.

Although many of the above interventions apply to smaller drinking establishments, there are also larger venues where alcohol-related aggression can be a substantial problem. Professional sports venues are a good example of this. Several of the abovementioned interventions would be equally applicable on larger scales. An example of an AMM-derived intervention specific to a sports venue would be the random and frequent interjection of the previously mentioned slogan Drink; Fight; Go to Jail on a large screen or on the perimeter boards. Additional methods of communicating these simple nonviolent messages might also prove useful. Vendors and other stadium workers who travel throughout the venue could wear T-shirts that have aggression–consequence linked slogans such as the one mentioned above. Large signs with similar messages could also be placed next to concession stands where alcohol is sold.

Clinical Interventions

Outside of public settings, the most likely location for alcohol-related intimate partner violence or child abuse is in the home (Leonard, Quigley, and Collins, 2002). AMM-informed prevention strategies could be adapted from those used in the public settings, although this approach presents several challenges, most notably the implausibility of displaying antiviolence cues (e.g., mirrors, video cameras, signs) throughout the home as well as the lack of independent bystanders to help redirect the inebriate's attention toward nonprovoking/inhibitory cues. Thus, AMM-informed interventions designed for domestic settings may be most effective to the extent that they incorporate a two-part approach. First, individual, couple, or family therapy could be used to build an internal reservoir of aggression-reducing skills that would capitalize upon our previously proposed mechanisms (i.e., decreasing negative affect, anger, and hostile rumination, as well as increasing self-awareness and empathy). Second, individualized plans could be developed that would employ physical cues of nonviolence as well as partners or other family members as agents of attentional redirection.

The psychotherapy literature is rich with evidenced-based interventions for individuals, couples, and families to modify hostile thoughts and regulate negative affects. Of particular relevance to the AMM, however, are therapeutic techniques, such as acceptance and commitment therapy, which have been shown to increase dispositional mindfulness (Hayes, Strosahl, and Wilson, 1999). As noted above, enhancing mindfulness should increase the likelihood that the intoxicated myopic can redirect his/her attention toward nonaggressive cues. Consistent with this view, a recent study found that heavy episodic drinking increased the perpetration of sexual aggression toward one's partner among men with lower, but not higher, levels of dispositional mindfulness (Gallagher, Hudepohl, and Parrott, 2010). Consistent with the AMM, it was reasoned that heavy episodic drinking did not increase sexual aggression in highly mindful men because they were better able to shift attentional focus away from sexually aggressive cues (e.g., desire to have sex) and toward nonaggressive cues (e.g., social proscriptions against aggression, resistance from one's partner to have sex).

Despite the acquisition of these skills, it will likely still be necessary to develop individualized methods to redirect the inebriate's attention toward nonaggressive cues in the home. To maximize the likelihood of implementation, these methods will need to be discreet yet still sufficiently salient for the at-risk individual. For instance, one could wear a nondescript wristband that has a personal meaning (i.e., a nonaggressive message) only to the person wearing it. Likewise, a decorative item in the house could also hold a symbolic nonaggressive meaning. Similar to the chips used in Alcoholics Anonymous to mark recovery goals, chips could be carried or worn to remind the person of his or her commitment to nonviolence. Finally, a therapist could work to develop cool-down statements that partners or family members could use in a conflict situation. Similar to the cool-down room in public settings, such statements would function to remind individuals to consider nonaggressive options or to move to a different setting in the house where distraction is more likely.

CONCLUSIONS AND DIRECTIONS FOR FUTURE RESEARCH

This chapter demonstrates that the AMM is an influential theoretical framework for alcohol-related aggression. It is important to note that we expanded the model by proposing five putative mechanisms (i.e., negative affect, angry affect, hostile cognitive rumination, self-awareness, and empathy) to explain how the AMM is specifically involved in the alcohol–aggression relation and for future researchers to test and expand upon it themselves. As was noted repeatedly throughout the chapter, its central message is that alcohol constricts attentional capacity and, as a result, aggression will ensue if the most salient stimuli in one's environment are hostile. As such, the chief message is that, in order to avoid a violent response, one must break the link between the hostile provocation and the violent response, particularly in intoxicated persons.

Given this, research is needed to extend the aggression-reducing effect of distraction from the confines of the laboratory to real-world settings. The study by Giancola *et al.* (2011) provides preliminary data to show that this is a highly attainable goal. Moreover, future work might be aimed at developing and testing distraction techniques that target the five intermediary mechanisms proposed above. Finally, given that acute alcohol consumption appears to only facilitate aggression in a subset of individuals, research should also be directed at identifying which individual difference variables create the greatest risk for alcohol-related violence within the context of the AMM.

ACKNOWLEDGMENT

This research was supported by grants R01-AA-017431 and R01-AA-020005 from the National Institute on Alcohol Abuse and Alcoholism awarded to Peter R. Giancola, PhD.

REFERENCES

Abbey, A. (2002) Alcohol-related sexual assault: A common problem among college students. *Journal of Studies on Alcohol*, (Suppl 14), 118–128.

Aviles, F., Earleywine, M., Pollock, V. *et al.* (2005) Alcohol's effect on triggered displaced aggression. *Psychology of Addictive Behaviors*, **19**, 108–111.

Bailey, D.S., Leonard, K.E., Cranston, J.W., and Taylor, S.P. (1983) Effects of alcohol and self-awareness on human physical aggression. *Personality and Social Psychology Bulletin*, **9**, 289–295.

Berkowitz, L. (1990) On the formation and regulation of anger and aggression: A cognitive-neoassociationistic analysis. *American Psychologist*, **45**, 494–503.

Berkowitz, L. (1993) *Aggression: Its Causes, Consequences, and Control*. New York: McGraw Hill.

Berman, M., Bradley, T., Fanning, J., and McCloskey, M. (2009) Self-focused attention reduces self-injurious behavior in alcohol-intoxicated men. *Substance Use and Misuse*, **44**, 1280–1297.

Bjorkqvist, K., Osterman, K., and Kaukiainen, A. (2000) Social intelligence – empathy = aggression? *Aggression and Violent Behavior*, **5**, 191–200.

Borders, A. and Giancola, P.R. (2011) Trait and state hostile rumination facilitate alcohol-related aggression. *Journal of Studies on Alcohol and Drugs*, **72**, 545–554.

Borders, A., Smucker-Barnwell, S., and Earleywine, M. (2007) Alcohol aggression expectancies and dispositional rumination moderate the effect of alcohol consumption on alcohol-related aggression and hostility. *Aggressive Behavior*, **33**, 327–338.

Boyatzis, R. (1975) The predisposition toward alcohol-related interpersonal aggression in men. *Journal of Studies on Alcohol*, **36**, 1196–1207.

Bushman, B. (1993) Human aggression while under the influence of alcohol and other drugs: An integrative research review. *Current Directions in Psychological Science*, **2**, 148–152.

Bushman, B. (1997) Effects of alcohol on human aggression: Validity of proposed explanations. In M. Galanter (ed.), *Recent Developments in Alcoholism, Volume 13: Alcohol and Violence* (pp. 227–243). New York: Plenum Press.

Bushman, B. and Cooper, H. (1990) Effects of alcohol on human aggression: An integrative research review. *Psychological Bulletin*, **107**, 341–354.

Bushman, B.J. (2002) Does venting anger feed or extinguish the flame? Catharsis, rumination, distraction, anger, and aggressive responding. *Personality and Social Psychology Bulletin*, **28**, 724–731.

Bushman, B.J., Bonacci, A.M., Pedersen, W.C. *et al.* (2005) Chewing on it can chew you up: Effects of rumination on triggered displaced aggression. *Journal of Personality and Social Psychology*, **88**, 969–983.

Carver, C.S. (1975) Physical aggression as a function of objective self-awareness and attitudes toward punishment. *Journal of Experimental Social Psychology*, **11**, 510–519.

Carver, C.S. and Scheier, M.F. (1978) Self-focusing effects of dispositional self-consciousness, mirror presence, and audience presence. *Journal of Personality and Social Psychology*, **36**, 324–322.

Carver, C.S. and Scheier, M.F. (1981) *Attention and Self-Regulation: A Control-Theory Approach to Human Behavior*. New York: Springer-Verlag.

Cheong, J. and Nagoshi, C. (1999) Effects of sensation seeking, instruction set, and alcohol/ placebo administration on aggressive behavior. *Alcohol*, **17**, 81–86.

Chermack, S. and Taylor, S. (1995) Alcohol and human physical aggression: Pharmacological versus expectancy effects. *Journal of Studies on Alcohol*, **56**, 449–456.

Collins, J. (1988) Suggested explanatory frameworks to clarify the alcohol use/violence relationship. *Contemporary Drug Problems*, **15**, 107–121.

Cowan, N. (1999) An embedded-processes model of working memory. In A. Miyake and P. Shah (eds), *Models of Working Memory: Mechanisms of Active Maintenance and Executive Control* (pp. 62–101). New York: Cambridge University Press.

Cowan, N. (2000) The magical number 4 in short-term memory: A reconsideration of mental storage capacity. *Behavioral and Brain Sciences*, **24**, 87–185.

Denson, T.F., Aviles, F.E., Pollock, V.E. *et al.* (2008) The effects of alcohol and the salience of aggressive cues on triggered displaced aggression. *Aggressive Behavior*, **34**, 25–33.

Dermen, K. and George, W. (1989) Alcohol expectancy and the relation between drinking and physical aggression. *Journal of Psychology*, **123**, 153–161.

Duke, A.A., Giancola, P.R., Morris, D.H. *et al.* (2011) Alcohol dose and aggression: Another reason why drinking more is a bad idea. *Journal of Studies on Alcohol and Drugs*, **72**, 34–43.

Duval, S. and Wicklund, R.A. (1972) *A Theory of Objective Self-Awareness*. New York: Academic Press.

Fishbein, D. (2003) Differential susceptibility to comorbid drug abuse and violence. *Journal of Drug Issues*, **28**, 859–891.

Gallagher, K.E., Hudepohl, A.D., and Parrott, D.J. (2010) Power of being present: The role of mindfulness on the relation between men's alcohol use and sexual aggression toward intimate partners. *Aggressive Behavior*, **36**, 405–413.

George, W. and Norris, J. (1991) Alcohol, disinhibition, sexual arousal, and deviant sexual behavior. *Alcohol Health and Research World*, **15**, 133–138.

Giancola, P., Josephs, R., Parrott, D., and Duke, A. (2010) Alcohol myopia revisited: Clarifying aggression and other acts of disinhibition through a distorted lens. *Perspectives on Psychological Science*, **5**, 265–278.

Giancola, P.R. (2002) Irritability, acute alcohol consumption, and aggressive behavior in men and women. *Drug and Alcohol Dependence*, **68**, 263–274.

Giancola, P.R. (2003) The moderating effects of dispositional empathy on alcohol-related aggression in men and women. *Journal of Abnormal Psychology*, **112**, 275–281.

Giancola, P.R. (2004a) Executive functioning and alcohol-related aggression. *Journal of Abnormal Psychology*, **113**, 541–555.

Giancola, P.R. (2004b) Difficult temperament, acute alcohol intoxication, and aggressive behavior. *Drug and Alcohol Dependence*, **74**, 135–145.

Giancola, P.R. (2006) The influence of subjective intoxication, breath alcohol concentration, and expectancies on the alcohol-aggression relation. *Alcoholism: Clinical and Experimental Research*, **30**, 844–850.

Giancola, P.R. and Corman, M.D. (2007) Alcohol and aggression: A test of the attention-allocation model. *Psychological Science*, **18**, 649–655.

Giancola, P.R., Duke, A.A., and Ritz, K.Z. (2011) Alcohol, violence, and the alcohol myopia model: Preliminary findings and implications for prevention. *Addictive Behaviors*, **36**, 1019–1022.

Giancola, P.R., Godlaski, A.J., and Parrott, D.J. (2005) "So I can't blame the booze?" Dispositional aggressivity negates the moderating effects of expectancies on alcohol-related aggression. *Journal of Studies on Alcohol*, **66**, 815–824.

Graham, K. (1980) Theories of intoxicated aggression. *Canadian Journal of Behavioral Sciences*, **12**, 141–158.

Greenfeld, L. and Henneberg, M. (2001) Victim and offender self-reports of alcohol involvement in crime. *Alcohol Research and Health*, **25**, 20–31.

Hayes, S.C., Strosahl, K., & Wilson, K.G. (1999) *Acceptance and Commitment Therapy: An Experiential Approach to Behavior Change*. New York: Guilford Press.

Heppner, W.L., Kernis, M.H., Lakey, C.E. *et al.* (2008) Mindfulness as a means of reducing aggressive behavior: Dispositional and situational evidence. *Aggressive Behavior,* **34,** 486–496.

Homel, R., Carvolth, R., Hauritz, M. *et al.* (2004) Making licensed venues safer for patrons: What environmental factors should be the focus of interventions? *Drug and Alcohol Review,* **23,** 19–29.

Hull, J. (1981) A self-awareness model of the causes and effects of alcohol consumption. *Journal of Abnormal Psychology,* **90,** 586–600.

Hull, J. and Bond, C. (1986) Social and behavioral consequences of alcohol consumption and expectancy: A meta-analysis. *Psychological Bulletin,* **99,** 347–360.

Hull, J.G., Levenson, R.W., Young, R.D., and Sher, K.J. (1983). Self-awareness-reducing effects of alcohol consumption. *Journal of Personality and Social Psychology,* **44,** 461–473.

Ito, T., Miller, N., and Pollock, V. (1996) Alcohol and aggression: A meta-analysis of the moderating effects of inhibitory cues, triggering events, and self-focused attention. *Psychological Bulletin,* **120,** 60–82.

Josephs, R. and Steele, C. (1990) The two faces of alcohol myopia: Attentional mediation of psychological stress. *Journal of Abnormal Psychology,* **99,** 115–126.

Kabat-Zinn, J. (2003). Mindfulness-based interventions in context: Past, present, and future. *Clinical Psychology: Science and Practice,* **10,** 144–156.

Kassel, J. and Shiffman, S. (1997) Attentional mediation of cigarette smoking's effect on anxiety. *Health Psychology,* **16,** 359–368.

Kassel, J. and Unrod, M. (2000) Smoking, anxiety, and attention: Support for the role of nicotine in attentionally mediated anxiolysis. *Journal of Abnormal Psychology,* **109,** 161–166.

Lau, M., Pihl, R., and Peterson, J. (1995) Provocation, acute alcohol intoxication, cognitive performance, and aggression. *Journal of Abnormal Psychology,* **104,** 150–155.

Leonard, K. (1989) The impact of explicit aggressive and implicit nonaggressive cues on aggression in intoxicated and sober males. *Personality and Social Psychology Bulletin,* **15,** 390–400.

Leonard, K. and Senchak, M. (1993) Alcohol and premarital aggression among newlywed couples. *Journal of Studies on Alcohol,* (Suppl 11), 96–108.

Leonard, K.E. (2002). Alcohol's role in domestic violence: A contributing cause or an excuse? *Acta Psychiatrica Scandinavica,* **106**(S412), 9–14.

Leonard, K.E., Quigley, B.M., & Collins, R.L. (2002). Physical aggression in the lives of young adults – Prevalence, location, and severity among college and community samples. *Journal of Interpersonal Violence,* **17,** 533–550.

MacDonald, T., Fong, G., Zanna, M., and Martineau, A. (2000a) Alcohol myopia and condom use: Can alcohol intoxication be associated with more prudent behavior? *Journal of Personality and Social Psychology,* **78,** 605–619.

MacDonald, T., MacDonald, G., Zanna, M., and Fong, G. (2000b) Alcohol, sexual arousal, and intentions to use condoms in young men: Applying alcohol myopia theory to risky sexual behavior. *Health Psychology,* **19,** 290–298.

MacDonald, T., Zanna, M., and Fong, G. (1995) Decision making in altered states: Effects of alcohol on attitudes toward drinking and driving. *Journal of Personality and Social Psychology,* **68,** 973–985.

Mann, T. and Ward, A. (2004) To eat or not to eat: Implications of the attentional myopia model for restrained eaters. *Journal of Abnormal Psychology,* **113,** 90–98.

Miller, P. and Eisenberg, N. (1988) The relation of empathy to aggressive and externalizing/antisocial behavior. *Psychological Bulletin,* **102,** 324–344.

Miller, T.R., Levy, D.T., Cohen, M.A., and Cox, K.L.C. (2006) Costs of alcohol and drug-involved crime. *Prevention Science,* **7,** 333–342.

Murdoch, D., Pihl, R., and Ross, D. (1990) Alcohol and crimes of violence: Present issues. *International Journal of the Addictions,* **25,** 1065–1081.

Murphy, C., Winters, J., O'Farrell, T. *et al.* (2005) Alcohol consumption and intimate partner violence by alcoholic men: Comparing violent and nonviolent conflicts. *Psychology of Addictive Behaviors,* **19,** 35–42.

Noel, N.E., Maisto, S.A., Johnson, J.D., and Jackson, L.A. (2009) The effects of alcohol and cue salience on young men's acceptance of sexual aggression. *Addictive Behaviors*, **34**, 386–394.

Nyaronga, D., Greenfield, T.K., and McDaniel, P.A. (2009) Drinking context and drinking problems among Black, White, and Hispanic men and women in the 1984, 1995, and 2005 U.S. National Alcohol Surveys. *Journal of Studies on Alcohol and Drugs*, **70**, 16–26.

Parrott, D.J. and Giancola, P.R. (2004) A further examination of the relation between trait anger and alcohol-related aggression: The role of anger control. *Alcoholism: Clinical and Experimental Research*, **28**, 855–864.

Parrott, D.J. and Zeichner, A. (2002) Effects of alcohol and trait anger on physical aggression. *Journal of Studies on Alcohol*, **63**, 196–204.

Pernanen, K. (1976) Alcohol and crimes of violence. In B. Kissin and H. Begleiter (eds), *The Biology of Alcoholism: Social Aspects of Alcoholism* (Vol. 4, pp. 351–444). New York: Plenum Press.

Phillips, J.P. and Giancola, P.R. (2008) Experimentally-induced anxiety attenuates alcohol-related aggression in men. *Experimental and Clinical Psychopharmacology*, **16**, 43–56.

Pihl, R. and Peterson, J. (1995) Drugs and aggression: Correlations, crime and human manipulative studies and some proposed mechanisms. *Journal of Psychiatry and Neuroscience*, **20**, 141–149.

Pihl, R., Peterson, J., and Lau, M. (1993) A biosocial model of the alcohol-aggression relationship. *Journal of Studies on Alcohol*, (Suppl 11), 128–139.

Quigley, B., Corbett, A., and Tedeschi, J. (2002) Desired image of power, alcohol expectancies and alcohol related aggression. *Psychology of Addictive Behaviors*, **16**, 318–324.

Quigley, B.M. and Leonard, K.E. (1999) Husband alcohol expectancies, drinking, and marital-conflict styles as predictors of severe marital violence among newlywed couples. *Psychology of Addictive Behaviors*, **13**, 49–59.

Quigley, B.M. and Leonard, K.E. (2006) Alcohol expectancies and intoxicated aggression. *Aggression and Violent Behavior: A Review Journal*, **11**, 484–496.

Sayette, M. (1999) Cognitive theory and research. In K. Leonard and H. Blane (eds), *Psychological Theories of Drinking and Alcoholism* (pp. 247–291). New York: Guilford Press.

Scheier, M.F., Fenigstein, A., and Buss, A.H. (1974) Self-awareness and physical aggression. *Journal of Experimental Social Psychology*, **10**, 264–273.

Silvia, P.J. (2002) Self-awareness and emotional intensity. *Cognition and Emotion*, **16**, 195–216.

Smucker-Barnwell, S., Borders, A., and Earleywine, M. (2006) Aggression expectancies and dispositional aggression moderate the relationship between alcohol consumption and alcohol related violence. *Aggressive Behavior*, **32**, 517–525.

Steele, C. and Josephs, R. (1988) Drinking your troubles away II: An attention-allocation model of alcohol's effect on psychological stress. *Journal of Abnormal Psychology*, **97**, 196–205.

Steele, C. and Josephs, R. (1990) Alcohol myopia: Its prized and dangerous effects. *American Psychologist*, **45**, 921–933.

Steele, C. and Southwick, L. (1985) Alcohol and social behavior I: The psychology of drunken excess. *Journal of Personality and Social Psychology*, **48**, 18–34.

Steele, C.M., Critchlow, B., and Liu, T.J. (1985) Alcohol and social behavior II: The helpful drunkard. *Journal of Personality and Social Psychology*, **48**, 35–46.

Taylor, S. and Leonard, K. (1983) Alcohol and human physical aggression. In R. Geen and E. Donnerstein (eds), *Aggression: Theoretical and Empirical Reviews*, Vol. 2 (pp. 77–101). New York: Academic Press.

Testa, M., Livingston, J., and Collins, L. (2000) The role of women's alcohol consumption in evaluation of vulnerability to sexual aggression. *Experimental and Clinical Psychopharmacology*, **8**, 185–191.

Ward, A. and Mann, T. (2000) Don't mind if I do: Disinhibited eating under cognitive load. *Journal of Personality and Social Psychology*, **78**, 753–763.

Ward, A., Mann, T., Westling, E.H. *et al.* (2008) Stepping up the pressure: Arousal can be associated with a reduction in male aggression. *Aggressive Behavior*, **34**, 584–592.

Welte, J. and Wieczorek, W. (1999) Alcohol, intelligence and violence crime in young males. *Journal of Substance Abuse*, **10**, 309–319.

Westling, E., Mann, T., and Ward, A. (2006) Self-control of smoking: When does narrowed attention help? *Journal of Applied Social Psychology*, **36**, 2115–2133.

Wicklund, R.A. and Duval, T.S. (1971) Opinion change and performance facilitation as a result of objective self-awareness. *Journal of Experimental Social Psychology*, **7**, 319–342.

Zeichner, A., Pihl, R., Niaura, R., and Zacchia, C. (1982) Attentional processes in alcohol-mediated aggression. *Journal of Studies on Alcohol*, **43**, 714–723.

Zhang, L., Wieczorek, W., and Welte, J. (1997) The nexus between alcohol and violent crime. *Alcoholism: Clinical and Experimental Research*, **21**(7), 1264–1271.

Chapter 4

ALCOHOL AND VIOLENCE IN EVOLUTIONARY PERSPECTIVE

RUSSIL DURRANT

Institute of Criminology, School of Social and Cultural Studies, Victoria University of Wellington, Wellington, New Zealand

INTRODUCTION

The relationship between alcohol and violence is well established. A large body of research clearly supports the idea that the consumption of alcohol is associated with an increased risk for aggression and violence (Exum, 2006; Rossow, 2001; Shaw *et al.*, 2006; Wells, Graham, and West, 2000). Considerable progress has also been made in delineating some of the important proximate biological, psychological and situational factors that can account for this relationship. Alcohol reliably impairs self-regulatory capacities and effectively narrows attention to the most salient cues in the environment (Giancola *et al.*, 2010). This subsequently increases the risk for violence, especially for individuals with antisocial characteristics (Giancola, 2002; Moeller and Dougherty, 2001) in particular kinds of drinking environments (Leonard, Quigley, and Collins, 2003) as they are most likely to focus on provocative cues that result in aggressive responses. Despite considerable progress in our understating of the proximate mechanisms underpinning alcohol-related violence, I will argue in this chapter that we can further our understanding of this phenomenon by taking an evolutionary perspective.

First, a brief general overview of evolutionary approaches to understanding human behaviour is provided. Then, evolutionary approaches to explaining aggression and violence are outlined, with a particular focus on how an evolutionary approach can help us to understand the important gender, age and social factors that are associated with violent offending. I then turn to a discussion of evolutionary approaches to understanding drug use, in general, and the consumption of alcohol, in particular. It will be argued that the attraction of psychoactive substances such as alcohol reflects the action of these substances on

Alcohol-Related Violence: Prevention and Treatment, First Edition. Edited by Mary McMurran.
© 2013 John Wiley & Sons, Ltd. Published 2013 by John Wiley & Sons, Ltd.

evolved motivational systems in the brain. An evolutionary framework for understanding alcohol-related violence is then provided, in which four evolutionary
'pathways' are outlined. These four pathways are then employed to provide a
discussion of how an evolutionary approach can help us more effectively manage
alcohol-related violence so as to reduce overall harm. Throughout this chapter,
the focus will be on alcohol-related violence between predominantly male strangers and acquaintances. This is not to downplay the importance of alcohol-related
violence in other contexts (e.g., between intimate partners and among family
members). However, a significant proportion of alcohol-related violence occurs
between men (especially young men) who are strangers or acquaintances (Chaplin,
Flatley, and Smith, 2011; Felson, Burchfield, and Teasdale, 2007). Moreover, this
violence often occurs in public spaces, especially in and around licensed premises
(Graham and Homel, 2008).

EVOLUTIONARY APPROACHES TO UNDERSTANDING HUMAN BEHAVIOUR

Humans, like all other animals on the planet, are the product of evolution by
natural (and sexual) selection. Our opposable thumb, bipedal stance and colour
visual system are all the end product of evolutionary processes that have favoured
these characteristics because they improved survival and reproductive success in
the environments in which they evolved. Just as our physical traits can be
explained by evolutionary processes, so too, argue evolutionary behavioural scientists, can our psychological and behavioural characteristics. In other words,
many (but not all) of the psychological and behavioural characteristics that
humans possess can be understood to be evolved adaptations: characteristics
that owe their existence to the fact that they enhanced survival and reproductive
success in ancestral environments (Buss, 1995; Confer *et al.*, 2010; Durrant and
Ellis, 2003).

Evolutionary explanations have a long – and, at times, controversial – history
in the social and behavioural sciences (Plotkin, 2004). Although there is a growing
acceptance of evolutionary approaches in psychology, and evolutionary ideas
have become more prominent in other disciplines such as economics, political
science and medicine, many still remain sceptical of their value and they remain
largely neglected in some areas such as sociology and criminology (Barkow, 2006;
Walsh, 2006). Space precludes a detailed discussion of the various criticisms that
have been directed against evolutionary approaches to explaining human behaviour (see Confer *et al.*, 2010; Durrant and Ward, 2011; Ketelaar and Ellis, 2000), but
a few relevant points are worth noting. First, despite some claims to the contrary,
evolutionary approaches do not commit us to a deterministic view of human
nature in which our characteristics are fixed by our evolutionary history. Indeed,
most evolutionary social scientists emphasise the enormous flexibility of human
behaviour and how this flexibility can be explained by the interaction of evolved
psychological systems and specific physical, social and cultural environments.
Second, providing an evolutionary explanation for a specific human behaviour
does not, therefore, suggest that the behaviour is necessarily morally acceptable.

This is a particularly salient point given the now extensive literature on topics such as aggression, violence, rape and war (Durrant and Ward, 2011). Finally, it is essential to recognise the *type* of explanation provided by evolutionary social and behavioural scientists. Specifically, evolutionary explanations focus on distal or 'ultimate' causes – those that relate to the evolutionary function and history of the characteristic in question. Most behavioural scientists, in contrast, focus on the more proximate physiological, psychological, developmental, situational and cultural processes that give rise to the phenomenon of interest. What this means is that evolutionary explanations are best viewed as compatible rather than competing explanatory accounts (Confer *et al.*, 2010; Durrant and Ward, 2011).

Over the last two decades, a field of enquiry known as 'evolutionary psychology' has dominated evolutionary approaches to understanding human behaviour. As Durrant and Ellis (2003, p. 1) summarise, 'Evolutionary psychology is the application of the principles and knowledge of evolutionary biology to psychological theory and research. Its central assumption is that the human brain is comprised of a large number of specialised mechanisms that were shaped by natural selection over vast periods of time to solve recurrent information processing problems faced by our ancestors' (also see Buss, 1995; Confer *et al.*, 2010). This quote clearly illustrates the idea that evolutionary psychology draws from evolutionary theory but that its focus is human psychology. It also highlights several 'special assumptions' that are not necessarily held by all evolutionary scientists. First, for evolutionary psychologists, psychological mechanisms (rather than behaviour per se) are the main unit of analysis. Second, it is assumed that humans possess a large number of domain-specific psychological mechanisms (often referred to as 'modules') that have evolved to solve specific 'adaptive problems' in our ancestral past. Third, because the human mind is the product of selection pressures operating in ancestral environments, there are likely to be a number of 'mismatches' between our evolved psychology and the modern environment.

Evolutionary psychologists have contributed significantly to our understanding of various human behaviours, including aggression and violence (e.g., Buss and Shackelford, 1997; Daly and Wilson, 1988). However, it is important to recognise that evolutionary psychology is one of at least three – largely complementary – approaches to explaining human behaviour from an evolutionary perspective, the other two being human behavioural ecology and gene–culture co-evolutionary theory (Brown *et al.*, 2011; Ward and Durrant, 2011). Human behavioural ecologists, like evolutionary psychologists, also draw their explanatory resources from evolutionary theory. However, they tend to view human behaviour as extremely flexible and that, typically speaking, humans behave adaptively in a wide range of ecological and social contexts. They therefore are not so committed to the idea of the 'massively modular' human mind and are less likely to emphasise mismatches between current behaviour and past selective environments (Smith, Borgerhoff Mulder, and Hill, 2001). A third approach to the evolutionary study of human behaviour is referred to as the 'gene–culture co-evolutionary theory' (or sometimes, 'dual inheritance theory'). Three key assumptions characterise the gene–culture co-evolutionary perspective (Henrich and McElreath, 2007; Richerson and Boyd, 2005). First, the human capacity for culture is, itself, a product of evolution by natural selection. Second, the existence of culture and the developmental processes that allow individuals to acquire cultural attitudes, beliefs, norms and values provides for a second form of inheritance: cultural evolution. Third, genetic and cultural evolutionary processes can be dynamically related to each other. In other words, genetic changes can influence cultural practices and cultural evolution can create changes in the environment, which result in genetic changes (Richerson and Boyd, 2005).

In sum, there is a growing acceptance of evolutionary ideas in the social and behavioural sciences. Evolutionary approaches to understanding human psychology focus on how our psychological and behavioural characteristics have been shaped by natural and sexual selection and thus provide 'ultimate' explanations for human behaviour. They are therefore, in principle, compatible with explanations that focus on proximate biological, psychological and situational factors, and in our attempts to provide complete explanatory accounts, it is important to draw on both proximate and ultimate levels of analysis. Although there are a number of different approaches to applying evolutionary theory to human behaviour, these should largely be viewed as complementary rather than competing approaches (Brown *et al.*, 2011; Dunbar, 2006; Durrant and Ward, 2011). As will be outlined below, each of the three perspectives provides important insights into our understanding of violence and alcohol use while drawing from the common stock of evolutionary theory.

AGGRESSION AND VIOLENCE

When we turn to an examination of the research on aggression, violence and violent offending, four important findings clearly stand out. First, men are much more likely to engage in aggression and violence than are women. Although women may be more likely to participate in indirect aggression (Archer and Coyne, 2005), and population-based studies suggest that rates of intimate partner violence in Western societies may be roughly comparable for men and women (Archer, 2002), on virtually all other measures of aggression and violence, men are overwhelmingly likely to be the perpetrators (Archer, 2004, 2009a,b). This point is most vividly illustrated in homicide statistics. Somewhere in the region of 90% of all homicides are perpetrated by men (Brookman, 2010; Uniform Crime Reports, 2010; United Nations Office on Drugs and Crime, 2011). Men are also more likely to be the *victims* of homicide. For instance, in the United States in 2009, 84% of homicide victims were male (Uniform Crime Reports, 2010). In other words, the vast majority of homicides involve men killing other men (Daly and Wilson, 1997). Second, the use of aggression and violence is most common among *young* men. Again, homicide statistics provide the most compelling picture of this finding with rates of homicide perpetration *and* victimisation tending to peak between the ages of 15 and 29 (Brookman, 2010; United Nations Office on Drugs and Crime, 2011). Third, although the evidence base is perhaps less compelling, violent offending is more common among individuals from lower socio-economic backgrounds (Brookman, 2010; Daly and Wilson, 1988). Finally, it must be noted that rates of violent offending vary significantly cross-culturally and historically. According to the United Nations Global Study on Homicide, for instance, regional homicide rates range between 17.4 per 100,000 in Africa to 3.1 per 100,000 in Asia (United Nations Office on Drugs and Crime, 2011). Similarly, rates of homicide and other forms of violence vary enormously across time in the same location (Eisner, 2003; Pinker, 2011).

The available evidence clearly indicates that the capacity for aggression and violence is a ubiquitous feature of human societies cross-culturally and histori-cally (Keeley, 1996; McCall and Shields, 2008). The use of aggression is also common across a wide range of animal species. From an evolutionary perspective, it can be argued that the psychological and physiological mechanisms that under-lie aggression are biological adaptations: they have been selected for because they increased the survival and reproductive success of individuals in ancestral environments (Archer, 2009a; Buss and Shackelford, 1997; Daly and Wilson, 1988; Goetz, 2010). As Buss and Shackelford (1997) note, however, aggression is a context-sensitive strategy; that is, aggression is employed in a diverse range of specific situations in order to solve particular adaptive problems. These include the co-option of resources from others, defence against attack, predation, the negotiation of status and power hierarchies, and the deterrence of long-term mates from sexual infidelity. An evolutionary perspective can also help us to understand the pervasive patterns in violent offending described above.

In order to account for sex differences in violent offending – particularly the preponderance of male–male violence – we need to draw on the resources of sexual selection and parental investment theory (Archer, 2004, 2009b; Daly and Wilson, 1997). Sexual selection theory highlights how characteristics can be selected for if they increase the reproductive success of the individuals who possess them, even though they may reduce survival prospects. Of particular importance to understanding patterns in aggression and violence is intra-sexual selection: the competition among members of one sex for access to the other sex. The strength of sexual selection, and, thus, sex differences in intra-sexual competi-tion, depends critically on differences in parental investment. Briefly, the sex that invests more in offspring is hypothesised to be choosier in selecting a mate and to be more generally risk averse for the simple evolutionary reason that it has more to lose from risky decision making (Campbell, 2006; Durrant and Ellis, 2003; Trivers, 1972). In the vast majority of mammalian species, including humans, females invest significantly more in offspring than do males, and hence we should expect intra-sexual competition to be more intense among males. Indeed, the significant physical differences between men and women in strength and muscle mass clearly indicate an evolutionary history of male–male competition (Archer, 2009b; Lassek and Gaulin, 2009; Puts, 2010). From this perspective, then, the pre-ponderance of male–male violence that is clearly illustrated in statistics on violent offending can be viewed as the outcome of competition between rival males for status and resources (Archer, 2009b; Daly and Wilson, 1997; Puts, 2010). This does not mean that men always fight 'over women'; rather, males compete with each other for dominance, status and physical resources, which correlate reliably with mating opportunities and overall reproductive success, or at least would have in ancestral environments.

In order to account for important age and social class differences in violent offending, we need to consider how the strategic use of violence is more or less beneficial (from an evolutionary perspective) depending on age and social context. Life-history theory provides a useful evolutionary framework for understanding these differences. Life-history theory is centrally concerned with how organisms allocate resources at different stages in development and in response to different environmental conditions. Two important trade-offs that face organisms are the allocation of resources into current versus future reproduction, and the direction of effort into mating versus parenting (Chisholm, 1993; Kaplan and Gangestad, 2005). Life-history theory predicts that intra-sexual competition among human males for status and resources should be most intense during late adolescence and young adulthood because this is the period where men are attempting to establish status and when opportunities for mating are most prevalent. Thus, it is hypothesised that the heightened risk taking that occurs during adolescence (including various types of antisocial behaviour), and which is mediated by important neurodevelopmental changes in the brain (Galvan, 2010; Steinberg, 2007), reflects the preferential allocation of resources into mating rather than parenting effort. As men age, they are more likely to accrue resources and status and therefore preferentially channel their efforts into parenting rather than mating. Consistent with this perspective, we see a decrease in violence and risk-taking behaviour associated with getting married, obtaining stable employment and having children (Archer, 2009b; Daly and Wilson, 1988).

Life-history theory also predicts that the allocation of resources should be dependent on features of the social and physical environments. In other words, we should also expect *within*-species differences in certain life-history characteristics depending on particular environmental contexts. Specifically, it is argued that exposure to harsh and unpredictable environments during development results in an adaptive suite of changes that tend to result in an increase in risk-taking and antisocial behaviour commensurate with an allocation of resources into current rather than future reproductive efforts (Belsky, Steinberg, and Draper, 1991; Ellis *et al.*, 2009, 2012). Consistent with this so-called fast life-history strategy, research finds that males who grow up in unpredictable and dangerous environments (e.g., individuals from lower socio-economic backgrounds) tend to engage in more risk-taking and antisocial behaviours including violence, reproduce earlier and have lower life expectancies (Daly and Wilson, 1988; Kruger and Nesse, 2006; Nettle, 2010). These differences in risk-taking strategies in response to different environmental conditions are referred to by evolutionary scientists as 'conditional adaptations' because their expression depends on a specific set of conditions (Ellis *et al.*, 2012).

The substantial differences in rates of violent offending that are found historically and cross-culturally may, on the face of it, seem somewhat of a puzzle from an evolutionary perspective. However, evolutionary psychologists emphasise how human behavioural diversity can reflect the operation of universal psychological mechanisms in response to different environmental conditions (Confer *et al.*, 2010). Thus, consistent with the life-history perspective outlined above, part of the variation in violent offending across time and space is likely to reflect the operation of contingent adaptations that make risk-taking and violent behaviour more selectively advantageous under different conditions. The finding that measures of income inequality are positively associated with national homicide rates is consistent with this idea (Jacobs and Richardson, 2008; McCall and Nieuwbeerta, 2007). A complete explanation for regional and historical differences, however, also needs to take into account patterns in cultural evolution. More specifically, changes in the nature and prevalence of violent offending are likely to reflect, in part, differences in attitudes, beliefs, values and norms along with changing social-structural contexts (Eisner, 2003; Pinker, 2011).

In sum, an evolutionary approach to understanding violence provides an ultimate explanation that highlights how aggression and violence have been selected for during our evolutionary history. The use of violence is, however, a risky strategy, and thus the evolutionary advantages of using violence will depend critically on gender, age and environmental context. Of course, in order to provide a complete explanation for violent offending, it is essential that we integrate evolutionary approaches with explanations drawn from different levels of analysis, and thus it is important that we also attend to the proximate psychological, situational, social and cultural factors that influence violent behaviour.

ALCOHOL USE AND ABUSE

The evolutionary function of aggression and violence can help us to understand why violent crime is a recurrent feature of human societies. Another virtually ubiquitous characteristic of human societies is the use of psychoactive drugs, including alcohol (Courtwright, 2001; Durrant and Thakker, 2003; Heath, 2000; Rudgley, 1993). Although the use of drugs may result in beneficial outcomes in certain circumstances, drug use is responsible for a significant amount of harm to users in modern societies and, thus, from an evolutionary perspective, would appear to be a maladaptive behaviour. It is unlikely, therefore, that the use of alcohol and drugs has been specifically selected for. However, an evolutionary approach can be fruitfully employed to shed some light on the human tendency to use and abuse psychoactive substances (Durrant *et al.*, 2009; Lende, 2008; Nesse and Berridge, 1997).

An important starting point is the recognition that all drugs of abuse, including alcohol, act either directly or indirectly to increase levels of dopamine in the mesocorticolimbic dopamine system (Koob and Le Moal, 2008; Picciotto, 1998). It has been argued that this system (along with others) is critically involved in mediating experiences of reward that are associated with fitness-enhancing activities such as sex, feeding, drinking and positive social relations (Berridge and Kringelbach, 2008). In short, people use drugs because they 'feel good' and they have this capacity to generate positive emotional states because they act on reward systems in the brain that have evolved to signal to the organism the presence of reproductively relevant stimuli. By virtue of these psychopharmacological effects, drugs can also exert changes in motivational–emotional systems that result in the characteristic pattern of compulsive drug use seen among individuals addicted to drugs. According to Robinson and Berridge (2003), repeated drug use leads to a sensitisation of the motivational systems underlying 'incentive salience' that leads to the pathological wanting of drugs.

Although alcohol also acts to increase levels of dopamine in the mesocorticol-imbic dopamine system, the extremely widespread use of alcohol (historically and cross-culturally) makes this particular substance a somewhat unusual case. In part, this reflects that fact that alcohol is easily obtained from a large variety of organic sources including fruit, grains, milk and even cactus (Durrant and Thakker, 2003; Heath, 2000). Alcohol is also somewhat unusual among psychoactive drugs in that it also provides a – potentially valuable – source of calories. Indeed, Dudley (2002) has argued that humans would have been exposed to the low levels of alcohol present in overripe fruit throughout their evolutionary history and so may have evolved specific olfactory and gustatory preferences for alcohol. Of course, as Dudley (2002) also points out, the ready availability of large amounts of high-proof alcohol is clearly an evolutionary novelty, and thus it is unlikely that humans are adapted to the drinking patterns that we see in many modern societies.

As with violence, the use of alcohol is clearly patterned by age, gender, socio-economic status and culture. Indeed, as Hill and Chow (2002) note, many of the patterns are highly similar: risky drinking is most prevalent for young, single men aged 18–29. Plausibly, these findings reflect the idea that problem drinking is a manifestation of general risk taking that is most prevalent among young men for the evolutionary reasons outlined above. There are also enormous cross-cultural differences in the use of alcohol (Durrant and Thakker, 2003; Heath, 2000; MacAndrew and Edgerton, 1969). Many cultural groups, of course, officially proscribe the use of alcohol (e.g., Mormons, Muslims), whereas others allow alcohol use but strongly condemn drunkenness. Among some cultural groups (e.g., most English-speaking Western nations), in contrast, there are norms that *prescribe* drinking, and those individuals that drink lightly or abstain can be viewed as deviant. Paton-Simpson (2001), for instance, describes how the heavy consumption of alcohol in social contexts in New Zealand is largely obligatory for young men, and those that do not conform to these norms may be subject to ridicule and abuse. These cultural differences reflect the fact that, although there may be an evolutionary basis to the consumption of alcohol and other drugs, their use is also heavily regulated by cultural attitudes, beliefs and norms.

ALCOHOL-RELATED VIOLENCE

The term 'alcohol-related violence' refers to the finding that the consumption of alcohol and violent behaviour tend to be associated with one another (Dingwall, 2006). Two causal models can potentially explain this relationship: (1) the consumption of alcohol causes (i.e., increases the risk or probability) for violent behaviour; and (2) the use of alcohol and violent behaviour arise from shared risk factors. These two models are, of course, not mutually exclusive, and the available research indicates that both models contribute to our understanding of the association between alcohol and violence.

The first model emphasises the importance of understanding the psychopharmacological effect of alcohol on the human brain and how this might increase the propensity to engage in violent behaviour. One prominent theoretical framework suggests that alcohol use increases the risk for violence because 'alcohol consumption impairs controlled effortful cognitive processing' (Giancola *et al.*, 2010, p. 266) and effectively narrows attention to salient cues in the environment. Given the strong, robust relationship between self-regulatory capacities and violence (de Ridder *et al.*, 2011; Rebellon, Straus, and Medeiros, 2008), it is not surprising that a substance that, when taken in sufficient quantities, impairs these capacities increases the risk for violent behaviour. Of course, most drinking episodes do not result in violence and many people drink alcohol on a regular basis without ever becoming aggressive. This clearly suggests the importance of identifying moderating variables that influence the association between alcohol and violence. These appear to include a range of psychological and situational factors such as antisocial personality, alcohol-related expectancies, irritability, low empathy, anxiety and drinking contexts conducive to violence (Giancola, 2002; Giancola *et al.*, 2010; Leonard *et al.*, 2003; McMurran, 2011). It also seems to be the case that individuals who are more prone to engaging in aggressive and violent behaviours are also at a higher risk for alcohol abuse and dependence, suggesting that the relationship between alcohol and violence emerges, in part, because of shared risk factors (Dingwall, 2006).

In sum, although more research is needed to clarify the important mediating and moderating variables that can explain the relationship between alcohol and violence, considerable progress has been made in identifying these important proximate processes. In this section, it is argued that our understanding of alcohol-related violence can be further advanced by considering some of the ultimate mechanisms that give rise to this relationship. Drawing from work in evolutionary medicine (e.g., Gluckman, Beedle, and Hanson, 2009; Nesse and Stearns, 2008), I suggest that problem behaviours such as alcohol-related violence can be understood in terms of the outcome of four distinct evolutionary pathways (see Figure 4.1): evolutionary adaptation, conditional adaptation, evolutionary mismatch and cultural evolution. It is argued that each of these pathways contributes to alcohol-related violence and can, as discussed in the next section, become targets for intervention efforts.

Pathway 1: Evolutionary Adaptation

The first pathway suggests that problem behaviours can arise, in part, due to the operation of evolved psychological adaptations operating as they were 'designed to' by natural and/or sexual selection in response to relevant environmental inputs. In other words, although we may consider the behaviour to be problematic or harmful, it may actually reflect the 'normal' operation of evolved cognitive, motivational and emotional systems. Consider an analogy from the field of evolutionary medicine. Many individuals will consider the higher fever, runny nose, vomiting and body aches that accompany a bout of influenza as highly undesirable, but plausibly, they reflect the natural operation of evolved physiological mechanisms in response to infectious agents (Nesse and Stearns, 2008). Similarly, a considerable amount of alcohol-related violence can be understood in terms of the fact that young men have been selected for intra-sexual competition that has, in part, involved acts of physical aggression and violence. From this perspective,

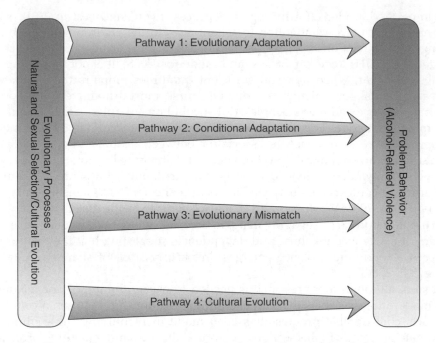

Figure 4.1 Four evolutionary pathways for understanding problem behaviours.

the association between alcohol and violence arises because (1) alcohol reduces the capacity for self-regulation and thus 'lowers the threshold' for the use of aggression in response to specific cues such as provocation; and (2) alcohol use brings large numbers of similarly aged men (and women) together in social contexts (bars, night clubs and other drinking establishments) that are likely to foster intra-sexual competition.

Research by McMurran *et al*. (2010, 2011) suggests that a significant majority of episodes of alcohol-related violence among young men reflect the pursuit of 'social dominance goals' and often occur in response to perceived provocations and threats. Consistent with work on the situational antecedents of homicide among young men (Luckenbill, 1977; Polk, 1995,1999), alcohol-related violence in this research often arose from an escalating series of provocative exchanges over what appears to be seemingly trivial matters (e.g., small debts, name-calling, arguments) that often occurred in public spaces in front of others. From an evolutionary perspective, status and reputation are important commodities that, in some contexts, may be worth fighting for – particularly when there is an audience of peers present. As one participant in McMurran *et al*.'s (2010, p. 74) study indicated,

> The fight was worth doing. . . . I feel proud. I can laugh about it when I get out. This gives me a reputation and people will respect me. I felt satisfied for winning the fight and I felt like I was in control. It was good for my rep [reputation].

Pathway 2: Conditional Adaptation

The second pathway is similar to the first except that it reflects the operation of *conditional psychological adaptations* operating as they were designed to by natural and/or sexual selection in response to specific environmental inputs, which also include relevant developmental environments. This pathway draws on life-history theory and is therefore relevant to understanding why alcohol-related violence is more prevalent among individuals who are more likely to have been exposed to harsh and unpredictable environments such as those that characterise lower socio-economic neighbourhoods. As noted earlier, these early stressful environments tend to result in the adaptive development of a suite of 'fast' life-history strategies that focus on immediate rewards and mating rather than parenting effort (Ellis *et al.*, 2012). These individuals, therefore, are especially prone to engage in risky behaviour, which may include violence, drug use and heavy drinking. Understanding the role of life-history factors is, therefore, important in explaining some of the important common causal factors that explain the association between alcohol use and violence (e.g., risk taking, impulsivity) as well as some of the importing moderating factors (e.g., antisocial traits and characteristics) that make alcohol-related violence more likely for some individuals than others.

Pathway 3: Evolutionary Mismatch

This pathway suggests that part of the relationship between alcohol use and violence arises due to an evolutionary mismatch between evolved psychological mechanisms and novel features of the contemporary environment. Examples of mismatches in evolutionary medicine are relatively easy to find. For instance, although preferences for food high in sugar and fat content probably contributed to reproductive fitness in ancestral environments where food availability was patchy, in many modern environments, these preferences contribute significantly to problems such as diabetes, tooth decay and obesity (Turner *et al.*, 2008).

Similarly, although low levels of alcohol consumption may have been a relatively long-standing feature of human evolutionary history (Dudley, 2002), it is clear that the ready availability of high alcohol content beverages is a novel feature of the human environment. Given the enduring appeal of alcohol and other drugs that act on evolved motivational systems, it is not surprising that alcohol use and alcohol-related problems are widespread in many Western countries. The development of alcoholic drinks high in sugar content (e.g., the so-called *alcopops*) has added an additional novel aspect by tapping into evolved human gustatory preferences. The widespread availability of alcohol means that, because of alcohol's psychopharmacological effect on the human nervous system, violence becomes more likely. In short, humans have not evolved in contexts where motivations to engage in intra-sexual competition are coupled with the ready availability of a psychoactive substance that has the capacity to reduce self-control.

Another – somewhat less widely recognized – novel feature of modern Western environments is age segregation (Ellis *et al.*, 2012). In ancestral environments (and among extant hunter-gatherer groups), individuals of all ages interacted in social and work contexts. In contrast, in modern Western societies, age segregation is the norm. This is most starkly illustrated in schooling environments but also tends to be a feature of recreational and leisure activities including parties and other contexts where young people gather to consume alcohol. There is some evidence that aggression is less prevalent in mixed-age groups, particularly those that include young children and infants (Gray, 2011). Age-segregated socialisation may also heighten alcohol-related violence as it places large numbers of young men in social contexts that, in effect, maximises opportunities for intra-sexual competition. In sum, the regular consumption of a 'cognitively impairing' psychoactive substance in the context of (often) age-segregated socialisation provides a novel evolutionary environment that furnishes recurrent opportunities for conflicts to emerge between young men.

Pathway 4: Cultural Evolution

The final pathway suggests that alcohol-related violence is also, partly, the result of cultural evolution and/or gene–culture co-evolutionary processes. As noted above, the relative prevalence of violence among young men and the consumption of alcohol both vary cross-culturally and historically. This suggests that alcohol-related violence is partly the product of social-structural and cultural factors in combination with evolved psychological mechanisms.

Historical and cross-cultural variations in homicide rates between young men are likely to be the result of a number of interacting factors (Pinker, 2011). One important social-structural factor is the presence of reliable third-party enforcement of social norms and legal sanctions. Wherever individuals are required to 'take the law into their own hands', then norms that favour the ready use of violence to obtain respect and to resolve conflicts are likely to evolve. The existence of norms favourable to the use of violence has, variously, been used to explain the high rates of violence among men in Europe in the middle ages (Eisner, 2003), in deprived neighbourhoods in the United States (Anderson, 1999) and among Southern White males (Nisbett, 1993). Drawing from the work of Norbert Elias, Pinker (2011) also emphasises the importance of norms favour self-control in the decline in male–male violence in Europe over the last 500 years.

As noted above, there are also clearly significant cross-cultural and historical differences in the use of alcohol and in the prevalence of alcohol-related violence. Although these differences are likely to reflect a number of factors, including the availability of alcohol, they are also clearly shaped by group level norms, values and attitudes towards drinking (Heath, 2000). In other words, although humans are likely to be drawn to the use of alcohol and other drugs for the evolutionary reasons outlined above, *how* they use such substances depends, in part, on the local norms that guide appropriate patterns of use. In contemporary English-speaking Western countries, heavy drinking, especially among young people, is both acceptable and – in some contexts – expected. Cultural beliefs about the expected and acceptable patterns of behaviour while intoxicated may also influence the prevalence of alcohol-related violence (Durrant and Thakker, 2003; Heath, 2000). MacAndrew and Edgerton (1969), for example, argued that there are important cultural norms that prescribe what is acceptable behaviour when intoxicated, and some research suggests that people's *expectations* about alcohol's effect may subsequently influence their behaviour when intoxicated (e.g., Smucker-Barnwell, Borders, and Earlywine, 2006).

IMPLICATIONS FOR THE MANAGEMENT OF ALCOHOL-RELATED VIOLENCE

A number of strategies have the potential to reduce alcohol-related violence. These include legislative changes that influence the availability of alcoholic beverages; situational crime prevention initiatives that focus on drinking environments; social crime prevention approaches that target individuals, families and communities; individual-based interventions; and attempts to change cultural norms and values regarding alcohol use. In this section, these general approaches are discussed in the light of the evolutionary framework for understanding alcohol-related violence presented in the previous section. Ultimately, the implementation of particular initiatives should be based on their proven effectiveness in reducing alcohol-related violence. It also makes sense that strategies to reduce alcohol-related violence focus on some of the more important proximate psychological and situational factors that have been identified. However, an evolutionary approach can also help us to understand why alcohol-related violence arises and what approaches are most likely to be effective.

English-speaking Western countries have favoured the use of legislative strategies in an attempt to reduce the problems that arise from the use of psychoactive drugs such as cannabis, cocaine and heroin. Tobacco, too, has been subject to a consistent series of legislative reforms over the last two decades. In contrast, the market in alcohol has become increasingly deregulated in many Western countries (Dingwall, 2006). Outright prohibition of alcohol is unlikely to find favour with politicians, policy makers or the public and, by creating an unregulated black market for alcohol, may be as likely to increase as to decrease alcohol-related violence. However, the evolutionary framework provided in the previous section does suggest that a number of legislative changes may be effective in reducing alcohol-related problems. Importantly, the recognition that there is a mismatch between evolved motivational–emotional systems and the ready availability of alcohol in most Western societies leads to a heightened appreciation that alcohol is 'no ordinary commodity' (Babor *et al.*, 2003). Consistent with this view, legislative initiatives that control the affordability, availability and promotion of alcohol should contribute to a reduction in alcohol-related problems (including violence) (Babor *et al.*, 2003). Furthermore, the recognition that adolescence is a period in human development that involves an increase in risk taking and intra-sexual competition encourages the setting of a legal drinking age as old as can be publicly acceptable.

Given that risk-taking behaviour and intra-sexual competition over status and resources are likely to be a relatively enduring feature of interactions among young men, initiatives that can effectively change features of the environment may be more realistic targets for intervention. Situational crime prevention strategies that alter the nature of drinking environments offer some plausible suggestions. Importantly, initiatives that decrease the likelihood of provocation (or perceived provocation) will reduce some of the situational 'triggers' for violence in public drinking environments. For example, reducing crowding, cutting waiting times to enter bars, improved lighting, and maintaining reasonable temperature and noise levels are likely to result in lower levels of frustration and conflicts among patrons (Graham and Homel, 2008). The effective enforcement of rules in public drinking establishments, including the swift intervention in conflicts before they escalate, may also be effective by setting local norms regarding appropriate behaviour. By preventing minor conflicts from getting out of hand, appropriately trained bar staff can also defuse violence, thus allowing protagonists to 'save face' and therefore not experience a loss in status (Graham and Homel, 2008). The evolutionary framework outlined above also suggests that drinking establishments that encourage a wide age range of patrons may be less prone to violence, although this might be difficult to implement in practice.

A good deal of research indicates that social crime prevention initiatives can be effective in reducing criminal and antisocial behaviour including problem drug use and violence (Farrington and Welsh, 2007). An evolutionary framework that draws on life-history theory and the idea of conditional adaptation provides an ultimate explanation for why such programmes can be effective. By changing important social contexts so as to improve the quality of developmental environments, social crime prevention initiatives can help to divert individuals from the development of fast life-history strategies associated with risk-taking and antisocial behaviours (see Ellis *et al.*, 2012). Of course, making meaningful and widespread changes in social-structural environments is not an easy task. However, as Ellis *et al.* (2012, p. 12) argue,

> Because these [life-history strategies] are powerful evolved responses that promoted lineage survival during our natural selective history, Band-aid interventions . . . are unlikely to effect change at a foundational level . . . Prevention and treatment programmes instead need to address causative environmental conditions. This means altering the social contexts of disadvantaged children and adolescents in ways that, through changes in their experiences, induce an understanding that they can lead longer, healthier, more predictable lives.

Making meaningful changes in social-structural conditions, although clearly desirable, represents a long-term strategy for reducing crime (including alcohol-related violence). It is also important, therefore, that we target individuals who have problems with violence, alcohol use and alcohol-related violence. A good deal of research supports the effectiveness of both alcohol and violent offender treatment programmes, although there is clearly some scope for improving outcomes (McGuire, 2006, 2008). Treatment programmes that target offender cognition in ways that improve self-regulatory capacities are consistent with an evolutionary approach as they are able to furnish at-risk individuals with the cognitive resources that help them to inhibit strong risk-taking proclivities. Relapse prevention plans that involve keeping individuals away from high-risk environments (e.g., public drinking establishments) are also likely to be effective because they help to remove some of the key situational triggers to alcohol-related violence. Finally, by considering the evolutionary origins of violence and drug use, it may be possible to develop intervention programmes that help individuals to pursue what Ward and Stewart (2003) call *primary human goods* (e.g., agency, mastery, pleasure, relatedness and knowledge) through nonharmful means (Ward and Maruna, 2007). Indeed, an extensive literature on 'natural recovery' from drug and alcohol problems highlights the importance of positive life experiences such as marriage, children and gainful employment in facilitating desistance (Klingemann and Sobell, 2007). As Ward and Durrant (2011, p. 202) note, 'A trend towards incorporating approach goals and trying to help offenders capitalize on their strengths and core commitments has recently emerged and is consistent with evolutionary theory. The points of connection arising from strength-based theories include their promotion of a suite of motivational adaptations (e.g., disposition to seek primary goods) alongside general and specific cognitive skills'.

Finally, the suggestion that alcohol-related violence can be understood, in part, as a consequence of cultural evolutionary processes encourages efforts to develop effective community interventions and social marketing approaches to targeting alcohol-related norms, attitudes and beliefs. Changing norms relating to drinking is no easy task, especially if we recognise that such norms may be more strongly held by specific groups in society. Efforts that highlight the risks of heavy drinking may, however, be less effective if problem drinking is, in part, driven by risk-taking proclivities as an evolutionary analysis suggests. More effective approaches may be to link status with prosocial behaviours and the effective *control* of violence and drinking. Sustained efforts to alter societal attitudes, beliefs and norms relating to tobacco use over the last three decades suggest that such change is possible. Whether or not they can be achieved in a deregulated environment that permits the widespread advertisement of alcohol beverages, however, remains an important question for policy makers.

SUMMARY

Alcohol-related violence is responsible for a significant amount of harm in society. Although considerable progress has been made in understanding the proximate causal mechanisms that link alcohol use with violence, I have argued that our understanding of this phenomenon can be further enhanced by taking an evolutionary approach that highlights the importance of ultimate causal mechanisms as well. More specifically, I have suggested that alcohol-related violence can be understood in terms of the action of four 'evolutionary pathways': evolutionary adaptation, conditional adaptation, evolutionary mismatch and cultural evolution. These different pathways highlight the fact that alcohol-related violence can be viewed as the product of evolved psychological mechanisms and processes (which, critically, differ by sex, age and life-history environments) operating in concert with specific situational, social and cultural environments. Furthermore, I have suggested that this evolutionary framework can help us to further understand how effective strategies for managing alcohol-related violence work. Throughout this chapter, I have focussed on alcohol-related violence that occurs largely among men in social contexts. There is, however, scope to extend this analysis to consider alcohol-related violence that occurs in other situations (e.g., family and intimate partner violence).

REFERENCES

Anderson, E. (1999) *Code of the Street: Decency, Violence, and the Moral Life of the Inner City*. New York: Norton.

Archer, J. (2002) Sex differences in physically aggressive acts between heterosexual partners: A meta-analytic review. *Aggression and Violent Behaviour*, **7**, 313–351.

Archer, J. (2004) Sex differences in aggression in real-world settings: A meta-analytic review. *Review of General Psychology*, **8**, 291–322.

Archer, J. (2009a) The nature of human aggression. *International Journal of Law and Psychiatry*, **32**, 202–208.

Archer, J. (2009b) Does sexual selection explain human sex differences in aggression? *Behavioral and Brain Sciences*, **32**, 249–311.

Archer, J. and Coyne, S.M. (2005) An integrated review of indirect, relational, and social aggression. *Personality and Social Psychology Review*, **9**, 212–230.

Babor, T.F., Caetano, R., Casswell, S. *et al.* (2003) *Alcohol: No Ordinary Commodity – Research and Public Policy*. Oxford: Oxford University Press.

Barkow, J.H. (2006) Introduction: Sometimes the bus does wait. In J.H. Barkow (ed.), *Missing the Revolution: Darwinism for Social Scientists* (pp. 3–60). Oxford: Oxford University Press.

Belsky, J., Steinberg, L., and Draper, P. (1991) Childhood experience, interpersonal development, and reproductive strategy: An evolutionary theory of socialization. *Child Development*, **62**, 647–670.

Berridge, K.C. and Kringelbach, M.L. (2008) Affective neuroscience of pleasure: Reward in humans and animals. *Psychopharmacology*, **199**, 457–480.

Brookman, F. (2010) Homicide. In F. Brookman, M. Maguire, H. Pierpoint, and T. Bennett (eds), *Handbook on Crime* (pp. 217–245). Cullompton, Devon: Willan Publishing.

Brown, G.R., Dickens, T.E., Sear, R., and Laland, K.N. (2011) Evolutionary accounts of behavioural diversity. *Philosophical Transactions of the Royal Society*, **366**, 313–324.

Buss, D.M. (1995) Evolutionary psychology: A new paradigm for psychological science. *Psychological Inquiry*, **6**, 1–49.

Buss, D.M. and Shackelford, T.K. (1997) Human aggression in evolutionary psychological perspective. *Clinical Psychology Review*, **17**, 605–619.

Campbell, A. (2006) Sex differences in direct aggression: What are the psychological mediators? *Aggression and Violent Behavior*, **11**, 237–264.

Chaplin, R., Flatley, J., and Smith, K. (2011) *Crime in England and Wales 2010/11: Findings from the British Crime Survey and Police Recorded Crime*. London: Home Office. Retrieved November 5, 2011, from http://www.homeoffice.gov.uk/publications/science-research-statistics/research-statistics/crime-research/hosb1011/hosb1011?view=Binary

Chisholm, J.S. (1993) Death, hope, and sex: Life history theory and the development of reproductive strategies. *Current Anthropology*, **34**, 1–24.

Confer, J.C., Easton, J.A., Fleischman, D.S. *et al.* (2010) Evolutionary psychology: Controversies, questions, prospects, and limitations. *American Psychologist*, **65**, 110–126.

Courtwright, D.T. (2001) *Forces of Habit: Drugs and the Making of the Modern World*. Cambridge, MA: Harvard University Press.

Daly, M. and Wilson, M. (1988) *Homicide*. Hawthorne, NY: Aldine.

Daly, M. and Wilson, M. (1997) Crime and conflict: Homicide in evolutionary psychological perspective. *Crime and Justice*, **22**, 51–100.

de Ridder, D.T.D., Lensvelt-Mulders, G., Finkenauer, C. *et al.* (2011) Taking stock of self-control: A meta analysis of how trait self-control relates to a wide range of behaviors. *Personality and Social Psychology Review*, **16**, 78–89.

Dingwall, G. (2006) *Alcohol and Crime*. Cullompton, Devon: Willan Publishing.

Dudley, R. (2002) Fermenting fruit and the historical ecology of ethanol ingestion: Is alcoholism in modern humans an evolutionary hangover? *Addiction*, **97**, 381–388.

Dunbar, R.I.M. (2006) Evolution and the social sciences. *History of the Human Sciences*, **20**, 29–50.

Durrant, R., Adamson, S., Todd, F., and Sellman, D. (2009) Drug use and addiction: An evolutionary perspective. *Australian and New Zealand Journal of Psychiatry*, **43**, 1049–1056.

Durrant, R. and Ellis, B.J. (2003) Evolutionary psychology. In M. Gallagher and R.J. Nelson (eds), *Handbook of Psychology: Biological Psychology*, Vol. 3 (pp. 1–33). Hoboken, NJ: John Wiley & Sons, Inc.

Durrant, R. and Thakker, J. (2003) *Substance Use and Abuse: Cultural and Historical Perspectives*. Thousand Oaks, CA: Sage Publications.

Durrant, R. and Ward, T. (2011) Evolutionary explanations in the social and behavioural sciences: Introduction and overview. *Aggression and Violent Behavior*, **16**, 361–370.

Eisner, M. (2003) Long-term historical trends in violent crime. *Crime and Justice*, **30**, 83–142.

Ellis, B.J., Del Giudice, M., Dishion, T.J. *et al.* (2012) The evolutionary basis of risk adolescent behaviour: Implications for science, policy, and practice. *Developmental Psychology*, **48**, 598–623.

Ellis, B.J., Figueredo, A.J., Brumbach, B.H., and Schlomer, G.L. (2009) Fundamental dimensions of environmental risk: The impact of harsh versus unpredictable environments on the evolution and development of life history strategies. *Human Nature*, **20**, 204–268.

Exum, M.L. (2006) Alcohol and aggression: An integration of findings from experimental studies. *Journal of Criminal Justice*, **34**, 131–145.

Farrington, D.P. and Welsh, B.C. (2007) *Saving Children from a Life of Crime: Early Risk Factors and Effective Interventions*. Oxford: Oxford University Press.

Felson, R.B., Burchfield, K.B., and Teasdale, B. (2007) The impact of alcohol on different types of violent incidents. *Criminal Justice and Behavior*, **34**, 1057–1068.

Galvan, A. (2010) Adolescent development of the reward system. *Frontiers in Human Neuroscience*, **4**, 1–9.

Giancola, P.R. (2002) Irritability, acute alcohol consumption and aggressive behavior in men and women. *Drug and Alcohol Dependence*, **68**, 263–274.

Giancola, P.R., Josephs, R.A., Parrott, D.J., and Duke, A.A. (2010) Alcohol myopia revisited: Clarifying aggression and other acts of disinhibition through a distorted lens. *Perspectives on Psychological Science*, **5**, 265–278.

Gluckman, P., Beedle, A., and Hanson, M. (2009) *Principles of Evolutionary Medicine*. Oxford: Oxford University Press.

Goetz, A.T. (2010) The evolutionary psychology of violence. *Psicothema*, **22**, 15–21.

Graham, K. and Homel, R. (2008) *Raising the Bar: Preventing Aggression in and Around Bars, Pubs and Clubs*. Cullompton, Devon: Willan Publishing.

Gray, P. (2011) The special value of children's age-mixed play. *American Journal of Play*, **3**, 500–522.

Heath, D.B. (2000) *Drinking Occasions: Comparative Perspectives on Alcohol and Culture*. Brunner/Mazel: Taylor & Francis Group.

Henrich, J. and McElreath, R. (2007) Dual-inheritance theory: The evolution of human cultural capacities and cultural evolution. In R.I.M. Dunbar and L. Barrett (eds), *The Oxford Handbook of Evolutionary Psychology* (pp. 555–568). Oxford: Oxford University Press.

Hill, E.M. and Chow, K. (2002) Life-history theory and risky drinking. *Addiction*, **97**, 401–413.

Jacobs, D. and Richardson, A.M. (2008) Income inequality and homicide in the developed nations from 1975–1995. *Homicide Studies*, **12**, 28–45.

Kaplan, H.S. and Gangestad, S.W. (2005) Life history theory and evolutionary psychology. In D.M. Buss (ed.), *The Handbook of Evolutionary Psychology* (pp. 68–95). Hoboken, NJ: John Wiley & Sons, Inc.

Keeley, L.H. (1996) *War before Civilization: The Myth of the Peaceful Savage*. New York: Oxford University Press.

Ketelaar, T. and Ellis, B.J. (2000) Are evolutionary explanations unfalsifiable? Evolutionary psychology and the Lakatosian philosophy of science. *Psychological Inquiry*, **11**, 1–22.

Klingemann, H. and Sobell, L.C. (2007) *Promoting Self-Change from Addictive Behaviors: Practical Implications for Policy, Prevention, and Treatment*. Zurich: Springer.

Koob, G.F. and Le Moal, M. (2008) Addiction and the brain antireward system. *Annual Review of Psychology*, **59**, 29–53.

Kruger, D.J. and Nesse, R.M. (2006) An evolutionary life-history framework for understanding sex differences in human mortality rates. *Human Nature*, **17**, 74–97.

Lassek, W.D. and Gaulin, S.J.C. (2009) Costs and benefits of fat-free muscle mass in men: Relationship to mating success, dietary requirements, and native immunity. *Evolution and Human Behavior*, **30**, 322–328.

Lende, D.H. (2008) Evolution and modern behavioral problems: The case of addiction. In W.R. Trevathan, E.O. Smith, and J.J. McKenna (eds), *Evolutionary Medicine and Health: New Perspectives* (pp. 277–290). New York: Oxford University Press.

Leonard, K.E., Quigley, B.M., and Collins, R.L. (2003) Drinking, personality, and bar environmental characteristics as predictors of involvement in barroom aggression. *Addictive Behaviors*, **28**, 1681–1700.

Luckenbill, D.F. (1977) Criminal homicide as a situated transaction. *Social Problems*, **25**, 176–186.

MacAndrew, C. and Edgerton, R.B. (1969) *Drunken Comportment: A Social Explanation*. Chicago: Aldine.

McCall, G.S. and Shields, N. (2008) Examining the evidence from small-scale societies and early prehistory and implications for modern theories of aggression and violence. *Aggression and Violent Behavior*, **13**, 1–9.

McCall, P.L. and Nieuwbeerta, P. (2007) Structural covariates of homicide rates: A European city cross-national comparative analysis. *Homicide Studies*, **11**, 167–178.

McGuire, J. (2006) General offending behaviour programmes: Concept, theory, and practice. In C.R. Holin and E.J. Palmer (eds), *Offending Behaviour Programmes: Development, Application and Controversies*. John Wiley & Sons, Inc.

McGuire, J. (2008) A review of effective interventions for reducing aggression and violence. *Philosophical Transactions of the Royal Society B*, **363**, 2577–2597.

McMurran, M. (2011) Anxiety, alcohol intoxication, and aggression. *Legal and Criminological Psychology*, **16**, 357–371.

McMurran, M., Jinks, M., Howells, K., and Howard, R.C. (2010) Alcohol-related violence defined by ultimate goals: A qualitative analysis of the features of three different types of violence by intoxicated young male offenders. *Aggressive Behavior*, **36**, 67–79.

McMurran, M., Jinks, M., Howells, K., and Howard, R.C. (2011) Investigation of a typology of alcohol-related violence defined by ultimate goals. *Legal and Criminological Psychology*, **16**, 75–89.

Moeller, F.G. and Dougherty, D.M. (2001) Antisocial personality disorder, alcohol, and aggression. *Alcohol Research and Health*, **25**, 5–11.

Nesse, R.M. and Berridge, K.C. (1997) Psychoactive drug use in evolutionary perspective. *Science*, **278**, 63–66.

Nesse, R.M. and Stearns, S.C. (2008) The great opportunity: Evolutionary applications to medicine and public health. *Evolutionary Applications*, **1**, 28–48.

Nettle, D. (2010) Dying young and living fast: Variation in life history across English neighborhoods. *Behavioral Ecology*, **21**, 387–395.

Nisbett, R.E. (1993) Violence and U.S. regional culture. *American Psychologist*, **48**, 441–449.

Paton-Simpson, G. (2001) Socially obligatory drinking: A sociological analysis of norms governing minimum drinking levels. *Contemporary Drug Problems*, **28**, 133–177.

Picciotto, M.R. (1998) Common aspects of the action of nicotine and other drugs of abuse. *Drug and Alcohol Dependence*, **51**, 165–172.

Pinker, S. (2011) *The Better Angels of Our Nature: Why Violence Has Declined*. London: Penguin.

Plotkin, H. (2004) *Evolutionary Thought in Psychology: A Brief History*. Oxford: Blackwell.

Polk, K. (1995) Lethal violence as a form of masculine conflict resolution. *Australian and New Zealand Journal of Criminology*, **28**, 93–115.

Polk, K. (1999) Males and honor contest violence. *Homicide studies*, **3**, 6–29.

Puts, D.A. (2010) Beauty and the beast: Mechanisms of sexual selection in humans. *Evolution and Human Behavior*, **31**, 157–175.

Rebellon, C.J., Straus, M.A., and Medeiros, R. (2008) Self-control in global perspective: An empirical assessment of Gottfredson and Hirschi's theory within and across 32 national settings. *European Journal of Criminology*, **5**, 331–362.

Richerson, P.J. and Boyd, R. (2005) *Not by Genes Alone: How Culture Transformed Human Evolution*. Chicago: Chicago University Press.

Robinson, T.E. and Berridge, K.C. (2003) Addiction. *Annual Review of Psychology*, **54**, 25–53.

Rossow, I. (2001) Alcohol and homicide: A cross-cultural comparison of the relationship in 14 European countries. *Addiction*, **96**(Suppl 1), S77–S92.

Rudgley, R. (1993) *The Alchemy of Culture: Intoxicants in Society*. London: The British Museum Press.

Shaw, J., Hunt, I.M., Flynn, S. *et al.* (2006) The role of alcohol and drugs in homicides in England and Wales. *Addiction*, **101**, 1117–1124.

Smith, E.A., Borgerhoff Mulder, M., and Hill, K. (2001) Controversies in the evolutionary social sciences: A guide for the perplexed. *Trends in Ecology and Evolution*, **16**, 128–135.

Smucker-Barnwell, S., Borders, A., and Earlywine, M. (2006) Aggression expectancies and dispositional aggression moderate the relationship between alcohol consumption and alcohol related violence. *Aggressive Behavior*, **32**, 517–525.

Steinberg, L. (2007) Risk taking in adolescence: New perspectives from brain and behavioural science. *Current Directions in Psychological Science*, **16**, 55–59.

Trivers, R.L. (1972) Parental investment and sexual selection. In B. Campbell (ed.), *Sexual Selection and the Descent of Man, 1871–1971* (pp. 136–179). Chicago: Aldine.

Turner, B.L., Maes, K., Sweeney, J., and Armelagos, G.J. (2008) Human evolution, diet, and nutrition: When the body meets the buffet. In W.R. Trevathn, E.O. Smith, and J.J. McKenna (eds), *Evolutionary Medicine and Health: New Perspectives* (pp. 55–71). New York: Oxford University Press.

Uniform Crime Reports (2010) Crime in the United States, 2009. U.S. Department of Justice. Retrieved from November 5, 2011, http://www.fbi.gov/about-us/cjis/ucr/ucr

United Nations Office on Drugs and Crime (2011) *Global Study on Homicide: Trends, Contexts, Data*. Retrieved November 5, 2011, from http://www.unodc.org/documents/data-and-analysis/statistics/Homicide/Globa_study_on_homicide_2011_web.pdf

Walsh, A. (2006) Evolutionary psychology and criminal behaviour. In J.H. Barkow (ed.), *Missing the Revolution: Darwinism for Social Scientists* (pp. 225–268). Oxford: Oxford University Press.

Ward, T. and Durrant, R. (2011) Evolutionary behavioural science and crime: Aetiological and intervention implications. *Legal and Criminological Psychology*, **16**, 193–210.

Ward, T. and Maruna, S. (2007) *Rehabilitation: Beyond the Risk Paradigm*. London: Routledge.

Ward, T. and Stewart, C.A. (2003) Criminogenic needs and human needs: A theoretical model. *Psychology, Crime and Law*, **9**, 125–143.

Wells, S., Graham, K., and West, P. (2000) Alcohol-related aggression in the general population. *Journal of Studies on Alcohol*, **61**, 626–632.

Chapter 5

ALCOHOL AND VIOLENCE IN DEVELOPMENTAL PERSPECTIVE

RICK HOWARD AND MARY MCMURRAN

Institute of Mental Health, University of Nottingham, Nottingham, England

INTRODUCTION

The purpose of this chapter is to describe the developmental risk factors that lead to an increased likelihood of adult alcohol-related violence. This is not a straight-forward enterprise. In each individual case, a unique set of risk factors pertains over time, and, additionally, a range of protective factors may also be present. These risk and protective factors operate on a range of levels and include individual characteristics, family functioning, school bonding and academic attainment, peer associations, leisure pursuits and employment. Furthermore, there is an interactive effect between the at-risk individual and his or her social environment, which may exacerbate or mitigate problems. The developmental trajectory of interest starts in infancy – or even *in utero* – and continues into adulthood, and so there is a long story to be told. Our aim is to describe some of the major risk factors for alcohol-related violence across this developmental pathway. To examine alcohol use in relation to violence, we will organise our material in three sections: childhood, adolescence and early adulthood. In each section, we will examine risk factors in the intrapersonal, interpersonal and social domains. Before we do this, it is important to clarify our position on a number of key points – the construct of violence, the construct of antisocial personality and gender issues.

Violence

In this chapter, we define aggression as any behaviour intended to harm a living being who is motivated to avoid harm (Baron and Richardson, 1994); violence is

Alcohol-Related Violence: Prevention and Treatment, First Edition. Edited by Mary McMurran.
© 2013 John Wiley & Sons, Ltd. Published 2013 by John Wiley & Sons, Ltd.

Table 5.1   Howard's quadripartite model of violence.

		Appetitive	Aversive
Impulsive	Goal	Enhancement of positive affect by infliction of harm and suffering	Reduction of negative affect through removal of interpersonal threat
	Affect	Positive	Negative
	Emotion	Exhilaration/Excitement; desire to maximise excitement	Fear, distress, Desire to eradicate threat
	Anger type	"Thrill-seeking anger"	Explosive/reactive anger
Controlled	Goal	Achievement of positive outcome/reinforcement	Removal of interpersonal threat/grievance by considered, premeditated action
	Affect	Positive	Negative
	Emotion	Pleasant anticipation; desire for positive outcome	Vengefulness; desire to "get even" with source of grievance
	Anger type	"Coercive anger"	Vengeful/ruminative anger

aggression that has extreme harm as its goal (Anderson and Bushman, 2002). We recognise the motivational heterogeneity of violence, and in this chapter, we focus on impulsive violence. Howard (2009, 2011) has proposed a motivational model of violence in which an act of violence may be either impulsive or controlled and, within each of these categories, is either appetitively or aversively motivated (see Table 5.1). This yields four violence types, each associated with the achievement of a particular goal. Each of these types of violence is associated with a particular affective state (positive or negative) and a particular constellation of emotions: fear, distress and explosive/reactive anger in the case of aversively motivated violence carried out impulsively; spite, vengefulness and vengeful/ruminative anger in the case of aversively motivated violence carried out in a controlled way; exhilaration, excitement and thrill-seeking anger in the case of appetitively motivated violence carried out impulsively; and pleasant anticipation and coercive anger in the case of appetitively motivated violence carried out in a controlled way. This model has been partially validated in antisocial and prosocial youth (Bjørnebekk and Howard, 2012).

Most alcohol-related violence is associated with impulsiveness; hence, the focus here will be on the two types of impulsive violence in Howard's model: impulsive violence, which is appetitively motivated, and that which is aversively motivated. The hallmarks of an impulsive act of violence are as follows. First, the act is based on a minimal or automatic (even unconscious) cognitive appraisal of some environmental trigger, such as a threat or challenge (particularly social). Second, the act is accompanied by the experience of, and failure to control, strong emotional impulses (Shapiro, 1965). The affect may be either positive or negative. This is automatic affect, which occurs rapidly, may not be conscious, and directly initiates an action (Baumeister *et al.*, 2007). Third, because of lack of control, the act is carried out recklessly and without regard of long-term consequences.

Antisocial Personality

The predictors of later antisocial personality and criminal behaviour are most robustly identified through longitudinal studies that begin with a cohort of individuals who are followed up over time to identify which individuals commit what crimes and what factors explain this. Longitudinal studies have identified many childhood risk factors for later offending (see Farrington, 2009), but our focus here is on those relevant to alcohol-related violence. We recognise that antisocial personality summarises the syndrome of adult problem behaviours that include heavy drinking and aggression. While heavy drinking is not a specific diagnostic criterion, it is highly prevalent in this group (Coid *et al.*, 2006). In the *Diagnostic and Statistical Manual of Mental Disorders, Fourth Edition, Text Revision* (DSM-IV-TR) (American Psychiatric Association, 2000), the criteria for antisocial personality disorder are failure to conform to social norms, deceitfulness, impulsivity, irritability and aggressiveness, recklessness, irresponsibility, and lack of remorse. One essential criterion for a diagnosis of antisocial personality disorder is evidence of conduct disorder (CD) in childhood. The DSM-IV-TR description of CD is 'a repetitive and persistent pattern of behavior in which the basic rights of others or major age-appropriate societal norms or rules are violated' (p. 98). The specific criteria are evidence of aggression, destructiveness, deceitfulness and rule breaking.

Antisocial personality disorder often co-occurs with borderline personality disorder, particularly in clinical and forensic samples (Becker *et al.*, 2000; Coid *et al.*, 2009). Borderline personality disorder, particularly when associated with antisocial traits, is associated with a high risk of violence (Newhill, Eack, and Mulvey, 2009; Newhill, Vaughn, and DeLisi, 2010). Borderline personality disorder is associated with the four I's: instability (of relationships, self-image and mood), impulsivity and inappropriate or intense anger. Antisocial and borderline personality disorders share genetic and environmental risk factors over and above those common to all cluster B personality disorders (Torgersen *et al.*, 2008). The trait-based ratings of personality disorder proposed for DSM-5 explicitly recognises trait-level commonality between antisocial and borderline personality disorders by proposing that they share traits of hostility and impulsivity (American Psychiatric Association, 2011). In other words, both are associated with an extreme position on a dimension of personality disorder called 'hostile impulsivity', reflecting emotional under-control, belligerence and non-compliance (Blackburn, 2009). Antisocial outcomes ranging from the relatively benign (e.g., financial crisis, homelessness, trouble with the police) to the more malign (e.g., frequent violence, particularly when intoxicated) occur significantly more frequently when adult antisocial personality co-occurs with borderline personality disorder than when it occurs alone (Freestone *et al.*, under review). Moreover, antisocial/ borderline co-morbidity is associated with more severe childhood CD than is antisocial personality alone (Freestone *et al.*, under review; Howard, Huband, and

Duggan, 2012). Therefore, when we attempt to trace the developmental antecedents of adult antisocial personality, we conceive of this more broadly than just antisocial personality disorder.

There is strong continuity of antisocial behaviour over time, and we are interested in those processes across the life span by which the key features of CD might persist into adult antisocial personality broadly conceived. While there is considerable continuity, there is also variability; while on average only about half of children with CD become antisocial adults (Kendall *et al.*, 2009), the proportion varies between 30% and 60% depending on the particular sample studied (Kjelsberg, 2006). It is important to understand the reasons for this variability to inform prevention and intervention strategies. Differences between people in early alcohol use may contribute to this variability since both antisocial and borderline personality disorders are associated with a history of early alcohol abuse (Bakken, Landheim, and Vaglum, 2004; Thatcher, Cornelius, and Clark, 2005).

Gender Issues

The problem behaviours relevant to this chapter are more common among men than women. Fewer women are heavy drinkers; fewer women commit acts of criminal violence; and women are less likely to be violent when intoxicated (Institute of Alcohol Studies, 2010; McMurran *et al.*, 2011b). Antisocial personality is also more common among men than women (Coid *et al.*, 2006). However, in a systematic review of the role of alcohol in women's offending, McMurran *et al.* (2011b) summarised the situation as follows. Although there are different base rates of violence for men and women, drinking increases the likelihood of violent offending for both sexes, and the risk of violence after drinking is elevated equally for both sexes. A large portion of the risk for alcohol misuse and offending occurs because of shared risk factors. However, after accounting for these, there remains a small but direct effect of heavy alcohol use on violent crime, and this is similar for males and females. Therefore, it is probable that the content of this chapter regarding alcohol-related violence applies similarly to both men and women.

EARLY CHILDHOOD EXTERNALISING DISORDERS

Children who are at risk for developing antisocial personality disorder are identifiable very early on in life. A difficult temperament in infancy, which is characterised by irregularities in eating and sleeping, inflexibility to changes in the environment and frequent negative moods, is associated with later externalising behaviour problems (Loeber, Stouthamer-Loeber, and Green, 1991; Sanson *et al.*, 1991). At the age of 3 years, children who were under-controlled, that is, those who were impulsive, restless and distractible, were more likely at 21 years to meet the diagnostic criteria for antisocial personality disorder (Caspi *et al.*, 1996). In the latter study, early under-control was also associated with later alcohol-related problems. Difficult temperament and under-control are predictive of later externalising (disruptive) disorders, as opposed to internalising disorders (i.e., depression, anxiety, phobias and psychosomatic disorders). Externalising disorders include oppositional defiant disorder (ODD), attention deficit hyperactivity disorder (ADHD) and CD.

In childhood, ODD, ADHD and CD are highly co-morbid disorders, and CD is also highly co-morbid with early-onset alcohol and other substance use disorders; therefore, disentangling their individual contributions to adult antisocial behaviour, and violence in particular, is difficult. However, progress has been made in identifying their individual contributions to adult antisociality, and to violence in particular. First, a recent analysis by Fergusson, Boden, and Horwood (2010) of long-term antisocial outcomes using prospective data from the Christchurch, New Zealand longitudinal study showed that, when the presence of CD was controlled, ADHD predicted only poor adult educational attainment. In contrast, when co-morbid childhood conditions were controlled, childhood CD still predicted adult antisocial outcomes, and violence in particular. Second, data from the same longitudinal study showed that adolescent-onset alcohol abuse predicted violent offending both in late adolescence (age 15–21) and in early adulthood (age 21–25) even when confounding background and individual factors, including CD, were controlled (Wells, Horwood, and Fergusson, 2004). This confirms the finding from the Cambridge, UK longitudinal study that adolescent-onset alcohol abuse and dependence is a significant risk factor for life-course persistent antisocial behaviour (Farrington, Ttofi, and Coid, 2009).

Childhood CD is, therefore, a childhood risk factor for adult antisociality, and violence in particular, and also later alcohol misuse. DeBrito and Hodgins (2009) go so far as to assert that '. . . almost all children and adolescents with CD will abuse alcohol and/or drugs . . . ' (p. 139). Nonetheless, several studies have identified individuals with a history of childhood CD who showed no significant history of alcohol abuse or dependence. These individuals, in comparison with those showing CD with co-occurring early alcohol abuse or dependence, show a lower degree of lifetime alcohol and adult antisocial problems (Finn et al., 2009) and, in mentally disordered offenders, less violence in their criminal history (Khalifa et al., in press). This suggests that CD is predictive of violence most strongly when it occurs in conjunction with adolescent alcohol use. Conduct disordered children who become antisocial as adults do so, at least in part, as a result of their early alcohol abuse, which both exacerbates and partly mediates the effects of CD on adult antisocial behaviour (Howard et al., 2012; Khalifa et al., in press). Furthermore, there is continuity in heavy drinking from adolescence through to young adulthood so that those showing CD as children who subsequently abuse alcohol in adolescence will, by the time they reach young adulthood, show both frequent and hazardous drinking (Buchmann et al., 2009).

Since, as we have seen above, adult antisociality (and violence in particular) is associated with co-occurring antisocial and borderline personality disorder, we need to consider childhood antecedents of adult borderline pathology. Important among these is childhood abuse and neglect (e.g., Van der Kolk et al., 1991). A study by Brodsky et al. (2001) investigated the relationship of reported childhood physical and sexual abuse to impulsivity, aggression and suicidal behaviour in a sample of 136 clinically depressed adults. Borderline personality disorder was highly co-morbid with depression in this sample and was associated with a history of child abuse. Impulsivity and aggression scores were significantly higher in those with a history of child abuse than in those without such a history, and were higher in those patients with a co-morbid borderline personality disorder diagnosis than in those without this co-morbidity. Brodsky *et al.* (2001) considered the possibility that the experience of physical or sexual abuse in childhood constitutes an environmental factor that influences the development of both trait impulsivity and aggression; alternatively, impulsivity may be an inherited trait that is worsened by experiences of abuse. Given the dynamic nature of impulsiveness, we would argue that both may be true: impulsiveness both predisposes to child abuse, and the latter exacerbates the risk for later externalising, as well as internalising, behaviour in adolescence.

In the section that follows, we review the role of impulsiveness in early adolescence as it relates to alcohol use and violence, and then go on to examine the interaction between the impulsive individual and his or her social environment. Before doing so, we will first summarise the story so far. Childhood CD predicts both early-onset alcohol use and adult antisocial behaviour, particularly violence. This suggests that early-onset drinking and antisocial behaviour are, in part, explained by a common factor. What is required – and we will attempt to provide this – is an account of how CD and early alcohol abuse translate into adult alcohol use and the violence associated with it. Impulsiveness is a key intervening variable, both as a predisposition to alcohol use and as a consequence of it, and is linked to a history of child abuse that predisposes to adult borderline personality disorder.

LATE CHILDHOOD AND EARLY ADOLESCENCE

In this section, we trace one major route into alcohol use and antisocial behaviour as an interaction between core features of impulsiveness and poor external controls.

Impulsiveness

Impulsiveness may be defined as a predisposition towards inappropriately rapid, unplanned or premature reactions to internal and external stimuli, without due regard to possible negative consequences (Moeller *et al.*, 2001). There are many behavioural expressions of impulsiveness, and these include both alcohol use and aggression (Enticott and Ogloff, 2006).

Stimulated by the development of the UPPS scales by Whiteside and Lynam (2001), there has, in recent years, been an increasing recognition of the multifaceted nature of impulsiveness and of the different personality pathways leading to impulsive behaviour. UPPS recognises four such pathways: urgency, lack of perseverance, lack of premeditation and sensation seeking. The first pathway, *negative urgency*, assesses an individual's tendency to give in to strong impulses, specifically when accompanied by negative emotions such as depression, anxiety or anger. A revised UPPS (UPPS-P) has recently incorporated a *positive urgency* scale that taps the tendency to act rashly when experiencing extreme positive emotion (Lynam, 2011). The next pathway, *lack of perseverance*, assesses an individual's ability to persist in completing jobs or obligations despite boredom and/or fatigue. The third pathway, *lack of premeditation*, assesses an individual's ability to think through the potential consequences of his or her behaviour before acting. The final pathway, *sensation seeking*, measures an individual's preference for excitement and stimulation.

Recent studies have begun to identify which of the UPPS pathways is related to alcohol use and the problems associated with it. Most interest has focused on the urgency (positive and negative) and sensation-seeking pathways. Pertinent to our current concern with alcohol use in those with antisocial personality, negative urgency is abnormally high in alcohol-dependent individuals with co-morbid antisocial traits (Whiteside and Lynam, 2003). Negative urgency is related to the degree of alcohol-related problems in young adults (Magid and Colder, 2007; Shin, Hong, and Jeon, 2012) and is linked to high levels of drinking driven by negative reinforcement (Anestis, Selby, and Joiner, 2007). Findings therefore suggest that problematic alcohol use represents an attempt to cope with negative emotions. However, although less widely studied, positive urgency has also been linked to alcohol problems (e.g., Cyders *et al.*, 2009). These results suggest that alcohol misuse in young adults represents dysfunctional coping with both negative and positive emotional states, and that such dysfunctional coping may be particularly prominent in the presence of antisocial traits and may manifest in alcohol-related violence.

McMurran (2011) suggested that antisocial individuals who are socially anxious may use alcohol to reduce anxiety and to facilitate social interaction. Alcohol intoxication reduces anxiety by reducing attentional capacity, thus causing people to focus on immediate pleasurable cues and to ignore distal anxiety-provoking cues. This effect of alcohol has been called 'alcohol myopia' (Giancola *et al.*, 2010; see Giancola Chapter 3). However, this same process can cause attention to focus on threat cues and to miss inhibitory cues. This is particularly relevant in drinking venues that are trouble hot spots. When the attention of antisocial individuals is focused on threat cues, then the likelihood of an aggressive response is increased.

Another facet of impulsiveness, sensation seeking, is particularly germane to alcohol-related violence. In a recent review of the relationship between impulsiveness in childhood and adult antisocial (particularly violent) behaviour, the sensation-seeking aspect of impulsiveness was found most clearly to predict adult violence (Jolliffe and Farrington, 2009). UPPS sensation seeking has been found to predict both increased frequency of alcohol use as well as alcohol-related problems in young people (Cyders *et al.*, 2009; Shin *et al.*, 2012). As suggested by Shin *et al.* (2012), UPPS sensation seeking may relate to alcohol use through a drive for increased stimulation and positive affect. Consistent with this, Lynam (2011) reported a high positive correlation (.66) between UPPS sensation seeking and the fun-seeking subscale of Carver and White's (1994) behavioural activation scale (BAS), whose items reflect a desire for new rewards and a willingness to approach something rewarding on the spur of the moment. These results suggest that alcohol use in young people may initially be driven by a quest for positive affective states, for example, excitement and exhilaration. Later, however, excessive drinking and problems associated with it may be associated with dysfunctional coping, both with negative emotional states (high urgency) and with positive emotional states (positive urgency). The association between positive urgency – the tendency to act impulsively in the context of positive affective states like excitement and exhilaration – and drinking problems highlights the role played by positive affective states in problematic alcohol use. The quest for enhanced positive affect is a common motive for alcohol use in young people (Comeau, Stewart, and Loba, 2001; Cooper *et al.*, 1995).

Reward Sensitivity and Rash Impulsiveness: Dual Brain Systems

Dawe, Gullo, and Loxton (2004) have presented evidence supporting a distinction between two independent impulsivity-related traits – 'reward sensitivity' and 'rash impulsiveness'. Reward sensitivity reflects individual variation in sensitivity to rewarding stimuli in the environment, while rash impulsiveness reflects a tendency to act rashly and without consideration of consequences. They argue that reward sensitivity is more important in the initial use of substances, while rash impulsiveness is more important in the subsequent loss of control over substance use.

This distinction bears a striking similarity, both conceptually and in terms of underlying neural substrates, to that drawn by Albert and Steinberg (2011) between two neural systems with different developmental trajectories: a social-emotional reward system and a cognitive control system. Coincident with the dramatic structural and functional changes in the human brain following puberty, the social-emotional reward system develops in a curvilinear fashion, with maximum sensitivity to social/emotional stimuli occurring in early/mid-adolescence. The cognitive control system, in contrast, develops more slowly and in a linear fashion over the course of adolescence and into early adulthood. This is illustrated in Figure 5.1. There is a time window during mid-adolescence (roughly between ages 13 and 15 years) when the social-emotional reward system shows maximum sensitivity, and there is heightened motivation for reward-seeking, unconstrained by a still immature cognitive control system that shows maturational lag. According to Albert and Steinberg (2011), synaptic pruning and increased myelination in late adolescence and early adulthood support a gradual improvement in the efficiency of the cognitive control system, which continues to develop well into the 20s. Driven by the motivation to seek rewards, risk taking occurs maximally during this mid-adolescent period, and part of that risk taking involves experimentation with drugs and alcohol. Those with CD would be expected to show a heightened sensitivity of the social-emotional reward system, leading them to seek out excitement and to engage in risky behaviours, including risky use of alcohol. Significantly, the mean age of onset of adolescent alcohol abuse in adolescents with a history of CD is around 16 years (Howard *et al.*, 2012). The consequence of excessive alcohol use, as proposed by Howard (2006), will be impaired and/or delayed development of neural substrates of the cognitive control system. Evidence has accumulated to indicate that adolescent alcohol abuse is associated with structural brain changes, including those in the prefrontal

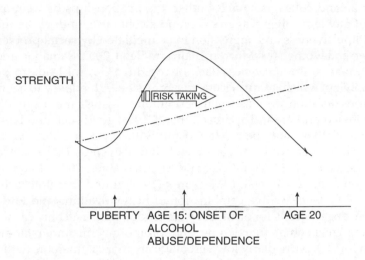

STRENGTH

RISK TAKING

PUBERTY   AGE 15: ONSET OF   AGE 20
          ALCOHOL
          ABUSE/DEPENDENCE

Figure 5.1   Developmental trajectory of the socio-emotional reward system (continuous line) and of the cognitive control system (broken line) (after Albert and Steinberg, 2011). The socio-emotional reward system reaches maximum strength in early/mid-adolescence and drives risk taking. Strengthening of the cognitive control system develops more slowly and linearly throughout adolescence and continues into young adulthood.

cortex (De Bellis *et al.*, 2005, 2008). Disruption of the cognitive control system will then result in a chronic inability to control emotional impulses (Dawe *et al.*'s rash impulsiveness) and hence a proneness to engage in impulsive violence. It will, in particular, result in deficits in executive function and, particularly, in problem solving, which will be reviewed next.

Problem Solving

The executive functions of the brain are those involved in self-regulation and include attention, abstracting relevant information, reasoning and problem solving. Executive functioning is poorer in violent offenders and in men with antisocial personality disorder compared with non-violent offenders and non-offenders (Giancola, 2000; Hoaken, Shaughnessy, and Pihl, 2003). Poor executive functioning may be related to aggression through impulsiveness; that is, people with poor executive functioning are less able to inhibit behaviour, including aggression. However, there is evidence that people with low executive functioning are more aggressive because they are unable to cope with the number of response options in a risky situation, they fail to access socially appropriate responses, and they make default aggressive responses when provoked (Hoaken *et al.*, 2003); that is, they are poor at social problem solving. Social problem solving is the ability to recognise, define and solve problems in the interpersonal domain – skills that are the essence of executive functioning (Zelazo *et al.*, 1997).

McMurran and colleagues have studied the relationships between impulsiveness, social problem solving, aggression and alcohol use, finding the relationship between impulsiveness and aggression to be mediated by social problem solving in both men and women (McMurran, Blair, and Egan, 2002; Ramadan and McMurran, 2005); that is, impulsiveness/lack of cognitive control leads to poor social problem solving, which, in turn, leads to aggression. A tendency to act rashly and without consideration of consequences militates against the acquisition of the more considered and planful approach that typifies good social problem solving.

Additionally, there may be a relationship with IQ, particularly verbal intelligence, which is negatively correlated with impulsiveness (Lynam, Moffitt, and Stouthamer-Loeber, 1993; Vigil-Colet and Morales-Vives, 2005). In a longitudinal study of young men, Welte and Wieczorek (1999) found that both drinking and IQ predicted violence, with a combination of heavy drinking and low verbal IQ being the strongest predictor of all. They concluded that, if alcohol causes violence by reducing intellectual functioning and promoting misunderstandings, then those with low IQ, particularly low verbal IQ, are more vulnerable to the negative consequences of alcohol. Low intelligence, especially poor verbal intelligence, may militate against the acquisition of good social problem-solving skills.

Miller, Collins, and Kent (2008) have highlighted the importance of possible linguistic abnormalities associated with impulsive aggression. They suggest that the language processing regions of the brain may mediate executive abilities important to the regulation of aggressive impulses, such as deductive reasoning, cognitive restraint and cognitive modulation of emotion. Abnormalities in language processing regions may exacerbate the impairments of frontally mediated self-regulatory functions caused by excessive drinking during adolescence (Howard, (2006). These impairments, in turn, would lead to impulsiveness and a deviant and disinhibited lifestyle, increasing the likelihood of antisocial behaviour, including impulsive aggression, throughout adulthood. Indeed, the younger the age at which alcohol use starts, the greater is the degree of violent recidivism and lifetime aggression (Gustavson *et al.*, 2007). Alcohol intoxication also increases the risk of head injury, through fighting and accidental blows, which may further impair brain functioning (Solomon and Molloy, 1992).

The Social Impact of Impulsiveness

The role of family management in the development of criminal behaviour is well evidenced. Poor supervision, punitive disciplining and erratic application of punishments are strong predictors of later criminal behaviour (see review by Farrington, 2009). Poor family management may in part be a result of the difficulties posed in managing a behaviourally disinhibited child, difficulties that can be exacerbated when family resources are stretched and family management skills are poor.

The roots of externalising problems are to be found in infancy, or even in foetal development. There may be heritable neuropsychological problems. Additionally, neural development may be affected during pregnancy, for example, by excessive smoking or drinking or by brain injury due to birth complications (Moffitt, 1993;

Murray *et al.*, 2010; Sayal *et al.*, 2009). The difficult child may be ignored by parents, and parental unresponsiveness has been conceptualised by attachment theorists as hindering the development of self-regulation in that a child who receives less contingent care may act more disruptively to gain parental attention (Shaw and Bell, 1993).

In a longitudinal study of a community sample, Hill *et al.* (2001) found that young people who scored high on behavioural disinhibition were at risk for later alcohol abuse if they came from consistently poorly managed families. Young people who came from well-managed family environments were not at risk of developing alcohol problems, even if they were high on behavioural disinhibition. To explain this, it is necessary to examine the likely outcomes of the interaction between behavioural disinhibition and poor family management.

The disinhibited child who is poorly controlled is more likely to be disruptive in the classroom and aggressive in social interactions (Coie, Dodge, and Kupersmidt, 1990). This leads to poor academic attainment and rejection by prosocial peers, both of which are predictive of delinquency (Coie *et al.*, 1990; Farrington, 2005). School experiences of failure and rejection are likely to increase the risk of truancy, which is also predictive of delinquency, probably because truants associate with delinquent and substance-using peers (Sher and Trull, 1994). Under these circumstances, the young person is unlikely to learn prosocial ways of social interaction. Additionally, poor performance at school is predictive of poor job stability in adulthood, which is a major risk factor for criminality in later life (Le Blanc, 1994). The wider social context also needs to be considered. Jones and Lynam (2009), for example, found that impulsiveness (particularly excitement seeking in young men) was more strongly correlated with offending among individuals who perceived their neighbourhoods to be low, rather than high, in supervision.

A life of uncontrolled externalising problems is essentially one wherein opportunities for prosocial activities diminish and opportunities for antisocial activities increase. In late childhood and early adolescence, because the purchase of alcohol and drinking in certain places is illegal, alcohol use is, by definition, a delinquent activity that features among a range of problem behaviours. In later adolescence, alcohol use becomes legal, and it is no longer a delinquent activity by definition. Alcohol-related antisocial behaviours then become the focus. Also, when people reach the legal age for drinking, there is a move to drinking in licensed social venues, and the context in which drinking occurs presents particular risks. In the next section, we shall look at the risk in the late adolescent and early adult phase of life.

LATE ADOLESCENCE AND EARLY ADULTHOOD

As Loeber *et al.* (2000) have suggested, CD and substance use likely act reciprocally with each other so that by late adolescence or early adulthood, alcohol abuse will have become woven into the fabric of disordered conduct. Once a pattern of excessive alcohol is established in late adolescence, it persists into early adulthood, as shown in a recent prospective study by Buchmann *et al.* (2009). Those who had shown disinhibitory psychopathology as children and who subsequently abused alcohol during their adolescence engaged in more frequent and more hazardous drinking by the time they reached young adulthood. This, in turn, will place them at an increased risk for violence due to the effects of alcohol intoxication, as well as contextual factors. The consequences of having a cognitive control system that has been functionally impaired or maturationally delayed as a result of exposure to excessive alcohol will, as Albert and Steinberg (2011) suggested, be a lack of *coordination* between cognition and affect: the cross talk between emotion and cognition that normally guides adaptive goal-directed behaviour and decision making will be lacking. The individual who has abused alcohol during adolescence will, when entering young adulthood, arguably be 'stuck' developmentally in adolescence. We will next investigate the acute effects of alcohol intoxication since these have an important bearing on why a young adult, particularly a young adult male with a history of alcohol abuse in adolescence, might become violent when intoxicated.

Acute Intoxication

Alcohol intoxication has a direct main effect on aggression, even after controlling for other factors (see McMurran, Chapter 11). When given to animals at doses that do not sedate or impair motor function, alcohol – like other anti-anxiety drugs – increases aggression, for example, in situations where two animals, usually males that have been previously isolated, are paired together and aggress towards each other (Gray, 1987). In common with other anti-anxiety drugs, alcohol has behaviourally disinhibiting effects both in animals (Gray, 1987) and in humans (Fillmore and Weafer, 2011). The latter authors reviewed evidence indicating that such alcohol-induced inhibitory deficits are particularly manifest in situations where rapid suppression of an action is required, and where an approach response is primed and prepotent. Thus, in a situation where angry aggression was primed by a suitable eliciting cue (e.g., interpersonal threat), alcohol, even at low doses, would prevent inhibition of the attack. Moreover, the slower recovery of inhibitory mechanisms relative to activational mechanisms results in behaviour being biased towards activation ('activational bias'), favouring the emission of approach responses such as angry aggression.

Fillmore and Weafer suggest that inhibitory mechanisms likely operate in a 'bottom-up' fashion to disrupt higher-order attentional and cognitive functions. A consequence of this might be alcohol myopia, the alcohol-induced tendency to attend primarily to salient and proximal environmental cues such as a threat or an insult (see Giancola, Chapter 3; Giancola *et al.*, 2010). Cues that trigger an angry/aggressive response will capture the attentional spotlight, while other, particularly inhibitory, cues may suffer attentional neglect. The attention of the aggressor will be strongly focused on the immediate environmental cue (the perceived threat), and his/her actions will be less affected by distal inhibitory cues (the adverse consequences of attacking the other person). Impulsive individuals were reported by Fillmore and Weafer to be especially sensitive to the disinhibiting effects of alcohol.

Self-monitoring for errors is another important aspect of executive function that is disrupted by alcohol intoxication. When an individual performs a simple reaction-time task where the possibility of motor errors is high, and he or she makes a motor error, the brain evinces a small negative-going electrical potential called 'error-related negativity' (ERN). The larger the ERN, the greater is the degree of behavioural adjustment following an error. Importantly, Hall, Bernat, and Patrick (2007) found that ERN was smaller in amplitude in externalisers, that is, individuals showing a general vulnerability to the development of impulse control problems, than in non-externalisers. ERN amplitude is also depressed when individuals imbibe alcohol (e.g., Bartholow *et al.*, 2012; Ridderinkhof *et al.*, 2002). In the Bartholow *et al.* (2012) study, subjects given alcohol were as aware as those given placebo or controls of their errors, but, unlike the comparison groups, they showed less negative affect after consuming alcohol. Furthermore, they were impaired in their behavioural adjustment following errors. Importantly, the effect of alcohol on behavioural adjustment was mediated by the reduction in negative affect and reduced ERN. Bartholow *et al.* (2012) proposed that the ERN appears to function as an alarm signal to the cognitive control system, warning it that a control failure has occurred and that behavioural adjustment is called for. The effect of alcohol in an impulsive individual, in whom this alarm signal is already muffled, will be to further compromise an already impaired cognitive control system.

The effects of alcohol, including its intoxicating effects, will always depend in part on the context in which it is imbibed. It is to this context that we now turn.

The Drinking Context

Impulsive violence can be construed as an extreme form of risky behaviour that has beneficial immediate consequences, for example, eradication of an inter-personal threat or achievement of excitement, but detrimental long-term consequences, for example, arrest, conviction and incarceration. Contextual factors are of critical importance in moderating the expression of emotion, cognition and behaviour in relation to risky behaviours (Steinberg, 2008). Impulsive violence is no exception: contextual factors influence the expression of violence, ranging from the more proximal (i.e., immediate environmental) to the more distal (i.e., societal and cultural influences) constraints and promoters. Contextual factors vary across countries and cultures. In some Scandinavian countries, for example, attitudes towards alcohol consumption are restrictive, retail outlets for the purchase of alcoholic beverages are controlled, and the price of alcohol is high. In contrast, in the United Kingdom, where attitudes to alcohol consumption are permissive, alcoholic beverages are both easy and cheap to purchase.

Risky behaviours engaged in by adolescents and young adults, including excessive drinking and delinquency, including acts of violence, typically occur in groups (Steinberg, 2007, 2008). Albert and Steinberg (2011) have suggested that the facilitative effect on risk taking exerted by the presence of peers is mediated by the socio-emotional reward system (see Figure 5.1). Importantly, they suggest that contextual affective stimuli, such as a crowd of friends' smiling faces at a party, can sensitise the brain's socio-emotional reward system to the effects of *unrelated* incentive stimuli. In the context of alcohol intoxication, the effect of contextual affective stimuli would be to enhance alcohol myopia, causing attention to focus on proximal cues that represent the promise of excitement. What is true of the appetitive motivational system likely holds equally true of the aversive motivational system. Entering a social milieu perceived as hostile and threatening would, following Albert and Steinberg's argument, sensitise the brain's aversive motivational system to unrelated aversive cues. As a consequence of alcohol myopia, attention will be focused on aversive cues such as a social threat, which will trigger angry aggression and, potentially, a violent act.

In early adolescence, when people are legally underage for purchasing and drinking alcohol, drinking is often unsupervised, for example, in public places or at home when parents are absent (Bellis *et al.*, 2007). Lack of supervision can mean that trouble can develop unhindered and the consequences of problems are not quickly dealt with, thus increasing the level of harm. In late adolescence, when individuals reach the legal age for drinking unaccompanied in commercial venues, contextual factors relating to bars and clubs come into play in explaining drinking and aggression. Factors to do with the drinking setting, such as bars and clubs, are covered by Forsyth (see Chapter 7). However, the probability of aggression in such venues is likely increased regardless of the occurrence of drinking in that the congregation in bars and clubs of youths who lead a similarly deviant and disinhibited lifestyle in itself creates a risk for violent encounters.

Triggers for Alcohol-Related Violence

We have seen in a previous section that alcohol-related violence is intimately bound up with impulsiveness and that much of the violence and aggression perpetrated by intoxicated individuals will be of an impulsive nature. Nonetheless, recall that impulsive violence may be either appetitively or aversively motivated. If the violence is aversively motivated, the trigger is said to be a *directly perceived interpersonal threat*, and the goal of the violent act and its associated angry affect (explosive/reactive anger) is to *remove the interpersonal threat and thereby to reduce the negative affect*. Due to alcohol myopia, the attention of the aggressor will be strongly focused on the immediate environmental cue (the perceived threat) and his/her actions will be less affected by distal inhibitory cues (e.g., the adverse consequences of attacking the other person).

In contrast to aversively motivated violence, the goal of appetitively motivated impulsive violence, involving the infliction of harm or suffering on another person, is to maintain or enhance a state of positive affect, characterised by exhilaration and excitement. The trigger in this case is anything that offers the prospect of excitement, be it something sexually provocative or something that just promises excitement. Alcohol myopia will operate here too, resulting in attention being overly focused on proximal cues that are salient and promise excitement, to the detriment of attending to less proximal cues. Once aroused, a state of excitement can easily spiral out of control due to a failure of self-regulation that is compounded by excessive drinking. Tragesser *et al.* (2008) showed that impulsive, dissocial young men used alcohol primarily as a means of enhancing positive emotional states, suggesting that the failure to self-regulate may be self-induced.

A recent study investigating the triggers of alcohol-related violence reported by young offenders identified both aversive and appetitive motivations (McMurran, Hoyte, and Jinks, 2012). Six broad themes were identified. *Being offended by someone* was a common trigger, which is similar to the findings of Graham and Wells (2003), who, in their study of barroom violence, also observed this type of trigger and defined it as a grievance motive. Grievances are influenced by 'macho' or hypermasculine values, defined as the need to prove oneself hard and tough, that are associated with drinking, aggression and other forms of antisocial behaviour (Archer, 2010; Beesley and McGuire, 2009). *Perception of threat* was a trigger for violence, specifically fearing that others were likely to attack and acting first to assume an advantage. Feeling *distress* was a theme typified by being in a negative emotional state from previous events, for example, seeing an ex-girlfriend with another man.

A theme of opportunistic, acquisitive offending was reported, namely, *seeing an opportunity for material gain*. The motivation behind alcohol-related acquisitive offending appeared to be to do with wanting to buy more alcohol to enable continued drinking and socialising after their money ran out. When an individual with antisocial values is intoxicated, the appearance of a likely target for robbery can trigger violence. A theme of *seeing others in need of help* described fighting to assist someone in trouble. In their barroom study, Graham and Wells (2003) also found that some people viewed it 'a moral imperative to support a 'buddy' in a fight' (p. 558). *Wanting a fight* was reported, albeit rarely. The desire to fight is fuelled by a number of rewards, including feelings of excitement during the fight, maintaining a reputation and gaining respect from peers (Graham and Wells, 2003; McMurran *et al.*, 2011a).

Personality Disorder

Among the personality disorders described by DSM-IV-TR (American Psychiatric Association, 2000), cluster B personality disorders, particularly antisocial and borderline personality disorders, have been most closely linked to both violence and substance abuse (e.g., Coid *et al.*, 1999). In a recent study by Freestone *et al.* (under review), alcohol dependence was particularly associated with co-morbidity between adult antisocial personality and borderline personality disorder and was significantly higher in an antisocial/borderline co-morbid group compared with those with adult antisocial or adult borderline alone. Of particular relevance to alcohol-related violence, being male, alcohol dependent and having a history of CD all independently contributed to the risk of being violent when intoxicated (odds ratios were 2.96, 2.95 and 2.76, respectively). As outlined earlier in this chapter, adult antisocial personality with co-morbid borderline personality disorder represents a critical pattern of co-morbidity associated with a particular set of genetic and environmental risk factors (Torgersen *et al.*, 2008). Among likely candidates as common risk factors can be included a difficult childhood temperament; a childhood characterised by deprivation, abuse and neglect; and an adolescence characterised by disruptive behaviour, poor academic achievement and excessive risk taking, particularly in regard to alcohol. Given the well-documented continuity of excessive alcohol use from adolescence through to young adulthood, we have a pathway leading from a genetic vulnerability to difficult temperament to childhood deprivation and abuse, childhood CD, and through adolescent alcohol abuse to adult antisocial/ borderline co-morbidity with its associated risk of repetitive, drunken violence.

CLINICAL IMPLICATIONS

The foregoing information strongly points to the need for efforts to be directed towards prevention. Given that heavy drinking and offending share many early risk factors, the same prevention approaches are likely to influence both outcomes (see also Forrester and Glynn, Chapter 8). Indeed, risk factors tend to be similar for a number of outcomes, including violent and non-violent offending, mental health problems, drug use and unemployment, and so prevention approaches are likely to have wide-ranging benefits (Farrington and Welsh, 2006). Prevention approaches include those operating at the individual, family and system levels (see review by Farrington and Welsh, 2007).

Programmes operating at the individual level include preschool intellectual enrichment and child skills training. Intellectual enrichment programmes target the risk factors of low intelligence and attainment by improving cognitive skills, school readiness, and social and emotional development. Social competence programmes target the risk factors of impulsivity, low empathy and self-centeredness and aim to teach children appropriate social skills, effective problem solving and emotion control. Programmes operating at the family level include parent management training. This includes training and educating parents in monitoring behaviour over long periods, stating clear house rules, making rewards and punishments contingent on behaviour, and negotiating disagreements so that conflicts do not escalate, and home support visits. School-based programmes include targets of classroom and discipline management, and increasing pupils' self-control and social competence through cognitive-behavioural or behavioural instructional methods. After-school programmes that provide prosocial opportunities for young people in the after-school hours can also reduce delinquency.

In late childhood and early adolescence, efforts to reduce the likelihood of later problematic drinking are important. In this regard, alcohol education, parental monitoring and community-based prevention are the foremost strategies. Educational approaches based on the premise that information about alcohol and the consequences of drinking will change attitudes and behaviour have been found to be ineffective in preventing problems, as have 'affective education' programmes, that include broader issues of personal development (Babor *et al.*, 2010). Regarding parental monitoring, both harm-minimisation and zero-tolerance approaches have their proponents. Parental provision of alcohol to children in a family environment allows for supervision, so that children are less likely to drink in risky unsupervised circumstances (Bellis *et al.*, 2007). Additionally, parents can encourage self-control and convey appropriate attitudes to alcohol. By contrast, zero-tolerance approaches suggest that alcohol use should be discouraged by parents and guardians. In light of the adverse effects of alcohol on the adolescent brain (De Bellis *et al.*, 2005, 2008; McQueeny *et al.*, 2009), this is a supportable position. Comparing these two approaches, McMorris *et al.* (2011) found that adult-supervised alcohol use resulted in higher levels of harmful alcohol consequences, contrary to predictions derived from a harm-minimisation approach. Community-based prevention programmes appear to hold promise for reducing alcohol consumption and alcohol-related injuries (e.g., Holder et al., 2000). These combine policy setting, media advocacy and community enforcement of drinking regulations.

Prevention of alcohol-related violence in later adolescence and adulthood is also important. Policy, policing and creating safer drinking environments are all clearly important, as described by Dingwall (Chapter 6) and Forsyth (Chapter 7). Treatments for alcohol-related violence in late adolescence and adulthood are comprehensively covered in Part IV of this book.

CONCLUDING COMMENTS

We have attempted to outline a developmental trajectory leading from childhood and adolescence to a heightened risk of alcohol-related violence in adulthood. We have suggested that the quest for excitement and exhilaration that drives early experimentation with alcohol (and other drugs) in early and mid-adolescence coincides with the rapid development, following puberty, of the socio-emotional reward system described by Albert and Steinberg (2011). This system will likely be particularly sensitive in children with disinhibitory psychopathology, making them at high risk for abusing alcohol in early and mid-adolescence. Excessive alcohol use from mid-adolescence will result in delayed and/or faulty maturation of the cognitive control system described by Albert and Steinberg (2011) that develops in late adolescence and supports mature self-regulation. Incomplete or delayed maturation of this system will result in a variety of self-regulatory deficits, including deficiencies in social problem solving, error monitoring and behavioural inhibition. Most importantly, late or incomplete maturation of this system will impair the integration of cognition and affect, which will not function synchronously. In particular, the ability to adaptively utilise affective information to guide decision making will be compromised. This deficit will be especially manifest in the interpersonal domain, where poor integration of affect with cognition will compromise effective social problem solving. It will also manifest in what Dawe *et al.* (2004) refer to as rash impulsiveness, which importantly will include an inability to control emotional impulses. An angry affect will easily be elicited by triggers of angry aggression such as interpersonal threat and, once elicited, will be poorly controlled. But impulsive violence can also be triggered by cues that promise excitement. Alcohol intoxication will greatly enhance sensitivity to such cues, while inhibitory cues will be neglected. Alcohol intoxication will further impair self-regulation in individuals whose powers of self-regulation are already compromised by virtue of exposure to excessive amounts of alcohol in adolescence. Since there is continuity of excessive alcohol use from adolescence into young adulthood, and the cognitive control system will still be maturing well into the 20s, the risk of violence will continue to increase through early adulthood. Individuals with such a developmental trajectory will stand on the threshold of a career of life-course persistent criminality and violence. However, lest the reader thinks we paint too bleak a picture, the many innovative and promising interventions for preventing and reducing alcohol-related violence covered elsewhere in this text offer grounds for optimism.

REFERENCES

Albert, D. and Steinberg, L. (2011) Peer influences on adolescent risk behaviour. In M.T. Bardo, R. Milich, and D.H. Fishbein (eds), *Inhibitory Control and Drug Abuse Prevention* (pp. 211–226). New York: Springer.

American Psychiatric Association (2000) *Diagnostic and Statistical Manual of Mental Disorders, Fourth Edition, Text Revision*. Arlington, VA: APA.

American Psychiatric Association (2011) DSM-5 development. *T04 Antisocial Personality Disorder (Dyssocial Personality Disorder) and T00 Borderline Personality Disorder*. June 2011 update. Retrieved December 12, 2011, from http://www.dsm5.org/proposedrevision/pages/proposedrevision.aspx?rid=17

Anderson, C.A. and Bushman, B.J. (2002) Human aggression. *Annual Review of Psychology*, **53**, 27–51.

Anestis, M.D., Selby, E., and Joiner, T. (2007) The role of urgency in maladaptive behaviors. *Behaviour Research and Therapy*, **45**, 3018–3029.

Archer, J. (2010) Derivation and assessment of a hypermasculine values questionnaire. *British Journal of Social Psychology*, **49**, 525–551.

Babor, T., Caetano, R., Casswell, S. *et al.* (2010) *Alcohol: No Ordinary Commodity – Research and Public Policy* (2nd edn). New York: Oxford University Press.

Bakken, K., Landheim, A.S., and Vaglum, P. (2004) Early and late onset groups of substance misusers: Differences in primary and secondary psychiatric disorders. *Journal of Substance Use*, **9**, 224–234.

Baron, R.A. and Richardson, D.R. (1994) *Human Aggression* (2nd edn). New York: Plenum.

Bartholow, B.D., Henry, E.A., Lust, S.A. *et al.* (2012) Alcohol effects on performance monitoring and adjustment: Affect modulation and impairment of evaluative cognitive control. *Journal of Abnormal Psychology*, **121**, 173–186.

Baumeister, R.F., Vohs, K.D., DeWall, C.N., and Zhang, L. (2007) How emotion shapes behavior: Feedback, anticipation, and reflection, rather than direct causation. *Personality and Social Psychology Review*, **11**, 167–203.

Becker, D.F., Grilo, C.M., Edell, W.S., and McGlashan, T.H. (2000) Co-morbidity of borderline personality disorder with other personality disorders in hospitalized adolescents and adults. *American Journal of Psychiatry*, **157**, 211–216.

Beesley, F. and McGuire, J. (2009) Gender-role identity and hypermasculinity in violent offending. *Psychology, Crime and Law*, **15**, 251–268.

Bellis, M.A., Hughes, K., Morleo, M. *et al.* (2007) Predictors of risky alcohol consumption in schoolchildren and their implications for preventing alcohol-related harm. *Substance Abuse Treatment, Prevention, and Policy*, **2**, 15.

Bjørnebekk, G. and Howard, R.C. (2012) Sub-types of angry aggression: Validating a motivation-based typology of aggression and violence in Norwegian antisocial youth. *Behavioral Sciences and the Law*, **30**, 167–180.

Blackburn, R. (2009) Sub-types of psychopath. In M. McMurran and R.C. Howard (eds), *Personality, Personality Disorders and Violence* (pp. 113–132). Chichester: Wiley-Blackwell.

Brodsky, B.S., Oquendo, M., Ellis, S.P. *et al.* (2001) The relationship of childhood abuse to impulsivity and suicidal behavior in adults with major depression. *American Journal of Psychiatry*, **158**, 1871–1877.

Buchmann, A.F., Schmid, B., Blomeyer, D. *et al.* (2009) Impact of age at first drink on vulnerability to alcohol-related problems: Testing the marker hypothesis in a prospective study of young adults. *Journal of Psychiatric Research*, **43**, 1205–1212.

Carver, C.S. and White, T.L. (1994) Behavioral inhibition, behavioral activation, and affective responses to impending reward and punishment: The BIS/BAS scales. *Journal of Personality and Social Psychology*, **67**, 319–333.

Caspi, A., Moffitt, T.E., Newman, D.L., and Silva, P.A. (1996) Behavioral observations at age 3 years predict adult psychiatric disorders: Longitudinal evidence from a birth cohort. *Archives of General Psychiatry*, **53**, 1033–1039.

Coid, J., Kahtan, N., Gault, S., and Jarman, B. (1999) Patients with personality disorder admitted to secure forensic psychiatry services. *British Journal of Psychiatry*, **175**, 528–536.

Coid, J., Moran, P., Bebbington, P. *et al.* (2009) The co-morbidity of personality disorder and clinical syndromes in prisoners. *Criminal Behaviour and Mental Health*, **19**, 321–333.

Coid, J., Yang, M., Tyrer, P. *et al.* (2006) Prevalence and correlates of personality disorder in Great Britain. *British Journal of Psychiatry*, **188**, 423–431.

Coie, J.D., Dodge, K.A., and Kupersmidt, J. (1990) Peer group behavior and social status. In S.R. Asher and J.D. Coie (eds), *Peer rejection in childhood* (pp. 178–201). New York: Cambridge University Press.

Comeau, N., Stewart, S.H., and Loba, P. (2001) The relations of trait anxiety, anxiety sensitivity, and sensation-seeking to adolescents' motivations for alcohol, cigarette and marijuana use. *Addictive Behaviors*, **26**, 803–825.

Cooper, M.L., Frone, M.R., Russell, M., and Mudar, P. (1995) Drinking to regulate positive and negative emotions: A motivational model of alcohol use. *Journal of Personality and Social Psychology*, **69**, 990–1005.

Cyders, M., Flory, K., Rainer, S., and Smith, G. (2009) The role of personality dispositions to risky behaviour in predicting first-year college drinking. *Addiction*, **104**, 193–202.

Dawe, S., Gullo, M.J., and Loxton, N.J. (2004) Reward drive and rash impulsiveness as dimensions of impulsivity: Implications for substance misuse. *Addictive Behaviors*, **29**, 1389–1405.

De Bellis, M.D., Van Voorhees, E., Hooper, S.R. *et al.* (2008) Diffusion tensor measures of the corpus callosum in adolescents with adolescent onset alcohol use disorders. *Alcohol: Clinical and Experimental Research*, **32**, 395–404.

De Bellis, M.D., Narasimhan, A., Thatcher, D.L. *et al.* (2005) Prefrontal cortex, thalamus, and cerebellar volumes in adolescents and young adults with adolescent-onset alcohol use disorders and comorbid mental disorders. *Alcoholism: Clinical and Experimental Research*, **27**, 1590–1600.

DeBrito, S.A. and Hodgins, S. (2009) Antisocial personality disorder. In M. McMurran and R.C. Howard (eds), *Personality, Personality Disorder and Violence* (pp. 133–153). Chichester: Wiley-Blackwell.

Enticott, P.G. and Ogloff, J.R.P. (2006) Elucidation of impulsivity. *Australian Psychologist*, **41**, 3–14.

Farrington, D.P. (2005) Childhood origins of antisocial behaviour. *Clinical Psychology and Psychotherapy*, **12**, 177–190.

Farrington, D.P. (2009) Psychosocial causes of offending. In M.G. Gelder, J.J. López-Ibor, N.C. Andreasen, and J. Geddes (eds), *New Oxford Textbook of Psychiatry* (2nd edn). (pp. 1908–1916). Oxford: Oxford University Press.

Farrington, D.P., Ttofi, M.M., and Coid, J.W. (2009) Development of adolescence-limited, late-onset, and persistent offenders from age 8 to age 48. *Aggressive Behavior*, **35**, 150–163.

Farrington, D.P. and Welsh, B.C. (2006) *Saving Children from a Life of Crime: Early Risk Factors and Effective Interventions*. New York: Oxford University Press.

Farrington, D.P. and Welsh, B.C. (2007) Saving children from a life of crime. *Criminology and Public Policy*, **6**, 871–880.

Fergusson, D.M., Boden, J.M., and Horwood, J. (2010) Classification of behaviour disorders in adolescence: Scaling methods, predictive validity, and gender differences. *Journal of Abnormal Psychology*, **119**, 699–712.

Fillmore, M.T. and Weafer, J. (2011) Impaired inhibitory control as a mechanism of drug abuse. In M.T. Bardo, R. Milich, and D.H. Fishbein (eds), *Inhibitory Control and Drug Abuse Prevention* (pp. 85–100). New York: Springer.

Finn, P.R., Rickert, M.E., Miller, M.A. *et al.* (2009) Reduced cognitive ability in alcohol dependence: Examining the role of covarying externalizing psychopathology. *Journal of Abnormal Psychology*, **118**, 100–116.

Freestone, M., Howard, R.C., Coid, J.W., and Ullrich, S. (under review) Adult antisocial syndrome with comorbid borderline pathology: Association with antisocial and violent outcomes. *Personality Disorders: Theory, Research and Treatment*.

Giancola, P.R. (2000) Executive functioning: A conceptual framework for alcohol-related aggression. *Experimental and Clinical Psychopharmacology*, **8**, 576–597.

Giancola, P.R., Josephs, R.A., Parrott, D.J., and Duke, A.A. (2010) Alcohol myopia revisited: Clarifying aggression and other acts of disinhibition through a distorted lens. *Perspectives on Psychological Science*, **5**, 265–278.

Graham, K. and Wells, S. (2003) Somebody's gonna get their head kicked in tonight! *British Journal of Criminology*, **43**, 546–566.

Gray, J.A. (1987) *The Neuropsychology of Anxiety*. Oxford: Oxford University Press.

Gustavson, C., Ståhlberg, O., Sjödin, A.-K. *et al.* (2007) Age at onset of substance abuse: A crucial covariate of psychopathic traits and aggression in adult offenders. *Psychiatry Research*, **153**, 195–198.

Hall, J.R., Bernat, E.M., and Patrick, C.J. (2007) Externalizing psychopathology and the error-related negativity. *Psychological Science*, **18**, 326–333.

Hill, K.G., Hawkins, D.J., Bailey, J.A. *et al.* (2001) Person-environment interaction in the prediction of alcohol abuse and alcohol dependence in adulthood. *Drug and Alcohol Dependence*, **110**, 62–69.

Hoaken, P.N.S., Shaughnessy, V.K., and Pihl, R.O. (2003) Executive cognitive function and aggression: Is it an issue of impulsivity? *Aggressive Behavior*, **29**, 15–30.

Holder, H.D., Gruenewald, P.J., Ponicki, W.P. *et al.* (2000) Effect of community-based interventions on high-risk drinking and alcohol-related injuries. *Journal of the American Medical Association*, **284**, 2341–2347.

Howard, R.C. (2006) How is personality disorder linked to dangerousness? A putative role for early-onset alcohol abuse. *Medical Hypotheses*, **67**, 702–708.

Howard, R.C. (2009) The neurobiology of affective dyscontrol: Implications for understanding "dangerous and severe personality disorder." In M. McMurran and R.C. Howard (eds), *Personality, Personality Disorder and Violence* (pp. 157–174). Chichester: Wiley-Blackwell.

Howard, R.C. (2011) The quest for excitement: A missing link between personality disorder and violence? *Journal of Forensic Psychology and Psychiatry*, **22**, 692–705.

Howard, R.C., Finn, P.E., Gallagher, J., and Jose, P. (2012) Adolescent-onset alcohol abuse exacerbates the influence of childhood conduct disorder on late adolescent and early adult antisocial behaviour. *Journal of Forensic Psychiatry and Psychology*, **23**, 7–22.

Howard, R.C., Huband, N., and Duggan, C. (2012) Adult antisocial syndrome with comorbid borderline pathology: Association with severe childhood conduct disorder. *Annals of Clinical Psychiatry*, **27**, 127–134.

Institute of Alcohol Studies (2010) *Alcohol and crime*. St. Ives, Cambridgeshire: Institute of Alcohol Studies.

Jolliffe, D. and Farrington, D.P. (2009) A systematic review of the relationship between childhood impulsiveness and later violence. In M. McMurran and R.C. Howard (eds), *Personality, Personality Disorder and Violence* (pp. 41–61). Chichester: Wiley-Blackwell.

Jones, S. and Lynam, D.R. (2009) In the eye of the impulsive beholder: The interaction between impulsivity and perceived informal social control on offending. *Criminal Justice and Behavior*, **36**, 307–321.

Kendall, T., Pilling, S., Tyrer, P. *et al.* (2009) Borderline and antisocial personality disorders: Summary of NICE guidance. *British Medical Journal*, **338**, b93.

Khalifa, N., Duggan, C., Lumsden, J., and Howard, R C. (in press) The relationship between childhood conduct disorder and adult antisocial behavior is partially mediated by early-onset alcohol abuse. *Personality Disorders: Theory, Research and Treatment*.

Kjelsberg, E. (2006) Exploring the link between conduct disorder in adolescence and personality disorders in adulthood. *Psychiatric Times*, **23**, 22–24.

Le Blanc, M. (1994) Family, school, delinquency, and criminality: The predictive power of an elaborated social control theory for males. *Criminal Behaviour and Mental Health*, **4**, 101–117.

Loeber, R., Burke, J.D., Lahey, B.B. *et al.* (2000) Oppositional defiant and conduct disorder: A review of the past 10 years, part 1. *Journal of the American Academy of Child and Adolescent Psychiatry*, **39**, 1468–1484.

Loeber, R., Stouthamer-Loeber, M., and Green, S.M. (1991) Age at onset of problem behaviour in boys, and later disruptive and delinquent behaviours. *Criminal Behaviour and Mental Health*, **1**, 229–246.

Lynam, D., Moffitt, T., and Stouthamer-Loeber, M. (1993) Explaining the relation between IQ and delinquency: Class, race, test motivation, school failure or self-control? *Journal of Abnormal Psychology*, **2**, 187–196.

Lynam, D.R. (2011) Impulsivity and deviance. In M.T. Bardo, R. Milich, and D.H. Fishbein (eds), *Inhibitory Control and Drug Abuse Prevention* (pp. 145–160). New York: Springer.

Magid, V. and Colder, C.R. (2007) The UPPS impulsive behavior scale: Factor analysis and relation with alcohol involvement. *Personality and Individual Differences*, **43**, 1927–1937.

McMorris, B.J., Catalano, R.F., Kim, M.J. *et al.* (2011) Influence of family factors and supervised alcohol use on adolescent alcohol use and harms: Similarities between youth in different alcohol policy contexts. *Journal of Studies on Alcohol and Drugs*, **72**, 418–428.

McMurran, M. (2011) Anxiety, alcohol intoxication, and aggression. *Legal and Criminological Psychology*, **16**, 357–351.

McMurran, M., Blair, M., and Egan, V. (2002) An investigation of the correlations between aggression, impulsiveness, social problem-solving, and alcohol use. *Aggressive Behavior*, **28**, 439–445.

McMurran, M., Hoyle, H., and Jinks, M. (2012) Triggers for alcohol-related violence in young male offenders. *Legal and Criminological Psychology*. DOI: 10.1111/j.2044-8333.2011.02010.x.

McMurran, M., Jinks, M., Howells, K., and Howard, R. (2011a) Investigation of a typology of alcohol-related violence defined by ultimate goals. *Legal and Criminological Psychology*, **16**, 75–89.

McMurran, M., Riemsma, R., Manning, N. *et al.* (2011b) Interventions for alcohol-related offending by women: A systematic review. *Clinical Psychology Review*, **31**, 909–922.

McQueeny, T., Schweinsburg, B.C., Schweinsburg, A.D. *et al.* (2009) Altered white matter integrity in adolescent binge drinkers. *Alcohol: Clinical and Experimental Research*, **33**, 1278–1285.

Miller, L., Collins, R.L., and Kent, T.A. (2008) Language and the modulation of impulsive aggression. *Journal of Neuropsychiatry and Clinical Neurosciences*, **20**, 261–273.

Moeller, F.G., Barratt, E.S., Dougherty, D.M. *et al.* (2001) Psychiatric aspects of impulsivity. *American Journal of Psychiatry*, **158**, 1783–1793.

Moffitt, T. (1993) Adolescence-limited and life-course-persistent antisocial behaviour: A developmental taxonomy. *Psychological Review*, **100**, 674–701.

Murray, J., Irving, B., Farrington, D.P. *et al.* (2010) Very early predictors of conduct problems and crime: Results from a national cohort study. *Journal of Child Psychology and Psychiatry*, **51**, 1198–1207.

Newhill, C.E., Eack, S.M., and Mulvey, E.P. (2009) Violent behavior in individuals with borderline personality disorder. *Journal of Personality Disorders*, **23**, 541–554.

Newhill, C.E., Vaughn, M.G., and DeLisi, M. (2010) Psychopathy scores reveal heterogeneity among patients with borderline personality disorder. *Journal of Forensic Psychiatry and Psychology*, **21**, 202–220.

Ramadan, R. and McMurran, M. (2005) Alcohol and aggression: Gender differences in their relationships with impulsiveness, sensation-seeking and social problem solving. *Journal of Substance Use*, **10**, 215–224.

Ridderinkhof, K.R., de Vlugt, Y., Bramlage, A. *et al*. (2002) Alcohol consumption impairs detection of performance errors in mediofrontal cortex. *Science*, **298**, 2209–2211.

Sanson, A., Oberklaid, F., Pedlow, R., and Prior, M. (1991) Risk indicators: Assessment of infancy predictors of preschool behavioural adjustment. *Journal of Child Psychology and Psychiatry*, **32**, 609–626.

Sayal, K., Heron, J., Golding, J. *et al*. (2009) Binge pattern of alcohol consumption during pregnancy and childhood mental health outcomes: Longitudinal population-based study. *Pediatrics*, **123**, 289–296.

Shapiro, D. (1965) *Neurotic Styles*. New York: Basic Books.

Shaw, D.S. and Bell, R.Q. (1993) Developmental theories of parental contributors to anti-social behaviour. *Journal of Abnormal Child Psychology*, **21**, 493–518.

Sher, K.J. and Trull, T.J. (1994) Personality and disinhibitory psychopathology: Alcoholism and antisocial personality disorder. *Journal of Abnormal Psychology*, **103**, 92–102.

Shin, S.H., Hong, H.G., and Jeon, S.-M. (2012) Personality and alcohol use: The role of impulsivity. *Addictive Behaviors*, **37**, 102–107.

Solomon, D.A. and Molloy, P.F. (1992) Alcohol, head injury, and neuropsychological function. *Neuropsychological Review*, **3**, 249–280.

Steinberg, L. (2007) Risk taking in adolescence: New perspectives from brain and behavioural science. *Current Directions in Psychological Science*, **16**, 55–59.

Steinberg, L. (2008) A social neuroscience perspective on adolescent risk-taking. *Developmental Review*, **28**, 78–106.

Thatcher, D.L., Cornelius, J.R., and Clark, D.B. (2005) Adolescent alcohol use disorders predict borderline personality. *Addictive Behaviors*, **30**, 1709–1724.

Torgersen, S., Czajkowski, N., Jacobson, K..T. *et al*. (2008) Dimensional representations of DSM-IV cluster B personality disorders in a population-based sample of Norwegian twins: A multivariate study. *Psychological Medicine*, **14**, 1–9.

Tragesser, S.L., Trull, T.J., Sher, K.J., and Park, A. (2008) Drinking motives as mediators in the relation between personality disorder symptoms and alcohol use disorder. *Journal of Personality Disorders*, **22**, 525–537.

Van Der Kolk, B.A., Hostetler, A., Herron, N., and Fisler, R.E. (1991) Trauma and the development of borderline personality disorder. *Psychiatric Clinics of North America*, **17**, 715–730.

Vigil-Colet, A. and Morales-Vives, F. (2005) How impulsivity is related to intelligence and academic achievement. *Spanish Journal of Psychology*, **8**, 199–204.

Wells, J.E., Horwood, L.J., and Fergusson, D.M. (2004) Drinking patterns in mid-adolescence and psychosocial outcomes in late adolescence and early adulthood. *Addiction*, **99**, 1529–1541.

Welte, J.W. and Wieczorek, W.F. (1999) Alcohol, intelligence, and violent crime in young males. *Journal of Substance Abuse*, **10**, 309–319.

Whiteside, S.P. and Lynam, D.R. (2001) The five factor model and impulsivity: Using a structural model of personality to understand impulsivity. *Personality and Individual Differences*, **30**, 669–689.

Whiteside, S.P. and Lynam, D.R. (2003) Understanding the role of impulsivity and externalizing psychopathology in alcohol abuse: Application of the UPPS impulsive behaviour scale. *Experimental and Clinical Psychopharmacology*, **11**, 210–217.

Zelazo, P.D., Carter, A., Reznick, J.S., and Frye, D. (1997) Early development of executive function: A problem-solving framework. *Review of General Psychology*, **1**, 198–226.

PART III

PREVENTION

Chapter 6

ALCOHOL-RELATED VIOLENCE AS ALCOHOL-RELATED CRIME: POLICING, POLICY AND THE LAW

GAVIN DINGWALL

De Montfort University, Leicester, England

INTRODUCTION

Any study on alcohol use and its link to violence benefits from a consideration of the way in which the law, and, in particular, the criminal justice system, responds to alcohol-related violence. Violence is generally perceived as a harm that warrants criminalisation. But the limits of the criminal law, and hence the criminal justice system, have to be recognised from the outset. An offence is a defined (though sometimes contested) legal construct and the definitional process means that only certain forms of violence constitute criminal activity: certain types of sporting activity, for example, are permissible. Even if the theoretical availability of a legal response does exist, comparatively few crimes are reported to the police (Home Office, 2011); not all crimes reported are subsequently recorded (Maguire, 2007), and, of those that are, the vast majority do not lead to a conviction (Ashworth, 2007). The British Crime Survey, which is designed to measure criminal incidents that do not come to official attention, found that violence is one of the categories least likely to be reported (Home Office, 2011). In cases of minor assault, 34% of incidents were reported and, even in cases of wounding, only 56% of incidents came to the attention of the police. It has been estimated that, of all the crimes reported by respondents in the British Crime Survey, only 2% lead to a conviction (Ashworth, 2007).

These initial observations are important for two reasons. First, it is necessary to counter the assumption that all violent individuals commit a crime and can be dealt with by the criminal justice system. Second, even where an offence occurs, criminal justice intervention ensues only in a minority of cases. Any response to

Alcohol-Related Violence: Prevention and Treatment, First Edition. Edited by Mary McMurran.
© 2013 John Wiley & Sons, Ltd. Published 2013 by John Wiley & Sons, Ltd.

alcohol-related violence that is overly dependent upon the criminal law will be necessarily limited. One of the contentions of this chapter is that, despite an extensive debate amongst policy makers and academics, any changes to criminal justice strategy are likely to achieve, at best, modest results. This does not mean that the quest for effective and just responses should be abandoned – it is vital that a system reliant upon punishment and coercion is subjected to rigorous critique – it is instead a plea for realism.

Many of the issues presented in this chapter are not new. Historically, there have been many claims that alcohol use leads to societal and moral degradation, including criminality. One of the most important criminal justice agencies emerged in this context. The birth of probation had strong links to the temperance movement (Bochel, 1976). At the same time that progressive opinion recognised that an attempt to address alcohol misuse may impact positively on criminality, there was a realisation that intoxication presented problems for criminal law doctrine. The dexterous attempts to offer public protection without abandoning basic tenets of criminal liability can largely be attributed, at least in the British context, to the growing belief that the mandatory death penalty for murder was inappropriate if the offender killed whilst intoxicated. A perceived lack of effectiveness and justice resulted in changes to both the criminal justice system and the law.

However, there have been significant changes in drinking behaviour over the past 20 years in the United Kingdom. Alcohol use has fallen, though consumption amongst some groups, in particular, young women, has risen (Smith and Foxcroft, 2009), leading to what Measham and Brain (2005) have called a new culture of intoxication. The drinking environment has also changed over the past decade in Britain. Traditional pubs, particularly 'locals', are struggling to remain open, whilst large, chain pubs concentrated in city centres are becoming ubiquitous. The concentration of large licensed premises in small geographical areas poses new challenges for the police. Young drinkers make less use of licensed premises than previously and increasingly drink outside or in houses (Bellis *et al.*, 2007). Informal control of excessive behaviour by older drinkers and licensees may have been replaced by more formal responses if underage drinking is public and visible. These have implications for the law, policy and policing, which are the focus of this chapter.

The next section will consider the link between intoxication and violent offending, primarily with reference to victim surveys. Attention will then turn to policing strategies where the two most important strategies – zero-tolerance and problem-oriented policing – will be analysed. How the criminal law responds to those who offend whilst intoxicated is highly contentious, and the underlying issues will be outlined in the section following. A comparison of four distinctive international approaches will be provided. Sentencing issues will be addressed in the penultimate section. The final section offers some tentative suggestions about the role that the criminal justice system can play in combating alcohol-related violence. It will be suggested that legal responses need to be viewed as part of a broader strategy to combating alcohol-related violence. Nonetheless, legal responses are a vital component of such a strategy and demand careful consideration.

ALCOHOL AND CRIME

A considerable amount is known about the extent of alcohol-related violence. The Home Office undertook detailed research into alcohol-related violence in 2003 (Budd, 2003), drawing upon data from the 1996, 1998 and 2000 British Crime Surveys. The British Crime Survey was designed to uncover the 'dark figure' of crime; those offences that are not reported to the police or that are not subsequently recorded. Respondents who report that they have experienced violence are asked supplementary questions including whether the attacker was 'under the influence of drink' at the time. As the study author recognised, the use of this question is problematic as it calls for a subjective assessment of the offender at the time of the incident. Two aspects of the study will be outlined here: the extent of alcohol-related violence and the nature of alcohol-related violence. Brief reference will be made to the times of such incidents and the location of such incidents in the section on policing.

In the 2009/2010 survey, the assailant was adjudged to be under the influence of drink in 50% of violent incidents (Flatley et al., 2010), but there was marked variance depending upon the relationship between the parties. Where they were strangers, 65% of offenders were judged to be 'under the influence of alcohol' compared to 37% of domestic incidents and 52% of incidents between acquaintances. This may reflect, to some degree at least, victims' attempts to rationalise a random attack by a stranger.

Most alcohol-related violence is comparatively minor and involves the victim being grabbed/pushed or punched/slapped (Budd, 2003). Weapons were 'used' in 19% of alcohol-related incidents involving acquaintances and strangers, although the word 'used' has been put in inverted commas here because the report states that no one was actually hit by a weapon – a conclusion that defies belief, not least as many victims reported injuries consistent with the use of glass as a weapon. Serious injury was rare, but a very high proportion of victims reported being emotionally affected by the incident.

A localised study of hospital admissions for alcohol-related violence in South Wales found that 30% of those admitted suffered serious injuries, in two cases, the injuries were classed as 'life threatening', and that a glass or bottle had been used in 10% of cases (Maguire and Nettleton, 2003). Statistics obtained in a hospital setting would naturally result in a higher proportion of serious injuries, but this study shows that a significant proportion of alcohol-related violence resulting in serious injury escapes the attention of the police. The statistics also throw doubt on the claim that no injuries were caused by glasses or bottles in the British Crime Survey analysis.

Findings of this nature are not limited to England and Wales. It has been calculated that 'alcohol-caused' violence (an extremely problematic concept) resulted in 124 deaths with a calculated total loss of 4,381 years of life and 26,882 hospital bed days in Australia in 1997 (Chikritzhs et al., 1999). A localised Australian study concentrating on the Sydney Local Government Area reported that 57.5% of the total number of non-domestic violence assaults were identified as being alcohol-related and that between 2004 and 2007, the rate of non-domestic violence assaults classified as alcohol-related increased by an average of 11.1% a year (New South Wales Sentencing Council, 2009). In this same area, 50.1% of domestic violence incidents were identified as being alcohol-related.

Those who engage in certain forms of drinking display a heightened risk of offending. This is particularly marked for men. Coleman and Cater (2005) found that underage males and females report equal incidents of alcohol-related harm; however, there are substantial differences in the types of harm reported. Women most commonly report unwanted sexual activity, whilst men cited fighting, by definition a criminal activity, as the most likely adverse consequence. Richardson and Budd (2003) also found a stronger link between binge drinking and fighting amongst men: male binge drinkers were more than 10 times more likely than female binge drinkers to admit to having been in a fight. Overall, 49% of male binge drinkers admitted criminal behaviour compared to 22% of female binge drinkers. A contrast has to be drawn between the activities of binge drinkers and those of other regular drinkers. Studies have consistently found that the association between alcohol use and crime is far weaker for regular but non-binge drinkers (e.g., Richardson and Budd, 2003; Viner and Taylor, 2007). Viner and Taylor (2007) concluded that

> [Associations between binge drinking and crime] may be explained by behaviours or temperamental factors previously reported to be associated with adolescent binge drinking, including impulsive acts and violence (p. 906).

Alcohol use or excessive alcohol use per se is not then the key issue for criminal justice agencies. Instead, it is the consequences of binge drinking that frequently become a criminal justice concern, not least for the police.

POLICING STRATEGIES

How alcohol-related crime and disorder is policed depends in part upon broader policing priorities. As the research by Budd (2003) and others demonstrates, much alcohol-related crime is comparatively minor and does not warrant the expenditure of considerable resources. Some alcohol-related crime, however, is either intrinsically serious – including incidents involving significant injury – or could lead to more serious harm occurring. Any strategy has then to recognise that most alcohol-related offending is low priority whilst simultaneously being mindful that this is not always the case. There are also practical limitations. Given the number of intoxicated individuals present in a city centre at night, low-level offences can only be enforced selectively since processing such individuals diverts officers from other duties. Policing is the art of the possible and officers have to make value judgements about evolving situations. Circumstances may also dictate a differential approach; for example, an officer deployed in a rural town may operate without the same backup as a colleague in a city centre. Even so, frontline police officers spend a considerable proportion of their time responding to alcohol-related incidents. Palk, Davey, and Freeman (2007) reported that frontline officers in Queensland, Australia, spent 25% of their time dealing with such incidents, although this included non-criminal incidents such as accidents.

Two broad strategies have been employed as a response to alcohol-related crime and disorder – zero-tolerance policing and problem-oriented policing. Problem-oriented policing has, on occasion, concentrated exclusively on alcohol-related crime and disorder, based on the view that alcohol-related crime is a discrete problem. By contrast, zero-tolerance strategies view drunkenness as one manifestation of antisocial behaviour, and these approaches are based upon a perceived causal link between policing minor alcohol-related crime and the reduction of more serious forms of criminality.

Zero-Tolerance Policing

Zero-tolerance policing seeks to remove, or in practice reduce, the discretion afforded to individual officers by demanding that all offending is enforced. The model rests on an assumption that a robust response to minor offending results in an environment where more serious criminal activity is curtailed (Kelling and Coles, 1997; Skogan, 1990; Wilson and Kelling, 1982). Its theoretical basis is found in the so-called broken window hypothesis: put simply, a failure to respond to minor crime and antisocial behaviour leads to a perceived abandonment of the area by law enforcers and a vacuum that will be filled by criminals. Drunkenness, and its associated antisocial behaviour, should lead to arrest under this model as it is symbiotic of lawlessness.

When one considers the political interest that zero tolerance generates, it is surprising how infrequently it has been implemented (Hopkins Burke, 2002). By far, the best-known scheme operated in New York under Chief Bratton. In the United Kingdom, Cleveland adopted the model and it was used selectively in certain locations in London and Glasgow. Testing the hypothesis that the enforcement of minor crime leads to a fall in serious crime is fraught with difficulty. Crime did fall markedly in areas operating zero-tolerance approaches in the United States and in the United Kingdom (Bratton, 1997; Fagan and Davies, 2001). Successful reductions in crime, though, were often short-lived (Hopkins Burke, 2002). More significantly, there were simultaneous falls in the crime rate in comparable American cities and in police forces neighbouring Cleveland (Innes, 1999). Evaluation is made more difficult in that other policing initiatives were introduced in New York at the same time (Mawby, 2008). Some of these, such as the greater use of crime mapping, are also common in forces using a problem-oriented strategy. It is generally accepted that the adoption of zero tolerance has not been the sole reason crime fell and other factors, for example, changes in the pattern of drug usage (Bowling, 1999), have been offered as alternative explanations.

Experience suggests that a zero-tolerance approach is likely to inflame relationships between the police and certain minority groups. Street drinkers are likely to find themselves subjected to far more intrusive and antagonistic interaction with the police. Similarly, young drinkers, who are more likely to drink outside following the stricter enforcement of licensing laws, may be drawn into the criminal justice system for minor breaches of the law. Questions need to be asked about whether this is appropriate, not least as empirical support is lacking for the claim that responding to minor crime and disorder in this fashion reduces serious offending.

In the absence of empirical support, and mindful of the significant financial implications associated with dealing with minor offending in this way, what is the enduring political attraction of zero tolerance? Reclaiming the streets for the law-abiding has rhetorical appeal even if it distorts the 'dangers' posed by the antisocial and the minor criminal (Newburn and Jones, 2007). Certainly, the logic behind zero tolerance can be explained succinctly; it involves an intuitive chain of reasoning and evidence for success can be provided (without the caveats expressed above). There is also an underlying frustration that politicians have increasingly recognised: too many people, and often those living in disadvantaged areas, are affected by antisocial behaviour. Sending out a message that low-level criminality will not be tolerated may be welcome in itself, even if the evidence of a causal link to more serious crime is suspect. The default position, in other words, also has political appeal.

Problem-Oriented Policing

Whilst zero-tolerance policing offers a uniform remedy to law breaking, resting as it does on the hypothesis that different types of offending are linked, problem-oriented policing starts from three very different premises. First, the universal is rejected in favour of the specific. The police response is tailored to a particular, narrowly defined problem. Determining the response requires a forensic appraisal of the problem and subsequent consideration of potential strategies. Second, the rigorous enforcement of minor infractions does not necessarily form part of that response. Finally, police involvement often coexists with the work of professionals in fields such as education and health care. This contrasts with zero tolerance, where police activity by itself is believed capable of effecting change. Problem-oriented approaches stress the futility of strategies which fail to address the underlying causes of crime (Matthews, 1992).

Alcohol-related crime and disorder has been seen as an area that lends itself to a problem-oriented approach (Doherty and Roche, 2003; Shepherd, 1994). Police intervention may be necessary in certain situations but is unlikely to address broader issues associated with problematic drinking behaviour either at an individual or at a community level. As with emergency medical intervention, those who respond to alcohol-related crime and disorder often have a transitory involvement in the lives of those with ongoing needs. Alcohol-related crime and disorder is often located in particular readily identifiable geographical 'hot spots', commonly in city centres. Moreover, incidents in these locations are often very time specific: typically, they occur in the early hours of Saturday and Sunday. Budd's (2003) study, based on three sweeps of British Crime Survey data, found that 61% of violent incidents involving acquaintances and 54% involving strangers occurred on weekend evenings or nights. Only 17% of assaults on strangers by those judged to have been sober and 5% of assaults by a sober acquaintance took place at this time.

Targeting hot spots at these times seems commonsensical, but the question then arises as to how best to respond. This involves deconstructing the problem further. For example, taxi ranks are often flash points, especially if individuals attempt to jump the queue, and one possible remedy would be to employ 'taxi wardens' at key times to ensure order. Zero-tolerance approaches would be impractical in this context, given the number of people drinking and the proportion of those who could be arrested for a drunkenness offence. In other situations, a zero-tolerance approach to alcohol-related offences may be justifiable, for example, in the vicinity of major sporting events where the consumption of alcohol is frequently banned. Arguably, the most significant development, however, is the realisation that the police must be part of a broader response to alcohol-related crime and disorder. Greater cooperation between a variety of public agencies as well as private interest groups such as licensees is increasingly regarded as crucial.

It is worth expanding on this point further given this collection's contribution to understanding the range of responses to alcohol-related violence. There is an evident danger that policy makers concentrate on discrete solutions without consideration of the broader picture. This is largely inescapable given individual job descriptions. It is often forgotten that the same criticism can be made of academic commentators whose areas of specialism are frequently narrow; it would be difficult to find an individual equally conversant with debates in policing, health policy and education, for example. The value of a multi-authored work such as this is that it synthesises the contributions of those from a variety of backgrounds and, hopefully, informs meaningful subsequent discussion.

The scheme in the Welsh capital, Cardiff, provides the best example of a problem-oriented approach designed specifically as a response to alcohol-related crime and disorder. The Tackling Alcohol-Related Street Crime (TASC) project was launched in 2000 after it was recognised that there was a serious problem with violence and disorder at certain city centre 'hot spots' (Maguire and Nettleton, 2003). Nine strategies were employed:

- focussed dialogue between the police and representatives of the licensed trade,
- measures aimed at improving the quality of work by door stewards,
- attempts to influence licensing policy,
- measures aimed at publicising the problem of alcohol-related violence,
- targeted policing of hot spots,
- a cognitive behavioural programme for repeat offenders,
- training for bar staff,
- alcohol education for school children and
- support for victims of alcohol-related violence admitted to hospital.

Many of these strategies did not involve the police. The Probation Service worked with Cardiff University to implement the cognitive behavioural programme. Courses for bar staff were organised by the University of Wales Institute, Cardiff (UWIC; now Cardiff Metropolitan University). The organisation of support for victims of violence was administered by a specially trained nurse working in the Accident and Emergency Department of Cardiff's main hospital. Part of the nurse's role was to encourage the reporting of alcohol-related crime, but the information gathered in the hospital setting was valuable in refining the approach as a more nuanced picture of the problem developed.

The involvement of licensees, which was seen as especially important, was fraught to begin with. There was, for example, hostility to a 'name and shame' policy, which would identify premises where an incident had occurred. Licensees felt that this could be misleading and unfair, and, in light of these objections, the proposal was abandoned. As part of this liaison, police shared information, for example, about known 'troublemakers' prior to a football match. One matter of concern is that the strategy had little impact on licensing policy. The TASC team objected to a number of new applications in the areas in question, but the licenses were still granted. This decision complicates an evaluation of the strategy. Nonetheless, Maguire and Nettleton (2003) concluded that

> Over the 18-month evaluation period when the TASC project was in operation, there was a decrease in the numbers of violent incidents known to have occurred in the targeted area. The first year of full implementation saw a fall of four per cent and the next six months saw little change. This reduction took place despite a significant rise in licensed premise [sic] capacity in the area, and despite increases in recorded incidents of violence against the person elsewhere in South Wales. The best estimate is that in its first year of operation, the impact of TASC was to reduce the expected level of violent incidents by eight per cent (i.e., by about 100 incidents) (p. 59).

INTOXICATION AS A 'DEFENCE' TO CRIME

One of the key issues for this chapter is the extent to which intoxication can provide a defence for a violent offender. Few areas of the criminal law are as conceptually problematic. At heart, there is a fundamental tension between widely accepted tenets of criminal liability (most notably, that the defendant has to satisfy all of the elements of the offence) and the understandable desire to convict those responsible for acts of violence both because a degree of culpability is seen to attach to intoxication and because punishment is seen as a necessary deterrent (see further Dingwall, 2006, pp. 90–91; Tolmie, 1999). A desire to convict is especially evident when, as is usual, the intoxication was self-induced and voluntary. (Involuntary intoxication will be excluded from the discussion due to its rarity and the fact that the law is largely settled.) Given the extensive nature of the debate, this section expands upon the underlying issues, which are essential to understanding the legal problems, before consideration is given to four diverse solutions.

Criminal offences usually stipulate both a prohibited harm (commonly referred to as the *actus reus*) and a state of mind that the offender must have exhibited at the time (the *mens rea*). Both elements must be proved for a conviction. When intoxication is present and the harm has occurred, the debate centres upon whether intoxication should be considered when determining if the defendant satisfied the *mens rea* for the offence. The dilemma is not whether the offence would have taken place if the defendant had been sober. What is in dispute is how to respond to situations where there is evidence to support the accused's claim that he was so intoxicated that he had no recollection of carrying out the harm (Dingwall, 2006; Lynch, 1982); in effect, this amounts to a denial of *mens rea*. The argument is not whether intoxication should be a defence akin to self-defence, as is sometimes claimed erroneously, but whether evidence of intoxication should be admissible in order to challenge an essential part of the prosecution case. A further common misperception should also be addressed: acquittal would not be automatic as the evidence would only have the potential to be determinative. Juries could consider the evidence and conclude that the defendant satisfied the *mens rea* for the offence even if alcohol use was present.

Violent offences usually require the offender to have either intended or to have been reckless about causing the specified injury. Both intention and recklessness are potentially problematic when evidence of intoxication exists. Intention encompasses purpose or aim, and there is considerable theoretical debate about the extent to which it extends to foresight of extreme probability when the defendant's stated aim is different. What is beyond dispute, though, is that intention is subjective: if it cannot be proved that the defendant intended to cause the harm, then an acquittal must follow. If someone was so intoxicated that he could not form intent, and since this is a fundamental requirement of the offence, doctrine would suggest that he must be acquitted. Recklessness is no less problematic. There is a long-standing dispute about whether recklessness should be viewed as an objective or a subjective concept; however, the jurisprudential trend is towards a subjective interpretation: to be reckless, a defendant has to consciously take an unjustified risk. Principle again suggests that an individual who was so intoxicated that he was unable to perceive a risk should be acquitted. It will come as no surprise that the courts have balked at the implications of the above, mindful that implementation would result in the possibility of intoxication excusing crime. Although intoxication would not amount to a proper defence (at least in this author's opinion), evidence of intoxication could successfully rebut the prosecution case; legalistic distinctions count for little if injustice is perceived. Experience from Australia and Canada has certainly shown that an acquittal on this ground can lead to genuine outrage. Balancing doctrine with perceived notions of justice and public protection has resulted in a number of approaches being adopted internationally, some of which have entailed lavish degrees of judicial creativity. Four of the most interesting approaches will be considered in turn.

Intoxication Is Irrelevant

This position is the easiest to state and the hardest to defend doctrinally. Evidence of intoxication is deemed irrelevant in all cases and must not be considered when determining if the accused satisfied the *mens rea* (see further Dingwall, 2006, pp. 93–99). Considerable mental dexterity is required by the fact finder when there is evidence that the defendant had been drinking due to the partial (and largely hypothetical) calculation that must be undertaken. The approach ultimately rests upon the fiction that someone can intend to do something when, factually, this was an impossibility. Nowadays, this approach is most commonly associated with Scotland, although it represents the traditional position in most common law countries (McAuley, 1997; McCord, 1992; Singh, 1933). The Scottish courts justify this approach on policy grounds, arguing that any alternative would be 'a perilous doctrine' (*HM Advocate v. Savage* [1923] JC 49 at 50).

Montana, and certain other states in the United States, adopts the same rule. The legality of such an approach was challenged in the US Supreme Court (*Montana v. Egelhoff* 518 US 37 (1996)) on the basis that the exclusion of fundamental evidence was unconstitutional as it violated due process. The Supreme Court held that the law was not unconstitutional as there was no fundamental right to have evidence of intoxication admitted.

Intoxication Is Potentially Relevant for Most Offences

For the reasons outlined above, an approach that allows for the consideration of evidence of intoxication is most consistent with legal principle, yet it is only comparatively recently that the courts in some common law jurisdictions, notably, Canada (*Daviault* (1994) 93 CCC (3rd) 21), New Zealand (*Kamipeli* [1975] 2 NZLR 610) and parts of Australia (*O'Connor* [1980] HCA 17), have recognised this. The reasoning of the Court of Appeal in New Zealand in the case of *Kamipeli* [1975] 2 NZLR 610 is convincing: society may need protection from drunken violence, but, as society also needs protecting from other types of crime, what is unique about alcohol-related offending that justifies departure from the standard requirements of criminal law? Acquittals on the basis of intoxication are an inevitable consequence, and these have on occasion proved highly contentious (Gough, 2000), particularly in cases of violence. Nowhere was this more evident than in Canada following the infamous *Daviault* (1994) 93 CCC (3d) 21 decision.

Henri Daviault, a chronic alcoholic, went to get alcohol for a friend of his wife. The friend was 65 years old and semi-paralysed. Daviault brought a large bottle of brandy to the house, and, after drinking half a glass, his wife's friend passed out. Whilst she was asleep, Daviault, who had already drunk at least seven beers, finished the bottle of brandy. He subsequently sexually assaulted the woman but maintained that he had no recollection of events that night. His claim was supported by expert evidence from a pharmacologist, who testified that the level of intoxication present meant that Daviault would have been unlikely to have been aware of his actions or to have been functioning normally. This evidence led the trial judge to rule that Daviault could be acquitted on the basis that the *mens rea* for the offence had not been made out. The subsequent acquittal was overturned by the Quebec Court of Appeal on the basis that evidence of intoxication could not be used to negate *mens rea* for a crime of general intent (see section on Intoxication Is Potentially Relevant for Some Offences). The question that was determined by the Canadian Supreme Court can be stated simply: could evidence of intoxication be considered in all cases where the 'state of drunkenness . . . is so extreme that an accused is in a condition that closely resembles automatism or a disease of the mind'?

At one level, the Supreme Court's ruling is narrow in that it considers whether the approach taken by the Quebec Court of Appeal was consistent with two sections of the Canadian Charter of Rights and Freedoms. More widely, though, the

Court's reasoning is highly instructive, as is the subsequent reaction. Two specific points of Canadian law were addressed. Section 7 of the Charter relates to the principle of fundamental justice, and it was held that this included the requirement that the Crown prove *mens rea*. The ruling in the Quebec Court of Appeal was inconsistent with this. Second, Section 11(d), which provides for a presumption of innocence, was inconsistent with an approach that equated voluntary intoxication with the stated *mens rea* for an offence. The Supreme Court held that those whose intoxication was akin to automatism could rely upon evidence of intoxication and that this evidence could lead to an acquittal.

This decision led to rapid legislative reform. Section 33.1 of the Criminal Code was amended so as to stipulate that an individual could not rely on self-induced intoxication as a defence in cases of violence if the accused departed markedly from the standard of care generally recognised in Canadian society. It is very much a moot point whether this amendment is consistent with the Charter, not least as it was specifically designed to minimise the effects of a Supreme Court judgement which considered the implications of the Charter on the law relating to intoxication and criminal liability. Section 33.1 would still, for example, appear to violate Section 7 of the Charter as the Crown would not be required to prove that the accused satisfied the *mens rea* for the offence in question. The Supreme Court of Ontario (*Dunn* (1999) 28 CR (5th) 295) and the Supreme Court of the North West Territories (*Brenton* (1999) 28 CR (5th) 308) have held the provisions to be unconstitutional, whilst the Supreme Court of British Columbia has held that the revisions are compatible (*Vickberg* (1998) 11 CR (5th) 164).

Intoxication Is Potentially Relevant for Some Offences

Another offence-specific model is found in England and Wales. Whilst the Canadian approach distinguishes between violent and non-violent offences, the English approach does not depend on the nature of the harm. Intoxication is potentially relevant for one category of offence, those requiring a 'specific' intent, but is of no relevance for the remaining category of 'basic' intent offences (see further Dingwall, 2006, pp. 99–110). How an offence is classified is pivotal to such an approach, but English law lacks a uniformly accepted formula (Williams, 1983). The leading case of *DPP v. Majewski* [1977] AC 443, which confirmed the distinction between 'basic' and 'specific' intent offences, demonstrated this confusion when different judges offered diverse, and incompatible, tests. What has emerged in practice is that offences requiring proof of intent are classified as 'specific' intent offences. Evidence of intoxication can be considered when deciding whether such intent existed. Offences which that do not require intention but can be committed recklessly are classified as 'basic' intent offences, the effect of which is that evidence of intoxication must be ignored when determining whether the defendant is guilty. The American Model Penal Code also draws a distinction on the basis of whether recklessness can satisfy *mens rea*; Section 2.08(2) providing:

> [When] recklessness establishes an element of the offence, if the actor, due to self-induced intoxication, is unaware of a risk of which he would have been aware had he been sober, such awareness is immaterial.

The approach taken with 'specific' intent offences is consistent with the general principle. More problematic is the claim that intoxication has no relevance to recklessness. In England and Wales, recklessness demands a subjective appreciation of risk (*R v. G* [2004] 1 AC 1034); if intoxication results in a failure to perceive risk, the exclusion of potentially probative evidence cannot be justified. It is difficult to find consistency in terms of the methodology of offence classification or of doctrinal purity in the English approach. As a consequence, the English approach has been extensively (e.g., Cavender, 1989; Farrier, 1976; Smith, 1976; Virgo, 1993), though not uniformly (Colvin, 1981; Dashwood, 1977), criticised. Perhaps it is best to think of this model as an uneasy compromise between principle and public protection, although the judges in *Majewski* stated explicitly that they would jettison principle in the event of conflict.

There are a considerable number of violent offences in England and Wales that are distinguished largely by the injury caused. Although murder and wounding or causing grievous bodily harm with intent to do grievous harm or to resist apprehension (s.18 Offences against the Person Act 1861) are offences of 'specific' intent, as are all offences of attempt, the majority of violent offences (including wounding or inflicting grievous bodily harm, assault occasioning actual bodily harm, and assault and battery) are offences of 'basic' intent. Intoxication will rarely lead to an acquittal in England and Wales for two reasons: most violence is of a comparatively minor nature (Budd, 2003), and the appropriate offence will be one of 'basic' intent; and, where injury is more serious, the offences of 'specific' intent are effectively underwritten by an offence of 'basic' intent.

'Intoxicated Harm' as a Distinct Offence

A radical alternative is the German offence of 'total intoxication' (Strafgesetzbuch, StGB, Section 323a):

> (1) Whoever intentionally or negligently get [sic] intoxicated with alcoholic beverages or other intoxicants, shall be punished with imprisonment for not more than five years or a fine, if he commits an unlawful act while in this condition and may not be punished because of it because he lacked the capacity to be adjudged guilty due to the intoxication, or this cannot be excluded.

Offences of this nature are not limited to continental jurisdictions. Section 268(5) of the South Australian Criminal Law Consolidation Act 1935 provides that someone may be convicted of criminal negligence where:

> (a) the objective elements of an alleged offence are established against a defendant but the defendant's consciousness was (or may have been) impaired by self-induced intoxication to the point of criminal irresponsibility at the time of the alleged offence; and
> (b) the defendant's conduct resulted in serious harm (but not death);
> (c) the defendant is not liable to be convicted of the offence under subsection (1) or (2); and

(d) the defendant's conduct, if judged by the standard appropriate to a reasonable and sober person in the defendant's position, falls so short of that standard that it amounts to criminal negligence.'

In England and Wales, the Committee on Mentally Abnormal Offenders (England and Wales) (1975) proposed the introduction of an offence of 'dangerous intoxication', where it could be proved that the offender satisfied the *actus reus* of a specified 'dangerous offence' (paras. 18.54–18.55), a category that included violent offences, and that the offender became intoxicated voluntarily. The proposal was justified on the basis that there was no convincing reason to exclude evidence of intoxication when dealing with a 'basic' intent offence. Five years later, the introduction of an offence of 'dangerous intoxication' was rejected by the Criminal Law Revision Committee (1980) in its report on offences against the person. Their central concern was that such an offence would fail to recognise the harm caused:

> It would be unfair for a defendant who has committed a relatively minor offence while voluntarily intoxicated to be labelled as having committed the same offence as the defendant who has killed (para. 261).

Four other reasons, primarily of a pragmatic nature, were given. First, it was believed that the availability of such an offence would complicate jury decision making. Second, difficulties would arise when some of the jury believed that the defendant had acted recklessly, whilst others wished to convict him of the new offence. Opinion could divide upon whether the defendant consciously took a risk by becoming intoxicated or consciously took a risk of a particular harm occurring. Third, given that the likely penalty would be lower, defendants would be encouraged to raise intoxication as an issue, thereby prolonging trials. Finally, there was a concern that the general public would not understand the law, a matter of some irony given the uncertainty associated with the current English approach.

The attraction of creating a distinct offence is that the harm for which punishment is justified is more honestly identified, that is, putting oneself in a state from which a criminal harm resulted. A conviction for this offence may be preferable to an acquittal for the original offence and, depending on the punishment imposed, may offer a degree of public protection. A distinct offence also has the virtue that the law does not rest on the fiction present in the Scottish approach or on the inconsistencies found in England and Wales. Nonetheless, there are concerns associated with the creation of an offence of this nature. If the crux of the offence rests on voluntary intoxication, why is there a requirement that harm ensues? Although it is seldom acknowledged, moral luck is omnipresent in the criminal law. Violence provides perhaps the best example as identical conduct can result in a radically different injury. Offences criminalising total intoxication or dangerous intoxication recognise this by identifying the culpable behaviour but then seemingly undermine this coherence by reintroducing unintended harm as a criterion.

SENTENCING ALCOHOL-RELATED CRIME

Few offenders can rely upon alcohol use as a means of avoiding criminal liability whichever approach applies as the intoxication is seldom sufficient to negate *mens rea* (Dingwall, 2006; Lynch, 1982). Trials are also commonly forfeited by defendants who can mount no plausible defence or who are attracted by a sentence discount. In practice then, it is at the sentencing stage when the need for a considered response to those who offend whilst intoxicated is most pressing. Unlike attributing criminal liability, scant attention has been paid to this in the academic literature or by the courts. This can be explained in part by the relative lack of research into sentencing generally; all students of law are required to study criminal law, few even have the option of studying sentencing. Moreover, an intriguing doctrinal question allied to comparatively few important judgements is a potent combination for many legal scholars. In comparison, few sentencing cases are even reported and, of those that are, most are fact specific and raise no issues of general applicability.

The underlying concern remains relevance: should alcohol intoxication be considered at the sentencing stage? And, if so, what impact should it have? The traditional common law position was that intoxication should be excluded from the sentencing decision (*Bradley* (1980) 2 Cr.App.R.(S.) 12). This conclusion appears to have been drawn on pragmatic grounds, and it was never fully articulated why an intoxicated individual should be treated identically to a sober individual when there are self-evident differences (Dingwall and Koffman, 2008). More recently, there has been official recognition that prior alcohol use should not be 'rewarded' with a lesser sentence. The primary sentencing legislation in England and Wales, the Criminal Justice Act 2003, did not address intoxication, although subsequent guidance from the Sentencing Guidelines Council (England and Wales) (2004, para. 1.22) has stated that prior alcohol consumption should be regarded as an aggravating factor. This is a contentious, though arguable, stance. What is regrettable is that this, like the effect of many other factors, is taken as a given and no explanation is provided.

A more developed approach can be found in New South Wales where the courts have attempted to distinguish situations where intoxication should mitigate sentence from situations where it should aggravate. In *Coleman v. The Queen* (1990) 47 A Crim R 306 at 327, it was stated that

> The degree of deliberation shown by an offender is usually a matter to be taken into account; such intoxication would therefore be relevant in determining the degree of deliberation involved in the offender's breach of the law. In some circumstances, it may aggravate the crime because of the recklessness with which the offender became intoxicated; in other circumstances, it may mitigate the crime because the offender has by reason of that intoxication acted out of character.

What is rare is that the New South Wales jurisprudence is clear that in appropriate situations, intoxication can act as mitigation and then articulates when such a situation arises. Intoxication in itself is insufficient which rules out a uniform approach to all cases involving drunkenness; instead, alcohol use may support another factor that is seen to reduce culpability. This reasoning is expanded upon in *Walters v. The Queen* [2007] NSWCCA 219 at [38]:

> The fact that an offender was intoxicated at the time of committing an offence is not of itself a reason for mitigating the sentence which should be imposed on the offender. However, the fact that an offender was intoxicated at the time of committing the offence may be taken into account as mitigating the objective criminality of the offence, insofar as it indicates that the offence was impulsive and unplanned and that the offender's capacity to exercise judgement was impaired.

The courts in New South Wales have also considered when intoxication should be aggravating and when it should be viewed neutrally. If an offender has a history of offending whilst intoxicated and is therefore aware of the potential consequences of drinking, the courts will increase sentence on the grounds that the offender's conduct was reckless (NSW: para. 3.31). Where the intoxication merely provides a context for the offence, it will be regarded as a neutral factor (NSW: para. 3.22).

The effect intoxication should have on sentence depends upon the underlying purpose of the sentence. If rehabilitation is prioritised, for example, intoxication may well be directly relevant (though one needs to guard against the assumption that a sentence should automatically be increased on this basis). Similarly, a desire to deter drunken violence may justify a sentence increase. It is more problematic to decide upon the weight, if any, that should attach to intoxication if the primary aim is retribution (see further Dingwall and Koffman, 2008). Imposing a proportionate sentence necessitates a quantification of the seriousness of the offence, which is determined in turn by the offender's culpability. The question, then, is whether intoxication impacts on culpability and, if so, how?

Dingwall and Koffman (2008) have suggested that intoxication should mitigate a sentence if the offender has not offended whilst intoxicated before. Thereafter, it should be treated as a neutral factor. Their argument rests on two assumptions. First, that a differential approach can be justified for a first offender. Second, that someone who has offended before whilst intoxicated has the same culpability as a sober offender. This requires further consideration, not least because the authors recognise that the two states are qualitatively different. Repetition on the offender's part, it is claimed, demonstrates an unwillingness to modify his or her behaviour despite knowledge that drinking had led to offending in the past. The culpability that attaches to deliberately becoming intoxicated with this background knowledge equates to a sober decision to offend. The alternative position, that intoxication should aggravate the sentence, is rejected on the basis that a failure to modify behaviour is not more culpable than a decision to offend. In a response to this argument, Padfield (2011) expressed concern that sentence levels would rise as a result. Padfield, who is both an academic and a sentencer, argued that sentencers are willing to treat some of those who offend whilst intoxicated leniently, particularly those who express a genuine willingness to seek treatment. She submits that

> No one should encourage disproportionate sentences, but a fixation on seeking to identify aggravating and mitigating factors in order to fix 'offence serious-ness' may lead to an unduly blinkered approach. Desert should certainly fix the upper limits of a sentence, but not necessarily its precise details (Padfield, 2011, p. 96)

There is agreement that aggravating a sentence due to intoxication is problem-atic, but Padfield would allow mitigation in a wider set of circumstances than Dingwall and Koffman. Another area of disagreement relates to the desirability of having a uniform approach as opposed to a more flexible system that allows courts to determine the consequences of intoxication in sentencing on a case-by-case basis. Padfield favours more discretion than Dingwall and Koffman, arguing that it is necessary to allow the courts to distinguish between different categories of intoxicated offender. These issues are of particular importance with regard to many moderately serious offences of violence where a decision to treat intoxica-tion as aggravation or mitigation may determine whether a custodial sentence is imposed. This may, in turn, determine what assistance, if any, an offender receives to address any underlying alcohol problems. The design, implementation and effectiveness of these programmes are discussed elsewhere in this volume.

CONCLUSION: RECOGNISING THE LIMITS OF THE LAW

A desire to use the criminal law in order to protect the public from violence or to deter individuals from assaulting others is a consistent theme in political dis-course and judicial reasoning. No one would deny that these are worthy aims, but, if these claims are to serve as the justification for using the criminal law, the potential of the law to achieve these outcomes has to be tested. Is there any proof, for example, that the Scottish approach to criminal liability, which excludes con-sideration of evidence of intoxication, has any deterrent effect? It would seem naive to conclude that the citizens of Edinburgh are any safer than the citizens of London, Auckland or Berlin, all of which operate under different legal regimes. This conclusion should hardly come as a surprise. Deterrence rests upon a degree of rationality: potential offenders would have to be aware of the consequences of offending (or, at least, the possible consequences of offending) and then calculate whether the 'benefits' of offending are outweighed by these consequences. The artificiality of this process explains the general failure of research to find that the availability of particular penalties impacts on crime rates (von Hirsch *et al.*, 1999). It is surely absurd to suggest that an intoxicated individual could make any sort of pragmatic calculation along these lines. Deterrence and public protection are often invoked too easily to justify criminalisation and/or a particular sentencing option. The likely impact is further minimised by the tiny proportion of violent incidents dealt with by sentencers (Home Office, 2011).

A more realistic assessment would be that many individuals who offend do so when intoxicated and that such individuals need to be sentenced appropriately, but that a broader, multi-agency response to alcohol-related violence will yield a far greater long-term benefit. How then should intoxicated offenders be dealt with? If deterrent arguments are rejected, the focus shifts towards retribution and the fundamental question of whether the intoxicated individual deserves punishment for his or her actions. A distinction can be drawn both with the sober offender (or, at least, with the sober offender who intended or was reckless about causing the prohibited harm) and with an individual who acts as an automaton in other circumstances. The essential distinction, given that the harm remains constant, relates to culpability. Three possible positions could be taken: intoxication should be regarded as an aggravating factor; intoxication should be regarded as mitigation; or intoxication should be viewed neutrally (Dingwall and Koffman, 2008). What strikes the present author is that the culpability (if any exists) relates not to the causing of the prohibited harm but to the voluntary process of intoxication. Many people may regard deliberate intoxication as a morally culpable behaviour, but it is not generally regarded as behaviour warranting a criminal sanction. If culpability does attach to intoxication, then again, three possibilities need to be considered: that such conduct, even if morally reprehensible, should not justify the use of the criminal law; that intoxication does warrant criminalisation, at least in some contexts, and the appropriate response is to enforce minor offences relating to drunkenness; finally, intoxication again warrants criminalisation but only if a criminal harm has occurred. The last possibility equates to the German approach. There are certain attractions to this type of offence, yet it has to be asked whether criminalisation should hinge on an arbitrary result.

Viewed objectively, debate on legal responses to alcohol-related crime has been patchy and has not necessarily focussed on the areas of greatest practical importance. Policing alcohol-related crime and disorder has received greater attention in the last 10 years. It is suggested that a growing political realisation that these activities constituted a significant social problem (Prime Minister's Strategy Unit, 2003), allied to the fact that two distinctive policing models were in operation, resulted in a need for comparative evaluation. The interest of criminal lawyers is perhaps more difficult to explain given the paucity of cases where the level of intoxication could arguably be sufficient to affect *mens rea*. Certainly, the attempts by the courts to balance pragmatism with principle deserve scrutiny, but the distinction between different approaches is to a large extent academic (Dingwall, 2006). What the case law from Canada does demonstrate, though, is the sense of injustice that can be felt if violent individuals are not held criminally liable due to intoxication. By way of contrast, sentencing has attracted little attention (but see Dingwall and Koffman, 2008; New South Wales Sentencing Council, 2009; Padfield, 2011). Determining the effect, if any, that intoxication should have on sentence is inherently difficult, but it is for this reason that debate has to take place. Courts do process many violent offenders who were drunk at the time, but it has to be recognised that these individuals constitute the minority. The limitations of the law must be recognised.

REFERENCES

Ashworth, A. (2007) Sentencing. In M. Maguire, R. Morgan, and R. Reiner (eds), *The Oxford Handbook of Criminology*, 4th edn (pp. 990–1023). Oxford: Oxford University Press.

Bellis, M.A., Hughes, K., Morleo, M. *et al*. (2007) Predictors of risky alcohol consumption in schoolchildren and their implications for preventing alcohol-related harm. *Substance Abuse Treatment, Prevention, and Policy*, **2**, 15.

Bochel, D. (1976) *Probation and After-Care: Its Development in England and Wales*. Edinburgh: Scottish Academic Press.

Bowling, B. (1999) The rise and fall of New York murder: Zero tolerance or crack's decline? *British Journal of Criminology*, **39**, 531–554.

Bratton, W.J. (1997) Crime is down in New York City: Blame the police. In N. Dennis (ed.), *Zero Tolerance: Policing a Free Society* (pp. 29–43). London: Institute for Economic Affairs.

Budd, T. (2003) *Alcohol-Related Assault: Findings from the British Crime Survey*. London: Home Office.

Cavender, S.J. (1989) The Lords against *Majewski* and the law. *Bracton Law Journal*, **21**, 9–16.

Chikritzhs, T., Jonas, H., Heale, P. *et al*. (1999) *Alcohol-Caused Deaths and Hospitalisations in Australia, 1990–1997*. National Alcohol Indicators Bulletin No.1. Perth, Western Australia: National Drug Research Institute.

Coleman, L. and Cater, S. (2005) Underage "binge" drinking: A qualitative study into motivations and outcomes. *Drugs: Education, Prevention and Policy*, **12**, 125–136.

Colvin, E. (1981) A theory of the intoxication debate. *Canadian Bar Review*, **59**, 750–779.

Committee on Mentally Abnormal Offenders (England and Wales) (1975) *Report of the Committee on Mentally Abnormal Offenders*. Cmnd.6244. London: HMSO.

Criminal Law Revision Committee (England and Wales) (1980) *Offences Against the Person*. Cmnd.7844. London: HMSO.

Dashwood, A. (1977) Logic and the Lords in *Majewski*. *Criminal Law Review*, [1977], 532–541.

Dingwall, G. (2006) *Alcohol and Crime*. Cullompton, Devon: Willan Publishing.

Dingwall, G. and Koffman, L. (2008) Determining the impact of intoxication in a desert-based sentencing framework. *Criminology and Criminal Justice*, **8**, 335–348.

Doherty, S.J. and Roche, M. (2003) *Alcohol and Licensed Premises: Best Practice in Policing*. Payneham, South Australia: Australian Centre for Policing Research.

Fagan, J. and Davies, G. (2001) Street stops and broken windows. *Fordam Urban Law Review*, **28**, 457–504.

Farrier, D. (1976) Intoxication: Legal logic or common sense? *Modern Law Review*, **39**, 578–581.

Flatley, J., Kershaw, C., Smith, K. *et al*. (2010) *Crime in England and Wales 2009/10* Home Office Statistical Bulletin 12/10.

Gough, S. (2000) Surviving without *Majewski*? *Criminal Law Review*, [2000], 719–733.

Home Office (2011) *Crime in England and Wales 2010/2011: Findings from the British Crime Survey and Police Recorded Crime*. London: Home Office.

Hopkins Burke, R. (2002) Zero tolerance policing: New authoritarianism or new liberalism? *Nottingham Law Journal*, **11**, 20–35.

Innes, M. (1999) An iron fist in an iron glove? The zero tolerance policing debate. *Howard Journal of Criminal Justice*, **38**, 397–410.

Kelling, G. and Coles, C. (1997) *Fixing Broken Windows: Restoring Order and Reducing Crime in our Communities*. New York: New York University Press.

Lynch, A.C.E. (1982) The scope of intoxication. *Criminal Law Review*, [1982], 139–145.

Maguire, M. (2007) Crime data and statistics. In M. Maguire, R. Morgan, and R. Reiner (eds), *The Oxford Handbook of Criminology*, 4th edn (pp. 241–301). Oxford: Oxford University Press.

Maguire, M. and Nettleton, H. (2003) *Reducing Alcohol-Related Violence and Disorder: An Evaluation of the "TASC" Project*. London: Home Office.

Matthews, R. (1992) Replacing "broken windows": Crime, incivilities and urban change. In R. Matthews and J. Young (eds), *Issues in Realist Criminology* (pp. 19–50). London: Sage.

Mawby, R.C. (2008) Zero-tolerance policing. In T. Newburn and P. Neyroud (eds), *Dictionary of Policing*. Cullompton, Devon: Willan Publishing.

McAuley, F. (1997) The intoxication defence in criminal law. *Irish Jurist*, **32**, 243–296.

McCord, D. (1992) The English and American history of voluntary intoxication to negate mens rea. *Journal of Legal History*, **11**, 372–395.

Measham, F. and Brain, K. (2005) Binge drinking, British alcohol policy and the new culture of intoxication. *Crime, Media, Culture*, **1**, 262–283.

New South Wales Sentencing Council (2009) *Sentencing for Alcohol-Related Violence*. Sydney, New South Wales: NSW Sentencing Council.

Newburn, T. and Jones, T. (2007) Symbolizing crime control: Reflections on zero tolerance. *Theoretical Criminology*, **11**, 221–243.

Padfield, N. (2011) Intoxication as a sentencing factor: Mitigation or aggravation? J.V. Roberts (ed.), *Mitigation and Aggravation at Sentencing* (pp. 81–101). Cambridge: Cambridge University Press.

Palk, G., Davey, J., and Freeman, J. (2007) Policing alcohol-related incidents: A study of time and prevalence. *Policing: An International Journal of Police Strategies and Management*, **30**, 82–92.

Prime Minister's Strategy Unit (2003) *Alcohol Harm Reduction Project: Interim Analytical Report*. London: Prime Minister's Strategy Unit.

Richardson, A. and Budd, T. (2003) *Alcohol, Crime and Disorder: A Study of Young Adults*. London: Home Office.

Sentencing Guidelines Council (England and Wales) (2004) *Overarching Principles: Seriousness*. London: SGC.

Shepherd, J. (1994) Violent crime: The role of alcohol and new approaches to the prevention of injury. *Alcohol and Alcoholism*, **29**, 5–10.

Singh, R.U. (1933) History of the defence of drunkenness in English criminal law. *Law Quarterly Review*, **49**, 528–546.

Skogan, W. (1990) *Disorder and Decline: Crime and the Spiral of Decay in American Neighbourhoods*. New York: Free Press.

Smith, J.C. (1976) Comment on *Majewski*. *Criminal Law Review*, [1999], 375–378.

Smith, L.A. and Foxcroft, D.R. (2009) *Drinking in the UK: An Exploration of Trends*. York, UK: Joseph Rowntree Foundation.

Tolmie, J. (1999) Intoxication and criminal liability in New South Wales: A random patchwork? *Criminal Law Journal*, **23**, 218–237.

Viner, R.M. and Taylor, B. (2007) Adult outcomes of binge drinking in adolescence: Findings from a UK national birth cohort. *Journal of Epidemiology and Community Health*, **61**, 902–907.

Virgo, G. (1993) The Law Commission consultation paper on intoxication and criminal liability part 1: Reconciling principle and policy. *Criminal Law Review*, [1993], 415–425.

von Hirsch, A., Bottoms, A., Burney, E., and Wikstrom, P.-O. (1999) *Criminal Deterrence and Sentence Severity: An Analysis of Recent Research*. Oxford: Hart Publishing.

Williams, G. (1983) *Textbook of Criminal Law* (2nd edn). London: Stevens.

Wilson, J.Q. and Kelling, G. (1982) Broken windows: The police and neighbourhood safety. *Atlantic Monthly*, **29**, 29–38.

Chapter 7

BARROOM APPROACHES TO PREVENTION

ALASDAIR J.M. FORSYTH

Scottish Centre for Crime and Justice Research, and the Institute for Society and Social Justice Research, Glasgow Caledonian University, Glasgow, Scotland

INTRODUCTION

Barrooms are an obvious setting for alcohol-related violence prevention. Pubs, nightclubs and other licensed premises are locations where a great deal of alcohol-related disorder takes place. Consequently, barrooms are also important settings for interventions aimed at reducing harm. Additionally, the public nature of barrooms makes these ideal venues in which to conduct research aimed at understanding alcohol-related aggression and for making assessments of the effectiveness of alcohol policy reforms, including violence reduction interventions.

Interventions affecting barrooms can vary in scale, from macro legislation covering whole jurisdictions through to the micro 'house rules' of individual premises. These have included both 'control of consumption' policies to limit access to alcohol and 'harm reduction' policies to foster safer drinking. This chapter will focus on barroom-level interventions which are designed to reduce alcohol-related violence harm, that is, on measures taken by or within barroom premises rather than on policies directed towards broader alcohol licensing law and policing.

By referring to a growing body of research evidence, this chapter will first look at the factors that govern barroom violence risk. Next, examples from barroom observational research will be provided to illustrate how these factors interact with each other and with prevention strategies. Finally, the difficulties in attributing success to specific barroom violence prevention interventions will be discussed as these are invariably affected by wider changes in the alcohol landscape.

Alcohol-Related Violence: Prevention and Treatment, First Edition. Edited by Mary McMurran.
© 2013 John Wiley & Sons, Ltd. Published 2013 by John Wiley & Sons, Ltd.

RESEARCHING BARROOM VIOLENCE

Studies investigating the link between alcohol consumption and violence have found a strong association between barrooms, their density, sales, peak hours, and recorded disorder or injuries. Barrooms can be described as 'hot spots' for violence, with most disorder occurring where and when most alcohol is consumed (Block and Block, 1995; Briscoe and Donnelly, 2001; Stockwell, Somerford, and Lang, 1992).

Research assessing barroom violence has involved retrospective analysis of crime statistics, such as police records or population surveys, and alcohol consumption data, augmented by interviews with either bar staff, patrons or other 'expert' stakeholders (e.g., Finney, 2004; Hadfield, 2009; Hope, 1986). But in being hot spots for violence, and coupled with their public nature, barrooms offer researchers a unique opportunity to study violence in real time, *in situ*, by participant observation (Graves *et al.*, 1981; Homel *et al.*, 1999). Thus, the majority of research into barroom aggression has involved some form of direct observation (Hughes *et al.*, 2011), often combined with interviews and crime statistics.

A large body of barroom observational research has followed a template pioneered by Kathryn Graham and colleagues in Canada (Graham *et al.*, 1980). Graham's method has entailed sending trained observers into barrooms not only to study the actual incidents of aggression they witness but also equally importantly to assess how normal service and sub-aggressive behaviours might relate to violent disorder in terms of precursors, prediction and prevention (Graham and Homel, 1997).

Over the past three decades, Graham's technique has been revisited and refined to produce validated instruments (checklists) for observers making assessments of risk factors for disorder within barrooms. Graham's work has informed the Safer Bars programme of Toronto's Centre for Addiction and Mental Health, which aims to reduce the risk of aggression and violence in bars (Graham, 1999, 2000; Graham *et al.*, 2004). The Safer Bars programme has, in turn, informed comparable alcohol-related disorder research, staff training and violence prevention around the world.

Outwith Canada, the bulk of barroom violence research has been conducted in Australia and in the United States, although more recently, similar research has begun to be conducted in Europe (Hughes *et al.*, 2011). Despite widespread differences in alcohol legislation or drinking culture, many of the findings of Graham and colleagues are now being replicated elsewhere, and a common global range of risk factors for violence in and around licensed premises is emerging (for reviews, see Graham and Homel, 2008, and Green and Plant, 2007).

Some risk factors have been found almost universally to increase both the incidence and severity of violence, in particular, cheap alcohol and a permissive atmosphere characterised by tolerance of rowdy, sub-aggressive behaviours (Graham and Homel, 2008; Hughes *et al.*, 2011). However, identifying preventive factors other than the absence of high-risk factors has proven more elusive. This may be in part because some factors that are preventative of alcohol-related violence in certain circumstances are predictive of it in others and because overall risk is dependent on the interaction of many factors.

Broadly speaking, three types of risk factors can be identified: (1) the physical barroom environment, (2) patron types and their behaviours, and (3) bar management and staffing practices. All three factors can interact with, or counteract, one another such that, for example, a change in staffing practice may either exacerbate or override an existing environmental risk. Risk factors tend to cluster within bars (Quigley, Leonard, and Collins, 2003) and these clusters may differ between local bars and/or national drinking cultures. The following sections will outline the ways in which reducing violence around barrooms is dependent on balancing a full ecological system (Graham, West, and Wells, 2000) and why no single measure is guaranteed to reduce problems without due consideration of how this will impact on other risk factors.

Making Safer Barroom Environments

Redesigning the physical nature of barrooms arguably presents the most straight-forward opportunity to lower violence risk. However, even the relative riskiness of such 'set-in-stone' features can be difficult to assess. The largest barroom premises are likely to experience more violent incidents simply because they have the most patrons. Inevitably, this means the effect of premises size on violence risk is difficult to measure. Larger premises will tend to be at the top of any violence 'league tables' (crime statistics) recorded from within any licensing jurisdiction. Therefore, any assessments of relative barroom risk using recorded crime data should first take account of venue size. But larger venues are likely to accommodate larger groups or crowds, and so size may in itself be a risk factor (Casswell, Zhang, and Wyllie, 1993; Graves *et al.*, 1981), at least in terms of scale-severity of group disorder. In contrast, smaller venues can more easily become crowded, and crowding is thought to be a more important risk factor than size (Homel and Clark, 1994; St John-Brooks and Winstanley, 1998). Yet attempts to reduce crowding, such as external queues/line-ups or security staff turning customers away to limit numbers, may aggravate (potential) patrons.

Level of crowding and violence risk is not one-directional. Venues that struggle to attract patrons may be less likely to turn away potentially aggressive or intoxicated patrons, and may be more likely to over-serve to retain their custom (Wallin, Gripenberg, and Andréasson, 2002). Too much space, with unrestricted patron movement, may provide room for horseplay, 'table-hopping' (joining other drinkers uninvited), fighting or other inappropriate behaviours, and for rowdy groups to dominate with less likelihood of bystander intervention. Yet busy barrooms may conceal potential problems from staff supervision.

The layout of barroom premises governs patrons' movement and how they enter and exit a venue. Barrooms where movement is constricted have been demonstrated to experience more disorderly incidents (Leonard, Collins, and Quigley, 2003), with mapping of fights indicating that these tend to occur more frequently at certain 'pinch points', such as stair foots/stair heads, passageways, raised platforms, cloakrooms and toilets (which are often also blind spots for staff supervision). This is thought to occur because congestion, or sudden stops to patron flow, can result in increased bumping, drink spillage and frustration, for example, while waiting to be served at the bar (Koleczko and Garcia-Hansen, 2011; St John-Brooks and Winstanley, 1998).

Crowding and congestion can also impact upon levels of barroom (dis)comfort. Uncomfortable barrooms have been shown to experience an increased likelihood of violent disorder (Homel and Clark, 1994; Leonard *et al.*, 2003). Factors such as uncomfortable seating, noise, smokiness, inclement temperature, odours, poor lighting, inadequate ventilation, and wet or sticky surfaces can all increase irritability or aggression amongst patrons and impede the staff's ability to supervise their behaviours (Koleczko and Garcia-Hansen, 2011; MacIntyre and Homel, 1997; St John-Brooks and Winstanley, 1998).

Crowding and comfort levels will also be influenced by premises type. Small local pubs may include seating, tables, open fires and other relaxing fixtures to create a setting designed for convivial conversation. Nightclubs and other entertainment venues with more energetic goals are likely to include features such as standing areas, dance floors or stages (for live shows), all of which increase the likelihood of crowding, congestion, bumping, longer trips to the bar, noise and other sources of irritation (Koleczko and Garcia-Hansen, 2011). Venues with a lack of seating ('vertical drinking establishments') may encourage rapid alcohol consumption and increase movement both within and between premises.

Too much seating has also been linked to increased disorder (Graham *et al.*, 1980), presumably because patrons linger longer and consume more alcohol. Furniture may restrict both patron movement and staff supervision (Brookman and Maguire, 2003). It may also be an injury hazard, which can exacerbate violence once it has begun. Similarly, the presence of stairs, escalators, lift/elevators, balconies/mezzanine landings, water features, naked flames, glassware or other sharps can all easily turn a minor incident into something more serious. This might especially be the case with objects that can be used as weapons.

Glass vessels and bottles have been found to be the most commonly used instruments of violence in drinking environments (Coomaraswamy and Shepherd, 2003). Broken glass also poses a health and safety hazard to both law-abiding patrons and bar staff (Luke *et al.*, 2002; Warburton and Shepherd, 2000). The replacement of glass with aluminium or plastic drinks containers has an obvious potential to reduce the severity of barroom injuries. A pilot of polycarbonate glass (PCB – an 'unbreakable' plastic used in motorcycle helmet visors and riot shields) by an English constabulary found patrons and staff to be largely positive about this medium (Anderson *et al.*, 2009). Yet there has been resistance to the removal of glassware from both the licensed trade industry and older consumers who view glass as sophisticated (Anderson *et al.*, 2009; Forsyth, 2008). In the extreme, research funded by the British glass industry concluded that the removal of glassware for violence reduction purposes could create *a self-fulfilling prophecy* where hostile patrons might be encouraged to fight if they felt that this would be less injurious (Winder and Wesson, 2006).

The main counter-argument to removing glassware is that its absence can set an impression that violence has taken place before or that it is expected (Leather and Lawrence, 1995). This may also true of other 'health and safety' or violence prevention measures, such as tables chained to the floor, window grills, security mirrors and CCTV. In contrast, the presence of fragile glassware, other breakables, open fireplaces or expensive ornamentation may give the impression that violence is not anticipated or tolerated (Graham and Homel, 1997). The presence of such features can also modify patrons' behaviours by reducing risk factors such as movement or horseplay (rowdy behaviour), and can make them feel that the management believes that they can be trusted. Delicate ornamentation may also make a bar more attractive. Overtly safety-conscious, solid, fixed or cheap (to replace) fittings may give a functional but aesthetically unattractive impression to potential customers.

Unattractive surroundings such as shabby decor, dirt, clutter, uncollected finished drinks, litter and poor toilet order have also been found to be predictive of violent disorder (Leather and Lawrence, 1995). Unclean barrooms may give patrons an impression of permissiveness of disorder, even attracting a rowdier clientele while deterring more sober customers (Leonard et al., 2003; St John-Brooks and Winstanley, 1998). Clean, comfortable barrooms have been shown to experience fewer problems (Homel et al., 2004). 'Upscale' exclusive premises with expensive fittings (or entrance fees) may deter some potentially troublesome customers, making those inside behave in an orderly fashion so as not to lose their privilege of having been allowed entry. Indeed, in many ways, premises type dictates patron type.

Orderly Patrons Make Orderly Barrooms

Patron type is often overlooked when assessing barroom violence risk. It should be obvious that bars located in communities with higher levels of violence, and its correlates (e.g., socio-economic or alcohol problems), should have more violent patrons (MacCallum et al., 2000; Wright and Kariya, 1997). In common with the largest premises, pubs or nightclubs serving the most disadvantaged patrons are likely to be at the top of any recorded crime league tables regardless of how responsibly these barrooms are managed.

To draw analogy from education research, the 'worst' schools (e.g., in terms of exam results league tables) often have the 'best' teachers. This is because the worst schools tend to serve the poorest neighbourhoods where teachers have a more difficult job to do, than, say, in schools serving affluent neighbourhoods where the pupils (or their parents) make it easier for even the worst teachers to appear successful. The same is true of bars serving disadvantaged communities, and as with schools, assessments should be made according to 'value added', that is, whether or not the barroom concerned is experiencing more or less violence than would be expected given the demographics of its patrons/ neighbourhood.

Elevated levels of barroom violence have been found in and around premises serving a low-income clientele (Graham and Homel, 2008; MacDonald et al., 1999; Roche et al., 2001), including those that cater to populations prone to alcohol problems ('skid row' bars). These are the same social groups in which violence is concentrated. Thus, violence in a barroom may only be a marker for the wider social problems of its clientele, which may, in turn, be governed by patrons' level of disadvantage, their age and gender.

Violence is often seen as a predominantly male activity, to the extent that much research into barroom aggression has traditionally focused only on men (Graham and Wells, 2003; Leonard *et al.*, 2003; Tomsen, 1997). Bars that cater predominantly to male patrons have been found to experience more violence (Graham and Wells, 2001; Homel and Clark, 1994; Lang *et al.*, 1995; Stockwell, Lang, and Rydon, 1993).

Alcohol consumption in many cultures is associated with masculinity (Benson and Archer, 2002). Graham and Homel (2008) concluded that 'Young men and the macho culture [is] the single most common source of conflict in many drinking contexts'. Barrooms characterised by a hyper-masculine culture, of male honour and risk taking, have consistently been found to be more violent. Participants within this hyper-masculine barroom culture can see fighting as an integral part of a good night out (Moore, 1990; Tomsen, 1997).

Graham and Wells (2003) interviewed young Canadian males who had been involved in barroom aggression, describing a proportion of these as 'recreational fighters', that is, patrons who would deliberately provoke barroom fights, for example, by making an exaggerated response to a minor incident (e.g., bumping). Graham and Wells even describe this behaviour as a 'rite of passage' amongst young males with a predisposition for violence. Subsequent research by the same Canadian team (Wells *et al.*, 2011) found that young males' involvement in violence could be predicted by their frequency of barroom attendance and heavy episodic drinking. This was true for both perpetrators and victims, but perpetrators could be distinguished from victims because they held more hyper-masculine values and scored higher on trait aggression.

With pubs often being seen as traditional masculine space (Leyshon, 2008; Measham, 2004), some aggressive males may view (certain) barrooms as acceptable arenas for macho behaviour. One potential solution to this could be the feminisation of the barroom environment, although the effects of this may become confounded with making premises more comfortable or upscale (Graham *et al.*, 1980; Homel and Clark, 1994). Barroom violence between females is relatively under-researched, perhaps because its occurrence, severity and nature vary between drinking cultures. In Canada, for example, compared to males, violence committed by females has been found to be less frequent, less severe (e.g., pushing rather than punching), involving single combatants, often known to each other, is usually intergender (i.e., between female and male 'couples') and with defensive intent on the woman's part (Graham and Homel, 2008; Graham and Wells, 2001). In the United States and in Australia, gendered alcohol aggression research has focused on the risk of victimisation of women in bars (De Crespigny, 2001; Parks, 1999).

Recent research from the United Kingdom has identified females, including groups of females, as the aggressors in acts of more serious alcohol-related violence directed at other women who may be strangers to them (Forsyth, Cloonan, and Barr, 2005; Forsyth and Lennox, 2010; Parker and Williams, 2003; Spence, Williams, and Gannon, 2009; Winder and Wesson, 2006). Whether this is a new trend (the 'ladette hypothesis') related to wider social changes, or merely reflecting a long-standing behaviour that has only recently begun to receive research attention as greater numbers of women drink in nondomestic settings, is not yet fully understood. At the barroom level, a broadly similar range of predictors are associated with female-to-female violence as for male conflicts (e.g., permissiveness, dancing), with 'flirtatious' behaviour by other females identified as a unique trigger for aggression between women patrons (Collins, Quigley, and Leonard, 2007; Forsyth and Lennox, 2010; Spence *et al.*, 2009).

Another demographic commonly associated with, and targeted in, research aimed at preventing alcohol-related violence is youth (e.g., Engineer *et al.*, 2003; Parker and Williams, 2003; Richardson and Budd, 2003). Bars catering to younger drinkers (e.g., under 25 years old) do experience higher levels of violence (Lang *et al.*, 1995; Stockwell *et al.*, 1993). Indeed, much barroom violence research has specifically been conducted within premises catering to youthful drinkers, arguably in the expectation that bars with an elderly clientele would not be such a good investment of the researchers' time. The presence of younger drinkers correlates with violence, but this finding may be confounded with a lax door policy, a permissive drinking environment and the premises types favoured by the youth (e.g., in terms of music, dancing and sexual activity).

Perhaps the most volatile patron type is a mixed clientele. The night-time economy often creates situations where socially divergent groups, who may never otherwise mix, meet and they do so while becoming intoxicated. For example, premises with a large proportion of underage females but overage males have been found to experience more violent disorder (Forsyth, 2006; Graham *et al.*, 1980), but is this down to something intrinsic to this demographic mix or merely lax door policy in that neither group may be able to gain entry elsewhere? Barrooms that have large numbers of either lone customers (perhaps problem drinkers) or large groups (e.g., male 'wolfpacks') have been associated with increased violence risk (Stockwell *et al.*, 1993). Certain occasions or events may bring particularly troublesome groups, such as 'hen' or 'stag nights' ('bachelor parties'), work nights out, public holidays, and music or sporting events (Koleczko and Garcia-Hansen, 2011).

Barrooms are places where people meet. This includes patrons who are 'scoping' or 'pulling' potential sexual partners. As a club designer quoted by Koleczko and Garcia-Hansen (2011) stated, 'In the end this is about male and females interacting, no matter what anyone says about the music and all that stuff, the bottom line it's courtship'. But levels of this behaviour do vary, and dancing clubs, where patrons engage in such activity, have been found to experience more violence (Lang *et al.*, 1995; Purcell and Graham, 2005; Wells, Graham, and Trembly, 2009a). Nightclubs characterised by 'dance drug' use (e.g., Ecstasy as opposed to alcohol) have been found to be *less* violent perhaps because of the relative absence of sexual competition at these venues (Forsyth, 2009; Henderson, 1996; Hunt, Maloney, and Evans, 2010; Purcell and Graham, 2005).

Elevated levels of sexual activity are likely to coexist with other risk factors in bars, such as youthful patrons, permissiveness, music and dancing. Alcohol may exacerbate this risky activity, but it is also the case that sexual competition would happen elsewhere if licensed premises did not exist (Homel *et al.*, 2004). Given that people will socialise in this way, barrooms that cater to a courtship clientele are clearly amongst those that require the most careful violence prevention management.

Responsible Bar Management and Server Practice

Barroom management (and local licensing/zoning policy) will decide what type of premise a venue will operate as, for example, a pub, hotel, nightclub, restaurant or a hybrid of these. Premises type sets behavioural norms that influence alcohol consumption and violence risk. Bars that function more as restaurants have been found to experience the least violence, while bars that function more as nightclubs experience the most violence (Stockwell *et al.*, 1992). Therefore, as with venue size or patron demographics, premises type should always be taken into account when making value-added assessments of a barroom's position within a jurisdiction's crime rate league table.

Although part of this gradient from restaurants to nightclubs might be explicable by differences in patron types (e.g., age) and physical environments (e.g., crowding), premises types with later opening hours are those likely to experience more violence (Stockwell *et al.*, 1992). For this reason, hotels experience more alcohol-related disorder than might otherwise be expected (Lang *et al.*, 1995). Although a late opening hour may in itself be a risk factor, this is most likely because patrons will have had more time to become intoxicated. Patrons involved in late-night barroom violence may have begun drinking elsewhere, a practice variously known as pre-gaming, preloading or front-loading (Forsyth, 2010; Hughes *et al.*, 2008; Wells, Graham, and Purcell, 2009b). Movement between premises ('barhopping') may be an additional risk (Felson *et al.*, 1997), but it may also incur some off-premise sobering-up time.

How a barroom is managed, its opening hours, door policy, drinks prices and entertainments, can define its attractions, clientele and reputation, as can how house rules are applied (permissiveness) and how trouble is dealt with. Once established, a clientele or reputation can be difficult to remove. Reputation is likely to influence disorder risk, and, in the worst cases, certain establishments may have a reputation for violence, attracting yet more aggressive patrons (Graham and Wells, 2003).

A bar's clientele or reputation can be managed by enforcing an exclusive door policy (who can/cannot enter or be served). This can also be achieved by a more subtle manipulation of economic and social factors, such as appealing to a niche demographic or subculture (e.g., students, tourists, sports fans, 'goths' and LGBT patrons), or by creating a certain ambiance via adjustments to bar prices or beverage brand range and decor (e.g., by marketing a bar as 'budget' priced or upscale).

Bar prices can also influence levels of alcohol-related disorder more directly through their effect on intoxication levels. Higher prices are likely to reduce the amount and rate of consumption, whereas cheaper prices may attract customers more interested in alcohol than the social aspects of the barroom experience. Drinks promotions (discount prices) have been found to be a factor in alcohol-related violence (Moore, Brennan, and Murphy, 2011; Scott, 2002; Stockwell *et al.*, 1993), for example, 'happy hours' (variable prices) can encourage rapid consumption (Babor *et al.*, 1978; Graham and Homel, 1997). 'Irresponsible' promotional practices are likely to be indicative of bars that are also more permissive in other ways (Stockwell *et al.*, 1993).

Beverage type can influence intoxication. Some bars may serve higher alcohol by volume (ABV) beverage ranges (e.g., premium beers, white ciders, fortified wines, and deluxe or blue-label spirits) than others. Some bars may encourage beverages to be purchased in larger measures (e.g., as double spirits or wine goblets). Beverages intended for immediate consumption (e.g., shots/shooters or neat spirits) risk intoxication as do beverages with unknown ABV, such as cocktails and novelty drinks (e.g., test tubes or alcoholic gels). Recently, caffeinated alcoholic beverages and energy drinks used as mixers have become associated with risk behaviours (O'Brien *et al.*, 2008), perhaps because of this stimulant's antagonism ('masking effect') of perceived intoxication level, although the effect of caffeine–alcohol interactions on aggression remains to be researched.

Providing a range of nonalcoholic beverages, such as soft drinks, milk, water or hot drinks (e.g., tea and coffee) as an alternative would seem an obvious strategy to reduce both rate of alcohol consumption and level of intoxication. Unfortunately, some bars may not encourage this, especially later at night when barroom research has observed nonalcoholic beverages being consumed only by patrons under the influence of illicit drugs (in nightclubs; Forsyth, 2006) or by those already intoxicated with alcohol attempting to temporally sober up (in pubs; Forsyth *et al.*, 2005).

Bar-food provision has a similar potential to reduce intoxication by slowing both drinking and alcohol absorption rates (Finnigan, Hammersley, and Millar, 1999). However, observational research has found that even where food is available, it is unlikely to be consumed on-premise later in the evening by already intoxicated patrons, for example, in dancing clubs (Forsyth, 2006). Providing food to drunken patrons carries its own risks by increasing the likelihood of spillages or clutter and by introducing potential weaponry (e.g., cutlery). Nevertheless, licensed premises where patrons do consume food have been found to be less violent (Graham *et al.*, 1980; Homel *et al.*, 1999; Scott, 2002). This is despite the presence of knives, which, unlike glass alcohol containers, are seldom used as barroom weapons. In contrast to drinking, eating, especially full, sit-down meals, sets behavioural standards/norms that are not associated with violence (although this may not be the case with takeaway food purchased later, elsewhere in the night-time economy). On-premise dining is also likely to provide distraction and diversion from drinking and aggression.

The provision of entertainment is another way to provide distraction and diversion from drinking and alcohol-related violence. However, entertainment such as music, TV, games, dancing or live acts can lengthen time spent on premises, thus increasing alcohol consumption. Entertainment-licensed premises are often allowed to open later, and they may also attract younger patrons (Homel and Clark, 1994). Types of entertainment are in part governed by physical venue types. Larger venues, such as nightclubs or 'superpubs', may have purpose-built stages for live acts and designated dance floors with DJ booths, complete with lighting and sound systems. Smaller venues may be restricted to televised action, piped music, jukeboxes, slot machines and bar games.

Barroom games, such as darts, cards, dominoes, pub quizzes and competitions, need to be carefully managed, with visible house rules to prevent things from becoming overly competitive and to discourage illegal gambling. Pool tables have been found to be related to a large proportion of barroom violence (Marsh and Kibby, 1993), particularly amongst young males. This may also be the case with karaoke amongst female patrons (Forsyth and Cloonan, 2008). Televised entertainment may encourage rowdy or (sub-)aggressive behaviours (Graham *et al.*, 2000), but is this down to the direct effects of what patrons are viewing, or the clientele a particular TV show attracts (e.g., football screenings in specialised sports bars)?

Music is perhaps the most obvious form of barroom entertainment, one that illustrates its often paradoxical effects on violence risk. The choice of music played by a barroom can define its clientele by attracting niche patron types, who chose which premise to enter from across the 'soundscape' of the night-time economy. Once inside, music has been demonstrated to influence alcohol consumption and, hence, intoxication levels. This can be achieved by its mere presence or absence (Drews, Vaughn, and Anfiteatro, 1992), by its volume level (Guéguen *et al.*, 2008), tempo (McElrea and Standing, 1992), emotion (Bach and Schaefer, 1979), genre (Forsyth, 2009) and drink-related lyrical content (Jacob, 2006).

Music can also influence aggressive behaviour more directly via its effects upon patrons' movement and mood (Graham *et al.*, 1980). The lyrical content of some songs can trigger violence, for example, where a song is associated with a local football team (Hadfield, 2006). Dancing often accompanies music, especially when alcohol consumption loosens patrons' inhibitions. Dancing, especially 'off-floor dancing', can make bars seem more permissive and rowdy, with more bumping, barging and horseplay (Graham *et al.*, 2000). In some bars, music and dancing may be sexualised, further increasing disorder risk (Forsyth, 2009).

Music-related noise, especially poor quality sound or musicianship, may increase patron hostility (Homel and Tomsen, 1993) and make the staff less able to hear when trouble is brewing. Yet in other circumstances, music can prevent violent disorder, even quell it. For example, playing songs unpopular with troublemakers can encourage them to leave (Forsyth, 2009; Forsyth and Cloonan, 2008). Homel and Tomsen (1993) noted that good quality bands can control large venues by keeping patrons entertained. Hadfield (2006) noted how, by varying their music (set lists), DJs can signal to patrons when it is time to converse, time to dance, time to visit the bar, even when it is almost time to leave, thus reducing congestion at closing time. Whether this 'sonic governance' (Hadfield, 2009) is conducted purposively to prevent violence, or merely to increase bar sales (and keep entertainers in employment), has not yet been researched.

There is a dearth of training available to or codes of practice designed for barroom entertainers. How do they simultaneously market alcohol and bars while acting as peacekeepers ('soft policing')? The same might be said of bar staff; how do they weigh up reducing violence risk (and wider health concerns) with doing their paid job of serving customers alcohol? Fortunately, there are many alcohol server responsibility and training programmes, and these have received much research attention and evaluation.

Over-serving of alcohol is predictive of engagement in violence and other problems (Lang *et al.*, 1995; Stockwell *et al.*, 1993). Although extremely intoxicated
patrons are unlikely to be capable of violence (Graham *et al.*, 2006), such persons
are left vulnerable as potential victims. Responsible beverage service (RBS) training is perhaps the most high-profile intervention aimed at reducing barroom
violence (Homel *et al.*, 1999). In essence, RBS is about encouraging bar staff not
to over-serve alcohol and, in turn, lowering levels of intoxication and numbers of
drunken patrons to prevent barroom violence.

RBS training programmes can conflict with the customer service training programmes, which bar staff may also receive (often provided by the drinks industry), in that when serving this commodity – 'the customer is *not* always right'.
Nevertheless, both training types have commonalities, for example, in teaching
that staff who are rude or slow can increase patron frustration and hostility (St
John-Brooks and Winstanley, 1998). Friendly staff are likely to have friendly customers; hostile staff have hostile customers. Staff socialising too much with
patrons, or too little, has been identified as increasing disorder risk (Graham
et al., 1980).

RBS can also focus on violence reduction more directly by training bar servers
in conflict management techniques for when there is trouble and also in more
subtle psychological techniques designed to prevent it from happening in the first
place. To this end, simple measures such as monitoring and being seen monitoring
the barroom can have a 'panopticon effect', modifying patrons' behaviour accordingly (Jeffs and Saunders, 1983; McKnight and Streff, 1994). Persons who believe
they are being watched are less likely to engage in illegal behaviours. RBS training
can advise on how best to achieve this, for example, by altering the physical layout
or design of a barroom to assist staff supervision of patrons' activities (Brookman
and Maguire, 2003). Greater staff numbers (i.e., higher staff to patron ratios) can
improve patron supervision and also reduce queuing or crowding and related
frustrations (Richardson and Budd, 2003). Again, a balance is required. Too many
staff, being overzealously watchful, interfering or imposing too many rules, may
prove counterproductive (Graves *et al.*, 1981; Hobbs *et al.*, 2003; Homel and Clark,
1994; Maguire and Nettleton, 2003; Scott, 2002).

Server training programmes have been positively received by bar staff as they
provide accreditation for their difficult job (Graham, Jelley, and Purcell, 2005).
Training is, however, no substitute for experience. Older, more experienced staff
are likely to be better at dealing with situations they have encountered before,
while younger, inexperienced staff have been found to be more likely to over-
serve (Toomey *et al.*, 2004). Perhaps the best bar staff are a mixed team in terms
of age, gender and experience. RBS aims to improve team coordination and communication with other staff types as well as the police and emergency services.

Some staff may be fearful of calling the police when there is trouble because
this effectively puts their bar into the recorded violence league table (Lister *et al.*,
2000). But good communication with the police should prevent this counting
against a bar in any subsequent legal proceedings. A good rapport can be built
by encouraging informal police visits, which may in themselves deter trouble
(Jeffs and Saunders, 1983), although too many such visits may harm a bar's reputation. External communication should also extend to other licensed premises

(e.g., via 'pubwatch' schemes) to warn of troublemakers in the area rather than sending such people away towards a rival business's bar. Research has found groups of adjacent pubs and nightclubs (with different parent companies) forming organic communities by informally sharing security resources and intelligence (Forsyth et al., 2005).

Training is equally important where barroom security staff are concerned (Lister et al., 2001; Maguire and Nettleton, 2003). Unofficial, untrained or hostile security staff have been found to actually increase violence (Hobbs et al., 2003; Homel and Clark, 1994; Wells, Graham, and West, 1998). The presence of (large numbers of) security staff might set an expectancy of trouble or might be seen as a challenge by violent individuals (Leather and Lawrence, 1995). On the other hand, there is some evidence that the mutual masculine respect between formidable security staff and potentially aggressive males can impose order without any loss of face (Tomsen, 2005).

Research has noted that barroom security is a male-dominated profession (Hobbs et al., 2003). This can foster a hyper-masculine barroom culture (Homel and Clark, 1994). More female security staff could reduce this risk. Increasing the presence of female security staff should also reflect the (growing) numbers of women participating in barroom culture. Night-time economies with more women drinkers are more likely to experience more female-to-female violence. Such conflicts are not easy for all-male security teams to resolve as, for example, any physical intervention may put them at risk of accusations of sexual assault. Female security staff are also needed to patrol female toilets and to conduct door searches of women entering premises (Forsyth and Lennox, 2010; Hobbs, O'Brien, and Westmarland, 2007).

The presence of professional, trained security staff can prevent or deter violence in a barroom. However, effective security may simply displace violence elsewhere, to other premises and to off-trade outlets where alcohol is purchased for unsupervised consumption in domestic settings or on the street. Indeed, as will be discussed in later sections, displacement is a caveat to all 'successful' barroom violence prevention interventions.

To illustrate how all these risk factors interact, and also some of the difficulties in making assessments of the effectiveness of violence prevention interventions, the next section will provide some illustrative examples from actual barroom observational research.

BARROOM RISK AND VIOLENCE PREVENTION OBSERVED

This section will present some findings from barroom observational research conducted inside pubs in the city centre of Glasgow, Scotland, during a project funded by the local health authority (Forsyth et al., 2005). This 'Glasgow Pub Study' was conducted in partnership with Alcohol Focus Scotland, who ran the local ServeWise RBS training programme, itself informed by the Canadian Safer Bars model. Thus, observing RBS was central to the project, and the eight bars selected for study were evenly divided between those that had undergone external server responsibility training and those that had not.

In the Glasgow Pub Study, two teams of two observers (one male, one female in each) assessed every pub twice (Friday and Saturday nights) using Kathryn Graham's Canadian methods and checklist of risk factors (Graham, 1999, 2000; Graham *et al.*, 2004). Fewer aggressive incidents were witnessed in the pubs that had undergone RBS training, and a lower level of sub-aggressive behaviour was observed in these bars, compared with those that had not undergone RBS training. Using the Safer Bars checklist, the RBS-trained pubs were assessed as being at less risk of violence and were subsequently found to have lower recorded crime rates.

When making their assessments, observers in the Glasgow Pub Study did not know why each pub had been selected (e.g., training status or crime rate), yet during observations, many of the barroom risk factors for violent disorder identified in research conducted elsewhere were significantly more apparent within the bars that had not undergone RBS training, including physical features (e.g., congestion or dirtiness), patron types (wolfpacks or sexualised behaviour) and management practice (e.g., permissiveness or hostile staff). Further, different risk and preventive factors tended to coexist, and interacted differently, within each pub. These complexities can be illustrated by contrasting observations (field notes) made between different barrooms.

The first field note (below) concerns the *Red Lion*, a budget chain pub located beside a large number of transport nodes. This pub had the highest crime rate of any premise (licensed or otherwise) in the city centre during the hours of observation (9 p.m. to midnight at weekends). As such, at least on paper (i.e., without an observational visit), the *Red Lion* might be considered as the sort of establishment where an intervention to reduce violence should be made. Indeed, as the following field note illustrates, many of the risk factors for alcohol-related barroom violence identified in the literature (described in the previous section) were present here:

> Served already very drunk patrons and let intoxicated ones in (and remain) - even one old man who had wet himself. Lots of 'horseplay' went on without staff commenting or even looking . . . Many single alcoholics (one man emptied leftover drinks into his glass). People straight from work - had tool belt, helmet. Rowdier than other bars, some people obviously just in to get a one-night stand openly snogging [kissing etc.]. Waves of people, only a quarter or less stayed all night. Younger clubbers in for a quick cheap fix of alcohol. (*Red Lion*, Female Observer)

From the above field note, it can be seen that in the *Red Lion*, there was a high level of permissiveness of rowdy behaviour and service to intoxicated customers. Although over-serving was relatively normative in the eight pubs sampled, here it extended to tolerance of 'minesweeping' (patrons consuming abandoned drinks). This high level of permissiveness was reflected in a door policy that allowed persons to enter who may well have been refused service elsewhere (e.g., single alcoholics) and those in possession of potential weapons (e.g., tool belt and helmet). The amount of movement was also noteworthy, as was the diversity of patron types, both of which may have been a reflection of the *Red Lion*'s location beside many transport nodes. There is evidence of pub-hopping here in that persons were entering the *Red Lion* having become intoxicated elsewhere, while other patrons were intending to move elsewhere (e.g., nightclubs) after becoming intoxicated (i.e., preloading). This was the most inexpensive of the pubs visited, and the above observation notes 'a cheap fix of alcohol' as an attraction, implying that this pub was not a setting for social drinking but for price-determined consumption.

The patron types who frequented the *Red Lion* may have been a reflection of its low prices. This was acknowledged by the manager of this establishment, who, when interviewed by the author after observations had ceased, stated 'Obviously at £1.59 a pint [large beer] we don't attract city people [financial sector employees]'. Rather, he saw his pub as serving a niche market who could not otherwise afford to drink on-trade. In his view, increasing his prices might effectively exclude poor people from any affordable on-trade city centre drinking. It might encourage off-trade consumption, including preloading, and perhaps also city centre street drinking.

Enforcing changes upon the *Red Lion* might simply result in the displacement of its customers and their attendant problems elsewhere, for example, to other nearby pubs which may not have staff used to dealing with this patron type. Ultimately, closing the *Red Lion*, simply on the grounds that it was top of the crime league table, would inevitably result in another pub becoming the city's worst (e.g., the next closest to the nearby city centre transit nodes), risking a domino effect. At present, from a policing point of view, the clientele of the *Red Lion* might be seen as contained within this one location from which they can easily be dispersed. It was noteworthy that the *Red Lion* was the only observed pub where the police made regular informal visits.

Price was not the only factor impacting upon risk behaviour observed during the Glasgow Pub Study. This is exemplified by another of the pubs in the sample, the *White Horse*, which was a club-like superpub or a vertical drinking establishment. Like the *Red Lion*, serving staff at the *White Horse* had only undergone their company's customer service training package. Here, the clientele was more affluent than the *Red Lion*, consisting mainly of single-sex groups in their 20s. Despite these differences, this pub was also assessed as being at high risk for disorder, although in the case of the *White Horse*, this was because of a very different range of risk factors, as the field note below illustrates:

> [T]he 'White Horse's' theme is 'manufactured party' instant party atmosphere from the moment you walk in. Flashing lights <u>very</u> loud music, TVs displaying raunchy videos, females in bar dancing together, obvious power drinking (very fast) all contribute towards this atmosphere upon arrival. You feel obliged to participate and by not participating in getting drunk you feel 'out of place'. Everyone there is intending to get drunk as quickly as possible – the variety of designer alcohol available contributes towards this, as well as the way in which it can be drunk (via glass, pitcher, bottle, test tube, shooter, flavours etc). It is a marketing fantasy come true and the punters [patrons] love it. (*White Horse*, Male Observer – emphasis his)

The above field note highlights how this pub's environment had been orchestrated in a way that encouraged alcohol consumption. At the *White* Horse, music and other distractions were being used as a marketing tool to sell alcohol, rather than low price. The *designer alcohol* sold here was not cheap, and it is easy to see how patrons might spend beyond their initial intention or financial means. Whereas some of the patrons of the *Red Lion* might be no strangers to violence whether drunk or sober (there, both observers and the interviewed manager commented on their scarred faces), this may not have been the case with *White Horse* patrons, some of whom might become caught up in alcohol-related disorder that they would have avoided had they gone elsewhere. The above field note also exemplifies many of the barroom environmental risks described in earlier sections, including an abundance of glassware, noise and variable lighting and (sexualised) dancing, which can foster violence triggers such as congestion, bumping and spillage, while also restricting the staff's ability to supervise or intervene.

The risk factors for violence observed in the *White Horse* differed greatly from those observed in the *Red Lion*. In the *Red Lion*, these were characterised by a troublesome clientele attracted by the permissive serving of cheap alcohol. In the *White Horse*, aggressive alcohol marketing techniques and their influence on patrons' behaviour elevated violence risk. Comparing these two high-risk pubs illustrates why different premises are unlikely to be equally responsive to the same barroom-level intervention.

By way of contrast, the *Railway* pub was assessed as being at low risk for violence by the Glasgow Pub Study. This bar had a much lower crime rate than the *Red Lion* or the *White Horse*, and its licensee had participated in an RBS training programme. Observations inside the *Railway* reflected these differences, as the following field note illustrates:

> [This pub] is attempting to be a sophisticated upmarket bar. Lots of soft light, candle lit tables, reclining chairs with designer 70s chic. The music has NO lyrics and is purely background music pitched at a level you don't really notice it until you stop talking (it is actually loud-less enough to converse). The male toilets were the best I have seen in Glasgow – black and white marble / tiles – really clean. . . . My attention was focussed on the doorman . . . I suspect the policy may have been over 25s only – or the bar is attempting to keep the atmosphere safe for the over 25s who want to relax. (*Railway*, Male Observer)

Superficially, the *Railway* may be seen as a responsible bar where management practice was successfully preventing violence. The overall cleanliness of this pub and the presence of candles might be considered as sending out a message that disorder was not expected. The *Railway*'s music policy encouraged socialisation rather than speed drinking, as at the *White Horse*, and the door policy was much less permissive than at the *Red Lion*.

The problem with this upscale approach is that it is essentially based on social exclusion. Not all bars can adopt this strategy. If they did, then there is a danger of swelling the ranks of who Hobbs *et al.* (2002) dubbed the 'legion of the banned', denying young people access to safer drinking environments, arguably forcing them towards off-trade consumption or establishments such as the *Red Lion*.

A final example from the Glasgow Pub Study, the *Crown* had adopted a more inclusive door policy than the *Railway*. The *Crown* had undergone the highest level of external server training (ServeWise) in the sample (licensee and staff). Despite a relatively permissive party (pre-club) atmosphere, this was the only pub where no aggressive incidents were witnessed during observations, and it had the lowest crime rate in the sample (zero violent crime in the previous 23 months). As the following field note illustrates, observers felt safe in this barroom:

> [Staff] all monitoring the bar constantly and acknowledging customers with eye contact when they were waiting to be served. All staff were very friendly and socialised with customers and each other. I think this added to the party atmosphere of the bar without affecting speed or efficiency of service. They regularly emptied ash trays and collected glasses from tables around the bar . . . Everyone seemed to be in a good mood possibly because it was a sunny day possibly because of altered brain chemistry. Not a hint of trouble. Easily the most pleasant bar I have researched. (*Crown*, Male Observer)

Although it is not possible from the above observation to ascribe the staffing practices of the *Crown* to external server responsibility training, the various ways by which the serving staff acknowledged customers would seem consistent with RBS training programmes designed to reduce patron frustration. It also indicates that the staff are mindful of patrons' behaviours, sending a panopticon-effect message that they are being watched. This can also be achieved by floor staff visiting tables (e.g., if they are becoming disorderly), and the way in which the *Crown*'s floor staff were observed clearing tables is consistent with the model that orderly premises have orderly patrons.

From Risk Factors to Violence Triggers

To some, table wiping, attractive decor (e.g., candles) and keeping a barroom clean may seem unlikely to impact on levels of violence, but these factors can interact with more obvious risks, such as drunken patrons, to influence violence. An example of how multiple barroom factors (environment, patron types and management) can interact to trigger violent behaviour is provided by the field note below made during the Glasgow Pub Study:

> P1 [Patron #1, a drunk male] had been sitting on end of table with group of males but didn't look like he was with them. P1 goes over to next table and talks to P2 to P4 [3 younger females patrons]. P1 pours / throws beer from bottle at P2, P3 and P4 and walks away to leave. P2 [Patron #2, a heavily-pregnant smoker] stands up and lobs [throws] empty wine bottle after him. (*Red Lion*, Female Observer)
>   . . . about 15 minutes after the bottle throwing incident a number of the bar staff came to clean a pool of vomit from a table near to the incident. As I had not seen anybody throw up I can only assume it had stood there for some time prior to being cleaned! (*Red Lion*, Male Observer)

The above incident combines several risk factors that may facilitate violence. The over-serving of cheap alcohol and permissive atmosphere of the *Red Lion* may be implicated because the incident involved drunken patrons, including both the table-hopping male and the heavily pregnant smoker (who continued to be served post-incident). This incident also may have arisen from the lack of cleanliness within the *Red Lion*, in that if vomit is left lying around unattended, it may feel more permissible (in the mind of an intoxicated patron) to throw beer around, which quickly escalates to bottle throwing, itself made possible by floor staff leaving empty glassware unattended.

This section has provided a snapshot of events in only a few pubs (i.e., one premises type), in one city centre, to illustrate the complicated interconnectedness of the factors known to influence violence risk in barroom settings. When interactions with other types of licensed premises (e.g., off-trade outlets) and policy factors external to the barroom environment (e.g., changes in wider alcohol policy, fashion, economics or demographics) are considered, the extent of the challenge facing barroom violence prevention is revealed. The final section will describe these confounding factors and how they interact to make assessments of barroom-level interventions difficult to evaluate.

IMPLICATIONS FOR RESEARCH AND PRACTICE

Despite an obvious logic behind their rationale, supported by some empirical observational research evidence (see previous section on Barroom Risk and Violence Prevention Observed), evaluations of barroom-level interventions have produced mixed results. This section will discuss why this might be the case and what the implications of this are for research and practice.

Why Might Barroom-Level Evaluations Fail?

Evaluations of interventions in or around barrooms are prone to the same caveats as all violence research, including how crime is recorded, under-reporting and displacement. For example, high-profile anti-violence campaigns may foster a greater willingness amongst witnesses to report barroom disorder. Proactive police operations resulting in increased arrests or the closure of bars can give the impression things have become worse. Interventions tend to take place at a perceived crime peak, increasing the likelihood of natural return to the mean (Graham, 2011). Also, violence recorded within bars may simply reflect wider changes within a jurisdiction, such as demographic trends, economic recession, policing priorities, societal tolerance and alcohol policy.

A recent review evaluating interventions for disorder and severe intoxication in and around licensed premises by Brennan *et al.* (2011) identified 15 such studies, only 3 of which were randomised control trials (RCTs). The review concluded that the evidence base was weak and noted that different evaluations had found contradictory outcomes for the same intervention. An earlier Cochrane Review by Ker and Chinnock (2008) of interventions in the alcohol server setting for preventing injuries concluded that there was evidence that barroom-level measures could prevent injury, but that the evidence was inconclusive or conflicting as to whether this was as a result of changes to server practice influencing intoxication levels.

To those familiar with the complexities of the barroom environment, these conclusions should hardly be surprising. As is suggested throughout this chapter, single interventions will have different effects across different premises, in different drinking cultures, and can be affected by changing alcohol policies or socio-economic conditions. The same factors may either be predictive or preventative of violent disorder, depending on a barroom's internal or external circumstances, and factors may impact differently upon violence incidence and violence severity (e.g., removing breakables/glassware or security staffing level).

Evaluations need to be designed accordingly, or else there is danger that the presence of preventative factors in a barroom may be interpreted as causal rather than correlational with violence risk. For example, the presence of security measures may correlate with violence, but these measures are also indicative that management is taking steps to reduce harm (Quigley *et al.*, 2003). Thus, many of the issues raised in this chapter can be ambiguous and difficult to measure, let alone find proof of effectiveness.

The studies cited in this chapter are mainly natural experiments carried out in the real world. There is much impracticality to conducting RCTs in the barroom environment. Compliance by premises and their staff needs to be ensured, and trials will inevitably be affected by unforeseen external events (e.g., changes in alcohol policy). For example, an RCT that introduced PCB drinking vessels across an English county was undermined by noncompliance and by participating bars ceasing trading during the trial (Anderson *et al.*, 2009).

One solution to this is to conduct artificial experiments, for example, by creating bar settings in laboratories. 'Bar lab' studies are also subject to criticism, such as the representativeness of patron types (e.g., students), ethics (e.g., intoxication) and ecological validity, in that drinkers will behave differently when faced with the cues, norms and intoxication expectancies (conditioning or placebo effects) of a real barroom (Wall, McKee, and Hinson, 2000).

Why Might Barroom-Level Interventions Fail?

Barroom-level interventions are controversial in that these are often seen as the preferable option by the drinks industry over externally imposed, but arguably more effective, control of consumption measures, such as alcohol price increases or opening-hour restrictions (St John-Brooks and Winstanley, 1998). In the view of social marketers or other antialcohol campaigners, this in itself implies that barroom-level interventions fail to reduce alcohol consumption; otherwise, the drinks industry would not be so supportive.

Is successful participation in interventions (e.g., RBS training) merely reflective of underlying responsible bar management and practice rather than the effect of the intervention itself (Graham and Homel, 1997)? RBS schemes will be ineffective if what trained staff have learned is not put into practice (Homel, Tomsen, and Thommeny, 1992). Some premises may only participate in safer barroom schemes to comply with regulations in order to give the illusion of social responsibility while actually only being concerned with maximising alcohol sales, leaving levels of intoxication unchanged (Homel and Clark, 1994; Lang *et al.*, 1998). An enduring problem with barroom-level interventions is that their positive effects reduce over time, for example, via staff turnover (Graham *et al.*, 2004).

To be effective, barroom-level interventions need to be monitored and enforced by an appropriate external authority (e.g., licensing board, police or environmental health officers). Taking the replacement of glass vessels as an illustrative example, all premises types in the jurisdiction affected must be included, ensuring that, in this example, if all barrooms serve alcohol in plastic vessels, then none will have the relative appearance of expecting disorder. Compliance should be enforced, in this example, by independent inspectors making spot checks, perhaps by using a polariscope to identify any annealed glass being passed off as safety glass.

Graham *et al.* (2000) concluded that the barroom is a 'full ecological system,' in which violence risk is governed not only by the effects of alcohol but also upon the drinkers' intoxication expectations, which are, in turn, governed by patrons' backgrounds, personalities and attitudes, themselves mediated by the drinking environment and societal norms. Koleczko and Garcia-Hansen (2011) concluded that barroom violence is a function of the 'total environment' because all the risk and protective factors are interconnected. These conclusions fit with Norman Zinberg's (1984) biopsychosocial template for controlled intoxication, specifically, 'drug' (in this case, alcohol, dosage and drinkers' physiology), 'set' (the mind-set, attitudes and expectancies of the bar patron or staff) and 'setting' (the physical barroom, its internal features and external location, combined with prevailing drinking culture and policy).

What goes on inside this ecological system is also interconnected to a range of external factors, too numerous to detail in this chapter. For example, alcohol can be sourced elsewhere, from other bars and, in particular, from the off-trade (Felson *et al.*, 1997). This will, in turn, be influenced by local geography (e.g., outlet densities, transport) by price differentials between bars or sectors (pubs/nightclubs and the off-trade) or by opening hours [e.g., later bar closing hours may foster pre- or front-loading from the off-trade, while early closing may encourage 'after-parties' or 'back-loading' after closing time with take-home/carryout alcohol (Forsyth, 2010)].

During evaluations, the impacts of barroom interventions elsewhere in the alcohol landscape need to be considered. Apparently, successful barroom measures may be counterproductive in other drinking contexts. In this scenario, bars which successfully introduce measures that reduce trouble on-premise may simply be displacing violence elsewhere. For example, the banning of happy hours is thought to have increased levels of drinking from the off-trade, including preloading before entering the night-time economy (Wells *et al.*, 2009b). A more holistic approach, in this case simultaneously banning irresponsible promotions in both the on- and off-trade sectors (or otherwise reducing price differentials), could reduce the likelihood of these unintended consequences.

Finally, it should never be forgotten that alcohol use in supervised barroom surroundings is preferable to consumption in unsupervised settings. This is true not only in terms of intoxication but also in terms of violence severity, assuming that in a barroom, there will always be someone present to intervene or call the emergency services. There is evidence that off-trade alcohol-related violence is more likely to escalate, resulting in more serious consequences (Forsyth, Khan, and McKinlay, 2010; Norstrom, 1998; Scribner *et al.*, 1999).

CONCLUSION

There is no overarching theory or model to reduce violence risk in barrooms. Instead, a range of strategies can be employed that are all interconnected with each other. No single factor on its own can prevent, or cause, barroom violence. It occurs from the interaction of multiple risk factors. Few of these risk factors are one-dimensional, and all are interconnected. There is no one-size-fits-all solution to barroom violence, and interventions need to be tailored to individual barroom circumstances. The absence of a 'magic bullet' single solution perhaps explains why no prevention package, evaluation or trial result has been globally adopted or proven to be an effective intervention. This is the case even before wider policy, fashion and cultural or socio-economic factors beyond the scope of barrooms (but greatly influencing what goes on inside these) are considered. We may never find a standard package of measures that can prevent barroom aggression, but carefully crafted interventions addressing specific problems within particular drinking cultures can be effective at preventing violence or at least reducing the severity of its consequences.

Case Study: The Glasgow 'Glass Ban'

On February 2, 2006, Glasgow City Council introduced a bylaw preventing premises holding an entertainment licence (i.e., nightclubs) from using (ordinary) annealed glassware (City of Glasgow Licensing Board, 2006). This was introduced in light of concerns over the use of glass vessels as weapons resulting in serious crime and injury within the city's barrooms. In 2005, 81 such incidents were recorded by the local Strathclyde Police. Initially, the policy applied only to city centre nightclubs, and there were exemptions for wine glasses, champagne flutes and vessels made from safety glass (i.e., toughened or tempered).

In late 2006, figures released by Glasgow's licensing board convener revealed that 59 glassings were treated by local hospitals' emergency departments in the year prior to the ban (37 of which had occurred in entertainment-licensed premises) compared to only five such incidents in the first 6 months after the ban. At this time, the policy was extended to entertainment-licensed premises outside the city centre, although an attempt to introduce it to pubs was successfully challenged by the local licensed trade industry.

In 2009, Strathclyde Police recorded 52 cases of glassing in serious violence (homicide, attempt homicide and serious assault occasioning permanent disfigurement, permanent impairment or endangerment of life) within or nearby licensed premises in the Glasgow (Strathclyde) region. These cases comprised 33 at pubs, 8 at nightclubs, 6 in hotels and 2 in restaurants, of which 12 pubs and 4 nightclubs were located in the city centre – 3 years after the initial ban was introduced there.

By late 2010, all licensed premises in the Glasgow region were being encouraged to use alternatives to ordinary (annealed) glass vessels where possible. Changes in Scottish licensing law under the Licensing (Scotland) Act 2005, effective October 2009, meant that licensees now had a duty to 'help prevent crime and disorder' and to 'enhance public safety' (Scottish Parliament, 2005). Failure to meet these responsibilities could include circumstances where a glassing had taken place, despite safer drinking vessels being available, thus placing the onus on licensees to remove annealed glassware in order to ensure they retain their licence to sell alcohol.

ACKNOWLEDGEMENTS AND DISCLAIMER

Thanks to Peter Doyle, Katie Hunter, Sarah Menzies, Tony McKee and Steve Parkin for conducting the barroom observations described in this chapter, and also to Alcohol Focus Scotland and the eight pubs that participated in research funded by the Greater Glasgow NHS Board. The views expressed in this chapter are those of the author alone.

REFERENCES

Anderson, Z., Whelan, G., Hughes, K., and Bellis, M.A. (2009) *Evaluation of the Lancashire Polycarbonate Glass Pilot Project*. Liverpool: Liverpool John Moores University.

Babor, T.F., Mendelson, J.H., Greenberg, I., and Kuehnle, J. (1978) Experimental analysis of the "happy hour": Effects of purchase price on alcohol consumption. *Psychopharmacology*, **58**, 35–41.

Bach, P.J. and Schaefer, J.M. (1979) The tempo of country music and the rate of drinking in bars. *Journal of Studies on Alcohol*, **40**, 1058–1059.

Benson, D. and Archer, J. (2002) An ethnographic study of sources of conflict between young men in the context of the night out. *Psychology, Evolution and Gender*, **4**, 3–31.

Block, R.L. and Block, C.R. (1995) Space, Place, and Crime: Hot spot areas and hot places of liquor-related crime. In J.E. Eck and D. Weisburd (eds), *Crime and Place* (pp. 145–184). Monsey, NY: Criminal Justice Press; Washington, DC: Police Executive Research Forum.

Brennan, I., Moore, S.C., Byrne, E., and Murphy, S. (2011) Interventions for disorder and severe intoxication in and around licensed premises, 1989–2009. *Addiction*, **106**, 706–713.

Briscoe, S. and Donnelly, N. (2001) *Assaults on Licensed Premises in Inner-Urban Areas*. Sydney: New South Wales Bureau of Crime Statistics and Research.

Brookman, F. and Maguire, M. (2003) *Reducing Homicide: Summary of a Review of the Possibilities*. RDS Occasional Paper, No 84. London: Home Office.

Casswell, S., Zhang, J.F., and Wyllie, A. (1993) The importance of amount and location of drinking for the experience of alcohol related harms. *Addiction*, **88**, 1519–1526.

City of Glasgow Licensing Board (2006) *Amended Policy Relative to the Use of Toughened Glass and/or Plastic in Public House and Entertainment Licensed Premises*. Glasgow: City of Glasgow Licensing Board.

Collins, R.L., Quigley, B.M., and Leonard, K.E. (2007) Women's physical aggression in bars: An event-based examination of precipitants and predictors of severity. *Aggressive Behavior*, **33**, 304–313.

Coomaraswamy, K.S. and Shepherd, J.P. (2003) Predictors and severity of injury in assaults with bar glasses and bottles. *Injury Prevention*, **9**, 81–84.

De Crespigny, C. (2001) Young women, pubs and safety. In P. Williams (ed.), *Alcohol, Young Persons and Violence* (pp. 31–46). Canberra: Australian Institute of Criminology.

Drews, D.R., Vaughn, D.B., and Anfiteatro, A. (1992) Beer consumption as a function of music and the presence of others. *Journal of Pennsylvania Academy of Science*, **65**, 134–136.

Engineer, R., Phillips, A., Thompson, J., and Nicholls, J. (2003) *Drunk and Disorderly: A Qualitative Study of Binge Drinking among 18 to 24 Years Olds*. Home Office Research Study No. 262. London: Home Office.

Felson, M., Berends, R., Richardson, B., and Veno, A. (1997) Reducing pub hopping and related crime. In R. Homel (ed.), *Crime Prevention Studies: Reducing Crime, Public Intoxication and Injury*, Vol. 7 (pp. 115–132). Monsey, NY: Criminal Justice Press.

Finney, A. (2004) *Violence in the Night-Time Economy: Key Findings from the Research*. Home Office Findings 214. London: Home Office.

Finnigan, F., Hammersley, R., and Millar, K. (1999) The effects of meal composition on blood alcohol, psychomotor performance and subjective state. *Appetite*, **31**, 361–375.

Forsyth, A.J.M. (2006) *Assessing the Relationships between Late Night Drinks Marketing and Alcohol-Related Disorder in Public Space*. London: Alcohol Education Research Council.

Forsyth, A.J.M. (2008) Banning glassware from nightclubs in Glasgow (Scotland): Observed impacts, compliance and patron's views. *Alcohol and Alcoholism*, **43**, 111–117.

Forsyth, A.J.M. (2009) "Lager, lager shouting": The role of music and DJs in nightclub disorder. *Addiciones*, **21**, 327–345.

Forsyth, A.J.M. (2010) Front, side and back-loading: Reasons for drinking alcohol purchased off-premises before during and after attending nightclubs. *Journal of Substance Use*, **15**, 31–41.

Forsyth, A.J.M. and Cloonan, M. (2008) Alco-pop? The use of popular music in Glasgow pubs. *Popular Music and Society*, **31**, 57–78.

Forsyth, A.J.M., Cloonan, M., and Barr, J. (2005) *Factors Associated with Alcohol-Related Problems within Licensed Premises*. Glasgow: Greater Glasgow NHS Board.

Forsyth, A.J.M., Khan, F., and McKinlay, W. (2010) The use of off-trade glass as a weapon in violent assaults by young offenders. *Crime Prevention and Community Safety: An International Journal*, **12**, 233–245.

Forsyth, A.J.M. and Lennox, J.C. (2010) Gender differences in the choreography of alcohol-related violence: An observational study of aggression within licensed premises. *Journal of Substance Use*, **15**, 75–88.

Graham, K. (1999) *Safer Bars: Assessing and Reducing Risks of Violence*. Toronto: Centre for Addiction and Mental Health.

Graham, K. (2000) *Safer Bars: Training Manual for Observers on the Safer Bars Study*. Toronto: Centre for Addiction and Mental Health.

Graham, K. (2011) Commentary on Brennan *et al.* (2011). Towards more interpretable evaluations. *Addiction*, **106**, 714–715.

Graham, K. and Homel, R. (1997) Creating safer bars. In M. Plant, E. Single, and T. Stockwell (eds), *Alcohol: Minimising the Harm – What Works?* (pp. 171–192). London: Free Association Books.

Graham, K. and Homel, R. (2008) *Raising the Bar: Preventing Aggression in and around Bars, Pubs and Clubs*. Cullompton, Devon: Willan.

Graham, K., Jelley, J., and Purcell, J. (2005) Training bar staff in prevention and managing aggression in licensed premises. *Journal of Substance Use*, **10**, 48–61.

Graham, K., La Roque, L., Yetman, R. *et al.* (1980) Aggression and barroom environments. *Journal of Studies on Alcohol*, **41**, 277–292.

Graham, K., Osgood, D.W., Wells, S., and Stockwell, T. (2006) To what extent is intoxication associated with aggression in bars? A multilevel analysis. *Journal of Studies on Alcohol*, **67**, 382–390.

Graham, K., Osgood, D.W., Zibrowski, E. *et al.* (2004) The effect of the Safer Bars programme on physical aggression in bars: Results of a randomized controlled trial. *Drug and Alcohol Review*, **23**, 31–41.

Graham, K. and Wells, S. (2001) The two worlds of aggression for men and women. *Sex Roles: A Journal of Research*, **45**, 595–622.

Graham, K. and Wells, S. (2003) "Somebody's gonna get their head kicked in tonight": Aggression among young males in bars – A question of values. *British Journal of Criminology*, **43**, 546–566.

Graham, K., West, P., and Wells, S. (2000) Evaluating theories of alcohol-related aggression in bars. *Addiction*, **95**, 847–864.

Graves, T.D., Graves, N.B., Semu, V.N., and Sam, I.A. (1981) The social context of drinking and violence in New Zealand's multi-ethnic pub settings. In T.C. Harford and L.S. Gaines (eds), Research Monograph No. 7, *Social Drinking Contexts* (pp. 103–120). Rockville, MD: NIAAA.

Green, J. and Plant, M. (2007) Bad bars: A review of risk factors. *Journal of Substance Use*, **13**, 157–189.

Guéguen, N., Jacob, C., Le Guellec, H. *et al.* (2008) Sound level of environmental music and drinking behavior: A field experiment with beer drinkers. *Alcoholism Clinical and Experimental Research*, **32**, 1795–1798.

Hadfield, P. (2006) *Bar Wars: Contesting the Night in Contemporary British Cities*. Oxford: Oxford University Press.

Hadfield, P. (2009) *Nightlife and Crime: Social Order and Governance in International Perspective*. Oxford: Oxford University Press.

Henderson, S. (1996) "E" types and dance divas: Gender research and community prevention. In T. Rhodes and R. Hartnoll (eds), *AIDS Drugs and Prevention: Perspectives on Individual and Community Action* (pp. 66–85). London: Routledge.

Hobbs, D., Hadfield, P., Lister, S., and Winlow, S. (2002) "Door lore": The art and economics of intimidation. *British Journal of Criminology*, **42**, 352–370.

Hobbs, D., Hadfield, P., Lister, S., and Winlow, S. (2003) *Bouncers: Violence and Governance in the Night-time Economy*. Oxford: Oxford University Press.

Hobbs, D., O'Brien, K., and Westmarland, L. (2007) Connecting the gendered door: Women, violence and doorwork. *British Journal of Sociology*, **58**, 21–38.

Homel, R., Burrows, T., Gross, J. *et al.* (1999) *Preventing Violence – A Review of the Literature on Violence and Violence Prevention. A report prepared for the Crime Prevention Division of the New South Wales Attorney General's Department*. Queensland: Griffiths University.

Homel, R., Carvolth, R., Hauritz, M. *et al.* (2004) Making licensed venues safer for patrons: What environmental factors should be the focus of interventions? *Drug and Alcohol Review*, **23**, 19–29.

Homel, R. and Clark, J. (1994) The prediction and prevention of violence in pubs and clubs. In R.V. Clarke (ed.), *Crime Prevention Studies*, Vol. 3 (pp. 1–46). Monsey, NY: Criminal Justice Press.

Homel, R. and Tomsen, S. (1993) Hot spots for violence: The environment of pubs and clubs. In H. Strang and S.-A. Gerull (eds), *Homicide: Patterns, Prevention and Control Canberra* (pp. 53–66). Canberra: Australian Institute of Criminology.

Homel, R., Tomsen, S., and Thommeny, J. (1992) Public drinking and violence – Not just an alcohol problem. *Journal of Drug Issues*, **22**, 679–697.

Hope, T. (1986) *Liquor Licensing and Crime Prevention*. Home Office Research Bulletin Number 20. London: Home Office.

Hughes, K., Anderson, Z., Morleo, M., and Bellis, M.A. (2008) Alcohol, nightlife and violence: The relative contributions of drinking before and during nights out to negative health and criminal justice outcomes. *Addiction*, **103**, 61–65.

Hughes, K., Quigg, Z., Eckley, L. *et al.* (2011) Environmental factors in drinking venues and alcohol-related harm: The evidence base for European intervention. *Addiction*, **106**(Suppl. 1), 37–46.

Hunt, G., Maloney, M., and Evans, K. (2010) *Youth, Drugs, and Nightlife*. Abingdon: Routledge.

Jacob, C. (2006) Styles of background music and consumption in a bar: An empirical evaluation. *International Journal of Hospitality Management*, **25**, 716–720.

Jeffs, B. and Saunders, W. (1983) Minimizing alcohol-related offences by enforcement of the existing licensing legislation. *British Journal of Addiction*, **78**, 67–77.

Ker, K. and Chinnock, P. (2008) Interventions in the alcohol server setting for preventing injuries. *Cochrane Database of Systematic Reviews*, (16), 3.

Koleczko, K. and Garcia-Hansen, V. (2011) Dangers of the after-dark wonderlands: Part B – A review of the impact of the physical environment design on nightclub violence. In *The First International Postgraduate Conference on Engineering, Designing and Developing the Built Environment for Sustainable Well-Being* (pp. 13–18). Brisbane: Queensland University of Technology.

Lang, E., Stockwell, T., Rydon, P., and Beel, A. (1998) Can training bar staff in responsible serving practices reduce alcohol related harm? *Drug and Alcohol Review*, **17**, 39–50.

Lang, E., Stockwell, T., Rydon, P., and Lockwood, A. (1995) Drinking settings and problems of intoxication. *Addiction Research*, **3**, 141–149.

Leather, P. and Lawrence, C. (1995) Perceiving pub violence: The symbolic influence of social and environmental factors'. *British Journal of Social Psychology*, **34**, 395–407.

Leonard, K.E., Collins, R.L., and Quigley, B.M. (2003) Alcohol consumption and the occurrence and severity of aggression: An event-based analysis of male to male barroom violence. *Aggressive Behavior*, **29**, 346–365.

Leyshon, M. (2008) "We're stuck in the corner": Young women, embodiment and drinking in the countryside. *Drugs: Education, Prevention and Policy*, **15**, 267–289.

Lister, S., Hadfield, P., Hobbs, D., and Winlow, S. (2001) Accounting for bouncers: Occupational licensing as a mechanism for regulation. *Criminal Justice*, **1**, 363–384.

Lister, S., Hobbs, D., Hall, S., and Winlow, S. (2000) Violence in the night-time economy; bouncers: The reporting, recording and prosecution of assaults. *Policing and Society*, **10**, 383–402.

Luke, L.C., Dewar, C., Bailey, M. *et al.* (2002) A little nightclub medicine: The healthcare implications of clubbing. *Emergency Medicine Journal*, **19**, 542–545.

MacCallum, H., Morrison, A., Stone, D.H., and Murray, K.J. (2000) Non-fatal head injury among Scottish young people: The importance of assault. *Journal of Epidemiology and Community Health*, **54**, 77–78.

Macdonald, S., Wells, S., Giesbrecht, N., and Cherpitel, C.J. (1999) Demographic and substance use factors related to violent and accidental injuries: Results from an emergency room study. *Drug and Alcohol Dependence*, **55**(1–2), 53–61.

MacIntyre, S. and Homel, R. (1997) Danger on the dance floor: A study of interior design, crowding and aggression in nightclubs. In R. Homel (ed.), *Policing for Prevention: Reducing Crime, Public Intoxication and Injury*, Vol. 7 (pp. 91–113). Monsey, NY: Criminal Justice Press.

Maguire, M. and Nettleton, H. (2003) *Reducing Alcohol-related Violence and Disorder: An Evaluation of the "TASC" Project*. Home Office Research Study 265. London: Home Office.

Marsh, P. and Kibby, K.F. (1993) *Drinking and Public Disorder, A Report of Research Conducted by MCM Research for the Portman Group*. London: Portman Group.

McElrea, H. and Standing, L. (1992) Fast music causes fast drinking. *Perceptual and Motor Skills*, **75**, 362.

McKnight, A. and Streff, F. (1994) The effect of enforcement upon service of alcohol to intoxicated patrons of bars and restaurants. *Accident Analysis and Prevention*, **26**, 79–88.

Measham, F. (2004) Play space: Historical and socio-cultural reflections on drugs, licensed leisure locations, commercialisation and control. *International Journal of Drug Policy*, **15**, 337–345.

Moore, D. (1990) Drinking, the construction of ethnic identity and social process in a Western Australia youth subculture. *British Journal of Addiction*, **85**, 1265–1279.

Moore, S.C., Brennan, I., and Murphy, S. (2011) Predicting and measuring premises-level harm in the night time economy. *Alcohol and Alcoholism*, **43**, 357–363.

Norstrom, T. (1998) Effects on criminal violence of different beverage types and private and public drinking. *Addiction*, **93**, 689–699.

O'Brien, M.C., Thomas, P., McCoy, M.S. *et al.* (2008) Caffeinated cocktails: Energy drink consumption, high-risk drinking and alcohol-related consequences among college students. *Academic Emergency Medicine*, **15**, 453–460.

Parker, H. and Williams, L. (2003) Intoxicated weekends: Young adults' work hard-play hard lifestyles, public health and public disorder. *Drugs: Education, Prevention and Policy*, **10**, 345–368.

Parks, K.A. (1999) Women's bar-related victimization: Refining and testing a conceptual model. *Aggressive Behaviour*, **25**, 349–364.

Purcell, J. and Graham, K. (2005) A typology of Toronto nightclubs at the turn of the millennium. *Contemporary Drug Problems*, **32**, 131–167.

Quigley, B.M., Leonard, K., and Collins, L. (2003) Characteristics of violent bars and bar patrons. *Journal of Studies on Alcohol*, **64**, 765–772.

Richardson, A. and Budd, T. (2003) *Alcohol, Crime and Disorder: A Study of Young Adults*. Home Office Research Study 263. London: Home Office.

Roche, A.M., Watt, K., McClure, R. *et al.* (2001) Injury and alcohol: A hospital emergency department study. *Drug and Alcohol Review*, **20**, 155–166.

Scott, M.S. (2002) *Assaults in and Around Bars, COPS Problem-Orientated Guides for Police Series No.1*. Washington, DC: US Department of Justice.

Scottish Parliament (2005) *Licensing (Scotland) Act 2005*. Edinburgh: Scottish Parliament.

Scribner, R., Cohen, D., Kaplan, S., and Allen, S.H. (1999) Alcohol availability and homicide in New Orleans: Conceptualised considerations for small area analysis of the effect of alcohol outlet density. *Journal of Studies on Alcohol*, **60**, 310–317.

Spence, C., Williams, S., and Gannon, T. (2009) "It's your round!" Female aggression in licensed premises. *Psychology Crime and Law*, **15**, 269–284.

St John-Brooks, K. and Winstanley, K. (1998) *Keeping the Peace: A guide to the Prevention of Alcohol Related Disorder, Produced by Working Solutions for the Portman Group*. London: Portman Group.

Stockwell, T., Lang, E., and Rydon, P. (1993) High risk drinking wettings: The association of serving and promotional practices with harmful drinking. *Addiction*, **88**, 1519–1526.

Stockwell, T., Somerford, P., and Lang, E. (1992) The relationship between license type and alcohol-related problems attributed to licensed premises in Perth, Western Australia. *Journal of Studies on Alcohol*, **53**, 495–498.

Tomsen, S. (1997) A top night out: Social protest, masculinity and the culture of drinking violence. *British Journal of Criminology*, **37**, 90–102.

Tomsen, S.A. (2005) Boozers and bouncers: Masculine conflict, disengagement and the contemporary governance of drinking-related violence and disorder. *Australian and New Zealand Journal of Criminology*, **38**, 283–297.

Toomey, T.L., Wagenaar, A.C., Erickson, D.J. *et al.* (2004) Illegal alcohol sales to obviously intoxicated patrons at licensed establishments. *Alcoholism: Clinical and Experimental Research*, **28**, 769–774.

Wall, A.M., McKee, S.A., and Hinson, R.E. (2000) Assessing variation in alcohol outcome expectancies across environmental context: An examination of the situational-specificity hypothesis. *Psychology of Addictive Behaviours*, **14**, 367–375.

Wallin, E., Gripenberg, J., and Andréasson, S. (2002) Too drunk for a beer? A study of overserving in Stockholm. *Addiction*, **97**, 901–907.

Warburton, A.L. and Shepherd, J.P. (2000) Effectiveness of toughened glassware in terms of reducing injury in bars: A randomised controlled trial. *Injury Prevention*, **6**, 36–40.

Wells, S., Graham, K., and Purcell, J. (2009b) Policy implications of the widespread practice of "pre-drinking" or "pre-gaming" before going to public drinking establishments: Are current prevention strategies backfiring? *Addiction*, **104**, 4–9.

Wells, S., Graham, K., Tremblay, P.F., and Magyarody, N. (2011) Not just the booze talking: Trait aggression and hypermasculinity distinguishing perpetrators from victims of male barroom aggression. *Alcoholism: Clinical and Experimental Research*, **35**, 613–620.

Wells, S., Graham, K., and Trembly, P.F. (2009a) "Every male in there is your competition": Yong men's perceptions regarding the role of drinking setting in male-to-male barroom aggression. *Substance Use and Misuse*, **44**, 1434–1462.

Wells, S., Graham, K., and West, P. (1998) The good, the bad, and the ugly: Responses by security staff to aggressive incidents in public drinking settings. *Journal of Drug Issues*, **28**, 817–836.

Winder, B. and Wesson, C. (2006) *Last Orders for Alcohol Related Violence: Exploring Salient Factors in UK Pubs and Other Late Night Venues*. Report to British Glass. Nottingham: Nottingham Trent University.

Wright, J. and Kariya, A. (1997) Aetiology of assault with respect to alcohol, unemployment and social deprivation: A Scottish accident and emergency department case-control study. *Injury*, **28**, 369–372.

Zinberg, N.E. (1984) *Drug Set and Setting: The Basis for Controlled Intoxicant Use*. New Haven and London: Yale University Press.

PART IV

TREATMENT

Chapter 8

INTERVENTIONS WITH CHILDREN AND FAMILIES

DONALD FORRESTER

Tilda Goldberg Centre for Social Work and Social Care Research, University of Bedfordshire, Luton, England

GEORGIA GLYNN

Institute of Applied Social Research, University of Bedfordshire, Luton, England

INTRODUCTION

Alcohol-related violence in families is one of the largest and most harmful social problems in the United Kingdom. Unfortunately, it is also one of the best hidden, with both violence and alcohol misuse in the family tending to be kept secret. In this chapter, we start by considering the extent and nature of the problem and by reviewing some conceptual and definitional issues. We then look at family interventions to reduce harm to children.

EXTENT AND NATURE OF ALCOHOL-RELATED VIOLENCE IN THE FAMILY

The very large numbers of children in Britain living with one or more parents who misuse alcohol has only become obvious comparatively recently. Estimates from Alcohol Concern suggest that between 900,000 and 1.4 million children live with a parent with a serious alcohol problem (Brisby, Baker, and Hedderwick, 1997). More recently, Manning *et al.* (2009) analysed existing datasets and found even larger numbers of children living with parents whose drinking might be causing problems: they found that 29% of children were living with at least one 'binge' drinker (using more than six units for a woman or eight for a man in 1 day), estimated in total to be 3,388,782 children in the United Kingdom.

Alcohol-Related Violence: Prevention and Treatment, First Edition. Edited by Mary McMurran.
© 2013 John Wiley & Sons, Ltd. Published 2013 by John Wiley & Sons, Ltd.

These studies establish that very large numbers of children live with parents whose use of alcohol may be problematic, whether that is because of binge drinking, drinking that may increase the risk of health or social harms, or because the parent is dependent on alcohol. Living with one or more parents with an alcohol problem has long been shown to be associated with problems for children. Children whose parents misuse alcohol are more likely to have difficulties at school, to exhibit behavioural or emotional problems, and to develop alcohol misuse problems in adult life. Furthermore, children of parents with alcohol problems are very overrepresented in groups of adults with serious problems, such as psychiatric or prison populations (Cleaver, Unell, and Aldgate, 1999; Velleman and Orford, 1999).

Parental alcohol misuse is therefore a risk factor for children. However, it is a risk factor that is mediated by an interplay of protective and other risk factors. In a classic study that examined a cohort of 244 adults of which 164 were the children of problem drinkers, Velleman and Orford (1999) found that parental alcohol misuse had a complex relationship to poor outcomes. Crucially, where parental alcohol misuse did not result in disruption to family life, it did not tend to be associated with long-term harm. Where alcohol was associated with violence in the home, it had particularly harmful effects on children. Velleman and Orford also outlined a variety of resilience factors that were associated with some children coping despite disruption caused by alcohol misuse. As found in studies of a variety of familial risk factors (such as parental mental health problems), intelligent children, those with good coping strategies and those with good relationship/s with one or more adults, tended to be better able to cope with family disruption. Even where children had developed problems, many appeared able to overcome them as they moved into adulthood. Children who developed positive and supportive primary relationships, found jobs or careers they enjoyed, and those who had supportive friends were more likely to make successful transitions to adulthood. Where parental alcohol misuse is associated with violence or abuse, the outcomes for children are far worse. Indeed, in Velleman and Orford's study, the presence of violence was the single biggest risk factor linked to poor outcomes for children affected by parental alcohol misuse.

Research with British samples has identified a strong association between alcohol misuse and family violence. Gilchrist *et al.* (2003) found that alcohol features in 62% of domestic violence incidents and 48% of domestic violence perpetrators were dependent on alcohol. Finney (2004) found that use of alcohol can increase the severity of violence. Manning *et al.* (2009) highlighted that, in Scotland, 2.5% of children live in homes where violence had occurred between adults after the perpetrator had been drinking. In total, it is estimated that 750,000 children witness domestic violence a year (Cleaver *et al.*, 1999), and it has been shown to have a negative impact on children. In a meta-analytic review, Wolfe *et al.* (2003) found that children suffered emotional and behavioural problems as a result of domestic violence. Children who experience both parental alcohol misuse and domestic abuse face an increased risk that their own lives will be negatively affected in these same areas (Cleaver *et al.*, 1999). Children can further be negatively affected if their parents' capacity to care for them is reduced as a result of alcohol problems (Cleaver *et al.*, 2006). Cleaver *et al.* (2007), in their case file study, found that 31.3% of children who were experiencing domestic abuse and parental substance misuse had severe unmet needs. In summary, children living in families where alcohol-related violence is present face greater adversity, and their chances of leading normal, healthy adult lives can be jeopardised by a multitude of problems that this situation brings for those involved.

CONCEPTUAL AND DEFINITIONAL ISSUES

Neither alcohol misuse nor violence in the home is a simple concept: each covers a variety of different features. Alcohol misuse may include regular heavy drinking and/or binges – and here binge refers to periods of very heavy drinking leading to severe intoxication and usually unconsciousness – rather than the more recent public health formulation of more than eight units in 1 day for men and six units for women (NHS Choices, 2010). Some patterns of misuse involve physical or psychological dependency on alcohol; however, this is not necessary for alcohol to be regularly involved in violence.

The focus of this book – and therefore this chapter – is on alcohol-related violence; however, this is only one manifestation of broader patterns of abusive behaviour. In general terms, domestic abuse can be defined as '. . . physical, sexual, psychological or financial violence that takes place within an intimate or family-type relationship and that forms a pattern of coercive and controlling behaviour . . . Domestic violence may include a range of abusive behaviours, not all of which are in themselves inherently "violent"' (Women's Aid, 2009, p. 2). It is characterised by the misuse of power rather than by violence; however, the use and threat of violence tends to be a key element of domestic abuse.

This is a broad definition of domestic abuse. There are probably different patterns of abusive behaviour. In fact, 'domestic violence' or 'domestic abuse' incorporates a wide variety of experiences. These share the misuse of power and tend to involve violence, but in other respects, they may be rather different. Despite this, there are sufficient commonalities – particularly in relation to identification and engagement – for it to be helpful to consider them together in this chapter.

A further dimension of domestic abuse to be considered is gender. Domestic abuse tends to be focussed on male perpetrators and female victims in heterosexual relationships – and that is the primary focus of the current chapter. Abuse is not confined to heterosexual relationships, and it is important to recognise that violence and abuse may be a feature of a lesbian or gay relationship. However, while abuse can take place in same-gender relationships, it is not a gender-neutral activity. Domestic abuse is one of the sites where male power and its misuse are most apparent. This chapter recognises this by referring to perpetrators as men and victims of abuse as women. This is not to say that men cannot experience mistreatment nor that women cannot be violent. Many men report being verbally and physically mistreated by female partners (Hester, 2009). Indeed, there are some studies that suggest rather similar rates of physical abuse in intimate relationships. However, Dobash and Dobash (2004, p. 343) found '. . . women's violence differs from that perpetrated by men in terms of nature, frequency, intention, intensity, physical injury and emotional impact'. When serious incidents of violence and abuse are considered, the vast majority involve abuse by men of women. The British Crime Survey identified that of the individuals reporting four or more serious incidents of interpersonal violence (including domestic violence and sexual abuse), 89% were women (Walby and Allen, 2004). This suggests that while a man reporting abuse by a woman should be taken seriously, it would be a misrepresentation of the nature of domestic abuse not to recognise that serious violence in the home tends to be perpetrated by men on women.

A specific conceptual issue is about the nature of the relationship between alcohol misuse and violence in the home. Surveys of perpetrators and victims of violence in the home suggest substantial numbers believe alcohol is a key factor associated with violence. Yet the picture is more complex than this. Many people drink without becoming violent. Most perpetrators of violence have also been violent when not under the influence of alcohol (Galvani, 2001). Some key figures in the field, therefore, argue that alcohol is used as a legitimating story to excuse or 'allow' violence, which absolves the perpetrators responsibility for the violence (Galvani, 2007). Humphreys *et al.* (2005) state that drinking alcohol does not cause an individual to become violent to a partner. Instead, 'the relationship between the substance and domestic abuse combines the effects of the substance specific expectations, gender roles, cultural learning, the social environment, relationship dynamics and individual choice' (Galvani, 2007, p. 175).

It is therefore certainly not as simple as requiring the alcohol problem to be dealt with in order to eliminate violence. Instead, a more complex approach may be required that targets not just alcohol and violence but also underlying belief systems and the reasons for their existence. Unfortunately, there is still comparatively limited robust research in this area. Nonetheless, this chapter attempts to identify some key elements of good practice in identifying and engaging with individuals in families where there is alcohol-related violence.

DOMESTIC ABUSE AND CHILD PROTECTION

The first author's interest in this area arose from his practice and then research in relation to parental substance misuse and child protection. His studies have consistently found that alcohol-related violence is one of the most under-recognised risk factors for poor outcomes in children. This can be illustrated through two research studies he has been involved in.

Forrester and Harwin (2006, 2011) identified all families allocated a social worker in four London local authorities and then followed up the children to explore their outcomes 21 months later. Overall, the families had very serious levels of problems: in addition to drug and/or alcohol problems, there were high levels of violence; almost all lived in serious poverty with many being homeless; and most had had ongoing contact with social services for some years. At follow-up, the factors associated with children having poor outcomes were explored statistically and qualitatively. A regression analysis found four factors were particularly strongly associated with poor welfare outcomes at follow-up.

The two most important factors predicting poor outcomes for children were alcohol misuse (as opposed to drugs) and violence in the home.

This statistical finding was compounded by a second. One of the factors that was most important in *reducing* the likelihood of children entering care was violence in the home. Thus, violence not only made poor outcomes more likely for children but it also made it *less* likely that children would be protected by removal. On the face of it, this is a very surprising finding: we know from a range of research that violence is a risk factor associated with poor outcomes for children (Cleaver *et al.*, 1999). That was confirmed as true for this specific sample of very vulnerable families. Yet social workers seemed less likely to use protective powers where there was violence.

Qualitative analysis of interviews suggested that this was because gaining access to families and working with them effectively was particularly difficult where there was violence. As one experienced worker put it with refreshing honesty,

> I was allocated the case at a meeting and somebody said, 'You better watch out for them'. I didn't do anything about that other than just stew on it for several weeks and did nothing. In hindsight it's actually been quite difficult to say, because (pause). So then you end up in the double bind of you've not done anything, and you're not doing anything (Forrester and Harwin, 2011, p. 212).

This worker was afraid. Being afraid of working with violent men was not unusual – it was the norm. The effectiveness of violence as a controlling strategy is not confined to women and children. This quote demonstrates how effective it can be at limiting professional involvement in families. This impact is increased by the power it has to silence the victims of violence. Thus, women and children living with a violent man may find talking about such issues very difficult. A crucial issue for professionals to consider is this: if I feel afraid, with all the power of my professional role, how must the woman and children in this home feel? And how should that shape my response to them?

A more recent study has identified another crucial issue in working with alcohol-related violence, namely, the fact that it appears to be considered by some women to be a normal part of their lives (Forrester *et al.*, 2012). In this study, we talked to 26 women who had been known to social services for serious child protection concerns and misuse of drugs or alcohol. One of the key findings was the ubiquitous and corrosive nature of alcohol-related violence in the sample. Violence was a feature of life in 80% of the families. The level of violence varied; however, in most families, it was very severe, with several women reporting serious injuries such as broken bones or other hospitalisations. One woman reported entering refuges 35 times in 10 years before her partner committed suicide. Another described being beaten outside the hospital when having a cigarette after having given birth to her baby hours before.

Yet what was most striking about these descriptions of violence was that they were generally presented not as shocking aberrations; they were spoken of as normal. Two-thirds of these women had grown up in families where there was violence and abuse of children. Even where this was not obviously the case, almost all appeared to have low self-esteem, in some instances verging on self-hatred. They then entered relationships with men who were violent and considered this to be normal or, in some sense, their own fault. These qualitative accounts are supported by quantitative research following up children for 20 years in the United States which has found strong relationships between being brought up in a violent home and not only being violent but also experiencing violence (Ehrensaft *et al.*, 2003). Ehrensaft *et al.* argue that experience of violence in childhood makes it more likely that children will find violence acceptable or normal in adult life, as well as operating to make it more likely that they will have other difficulties such as attachment problems and conduct issues. Unfortunately, the same cycle of disadvantage operates in relation to alcohol and drug misuse, which means that patterns of violence and alcohol misuse may reinforce one another in creating intergenerational disadvantage. The qualitative accounts in Forrester *et al.* (2012) provide compelling evidence for the need for professional involvement in families experiencing alcohol-related violence, but they simultaneously underscore some of the profound challenges involved in carrying out such work. The next sections consider key issues in how to identify and engage families (i.e., both adults and children) affected by alcohol-related violence.

IDENTIFYING ALCOHOL-RELATED VIOLENCE

Identifying alcohol-related violence is not about a simple checklist of 'things to look out for'. An understanding of the processes of stigma and silencing, controlling and normalising is at the heart of identifying alcohol-related violence. Reporting on violence or abuse at home is difficult for women and for children, especially because a feature of domestic abuse is isolation as the perpetrator cuts off the victim's ties and communication with family, friends and supportive professionals (Taylor, 2003). Even when there are clear injuries, the victims may provide cover stories to account for them. In many ways, therefore, the key issues are less about identification than about having professional responses that are open, caring, non-judgemental, and that realise that working with people to escape victimisation may require patience and empathy – even if referrals for the involvement of police or children's social services are necessary.

Given this, a crucial first place to start is by examining one's own values and feelings about working with families. In particular, if one has a positive experience of family life and positive views about the value of family life, then it can be difficult to face the unpalatable truth that, for all too many children and women, family life can be characterised by violence and abuse. There is, therefore, a danger in policies that focus uncritically on the 'family' – whether this is the government's 'Think Family' policy (Department of Children, Schools and Families, 2009) or the more subtle value judgements of parenting programmes that work on the assumption that parents want the best for one another and for the child. It is difficult to identify violence in the family – or indeed other types of child maltreatment – if one's core belief is that parents *always* want the best for children. Effective identification of alcohol-related violence – in common with other types of abuse and neglect – requires a more nuanced and difficult position in which families are considered not just as units but also as individuals in relationship, and which sees the interactions in families as being enormously important in giving support, for most of us, but also as sites for potential abuse or neglect. Identifying alcohol-related violence, therefore, requires an openness to the needs of individuals within families, rather than a focus simply on the family, and a critical appreciation of one's own values and the way they may shape perceptions.

Alcohol misuse and violence in the family are often kept secret by families as they tend to feel shame and stigma about the presence of such issues (Alcohol Concern, 2010; Toft, 2011). This shame is not confined to those whose drinking is problematic or who are violent. Indeed, the sense of shame and stigma can be just as great for those experiencing alcohol-related violence, and these feelings can be compounded by the silencing and controlling tactics of the abusive partner (Cleaver *et al.*, 1999). Therefore, women and children face many barriers to disclosure of alcohol-related violence. This has been demonstrated consistently by research that shows women do not report domestic abuse to the police as often as it occurs (Walby and Allen, 2004). Part of this is because women experiencing domestic abuse fear the removal of their children (Women's National Commission, 2010), which can be compounded if alcohol is a significant element of their situation.

Once one has understood one's own values, as well as the place of stigma and shame, it is worth considering some of the ways in which alcohol-related violence may present. These include the following:

- Disclosure
- Injury
- Behaviour

Disclosure

The key to any professional being able to intervene early in the lives of families is adequate training and effective multiagency working (Galvani, 2010). Many staff who work with the general public in various capacities, such as the police, psychologists, social workers, health visitors, teachers, alcohol workers and domestic violence workers, need to be able to respond appropriately to individuals who are experiencing alcohol-related violence. Women have reported feeling labelled and unsupported when they have sought help, and some say this has put them off ever seeking help again (Women's National Commission, 2010).

Part of working effectively is working within an organisation that allows workers to develop their understanding of the issue and encourages them to develop skills that enable them to work with families facing this problem. Of course, organisations can only work within their remit; however, it is vital that workers are confident enough to be able to recognise alcohol-related violence when it presents and do something with that recognition, be it referring to a specialist service or advising of possible options for the individual. At the very least, all organisations need to ensure that the safety of the victims is their priority (Galvani, 2010).

Galvani's (2010) paper outlines ways in which organisations can make changes to support people who are experiencing alcohol-related violence. It is highlighted that women (and children) may not disclose domestic abuse the first time they are asked about it, so openness to disclosure needs to be maintained throughout the professional interactions. Mullender (2004) advises that children who disclose domestic abuse should always be believed.

The language that professionals use when speaking about alcohol-related violence needs to be thought about. Women and children may not identify themselves as victims of domestic abuse. Galvani (2010) advises that organisations liaise with domestic violence agencies to find out how to ask the questions in the right way. Workers must also bear in mind that encouraging a disclosure in the presence of the perpetrator may place women and children at risk. Victim safety needs to be paramount, and it is not advised that this is jeopardised by supporting a disclosure in the presence of a potential perpetrator (Galvani, 2007).

Injury

One of the biggest opportunities for professionals to intervene is when a woman or a child presents with injuries resulting from alcohol-related violence. Injury from domestic abuse is one of the most common causes of injury in women (Campbell, 2002). Therefore, medical staff need to be skilled enough to be able to engage the victims in speaking about their experiences and knowledgeable about what to then do to help support the victims. Routine screening for domestic abuse in women presenting with certain injuries could aid this (see Galvani, 2006, for some appropriate screening tools). Once again, the language and who is present while this is being undertaken need to be considered. In addition, the physical ill health that women present with may not occur immediately after a domestic abuse incident. Women suffering from alcohol-related violence may present even after the abuse has ended (Campbell, 2002).

Behaviour

Not all domestic abuse reaches the level at which women and children are presenting in hospitals with severe physical injuries. In fact, most female victims report the psychological abuse suffered as the most damaging in the long term (Galvani, 2001, 2010). Therefore, frontline workers need to be aware of the other less obvious signs that a woman and her children may be experiencing alcohol-related violence. Women who have been victims of domestic abuse face a greater risk of suffering from mental health problems such as depression, self-harm and trauma symptoms (Golding, 1999; Humphreys and Thiara, 2003). Therefore, mental health professionals should be able to support such individuals. Humphreys and Thiara (2003) found that women appreciated professionals who addressed domestic abuse in their lives and worked with them to support their own needs and those of their children. As outlined previously, children growing up in homes where domestic violence and parental alcohol abuse are occurring are at a greater risk of suffering from emotional and behavioural difficulties (Wolfe *et al.*, 2003). Children's behaviour at school and extracurricular activities may indicate to staff that something may be happening at home that they need support with.

ENGAGING FAMILIES, VICTIMS AND PERPETRATORS

Once violence has been identified as an actual or potential problem, how to engage family members arises as a key issue. Two factors are central to the engagement of victims and perpetrators of alcohol-related violence: ambivalence and power. This section considers the nature of each of these and their implications for how one might engage both victims and perpetrators of alcohol-related violence.

Ambivalence

The key role of ambivalence is now widely recognised in relation to helping people with alcohol problems. On the face of it, somebody may be using alcohol in a way that is causing them and/or others clear harm. It may appear obvious that they should change. Yet, all too often, individuals struggle to change, and the well-meaning attempts to help by offering suggestions, confronting or explaining reasons why reducing alcohol use might be a good idea are rejected. The reasons for this ineffectiveness are perhaps best captured in the concept of 'ambivalence' as described in motivational interviewing (MI) (Miller and Rollnick, 2002), though similar concepts are present in most effective ways of helping people with alcohol problems. Individuals who are ambivalent feel two ways about changing. On the one hand, they may be very aware of good reasons why they should change: they can see the harm that their alcohol use is causing. Yet, simultaneously, they may also have profound reasons for not wanting to change. These may include positives about their drinking, for instance, it may help them cope with difficult emotions or with the impact of violence; or negatives about giving up drinking, for instance, they cannot imagine a life without alcohol or all their friends may drink heavily. Ironically, well-intentioned attempts to make the case for changing can all too often have the opposite effect: by arguing for one side of the ambivalence, the professional inadvertently tends to elicit from individuals their reasons for *not* changing. That is why interventions that have at various times been popular with professionals – such as confrontative or educational therapy – actually tend to make drinking worse (Miller and Wilbourne, 2002). At a more prosaic level, we can each think of behaviours we might want to change but have not – such as eating more healthily or exercising more often. Imagine if a professional came and tried to persuade you to carry out these changes. It is highly likely that you would feel a bit annoyed and very possible that you would find yourself outlining all the reasons why you should not change your behaviour.

MI is perhaps the most strongly supported way of working with alcohol problems and is increasingly being used to help engage individuals in other forms of treatment (Arkowitz *et al.*, 2008). At the heart of MI is an attempt to avoid creating resistance through empathic listening and an attempt to elicit arguments for change through directive questions and reflections. This cannot 'make' people change, but there is a strong evidence base that such an approach maximises the chances of change by increasing engagement and allowing people to explore whether they wish to change in a purposeful manner.

Ambivalence is widely recognised in the alcohol treatment field, yet there has been far less exploration of its place and implications in relation to working with domestic violence. In fact, ambivalence is a common feature in victims of violence in the home and is also likely to be a key issue in working with perpetrators of violence (as discussed below). The rather different nature of ambivalence for each is worth exploring. Professionals who have experience of victims of domestic violence often find themselves frustrated, and sometimes get angry, about the reluctance of victims of violence to leave abusive relationships or the fact that sometimes they return after having left. Understanding why this happens is the first step in more effective engagement.

It may be very obvious from the outside that a victim of violence should leave or should take other actions (such as ending a relationship or getting an injunction): she is suffering, the children are at risk, and leaving may seem the only sensible option. Yet, the woman may, in fact, be profoundly ambivalent. Some of this ambivalence is related to well-founded fears: abusive men can and do stalk women and assault or even kill them (Department of Health, 2005). In fact, one of the most risky times for a woman experiencing domestic violence is the period after she has left her partner (Lees, 2000). Therefore, it is not necessarily as simple as just leaving, or taking other actions to end a relationship. Injunctions, for instance, are hard to police. There may also be a welter of practical reasons why leaving seems difficult. Changing house and perhaps neighbourhood is difficult at any time; when children are involved, it becomes even more complicated. These are not insignificant barriers to changing.

Yet perhaps even more important may be the emotional ambivalence that victims feel about the perpetrator. In many respects, this ambivalence may reflect the perpetrator's behaviour: they may be violent, but at other times, their character or the relationship may be very appealing. Indeed, this appears particularly associated with alcohol-related violence, where alcohol misuse is used as a way of marking 'different' behaviour – when not drunk, the perpetrator may act completely differently. Taking an approach that tries to confront or educate the woman (or the child) in this situation is likely – as was found for alcohol treatment – to produce the contrary effect. In this respect, there seems to be much that the domestic violence field could learn from the better-developed evidence base for intervention in relation to alcohol problems. In particular, non-judgemental empathy, combined with skilled directive listening aimed at eliciting from the woman herself arguments for taking action, may be the most appropriate response.

Power and Protection

Yet, while high-level communication skills may help workers to work with ambivalence and maximise the likelihood of engagement and change, they are not a sufficient response on their own. Abuse is about the misuse of power. Violence is a key element of this. For this reason, it may be that therapeutic engagement may not be enough.

The necessity for thinking about individuals when working with families is most clear in relation to making child protection or police referrals. The needs of the perpetrator and the victim are often different. However, more complex and challenging to work with are when the actions of a victim (namely, the mother) appear likely to place not only her but also her children at risk of significant harm. It is important to understand the legal situation in such circumstances. However, even a good legal understanding does not obviate the need for careful and considered judgements about appropriate actions.

Professionals also need to be sensitive to cultural factors, and the interaction that plays out between power, control, gender and stigma in different communities (Galvani, 2006). The use of alcohol by perpetrators and victims can be stigmatised within the community, and so women may feel it is best not to say anything to anyone. Taylor (2003) demonstrated this in communities in East London. The fear of shame being brought on one's family can prove to be a big barrier to disclosure for women experiencing alcohol-related violence. This serves to further isolate the mother and her children through fear of being rejected by their community if they make a disclosure and people find out they have spoken outside of the community (Mullender *et al.*, 2002).

For children, there are relatively straightforward principles to be considered: if a child appears 'likely' to be at risk of 'significant harm', then a referral to children's services should be made. In England, amendments to the Children Act 1989 stated that the assessment of harm now includes children witnessing or hearing the ill treatment of others. For all professionals, the safety and well-being of children should be paramount. Insofar as this can be secured through work with the family, then it may not be necessary to make a referral. However, the immediate and long-term risks to children are such that it may well be necessary to make a referral.

Issues are rather less clear-cut in relation to women experiencing violence. In general terms, as adults, they have the right to make informed decisions. Yet, in practice, some fine judgements may need to be made. The safety of children is paramount, yet the best way of securing this is not always clear. Is it better to work to engage a woman and support her to leave a violent man while she and her children remain in a highly risky environment? What type of responses are child protection services likely to make? Will this actually help the children or their mother? What impact will the involvement of services with legal authority have on the relationship of the victim with other services? These are amongst the conundrums that any professional (or indeed non-professional) faces when working with alcohol-related violence. There are no easy procedural answers. Rather, what is required is an ability to balance the likely consequences of various courses of action. It is particularly important to be as open and clear with the victim as possible.

HELPING FAMILIES

Thus far, we have reviewed the extent and nature of alcohol-related violence and considered some key issues in engaging victims. In this final section, how to help families is considered.

Working with Children

How children cope growing up with alcohol-related violence is mediated by protective and risk factors present in their lives, and there is a great deal of variability between children growing up in similar circumstances (Velleman and Orford, 1999). Evans (2006) outlined the various resilience factors that can enable children to positively cope with alcohol and domestic abuse in the home and lead healthier and happier lives. These include support from inside and outside the home, a stable relationship with a non-drinking adult, a caring and healthy relationship with the parent(s), a good school life and positive self-esteem. Templeton *et al.* (2009) believe the primary protective factor for children living with alcohol misuse and violence is having a consistent and supportive person in one's life. Mullender (2004) provides some good ways in which professionals can work with children who have witnessed domestic abuse, including individual and group work that enables children to comprehend their experiences, share their feelings with and listen to other children with similar experiences, and work on how to be safe.

Research shows it is also important to support the relationship between women and their children after experiencing domestic abuse, as it often has been undermined by the perpetrator (Humphreys, Thiara, and Skamballis, 2011; Mullender *et al.*, 2002). Helping to rebuild communication between women and their children is important, as it has been shown that they often remain silent about what has happened and how they feel (Humphreys *et al.*, 2006).

Working with the Perpetrator and Families

One obvious way to help victims of violence is to help them to end the relationship with the perpetrator. If this is what the victim wishes, then it is always appropriate to support them to do so, though the risks involved during the period after ending a relationship need to be taken seriously. Where the victim is ambivalent or wishes to stay in the relationship, the professional has a responsibility to consider the risks to the woman and the children should the family remain intact. Even if the family separates, then the risks associated with contact with violent men need to be considered carefully.

Where the victim wishes to remain in the relationship, the question of how to help the family arises; and here, there are very significant problems arising from the research literature. There is little evidence supporting the effectiveness of any intervention aimed at reducing violence from men, and there are strong grounds for believing that women and children may be placed at risk during the process of therapy for the man. In this section, we consider the evidence for violence reduction, first, for therapies focussed on issues other than violence and then for perpetrator programmes. We then consider how such programmes might be improved before making recommendations for good practice in relation to victims when perpetrators are being worked with.

Non-Violence-Related Work

Often, families may be offered help that does not focus on violence. For example, if alcohol is an issue for the family, they may be offered alcohol counselling in the (explicit or implicit) belief that this will address the violence. Where alcohol use is related to violence, it is not appropriate for men to attend alcohol treatment without their perpetration of domestic abuse being addressed. This practice is not supported by research evidence (Respect, 2010) and has, in fact, shown to increase the risk women face from their partners (Galvani, 2010). The role of alcohol in the man's violence is also not sufficiently addressed in these interventions. Alcohol is not responsible for violence, and this belief needs to be altered in interventions with the perpetrator (Galvani, 2007). It is dangerous to send a man on an alcohol treatment programme and to expect abstinence from drinking will eradicate all violence (Galvani, 2010). The evidence has shown that domestic abuse does not go away afterward and, in fact, can put women in danger if they then think that their partner is now 'alcohol free and therefore violence free'. This opens up important questions for alcohol treatment, given the linkages between violence and alcohol problems. Are services ensuring that violent behaviour is addressed in their work with men with alcohol problems?

Alternatively, there are various ways of working with families or couples – such as many parenting programmes, family therapy approaches, some couple therapies or interventions such as social behaviour network therapy (Copello *et al.*, 2009) for alcohol use – that work with the family without explicitly recognising the possibility of violence and abuse as a feature of intrafamilial relationships. Galvani (2010) has written persuasively about the dangers of these approaches. First, they may lead to the victim believing that they are safe without addressing the underlying attitudes that contribute to alcohol-related violence. Second, they may fail to ensure that the perpetrators take responsibility for their violence (Galvani, 2007).

Working with Perpetrators

On the other hand, treatment programmes for violent men have in general rather poor outcomes. There are many perpetrator programmes to reduce and ideally eradicate their controlling and abusive behaviours and their patriarchal attitudes towards women and children. The Duluth model is an example of this. It draws from the experience of victims and holds perpetrators accountable while maintaining the safety of victims, utilising cognitive-behavioural, psycho-educational and feminist perspectives. Dobash *et al.* (2000) claim the Duluth model is one of the best domestic violence interventions in the world. However, research into perpetrator programmes continues to be divided and contentious (Paymar and Barnes, n.d.), and evaluations of programmes have found small reductions in violent behaviours or none at all (Babcock, Green, and Robie, 2004).

Various explanations have been offered for these poor results. Day *et al.* (2009) have suggested that there may be issues about whether programmes are delivered in the manner intended. This has also been offered as an explanation by defenders of the Duluth model (Paymar and Barnes, n.d.). On the face of it, this is not a convincing explanation: if one wanted to understand why a programme worked in one setting but did not work in others, then one possible reason would be that it was not delivered well. In relation to treatment programmes for violence, this does not seem to be the case. There is little robust evidence of programmes working, and the more rigorous the research, the smaller the impact of the programme (Day *et al.*, 2009).

An alternative explanation for these small impacts is that the approaches used are rather ineffective ways of working with problem behaviours. In this regard, there appear to be important lessons from the alcohol treatment field for violence treatment programmes to embrace. The types of approach reviewed by Babcock *et al.* (2004) are based on perpetrators acknowledging and taking responsibility for their actions. They are implicitly confrontational and explicitly educative. These approaches tend to have high drop-out rates and do not seem to reduce the likelihood of further violence. Such approaches were once dominant in the alcohol treatment field, where denial was seen as a symptom of the 'illness' of addiction. However, a substantial body of research indicated not only that confrontative and educative approaches were ineffective but also that they tended to increase the level of problem drinking (Miller and Wilbourne, 2002). Instead, approaches that focussed on client-centred engagement with a view to structured behaviour change are more likely to create positive changes. There is therefore a very real danger that the types of treatment offered for perpetrators of violence are ineffective and that they may actually make the situation worse.

There is some evidence that seeing perpetrators as 'men with needs' may be more effective. For instance, Musser *et al.* (2008) found that two sessions of MI offered prior to group intervention had a significant impact in increasing engagement with treatment. There are also promising indications from initial evaluations of approaches that take a more perpetrator-centred approach (Tollefson *et al.*, 2009). Working in an empathic and client-centred way with a man who perpetrates violence is probably the most effective way of reducing their subsequent violence. This is certainly true in relation to alcohol problems, and it is a pretty general finding across helping relationships for a range of problem behaviours (see Roth and Fonagy, 2005). Yet there has been a reluctance to take such an approach because there is perhaps a perception that it would involve 'colluding' with unacceptable violence. This is not an argument that bears much scrutiny. If one works empathically with someone with an alcohol or drug problem, an eating disorder, depression, or any other issue, this does not involve colluding or condoning the behaviour. Rather, it involves getting alongside the person to help him or her to form a plan for change. An irony may be that our justified anger at violence may lead us to offer services that are unlikely to be effective. A more promising approach is likely to involve more focus on developing effective therapeutic alliances with men who are abusive.

However, whatever approach is taken to helping perpetrators to change, it is crucially important to recognise that the victims of violence may be at risk during or after the treatment. As a result, treatment for perpetrators is not on its own enough. What is needed is a systemic response that places the needs and views of the victims of violence at the heart of effective helping. In this respect, the Duluth model has the right agenda. Support for victims is offered in tandem with treatment for perpetrators, and wider systems such as (crucially) criminal justice responses are focussed on supporting and protecting the victims of violence. While we have been critical of the nature of perpetrator treatment within this model, the systemic elements of the Duluth response are critical elements of effective responses to violence in the home. These include working with victims and at the same time with perpetrators and ensuring that safety strategies are operated simultaneously with help for perpetrators.

CONCLUSION

In this chapter, we have considered the issue of alcohol-related violence in the family and how best to respond to it. We started by highlighting how widespread and serious the problem is and how complex and challenging the issue is to respond to. Alcohol-related violence has psychological components, but to understand and respond effectively, it is necessary to also incorporate a broader focus that includes an awareness of ongoing risks and the ways in which wider systems and societal attitudes contribute to the problem and need to be taken into account in effective responses.

One of the points made more than once has been that simply treating the alcohol problem is not only likely to be ineffective for reducing violence but it may also actually be dangerous if the victim and others believe that reducing or preventing drinking will be protective in its own right. Nonetheless, a theme running through the chapter is that many of the key elements of responding effectively to alcohol problems should inform our responses to violence in the home. Thus, for instance, responses that have been found to be effective in helping those with alcohol problems – such as MI or various brief interventions – are likely to be helpful in engaging both victims and perpetrators of alcohol-related violence. It is important to recognise this, but it is equally important to emphasise that this is not enough on its own. Effective responses to alcohol-related violence certainly require skilled and client-centred communication, but they also require us to always consider the situation of the victims and appropriate ways in which we can listen to their views and ensure their safety and well-being. Ultimately, the best practice and policy responses to alcohol-related violence in the home are those that put the needs of the victims of violence first.

REFERENCES

Alcohol Concern (2010) *Swept under the Carpet: Children Affected by Parental Alcohol Misuse.* Retrieved November 3, 2011, from http://www.alcoholconcern.org.uk/assets/files/Publications/Swept%20under%20the%20carpet.pdf

Arkowitz, H., Westra, H., Miller, W., and Rollnick, S. (2008) *Motivational Interviewing in the Treatment of Psychological Problems.* New York: Guilford Press.

Babcock, J., Green, C., and Robie, C. (2004) Does batterers treatment work? A meta-analytic review of domestic violence treatment. *Clinical Psychology Review*, **23**, 1023–1053.

Brisby, T., Baker, S., and Hedderwick, T. (1997) *Under the Influence: Coping with Parents Who Drink Too Much.* London: Alcohol Concern.

Campbell, J. (2002) Health consequences of intimate partner violence. *The Lancet*, **359**, 1331–1336.

Cleaver, H., Nicholson, D., Tarr, S., and Cleaver, D. (2006) *The Response of Child Protection Practices and Procedures to Children Exposed to Domestic Violence or Parental Substance Misuse.* Retrieved September 26, 2011, from https://www.education.gov.uk/publications/eOrderingDownload/RW89-r.pdf

Cleaver, H., Nicholson, D., Tarr, S., and Cleaver, D. (2007) *Child Protection, Domestic Violence and Parental Substance Misuse: Family Experiences and Effective Practice.* London: Jessica Kingsley.

Cleaver, H., Unell, I., and Aldgate, J. (1999) *Children's Needs-Parenting Capacity. The Impact of Parental Mental Illness, Problem Alcohol and Drug Use, and Domestic Violence on Children's Development.* London: The Stationery Office.

Copello, A., Orford, J., Hodgson, R., and Tober, G. (2009) *Social Behaviour and Network Therapy for Alcohol Problems.* London: Routledge.

Day, A., Chung, D., O'Leary, P., and Carson, E. (2009) Programs for men who perpetrate domestic violence: An examination of the issues underlying the effectiveness of intervention programs. *Journal of Family Violence*, **24**, 203–212.

Department of Children, Schools and Families (2009) *Think Family Toolkit: Improving Support for Families at Risk: Strategic Overview.* Retrieved January 16, 2011, from https://www.education.gov.uk/publications/eOrderingDownload/Think-Family.pdf

Department of Health (2005) *Responding to Domestic Abuse: A Handbook for Health Professionals.* London: Department of Health.

Dobash, P. and Dobash, R. (2004) Women's violence to men in intimate relationships: Working on a puzzle. *British Journal of Criminology*, **44**, 324–349.

Dobash, R.E., Dobash, R.P., Cavanagh, K., and Lewis, R. (2000) *Changing Violent Men.* Thousand Oaks, CA: Sage.

Ehrensaft, M.K., Cohen, P., Brown, J. *et al.* (2003) Intergenerational transmission of partner violence: A 20-year prospective study. *Journal of Consulting and Clinical Psychology*, **71**, 741–753.

Evans, D. (2006) Children, alcohol and family violence. In F. Harbin and M. Murphy (eds), *Secret Lives: Growing with Substance: Working with Children Who Live with Substance Misuse.* Lyme Regis: Russell House Publishing.

Finney, A. (2004) *Alcohol and Intimate Partner Violence: Key Findings from Previous Research.* Findings 216. London: Home Office.

Forrester, D. and Harwin, J. (2006) Parental substance misuse and child care social work: Findings from the first stage of a study of 100 families. *Child and Family Social Work*, **11**, 325–335.

Forrester, D. and Harwin, J. (2011) *Parents Who Misuse Drugs or Alcohol: Effective Interventions in Social Work and Child Protection.* Chichester: Wiley-Blackwell.

Forrester, D., Holland, S., Williams, A., and Copello, A. (2012) *Final Report on the Evaluation of "Option 2" Intensive Family Preservation Service*. London: Alcohol Research UK.

Galvani, S. (2001) The role of alcohol in violence against women: Why should social work care? *Practice*, **13**, 5–20.

Galvani, S. (2006) *Safeguarding Children: Working with Parental Alcohol Problems and Domestic Abuse*. Alcohol Concern. Retrieved September 28, 2011, from http://www.alcoholandfamilies.org.uk/briefings/13.8.pdf

Galvani, S. (2007) Safety in numbers? Tackling domestic abuse in couples and network therapies. *Drug and Alcohol Review*, **26**, 175–181.

Galvani, S. (2010) *Factsheet: Grasping the Nettle: Alcohol and Domestic Violence*. Alcohol Concern. Retrieved September 21, 2011, from http://www.alcoholconcern.org.uk/assets/files/Publications/Grasping%20the%20nettle%20factsheet%20revised%20June%202010.pdf

Gilchrist, E., Johnson, R., Tikriti, R. *et al.* (2003) *Domestic Violence Offenders: Characteristics and Offending Related Needs*. Findings 217. London: Home Office.

Golding, J. (1999) Intimate partner violence as a risk factor for mental disorders: A meta-analysis. *Journal of Family Violence*, **14**, 99–132.

Hester, M. (2009) *Who Does What to Whom? Gender and Domestic Violence Perpetrators*. Bristol: University of Bristol in association with Northern Rock.

Humphreys, C., Mullender, A., Thiara, R., and Skamballis, A. (2006) Talking to my mum: Developing communication between mothers and children in the aftermath of domestic violence. *Journal of Social Work*, **6**, 53–63.

Humphreys, C., Regan, L., River, D., and Thiara, R. (2005) Domestic violence and substance use: Tackling complexity. *British Journal of Social Work*, **35**, 1303–1320.

Humphreys, C. and Thiara, R. (2003) Mental health and domestic violence: "I call it symptoms of abuse." *British Journal of Social Work*, **33**, 209–226.

Humphreys, C., Thiara, R., and Skamballis, A. (2011) Readiness to change: Mother-child relationship and domestic violence intervention. *British Journal of Social Work*, **41**, 166–184.

Lees, S. (2000) Marital rape and marital murder. In J. Hanmer and C. Itzin (eds), *Home Truths about Domestic Violence: Feminist Influences on Policy and Practice: A Reader*. London: Routledge.

Manning, V., Best, D., Faulkner, N., and Titherington, E. (2009) New estimates of the number of children living with substance misusing parents: Results from UK national household surveys. *BMC Public Health*, **9**, 377–389.

Miller, W.R. and Rollnick, S. (2002) *Motivational Interviewing: Preparing People for Change*. New York: Guilford Press.

Miller, W.R. and Wilbourne, P. (2002) Mesa grande: A methodological analysis of clinical trials of treatments for alcohol use disorders. *Addiction*, **97**, 265–277.

Mullender, A. (2004) *Tackling domestic violence: Providing Support for Children Who Have Witnessed Domestic Violence*. Home Office Development and Practice Report 33. London: Home Office.

Mullender, A., Hague, G., Imam, U. *et al.* (2002) *Children's Perspectives on Domestic Violence*. London: Sage.

Musser, P., Semiatin, J., Taft, C., and Murphy, C. (2008) Motivational interviewing as a pregroup intervention for partner-violent men. *Violence and Victims*, **23**, 539–557.

NHS Choices (2010) *Binge Drinking*. Retrieved September 19, 2011, from http://www.nhs.uk/livewell/alcohol/pages/bingedrinking.aspx

Paymar, M. and Barnes, G. (n.d.) *Countering Confusion about the Duluth Model*. Retrieved March 1, 2012, from http://www.theduluthmodel.org/pdf/CounteringConfusion.pdf

Respect (2010) *Respect Briefing Paper: Evidence of Effects of Domestic Violence Perpetrator Programmes on Women's Safety*. Retrieved January 16, 2012, from http://www.respect.uk.net/data/files/resources/respect_briefing_paper_on_the_evidence_of_effects_of_perpetrator_programmes_on_women_revised_18th_march_10.pdf

Roth, A. and Fonagy, P. (2005) *What Works for Whom? A Critical Review of Psychotherapy Research* (2nd edn). New York: Guilford.

Taylor, H. (2003) *Substance Misuse and Domestic Violence-Making the Links. An Evaluation of Service Provision in Tower Hamlets.* London: Tower Hamlets Domestic Violence Team.

Templeton, L., Velleman, R., Hardy, E., and Boon, S. (2009) Young people living with parental alcohol misuse and parental violence "no-one has ever asked me how I feel in any of this." *Journal of Substance Use,* **14**, 139–150.

Toft, C. (2011) *Embracing Alcohol, Domestic Violence and Families – A New Approach (Alcohol Concern).* Retrieved January 17, 2012, from http://www.alcoholconcern.org.uk/assets/ files/Embrace/Embracing%20alcohol,%20domestic%20abuse%20and%20families%20-%20a%20new%20approach.pdf

Tollefson, D., Webb, K., Shumway, D. *et al.* (2009) A mind-body approach to domestic violence perpetrator treatment: Program overview and preliminary outcomes. *Journal of Aggression, Maltreatment and Trauma,* **18**, 17–45.

Velleman, R. and Orford, J. (1999) *Risk and Resilience: Adults Who Were the Children of Problem Drinkers.* Newark: Harwood Academic Publishers.

Walby, S. and Allen, J. (2004) *Domestic violence, sexual assault and stalking: Findings from the British Crime Survey.* Home Office Research Study 276, London: Home Office.

Wolfe, D., Crooks, C., Lee, V. *et al.* (2003) The effects of children's exposure to domestic violence: A meta-analysis and critique. *Clinical Child and Family Psychology Review,* **6**, 171–187.

Women's Aid (2009) *Domestic Violence: Frequently Asked Questions Factsheet 2009.* Retrieved January 10, 2012, from http://www.womensaid.org.uk/domestic_violence_topic.asp?section=0001000100220041&sectionTitle=Domestic+violence+%28general%29

Women's National Commission (2010) *Listening to the Voices of Women Experiencing Problematic Substance Use and Gender-Based Violence: A Summary Briefing from the Still We Rise Report.* Retrieved October 1, 2011, from http://www.avaproject.org.uk/media/43594/ listening%20to%20the%20voices%20of%20women%20experiencing%20sm%20and%20gbv.pdf

Chapter 9

TREATMENTS FOR OFFENDERS OF INTIMATE PARTNER VIOLENCE

CAROLINE J. EASTON

Department of Psychiatry, Yale University School of Medicine, New Haven, Connecticut, USA

INTRODUCTION

To date, intimate partner violence (IPV) continues to be an escalating and pervasive public health problem in many societies across the world. The social, psychiatric, and medical consequences are devastating to the family as a whole (e.g., victims, children, and offenders). The estimated economic costs of IPV (e.g., physical assault, sexual assault, and stalking) exceed $5.8 billion each year (US Department of Health and Human Services, 2003). In fact, it is estimated that $4.1 billion of the costs of IPV consequences are directly related to medical and mental healthcare services, but the costs include nearly $.9 billion in lost work productivity of victims (US Department of Health and Human Services, 2003). However, the largest of IPV-related costs is health care, which accounts for more than two-thirds of the total costs (US Department of Health and Human Services, 2003). Although the largest and most prevalent proportion of the costs results from physical assault victimization (US Department of Health and Human Services, 2003), it is important to note that most studies rarely include costs related to verbal or psychological IPV victimization, which also contribute to healthcare and unemployment costs. In fact, verbal and psychological victimization alone occur in approximately 17% of IPV cases (Coker *et al.*, 2002), and this is not typically taken into account with total IPV cost estimations. Moreover, additional costs to the family and society as a whole drive this number up substantially when childcare needs, the child's mental health treatment, the offender's loss of income, and overall judicial and criminal justice costs are included. In sum, the social and economic cost is exorbitant and shines a beacon of light on the need for policy reform as it pertains to IPV interventions at a global level.

Alcohol-Related Violence: Prevention and Treatment, First Edition. Edited by Mary McMurran.
© 2013 John Wiley & Sons, Ltd. Published 2013 by John Wiley & Sons, Ltd.

Within the United States, the Bureau of Justice Statistics (2005) reported that 80% of IPV cases reported to the police in 2000 were male-to-female violence. Moreover, community surveys show that women are just as likely to engage in domestic violence as are men, although men are more likely to cause serious injury (Archer, 2000). In fact, contrary to the popular view of the aggressive male and passive female, a high percentage of IPV is reciprocal, and one of the best predictors of violence by either gender is the level of violence by one's partner (Archer, 2000; Wupperman *et al.*, 2009). More recently, a paradigm shift has occurred within the research community to assess bidirectional IPV that occurs within the dyad (Wupperman *et al.*, 2009). For the purposes of this chapter, IPV interventions will focus on male-to-female IPV, but some discussion will be presented regarding female-to-male IPV interventions.

The aims of this chapter are the following: (1) to provide an overview of IPV interventions (standard of care vs. evidence-based interventions), (2) to discuss alcohol-related violence and other drug-related violence, (3) to underscore the high co-occurrence of alcohol dependence among IPV offenders, and (4) to discuss co-occurring models of care in the treatment of alcohol-related disorders and IPV.

THE DULUTH MODEL OR DULUTH DERIVATIVES OF CARE

Research reviews have indicated that IPV interventions for male offenders have been costly and ineffective (e.g., Babcock, Green, and Robie, 2004; Babcock and La Taillade, 2000). Moreover, the research community has called for IPV intervention reform and highlighted the need to utilize empirically supported treatments and research rather than adherence to unsubstantiated etiological models or old standards of treatment (e.g., Easton *et al.*, 2008; Eckhardt *et al.*, 2006).

To date, the standards of care for IPV interventions have changed very little over the past 30 years. The treatment as usual ("TAU") approaches are known as "Duluth models" or "Duluth derivatives" of care. This is the most widely used approach among the criminal justice system. For example, men convicted of IPV are referred to batterer/IPV programs. The names "batterer" and/or "perpetrator" are terms most often used by proponents of a feminist approach in the treatment of IPV (e.g., "Duluth camp"). The terms used to define men who abuse are punitive, create a negative stereotype, and are often confrontational in nature. Many individuals treated by the Duluth model are, in fact, individuals that are not receiving treatment for legitimate behavioral health disorders (e.g., addiction and/or mental health disorders). In general, the Duluth Domestic Abuse Intervention Project was established by an activist group associated with a women's shelter in Duluth, Minnesota, and is grounded in feminist principles that view men as dominant over women (e.g., patriarchal dominance) and view men with IPV as attempting to "control" the female partner. The core of a perpetrator program is to change the behavior of men convicted or accused of domestic assault. The program uses a psychoeducation structure within which actual behaviors are identified and challenged by facilitators, who model alternative behaviors and alternative solutions to conflict.

The methodology is based on a two-part "map" of violent and nonviolent behaviors, displayed in a wheel format (the "power wheel or Duluth wheel").

One "wheel" divides violence and abuse into eight categories: coercion and threats, intimidation, economic abuse, gender privilege, isolation, using children, minimizing, and denying and blaming. On the other wheel, the respective target behavior shown for each category is negotiation and fairness, nonthreatening behavior, economic partnership, respect, shared responsibility, trust and support, responsible parenting, and honesty and accountability. It is also important to note that many of the Duluth model approaches are "presentence diversionary programs" in which psychiatric or addiction evaluations are not typically done. Many of the offenders are treated with this "one-size-fits-all" model of care.

There is very little empirical support regarding the effectiveness of the Duluth model in reducing violence, mental health symptoms, or substance use, which suggests that many offenders are likely to repeat the cycle of violence (Babcock et al., 2000). With that said, it is possible that this model would be more effective with a subpopulation of clients if more comprehensive psychiatric and addiction screens were an inherent part of this psychoeducational model of care. Meta-analytic reviews of outcomes for these approaches have consistently found them to be of very limited effectiveness, with effect sizes near zero (Babcock et al., 2000). In fact, McMurran and Gilchrist (2008) describe the importance of utilizing a "risk–needs approach" when assessing how to best treat men who are arrested for domestic violence. For example, McMurran and Gilchrist (2008) discuss the inherent problems in applying a Duluth model approach when anger and drinking might be better be addressed by interventions designed to treat anger and drinking as opposed to addressing solely "control issues" via the Duluth model. Moreover, failing to address other affective or behavioral targets may hinder progress in the field of IPV treatment and may further reinforce stagnation in the IPV field.

ALCOHOL-RELATED DISORDERS: A COMMON CO-OCCURRENCE

It has been well documented across studies that there is a high co-occurrence of alcohol misuse in IPV cases (Easton et al., 2007a; Leonard, 2005; Wupperman et al., 2009). Alcohol abuse disorders are involved in 40–60% of IPV incidents (Easton et al., 2007a; Easton, Swan, and Sinha, 2000a,b; Murphy and O'Farrell, 1996). Moreover, rates of both alcohol misuse and drug abuse occur in IPV offenses. For example, Brookoff, O'Brien, and Cook (1997) found that 92% of offenders self-reported or tested positive for some substance (e.g., alcohol, drugs, or some combination) on the day of the IPV incident. Several lines of evidence suggest that alcohol use plays a facilitative role in IPV by precipitating or exacerbating violence to the point where researchers have assertively stated that "we have reached the point where we should conclude that heavy drinking is a contributing cause of violence" (Leonard, 2005, p. 423).

Alcohol Consumption and IPV

A large percentage of IPV episodes involve alcohol consumption. Kaufman Kantor and Straus (1990) found severe violence to occur in 20% of males who were drinking just prior to the act of violence. Victims of IPV frequently report that the offender had been drinking (Bureau of Justice Statistics, 1998a) or using illicit drugs (Miller, 1990; Roberts, 1998). Miller (1990) reported that offenders of IPV typically use alcohol and have a dual problem with drugs. A strong relationship between substance use and perpetration of IPV has been found in primary healthcare settings (McCauley et al., 1995), family practice clinics (Oriel and Fleming, 1998), prenatal clinics (Muhajarine and D'Arcy, 1999), and rural health clinics (Van Hightower and Gorton, 1998). A more recent study found that offenders who had a dual problem with alcohol and drugs (e.g., tested positive for both alcohol and illicit drug use) had poorer responses to treatment compared with male offenders who abused alcohol alone (Easton et al., 2007a).

IPV and Substance Use: Evidence for a Proximal Effects Model

Leonard and Quigley (1999) have demonstrated a proximal effects model when discussing the relationship between IPV and alcohol use. Several studies suggest that alcohol and other drug use are associated with partner violence after controlling for factors thought to be associated with both behaviors, such as age, education, socioeconomic or occupational status, and race/ethnicity (e.g., Leonard et al. 1998; Pan, Neidig, and O'Leary, 1994). The relationship between alcohol use and violence remains strong after controlling for levels of general hostility (e.g., Leonard and Senchak, 1993) and normative views of aggression (Kaufman Kantor and Straus, 1990).

It is important to emphasize that, although alcohol-related disorders are the most prevalent among IPV offenses, offenders often have a dual problem with alcohol and illicit drug use. Regarding the proximal effects model, individuals who consume psychoactive alcohol and/or illicit drugs are more likely to engage in partner violence because intoxication facilitates violence, which may be mediated through the psychopharmacological effects of drugs on cognitive processing (Chermack and Taylor, 1995). It follows from this theory that alcohol and drug use (e.g., stimulant/cocaine use) should precede the episodes of IPV, and the episode of violence should occur close in time to the consumption of the drug. More recently, Leonard (2005) have shown that the proximal effects model appears to show greatest empirical support with heavy drinking. Hence, evidence-based interventions that target specifically alcohol use among men with histories of IPV have the potential to reach a larger population and lead to positive treatment outcomes (Easton et al., 2007b).

TREATMENTS FOR IPV

Standard Substance Abuse Treatment: Effects on IPV

Several studies suggest that treatment-associated reductions in substance use are related to reductions in violence. O'Farrell et al. (2003) examined partner violence in the year before and in the year after individually based, outpatient alcoholism treatment for male alcoholic patients, compared to a demographically matched nonalcoholic comparison group. In the year before treatment, 56% of the alcoholic patients had been violent toward their female partner, which was four times the rate of the comparison sample (14%). In the year after treatment, violence decreased significantly to 25% of the alcoholic sample but remained higher than the comparison group. In a parallel study, Fals-Stewart, Golden, and Schumacher (2003) examined partner violence among a sample of married or cohabiting men entering outpatient treatment for drug abuse. During the year before treatment, the prevalence of IPV was roughly 60% but dropped to 35% during the 1-year posttreatment follow-up period. In both studies, the treatments were standard twelve-step facilitation (TSF) interventions that did not address partner violence (e.g., Schumacher, Fals-Stewart, and Leonard, 2003). Nonetheless, participation in the programs resulted in significant reductions in interpersonal violence, consistent with what would be expected from the proximal effects model. Nevertheless, the levels of IPV during the posttreatment period for participants in both groups remained comparatively high. Because substance use is only one of several factors likely to influence the occurrence of IPV (other factors include negative mood states such as anger and hostility), interventions designed to address the other issues may further reduce IPV.

Couple-Based Psychotherapies

Several recent studies suggest that interventions targeting a reduction in substance use and ameliorating skill deficits have particular promise in this population. Behavioral couples therapy (BCT) has been demonstrated effective in several populations (Fals-Stewart, 2002; O'Farrell and Fals-Stewart, 2000). Although BCT was not designed specifically as an intervention for IPV, it has demonstrated efficacy in reducing alcohol and drug use and in improving dyadic functioning (for a review, see O'Farrell and Fals-Stewart, 2000). The effects of BCT on the frequency of maladaptive methods of conflict resolution used by male partners were examined during 12 weeks of treatment. Compared with standard treatment, men who received BCT reported more rapid reductions in the frequency of maladaptive methods of conflict resolution and, by the end of treatment, reported a lower frequency of maladaptive methods of conflict resolution. Changes in drinking and in the frequency of maladaptive methods of conflict resolution were both significant mediators of posttreatment frequency of IPV.

There are several BCT techniques that couples learn and practice both within and outside treatment. One example is utilizing a "sobriety contract" by which the substance-using partner verbally commits not to consume any alcohol or to take any illicit drugs that day (O'Farrell and Fals-Stewart, 2002). In return, the nonusing partner expresses verbal support for the substance-using partner. The nonusing partner records all information on a calendar. A second BCT example is the development of more effective communication skills. Active listening skills are taught to the dyad, and the couple takes turns in session to practice the newfound skills and to make reflective statements (O'Farrell and Fals-Stewart, 2002). A third and related BCT topic is helping the couple to engage in shared positive activities while minimizing negative interactions. One assignment, for instance, is entitled "Catch Your Partner Doing Something Nice," by which each partner points out one specific thing that she/he appreciated that the partner did each day; couples are taught to focus on compliments rather than on criticisms (O'Farrell and Fals-Stewart, 2002). Couples also are encouraged to contemplate leisure activities they both enjoy and to schedule time each week to do these activities together. Focusing on specific activities is most useful since many substance abusers are no longer engaged in many healthy activities. The final section in BCT focuses on relapse prevention. Each partner develops a "continuing recovery plan" to specify abstinence-based activities. Possible difficult or challenging situations are considered such that they are less likely to lead to relapse should they be encountered in the future.

Although there is ample evidence that BCT is effective with couples willing and motivated to participate in this treatment, it may not be applicable to all male participants with co-occurring substance abuse and IPV. In some cases, BCT may be contraindicated (e.g., the relationship is over; severe violence; protective orders are in place). Hence, there is a need for other evidenced-based approaches that do not rely on couples' interventions.

Cognitive-Behavioral Therapy (CBT) Approaches for Substance Abuse and IPV

Although the Babcock studies (Babcock and La Taillade, 2000; Babcock et al., 2004) and other meta-analytic reviews (Smedslund et al., 2007) state that CBT shows limited effectiveness in IPV outcomes, it is important to highlight that the majority of the studies included in the meta-analytic reviews were quasi-experimental (Babcock et al., 2004), not randomized controlled trials, and there was a lack of assessment and treatment of a co-occurring alcohol-related disorder. Moreover, IPV populations with co-occurring alcohol-related disorders did not receive any evidence-based addiction interventions (Easton et al., 2008). If CBT interventions are to be evaluated with IPV populations, well-designed randomized controlled trials with treatment fidelity measures are needed. In fact, contrary to the findings reported within the Babcock et al. (2000, 2004) and Smedslund et al. (2007) meta-analytic reviews, CBT has been repeatedly found to be effective at treating a range of substance abuse disorders (Carroll, 1996; DeRubeis and Crits-Christoph, 1998; Irvin et al., 1999; National Institute on Drug Abuse, 2009). Based on social learning theories of substance use disorders, CBT focuses on the implementation of effective coping skills for recognizing, avoiding, and coping with high-risk situations in an attempt to decrease the risk of alcohol and/or drug use. CBT is one of comparatively few empirically supported therapies that has been demonstrated to be effective across a range of substance use disorders, including alcohol-dependent populations (Morgenstern and Longabaugh, 2000; Project MATCH Research Group, 1997), marijuana-dependent populations (The Marijuana Research Treatment Group [MRTG], 2004), and cocaine-dependent populations (Carroll et al., 1994, 1998; Maude-Griffin et al., 1998; McKay et al., 1997; Monti et al., 1997). CBT is well accepted by the clinical community and can be implemented effectively by "real-world" clinicians (Morgenstern *et al.*, 2001; Sholomskas *et al.*, 2005). CBT's effectiveness across community mental health and addiction treatment facilities makes it a potential vehicle to target co-occurring addiction and IPV, and this should be compared with an equally intensive control condition in a well-designed randomized clinical trial.

Substance Abuse–Domestic Violence (SADV) Behavioral Therapy

More recently, a SADV behavioral therapy approach was developed out of a community need for an integrated intervention. Men with co-occurring alcohol-related disorders and domestic violence problems are rarely motivated for one treatment program, let alone referral to separate programs located across town (Easton *et al.*, 2000a). Evidence suggests that cross referrals to separate agencies do not work (Easton *et al.*, 2000b). SADV is grounded in evidenced-based treatments (e.g., CBT for substance users) with additional sessions that pertain to the target population (negative mood states, communication skills, and conflict resolution skills training) from the Project Match Elective Session Modules (National Institute on Alcohol Abuse and Alcoholism, 1995), as well as key components such as behavioral contracts that are reinforced in therapy such as "no angry touching, no yelling/screaming, reduce substance use, and get out of the situation if you are under the influence or have the urge to lose control."

Defining Characteristics of SADV

SADV is an integrated treatment designed to target both substance use and aggressive behaviors within each session at one location. Cognitive-behavioral skills training in SADV is used to target substance use, interpersonal violence/conflict, and the relationship between the two. SADV interventions include understanding patterns of substance use, coping with craving, coping with aggressive behaviors, negotiating conflicts in healthier ways, problem-solving skills, drug refusal skills, and managing cognitions. First, participants are asked to monitor their substance use, as well as any difficulty they may be having controlling violent behavior and angry feelings, in order to highlight relationships between the two and to help patients understand behavior patterns (e.g., how substance use may trigger anger or violent behavior, and how anger or violence may lead to relapse to verbal and/or physical aggression). Second, skills are taught that are directly relevant to the reduction of IPV, including communication and management of anger. SADV differs from standard CBT for substance use in its dual focus on substance use and interpersonal violence and on the relationship between the two. SADV differs from BCT in the inclusion of specific skills for reducing and/or eliminating aggressive behaviors. SADV differs from TSF and drug counseling, which focus on alcohol and illicit substances (Mercer and Woody, 1999), in that there is also a focus is on interpersonal violence, skills training, and practice exercises (e.g., conflict resolution skills training, affect modulation skills training).

The key ingredients that distinguish SADV from other therapies and that must be delivered for adequate exposure to SADV include the following: (1) dual focus on treatment strategies for substance use and IPV (e.g., identify triggers for substance use and identify triggers for violence); (2) individualized training that emphasizes that complete abstinence from alcohol and/or illicit drugs is likely to lead to abstinence in IPV or reducing use will lead to reductions in IPV; (3) preparing unique coping skills for each client in preparation for high-risk situations (this essential ingredient emphasizes that a substance use slip or relapse does not need to result in violence); (4) increased emphasis on role plays and practice exercises in each session pertaining to anger management, communication, and conflict resolution skills training; (5) no requirement for the female partner be involved in the intervention but flexibility to allow for couples modules when feasible and therapeutically indicated.

To date, SADV has shown promising results in a recently completed randomized controlled study (Easton *et al.*, 2007b). Clients were referred by the court and were given a comprehensive battery of assessments and diagnosed with alcohol dependence via *Diagnostic and Statistical Manual of Mental Disorders, Fourth Edition* (DSM-IV) criteria using structured assessment instruments (for a review, see Easton *et al.*, 2007a). More specifically, alcohol-dependent men with a domestic violence arrest within the past 6 months were recruited and evaluated. Male participants were randomly assigned to either 12 weeks of the integrated SADV group treatment or 12 weeks of the group TSF. Of the 78 individuals who were eligible, 77 were randomized and 75 started treatment. Out of the 75 starters, 62 completed the full 12 weeks of treatment. Across treatments, participants completed an average of 9 of 12 offered sessions. There were no significant differences between the SADV and the TSF groups in the number of sessions attended. Follow-up interviews were conducted 6 months after randomization; the follow-up rate was 80% across conditions. Those receiving SADV showed significantly more days abstinent from alcohol use as compared with the TSF group. The SADV group also showed a significantly greater decline in aggressive behavior from pre- to posttreatment as compared with the TSF group. To date, this is one of the first integrated group treatments found to be efficacious. However, this study needs to be replicated with a larger sample of alcohol-dependent men with co-occurring physical violence in both individual and group treatment modalities.

In a more recent randomized controlled trial, which is yet to be published, the same investigators evaluated 63 substance-dependent IPV offenders, primarily alcohol-dependent men who abused cocaine and marijuana. The SADV approach was replicated within the context of an individual behavioral therapy approach with optional behavioral couples modules (SADV targeting both addiction and IPV, $N = 29$) and compared to an equally intensive drug counseling (DC) approach targeting addiction alone along with couples counseling modules ($N = 34$). This replication study assessed substance-dependent men who were arrested for IPV within the year prior to the initiation of treatment. The integrated SADV approach controlled for the limitations that were inherent within the first group therapy study (e.g., utilized continuous measures to control for severity of IPV; allowed for the inclusion of alcohol, cocaine, and marijuana use; controlled for contact hours with the female partners; and used more sensitive measures of IPV in addition to the widely used Conflict Tactic Scale (CTS-2 revised; Straus *et al.*, 1996). The results from this study suggested that individuals in the SADV condition did not have any differences in the number of sessions attended as compared to the DC approach. The individuals in the SADV condition had significantly more total days of abstinence from total aggressive behaviors (both physical and verbal aggression) across 84 days in treatment as compared to the DC condition. Moreover, on days of a drinking episode, individuals in the DC condition were nearly two times more likely to partake in aggressive behaviors compared with individuals in the SADV individual therapy approach. Again, larger sample sizes and replications of this design are needed.

FEMALE-TO-MALE PERPETRATION OF VIOLENCE

Although past research reports a smaller percentage of female-to-male physical aggression (Bureau of Justice Statistics, 1998a), it is important to understand the characteristics of women who are perpetrators of IPV and especially because recent literature reviews find that IPV is bidirectional in the dyad (Wupperman *et al.*, 2009). For example, Stuart *et al.* (2003) studied relationship aggression among women court-referred to a domestic violence intervention. This study recruited 35 women who were arrested for domestic violence. The results of the study showed that about half the women were classified as hazardous drinkers, one-quarter met criteria for alcohol abuse or dependence, and one-quarter had drug-related problems. This study also found that over a half of the women reported that their relationship partners were hazardous drinkers as well. These researchers also found that the group of women who were hazardous drinkers had more drug problems, relationship aggression, general violence, and marital dissatisfaction compared with the group of women with nonhazardous drinking. In another study by Stuart *et al.* (2004), they found that women's hazardous drinking status was important in predicting physical assault perpetration toward their partners. Stuart *et al.* (2004) state the importance of offering integrated substance abuse and anger management treatment among women who are arrested for domestic violence. Suffice to say, there is little research that evaluates men who are victims of domestic violence. Further investigation is needed in this area.

TYPOLOGIES OF MEN WHO ARE PHYSICALLY VIOLENT AND THE ROLE OF ANTISOCIAL PERSONALITY DISORDER

Other diagnostic issues come into play when considering how to classify subgroups of individuals who are offenders of IPV. As mentioned above, there are high rates of co-occurring substance abuse among perpetrators of IPV (Easton *et al.*, 2007a; Leonard, 2005). Moreover, it is more than likely that there are other psychiatric comorbidities on Axis I (e.g., anxiety and mood disorders) and Axis II (e.g., personality disorders) that would help community treatment providers match IPV offenders to the most clinically appropriate care. One group that has researched other co-occurring mental health-related pathologies in the form of typologies is that of Holtzworth-Munroe and colleagues (Holtzworth-Munroe and Meehan, 2004; Holtzworth-Munroe and Stuart 1994). These researchers describe three groups/typologies of batterers. The three descriptive dimensions of men with IPV include (1) family only (FO), (2) borderline–dysphoric (BD), and (3) generally violent–antisocial (GVA). FO batterers engage in the least severe form of marital violence, violence outside the home, and criminal behavior. These men evidence little or no psychopathology. BD batterers engage in moderate to severe abuse. Their violence is primarily confined to the wife or partner, although some extrafamilial violence might be evident. BD batterers are often psychologically distressed, demonstrate borderline personality characteristics, and abuse substances. GVA batterers engage in moderate to severe abuse and have the highest levels of extrafamilial aggression and criminal behavior. They are the most likely to have antisocial characteristics and problems with substance abuse. Holtzworth-Munroe and colleagues suggest that typologies 1 and 2 respond to treatment, while the GVA typology shows a limited response. While these researchers support the "typologies of batterers approach" described above, other approaches have yet to posit dimensional approaches. Further research is needed to study dimensional approaches.

PHARMACOLOGICAL AGENTS IN THE TREATMENT OF VIOLENCE

To date, few large-scale randomized trials have assessed the safety and efficacy of pharmacological agents in treating domestic violence offenders with and without substance-related problems. Regarding medication compliance, Timothy O'Farrell (2000) used BCT in patient populations receiving methadone maintenance, naltrexone, and HIV medications. These researchers assessed whether BCT would increase medication compliance, decrease substance use, and increase relationship adjustment. O'Farrell (2000) found that men in a methadone maintenance program who were assigned to BCT had fewer urine screens positive for drugs, better relationship adjustment, and greater reductions in drug use severity. Similarly, this group has found positive treatment outcomes for both addiction and IPV outcomes with naltrexone and IPV medications (O'Farrell and Fals-Stewart, 2000).

CLINICAL IMPLICATIONS AND FUTURE DIRECTIONS

Although BCT has been shown to be the most effective therapy to date for co-occurring addiction and IPV, it may have limited application to IPV in substance abuse treatment facilities. There is a need for an alternative approach for the following reasons: (1) it is not clinically feasible to involve all female partners in couples' treatment (e.g., female partner has left the relationship and has no involvement with the offender); (2) a male offender may refuse to have his partner participate in his treatment; (3) a female partner may refuse to participate in the offender's treatment; (4) there may be restraining or protective orders that limit contact between the offender and the victim; and (5) offenders and victims may separate and have no further contact. Thus, even if BCT may be an effective approach to address dual substance use and IPV, there is a clear need for an integrated IPV-substance abuse treatment that is *not solely* couple based (Easton *et al.*, 2007b). Moreover, additional randomized behavioral therapy trials are needed among the IPV population as research continues to lag in the development of both behavioral therapies and pharmacological treatments among substance-using offenders of domestic violence. Additional studies are needed that involve the following: (1) behavioral therapy approaches grounded in evidence-based theories; (2) well-controlled trials with sample sizes adequate to detect treatment effects; (3) comparisons of equally intensive behavioral therapy conditions; (4) manualized therapies with intensive treatment fidelity checks (e.g., adherence to the behavioral therapy manuals and competency in administering the therapy); (5) comprehensive batteries of reliable and validated demographic, addiction, and psychiatric assessments; (6) objective indicators of substance use (urine toxicology screens and breathalyzer analysis; (7) collateral data from partner, family, and criminal justice informants for IPV/aggressive behavior data; and (8) assessments of bidirectional aggression within the dyad.

Regarding the need to incorporate more clinical research that targets alcohol-related IPV, suggestions include assessing specific pharmacotherapy adjuncts and behavioral therapies already shown to decrease alcohol-related disorders. Perhaps these therapies will show reductions in IPV if IPV outcomes are assessed. For example, naltrexone or Antabuse, in conjunction with evidenced-based addiction behavioral treatments (e.g., CBT or TSF), has been shown to have positive treatment outcomes (reductions and/or abstinence in alcohol use) among clients with alcohol-related disorders.

Alternative approaches such as SADV show promise, and future investigations would include more randomized studies with larger samples of patients. Other directions include assessing SADV with and without various pharmacotherapies as adjunctive medication may further improve treatment outcomes with this population and may lead to prolonged abstinence from substance use and violence.

The following clinical guidelines can be ascertained from this chapter and are summarized below: (1) screen IPV men for mental health and substance-related disorders; (2) provide a thorough evaluation of the type and frequency of IPV (e.g., physical violence, psychological, verbal, sexual violence) utilizing the CTS-2 and/or Timeline Follow-Back for Violent and Aggressive Behaviors (Fals-Stewart *et al.*, 2000); (3) assess multiple domains of social and functional impairment in men and women with co-occurring substance abuse and domestic violence; (4) consider both pharmacological and evidenced-based behavioral treatment interventions; and 5) consider alternative treatment goals designed to motivate clients to reduce use as a form of harm reduction (reduction of alcohol use and/or reduction of drug use) when clients may not wish to completely abstain from alcohol and/or drug use.

In conclusion, IPV is a pervasive problem across the globe; male-to-female violence is the most prevalent IPV, while noting that IPV is often bidirectional within the relationship (Wupperman *et al.*, 2009). Additionally, high rates of substance use have been shown to co-occur among men who are physically violent toward their partners (Easton *et al.*, 2007a). Moreover, substance use has been shown to facilitate or exacerbate physical aggression (Leonard, 2005). Substance abuse treatment alone has been shown to decrease physical aggression among men who have co-occurring substance use and domestic violence problems (Easton *et al.*, 2007a). BCT has been shown to be an effective treatment approach for men in an intact relationship where both partners are willing to participate. BCT has been shown to decrease substance use, decrease violence, and increase marital satisfaction among couples (Easton *et al.*, 2007b). A CBT approach such as SADV shows promise as both a group and individual therapy intervention for decreasing substance use and physical aggression among substance-abusing men arrested for domestic violence.

REFERENCES

Archer, J. (2000) Sex differences in aggression between heterosexual partners: A meta-analytic review. *Psychological Bulletin*, **126**, 651–680.

Babcock, J.C., Green, C.E., and Robie, C. (2004) Does batterers' treatment work?: A meta-analytic review of domestic violence treatment outcome research. *Clinical Psychology Review*, **23**, 1023–1053.

Babcock, J.C., Jacobson, N.S., Gottman, J.M., and Yerington, T.P. (2000) Attachment, emotional regulation, and the function of marital violence: Differences between secure, preoccupied and dismissing violent and nonviolent husbands. *Journal of Family Violence*, **15**, 391–409.

Babcock, J.C. and La Taillade, J.J. (2000) Evaluating interventions for men who batter. In J. Vincent and E. Jourilles (eds), *Domestic Violence: Guidelines for Research-Informed Practice* (pp. 37–377). London: Jessica Kingsley.

Brookoff, D., O'Brien, K.K., and Cook, C.S. (1997) Characteristics of participants in domestic violence: Assessment at the scene of domestic assault. *Journal of the American Medical Association*, **277**, 1369–1373.

Bureau of Justice Statistics (1998a) *Violence by intimates* (NCJ Publication No. 167237). Washington, DC: US Department of Justice.

Bureau of Justice Statistics (1998b) *Alcohol and Crime: An Analysis of National Data on the Prevalence of Alcohol Involvement in Crime*. (NCJ Publication No. 168632). Washington, DC: US Department of Justice.

Bureau of Justice Statistics (2005) *Family Violence Statistics Including Statistics on Strangers and Acquaintances* (NCJ Publication No. 207846). Washington, DC: US Department of Justice.

Carroll, K.M. (1996) Relapse prevention as a psychosocial treatment approach: A review of controlled clinical trials. *Experimental and Clinical Psychopharmacology*, **4**, 46–54.

Carroll, K.M., Kadden, R.M., Donovan, D.M. *et al.* (1994) Implementing treatment and protecting the validity of the independent variable in treatment matching studies. Special Issue: Alcoholism treatment matching research: Methodological and clinical approaches. *Journal of Studies on Alcohol*, **12**, 149–155.

Carroll, K.M., Nich, C., Ball, S.A. *et al.* (1998) Treatment of cocaine and alcohol dependence with psychotherapy and disulfiram. *Addiction*, **93**, 713–728.

Chermack, S.T. and Taylor, S.P. (1995) Alcohol and human physical aggression: Pharmacological versus expectancy effects. *Journal of Studies on Alcohol*, **56**, 449–456.

Coker, A., Davis, K., Arias, I. *et al.* (2002) Physical and mental health effects of intimate partner violence for men and women. *American Journal of Preventive Medicine*, **23**, 260–268.

DeRubeis, R.J. and Crits-Christoph, P. (1998) Empirically supported individual and group psychological treatments for adult mental disorders. *Journal of Consulting and Clinical Psychology*, **66**, 37–52.

Easton, C., Lee, B., Wupperman, P., and Zonana, H. (2008) Substance abuse and domestic violence interventions: The need for theoretical based research. *The American Journal on Addictions*, **17**, 341–342.

Easton, C., Swan, S., and Sinha, R. (2000a) Prevalence of family violence in clients entering substance abuse treatment. *Journal of Substance Abuse Treatment*, **18**, 23–28.

Easton, C., Swan, S., and Sinha, R. (2000b) Motivation to change substance use among offenders of domestic violence. *Journal of Substance Abuse Treatment*, **19**, 1–5.

Easton, C.J., Mandel, D.L., Babuscio, T.A. *et al.* (2007a) Differences in treatment outcome between male alcohol dependent offenders of domestic violence with and without positive drug screens. *Addictive Behaviors*, **32**, 2151–2163.

Easton, C.J., Mandel, D.M., Hunkele, K. *et al.* (2007b) A cognitive behavioral therapy for alcohol dependent domestic violence offenders: An integrated substance abuse-domestic violence treatment approach (SADV). *The American Journal on Addictions*, **16**, 24–31.

Eckhardt, C., Murphy, C., Black, D., and Suhr, L. (2006) Intervention programs for perpetrators of intimate partner violence: Conclusions from a clinical research perspective. *Public Health Reports*, **121**, 369–381.

Fals-Stewart, W. (2002) Behavioral family counseling and naltrexone for male opioid dependent patients. *Journal of Consulting and Clinical Psychology*, **71**, 432–442.

Fals-Stewart, W., Golden, J., and Schumacher, J.A. (2003) Intimate partner violence and substance use: A longitudinal day-to-day examination. *Addictive Behaviors*, **28**, 1555–1574.

Fals-Stewart, W., O'Farrell, T.J., Freitas, T. *et al.* (2000) The timeline follow-back interview for substance abuse: Psychometric properties. *Journal of Consulting and Clinical Psychology*, **68**, 134–144.

Holtzworth-Munroe, A. and Meehan, J.C. (2004) Typologies of men who are martially violent: Scientific and clinical implications. *Journal of Interpersonal Violence*, **18**, 309–319.

Holtzworth-Munroe, A. and Stuart, G. (1994) Typologies of male batterers: Three subtypes and the differences among them. *Psychological Bulletin*, **116**, 476–497.

Irvin, J.E., Bowers, C.A., Dunn, M.E. *et al.* (1999) Efficacy of relapse prevention: A meta-analytic review. *Journal of Consulting and Clinical Psychology*, **67**, 563–570.

Kaufman Kantor, G. and Straus, M. (1990) The "drunken bum" theory of wife beating. In M.A. Straus and R.J. Gelles (eds), *Physical Violence in American Families: Risk Factors and Adaptations to Violence in 8,145 Families* (pp. 203–224). New Brunswick, NJ: Transaction Publishers.

Leonard, C., Puranik, C., Kuldau, J. *et al.* (1998) Normal variation in the frequency and location of human auditory cortex landmarks: Heschl's gyrus: Where is it? *Cerebral Cortex (New York, N.Y.: 1991)*, **8**, 397–406.

Leonard, K.E. (2005) Alcohol and intimate partner violence: When can we say that heavy drinking is a contributing cause of violence? *Addiction*, **100**, 422–425.

Leonard, K.E. and Quigley, B.M. (1999) Drinking and marital aggression in newlyweds: An event-based analysis of dinking and the occurrence of husband marital aggression. *Journal of Studies on Alcohol*, **60**, 537–545.

Leonard, K.E. and Senchak, M. (1993) Alcohol and premarital aggression among newlywed couples. *Journal of Studies on Alcohol. Supplement.*, **11**, 96–108.

Maude-Griffin, P.M., Hohenstein, J.M., Humfleet, G.L. *et al.* (1998) Superior efficacy of cognitive-behavioral therapy for crack cocaine abusers: Main and matching effects. *Journal of Consulting and Clinical Psychology*, **66**, 832–837.

McCauley, J., Kern, D.E., Kolodner, K. *et al.* (1995) The battering syndrome: Prevalence and clinical characteristics of domestic violence in primary care internal medicine practices. *Annals of Internal Medicine*, **123**, 737–746.

McKay, J.R., Alterman, A.I., Cacciola, J.S. *et al.* (1997) Group counseling versus individualized relapse prevention aftercare following intensive outpatient treatment for cocaine dependence. *Journal of Consulting and Clinical Psychology*, **65**, 778–788.

McMurran, M. and Gilchrist, E. (2008) Anger control and alcohol use: Appropriate interventions for domestic violence? *Psychology, Crime, and Law*, **14**, 107–116.

Mercer, D. and Woody, G. (1999) *Individual Drug Counseling. Treating Cocaine Addiction Therapy Manual 3*. (NIH Publication No. 99-4380). Rockville, MD: National Institute on Drug Abuse.

Miller, B. (1990) The interrelationships between alcohol and drugs and family violence. In M. De La Rosa and B. Gropper (eds), *Drugs and Violence: Causes, Correlates, and Consequences* (pp. 177–207). NIDA Research Monograph 103. Rockville, MD: National Institute on Drug Abuse.

Monti, P.M., Rohsenow, D.J., Michalec, E. *et al*. (1997) Brief coping skills treatment for cocaine abuse: Substance use outcomes at three months. *Addiction*, **92**, 1717–1728.

Morgenstern, J. and Longabaugh, R. (2000) Cognitive-behavioral treatment for alcohol dependence: A review of the evidence for its hypothesized mechanisms of action. *Addiction*, **95**, 1475–1490.

Morgenstern, J., Morgan, T.J., McCrady, B.S. *et al*. (2001) Manual-guided cognitive behavioral therapy training: A promising method for disseminating empirically supported substance abuse treatments to the practice community. *Psychology of Addictive Behaviors*, **15**, 83–88.

Muhajarine, N. and D'Arcy, C. (1999) Physical abuse during pregnancy: Prevalence and risk factors. *Canadian Medical Association Journal*, **160**, 1007–1011.

Murphy, C.M. and O'Farrell, T.J. (1996) Marital violence among alcoholics. *Current Directions in Psychological Science*, **5**, 183–186.

National Institute on Alcohol Abuse and Alcoholism (1995) *Cognitive Behavioral Coping Skills Therapy Manual: A Clinical Research Guide for Therapists Treating Individuals with Alcohol Abuse and Dependence*. Project Match Manual Series, Vol. 3. Bethesda, MD: NIAAA.

National Institute on Drug Abuse (2009) *Principles of Drug Abuse Treatment: A Research Based Guide*. Bethesda, MD: NIDA.

O'Farrell, T.J. (2000) Behavioral couples therapy for alcoholism and drug abuse. *Journal of Substance Abuse Treatment*, **18**, 51–54.

O'Farrell, T.J. and Fals-Stewart, W. (2000) Behavioral couples therapy for alcoholism and drug abuse. *Journal of Substance Abuse Treatment*, **18**, 51–54.

O'Farrell, T.J. and Fals-Stewart, W. (2002) Marital and family therapy. In R.K. Hester and W.R. Miller (eds), *Handbook of Alcoholism Treatment Approaches: Effective Alternatives* (pp. 188–212). New York: Allyn and Bacon.

O'Farrell, T.J., Fals-Stewart, W., Murphy, M. *et al*. (2003) Partner violence before and after individual based alcoholism treatment for male alcoholic patients. *Journal of Consulting and Clinical Psychology*, **71**, 92–102.

Oriel, K.A. and Fleming, M.F. (1998) Screening men for partner violence in a primary care setting. A new strategy for detecting domestic violence. *The Journal of Family Practice*, **46**, 493–498.

Pan, H.D., Neidig, P.H., and O'Leary, K.K. (1994) Predicting mild and severe husband-to-wife physical aggression. *The Journal of Applied Behavioral Science*, **36**, 108–122.

Project MATCH Research Group (1997) Matching alcohol treatments to client heterogeneity: Project MATCH posttreatment drinking outcomes. *Journal of Studies on Alcohol*, **58**, 7–29.

Roberts, A.R. (1998) *Battered Women and Their Families: Intervention Strategies and Treatment Approaches*, 2nd edn. New York: Springer Publishing Co.

Schumacher, J.A., Fals-Stewart, W., and Leonard, K.E. (2003) Domestic violence treatment referrals for men seeking alcohol treatment. *Journal of Substance Abuse Treatment*, **24**, 279–283.

Sholomskas, D.E., Syracuse-Siewert, G., Rounsaville, B.J., Ball, S.A., Nuro, K.F., and Carroll, K.M. (2005) We don't train in vain: A dissemination trial of three strategies of training clinicians in cognitive-behavioral therapy. *Journal of Consulting and Clinical Psychology*, **73**, 106–115.

Smedslund, G., Dalsbo, T.K., Steiro, A. *et al*. (2007) Cognitive behavioural therapy for men who physically abuse their female partner (Review). *Cochrane Database of Systematic Reviews*, (3), CD006048. DOI: 10.1002/14651858.CD006048.pub2.

Straus, M.A., Hamby, S.L., Boney-McCoy, S. *et al.* (1996) The Revised Conflict Tactics Scale (CTS2): Development and preliminary psychometric data. *Journal of Family Issues*, **17**, 283–316.

Stuart, G.L., Moore, T.M., Ramsey, S.E., and Kahler, C.W. (2003) Relationship aggression and substance use among women court-referred to domestic violence intervention programs. *Addictive Behaviors*, **28**, 1603–1610.

Stuart, G.L., Moore, T.M., Ramsey, S.E., and Kahler, C.W. (2004) Hazardous drinking and relationship violence perpetration and victimization in women arrested for domestic violence. *Journal of Studies on Alcohol*, **65**, 46–53.

The Marijuana Research Treatment Group (MRTG) (2004) Brief treatments for cannabis dependence: Findings from a randomized multisite trial. *Journal of Consulting and Clinical Psychology*, **72**, 455–466.

US Department of Health and Human Services, Centers for Disease Control and Prevention, National Center for Injury Prevention and Control (2003) *Costs of Intimate Partner Violence Against Women in the United States*. Atlanta, GA: US DHHS.

Van Hightower, N.R. and Gorton, J. (1998) Domestic violence among patients at two rural health care clinics: Prevalence and social correlates. *Public Health Nursing*, **15**, 355–362.

Wupperman, P., Amble, P., Devine, S. *et al.* (2009) Prevalence of violence and substance use among female partner of men in treatment of intimate-partner violence. *The Journal of the American Academy of Psychiatry and the Law*, **37**, 75–77.

Chapter 10

ALCOHOL ARREST REFERRAL

KATIE MCCRACKEN

OpCit Research, London, England

FRANCO SASSI

Organisation for Economic Co-operation and Development (OECD), Paris, France (Note: FS was affiliated with the London School of Economics and Political Science when this project started. The project is not part of OECD institutional work.)

INTRODUCTION

Alcohol is frequently involved in violent offences in the United Kingdom, including 37% of domestic violence incidents, 52% of cases of violence towards acquaintances and 65% of cases of violence towards people not known to the perpetrator (Flatley *et al.*, 2010). It is estimated that alcohol-related crime costs the economy of England and Wales between £8 and £13 billion per year (Home Office, 2010). Research has consistently shown links between crime and disorder, 'binge' drinking[1] and the night-time economy (Allen *et al.*, 2003; Hobbs *et al.*, 2003; Matthews and Richardson, 2005).

In Britain, interventions to tackle alcohol-related offending at the point following arrest have existed for some years. For example, the Criminal Justice Act 2003 allows judges and magistrates to issue community sentences requiring offenders to attend treatment for alcohol problems. However, referring to alcohol treatment at the point of arrest is a new approach. The Home Office piloted this approach in England and Wales between 2008 and 2011 by funding Alcohol Arrest Referral (AAR) schemes.

The AAR pilots were introduced in two tranches. The first set of pilots introduced schemes in six areas, the second tranche in another eight different areas.

---

[1]Binge drinking is defined in many ways but typically refers to people drinking more than six to eight units (equivalent of 2–3 pints of average strength lager or three to four 175-mL glasses of wine) of alcohol in a single session (Raistrick, Heather, and Godfrey, 2006).

Alcohol-Related Violence: Prevention and Treatment, First Edition. Edited by Mary McMurran.
© 2013 John Wiley & Sons, Ltd. Published 2013 by John Wiley & Sons, Ltd.

The schemes were introduced to explore ways of tackling the link between alcohol and offending, with the working hypothesis that by tackling low-level alcohol problems, then future offending linked to alcohol may be reduced. The pilots were introduced following favourable findings from brief interventions offered in healthcare settings and support given within the alcohol harm reduction strategy for England (Cabinet Office, 2004) and updated strategy (Department of Health and Home Office, 2007) for so-called brief interventions. The strategy describes brief interventions as a means of helping people to identify their harmful or hazardous drinking patterns and of advising them on ways of reducing alcohol consumption. Brief interventions are characterised primarily by their short length and may be delivered in one or more sessions but usually not beyond five (Babor *et al.*, 2006). They usually involve motivational interviewing as part of an assessment of needs (Raistrick *et al.*, 2006). Part of the logic behind early brief interventions for alcohol is that when people have just experienced problems linked to alcohol, they may be more receptive to changing their behaviour.

Whilst there is strong evidence for the effectiveness of brief interventions for reducing alcohol consumption in problematic drinking men in primary care settings, such as doctors' surgeries and emergency care (Kaner *et al.*, 2009), the AAR scheme intended to establish whether these successes could be replicated in a criminal justice context, specifically to reduce reoffending.

Clients were identified in police custody. The AAR involved a brief intervention session with an Alcohol Arrest Referral worker (AARw) and, in some cases, follow-up sessions arranged for a later date, if deemed necessary by the worker. If the client was assessed as having additional needs, they could be referred on to other services outside of the AAR scheme. The main elements of the AAR are summarised as follows: (1) the client's drinking patterns and needs are assessed; (2) information about the risks of alcohol consumption is provided to the client; (3) the clients are offered practical advice and techniques for reducing their alcohol consumption and for managing the risks of drinking; (4) if necessary, following assessment, the client is referred either for a follow-up brief intervention or to another agency for further assessment or treatment.

The AAR schemes were evaluated by independent researchers appointed by the Home Office, including the author of this chapter. This chapter outlines the findings from the evaluation of the second phase of pilots, which took place between November 2009 and March 2011. The elements of the evaluation reported here include analysis of the characteristics of those accessing the schemes, determining whether there was an impact on clients' re-arrest rates, assessing if any change in alcohol consumption occurred and identifying implementation and delivery lessons that may be applied to any future similar AAR schemes.

METHODOLOGY OF THE RESEARCH

The evaluation study included three main elements: a process assessment, an outcome assessment and a cost assessment. The evaluation took place between March 2009 and June 2010, with follow-up data on clients being collected until

December 2010. The main sources of data used for the evaluation were the AAR clients' alcohol intervention record (AIR), which all schemes used to assess the clients' needs, as well as to note police arrest records.

Completed AIRs were forwarded to the evaluation team. A total of 6,916 AIR forms were forwarded, covering the evaluation period of May/June 2009 to June 2010. After removing duplicate and incomplete forms, 4,739 AIRs were included in the analyses. The police custody records of these 4,739 cases were examined to examine the impact of the AAR on reoffending. Arrest rates were used as a proxy measure for reoffending because arrest data were the most readily accessible and up-to-date information available. Arrests for the AAR clients (the intervention group) were compared for the 6 months prior to the intervention and the 6 months following the intervention. The same analysis was undertaken for a comparison group (N = 4,711), which comprised arrestees from within the same police force area, 12 months prior to the AAR pilot's commencement, using offence type, age and gender, and month of arrest to match to the intervention group on an individual basis.

Statistical analyses were conducted to determine if there were significant differences in re-arrest outcomes between the intervention and comparison groups. Regression analyses were done to determine which characteristics of the intervention and comparison group were associated with higher or lower relative re-arrest rates. Throughout this chapter, the term 'significant' means that the result was statistically significant using the appropriate statistical test.

In addition to a comparison of police data, follow-up telephone interviews were attempted with AAR clients 6 months after the AAR took place. The purpose of these interviews was to identify changes in alcohol consumption and/or related behaviour or problems 6 months following the intervention. Of the 4,739 total intervention group sample, 1,943 individuals consented to take part in interviews and provided telephone numbers. From this group, 34% (N = 667) were interviewed. The telephone interviews were based on the AIR form, which the client had already completed at the time of the intervention. Although an analysis found that the 667 clients providing follow-up interviews were generally representative of all clients receiving the intervention in terms of age range, gender, ethnicity and offending history, the low response rate compared to the total population receiving AARs, and the lack of a comparison group, means that the findings about changes in alcohol consumption amongst arrest referral clients should be treated with caution.

OVERVIEW OF THE AAR PILOT SCHEMES AND CLIENT CHARACTERISTICS

Referral Routes into the Projects

AAR sites were given a degree of autonomy in setting up their AAR schemes to best meet local needs. Details of schemes' referral routes, the location of first AAR sessions and the average length of the first session are included in Table 10.1 and are discussed in more detail below.

Table 10.1   Referral routes and processes used by scheme.

Project	Main Referral Route	Main Location for Intervention Delivery[a]	Max. Number of Sessions Offered	Average Length of First Session (min)	Valid AIRs Used in Analysis	Percentage Male
A	Voluntary	Police custody	1	20	485	86
B	Voluntary	Police custody	2	53	1,443	82
C	Conditional bail	Non-custody venue	3	35	516	81
D	Voluntary	Police custody	3	42	495	91
E	Voluntary	Non-custody venue	3	26	645	89
F	Voluntary	Non-custody venue	3	48	250	84
G	Voluntary	Police custody	2	36	365	83
H	Voluntary	Police custody	3	18	540	88
Total					4,739	86

[a]The main location for the intervention delivery is based on where the initial AIR form was undertaken, which was gleaned from interviews with scheme partners.

Projects used two main referral routes, broadly described as voluntary or mandatory. Clients were offered the intervention if they were deemed by the arresting officer or the custody sergeant to be under the influence of alcohol when arrested. First interventions that were delivered in custody were done on a voluntary basis as they occurred before an arrestee was 'disposed' from custody. The AIR was completed at this point. Mandatory-type routes involved a client being referred as a condition of a conditional caution or conditional bail. Mandatory routes tended to be used for clients who were referred to an appointment outside of custody, particularly second appointments, although voluntary referrals may also be made to outside appointments.

Number of Sessions

Only one project (project A) limited its AAR scheme to one session only. Other projects offered further sessions if deemed appropriate by the AARw. First sessions lasted on average between 18 and 53 minutes (overall range 3–170).

Throughput of the AAR Schemes

During a 12-month period from May/June 2009 to June 2010 when the evaluation was undertaken, 6,916 AIR forms were submitted for evaluation purposes; of these, 4,739 were considered to be valid forms (68.5% of AIRs collected). Table 10.1 shows the number of valid AIRs submitted by the participating site during the 12-month period.

Table 10.2   AAR clients' arrest offences (N = 4,632).

Index Offence	Violence	Criminal Damage	Drink-Driving	Drugs	Drunk and Disorderly	Other	Public Order	Acquisitive
Total	1,713	462	487	154	782	305	167	562
Percentage of total	36	10	10	3	16	6	4	12

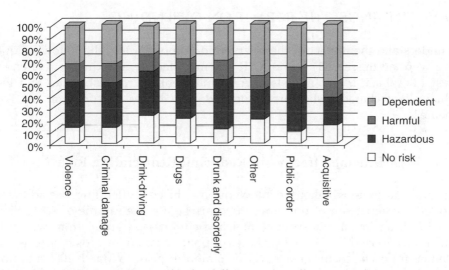

Figure 10.1   AUDIT category profile for different index offence types (N = 4,632).

AAR Clients

The overwhelming majority of clients were male (86%) and White (92%), with the average age being 31 years old. Data on the offence the client was arrested for at the time of the intervention (the 'index offence') were based on entries recorded on the AIR. Table 10.2 shows the breakdown of index offence types for AAR clients recorded by the AARw. At 36%, the highest proportion of offences was in the violence category (which included assault, common assault, attempted murder and violent disorder). Specific alcohol-related offences of drink-driving and drunk and disorderly accounted for just over a quarter of offences (26%).

Scores on the Alcohol Use Disorders Identification Test (AUDIT) (Babor *et al.*, 2001) were banded according the manual as follows: 0–7 is no risk; 8–15 identifies hazardous drinkers; 16–19 identifies harmful drinkers; and 20 or over identifies dependent drinkers. Figure 10.1 shows the proportions of AAR clients in different AUDIT score bands by offence type. It shows that the AUDIT profile of clients is broadly similar across index offence types, with the exception of a slightly elevated number of those with acquisitive index offences in the dependent category. This accords with research by McMurran and Cusens (2005), which showed that offenders with alcohol-related acquisitive convictions scored higher on the AUDIT than offenders with alcohol-related violence convictions and offenders with non-alcohol-related convictions. Overall, the largest proportion of clients was in the dependent drinker category (37%). This was followed closely by hazardous drinkers. There was little variation in these proportions across the eight schemes.

MAIN FINDINGS: THE IMPACT ON OFFENDING

To understand the impact of the intervention on offending, the following questions were addressed: (1) Is the AAR scheme effective in reducing reoffending rates? (2) Which, if any, models of AAR intervention, referral routes and individual client characteristics are associated with better outcomes in the AAR scheme?

Is the AAR Scheme Effective in Reducing Reoffending Rates?

The question about whether the intervention reduced reoffending was addressed through a comparison of police-recorded arrests for the sample of AAR clients ($N = 4,739$) against a retrospective matched comparison group from within the same police force ($N = 4,711$). Databases of police custody records of arrests were obtained for each scheme area, covering 6 months prior to March 2009 and up to December 2010 for the intervention group and 24 months up to September 2008 for the comparison group. Both comparison group and intervention group databases were given the same codes for offence type and were cleaned to remove duplicate arrest records.

Intervention group clients were matched to their own arrest records by using their initials and date of birth. The comparison group was matched to the intervention group on a case-by-case basis by offence type, gender, age band and month of arrest, and also according to whether the time of arrest occurred between 9 p.m. and 6 a.m., in order to act as a proxy for alcohol-related offending. For both the intervention and comparison group, all arrests prior and subsequent to the index offence were taken into account in the analysis, regardless of the time of arrest or the offence type.

Offending Histories of the Intervention and Comparison Group

Tables 10.3 and 10.4 provide a simple breakdown of the number of pre- and post-index offence arrests for the intervention and comparison groups. Analyses of arrest rates show that the majority of AAR clients (54%) and those within the comparison group (61%) had been arrested only once in the time period examined; that is, they had no pre- or post-index offence arrests.

Table 10.3 Pre- and post-index offence arrests for the intervention group (N = 4,739).

	Acquisitive	Criminal Damage	Drink-Driving	Drugs	Drunk and Disorderly	Public Order	Violence	Others	Total
Number of pre-index offence arrests	689	249	63	76	188	313	570	645	2,793
Percentage of total pre-index offence arrests	25	9	2	3	7	11	20	23	
Number of post-index offence arrests	748	193	28	83	207	261	498	923	2,946
Percentage of total post-index offence arrests	25	7	1	3	7	9	17	31	
Pre-post difference – N (percentage)	+59 (8.65)	−56 (22.5)	−35 (55.6)	+12 (15.8)	+19 (10.1)	−52 (16.6)	−72 (12.6)	+278 (43.1)	+153 (5.4)

Table 10.4 Pre- and post-index offence arrests for the comparison group ($N = 4,711$).

	Acquisitive	Criminal Damage	Drink-Driving	Drugs	Drunk and Disorderly	Public Order	Violence	Others	Total
Number of pre-index offence arrests	764	245	80	71	108	243	490	614	2,615
Percentage of total pre-index offence arrests	29	9	3	3	4	9	19	23	
Number of post-index offence arrests	724	165	69	49	109	195	407	746	2,464
Percentage of total post-index offence arrests	29	7	3	2	4	8	17	30	
Pre-post difference – N (percentage)	−40 (5.2)	−80 (32.8)	−11 (13.8)	−22 (31.0)	+1 (9.0)	−48 (19.8)	−83 (17.0)	+132 (21.5)	−151 (5.8)

A comparison of the distributions of the arrests per individual in the pre- and post-index offence phases shows very similar patterns in the intervention and comparison groups. Around 40% of individuals had arrests in the pre- and post-index offence phases. Only a few individuals had over five offences in either phase. This means, in general, that the population studied does not tend to have a substantial history of offending for the 6-month pre-index offence phase. It also precludes the possibility that any observed changes in the overall rates of arrests were being driven by a minority of people.

Overall, there were a higher number of arrests in the post-index offence phase for the intervention group compared with the pre-index offence phase, but fewer arrests in the comparison group. For the intervention group, the total number of arrests in the post-index offence phase had increased for acquisitive, drugs, drunk and disorderly, and other offences, compared to the number of arrests in the pre-index offence phase, whilst the number had decreased for the remaining categories. However, the only markedly higher number of post-index offence phase arrests was in the other category. Offence types in this category were extremely diverse and small in number, and this was the case in both the intervention and comparison groups. The number of arrests between the pre-index offence and post-index offence phases for other offence types increased in *both* the intervention and comparison samples, suggesting that changes in local police enforcement policy or other contextual factors are not responsible. In addition, as individuals in both comparison and intervention groups had arrests in a range of categories in both the pre-index offence and post-index offence phases, it is unlikely that certain offence types are driving either increases or decreases in the overall re-arrest rates.

Changes in Post-Index Offence Arrest Rates: Intervention versus Comparison Group

Differences in the number of post-index offences were calculated between the intervention and comparison groups. A difference in differences approach was also used to compare numbers of arrests before and after the index offence.

Overall, the intervention group had *more* arrests post-index offence than the comparison group. The difference in re-arrest rates between the two groups was 6%, and this result was significant in the *negative* direction. Scheme A alone showed a lower number of arrests post-index offence in the intervention group compared with the comparison group, and the difference was statistically significant in a positive direction.

A logistic regression, controlling for the effects of age, gender, month of index offence, index offence type and number of pre-index offence intervention arrests was conducted to examine the effects of intervention and comparison groups on arrest outcomes. In this analysis, the positive result for scheme A was no longer statistically significant, and the same applies for scheme G. Significant negative results for schemes C, E, F and H remained. An analysis entering only drunk and disorderly and drink-driving index offences was conducted to identify if results were different if only individuals arrested for de facto alcohol-related offence types were included. The result of this analysis was that, overall, the impact of

Table 10.5   Adjusted odds ratios (OR) for arrests (intervention vs comparison group).

Project	OR intervention vs. comparison	P value	Direction of result
A	0.78	0.164	Positive
B	1.17	0.081	Negative
C	1.67	0.001	Negative
D	1.30	0.144	Negative
E	7.60	<0.001	Negative
F	2.63	<0.001	Negative
G	1.41	0.104	Negative
H	2.015	<0.001	Negative

the intervention was statistically significant in a negative direction, although scheme A had a significant positive result after controlling for key variables.

Re-arrest Rates by Age and Gender

Re-arrest rates for the intervention and comparison groups overall were examined for differences in age and gender alone. Age and gender variables were combined in the analysis to explore how re-arrest patterns by age differed in men and in women and how gender-related patterns of re-arrest differ in different age groups. Analyses by age and gender showed mostly non-significant results in a negative direction; that is, there were lower re-arrest rates amongst the comparison group compared with the intervention group. This was the case across the samples, except for females aged 60 and above for whom the reverse was true, although this positive result was not significant. The only significant result was a higher re-arrest rate amongst the intervention group, compared with comparison, for males aged 40 and below. These results were replicated for each scheme area except for scheme A, which showed a lower re-arrest rate for the intervention group compared with the comparison group (i.e., results in the positive direction) for males aged between 30 and 50. Other age groups in scheme A's treated group also showed a reduction in arrests compared to the comparison group, but these findings were not significant.

Re-arrest Rates by Different Index Offence Types

Re-arrest rates for the different index offence categories were examined for the intervention and comparison groups overall to identify any differences in outcomes for specific offence types. This showed that there were fewer re-arrests for criminal damage and drink-driving offences for the intervention group compared with the comparison group, although results were not significant. For all other index offence categories, there were more re-arrests amongst the intervention group compared with the comparison group, although again results were not significant. Overall, there were no significant differences in re-arrest rates between those with a history of previous arrests and those with no history of previous arrests.

WHICH MODELS OF AAR INTERVENTIONS, REFERRAL ROUTES AND CLIENT CHARACTERISTICS ARE ASSOCIATED WITH BETTER OUTCOMES?

The second research question aimed to identify specifically what worked with whom. This was addressed in two ways. First, we analysed pre- and postintervention arrests for the full intervention group ($N = 4,739$), looking at both individual characteristics and differences between the schemes. This was done to test various hypotheses about the influence of demographic and other characteristics on differences in re-arrest rates. Second, we analysed the characteristics of a subsample of 667 clients at baseline and again 6 months later, when a follow-up interview was conducted. This dataset provided useful information on psychosocial changes 6 months following the intervention, which was not available for the larger sample of AAR clients.

Client Characteristics Associated with Re-arrest

Differences in re-arrest rates were examined by age, gender, AUDIT scores, index arrest offence type and which scheme clients accessed. A history of a previous arrest for any offence type was strongly associated with reoffending, regardless of AUDIT score, scheme area or any demographic variable. The odds of reoffending increased by approximately 80% for every additional offence in a client's 6-month previous history. Re-arrest is strongly positively correlated with AUDIT scores at baseline. Analysing AUDIT scores by band, those in the highest-risk category (scoring 20 plus) had 2.34 times greater odds of re-arrest than those in the no risk category (scoring 0–7), even after adjusting for the relative impacts of age, gender, index offence type and scheme area. Figure 10.2 shows the odds of

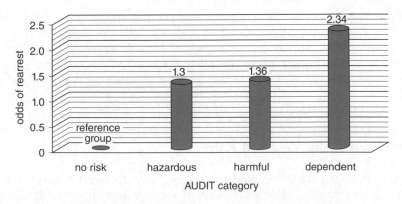

Figure 10.2 Odds of re-arrest by AUDIT score category ($N = 4,737$).

re-arrest for each AUDIT score category. This shows the marked increase in re-arrest odds for dependent drinkers, whilst those in the harmful and hazardous categories are similar. These findings suggest that dependent drinkers are less amenable to behavioural change than those in other categories.

Motivation to Reduce Alcohol Consumption and Re-arrest Rates

AAR clients were asked to assess their motivation to reduce alcohol consumption on a ladder of 0–10, where 0 was 'not at all motivated' and 10 was 'extremely motivated'. Although not a validated means of assessing motivation, it was used as a talking point during the intervention and was a useful indicator of clients' attitudes towards their consumption.

A simple analysis of client motivation to reduce alcohol consumption and reoffending shows that clients with higher levels of motivation are also more likely to be re-arrested. However, clients who are more motivated to reduce their consumption tend to have more severe alcohol-related problems, meaning that they are also at higher risk of offending. When differences between clients in their underlying probabilities of reoffending are accounted for (through baseline AUDIT scores), motivation is not associated with the probability of reoffending.

Employment and Re-arrest Rates

Overall, clients who were unemployed were almost twice as likely to reoffend as those who were in employment (38% vs. 20%). After adjusting for differences in age, sex, offending history, index offence types and scheme area, the odds of reoffending increased to approximately 77% for those who were unemployed.

Duration of the Intervention

The duration of the first intervention session was positively correlated with baseline AUDIT scores; clients who had higher AUDIT scores tended to receive longer interventions. However, the duration of the intervention was not associated with either a higher or lower likelihood of re-arrest, when taking into account that higher alcohol-related needs are associated with the longer session duration.

Referral Routes and Re-arrest Rates

Over three in four clients received the intervention through a voluntary rather than mandatory referral. However, referral route is not significantly associated with a different likelihood of re-arrest, either in a univariate correlation analysis or in an analysis adjusting for differences in other client characteristics.

Role Played by Alcohol in Arrest and Re-arrest Rates

Clients were asked to assess the role that alcohol played in their offence on a scale of 1–5, where 1 is 'no role at all' and 5 is a 'very big role'. The largest proportions of clients said that alcohol played a very big role (54%) followed by no role at all (16%). The relationship between the role alcohol played variable and re-arrest rates appears to be U-shaped, with higher re-arrest rates (over 30%) in those who report their offences being completely unrelated and those reporting it to be strongly related compared to those in the middle with arrest rates between 22% and 25%.

Although it is not possible to investigate the impact of other factors on re-arrest rates due to the absence of similar data for a comparison group, this finding is potentially interesting for practitioners given that a central purpose of motivational interviewing is to identify clients' ambivalence and to direct them towards a change in attitude (Miller and Rollnick, 2002). The effect of client ambivalence on the AAR's effectiveness may prove an interesting area for further exploration.

Findings from Follow-up Interview Data

Regression analyses were conducted on the 667 cases in the intervention sample to identify characteristics that were associated with changes in alcohol problems, as identified by the AUDIT, and re-arrest rates. Self-reported offending behaviour was also assessed. There was a mean reduction of 5.2 points (range −40 to +25) in the AUDIT score between baseline and follow-up, and three in four clients experienced a reduction in AUDIT scores. This is statistically significant but based on low numbers. One in two clients reported a reduction in their self-reported offences (different from police-recorded offences) between baseline and follow-up; 35% reported no change in offending; and 15% reported an increase. A mean reduction in self-reported offending between baseline and follow-up of 1.6 was observed (range −129 to +46).

Relationships between variables at baseline and follow-up data were further explored to investigate associations between offending and alcohol consumption. The average reduction achieved by women in both AUDIT score totals and self-reported offending was larger than that achieved by men (−7.1 vs. −4.8 in AUDIT scores and −2.3 vs. −1.5 in self-reported offending history). However, only the difference in AUDIT scores was statistically significant. Clients with higher AUDIT and self-reported offending scores tended to experience the highest and statistically significant reductions. There were no significant differences in either alcohol consumption or offending between clients referred on a voluntary or mandatory basis. Clients in better health experienced better outcomes in terms of AUDIT and self-reported offending rates than those in fair or poor health, once other factors were accounted for. This finding was consistently significant across all three outcome measures.

DISCUSSION

The key finding from this study is that, overall, across all schemes, the AAR intervention appears to be ineffective for the client group in terms of reducing reoffending. Although the results are less significant after adjusting for age, gender and index offence type, the direction of the results is still against the intervention. However, the evaluation had a clear limitation: the comparison group could not be matched for its level of alcohol consumption or alcohol 'risk' as these data are not available. Despite this, cases were matched on the basis of having a similar index offence type which occurred during night-time hours, which is normally associated with alcohol-related offending. This was not a perfect match for alcohol-related offending, and this limitation should be taken into consideration when interpreting the results. Nonetheless, confidence in the findings is strengthened because a similar overall finding of no effect was found for de facto alcohol-related offending (drink-driving and drunk and disorderly), where alcohol was certainly a factor in the arrest. The study was also protected against potential selection bias whereby only those with high-level alcohol issues would be 'selected' for the intervention. This is because the AAR intervention was widely offered to any arrestee where alcohol was deemed a factor in their arrest, regardless of offence type and perceived level of intoxication.

There was a key exception to the overall weight of the evidence, which poses interesting questions for further research. Notably, scheme A resulted, in some analyses, in reductions in arrests by the treatment group compared to the comparison group. Whilst this initial positive result was rendered insignificant following further controls for age and gender and other key variables, the headline analysis was for significant reductions for the intervention group. Furthermore, for drink-driving and drunk and disorderly offence types, scheme A showed a significant positive effect of the intervention, even after controlling for confounding variables.

There were two key differences with the way scheme A was run compared to other schemes. The first is that scheme A interventions were briefer and less numerous than other schemes: only one brief session was offered, and this was, on average, 20 minutes in duration. (Only one other scheme had shorter sessions, but in this case, a maximum of three sessions was offered.) Qualitative data from scheme A revealed that, where an arrestee was identified as having high-level alcohol needs, referral was made to an external alcohol treatment agency, but this was outside of the AAR scheme remit. Thus, once referred for specialist treatment, the client was managed through externally established treatment processes and staff.

The second factor was that the socio-economic profile of scheme A clients differed from other schemes in that they were more likely to be in employment. Qualitative data from scheme A and other scheme staff respondents suggest that being in employment may provide stronger motivation to change behaviour as, for these clients, there is more to lose by being involved in antisocial or criminal behaviour. An analysis of outcomes amongst the whole treated group found that unemployment at baseline was significantly linked to higher chances of re-arrest.

The results also showed a strong positive correlation between AUDIT score and re-arrest. Within the intervention group, those in the dependent AUDIT category were more than twice as likely to reoffend as those in the lowest-risk category, whilst hazardous and harmful drinkers were 30–36% more likely to reoffend than those in the lowest-risk AUDIT category. Given that large proportions of people arrested for alcohol-related offences scored within the dependent category, across all index offence types, the results indicate that custody suites may be good locations for targeting a potentially costly population group that has a high likelihood of reoffending. It further suggests that alcohol dependency may play a large role in many offence types and not just those that are, de facto, associated with alcohol. This finding provides a potential justification for targeting interventions at alcohol-dependent arrestees, even if it is not a brief intervention such as that used in the AAR scheme.

Implementing Custody-Based Alcohol Interventions

The AAR pilot scheme provided useful lessons for implementing custody-based alcohol interventions. A key point is that schemes generated a large throughput of clients over a 12-month period. Referrals or signposting to the AARw was done by police and other custody staff so cooperation and trusting working relationships were necessary for this to be achieved. A key lesson for the implementation of such a custody-based scheme is that the cooperation and support of senior police officers and police leaders within the custody setting is essential to motivate custody staff on whom referrals are dependent. A key overriding lesson from this research is, therefore, that it is possible to introduce effective working relationships between custody staff and alcohol agency workers in providing alcohol interventions.

Nonetheless, evidence from this study found that, overall, the AAR scheme did not achieve the desired effect, which was to reduce levels of reoffending. However, there was some evidence that the brief intervention resulted in reductions in AUDIT scores, and this mirrors international evidence on the effectiveness of brief interventions in non-criminal justice settings (Kaner et al., 2009). Despite the evidence for a reduction in alcohol-related problems, offending behaviour does not appear to be reduced following the intervention. The reasons for this require further exploration. Possible avenues for investigation on this question may include the wider levers for antisocial behaviour in night-time cultures, including complex social and psychological factors (Winlow and Hall, 2006), which may be used to develop safer drinking environments (see Forsyth, Chapter 7, in this volume).

However, the AAR client group included a large proportion of individuals in the other AUDIT categories of drinking risk, and the intervention did not appear to be effective for any category of AUDIT risk. This suggests two possibilities: (1) that brief alcohol interventions do not work with this specific client group (i.e., people who are arrested when intoxicated) or (2) that the content of the brief interventions is not commensurate with what is effective in practice. Regarding the first point, brief alcohol interventions may not address the criminogenic needs of those arrested. Knowledge of what works to reduce offending tells us that targeting criminogenic needs is important (Andrews and Bonta, 2003), and it may be that a person who is intoxicated upon arrest has treatment needs other than alcohol problems. Alternatively, it may be that brief interventions do not work because the level of dependence in this client group is too high. Evidence suggests that brief alcohol interventions are not effective for those with high-level alcohol needs (Raistrick *et al.*, 2006). Although the evidence from this study suggests that those with higher needs also tended to be more motivated to change, and they had longer AAR sessions, probably as a result of this higher motivation, this did not affect their re-arrest rates. It appears that these arrested high-risk drinkers do not respond to brief interventions. Future research is needed to explore differences in outcomes according to different drinking risk categories.

Regarding the second point, whilst a number of observations were undertaken of the brief intervention sessions, it was not possible to check the appropriateness of all interventions delivered. Furthermore, the schemes developed different intervention contents, which ranged widely in duration. Thus, it is possible that a number of interventions were delivered that did not conform with best practice in brief alcohol interventions.

CONCLUSION

Alcohol-related offending is a seriously harmful problem for society and individuals, and the principle of basing an intervention in custody settings appears to be supported through the experience of the AAR programme. The high levels of self-reported motivation to change alcohol consumption amongst higher needs clients identified in this study suggest that an AAR scheme could be an effective way of identifying and referring those with alcohol needs to further treatment. However, the intervention does not appear to be effective at reducing offending amongst this client group. Whilst the overall direction of the evidence does not support the continuation of the AAR process in its current form or for the current outcome measures, the research presents arguments for custody-based interventions that screen for alcohol needs and refer clients to appropriate support. This is a similar conclusion to Watt and colleagues' study of alcohol brief interventions for violent offenders in a Magistrates Court setting: that the positive effect of the intervention could not be detected above that of being sentenced and, therefore, alcohol screening might be a more effective intervention in itself (Watt, Shepherd, and Newcombe, 2008). It would appear that for people whose drinking brings them into contact with the criminal justice system, their specific problems may differ from those receiving brief interventions in other contexts such as healthcare settings. Further research is therefore needed to understand what this client groups' support needs are, which might help them to reduce their antisocial and criminal behaviour.

REFERENCES

Allen, J., Nicholas, S., Salisbury, H., and Wood, M. (2003) Nature of burglary, vehicle and violent crime. In C. Flood-Page and J. Taylor (eds), *Crime in England and Wales 2001/2002: Supplementary Volume*. Home Office Statistical Bulletin 01/03. London: Home Office.

Andrews, D.A. and Bonta, J. (2003) *The Psychology of Criminal Conduct*. Cincinnati, OH: Anderson.

Babor, T., Higgins-Biddle, J.C., Dauser, D. *et al.* (2006) Brief interventions for at-risk drinking: Patient outcomes and cost effectiveness in managed care organisations. *Alcohol and Alcoholism (Oxford, Oxfordshire)*, **41**, 624–631.

Babor, T.F., Higgins-Biddle, J.C., Saunders, J.B., and Monteiro, M.G. (2001) *AUDIT: The Alcohol Use Disorders Identification Test: Guidelines for Use in Primary Care* (2nd edn). Geneva: World Health Organization.

Cabinet Office (2004) *Alcohol Harm Reduction Strategy for England*. London: Cabinet Office Strategy Unit.

Department of Health and Home Office (2007) *Safe. Sensible. Social. The Next Steps in the National Alcohol Strategy*. London: Department of Health, Home Office, Department for Education and Skills, and Department for Culture, Media and Sport.

Flatley, J., Kershaw, C., Smith, K. *et al.* (2010) *Crime in England and Wales 2009/10*. Home Office Statistical Bulletin 12/10. London: Home Office.

Hobbs, R., Winlow, S., Lister, S., and Hadfield, P. (2003) Bouncers and the social context of violence: Masculinity, class and violence in the night-time economy. In E. Stanko (ed.), *The Meanings of Violence* (pp. 165–183). London: Routledge.

Home Office (2010) *Government reveals tough new powers tackle alcohol crime*. Retrieved July 27, 2010, from http://www.cjp.org.uk/news/archive/government-reveals-tough-new-powers-to-tackle-alcohol-crime-19-01-2010/

Kaner, E., Bland, M., Cassidy, P. *et al.* (2009) Screening and brief interventions for hazardous and harmful alcohol use in primary care: A cluster randomised controlled trial protocol. *BMC Public Health*, **9**, 287.

Matthews, S. and Richardson, A. (2005) *Findings from the 2003 Offending, Crime and Justice Survey: Alcohol-Related Crime and Disorder*. Home Office Research Findings 261. London: Home Office.

McMurran, M. and Cusens, B. (2005) Alcohol and violent and non-violent acquisitive offending. *Addiction Research and Theory*, **13**, 439–443.

Miller, W.R. and Rollnick, S. (2002) *Motivational Interviewing: Preparing People for Change* (2nd edn). New York: Guilford Press.

Raistrick, D., Heather, N., and Godfrey, C. (2006) *Review of the Effectiveness of Treatment for Alcohol Problems*. London: National Treatment Agency for Substance Misuse. Retrieved December 9, 2011, from http://www.nta.nhs.uk/uploads/nta_review_of_the_effectiveness_of_treatment_for_alcohol_problems_fullreport_2006_alcohol2.pdf

Watt, K., Shepherd, J., and Newcombe, R. (2008) Drunk and dangerous: A randomised controlled trial of alcohol brief intervention for violent offenders. *Journal of Experimental Criminology*, **4**, 1–19.

Winlow, S. and Hall, S. (2006) *Violent Night: Urban Leisure and Contemporary Culture*. Oxford: Berg.

Chapter 11

TREATMENTS FOR OFFENDERS IN PRISON AND THE COMMUNITY

MARY MCMURRAN

Institute of Mental Health, University of Nottingham, Nottingham, England

INTRODUCTION

In Britain, the overall cost of alcohol-related crime and antisocial behaviour is estimated at between £8 and £13 billion a year (Community Justice Portal, 2010). Offenders, as a group, are heavy drinkers. Using the Alcohol Use Disorders Identification Test (AUDIT; Babor *et al.*, 1992[1]) in a comprehensive survey of prisoners in England and Wales, 63% of male sentenced prisoners and 39% of female sentenced prisoners reported hazardous or harmful drinking during the year before coming into prison (Singleton, Farrell, and Meltzer, 1999). Hazardous drinking is a pattern of alcohol consumption that increases the risk of adverse consequences for the drinker's physical and mental health or of causing harm to others. Harmful use is when these adverse consequences are actually reported. The prevalence of hazardous or harmful drinking among prisoners compares with 33% and 16% in the general population for men and women respectively (Health and Social Care Information Centre, 2009).

Heavy alcohol consumption compromises both physical and mental health, and, clearly, offenders ought to be offered help to reduce their drinking so as to improve their overall well-being. From a criminal justice perspective, interventions that reduce alcohol-related crime are important. However, alcohol interventions for offenders are seriously underprovided and underdeveloped, at least in England and Wales. In a recent thematic report on alcohol services in prisons, the then Chief Inspector of Prisons commented on the lack of provision as a 'depressing picture' (HM Inspectorate of Prisons, 2010). A similarly fragmented picture of services provided by probation services was identified in a review of services for alcohol-abusing offenders (McSweeney *et al.*, 2009). Both reports comment on the

---

[1]The most recent version is Babor *et al.* (2001).

Alcohol-Related Violence: Prevention and Treatment, First Edition. Edited by Mary McMurran.
© 2013 John Wiley & Sons, Ltd. Published 2013 by John Wiley & Sons, Ltd.

lack of evidence-based alcohol interventions for offenders whose criminal behaviour is related to their use of alcohol.

While alcohol consumption may be associated with a range of offence types, including acquisitive offending (McMurran and Cusens, 2005), it is most strongly associated with violent crime (Flatley *et al.*, 2010; McMurran, 2005). The need to reduce the prevalence of alcohol-related violence in society has been repeatedly expressed over a long period of time (McMurran, 2006). Tackling the problem demands interventions at different levels, including legal restrictions on the production, sale and use of alcohol; making drinking environments safer; problem-oriented policing; punishment of offenders; and treatment of offenders (Babor *et al.*, 2010; Dingwall, 2006; McMurran, 2006). Indeed, taking account of both the population prevalence of hazardous drinking and the strong association with violence, reducing hazardous drinking through public health approaches has the potential to make a substantial impact on violent crime (Coid *et al.*, 2006). Alongside this, it is important to conduct interventions at the individual level. The focus in this chapter is specifically on interventions that aim to reduce alcohol-related violence with convicted offenders, specifically offenders convicted of non-sexual violence and violence occurring outside intimate relationships. (Sexual violence is covered in Chapter 12 and intimate partner violence in Chapter 9.) The first part of the chapter will consist of a review of research. The second part of the chapter will present evidence-based suggestions for the development of effective interventions for offenders who commit alcohol-related violence. Finally, issues relating to service provision will be addressed.

REVIEW OF RESEARCH

In order to review the body of research on treatments for alcohol-related violence efficiently, the approach taken here is a systematic review of systematic reviews. Systematic reviews are syntheses of the research relevant to a particular question. The methodology for conducting a systematic review is rigorous, including precise specification of the research question, explicitly stating the criteria for including and excluding studies and comprehensively searching the research literature. Systematic reviews are helpful in that they collate and interpret what can be a voluminous literature. Importantly, the systematic approach reduces the bias that can be evident in non-systematic reviews, where reviewers may be selective in what they choose to include. It seemed wise to begin a chapter on interventions for offenders who are violent when intoxicated by describing existing systematic reviews on the topic. Additionally, it seemed wise to search for these systematic reviews systematically, that is, to conduct a systematic review of systematic reviews.

The question was 'What systematic reviews exist on the topic of alcohol interventions aimed at reducing violent reoffending with convicted offenders?' The inclusion and exclusion criteria were as follows. The *population* under study included convicted male and female offenders. Reviews focusing on unconvicted arrestees were excluded (e.g., diversion schemes), and reviews on clinical populations that might have included convicted offenders were excluded (e.g., perpetrators of intimate partner violence). Included were reviews focusing on mentally disordered and non-mentally disordered offenders, who might be prisoners, probation service clients or patients. The *interventions* reviewed were alcohol interventions aimed at reducing violent reoffending. Drink-driving interventions were excluded. The *outcomes* included were measures of alcohol use, aggression or violence, and criminal convictions.

The search used combined terms for the following concepts: offender (offend* or prison* or probation*), treatment (treat* or interven*), alcohol (alcohol* or drink*) and review (review or meta-analysis). The following databases were searched: Embase, CINAHL, Medline, National Criminal Justice Reference Service (NCJRS), Cochrane, Campbell Collaboration and Web of Science. The search was conducted for English language publications between 1980 and 2011.

In total, 417 titles were retrieved from the database searches. After deduplication, 330 titles and abstracts remained and were screened for relevance. A total of 308 articles were excluded during the title and abstract screening stage. Of these, 18 were in languages other than English; 269 were not specifically related to alcohol interventions with offenders (e.g., illicit drug treatment programmes, non-offender samples, health outcomes); and 21 focused on drink-driving interventions. The remaining 22 potentially relevant studies were selected for further examination. Of these, 15 were reviews that were not systematic, and 3 were reviews that included alcohol interventions for offenders, but specific data on outcomes for offenders treated for alcohol problems were not presented. Four systematic reviews were identified for inclusion in this chapter. These focused on motivational interviewing (MI), young offenders, women offenders and alcohol-related violence interventions. Each review will be described in turn.

Motivational Interviewing

McMurran (2009) systematically reviewed the evidence of the impact of MI or motivational enhancement interventions with offenders. Of 19 studies identified, 10 addressed the effects of motivational interventions on substance users. Only two of these paid specific attention to alcohol use. Mendel and Hipkins (2002) reported an evaluation of an MI group treatment for alcohol problems with seven men with mild learning disabilities who were detained in a medium secure residential unit. After the three-session intervention, five of the men improved on a drinking Readiness to Change Questionnaire (Rollnick *et al.*, 1992) and on their self-efficacy to change alcohol consumption. No measures of actual alcohol consumption or offending were used. Harper and Hardy (2000) compared the outcomes of 18 MI-trained probation officers with 18 non-MI-trained probation officers working with offenders (85% men) with drug and alcohol problems. After a probation order lasting on average 16.5 months, the offenders whose probation officers were MI-trained showed greater improvement on an attitudes to crime questionnaire (the CRIME-PICS II; Frude, Honess, and Maguire, 1998) and a significant decrease in self-reported drug and alcohol problems. However, alcohol problems were not assessed separately, and, again, no measures of actual alcohol consumption or offending were used.

In non-offender populations, MI shows promise in reducing alcohol use, particularly for non-dependent drinkers (Vasilaki, Hosier, and Cox, 2006). It may be that MI could be effective in reducing drinking and alcohol-related violence in offender populations, and MI has the potential to do this in a cost-effective manner. However, well-designed treatment trials are needed to evaluate outcomes with offenders.

Young Offenders

Tripodi and Bender (2011) identified five studies of four types of treatment that used a control or comparison group to examine the effectiveness of treatment for alcohol use with juvenile justice clients aged between 12 and 19 years. Interventions were conducted in a variety of community settings (e.g., clinics, homes, schools). Four of the studies were randomised controlled trials (RCTs) and all examined changes in alcohol use at follow-up periods ranging from 3 to 18 months.

Two treatments showed no statistically significant effect on alcohol use, although a greater reduction in alcohol use was noted for the treated group. These were assertive continuing care (Godley et al., 2002, 2007) and multidimensional treatment foster care (Smith, Chamberlain, and Eddy, 2010). Assertive continuing care provides relapse prevention support to young people and their carers after they leave residential treatment for substance use. Multidimensional treatment foster care includes family management skills training for carers, skills training and supportive therapy for youth, and school-based behavioural interventions and academic support.

Only two studies showed statistically significant changes in alcohol measures. Friedman, Terras, and Glassman (2002) found a 24-session triple modality social learning intervention superior to basic residential treatment in reducing alcohol use at 6 months' follow-up, with a medium effect size (Hedges' g = .514). Henggeler, Pickrel, and Brondino (1999) found multisystemic therapy superior to treatment as usual in reducing alcohol use at 130-day follow-up, with a small to medium effect size (Hedges' g = .390), but no significant difference was apparent at 10 months' follow-up.

The triple modality social learning intervention is a classroom-based intervention that covers substance abuse prevention, violence prevention and values clarification. Multisystemic therapy is a home-based approach where clinicians work with the young person and his or her family to identify areas for change in a number of systems, including the home, school, peers and the community. The components include family therapy, parent training, individual goal-based work and collaborations with relevant individuals, such as teachers, neighbours and friends.

This review identifies psychosocial interventions for youth as promising. However, the review permits no clear conclusion with regard to what is most effective in reducing alcohol use. One issue is that programmes appear not to focus specifically on alcohol use. Programmes tackling 'substance misuse' tend to cater primarily to illicit drug users and, although problem drinkers may have access to these programmes, issues surrounding alcohol use may receive inadequate attention.

Women Offenders

McMurran *et al.* (2011) reviewed the literature to answer three questions: (1) What works in the treatment of women who commit alcohol-related offences? (2) What are the identifiable risk–needs factors for non-alcohol-dependent women who commit offences involving alcohol misuse? and (3) Are there differences between men's and women's alcohol-related offending and how might these inform the development of treatments specifically for women offenders? Only four intervention studies with comparison groups were identified. Three of these were for drink-driving, and the sole outcome measured in these studies was drink-driving reconviction; none measured alcohol use. The one study that did measure alcohol use was an RCT by Stein *et al.* (2010) aimed at reducing alcohol use and HIV infection. The participants were hazardous-drinking women prisoners who had a recent record of unprotected sex. A brief intervention, which consisted of a single motivational and goal-setting interview in prison and a second follow-up motivational interview in the community after release, was compared with assessment only. A statistically significant difference between the treatment and control groups was evident only on the number of drinking days at the 3-month follow-up [odds ratio (OR) = 1.96], but there was no difference between groups on the number of drinks drunk on drinking days. The effect was stronger for non-dependent women than for dependent women. Those in the treatment group reported significantly fewer problems related to drinking at 3 months. However, all effects had disappeared at 6-month follow-up.

This study indicates that brief interventions for women offenders may be effective in the short term for reducing drinking days although not for reducing the quantity consumed on a drinking day. The study focused on women who were also engaging in sexually risky behaviours, and these may not be representative of all women offenders with alcohol-related problems. Alcohol-related crime was not a focus of this study, either in the intervention or in the outcomes measured.

In their review, McMurran *et al.* (2011) commented that, while the rates of alcohol-related violence are substantially lower for women compared with men, nonetheless, drinking alcohol elevates the risk of violence for both men and women. This accords with laboratory studies of alcohol-related aggression, which suggest that alcohol does increase aggressive responding for both genders but that its effect is stronger for men than for women (Giancola *et al.*, 2009). It is likely that the mechanisms by which alcohol increases the likelihood of violence are common to both genders, for example, 'alcohol myopia' (Giancola, Chapter 3 in this volume; Giancola *et al.*, 2010), but that gender-related issues moderate the likelihood of an aggressive outcome. Moderators might include biological differences (e.g., higher testosterone levels in men), differing social constraints in expressing aggression, and better cognitive and verbal abilities in women (Bennett, Farrington, and Huesmann, 2005).

This suggests that interventions for women offenders whose violent offences are alcohol-related might not differ markedly from programmes offered to men in that similar risk factors need to be addressed. However, there is evidence that women offenders with alcohol problems have more social and psychological problems than men, and so programmes designed for men need to be adapted and extended to suit women offenders. A change in emphasis, with less focus on criminal attitudes and criminal peers and more focus on emotional triggers for drinking, is indicated (McMurran *et al.*, 2011). Women's psychological health needs to be addressed, whether within alcohol–violence treatment programmes or in interventions additional to this. The most pressing needs for women are domestic issues, such as child care and housing; abuse issues, such as trauma from past abuse and current intimate partner violence; psychological issues, such as mood disorders, eating disorders and drug use; and socio-economic factors such as poverty, isolation and unemployment (Adams, Leukefeld, and Peden, 2008; Corston, 2008).

Alcohol-Related Violence Interventions

One perspective on the treatment of intoxicated aggression is the need for 'interventions that not only employ standard treatment techniques (e.g., anger management), but also use knowledge of the effects of alcohol and the process of aggression in treating violent individual' (Graham *et al.*, 1998, p. 670). McMurran (2012a) conducted a systematic review of integrated interventions for non-sexual violence and alcohol use. Only four studies of two different interventions were identified. Of these two interventions, one was not delivered to convicted offenders; it was a brief intervention for violence and alcohol misuse delivered to adolescents in a US hospital emergency department (Cunningham *et al.*, 2009; Walton *et al.*, 2010).

A programme called Control of Violence for Angry Impulsive Drinkers (COVAID) was evaluated in two studies. COVAID is a 10-session structured cognitive-behavioural treatment programme aimed at reducing alcohol-related aggression by addressing alcohol consumption, aggression and the relationship between these in an anger–aggression system. First, a comparison of six male probation service clients with a history of repeated alcohol-related violence who completed COVAID was made with 10 comparable men who were referred but were not treated. Information about reconviction collected from the participants' probation officers 18.5 weeks after referral showed fewer reconvictions in the treated group (1 out of 6) compared with the untreated group (3 out of 10) [OR = .55, 95% confidence interval (CI) = .05–6.63] (McMurran and Cusens, 2003). Second, using a single-case methodology, 10 community clients with alcohol-related aggression problems recruited from social services, probation service, and a community alcohol and drug service were assessed on a number of psychometric measures before and after COVAID treatment (McCulloch and McMurran, 2008). Using Jacobson and Truax's (1991) methods of calculating the clinical significance and reliability of change, five participants showed clinically significant and reliable improvement on the Alcohol-Related Aggression Questionnaire

(ARAQ; McMurran *et al.*, 2006) and one clinically significant but not reliable change; seven showed a clinically significant but not reliable improvement on the Controlled Drinking Self-Efficacy Scale (CDSES; Sitharthan *et al.*, 2003). However, the mean weekly self-reported alcohol consumption for the first 5 weeks of treatment compared to the second 5 weeks did not change. Self-reported aggression was low throughout, and at a mean 29-week follow-up, there were no convictions for the eight participants for whom information was available. Note that not all of the participants in the latter study were offenders.

These reviews indicate that there are few well-designed outcome studies of interventions specifically addressing alcohol problems in convicted offender populations, at least in the four major domains addressed by the reviewers. This is perplexing since the prevalence of alcohol problems among offenders and the extent of alcohol-related crime are of significant societal concern (Flatley *et al.*, 2010; HM Inspectorate of Prisons, 2010). The dearth of research needs to be explained.

Why the Apparent Lack of Research?

One explanation for the lack of evaluations of interventions for alcohol-related violence is that offenders with alcohol problems are treated within programmes addressing substance use more generally. Both therapeutic communities and structured cognitive-behavioural therapies are provided in correctional services for substance users, with positive outcomes on recidivism, at least where people complete treatment (McMurran, 2007; Ministry of Justice, National Offender Management Service, 2010; Palmer *et al.*, 2011). One argument in support of directing offenders with alcohol problems into general substance use treatment programmes is that they often have problems with other drugs too (Parkes *et al.*, 2010), and so providing separate alcohol services may not meet their needs in the round. If this position is to be held, then evaluators of these programmes should, at the very least, record profiles of participants' alcohol and drug use separately. Ideally, alcohol consumption, drug use and crime should be all measured as treatment outcomes. However, the focus in substance use programmes is primarily on illicit drug use, and this may not serve the needs of offenders whose primary problem is related to alcohol use.

Unlike drug use, drinking is not an illegal activity in most countries, and treating offenders with problems relating to alcohol use needs to take this into account. Of course, alcohol is a major causal factor in health problems as well as crime problems. Offenders' health is an important consideration, but nonetheless, it is important to develop and evaluate interventions specifically aimed at reducing alcohol-related crime, specifically violent crime. The remainder of this chapter will focus on what might work with convicted offenders to reduce alcohol-related violence.

TARGETS FOR REDUCING ALCOHOL-RELATED VIOLENCE

The relationship between alcohol and violence can be explained only by attention to a multiplicity of factors. The risk of alcohol-related violence depends on the

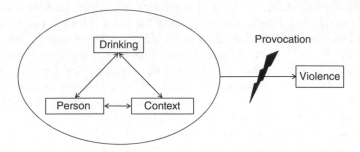

Figure 11.1 Factors explaining the alcohol–violence relationship.

characteristics of the person drinking (e.g., dispositional aggressiveness, expectations of aggressive outcomes after drinking); what sort of drink is being imbibed,
in what quantity and at what speed (i.e., the degree and speed of intoxication);
where the drinking is taking place and with whom; and whether or not that
person encounters a provocation (McMurran, 2012b). This complex interrelation-
ship of factors is represented in Figure 11.1. This diagram helps guide us to consider what the targets of interventions might be. The aim in this section is to
identify the treatment targets that would likely comprise an effective intervention
for alcohol-related violence. These are based on evidence of known risk factors.

Drinking

Interventions to reduce alcohol-related violence may simply aim to reduce the
level and frequency of intoxication. This is predicated on the assumption that
alcohol intoxication has a substantial direct effect on aggressive behaviour. Evidence from a number of different types of study does indeed tell us that alcohol
is a causal risk factor for violence, that is, 'a risk factor that can change, and, when
changed, cause(s) a change in risk for the outcome' (Murray, Farrington, and
Eisner, 2009, p. 4).

Population studies show that, as alcohol consumption increases, so does violence, even after controlling for confounding variables such as economic deprivation (Bye, 2010). The relationship is more evident in countries where heavy
episodic drinking (i.e., binge drinking) is common (Bye and Rossow, 2010; Room
and Rossow, 2001). In birth cohorts, compared with light drinkers, heavy drinkers
are three times more likely to have committed offences of violence, even after
controlling for confounding variables such as social disadvantage, family adversity and conduct problems (Fergusson, Lynskey, and Horwood, 1996). In a case
crossover study of violent offenders, drinking in the previous 24-hour period
increased the risk of committing a violent offence by 13 times (Håggard-Grann
et al., 2006).

There is also supportive evidence from laboratory studies. Exum (2006)
reviewed and integrated findings from seven meta-analyses of experimental

studies of alcohol on aggression. Experimental studies typically set up a competition (e.g., a reaction-time task) between participants, in which electric shocks of varying intensity are delivered to the loser. The experimental subject will both receive and deliver electric shocks, but the unseen competitor is fictional. The level of provocation is the level or duration of the shock administered by the competitor, and the dependent variable is the level or duration of the shock administered by the subject. Alcohol consumption is one variable that can be manipulated. Using a balanced placebo design, the pharmacological versus the expected effects of alcohol can be examined. In balanced placebo design studies, there are usually four conditions: (1) participants are told they will receive alcohol and are given alcohol (alcohol condition); (2) participants are told they will not receive alcohol and are given a non-alcoholic drink (control); (3) participants are told they will receive alcohol and are given a non-alcoholic drink (placebo); and (4) participants are told they will not receive alcohol and are given alcohol (anti-placebo). Overall, there is a significant direct effect of alcohol on aggression, and the effect of alcohol is more pronounced at high doses and when there are no non-aggressive response options. Alcohol mainly increases aggression at low levels of provocation; at high levels of provocation, aggression is likely regardless of alcohol. Most experimental research has been conducted with men, but research with women shows that they do respond aggressively in laboratory tasks, and alcohol does increase their aggression. However, this effect is not as pronounced as it is for men.

The evidence in support of alcohol as a causal risk factor for violence strongly suggests that reducing the frequency and level of intoxication will contribute to reducing violence, especially for men. According to a comprehensive review by the National Institute for Health and Clinical Excellence (2011), the psychosocial interventions that are most successful in reducing alcohol consumption are brief motivational and advice-giving interventions, cognitive-behaviour therapies, couple and family therapies, and social network therapies. Helping people to attend mutual self-help groups (e.g., Alcoholics Anonymous) is also indicated. Intensive structured community-based interventions (e.g., therapeutic communities) are indicated for people with moderate and severe alcohol dependence who have very complex needs, limited social support or who have not responded to community-based interventions.

Pharmacological Treatments

While the focus of this chapter is mainly upon psychosocial treatments, pharmacological treatments have a role to play, and it may be of interest to readers to summarise this area. Alcohol withdrawal syndrome develops after stopping or reducing heavy and prolonged alcohol use and is clearly relevant to newly detained offenders. Benzodiazepines reduce the severity of withdrawal (Amato, Minozzi, and Davoli, 2011). Dependent drinkers may benefit from medications to prevent relapse after detoxification. Medications variously reduce cravings (e.g., acamprosate), attenuate the pleasure response associated with drinking (naltrexone) or create unpleasant effects after drinking (e.g., disulfiram). A systematic review of RCTs found acamprosate to be associated with a lower risk of drinking and with greater duration of abstinence compared with a placebo in alcohol-dependent participants (Rösner *et al.*, 2010). A systematic review and meta-analysis has shown that, compared with a placebo group, 10% more of the alcohol-dependent adults in an outpatient treatment who received naltrexone remained abstinent, and 14% fewer relapsed to drinking over a 12-week period (Streeton and Whelan, 2001). Disulfiram (Antabuse) gives inconsistent results in helping patients to abstain from alcohol, although it may be useful in conjunction with other medications for reducing cravings (Suh *et al.*, 2006). The main problem with pharmacological therapies is non-adherence to the treatment regimen (Chick *et al.*, 2000). Pharmacotherapy is frequently conducted in conjunction with psychosocial therapies, and this may be the best way forward for most clients (Streeton and Whelan, 2001). Research into the effectiveness of pharmacotherapy for offenders who are alcohol dependent is urgently required (Cropsey, Villalobos, and St Clair, 2005).

Treatment Goals

The issue of treatment goals for offenders is an important consideration. Offenders in treatment may have one or more of the following goals: to abstain from alcohol, either for life or for a set period; to reduce alcohol consumption; to reduce the frequency and intensity of alcohol intoxication; and to change drinking habits, for instance, where and with whom drinking occurs. All of these changes to drinking may reduce the likelihood of violent crime. Some offenders may wish to reduce the likelihood of future violence without necessarily changing drinking at all.

While it may be medically advisable for people who are severely dependent on alcohol to abstain from alcohol, it is also true to say that it is possible for some dependent drinkers to adopt low-harm drinking patterns. In a large epidemiological study of adults, of those ever diagnosed as alcohol dependent, 30% showed non-abstinent recovery in the past year (Dawson *et al.*, 2005). However, the presence of a personality disorder decreased the odds of attaining non-abstinent recovery. This is an important observation, given that, in a review of prison surveys worldwide, 65% of men and 25% of women were diagnosable with a personality disorder (Fazel and Danesh, 2002).

The main issue, however, is that the vast majority of offenders are not dependent drinkers (Singleton *et al.*, 1999), yet they are responsible for a great amount of violence and disorder when intoxicated. Sobell and Sobell (2011) argue for the legitimacy of low-risk drinking goals for those who do not consider themselves to be 'alcoholics'. A similar argument for controlled drinking goals has been made for violent offenders, who are mainly young men who do not see themselves as dependent and who may not wish to aim for abstinence (McMurran, 2006).

Of course, while alcohol intoxication is an important causal factor for violence, it is clearly neither necessary nor sufficient for violence to occur. Sober people can be violent, and people can be drunk and not be violent. Indeed, even those who are sometimes violent when intoxicated are not so on every drinking occasion. This indicates that there are other contributory factors that could be targeted in interventions to reduce risk. These include the characteristics of the person who is drinking and the context in which drinking takes place.

The Person

In general, research has shown that people who are aggressive or violent after drinking have high dispositional or trait aggressiveness, that is, a tendency to behave aggressively across a range of situations (Giancola, 2006). What is needed, however, is social-cognitive research that elucidates the underlying mechanisms responsible for the development and maintenance of trait aggressiveness (Tremblay and Dozois, 2009). In this section, two cognitive domains relevant to alcohol-related aggression will be addressed – alcohol outcome expectancies and cognitive impairment.

Alcohol Outcome Expectancies

Alcohol outcome expectancies are the effects one expects to experience as a result of drinking (Goldman, Del Boca, and Darkes, 1999). Put simply, expectancies are a cognitive representations of an 'if–then' relationship: 'If I drink, then I will . . .'. The content of outcome expectancies develops from early in life through observation of how people relate and respond to alcohol and later through direct experience. Expectancies may be positive, such as alcohol enhancing social functioning, or negative, such as alcohol leading to loss of self-control or feelings of depression (Jones, Corbin, and Fromme, 2001; Leigh and Stacy, 2004). Greater endorsement of positive alcohol outcome expectancies is associated with higher levels of alcohol consumption, and greater endorsement of negative alcohol outcome expectancies is associated with lower levels of alcohol consumption (Fromme, Stroot, and Kaplan, 1993; Leigh and Stacy, 2004).

The expectancy 'If I drink, then I will become aggressive' might be expected to promote aggression, yet this has had mixed support. In a student sample, Quigley, Corbett, and Tedeschi (2002) found heavy drinking to be associated with violence in men but not in women, and the belief that alcohol leads to aggression personally was associated with alcohol-related violence. Again with students, Zhang, Welte, and Wieczorek (2002) found that heavy drinkers were more likely to have been drinking prior to acts of violence, and this was particularly true for those who held high aggression-related alcohol expectancies. In an experimental study using a competitive reaction-time task, male students who held high expectancies that alcohol increases aggression were more aggressive than those who expected alcohol to decrease aggression (George, Dermen, and Nochajski, 1989). These studies suggest that the alcohol–aggression outcome expectancy moderates the effect of alcohol on aggression. However, in an experimental study to test the alcohol–aggression outcome expectancy, Giancola (2006) controlled for dispositional aggressiveness. He found that alcohol–aggression expectancies predicted aggression for men but not in women but that this relationship disappeared after controlling for dispositional aggressiveness. Giancola (2006) concluded that intoxicated aggression, at least in men, is mainly the result of the pharmacological properties of alcohol in conjunction with an aggressive disposition.

It may be that expectancies of enhanced social confidence may be more relevant. In a study of young offenders, McMurran (1997) found alcohol-related violence to be associated with expecting changes in social behaviour after drinking. Similarly, in a study of young offenders, alcohol-related aggressiveness was measured by the Alcohol-Related Aggression Questionnaire (ARAQ) (McMurran *et al.*, 2006) in those serving sentences for violent offences that were not alcohol-related and in those serving sentences for violent offences that were alcohol-related. Outcome expectancies were measured by the Drinking Expectancy Questionnaire (DEQ) (Young and Oei, 1996), and expectancies were found to mediate between ARAQ score and group membership, and this was strongest for the increased confidence scale of the DEQ; that is, among violent offenders, those who are more prone to alcohol-related aggression, as measured by the ARAQ, are more likely to be perpetrators of alcohol-related violence if they expect alcohol to increase their social confidence. The increased confidence scale of the DEQ contains items about alcohol enabling the expression of feelings, increasing friendliness and promoting a 'who cares?' attitude. The DEQ increased confidence scale also predicts hazardous drinking; thus, drinking to increase confidence in social situations appears to be an important facet of young men's drinking and one that is associated with violence.

How might drinking to increase social confidence be associated with aggression and violence (see McMurran, 2011b)? One possible link is the effect of anxiety in combination with antisocial traits. Anxiety disorders and conduct disorders co-occur in youth, but the strength of this relationship decreases with age (Marmorstein, 2007). Anxiety appears to moderate the severity of conduct disorders in childhood, but the presence of anxiety and conduct disorder in adolescence is a marker for continued psychopathology (Russo and Beidel, 1994). One possible explanation for this may be that older adolescents find ways of coping with anxiety, and this may be alcohol use, which typically begins regularly in the teenage years. Alcohol may help people cope with anxiety, but at the same time, it may also make anxious people more aggressive.

To clarify the anxiety–conduct disorder relationship, Marmorstein (2007) investigated different types of anxiety by gender and found that the relationship between anxiety and externalising disorder was weaker for girls, and the association for them was strongest with generalised worry, whereas for boys, the strongest association was between conduct disorder and social phobia. Social anxiety may lead to social withdrawal as a means of coping, and it is this that buffers against serious antisocial conduct and aggression in the early years (Zara and Farrington, 2009). Some individuals may remain socially withdrawn into adulthood, but most will not. As we have seen, drinking to increase confidence in social situations appears to be an important facet of young offenders' drinking, and one that is associated with violence. Anxious antisocial individuals may drink in venues where aggression and violence are common, and they may be vigilant for threat cues in these social venues. The mechanism by which alcohol assuages anxiety is the same as that by which it increases the likelihood of aggression. Alcohol narrows the attentional capacity, and so, there is only the capacity for concentrating on whatever are the most salient cues in the immediate context. If anxious antisocial individuals are vigilant for aggression cues, then they are likely to find them. They may even interpret ambiguous cues as hostile (Dodge and Pettit, 2003). Consequently, they are likely to respond to perceived threat with defensive action. Defence in response to threat has been identified as a motive for alcohol-related aggression in young male offenders (McMurran et al., 2010).

A major clinical implication of anxiety as a risk factor for alcohol-related aggression is that it is important for clinicians to recognise that antisocial young people may be anxious. This high anxiety group may be responsive to treatment. Interventions to improve social confidence are obviously indicated. De Brito and Hodgins (2009) suggest the need for interventions to reduce their feelings of being threatened and their hyper-reactivity to stress. Strategies to distract from vigilance for non-specific threat, and to avoid or cope with threat when it does present, are likely to be helpful.

Cognitive Impairment

Alcohol intoxication impairs 'executive cognitive functioning', which is the overall term for the higher-order cognitive abilities. These include attention to external and internal cues, abstracting relevant information, storing these in working memory, reasoning, problem solving, planning and self-regulation. Violent offenders and men with antisocial personality disorder have poorer executive cognitive functioning than non-violent offenders and non-offenders (Giancola, 2000; Hoaken, Shaughnessy, and Pihl, 2003). These groups are the very people who are likely to drink heavily. Furthermore, Howard (2006) suggests that youngsters with early disinhibitory psychopathology (e.g., conduct disorder, attention deficit hyperactivity disorder) who drink heavily during adolescence cause permanent impairment to frontal lobe functioning that, in view of their personality traits, increases the likelihood of antisocial behaviour, including aggression, throughout adulthood.

One way of clarifying how poor executive cognitive functioning is related to aggression is through social problem solving. Social problem solving is the ability to recognise, define and solve problems in the interpersonal domain – skills that require higher-order cognitive abilities. This problem-solving framework adequately captures the processes of executive cognitive functioning (Zelazo et al., 1997). How is social problem solving related to and affected by drinking?

In a laboratory study of executive cognitive functioning and aggression, Hoaken, Shaughnessy, and Pihl (2003) found that participants with low executive cognitive functioning responded more aggressively to provocation than did those with high executive cognitive functioning, and that this effect was more pronounced for men than in women. Compared to those with high executive cognitive functioning, participants with low executive cognitive functioning took significantly *longer* to select the intensity of shock that would be delivered to their putative opponent in a competitive reaction-time task, which Hoaken et al. (2003) interpreted as indicating the importance of a social component: people with low executive cognitive functioning make poor social decisions in that they are aggressive, but they make these decisions slowly. People with low executive cognitive functioning are more aggressive because they are unable to cope with the number of response options, fail to access socially appropriate responses and make default aggressive responses when provoked; that is, they are poor at social problem solving. In studies of the relationships between impulsiveness, social problem solving, aggression and alcohol use, impulsivity and aggression have been identified as related via the mediator of social problem solving in both men and women (McMurran, Blair, and Egan, 2002; Ramadan and McMurran, 2005); that is, impulsivity leads to poor social problem solving, which, in turn, leads to aggression. Improving social problem solving is likely to be one useful aspect of any intervention to reduce alcohol-related aggression and violence (Huband *et al.*, 2007).

The Drinking Context

There is a considerable body of work on risks in the drinking context. This work largely drives risk reduction in and around licensed premises (see Forsyth, Chapter 7 in this volume). However, the individual can also set personal rules for avoiding trouble hot spots and for avoiding drinking with others who often get into trouble after drinking. Phrased positively (i.e., approach goals rather than avoidance goals), these personal rules might include choosing to visit safer bars and clubs, drinking with specific people who do not have a reputation for drunken violence, leaving pubs and clubs before long queues form for buses and taxis, and using suburban rather than urban fast-food outlets.

Provocations

Investigation of the provocations likely to be encountered in drinking contexts is also important. In a study of the triggers for incidents of alcohol-related aggression reported by convicted young male offenders, six themes were identified, each with different implications for treatment (McMurran, Hoyte, and Jinks, 2012c). *Being offended by someone* was the most common trigger in this sample. This is consistent with the view that alcohol-related aggression is understood primarily to be reactive aggression, which is an immediate, angry response to an insult or injury. In a study of barroom violence, Graham and Wells (2003) also observed this type of trigger and defined it as a grievance motive. They pointed out that the aggressor's definition of a grievance is influenced by 'macho' or hypermasculine values, which are the belief that it is necessary to be hard and tough to survive without being taken advantage of by others. Hypermasculine values are associated with drinking, aggression and other forms of antisocial behaviour (Archer, 2010; Beesley and McGuire, 2009; Wells *et al.*, 2011).). In dealing with triggers that fall into the category of *being offended*, interventions need to address hypermasculine values and introduce non-aggressive responses to perceived disrespect.

Opportunistic, acquisitive offending motives were also common in incidents of alcohol-related aggression, namely, *seeing an opportunity for material gain*. The motivation behind alcohol-related acquisitive offending is often to access more alcohol and other drugs (McMurran and Cusens, 2005). Although some young offenders may be dependent on alcohol, acquisitive offending appears to be more to do with wanting to continue drinking and socialising after the money has run out. When an individual with antisocial values is intoxicated, the appearance of a likely target for robbery triggers violence. Interventions for alcohol-related violence should aim to change the antisocial values that permit such behaviour and to counter the notion that alcohol provides an excuse for antisocial behaviour.

Young offenders report *seeing others in need of help* as a trigger for alcohol-related violence. This was commonly helping a friend who got himself into a fight. This has a note of valour to it; however, the actions involved in 'helping others' appear to add to the violence rather than to calm things down. In coping with seeing others in trouble, it may help to identify simple actions that could de-escalate a situation, such as distracting a friend from a perceived threat or removing a friend from a risky situation. In this way, helping others could be of genuine assistance.

Young offenders reported that alcohol-related violence was triggered by the *perception of threat* to themselves by others. This may be explained by the attention-allocation model of alcohol myopia (Giancola *et al.*, 2010; see Chapter 3 in this volume). Alcohol reduces attentional capacity, narrowing the range of cues to which a person can attend. In social situations, especially those where conflict is a possibility, attention focuses on threat cues, thus increasing the likelihood of aggression. Giancola (Chapter 3 in this volume) suggests teaching techniques for distraction from provocative cues and techniques for making inhibitory cues more salient.

Violence

Violence is a learned behaviour that can, as argued above, become a default choice for solving interpersonal problems when intoxicated. Introducing and entrenching alternative behaviours in the individual's repertoire are important. Improving anger and aggression control is one obvious intervention for reducing the likelihood of violence, whether intoxicated or not (Novaco, 2011), as is teaching people prosocial skills for handling interpersonal conflict (Botvin, Griffin, and Nichols, 2006). It is also important to introduce the notion that when emotions run high, the lowest-risk option is to walk away from a risky situation. To do this, the individual needs to be taught to recognise risk through awareness of rising levels of physiological arousal, to use this as a cue to leave the situation, to then reduce arousal through physical and cognitive calming techniques (e.g., deep breathing, calming self-talk) and to decide what to do next. Escape is likely to be considered as an option only if it can be done without losing face, and ways of avoiding feeling humiliated need to be addressed.

Summary

An evidence-based treatment programme aimed at reducing the likelihood of alcohol-related violence at the individual level would address alcohol intoxication, but there would be other targets too. The risk domains shown in Figure 11.1, elaborated upon in the foregoing section, direct us to what might usefully be addressed in treatment programmes. Addressing all aspects of the system would lead to a comprehensive intervention. However, as in alcohol services generally, a needs-matched approach is probably the most cost-efficient.

DEVELOPING SERVICES TO REDUCE ALCOHOL-RELATED VIOLENCE

Services for offenders with problems of alcohol-related violence need to be designed to meet a range of needs. People have different requirements depending upon their level and style of alcohol consumption, their reasons for drinking, the type and seriousness of the alcohol-related problems, their degree of dependence on alcohol and their treatment goals. Additionally, some service users will have a complex set of needs relating to co-occurring mental and physical health problems, relationship problems and social deprivation.

The National Treatment Agency for Substance Misuse (2006) of the Department of Health for England and Wales recommends four tiers of treatment provision, depending on the complexity of the problem. Tier 1 is screening, advice and onward referral, as appropriate. Tier 2 focuses on more in-depth alcohol-specific information, advice and support. Tier 3 includes a comprehensive assessment, care planning and review, evidence-based prescribing interventions, structured evidence-based psychosocial therapies and treatments for coexisting conditions. Tier 4 interventions include provision of residential, specialised alcohol treatments that are care planned and coordinated to ensure continuity of care and aftercare. Tiers 1 and 2 could be provided by specially trained prison and probation service workers. Tier 3 could be provided in prison and probation services by specialist outreach workers. Probation service clients could be referred out to tier 4 services, and tier 4 services could conceivably be provided in-house by prison services. Residential therapeutic communities for drug users are provided, and they have a good track record with drug-using offenders (Mitchell, Wilson, and MacKenzie, 2006), and specialist alcohol communities could be resourced. Within all tiers, interventions specific to alcohol-related violence could be included. For example, the COVAID intervention described earlier has been translated into a single-session version [Single Session-Control of Violence for Angry Impulsive Drinkers (SS-COVAID); McMurran and Delight, 2007], which would fit in tiers 1 and 2, whereas the longer version would fit in tiers 4 and 5.

CONCLUSION

Excessive alcohol use, in general, and alcohol-related violence, in particular, are significant problems in offender populations, yet alcohol interventions are under-developed and underevaluated (HM Inspectorate of Prisons, 2010; McSweeney *et al.*, 2009). There is a need to develop and offer a range of cost-effective approaches for problematic alcohol use generally, both to reduce risk and to enhance well-being. These would include motivational interventions, brief advice, cognitive-behavioural interventions, specialist assessment and management, and residential treatments. There is scope within each of these levels to focus specifically on alcohol-related violence. Tackling alcohol-related violence successfully will obviously reduce injury to victims and offenders and will make society safer. It will also reduce the burden of costs on a range of public services, including police, probation, prison and health. Resourcing the development, implementation and evaluation of interventions to reduce alcohol-related violence would be a sound investment.

REFERENCES

Adams, S., Leukefeld, C.G., and Peden, A.R. (2008) Substance abuse treatment for women offenders: A research review. *Journal of Addictions Nursing*, **19**, 61–75.

Amato, L., Minozzi, S., and Davoli, M. (2011) Efficacy and safety of pharmacological interventions for the treatment of the alcohol withdrawal syndrome. *Cochrane Database of Systematic Reviews*, (6), CD008537. DOI: 10.1002/14651858.CD008537.pub2.

Archer, J. (2010) Derivation and assessment of a hypermasculine values questionnaire. *The British Journal of Social Psychology*, **49**, 525–551.

Babor, T., Caetano, R., Casswell, S. *et al.* (2010) *Alcohol: No Ordinary Commodity. Research and Public Policy*. Oxford: Oxford University Press.

Babor, T.F., Fuente, J.R., Saunders, J.B., and Grant, M. (1992) *AUDIT: The Alcohol Use Disorders Identification Test: Guidelines for Use in Primary Care*. Geneva: World Health Organization.

Babor, T.F., Higgins-Biddle, J.C., Saunders, J.B., and Monteiro, M.G. (2001) *AUDIT: The Alcohol Use Disorders Identification Test: Guidelines for Use in Primary Care* (2nd edn). Geneva: World Health Organization. Retrieved October 12, 2011, from: http://whqlibdoc.who.int/hq/2001/who_msd_msb_01.6a.pdf

Beesley, F. and McGuire, J. (2009) Gender-role identity and hypermasculinity in violent offending. *Psychology, Crime and Law*, **15**, 251–268.

Bennett, S., Farrington, D.P., and Huesmann, L.R. (2005) Explaining gender differences in crime and violence: The importance of social cognitive skills. *Aggression and Violent Behavior*, **10**, 263–288.

Botvin, G.V., Griffin, K.W., and Nichols, T.D. (2006) Preventing youth violence and delinquency through a universal school-based prevention approach. *Prevention Science*, **7**, 403–408.

Bye, E.K. (2010) Alcohol and violence: Use of possible confounders in a time-series analysis. *Addiction*, **102**, 369–376.

Bye, E.K. and Rossow, I. (2010) The impact of drinking pattern on alcohol-related violence among adolescents: An international comparative analysis. *Drug and Alcohol Review*, **29**, 131–137.

Chick, J., Anton, R., Checinski, K. *et al.* (2000) A multicentre, randomized, double-blind, placebo-controlled trial of naltrexone in the treatment of alcohol dependence or abuse. *Alcohol and Alcoholism*, **35**, 587–593.

Coid, J., Yang, M., Roberts, A. *et al.* (2006) Violence and psychiatric morbidity in a national household population. *American Journal of Epidemiology*, **164**, 1199–1208.

Community Justice Portal (2010) *Government reveals tough new powers tackle alcohol crime*. Retrieved July 27, 2010, from http://www.cjp.org.uk/news/archive/government-reveals-tough-new-powers-to-tackle-alcohol-crime-19-01-2010

Corston, J. (2008) *The Corston Report: A Review of Women with Particular Vulnerabilities in the Criminal Justice System*. London: Home Office.

Cropsey, K.L., Villalobos, G.C., and St Clair, C.L. (2005) Pharmacotherapy treatment in substance-dependent correctional populations: A review. *Substance Use and Misuse*, **40**, 1983–1999.

Cunningham, R.M., Walton, M.A., Goldstein, A. *et al.* (2009) Three-month follow-up of brief computerized and therapist interventions for alcohol and violence among teens. *Academic Emergency Medicine*, **16**, 1193–1207.

Dawson, D.A., Grant, B.F., Stinson, F.S. *et al.* (2005) Recovery from DSM-IV alcohol dependence: United States, 2001–2002. *Addiction*, **100**, 281–292.

De Brito, S.A. and Hodgins, S. (2009) Antisocial personality disorder. In M. McMurran and R. Howard (eds), *Personality, Personality Disorder, and Violence* (pp. 133–153). Chichester: Wiley-Blackwell.

Dingwall, G. (2006) *Alcohol and Crime*. Cullompton, Devon: Willan

Dodge, K.A. and Pettit, G.S. (2003). A biopsychosocial model of the development of chronic conduct problems in adolescence. *Developmental Psychology*, **39**, 349–371.

Exum, M.L. (2006) Alcohol and aggression: An integration of findings from experimental studies. *Journal of Criminal Justice*, **34**, 131–145.

Fazel, S. and Danesh, J. (2002) Serious mental disorder in 23 000 prisoners: A systematic review of 62 surveys. *Lancet*, **359**, 545–550.

Fergusson, D.M., Lynskey, M.T., and Horwood, L.J. (1996) Alcohol misuse and juvenile offending in adolescence. *Addiction*, **91**, 483–494.

Flatley, J., Kershaw, C., Smith, K. *et al.* (2010) *Crime in England and Wales 2009/10*. Home Office Statistical Bulletin 12/10. London: Home Office.

Friedman, A.S., Terras, A., and Glassman, K. (2002) Multimodel substance use intervention program for male delinquents. *Journal of Child and Adolescent Substance Abuse*, **11**, 43–64.

Fromme, K., Stroot, E., and Kaplan, D. (1993) Comprehensive effects of alcohol: Development and psychometric assessment of a new expectancy questionnaire. *Psychological Assessment*, **5**, 19–26.

Frude, N., Honess, T., and Maguire, M. (1998) *CRIME-PICS II Manual*. Cardiff: Michael and Associates.

George, W.H., Dermen, K.H., and Nochajski, T.H. (1989) Expectancy set, self-reported expectancies and predispositional traits: Predicting interest in violence and erotica. *Journal of Studies on Alcohol*, **50**, 541–551.

Giancola, P.R. (2000) Executive functioning: A conceptual framework for alcohol-related aggression. *Experimental and Clinical Psychopharmacology*, **8**, 576–597.

Giancola, P.R. (2006) Influence of subjective intoxication, breath alcohol concentration, and expectancies on the alcohol-aggression relationship. *Alcoholism: Clinical and Experimental Research*, **30**, 844–850.

Giancola, P.R., Josephs, R.A., Parrott, D.J., and Duke, A.A. (2010) Alcohol myopia revisited: Clarifying aggression and other acts of disinhibition through a distorted lens. *Perspectives on Psychological Science*, **5**, 265–278.

Giancola, P.R., Levinson, C.A., Corman, M.D. *et al.* (2009) Men and women, alcohol and aggression. *Experimental and Clinical Psychopharmacology*, **17**, 154–164.

Godley, M.D., Godley, S.H., Dennis, M.L. *et al.* (2002) Preliminary outcomes form the assertive continuing care experiment for adolescents discharged from residential treatment. *Journal of Substance Abuse Treatment*, **23**, 21–32.

Godley, M.D., Godley, S.H., Dennis, M.L. *et al.* (2007) The effect of assertive continuing care on continuing care linkage, adherence, and abstinence following residential treatment for adolescents with substance use disorders. *Addiction*, **102**, 81–93.

Goldman, M.S., Del Boca, F.K., and Darkes, J. (1999) Alcohol expectancy theory: The application of cognitive neuroscience. In K.E. Leonard and H.T. Blane (eds), *Psychological Theories of Drinking and Alcoholism* (2nd edn). (pp. 203–246). New York: Guilford.

Graham, K., Leonard, K.E., Room, R. *et al.* (1998) Current directions in research on understanding and preventing intoxicated aggression. *Addiction*, **93**, 659–676.

Graham, K. and Wells, S. (2003) Somebody's gonna get their head kicked in tonight! *The British Journal of Criminology*, **43**, 546–566.

Hággard-Grann,U., Hallqvist, J., Lángström, N., and Möller, J. (2006) The role of alcohol and drugs in triggering criminal violence: A case cross-over study. *Addiction*, **101**, 100–108.

Harper, R. and Hardy, S. (2000) An evaluation of motivational interviewing as a method of intervention with clients in a probation setting. *British Journal of Social Work*, **30**, 393–400.

Health and Social Care Information Centre (2009) *Statistics on Alcohol: England, 2009*. Retrieved September 30, 2011, from http://www.ic.nhs.uk/webfiles/publications/alcoholeng2009/Final%20Format%20draft%202009%20v7.pdf

Henggeler, S.W., Pickrel, S.G., and Brondino, M.J. (1999) Multisystemic treatment of substance-abusing and dependent delinquents: Outcomes, treatment fidelity, and transportability. *Mental Health Services Research*, **1**, 171–184.

HM Inspectorate of Prisons (2010) *Alcohol Services in Prisons: An Unmet Need*. London: HM Inspectorate of Prisons.

Hoaken, P.N.S., Shaughnessy, V.K., and Pihl, R.O. (2003) Executive cognitive function and aggression: Is it an issue of impulsivity? *Aggressive Behavior*, **29**, 15–30.

Howard, R. (2006) How is personality disorder linked to dangerousness? A putative role for early-onset alcohol abuse. *Medical Hypotheses*, **67**, 702–708.

Huband, N., McMurran, M., Evans, C., and Duggan, C. (2007) Social problem solving plus psychoeducation for adults with personality disorder: A pragmatic randomised controlled trial. *The British Journal of Psychiatry*, **190**, 307–313.

Jacobson, N.S. and Truax, P. (1991) Clinical significance: A statistical approach to defining meaningful change in psychotherapy research. *Journal of Consulting and Clinical Psychology*, **59**, 12–19.

Jones, B.T., Corbin, W., and Fromme, K. (2001) A review of expectancy theory and alcohol consumption. *Addiction*, **96**, 57–72.

Leigh, B.C. and Stacy, A.W. (2004) Alcohol expectancies and drinking in different age groups. *Addiction*, **99**, 215–227.

Marmorstein, N.R. (2007) Relationships between anxiety and externalizing disorders in youth: The influences of age and gender. *Journal of Anxiety Disorders*, **21**, 420–432.

McCulloch, A. and McMurran, M. (2008) Evaluation of a treatment programme for alcohol-related violence. *Criminal Behaviour and Mental Health*, **18**, 224–231.

McMurran, M. (1997) Outcome expectancies: An important link between substance use and crime? S. Redondo, V. Garrido, J. Pérez, and R. Barbaret (eds), *Advances in Psychology and Law* (pp. 312–321). Berlin: De Gruyter.

McMurran, M. (2005) Drinking, violence, and prisoners' health. *International Journal of Prisoner Health*, **1**, 25–29.

McMurran, M. (2006) Controlled drinking goals for offenders. *Addiction Research and Theory*, **14**, 59–65.

McMurran, M. (2007) What works in substance misuse treatments for offenders? *Criminal Behaviour and Mental Health*, **17**, 225–233.

McMurran, M. (2009) Motivational interviewing with offenders: A systematic review. *Legal and Criminological Psychology*, **14**, 83–100.

McMurran, M. (2011) Anxiety, alcohol intoxication, and aggression. *Legal and Criminological Psychology*, **16**, 357–351.

McMurran, M. (2012a) Individual-level interventions for alcohol-related violence: A Rapid Evidence Assessment (REA). *Criminal Behaviour and Mental Health*, **22**, 14–28.

McMurran, M. (2012b) Youth, alcohol, and aggression. In F. Lösel, A. Bottoms, and D.P. Farrington (eds), *Young Adult Offenders: Lost in Transition?* London: Taylor and Francis.

McMurran, M., Blair, M., and Egan, V. (2002) An investigation of the correlations between aggression, impulsiveness, social problem-solving, and alcohol use. *Aggressive Behavior*, **28**, 439–445.

McMurran, M. and Cusens, B. (2003) Controlling alcohol-related violence: A treatment programme. *Criminal Behaviour and Mental Health*, **13**, 59–76.

McMurran, M. and Cusens, B. (2005) Alcohol and violent and non-violent acquisitive offending. *Addiction Research and Theory*, **13**, 439–443.

McMurran, M. and Delight, S. (2007) SS-. COVAID: Single Session-Control of Violence for Angry Impulsive Drinkers. Unpublished treatment manual. Macclesfield, Cheshire: Delight Training Services, Ltd.

McMurran, M., Egan, V., Cusens, B. et al. (2006) The alcohol-related aggression questionnaire. Addiction Research and Theory, 14, 323–343.

McMurran, M., Hoyte, H., and Jinks, M. (2012c) Triggers for alcohol-related violence in young male offenders. Legal and Criminological Psychology. DOI:10.1111/j.2044-8333. 2011.02010.x.

McMurran, M., Jinks, M., Howells, K., and Howard, R.C. (2010) Alcohol-related violence defined by ultimate goals: A qualitative analysis of the features of three different types of violence by intoxicated young male offenders. Aggressive Behavior, 36, 67–79.

McMurran, M., Riemsma, R., Manning, N. et al. (2011) Interventions for alcohol-related offending by women: A systematic review. Clinical Psychology Review, 31, 909–922.

McSweeney, T., Webster, R., Turnbull, P.J., and Duffy, M. (2009) Evidence-Based Practice? The National Probation Service's Work with Alcohol-Misusing Offenders. Ministry of Justice Research Series 13/09. London: Ministry of Justice.

Mendel, E. and Hipkins, J. (2002) Motivating learning disabled offenders with alcohol-related problems: A pilot study. British Journal of Learning Disabilities, 30, 153–158.

Ministry of Justice, National Offender Management Service (2010) What Works with Offenders Who Misusedrugs? London: Ministry of Justice.

Mitchell, O., Wilson, D.B., and MacKenzie, D.L. (2006) The effectiveness of incarceration-based drug treatment on criminal behavior. Campbell Systematic Reviews, 2006, 11. DOI: 10.4073/csr.2006.11.

Murray, J., Farrington, D.P., and Eisner, M.P. (2009) Drawing conclusions about causes from systematic reviews of risk factors: The Cambridge Quality Checklists. Journal of Experimental Criminology, 5, 1–23.

National Institute for Health and Clinical Excellence (2011) Alcohol-Use Disorders: The NICE Guideline on Diagnosis, Assessment and Management of Harmful Drinking and Alcohol Dependence. London: National Collaborating Centre for Mental Health. Retrieved November 18, 2011, from http://www.nice.org.uk/nicemedia/live/13337/53190/53190. pdf and http://www.nice.org.uk/nicemedia/live/13337/53194/53194.pdf

National Treatment Agency for Substance Misuse (2006) Models of Care for Alcohol Misusers (MoCAM). London: Department of Health/National Treatment Agency for Substance Misuse.

Novaco, R.W. (2011) Anger dysregulation: Driver of violent offending. Journal of Forensic Psychiatry and Psychology, 22, 650–668.

Palmer, E., Hatcher, R., McGuire, J. et al. (2011) Evaluation of the Addressing Substance-Related Offending (ASRO) program for substance-using offenders in the community: A reconviction analysis. Substance Use and Misuse, 46, 1072–1080.

Parkes, T., MacAskill, S., Brooks, O. et al. (2010) Prison health needs assessment for alcohol problems. Retrieved November 23, 2010, from http://www.ohrn.nhs.uk/resource/policy/PrisonHealthNeedsAssessmentAlcohol.pdf

Quigley, B.M., Corbett, A.B., and Tedeschi, J.T. (2002) Desired image of power, alcohol expectancies, and alcohol-related aggression. Psychology of Addictive Behaviors, 16, 318–324.

Ramadan, R. and McMurran, M. (2005) Alcohol and aggression: Gender differences in their relationships with impulsiveness, sensation seeking and social problem solving. Journal of Substance Use, 10, 215–224.

Rollnick, S., Heather, N., Gold, R., and Hall, W. (1992) Development of a short "readiness to change" questionnaire for use in brief, opportunistic, interventions among excessive drinkers. British Journal of Addiction, 87, 743–754.

Room, R. and Rossow, I. (2001) The share of violence attributable to drinking. Journal of Substance Use, 6, 218–228.

Rösner, S., Hackl-Herrwerth, A., Leucht, S. et al. (2010) Acamprosate for alcohol dependence. Cochrane Database of Systematic Reviews, (9): CD004332. DOI: 10.1002/14651858. CD004332.pub2.

Russo, M.F. and Beidel, D.C. (1994) Comorbidity of childhood anxiety and externalising disorders: Prevalence, associated characteristics, and validation issues. *Clinical Psychology Review*, **14**, 199–221.

Singleton, N., Farrell, M., and Meltzer, H. (1999) *Substance Misuse Among Prisoners in England and Wales*. London: Office for National Statistics.

Sitharthan, T., Job, R.F.S., Kavanagh, D.J. *et al.* (2003) Development of a controlled drinking self-efficacy scale and appraising its relation to alcohol dependence. *Journal of Clinical Psychology*, **59**, 351–362.

Smith, D.K., Chamberlain, P., and Eddy, J.M. (2010) Preliminary support for multidimensional treatment foster care in reducing substance use in delinquent boys. *Journal of Child and Adolescent Substance Abuse*, **19**, 343–358.

Sobell, M.B. and Sobell, L.C. (2011) Editorial: It is time for low-risk drinking goals to come out of the closet. *Addiction*, **106**, 1715–1717.

Stein, M.D., Caviness, C.M., Anderson, B.J. *et al.* (2010) A brief alcohol intervention for hazardously drinking incarcerated women. *Addiction*, **105**, 466–475.

Streeton, C. and Whelan, G. (2001) Naltrexone, a relapse prevention maintenance treatment of alcohol dependence: A meta-analysis of randomized clinical trials. *Alcohol and Alcoholism (Oxford, Oxfordshire)*, **36**, 544–552.

Suh, J.J., Pettinati, H.M., Kampman, K.M., and O'Brien, C.P. (2006) The status of disulfiram: A half of a century later. *Journal of Clinical Psychopharmacology*, **26**, 290–302.

Tremblay, P.F. and Dozois, D.J.A. (2009) Another perspective on trait aggressiveness: Overlap with early maladaptive schemas. *Personality and Individual Differences*, **46**, 569–574.

Tripodi, S.J. and Bender, K. (2011) Substance abuse treatment for juvenile offenders: A review of quasi-experimental and experimental research. *Journal of Criminal Justice*, **39**, 246–252.

Vasilaki, E.I., Hosier, S.G., and Cox, W.M. (2006) The efficacy of motivational interviewing as a brief intervention for excessive drinking: A meta-analytic review. *Alcohol and Alcoholism (Oxford, Oxfordshire)*, **41**, 328–335.

Walton, M.A., Chermack, S.T., Shope, J.T. *et al.* (2010) Effects of a brief intervention for reducing violence and alcohol misuse among adolescents: A randomized controlled trial. *Journal of the American Medical Association*, **304**, 527–535.

Wells, S., Graham, K., Tremblay, P.F., and Magyarody, N. (2011) Not just the booze talking: Trait aggression and hypermasculinity distinguish perpetrators from victims of male barroom aggression. *Alcoholism: Clinical and Experimental Research*, **35**, 613–620.

Young, R.M.C.D. and Oei, T.P.S. (1996) *Drinking Expectancy Profile: Test Manual*. Brisbane: The University of Queensland.

Zara, G. and Farrington, D.P. (2009) Childhood and adolescent predictors of late onset criminal careers. *Journal of Youth and Adolescence*, **38**, 287–300.

Zelazo, P.D., Carter, A., Reznick, J.S., and Frye, D. (1997) Early development of executive function: A problem-solving framework. *Review of General Psychology*, **1**, 198–226.

Zhang, L., Welte, J.W., and Wieczorek, W.W. (2002) The role of aggression-related alcohol expectancies in explaining the link between alcohol and violent behavior. *Substance Use and Misuse*, **37**, 457–471.

Chapter 12

TREATMENT FOR ALCOHOL-RELATED SEXUAL VIOLENCE[1]

RUTH E. MANN

National Offender Management Service, London, England

MARK FARMER

Staffordshire and West Midlands Probation Trust, Birmingham, England

INTRODUCTION

Most clinicians working with sexual offenders are well aware that alcohol is a prominent feature in many offences. Drawing on 1997 US prisoner survey data, for instance, Felson and Staff (2010) reported that alcohol is far more likely to have been implicated in homicide and assaults, including sexual assaults, than in offences such as robbery, burglary, drugs or theft crimes. Given this, it is rather surprising that most texts on the treatment of sexual offending pay little or no attention to the role of alcohol. Those that do tend to view alcohol as some sort of distraction from the 'real' reasons behind sexual offending. For instance, in an early influential text on the treatment of sexual offenders (Salter, (1988)), the only mention of alcohol is in a section headed 'Denial of Responsibility for Behaviors'. In this section, Salter discussed 'offenders [who] admit the behaviour was inappropriate but do not take full responsibility. This is sometimes blatant, as when an offender attributes the abusive behavior to alcohol and insists that he needs no treatment at all (as he does not plan to drink again) or at the most needs treatment for alcoholism' (p. 107). Finkelhor (1984), in an early descriptive model of the process of sexual offending, referred to the use of alcohol as an example of an action an offender can take to 'overcome internal inhibitions'. This implied that the use of alcohol is a conscious and rationally chosen strategy to enable offending

[1]Author Note: The views expressed in this chapter are those of the authors and not of National Offender Management Service (NOMS) or the Staffordshire and West Midlands Probation Trust.

and is therefore not a risk factor for sexual offending. This view mirrors a common belief in the domestic violence field which has led to the deliberate omission of alcohol-focused intervention with domestic violence offenders, despite strong evidence that alcohol consumption is a risk factor for this type of offending (see McMurran and Gilchrist, 2007). Even some of the more modern textbooks on the treatment of sexual offending (e.g., Marshall, Anderson, and Fernandez, 1999; Marshall *et al.*, 2006) make no mention of how to approach alcohol-related offending, and neither is there an index mention of alcohol in Ward, Polaschek, and Beech's (2006) collection on theories of sexual offending. It therefore appears that advice to clinicians on the treatment of alcohol-related sexual offending is markedly absent from most of the main sources of guidance. It is not clear whether perpetrators of sexual offending who also have histories of alcohol abuse or who were intoxicated when they offended require adjunctive treatment for drinking, or whether a recognition of the role of alcohol should be built into sex offender treatment programmes or whether it should be ignored altogether.

In this chapter, we will attempt to rectify the absence of guidance to clinicians by re-exploring the role that alcohol plays in some sexual offending. First, we will examine the extent to which sexual offending appears linked to alcohol use, in terms of both the problem drinking histories of known offenders and the extent to which offenders are intoxicated before offending. Second, we will summarise what is known about the effects of alcohol on factors relevant to sexual offending. Third, drawing on the preceding discussions, we will briefly examine existing models of the role of alcohol in sexual offending and propose some ways in which alcohol and sexual offending could be related. Lastly, with the intent to develop the effectiveness of offender rehabilitation, we will propose some ways in which the use of alcohol within sexual violence could be addressed within interventions for sexual offending.

If or when alcohol is implicated in sexual offending, a key question is whether it should be considered to be part of the cause of the offence. There have been similar debates in the domestic violence field (McMurran and Gilchrist, 2007). To start with, it may be helpful to briefly discuss the meaning of the term 'causal risk factor'. This term (see, e.g., Mann, Hanson, and Thornton, 2010) has been used to refer to a factor that (1) if present, raises the risk for recidivism, and (2) could plausibly be a cause of offending (e.g., it could be plausibly integrated into a theoretical account of how the offending occurred). Using these criteria, Mann *et al.*, in their account of the meta-analytic evidence about risk factors for sexual recidivism, identified 'lifestyle impulsiveness' as a strongly supported causal risk factor for sexual recidivism, with substance abuse history named as one of the indicators of this risk factor. By itself, substance abuse history has a small but significant relationship with sexual recidivism (Hanson and Morton-Bourgon, 2005). Mann *et al.* concluded that further theoretical work is needed to establish a deeper conceptualisation of the role of each apparent risk factor for sexual recidivism, and acknowledged that their categorisation approach, where some factors are considered to be indicators of others rather than risk factors in their own right, needs further examination. Hence, in this chapter, we will also try to further the theoretical understanding of alcohol use, both chronic and acute, in relation to sexual offending.

THE EXTENT OF ALCOHOL USE IN SEXUAL OFFENDERS

Studies of alcohol use in relation to sexual offending have mainly examined either the extent of chronic or historical alcohol abuse in those convicted of sexual offending, or the extent to which drinking is implicated in sexual offences (i.e., the proportion and type of sexual offences where drinking occurred in the lead-up to the offence). In both cases, most of the research has focused on those who offended against adults rather than on child molesters. This bias may reflect a genuine difference in the two populations, with drinking being less implicated in offences against children. The possibility of such a difference will be explored in the research summary below.

Alcohol Abuse Histories amongst Sexual Offenders

Research has generally revealed significant histories of alcohol abuse amongst convicted sexual offenders. It seems that sexual offenders often have serious problems with alcohol, and some studies have shown that they are more likely to have such problems than other offenders. However, there are difficulties in drawing robust conclusions across studies because of variations in the definition and measurement of historic alcohol abuse and also of sexual offending. Below, we will briefly consider findings from large-scale surveys of offenders, as well as some smaller-scale exploratory studies.

Surveys of Offenders

Peugh and Belenko (2001) analysed data from a large-scale 1991 US survey of inmates in state correctional facilities. They compared the 1,273 sexual offenders included in the survey to a group of 4,933 inmates who were incarcerated for a non-sexual violent crime. The sex offender sample included rapists, statutory rapists (i.e., where one of the parties is below the age of consent), sexual assaulters and men who had committed a lewd act with a child. Their sample therefore contained a mixture of men with adult victims and child victims, but the relative proportions within the sample were not reported. It was found that 30% of the sexual offenders had a history of treatment for alcohol abuse, comparable to 29% of non-sexual violent offenders. Peugh and Belenko also reported that offenders who had abused alcohol were significantly less likely than non-substance-misusing sex offenders to have victimised a minor or a child, suggesting that problem drinking is more of an issue for rapists than child molesters.

Långström, Sjöstedt, and Grann (2004) collected data on all adult male sex offenders released from prison between 1993 and 1997 in Sweden, a total nationwide sample of 1,215. They found that alcohol use disorder was the most frequent disorder for all sex offenders, but particularly so for rapists. Overall, 7.8% of all sex offenders in the study, 9.3% of the rapists and 3.4% of the child molesters were determined to have an alcohol problem. However, in this study, alcohol abuse was determined by hospital admission only. This raises a significant problem with the study in that it probably underestimated alcohol abuse because most people who abuse alcohol are not admitted to hospital. This may explain why the overall rate of alcohol abuse is lower than that found in other studies.

Singleton, Farrell, and Meltzer (1999) analysed data on substance misuse amongst prisoners in England and Wales using Office of National Statistics data gathered in 1997. They found that overall, 63% of male sentenced prisoners had an Alcohol Use Disorders Identification Test (AUDIT; Babor *et al.*, 2001) score of 8 or above, meaning that their drinking was hazardous or harmful. However, sentenced men who reported hazardous drinking histories were less likely to be sexual offenders. Six per cent of those who scored 8 or above on AUDIT were sex offenders, compared to 12% of those with an AUDIT score below 8.

Lastly, Debiden (2009) reported on substance misuse in a very large sample of offenders in England and Wales (total $N = 325,863$). The data were taken from the Offender Assessment System (OASys), a structured process designed to assess criminogenic need consistently across all those serving prison or community sentences. Of 16,055 sex offenders in the sample, 26.5% were classed as 'having need' in the alcohol section of OASys, compared against 59.5% of violent offenders, 36.7% of burglars, 43.1% of robbery offenders, 67% of criminal damage offenders and 17.7% of drug offenders. In OASys, 'need' in the alcohol section is defined as a need being identified in relation to any of the following items: Is current use a problem? Has there been binge drinking or excessive use in the last 6 months? Frequency and level of alcohol misuse in the past? Violent behaviour related to alcohol use at any time? A particular strength of this report is the large sample size and the fact that the sample included offenders sentenced to both custodial and community sentences. The findings are therefore likely to be representative of convicted sexual offenders in general rather than those who are at higher risk or are more serious in their offending. However, one problem with this research is that need is assessed by professionals working with offenders rather than researchers. Consequently, if professionals do not view alcohol abuse as a risk marker for sexual offending, then they might quite possibly have underestimated its significance in the offender assessment. It is possible therefore that despite the large sample size, the extent of alcohol abuse amongst sexual offenders is higher than indicated here.

According to the survey data, overall, it seems that alcohol abuse features in the histories of around one-quarter to one-third of sexual offenders. Where data were broken down by sex offender subtype (broadly, rapists vs. child molesters), it appears that a history of problem drinking is much more significant for rapists and is found only rarely with child molesters. The comparisons with non-sexual offenders vary, with US data indicating similar levels of problem drinking in sexual and non-sexual offenders, and the OASys study in England and Wales indicating far greater need amongst non-sexual offenders. However, the OASys finding may be misleading because, in this report, all sex offenders were classed together rather than being subdivided into rapists and child molesters. Whether or not sexual offenders have less serious alcohol histories than non-sex offenders, it is clear from these large-scale surveys that, overall, levels of problem drinking are higher in rapists than in the general population.

Exploratory Studies

Langevin and Lang (1990) reviewed studies published between 1965 and 1988 and reported that the percentage of sexual offenders reporting alcohol use ranged from 0% to 52% – the width of this range being accounted for by differing definitions of alcohol use and alcoholism. In their own study of 461 male sex offenders, the majority of whom were child molesters, using the Michigan Alcohol Screening Test (MAST; Selzer, 1971), Langevin and Lang found that over 85% of all sexual abusers reported alcohol use 'at some time in their lives'. Ten per cent reported using alcohol daily at the time of assessment, and 35% reported that they drunk alcohol daily at some point in their lives. In comparison to the 5% of all Canadians known to be alcoholics, 38% of paedophiles met the most stringent criterion for alcoholism (a score of 9 or over on the MAST), along with 23% of those who had sexually assaulted adult female strangers, 38% of incest offenders and 25% of exhibitionists. In contrast to most other studies, this study therefore indicated that sexual offenders with child victims, both intra- and extrafamilial, had higher rates of problem drinking than sexual offenders with adult victims. No information is given about how the sample was obtained, so it is hard to conjecture why this study yielded such a different outcome from others.

Abracen, Looman, and Anderson (2000) compared the frequency of alcohol abuse amongst sexual offenders with that of non-sexual violent offenders, again measuring problem drinking by administering the MAST. The study compared 72 rapists with 34 child molesters and 24 non-sexual violent offenders. Sexual offenders reported higher levels of alcohol abuse than the non-sexually violent offenders, with 45.8% of rapists and 41.2% of child molesters reporting a severe level of alcohol abuse, and 69.4% of rapists and 55.9% of child molesters reporting either moderate or severe MAST scores. Because the levels of alcohol abuse were significantly lower amongst the non-sexually violent group (4.2% severe, 41.7% moderate or severe), the authors argued that alcohol abuse may not be related to aggression in general but may be specifically related to sexual offending. Looman et al. (2004) built on Abracen et al.'s study by comparing a slightly larger sample of 95 offenders – 41 of whom were rapists, 25 child molesters and 29 violent offenders – on alcohol abuse histories, again measured by the MAST. The results supported Abracen et al.'s earlier findings in that the combined sexual offender group (i.e., rapists and child molesters) had significantly higher MAST scores than the violent offenders. Again, the authors concluded that alcohol abuse seemed to be related to sexual offending. However, in both studies, the samples were small and were obtained from a particular correctional facility that is mandated to provide treatment to high-risk sexual offenders, so the sample presumably represents a rather skewed and high-need subsample of sexual offenders.

Overall, the studies reviewed above could be taken to suggest that perpetrators of sexual abuse are more likely to have alcohol abuse histories than non-sexually violent offenders and certainly than the general non-criminal population. In this respect, the findings of these studies support the findings of the large-scale prisoner/offender surveys. But there are some dangers with this conclusion. The sexual offenders participating in these particular studies were often in some way atypical, such as being high-risk incarcerated offenders who had records of persistent antisocial behaviour where the sexual offences formed part of a considerable and more varied offending history. These populations might be different from low- or medium-risk sex offenders on community sentences, who in general only offend once and do not have other criminality markers. Furthermore, studies have used different methodologies to measure problem drinking. For example, the survey reported by Peugh and Belenko analysed self-report information about previous treatment for alcohol abuse; the OASys data in England and Wales were based on clinical ratings by probation officers; and Abracen *et al.* measured alcohol abuse via self-report using the MAST. Some critics have raised the concern in relation to self-report methods that sexual offenders might exaggerate their alcohol abuse histories in order to justify their behaviour (Finney, 2004). However, Looman *et al.* (2004) found that file information corroborated self-reported drinking levels amongst their sample of sexual offenders, and so offenders' self-reports of drinking may be valid, at least when they are asked for research purposes (McMurran, Hollin, and Bowen, 1990).

Considering these limitations, we believe that it is acceptable to conclude that alcohol abuse histories are found disproportionately in high-risk imprisoned men who have sexually assaulted adults. However, this does not enable a conclusion that such histories are part of the explanation for sexual offending. For instance, it is possible, but quite untested, that sexual offending causes alcohol abuse rather than the other way around or that both may be related to a third, unknown variable. Examining alcohol use at the time of offending may enable a greater understanding of the role of alcohol in sexual assault.

The Extent of Alcohol Consumption during Offence Events

A second line of investigation in relation to alcohol and sexual offending has been to examine the extent to which offenders are intoxicated at the time of their offences. This may be more important than studying chronic drinking problems because acute effects have been asserted to have a greater impact on aggressive behaviour generally (Giancola *et al.*, 2010). For example, Grubin and Gunn (1991) studied 142 men imprisoned for rape and found that 58% had been drinking in the 6 hours before the rape. This statistic matches the 57% of sex offenders who had been drinking before their offence found in an earlier and much larger US study, again with imprisoned rapists [Bureau of Justice Statistics (BJS) 1983, reported in Finney, 2004]. In a subsequent BJS (1991) survey reported by Peugh and Belenko (2001), 23% of sexual offenders were classified as 'under the influence of alcohol at the time of the offence' and a further 15% as under the influence of alcohol and drugs, meaning that in total, 38% of offenders were thought to have been drinking at the time of the offence. It is not possible to discern from the reports whether the two BJS surveys used identical definitions to classify participants as drinking/under the influence. However, it seems likely that the Peugh and Belenko study contained both rapists and child molesters, in comparison to the earlier BJS study from which Finney (2004) only reported figures for rapists. If rapists are more likely to be intoxicated whilst offending than child molesters, this may account for the difference in intoxication rates found in the different studies. Such a conclusion is supported by a small-scale Icelandic study, where 75% of rapists but only 13% of child molesters were found to have been intoxicated at the time of offending (Gudjonsson and Sigurdsson, 2000), indicating an important difference in the role alcohol might play in these different types of sexual offending.

Of particular relevance to our aims in this chapter are research findings that tell us about the types of sexual offences in which alcohol is most frequently implicated. Finney (2004) summarised these findings succinctly in relation to sexual assaults against adults:

- Alcohol-related sexual offences are most likely to occur between an offender and a victim who knew each other but not well (e.g., Abbey et al., 2001).
- Alcohol was consumed by the offender (and the victim) most frequently in date-situation rapes and least frequently in rapes involving intimates (Koss, Dinero, and Seibel, 1988)
- Alcohol-related sexual violence is most likely to occur in bars or at parties rather than in a home (Abbey et al., 2001)
- The majority of alcohol-related sexual violence incidents involve drinking by both the offender and the victim (Abbey et al., 2001) or by the offender alone, but rarely by the victim alone (Brecklin and Ullman, 2010).

It seems that alcohol features in certain types of sexual offending in particular: offences against adults that take place in social situations where alcohol is an established part of the situation, outside the home, where both perpetrator and victim have been drinking, and where there may have been some indication of sexual interest or attraction (but not sexual intention) already expressed. Intoxication appears to be most clearly implicated in acquaintance or date rapes rather than sexual aggression against strangers or intimates or children.

ALCOHOL AND ITS EFFECT ON OTHER SEXUAL RECIDIVISM RISK FACTORS

We noted earlier that alcohol abuse has a small but significant relationship with recidivism in sexual offenders (Hanson and Morton-Bourgon, 2005). Because most people who drink do not commit sexual offences, it is likely that alcohol promotes recidivism by interacting with, or exacerbating, other risk factors. Table 12.1 shows those psychologically meaningful causal risk factors that have been found, to date, to predict recidivism in sexual offenders (Mann et al., 2010). This list contains a number of factors that are potentially exacerbated by either chronic or acute alcohol use, possibly dramatically so. We will discuss these interactions in more detail below. We note at the outset of this discussion that the literature on the effects of alcohol sometimes distinguishes between pharmacological effects and psychological effects. The latter are often termed 'alcohol expectancy effects' and refer to the observation that individuals' experiences of alcohol are markedly influenced by the effect that they expect alcohol to have on them.

Table 12.1   Empirically supported psychological risk factors for sexual recidivism (from Mann *et al.*, 2010).

Sexual preoccupation
Any deviant sexual interest
Offence supportive attitudes
Emotional congruence with children
Lack of emotionally intimate relationships with adults
Lifestyle instability
General self-regulation problems
Poor cognitive problem solving
Resistance to rules and supervision
Grievance/hostility
Negative social influences

Numerous studies have reported attempts to disentangle the actual effects of alcohol from the expectancy-related effects, and this literature is replete with methodological critiques and complex laboratory designs. The difference between these types of effects is probably not clear-cut in that the pharmacological effects of alcohol act through psychological mechanisms, such as effects on information processing, as will be discussed below. Moreover, in relation to the specific alcohol–aggression expectancy (the belief that drinking will increase one's aggressive behaviour), the impact of such beliefs has been found to be non-significant when controlling for trait aggression (Giancola, 2006).

The Effects of Alcohol on Cognitive Processing and Executive Functioning

There is considerable evidence that a number of cognitive processes are adversely affected by alcohol, including recognition of inhibitory cues, the ability to consider consequences prior to acting, and the ability to detect and correct errors of behaviour. Furthermore, these effects seem to be more severe in people who have a pre-existing tendency to aggressivity, hostile rumination, sensation seeking and low levels of anger control (Giancola *et al.*, 2010), or who already have executive functioning difficulties (Giancola, 2004), all of which traits are commonly associated with sexual offending (e.g., Mann *et al.*, 2010). Executive functioning impairment will make it more likely that someone who has been drinking will have difficulty inhibiting and monitoring their behaviours, and will struggle to work out and adopt the most appropriate response to complex social situations. Both chronic alcohol use and acute intoxication can impair cognitive functioning. Although the findings mentioned above refer to the short-term effects of intoxication, there is also evidence that long-term drinking can prevent or damage neuropsychological development (see Howard and McMurran, Chapter 5, this volume).

It therefore appears likely that both chronic and acute alcohol use diminish problem-solving and other self-regulatory skills, exacerbating the kinds of deficits that have been identified as risk factors for sexual offending.

Effects of Alcohol on Sexual Arousal and Behaviour

Laboratory studies have demonstrated that alcohol (or alcohol expectancy) affects people's perception of their sexual drive. In general, men report increased subjective sexual arousal in response to sexual stimuli as their blood alcohol level rises, although their actual genital responses do not necessarily show the same increases and, in fact, tend to decrease as blood alcohol level rises past a certain point (Briddell and Wilson, 1976; Crowe and George, 1989; Prause, Staley, and Finn, 2011).

Another important question is whether alcohol increases arousal to deviant sexual stimuli. Several studies have indicated some relevant although subtle effects. For instance, it appears that men who have drunk alcohol show less discrimination between consenting and rape stimuli than do men who drank a placebo (e.g., Barbaree et al., 1983), view pictures of violent sexual encounters for longer than non-intoxicated men (e.g., George and Marlatt, 1986) and take longer to determine that a woman wants her partner to stop sexual activity (Marx, Gross, and Adams, 1999; Marx, Gross, and Juergens, 1997). Alcohol also seems to increase sexual risk taking (George and Stoner, 2000), probably due to a diminished tendency to pay attention to possible negative consequences of risky behaviour.

The belief (expectancy) that alcohol increases sex drive is frequently observed and may not always be distinguishable from the actual effect of alcohol – or may interact with it. For example, Abbey et al. (2012) reported on a study with an unconvicted community sample of young men drawn from the Detroit area of the United States ($N = 423$). They assessed (amongst other things) sexual aggression, misperception of women's sexual intent, alcohol expectancies and alcohol consumption in sexual situations at two interviews conducted 1 year apart. Forty-three per cent of the sample admitted having perpetrated some type of sexual aggression since the age of 14, and these participants were divided into three groups, according to whether they had been sexually aggressive before the first of the interviews only (desisters), whether they had been sexually aggressive both before and since the first interview (persisters) or whether they had been sexually aggressive since but not before the first interview (initiators). Persisters reported stronger beliefs that alcohol would increase their sex drive than desisters or initiators. Furthermore, all three groups reported stronger such beliefs than non-perpetrators. The authors concluded that expectancies about the effect of alcohol on sex drive were one of the key contributors to intoxicated sexual aggression, but emphasised that expectations, misperceptions and intoxication were closely interlinked phenomena. This study yielded considerable insight into the problem of unconvicted sexual assault, but findings would need to be replicated on convicted sexual aggressors in order to ensure their relevance to the treatment of known offenders.

It therefore appears that alcohol intoxication can potentially exacerbate at least two other established risk factors for sexual offending: sexual preoccupation, through the expectancy effect, and deviant sexual arousal, by diminishing inhibitions or exacerbating the likelihood of misperception.

Effects of Alcohol on Lifestyle Instability

Over time, heavy drinking may produce increases in sensation seeking and impulsivity, to the extent that these increases could be called a personality change (Quinn, Stappenbeck, and Fromme, 2011). Quinn *et al.* concluded that drinking 'may more generally increase propensities to prefer risky activities to safe ones and short term rewards to long term benefits, thereby contributing to more pervasive negative outcomes' (p. 553). Langevin and Lang (1990) listed a number of consequences of long-term substance abuse, including deterioration in health, dysfunctional family and marital relations and loss of employment. Such consequences of drinking are highly likely to contribute to decreased lifestyle stability, a known risk factor for sexual offending (Mann *et al.*, 2010).

Effect of Alcohol on Sexual Expectations

Another well-documented and relevant effect of alcohol is its perceived value as an enabler of sexual interaction. In one study of this issue, Lindgren *et al.* 2009 conducted a qualitative examination of 29 college students' perceptions about alcohol and sexual behaviour. They concluded that college students drank in order to find a sexual partner, believing that alcohol makes it easier to talk and act about sex. In particular, the participants in this study thought alcohol empowers people to set aside cultural or gender prohibitions to talk about sex. Men who drank assumed women who drank were more available (see also Kanin, 1985, and Scully, 1991, who have both reported that sexual assault perpetrators often label women who drink as promiscuous). Men who drank also believed that the act of drinking by itself signalled their interest in sex to women: 'According to these participants, simply holding a beer is a strategic, effective, method to indicate sexual interest without having to say or do anything else' (p. 10). Whilst the population studied in this research were US college students, and therefore their cultural context is dissimilar to most of those convicted of sexual offending, it is an intriguing and important possibility that some men believe that drinking is a signal of sexual readiness in both men and women. Such a belief could easily lead to misperceptions of sexual intent, a common feature particularly of acquaintance rape, as discussed further below.

Effect of Alcohol on (Mis)perception of Others' Sexual Intentions

Parkhill, Abbey, and Jacques-Tiura (2009) examined drinking and sexual coercion in a sample of 163 community men (i.e., a non-forensic sample) recruited for a study on dating experiences. Of these, 107 admitted having ever used a coercive strategy to force sex on women and so were included in the study. In line with Finney's (2004) conclusions noted earlier, the vast majority (96%) of the incidents of coercive sex had been perpetrated on an acquaintance. Parkhill *et al.* compared those who had been drinking heavily before sexual coercion (five or more drinks) to those who had been drinking lightly (one to four drinks) or not at all. The study found that those who drank heavily during the abusive incident had misperceived their victims' sexual intentions for a longer time (it is unfortunately not clear exactly how this was defined or how it was understood by the participants), employed more isolating and controlling behaviours, had been more physically forceful and committed assaults that were more severe. Parkhill *et al.* concluded that 'heavy drinking men may be so focused on their own sexual arousal and feelings of entitlement that they miss or ignore messages intended to convey the woman's lack of interest' (p. 3). They also noted that men who had drunk more heavily before coercing someone into sex were more likely to perceive their sexually forceful behaviour as serious, to take responsibility for it and to say that they had learned a lesson from it. Parkhill *et al.* speculated that these latter findings indicated that these men were able to admit their offending because the excuse of being drunk protected their ego. However, it is not clear why they favoured this explanation over other possible interpretations.

Abbey *et al.* (2012), as described above, further examined the relationship between drinking and misperception of sexual intention, concluding that there is an interaction between expectation, misperception and intoxication. Specifically, they proposed that intoxicated men with expectations of sexual gratification focus their attention on their own arousal and consequently are less attuned to, or actively ignore, signs of non-consent or even distress from a woman.

Conclusions: How Alcohol May Exacerbate Sexual Offending Risk Factors

These findings suggest that alcohol may exacerbate several dispositions related to sexual offending, such as self-regulation problems, lifestyle instability, deviant sexual arousal and sexual preoccupation. Such effects of alcohol seem to be stronger in people who have other characteristics associated with sexual offending, such as hostility, sensation seeking and mood disturbance.

MODELS OF THE ROLE OF ALCOHOL IN SEXUAL OFFENDING

As the brief review above shows, a developing literature indicates that many people convicted of sexual abuse have significant alcohol problems. It further appears that alcohol plays a more pertinent role in certain types of sexual offending compared with others. In this section, we consider and critique existing models that have been proposed to explain the role of alcohol in some sexual offending.

Seto and Barbaree (1995) proposed a 'disinhibition model' to explain the role of alcohol in sexual assault. They deconstructed 'disinhibition' into three stages. The first stage involves the effect of disinhibition expectancy. Those individuals who believe that alcohol is a disinhibitor are more likely to behave in a disinhibited way after drinking. The second stage of disinhibition involves the effect that alcohol ingestion has on one's perception of social norms. An individual can be disinhibited by the belief that drinking alcohol is associated with a set of more liberal norms about the acceptability of certain behaviours; that is, the individual believes, not irrationally, that some behaviours are severely censured if carried out by someone who is sober but are more tolerated when carried out by someone who is drunk. Seto and Barbaree referred to this as the 'excuse-giving function of alcohol' (p. 560). The third stage of disinhibition involves the pharmacological effect of alcohol, which, as we have seen, impairs an individual's ability to process inhibitory cues, such as expressions of non-consent, distress or resistance. Seto and Barbaree speculated that this effect of alcohol would be heightened in men whose processing may already be inhibited by other characteristics such as hostility towards women and rape-supportive attitudes.

This was an early model of the alcohol–sexual aggression link, and as such, it does not incorporate all the issues that we have reviewed above. First, this model applies only to those who were intoxicated at the time of offending. It does not attempt to incorporate the effects of longer-term problem drinking into its explanation of offending. Second, the model implies a mainly instrumental use of alcohol. It implies that intoxication was chosen as a strategy to deliberately self-disinhibit and avoid social censure. There is, in our view, evidence to support a wider interpretation of the role of alcohol in sexual offending than this model implies. Third, this model, whilst acknowledging the impact of alcohol upon cognitive processing, does not fully account for the further evidence that alcohol, either directly or through expectancies, affects sexual arousal, disinhibits sexual interest and leads to misperceptions of another person's reciprocal sexual interest. Put another way, the model appears better able to explain planned offending than opportunistic offending. A final critique of the model, although this is not necessarily the authors' fault, is that it has had little impact on practice. Seto and Barbaree concluded their article with some excellent suggestions for treatment goals for sexual offenders who were intoxicated whilst offending, but as we noted at the outset of this chapter, these have not been taken up into other published guidance on the treatment of sexual offenders.

Testa (2002) proposed a refined model of the alcohol–sexual aggression link that placed more emphasis on the situational aspect of alcohol-related sexual violence. Her model recognised two significant distal influences on alcohol-related sexual violence: long-term use/abuse of alcohol by the perpetrator and the presence of certain individual difference variables such as hypermasculinity and impulsivity. In Testa's model, these two distal influences raise the likelihood that the perpetrator frequents certain 'alcohol contexts' such as bars and parties where most people are likely to be intoxicated. Two key aspects of these alcohol contexts are that norms differ and that intoxicated women are also likely to be present, activating expectancy beliefs that women drink as a sexual cue, which leads to sexual misperception and, ultimately, sexual aggression.

Testa's model effectively integrates the psychological and social influences on alcohol-related sexual violence and, in our view, overcomes some of the limitations of Seto and Barbaree's model, especially in its acknowledgement of the process of opportunistic offending. However, as acknowledged by Testa herself, the model works best in explaining acquaintance rape. This model cannot account for other types of alcohol-related sexual violence, such as the drunken husband who rapes his wife.

Proulx and Beauregard's typology of sexually aggressive subtypes (see Proulx and Beauregard, 2009) makes headway in explaining how alcohol can be implicated in different ways in different types of sexual offending. In this typology, four types of sexual aggression are identified (sadistic, angry, opportunistic and compensatory), and alcohol consumption is specifically implicated in the offending of the angry and opportunistic types but not of the other two types. The angry type is primarily grievance motivated, and feelings of intense anger and revenge motivations are reported prior to offending; there is not usually a proneness to deviant sexual interests; offences are not planned, and the aim of aggression is catharsis. The opportunistic type is also not associated with deviant sexual interests and offending is unplanned, but in contrast to the angry type, there is neither anger nor a grievance. The role of alcohol in the opportunistic type is as a disinhibitor.

Whilst this typology offers another way of accounting for the contribution of alcohol to certain types of sexual offending, it does not give detailed proposals about the particular functions of alcohol. Of course, this was not the purpose of the typology; hence, its explication of the role of alcohol is rudimentary.

Alcohol-Related Pathways to Sexual Offending

We have reviewed some different ways of accounting for the role of alcohol in sexual offending, all of them useful and grounded in good experimental research. However, none of the models adequately explains the variety of relationships that alcohol may have with sexual offending. A comprehensive model would need to integrate the influence of historical alcohol abuse with situational intoxication, as well as alcohol's pharmacological and psychological effects on cognitive processing, sexual arousal, and beliefs about alcohol and sexual behaviour. Furthermore, a model needs to account for different types of sexual offending. In our view, there appear to be three main pathways through which alcohol could lead to sexual aggression.

The first pathway involves the role of chronic problem drinking in causing offending and is justified by the indication from the meta-analytic research that substance abuse has a small but robust relationship with recidivism (Hanson and Morton-Bourgon, 2005). It is proposed that chronic alcohol abuse exacerbates other risk factors for sexual recidivism, particularly social risk factors such as employment and family problems. The effects of long-term problem drinking are particularly severe in individuals with other risk factors for sexual recidivism such as antisociality, sensation seeking and dysfunctional coping. For example, long-term alcohol use will increase the desire for stimulation and positive affect, whilst simultaneously delaying or impairing the cognitive control system (see Howard and McMurran, Chapter 5, this volume).

The second pathway explains the role of alcohol in planned sexual offending. Our understanding of this pathway draws particularly on Seto and Barbaree's model described above. Alcohol is ingested deliberately for its disinhibiting effect. Three particular expectancies may account for the choice to drink alcohol as part of a plan to offend: the expectancy that alcohol leads to aggression, the expectancy that alcohol leads to sex and the expectancy that intoxication will reduce social censure later on. In this pathway, therefore, the *expectation* of disinhibition potentially plays more of a key role than any actual disinhibiting effect of alcohol.

The third pathway explains the role of alcohol in unplanned sexual offending and draws particularly on Testa's model of alcohol-related acquaintance rape and Giancola's account of the effect of alcohol on attention and cognitive processing (e.g., Giancola *et al.*, 2010). In this pathway, intoxication and offending are context specific. Alcohol's effect on sexual arousal, perceptions, interpretations and decision making interacts with expectancies and beliefs about alcohol as a sexual enabler and women who drink as sexually available and ready. Acquaintance rape may occur when the intoxicated perpetrator is intent on sexual gratification and is so focused on the immediate positive consequences that he desires to achieve and fails to adequately examine cues from potential partners that indicate lack of sexual willingness (the 'sexual misperception' variant of the pathway). The effect is essentially that of alcohol myopia (Giancola *et al.*, 2010), where, to put it simply, someone who is drunk can only focus on one thing, and if that thing is sexual gratification, inhibitory cues can go unnoticed. Stranger rape, or more violent acquaintance rape, may occur when the intoxicated perpetrator has a tendency to over-perceive threat or rejection, which is exacerbated by alcohol (the 'threat misperception' variant of the pathway; drawing upon the angry rapist type). Here, rape occurs in line with the well-documented relationship between alcohol and non-sexual aggression, where the alcohol myopia effect focuses attention upon aggression-provoking cues, especially in those who are dispositionally prone to aggressive thinking or in a state of negative affect.

Alcohol-related offences occurring in this unplanned way may or may not draw upon pre-existing aggressive sexual interests. In some cases, it is likely that the perpetrator has no deviant interest and, in other situations and/or when sober, no intention to ever commit a sexual offence.

ADDRESSING ALCOHOL USE IN TREATMENT PROGRAMMES FOR SEXUAL OFFENDING

Many of the researchers who have studied in one way or another the relationship between alcohol and sexual offending have called for a greater integration of treatment for problem drinking into sex offending treatment programmes, although their recommendations for how this should be done have been inconsistent. For instance, Seto and Barbaree (1995) concluded their review with a set of suggestions for intervention design, suggesting that treatment should address both alcohol-related expectancies and the effect of alcohol on the processing of inhibitory cues.

Peugh and Belenko (2001) concluded that 'Our analyses strongly suggest the need to improve assessment and treatment of substance abuse and related issues amongst incarcerated sex offenders' (p. 192). Abracen *et al.* (2000) proposed that 'treatment providers who work with violent offenders should have training in the area of substance abuse' (p. 272), but otherwise recommended that substance misuse can be satisfactorily dealt with through concomitant substance abuse programmes that complement other treatment services for sexual offenders. In contrast, Abbey (2011) focused on the need to integrate alcohol interventions into sex offender programmes rather than to provide separate programming, stressing 'the importance of developing integrated alcohol and sexual assault prevention and treatment programs that address both of these problems concurrently' (p. 487). This is pertinent because we have seen that the effect of alcohol abuse on sexual offending is not only a distal relationship relying on the long-term effects of chronic alcohol abuse on personality factors but is also implicated in the offence process itself.

The best evidence, to date, indicates that programmes for sexual offenders, as for other offenders, are most effective when they align with the risk, need and responsivity (RNR) principles (Andrews and Bonta, 2010; Hanson *et al.*, 2009). These principles dictate that programmes should target higher-risk offenders (the risk principle), address factors that have an empirical relationship with offending (the need principle) and adopt cognitive-behavioural methods (the responsivity principle). Mann *et al.* (2010) have recently summarised the literature that has examined the factors that sexual offending programmes should address – usually called criminogenic needs or psychological risk factors (see Table 12.1). Their list of evidence-based treatment targets did not include drinking as a specific risk factor but rather integrated substance misuse into the risk factor of lifestyle instability. Perhaps for this reason, a recent study of the content of North American treatment programmes did not even ask respondents whether they addressed drinking as part of their treatment programme (McGrath *et al.*, 2010). According to the RNR model, on current evidence, the treatment of problem drinking has no major place within a programme designed to address sexually aggressive behaviour.

However, there is now a movement towards incorporating greater individualisation within treatment programmes, even though the crucial importance of an overall structured approach remains clear (Mann, 2009). Greater individualisation means, in practice, carrying out individual formulations of each offender's needs and addressing these whilst retaining a strong and structured overall focus on criminogenic factors. Clearly, not all sexual offenders have histories of alcohol abuse and not all of them were drinking before they offended, so to include alcohol-focused treatment for everyone would be indicative of a poorly constructed programme, a one-size-fits-all approach that would be wasteful of time and resources and likely to alienate many participants by requiring them to undertake treatment for problems that they do not have. On the other hand, it does seem probable that for some offenders, risk factors for reoffending are exacerbated by drinking. To ignore a relationship between drinking and, for example, a failure to notice cues of sexual uninterest may not prepare the offender adequately for coping with future social and sexual interactions. Similarly, men who believe that women who see them drinking will understand their sexual intent, or men who believe that women who drink are signalling their own sexual availability, may continue to hold these troublesome beliefs if not explicitly addressed during treatment.

We contend that there is a particular need to move away from the narrow and stereotyped assumptions that offenders only drink to give themselves permission to commit a sexual offence (thus, the assumption that the desire to offend precedes the desire to drink) or that offenders only refer to their drinking as a way to excuse or justify their behaviour. Either of these propositions might be true. But there are other possible links between drinking and offending, and to ignore or discount them runs the risk of failing to fully prepare a client for future risky situations, and/or of alienating the client by failing to give credence to his own concerns about the role of drinking in his offending. We therefore offer the following suggestions for ways in which drinking could be addressed, for those for whom it is relevant, within an overall structured programme for sexual offending, assuming that the structure of the programme enables some room for individualisation (see Mann, 2009).

For Those Who Were Drinking in the Immediate Lead-up to the Offence

During the assessment phase, treatment providers should establish whether drinking took place prior to the offence. If so, they should consider explicitly the following questions:

- Were the offender and victim both drinking and, if so, what messages did the offender believe each was conveying to the other through their drinking?
- Does he habitually use alcohol as a way of expressing sexual intent?
- Does he believe that women who drink are expressing sexual availability or are promiscuous?
- Was he drinking on that occasion because he believed this would help him achieve a goal of sexual intercourse (not necessarily a goal of committing an offence)?
- Does drinking tend to increase his interest in pursuing sexual goals?
- Does drinking tend to increase his determination to obtain sexual gratification?
- Are sexual preoccupation, hostile rumination, impulsivity, poor problem solving or entitlement thinking also risk factors for this individual? If so, note that these may be particularly exacerbated by drinking.

The treatment provider can use this information to create a formulation about the relationship between alcohol and offending for each individual.

During the treatment phase, the treatment provider could address problems identified in the formulation as follows. For those who believe that drinking conveys a message of sexual intent or sexual availability, such beliefs could be treated as cognitive schemas, where a pre-existing belief is repeatedly drawn upon to assist with explaining new situations. Cognitive schemas tend to be utilised as heuristics for information processing, often without awareness or without questioning their actual validity. Such beliefs can be addressed through straightforward cognitive therapy or cognitive-behavioural techniques, including behavioural experimentation. In addition, Giancola et al. (2010) suggested that reducing the problematic underlying dispositions that interact with intoxication, such as reducing hostile rumination or increasing perspective taking, is likely to reduce the effect of alcohol myopia in future situations. They also suggested that enhancing mindfulness should reduce the effect of alcohol myopia, based on a study indicating that highly mindful men seemed better able to shift their focus away from sexual or aggressive cues than men with low levels of dispositional mindfulness (Gallagher, Hudepohl, and Parrott, 2010).

For those who drink in order to improve their chances of sexual gratification, the normality of this belief must be recognised. It is not some kind of belief unique to sex offenders nor is it a sign of 'cognitive distortion' to believe that if one drinks alcohol, one is more likely to successfully achieve sexual goals. There is clear evidence to support the notion that many people deliberately drink alcohol for exactly this purpose. Hence, it is likely to alienate treatment clients and reduce the therapist's credibility, to suggest otherwise. However, it may be that there are particular dangers with this belief in those who have other risk factors for sexual offending. Clients may also benefit from working through the consequences of this belief and identifying the ways in which it biased their information processing. This strategy will probably also be important with those for whom alcohol increases their interest in pursuing sexual goals and with those for whom alcohol increases their determination to obtain sexual gratification. In particular, it may be helpful for clients to better understand sexual and non-sexual cues, how to interpret them and the effect alcohol may have on their ability to do so.

For Those with Chronic Alcohol Abuse Histories

With chronic alcohol abusers, there may be no proximal link between the alcohol abuse and sexual offending. However, it may still be prudent to address rather than ignore chronic alcohol abuse, especially given Looman et al.'s speculation that there could be some relationship between chronic problem drinking and long-term emotionally focused coping and intimacy deficits. Additionally, offenders with problem drinking may find themselves socially excluded in a range of ways, or may have difficulty maintaining employment or other activities important within a busy, healthy lifestyle. Problem drinking may also prevent the development of protective factors, by leading to chaotic or weak social bonds, or may exacerbate other risk factors such as difficulty managing emotions and solving problems. Although most sexual offending treatment programmes major on teaching self-regulation strategies, it may be that participants in such programmes fail to realise that they can generalise these strategies from offending to other self-regulation challenges such as drinking. The difficulty in generalisation was illustrated in a recent small-scale qualitative study of violent (non-sexual) offenders (Box, 2012). In this study, men who had reoffended following comprehensive treatment all noted the role of alcohol or drug use in their relapse and explicitly stated that they had not realised they could apply the strategies they had learned for controlling their violence to their substance abuse.

We therefore propose that during the assessment phase, all sexual offenders are assessed for histories of problem drinking using a validated instrument such as the MAST. For those who disclose any history of problem drinking, it would be useful to examine the recency of problem drinking and their preparedness to manage problem drinking in the future. All those for whom problem drinking is a recent phenomenon should be directed to adjunctive treatment designed to explicitly address problem drinking.

CONCLUSIONS

Despite the research effort examining the link between alcohol abuse and sexual violence, the exact nature of the relationship between the two remains unclear. Nevertheless, we have been able to draw some conclusions from the literature that have implications for those providing sex offender treatment.

Certainly clinicians are advised to recognise that alcohol's relationship with abusive behaviour is not only that of a deliberately self-administered disinhibitor. In particular, we note evidence that perpetrators of sexual abuse, particularly rapists, are more likely to have histories of alcohol abuse (although we have noted a number of limitations in these studies that hamper our ability to generalise the results to all sexual offenders). Second, the literature on 'event level' studies indicates a pattern of alcohol abuse being present in certain types of sexual offending, particularly offences against known but not intimate adults in social situations. Third, we note that alcohol abuse may work to exacerbate or even create some of the factors that we know are linked to sexual aggression. These factors can be summed up as self-regulation problems and sexual preoccupation. Furthermore, there is evidence that, for some men, alcohol consumption may be interpreted as a sign of sexual intent in both men and women. Finally, there is evidence that alcohol consumption can result in some men missing or ignoring cues from a potential victim that signal they are not interested in sex. We therefore propose a three-pathway model to understanding the role of alcohol in sexual offending, namely, the impact of chronic alcohol abuse in exacerbating certain risk factors for sexual abuse; the use of alcohol as a deliberate disinhibitor in planned sexual abuse events; and the effect of alcohol on perceptions, interpretations and decision making in unplanned sexual offences.

It is somewhat surprising that addressing alcohol issues has not been given a higher priority in sex offender treatment programmes. This is partly explained by research into risk or criminogenic factors on which such programmes are based, which so far has failed to establish a link between alcohol use and sexual recidivism. This, however, may simply be because alcohol abuse was not amongst the range of factors tested in such research or because the role of alcohol is relevant only when situational rather than chronic, hence excluding it from research into dispositions related to reoffending.

Fortunately the thinking behind sex offender treatment is changing from a highly structured risk-based model to a more pluralist approach that enables psychological, biological and social factors to be addressed, depending on individual need, within a structured yet flexible treatment curriculum. Whilst chronic alcohol problems may well be best dealt with in specialist alcohol treatment additional to sex offender treatment programmes, we agree with Abbey (2011) that other alcohol-related issues should be addressed as part of sex offender treatment. These issues can be addressed in many cases by extending the scope of schema-based work within treatment to include work on beliefs about alcohol and sexual availability, recognising that alcohol consumption is an essentially normative behaviour but may have particular dangers for those who have pre-existing vulnerabilities towards abusive behaviour and ensuring clients are better prepared to understand relevant cues from others, particularly those that signal sexual uninterest. The recent focus within sex offender treatment on more individualised assessment and treatment approaches should enable this work to take place for those who need it, provided therapists are mindful of these issues.

REFERENCES

Abbey, A. (2011) Alcohol's role in sexual violence perpetration: Theoretical explanations, existing evidence and future directions. *Drug and Alcohol Review*, **30**, 481–489.

Abbey, A., Wegner, R., Pierce, J., and Jacques-Tiura, A.J. (2012) Patterns of sexual aggression in a community sample of young men: Risk factors associated with persistence, desistance and initiation over a 1-year interval. *Psychology of Violence*, **2**, 1–15.

Abbey, A., Zawacki, T., Buck, P.O. *et al.* (2001) Alcohol and sexual assault. *Alcohol Health and Research World*, **25**, 43–51.

Abracen, J., Looman, J., and Anderson, D. (2000) Alcohol and drug abuse in sexual and nonsexual violent offenders. *Sexual Abuse: A Journal of Research and Treatment*, **12**, 263–274.

Andrews, D.A. and Bonta, J. (2010) *The Psychology of Criminal Conduct*. Providence, NJ: Anderson Publishing.

Babor, T.F., Higgins-Biddle, J.C., Saunders, J.B., and Monteiro, M.G. (2001) *AUDIT: The Alcohol Use Disorders Identification Test*. Geneva: World Health Organization.

Barbaree, H.E., Marshall, W.L., Yates, E., and Lightfoot, L.O. (1983) Alcohol intoxication and deviant sexual arousal in male social drinkers. *Behaviour Research and Therapy*, **21**, 365–373.

Box, G. (2012) *Persistence and desistance from violence following a high intensity cognitive behavioural intervention in prison*, in preparation.

Brecklin, L.R. and Ullman, S.E. (2010) The roles of victim and offender substance use in sexual assault outcomes. *Journal of Interpersonal Violence*, **25**, 1503–1522.

Briddell, D.W. and Wilson, G.T. (1976) Effects of alcohol and expectancy set on male sexual arousal. *Journal of Abnormal Psychology*, **85**, 225–234.

Crowe, L.C. and George, W.H. (1989) Alcohol and human sexuality: Review and integration. *Psychological Bulletin*, **105**, 374–386.

Debiden, M. (2009) *A Compendium of Research and Analysis on the Offender Assessment System 2006–2009*. London: Ministry of Justice. Ministry of Justice Research Series 16/09.

Felson, R.B. and Staff, J. (2010) The effects of alcohol intoxication on violent versus other offending. *Criminal Justice and Behavior*, **37**, 1343–1360.

Finkelhor, D. (1984) *Child Sexual Abuse: New Theory and Research*. New York: The Free Press.

Finney, A. (2004) *Alcohol and Sexual Violence: Key Findings from the Research. Home Office Findings 215.* London: Home Office.

Gallagher, K.E., Hudepohl, A.D., and Parrott, D.J. (2010) The power of being present: The role of mindfulness on the relation between men's alcohol use and sexual aggression towards intimate partners. *Aggressive Behavior,* **36,** 405–413.

George, W.H. and Marlatt, G.A. (1986) The effects of alcohol and anger on interest in violence, erotica and deviance. *Journal of Abnormal Psychology,* **95,** 150–158.

George, W.H. and Stoner, S.A. (2000) Understanding acute alcohol effects on human behaviour. *Annual Review of Sex Research,* **11,** 92–124.

Giancola, P.R. (2004) Executive functioning and alcohol-related aggression. *Journal of Abnormal Psychology,* **113,** 541–555.

Giancola, P.R. (2006) Influence of subjective intoxication, breath-alcohol concentration and expectancies on the alcohol-aggression relation. *Alcoholism: Clinical and Experimental Research,* **30,** 844–850.

Giancola, P.R., Josephs, R.A., Parrott, D.J., and Duke, A.A. (2010) Alcohol myopia revisited: Clarifying aggression and other acts of disinhibition through a distorted lens. *Perspectives on Psychological Science,* **5,** 265–278.

Grubin, D. and Gunn, J. (1991) *The Imprisoned Rapist and Rape.* London: HSMO.

Gudjonsson, G.H. and Sigurdsson, J.F. (2000) Differences and similarities between violent offenders and sex offenders. *Child Abuse and Neglect,* **24,** 363–372.

Hanson, R.K., Bourgon, G., Helmus, L., and Hodgson, S. (2009) The principles of effective correctional treatment also apply to sexual offenders: A meta-analysis. *Criminal Justice and Behavior,* **36,** 865–891.

Hanson, R.K. and Morton-Bourgon, K.E. (2005) The characteristics of persistent sexual offenders: A meta-analysis of recidivism studies. *Journal of Consulting and Clinical Psychology,* **73,** 1154–1163.

Kanin, E.J. (1985) Date rapists: Differential sexual socialisation and relative deprivation. *Archives of Sexual Behavior,* **14,** 219–231.

Koss, M.P., Dinero, T.E., and Seibel, C.A. (1988) Stranger and acquaintance rape: Are there differences in the victim's experience? *Psychology of Women Quarterly,* **12,** 1–24.

Langevin, R. and Lang, R.A. (1990) Substance abuse among sex offenders. *Sexual Abuse: A Journal of Research and Treatment,* **3,** 397–424.

Långström, N., Sjöstedt, G., and Grann, M. (2004) Psychiatric disorders and recidivism in sexual offenders. *Sexual Abuse: A Journal of Research and Treatment,* **16,** 139–150.

Lindgren, K.P., Pantalone, D.W., Lewis, M.A., and George, W.H, (2009) College students' perceptions about alcohol and consensual sexual behavior: Alcohol leads to sex. *Journal of Drug Education,* **39,** 1–21.

Looman, J., Abracen, J., DiFazio, R., and Mallet, G. (2004) Alcohol and drug abuse among sexual and nonsexual offenders: Relationship to intimacy deficits and coping strategy. *Sexual Abuse: A Journal of Research and Treatment,* **16,** 177–189.

Mann, R.E. (2009) Sexual offender treatment: The case for manualisation. *Journal of Sexual Aggression,* **15,** 121–132.

Mann, R.E., Hanson, R.K., and Thornton, D. (2010) Assessing risk for sexual recidivism: Some proposals on the nature of psychologically meaningful risk factors. *Sexual Abuse: A Journal of Research and Treatment,* **22,** 172–190.

Marshall, W.L., Anderson, D., and Fernandez, Y.M. (1999) *Cognitive Behavioural Treatment of Sexual Offenders.* Chichester: John Wiley & Sons, Ltd.

Marshall, W.L., Fernandez, Y.M., Marshall, L.E., and Serran, G.A. (2006) *Sexual offender Treatment: Controversial issues.* Chichester: John Wiley & Sons, Ltd.

Marx, B.P., Gross, A.M., and Adams, H.E. (1999) The effect of alcohol on the responses of sexually coercive and non-coercive men to an experimental rape analogue. *Sexual Abuse: A Journal of Research and Treatment,* **11,** 131–145.

Marx, B.P., Gross, A.M., and Juergens, J.P. (1997) The effects of alcohol consumption and expectancies in an experimental date rape analogue. *Journal of Psychopathology and Behavioral Assessment,* **19,** 281–302.

McGrath, R.J., Cumming, G.F., Burchard, B.L. *et al.* (2010) *Current Practices and trends in Sexual Abuser Management: The Safer Society 2009 North American Survey.* Brandon, VT: Safer Society Press.

McMurran, M. and Gilchrist, E. (2007) Anger control and alcohol use: Appropriate interventions for perpetrators of domestic violence? *Psychology, Crime and Law*, **14**, 107–116.

McMurran, M., Hollin, C.R., and Bowen, A. (1990) Consistency of alcohol self-report measures in a male young offender population. *British Journal of Addiction*, **85**, 205–208.

Parkhill, M.R., Abbey, A., and Jacques-Tiura, A.J. (2009) How do sexual assault characteristics vary as a function of perpetrators' level of intoxication? *Addictive Behaviors*, **34**, 331–333.

Peugh, J. and Belenko, S. (2001) Examining the substance use patterns and treatment needs of incarcerated sex offenders. *Sexual Abuse: A Journal of Research and Treatment*, **13**, 179–195.

Prause, N., Staley, C., and Finn, P. (2011) The effects of acute ethanol consumption on sexual response and sexual risk-taking intent. *Archives of Sexual Behavior*, **40**, 373–384.

Proulx, J. and Beauregard, E. (2009) Decision making during the offending process: An assessment among subtypes of sexual aggressors of women. In A.R. Beech, L.A. Craig, and K.D. Browne (eds), *Assessment and Treatment of Sex Offenders* (pp. 181–198). Chichester: Wiley-Blackwell.

Quinn, P.D., Stappenbeck, C.A., and Fromme, K. (2011) Collegiate heavy drinking prospectively predicts change in sensation seeking and impulsivity. *Journal of Abnormal Psychology*, **120**, 543–556.

Salter, A.C. (1988) *Treating Child Sex Offenders and Victims: A Practical Guide.* Newbury Park, CA: Sage Publications.

Scully, D. (1991) *Understanding Sexual Violence: A Study of Convicted Rapists.* Boston: Unwin Hyman.

Selzer, M.L. (1971) The Michigan Alcoholism Screening Test: The quest for a new diagnostic instrument. *The American Journal of Psychiatry*, **127**, 1653–1658.

Seto, M.C. and Barbaree, H.E. (1995) The role of alcohol in sexual aggression. *Clinical Psychology Review*, **15**, 545–566.

Singleton, N., Farrell, M., and Meltzer, H. (1999) *Substance Misuse Among Prisoners in England and Wales.* London: Office for National Statistics.

Testa, M. (2002) The impact of men's alcohol consumption on perpetration of sexual aggression. *Clinical Psychology Review*, **22**, 1239–1263.

Ward, T., Polaschek, D.L.L., and Beech, A.R. (2006) *Theories of Sexual Offending.* Chichester: John Wiley & Sons, Ltd.

Chapter 13

TREATMENTS FOR OFFENDERS WITH DUAL DIAGNOSIS

AMY COHN

Center on Co-Occuring Disorders, Justice, and Multidisciplinary Research and Department of Mental Health Law and Policy and Department of Criminology, University of South Florida, Tampa, Florida, USA

KIM T. MUESER

Department of Occupational Therapy and Center for Psychiatric Rehabilitation, Boston University, Boston, Massachusetts, USA

INTRODUCTION

Serious mental illnesses (SMIs) such as bipolar disorder, schizophrenia, and treatment-refractory major depression and anxiety disorders have a high comorbidity with alcohol and drug use disorders (i.e., dual diagnosis, dual disorder, or co-occurring disorders). For example, the lifetime prevalence of substance use disorder in people with an SMI is approximately 50%, compared to about 15% in the general population (Kessler *et al.*, 2005; Mueser *et al.*, 1990; Regier *et al.*, 1990a). Alcohol and drug use are associated with a wide range of negative consequences among those with SMI, including relapse, impairment in functioning, family stress, housing instability, health problems, and violence and victimization (Chandler *et al.*, 2004; Drake and Brunette, 1998; Farkas and Hrouda, 2007; Fletcher *et al.*, 2007; Friedmann *et al.*, 2008; Gumpert *et al.*, 2010; Kerridge, 2009; Pelissier, Jones, and Cadigan, 2007; Roman and Travis, 2004; Ruiz *et al.*, 2012; Sacks, 2004). As a result of the legal repercussions and destabilizing effects of drug and alcohol use on the course and treatment of psychiatric illness, many individuals with a dual diagnosis become involved in the criminal justice system.

In terms of criminal justice involvement, problem drinking can result in very different criminal offenses than problem drug use, by the fact that the possession, consumption, or sale of certain psychoactive substances is illegal, while alcohol use (over the age of 21) is not punishable by law. Compared with alcohol-related

Alcohol-Related Violence: Prevention and Treatment, First Edition. Edited by Mary McMurran.
© 2013 John Wiley & Sons, Ltd. Published 2013 by John Wiley & Sons, Ltd.

offenses, drug-related offenses are usually harsher (felony), of longer duration, and are more likely to involve jail or prison time. This means that a substantial proportion of individuals involved in the justice system are drug users or have a drug use problem. However, despite apparently high rates of drug abuse and dependence in criminal justice populations, alcohol appears to be the most commonly used substance (Abram and Teplin, 1991; Teplin, 1994).

In addition to increasing involvement in the criminal justice system, alcohol and drug use disorders have been cited as primary risk factors linking violence committed by individuals with mental illness (Elbogen *et al.*, 2006; Fazel *et al.*, 2009; Hodgins *et al.*, 2008). Alcohol use, in particular, is associated with an increased frequency of violent and criminal behavior among individuals with a mental disorder, above and beyond the effects of drug use or abuse alone (Merricle and Havassy, 2008). Additionally, recent evidence suggests that same-day alcohol use is more prevalent than same-day drug use in individuals charged with a violent offense (Friend, Langhinrichsen-Rohling, and Eichold, 2011). However, most studies of dual diagnosis in offenders do not separate out alcohol use disorders from drug use disorders primarily due to their high comorbidity (Grant *et al.*, 2004). Further, studies have seldom focused on just violent behavior as the primary outcome. This may be, in part, because violence has a relatively low rate of occurrence among persons with SMI (Chloe, Teplin, and Abram, 2008), and therefore it is difficult to demonstrate significant associations of alcohol use (over drug use) on violence perpetration among those with SMI without large sample sizes.

IMPACT OF DUAL DIAGNOSIS IN THE CRIMINAL JUSTICE SYSTEM

Between ten percent and fifteen percent of individuals in jails and prisons have an SMI (Fazel, Bains, and Doll, 2005; Fazel and Danesh, 2002; Lamb, Weinberger, and Gross, 2004). Rates of dual diagnosis in justice-involved individuals are also high (Kerridge, 2009) and greater than those reported in the general population (Fazel and Danesh, 2002; Mallik-Kane and Visher, 2008; Teplin, 1994). Prevalence rates of co-occurring substance use disorders for justice-involved individuals with an SMI are approximately 80% for lifetime alcohol abuse or dependence and 60% for lifetime drug abuse or dependence (Abram and Teplin, 1991; Abram, Teplin, and McClelland, 2003). The combination of an alcohol and/or drug use disorder with SMI is more uniquely associated with violence perpetration and criminal behavior than either disorder alone (Arseneault *et al.*, 2000; Castillo and Fiftal Alarid, 2011; Douglas, Guy, and Hart, 2009; Teplin, Abram, and McClelland, 1994), and alcohol use appears to be a unique predictor of violence perpetration in justice-involved persons with SMI compared to the effects of drug use (Friend *et al.*, 2011; Merricle and Havassy, 2008).

There are several reasons why it is important to treat dual diagnosis in individuals involved in the criminal justice system. SMI and substance use disorders, both singly and in conjunction with each other, can have a negative impact on a variety of outcomes, including greater risk of HIV infection, substance use relapse, poor treatment prognosis, rehospitalization, depression, suicide, violence, and impaired social functioning (Drake and Brunette, 1998; Drake, Morrissey, and Mueser, 2006; Drake, Wallach, and McGovern, 2005; Drake *et al.*, 1998b; Pearson *et al.*, 2008; Peters, 2008; Webb *et al.*, 2011; Wilper *et al.*, 2009). Recent evidence also indicates that dual diagnoses confer greater risk for criminal outcomes, rearrest, technical violations following release from prison, and new offenses compared with the presence of just one mental health or substance use diagnosis (Baillargeon, Hoge, and Penn, 2010; Baillargeon *et al.*, 2009, 2010; Peters, 2008; Skeem *et al.*, 2009). These associations suggest that dual diagnosis is an important target for treatment before, during, and after involvement with the justice system (Osher, 2008; Osher and Steadman, 2007).

OVERALL "STATE OF THE SCIENCE"

Substantial work is needed in order to adapt current empirically based treatments for co-occurring alcohol or drug use disorders for individuals who are involved in the criminal justice system who have an SMI. The design, development, and implementation of dual diagnosis treatments in the justice system are complicated by several factors. First, empirically supported interventions that have been developed for dual diagnosis in the general population of people with SMI (Drake, O'Neal, and Wallach, 2008) have not incorporated important treatment targets for individuals involved in the criminal justice system, including risk factors for recidivism and criminogenic needs (Skeem, Manchak, and Peterson, 2011). Thus, modifications of existing empirically based treatments for dual diagnosis are needed for this population. Second, there have been limited resources available to undertake the modifications necessary to adapt and empirically validate dual diagnosis interventions for people with criminal justice involvement, resulting in a lack of access to such interventions for those in need (Osher and Steadman, 2007). As a related note, few, if any, empirically based treatments have been adapted to specifically treat co-occurring alcohol use disorders and SMI in the context of curtailing violence or recidivism for justice-involved persons.

A third obstacle to establishing effective interventions for dual diagnosis in the criminal justice system has been the broad heterogeneity of this population, reflecting a wide range of mental health and substance use treatment needs. While the broad group of individuals with SMI and comorbid substance use disorder (both alcohol and drug) may have a common set of treatment needs (e.g., medication management, psychoeducation about mental illness and substance abuse relapse), the needs of people with other types of dual diagnosis may be quite different, such as those with a primary anxiety disorder (e.g., posttraumatic stress disorder) or personality disorder (e.g., borderline personality disorder) and those with an alcohol versus drug use problem. For example, the fact that alcohol use disorders are more prevalent than drug use disorders in both the general population and in justice-involved samples highlights the importance of research focusing specifically on alcohol use problems in this group of individuals. However, few studies, to our knowledge, have examined the efficacy of adapted empirically based treatments for offenders with an alcohol use disorder and SMI. Lack of specificity regarding the nature and severity of co-occurring alcohol and/or drug use disorders with SMI makes generalizability of treatment outcome findings difficult, particularly as it relates to understanding the role of alcohol use in violence perpetration and criminal recidivism. For example, it remains unclear whether post-intervention reductions in violence are mediated by reductions in drinking, as opposed to drug use, over the course of treatment. Additionally, differences in treatment outcomes among people with a dual diagnosis may be related to diagnostic variability between subgroups of individuals rather than to components of the treatments.

A final challenge is that efforts to adapt and implement treatments for individuals with a dual diagnosis in the justice system are relatively new. Most research has not attempted to identify specific moderators or mediators of treatment outcome for alcohol use versus drug use disorders, or the effects of specific drug-only versus alcohol-only treatments. As mentioned earlier, this may be complicated by the fact that most studies group alcohol use disorders together with drug use disorders and include them into a broader category of substance use disorders, rather than examine alcohol use disorder as a predictor separate from drug use. The field is still trying to figure out what works before moving on to the "why" and "for whom" does it work. Additionally, because this line of research is in its infancy, there is limited research on the longer-term impact of these treatments on the quality of life of ex-offenders, health and mental health functioning, recidivism, and costs or cost savings, both in the criminal justice field and, more broadly, in health care. For example, preliminary evidence suggests that the cost of treating substance abuse and mental health in prison reduces the overall economic burden to society (Collins *et al.*, 2010; French, Popovici, and Tapsell, 2008). However, the rising cost of health care and the high burden placed on the justice system of treating the growing number of offenders with dual diagnoses underscore the need for more research on establishing effective and cost-effective interventions for this population.

DEFINITIONS AND TERMS

We use the term *offender* in this chapter to refer to an individual who is in prison or jail, or who is on probation or parole. The terms *dual diagnosis* and *dual disorders* have been used interchangeably in the research and clinical literature with the term *co-occurring disorders* and was also formerly referred to as *mentally ill chemically dependent* (MICA). Given the dearth of literature that has focused specifically on alcohol use disorders, as opposed more broadly to substance use disorders (both alcohol and drug use disorders), in offenders with a dual diagnosis, the term substance use disorder will be used to refer to any alcohol and/or drug use disorder throughout the rest of this chapter. A dual diagnosis, for the purposes of this chapter, broadly refers to the presence of a substance use disorder and another DSM-IV Axis I mental disorder, such as a mood disorder (major depression and bipolar disorder), anxiety disorder, or psychosis spectrum disorder (Peters and Hills, 1997). Axis I disorders are often associated with an Axis II personality disorder, such as borderline personality disorder and antisocial personality disorder

(ASPD) (American Psychiatric Association [APA], 2000). Sometimes, Axis II disorders are included in the definition of a major mental illness.

The association between aggression, violence, criminal behavior, and substance use disorders has been frequently highlighted in the dual disorder literature (Constantine *et al.*, 2010a; Douglas *et al.*, 2009; Elbogen and Johnson, 2009; Fletcher *et al.*, 2007; Gumpert *et al.*, 2010; Soyka, 2000; Wright *et al.*, 2002). Many of the characteristics associated with heightened risk for the presence of a comorbid SMI and substance use disorder are also indicators of violent and aggressive behavior and criminal recidivism (Castillo and Fiftal Alarid, 2011). It is important to highlight that violence is frequently cited as a common clinical correlate of alcohol and drug use in those with SMI, and that violence and alcohol use, in particular, frequently co-occur with each other (Constantine *et al.*, 2010a; Elbogen and Johnson, 2009; Elbogen *et al.*, 2006). However, despite the apparent overlap in risk factors for mental disorders, substance use disorders, and violent behavior, it is unclear what the direct associations are between specific diagnoses and increased rates of violence, arrest, and recidivism (Teplin, 1994; Teplin *et al.*, 1994). Some predisposing factors for these conditions have been identified, such as adverse childhood experiences like sexual abuse or neglect (Felitti *et al.*, 1998), and affiliation with delinquent peer networks (Moffitt, 1993). Therefore, underlying vulnerability processes that increase susceptibility to a dual diagnosis may also contribute to violent and criminal behavior. Regardless of the exact mechanisms, however, research findings overwhelmingly indicate higher rates of criminal behavior, violence, and rearrest among individuals with co-occurring disorders compared to those with one or no disorder (Baillargeon *et al.*, 2010a,b; Constantine *et al.*, 2010a,b; Smith and Trimboli, 2010).

SUBTYPES OF DUALLY DIAGNOSED OFFENDERS

A substantial body of literature suggests the presence of several subtypes or "diagnostic" clusters of offenders with a dual diagnosis. We focus primarily on two subgroups with co-occurring substance use disorders (alcohol and/or drug use disorders): (1) those with a substance use disorder and mood (depression, bipolar disorder) or anxiety disorder, and (2) those with a substance use disorder and schizophrenia spectrum disorder (Abram and Teplin, 1991; McCabe *et al.*, 2012), as these are most highly represented in criminal justice samples (Abram and Teplin, 1991; Fazel and Danesh, 2002; McCabe *et al.*, 2012). Below, we review prevalence estimates, etiological explanations, and distinguishing factors associated with the most prominent subtypes of dual diagnoses among criminal offenders.

Mood or Anxiety Disorder and Substance Use Disorder Cluster

Prevalence estimates of mood disorders, anxiety disorders, and alcohol and drug use disorders among offenders all surpass those in the general population (Grant, 1995; Grant and Hartford, 1995; Grant *et al.*, 2004; Hawthorne *et al.*, 2012; Kessler *et al.*, 1996b; Regier *et al.*, 1990b; Ruiz *et al.*, 2012; Teplin, 1994). For example, in the general the population, rates for a past-year Axis I diagnosis are 11% for any anxiety disorder, 9% for any substance use disorder (approximately 8% for an alcohol use disorder and 2% for a drug use disorder), 9% for depression, and 1% for bipolar disorder (Grant *et al.*, 2004). In contrast, among those in the jail or prison population, approximately 30% have a substance use disorder, between 7% and 21% major depression, and 3% bipolar disorder (Bean, Mierson, and Pinta, 1988; Diamond *et al.*, 2001; Motiuk and Porporino, 1991; Neighbors *et al.*, 1987). Similarly, the dual diagnosis of any substance use disorder with major depression, bipolar disorder, and/or anxiety disorders among justice-involved samples is also high and greater than estimates in the general population (Grant *et al.*, 2004; Kessler *et al.*, 1996b; Ruiz *et al.*, 2012). For example, in the general population, approximately 4% of individuals have a co-occurring mental disorder and substance use disorder. Among individuals in the general population with any substance use disorder in their lifetime, the prevalence of any lifetime mood or anxiety disorder is approximately 22% and 19%, respectively (Conway *et al.*, 2006), with major depression being the most prevalent mood disorder among those with any substance use disorder (approximately 33%), followed by bipolar disorder (approximately 12%) (Conway *et al.*, 2006; Kessler *et al.*, 1996a, 2005; Regier *et al.*, 1990a). Additionally, the comorbidity of any drug user disorder with mood and anxiety disorders in the general population is stronger than the comorbidity of alcohol use disorders in people with a mood and anxiety disorder (Grant *et al.*, 2004).

In contrast, nearly 75% of individuals in the jail and prison system report a lifetime Axis I mood or anxiety disorder with any comorbid substance use disorder (Steadman *et al.*, 2009). Specifically, the prevalence of substance use disorders among justice-involved individuals with depression ranges from 59% for those that have drug abuse/dependence to 81% for those with alcohol abuse/dependence; and the prevalence of substance use disorders for those with bipolar disorder ranges from 46% for drug abuse/dependence to 86% for alcohol abuse/dependence (Abram and Teplin, 1991). A crucial statistic that stands out from these findings is that the prevalence of comorbid alcohol use and mood disorders in offender samples is much higher than the prevalence of comorbid drug use and mood disorders. These data again illustrate the importance of specifically focusing on the dual diagnosis of alcohol abuse/dependence with other mental disorders in offender populations.

Dual diagnosis of mood or anxiety disorders with substance use disorders is also purported to have some of the most profound impact on treatment engagement and retention among individuals involved in the justice setting (Peters, 2008). Research has shown that individuals with a substance use disorder and mood disorder have more impaired social functioning, are at greater risk for substance abuse relapse, and respond more poorly to substance abuse treatment compared with those without a co-occurring mood disorder (Conner, Pinquart, and Gamble, 2009; Greenfield *et al.*, 1998; Hasin *et al.*, 2002; Ilgen and Moos, 2005, 2006; Mazza *et al.*, 2009).

Systematic investigations of the course and onset of substance use and mood or anxiety disorders suggest multiple pathways. First, symptoms of depression, anxiety, or mania can occur in the context of substance use. For example, since alcohol is a central nervous depressant, individuals who drink heavily over long periods of time can present to treatment with depression-like symptoms. Conversely, many stimulant-like substances, such as cocaine and methamphetamine, can induce acute levels of intoxication that mimic symptoms of mania (APA, 2000). A second pathway arises from the self-medication of depression or anxiety through the use of alcohol or drugs. For these individuals, substance use develops secondary to the onset of the mood or anxiety disorder, and is used to escape or avoid distress (Fergusson, Boden, and Horwood, 2011). Mental health symptoms that persist following abstinence from the substance may remit or decrease substantially once treated. Whereas recent evidence suggests a direct causal pathway from drug and alcohol use leading to depression but not anxiety (Fergusson *et al.*, 2011), the comorbidity of alcohol use and anxiety symptoms, as opposed to drug use and anxiety symptoms, has a reciprocal association with the mental health and substance use disorder each worsening the other (Fergusson *et al.*, 2011).

A third possible pathway is that the mood or anxiety disorder and substance use disorder may arise from a shared or common underlying pathway, such as an emotional or biological vulnerability that predisposes the individual to both disorders. This is often called the "third" or common pathway model (Kushner and Mueser, 1993). Possible examples of third variable models are childhood physical or sexual abuse or neglect, which increase vulnerability to both mental and substance use disorders. Yet another theory, the kindling model, suggests that the biological vulnerability to bipolar disorder can be triggered by substance use (Strakowski and DelBello, 2000; Strakowski *et al.*, 1996).

Schizophrenia Spectrum Disorder Cluster

Evidence also suggests that people with schizophrenia and a comorbid substance use disorder are an especially vulnerable group with high criminal justice involvement and particularly poor outcomes (Constantine *et al.*, 2010b; Hodgins, Toupin, and Côté, 1996; Kelly, 2009; Regier *et al.*, 1990a; Robins and McEvoy, 1992; Robins and Price, 1991; Soyka, 2000; Swanson *et al.*, 2006). They differ substantially from those with schizophrenia without a comorbid substance use disorder (Soyka, 2000) in that they are more likely to be male, have greater mood problems and higher rates of suicide, poorer medication adherence and treatment prognosis, and higher rates of relapse and hospitalization (Linszen, Dingemans, and Lenior, 1994; Novick *et al.*, 2010; Owen *et al.*, 1996; Tiet and Mausbach, 2007).

Studies have documented lifetime prevalence rates of substance use disorder in schizophrenia ranging from 2% for opioids to over 50% for alcohol (Mueser, Bellack, and Blanchard, 1992; Mueser *et al.*, 1990), and between 33% and 66% of individuals diagnosed with schizophrenia meet criteria for a substance use disorder at some point in their life (Koskinen *et al.*, 2010; Mueser, Yarnold, and Bellack, 1992; Regier *et al.*, 1990a; Swartz *et al.*, 2006). Elbogen and Johnson (2009) found that the combination of any alcohol or drug use disorder with psychosis comprised a greater risk of violence than psychosis without a substance use disorder; however, findings did not separate out the effects of alcohol use from drug use. Other studies report similar findings with more detailed results (Fazel *et al.*,

2009; Kelly, 2009; McCabe *et al.*, 2012). For example, using a large sample of individuals with SMI with an arrest history, McCabe *et al.* (2012) showed that the prevalence of any drug use disorder among those with a schizophrenia spectrum disorder was higher than the prevalence of any alcohol use disorder. Further, McCabe *et al.* (2012) showed that the risk of arrest for any violent crime among individuals with a schizophrenia spectrum disorder was significantly stronger for those with a co-occurring schizophrenia spectrum disorder and a drug use disorder than those with a co-occurring alcohol use disorder. When examining these findings, one should take into consideration that the increased risk of arrest related to drug use versus alcohol use is in part due to the lower prevalence or base rate of drug use disorders relative to alcohol use disorders. Thus, since alcohol abuse is more common, it is more difficult to demonstrate that it increases violence risk, relative to drug abuse.

Several reasons may underlie high rates of comorbidity between schizophrenia spectrum disorders and substance use disorders. One theory suggests that individuals with a schizophrenia spectrum disorder are biologically predisposed to developing a substance use disorder by a neurobiological deficit in the dopamine pathway that is implicated in both symptoms of psychosis (i.e., delusions, hallucinations) and the central reward system of the brain that underlies substance misuse (Green *et al.*, 1999, 2008; Roth, Brunette, and Green, 2005). Another hypothesis is that people with a schizophrenia spectrum disorder are more biologically sensitive to the negative effects of modest amounts of substance use, so that even "normative" use of alcohol or drugs may lead to negative consequences and, hence, a substance use disorder (Mueser, Drake, and Wallach, 1998).

Alternatively, the self-medication hypothesis suggests that substance use serves to alleviate the negative physical side effects of antipsychotic medications (Wilkins, 1997) or to lessen the intensity and distress of mental health symptoms such as hallucinations, depression, and anxiety (Khantzian, 1997). Other explanations include the use of substances to facilitate social interactions, the "third variable" hypothesis as previously discussed (e.g., childhood maltreatment), and schizophrenia triggered by cannabis or stimulant abuse (Allebeck *et al.*, 1993; Andréasson, Allebeck, and Rydberg, 1989; Andréasson *et al.*, 1987; Fernandez-Espejo *et al.*, 2008; Hall and Degenhardt, 2008; Semple, McIntosh, and Lawrie, 2005). We must note that all of the above explanations may also be highly impacted by the fact that alcohol is more readily available than many illegal drugs.

ASPD, Comorbid Substance Use Disorders and Schizophrenia Spectrum Disorders

It has often been the assumption that alcohol or drug use drives much or all of the violence that is perpetrated by individuals with a co-occurring substance use disorder and SMI (Elbogen and Johnson, 2009; Fazel *et al.*, 2009). However, while drug and alcohol abuse can contribute to violence, it is likely that the association is better explained by the third variable of ASPD (Hodgins, 2008; Hodgins *et al.*, 1996, 2008; Moran and Hodgins, 2004; Moffitt, 1993). ASPD is characterized by a long-standing pattern of aggression and violence dating back to childhood or adolescence (conduct disorder) and is the single greatest risk factor for the development of a substance use disorder, both in the general population and those with SMI.

ASPD and schizophrenia together also have a high rate of comorbidity (Abram and Teplin, 1991; Hodgins, Tiihonen, and Ross, 2005). In the DSM-IV (APA, 2000), ASPD is defined by a pervasive pattern of disregard for, and/or violation of, the rights of others that also includes chronic deviant behavior, deceitfulness, and lack of remorse. By definition according to DSM-IV (APA, 2000), ASPD in adulthood must be preceded by conduct disorder prior to the age of 15, which includes a persistent pattern of behavior that violates the basic rights of others, societal norms, or rules and is manifest by aggression toward people or animals, destruction of property, theft of deceit, and serious rule violation. Childhood conduct disorder and full ASPD are also established risk factors for the development of substance use disorders in the general population (e.g., Hesselbrock, Hesselbrock, and Stabenau, 1985, 1986; Hasin *et al.*, 2007) and may potentially link schizophrenia and criminal outcomes in a subset of individuals (Kessler *et al.*, 1996a; Mueser *et al.*, 2006; Regier *et al.*, 1990a). In fact, ASPD among individuals with schizophrenia spectrum disorders is associated with even higher rates of substance abuse comorbidity (Mueser *et al.*, 1999), and, among those with a dual disorder and ASPD, there is an more severe course of substance abuse (Mueser *et al.*, 1997, 2006), as well as a greater likelihood of committing violent crimes, and higher rates of criminogenic thinking (Hodgins, 2008).

ASPD is frequently diagnosed in criminal justice samples (Abram and Teplin, 1991; Fazel and Danesh, 2002; Ruiz *et al.*, 2012; Teplin, 1994), and the co-occurrence of ASPD in people with schizophrenia involved in the justice system can be upward of 65% (Abram and Teplin, 1991). Such individuals with co-occurring schizophrenia spectrum disorders and ASPD have more criminal involvement, more aggression, more severe alcohol and drug use problems, greater depression, lower educational attainment, and more impaired social functioning than those without co-occurring ASPD (Hasin *et al.*, 2007; McCabe *et al.*, 2012; Moran and Hodgins, 2004; Mueser *et al.*, 1997, 2006,2012). Individuals with ASPD and co-occurring SMI and substance use problems have unique treatment needs and represent particular challenges to evidence-based integrated treatment protocols, as discussed in more detail later in this chapter.

TREATMENT NEEDS AND PROBLEMS

Similar to individuals with a dual diagnosis (i.e., SMI and a substance use disorder) living in the community, dual diagnosis individuals involved in the justice system face significant mental health/substance abuse needs. These needs include psychiatric symptoms, potential for decompensation of psychiatric state, increased risk of harm to self or others, impaired functioning or loss of functioning, and crisis management. Additionally, substance use disorder carries with it several unique treatment needs/risks, which include craving, withdrawal, self-medication of symptoms, peer pressure to use, drug-seeking behavior, and increased potential for violence in the context of acute alcohol or drug intoxication. These areas should ideally be targeted in a single, integrated treatment program using an interdisciplinary team approach to concurrently treat and stabilize acute psychiatric symptoms, teach patients how to prevent substance use relapse, and teach illness self-management skills for both during and after incarceration (Bellack, Bennet, and Gearson, 2007; Dixon *et al.*, 2010; Drake *et al.*, 2008; Mueser, Noordsy, and Drake, 2003; Weiss and Connery 2011). Psychiatric symptomatology and substance use craving can be alleviated through the provision of different types of medication and coping skills training, whereas risk of relapse can be alleviated by teaching medication management skills, symptom monitoring, and developing a relapse prevention plan. Loss of functioning, social isolation, and peer pressure to use alcohol or other drugs can be addressed through psychoeducation about the causes and consequences of mental illness and increasing engagement in meaningful activities that improve quality of life and foster social connections with people who do not use substances. Finally, crisis situations and substance use relapse can be prevented or dealt with through a combination of developing relapse prevention plans and implementation of harm reduction strategies.

Given the unique associations that alcohol has to violence perpetration and SMI in justice-involved populations, treatment programs should also focus separately on the triggers and consequences associated with drinking versus drug use in offenders with a dual diagnosis. For example, even though alcohol has been cited as a major risk factor for violence and criminal behavior, many justice-involved individuals perceive drug use (but not drinking) as being a major factor in the crimes for which they were arrested (Lo and Stephens, 2002). Even at relatively low levels of intoxication, alcohol substantially decreases inhibition and impairs judgment, which may dramatically increase the occurrence of violent or disruptive behavior. There are several additional reasons why it is important to focus specifically on alcohol use in certain components of treatments for offenders with dual diagnosis: the genetic risks for alcohol abuse/dependence differ from those for drug abuse/dependence; the metabolism and pharmacokinetics of alcohol use differ substantially from drug use; and medications that are effective at treating alcohol dependence may not be useful at treating drug dependence or vice versa (Volkow and Skolnick, 2012).

In addition to these common mental illness and substance abuse treatment needs, people with a dual diagnosis who are involved in the criminal justice system face a unique set of treatment needs and problems related to criminogenic needs and risks associated with recidivism/reoffending. Criminogenic needs involve factors that influence crime and increase crime-related risk. They include violence, theft, antisocial behaviors, criminal thinking styles (e.g., the belief that the rules of society do not apply to the person), associating with criminal peers, and environmental or social/structural contexts that promote criminal activity. Some approaches to addressing criminogenic needs include cognitive-behavioral techniques, such as identifying alternatives to engaging in risky situations, anger management and coping skills training, recognizing and modifying antisocial thought patterns, learning to adopt an "anticriminal" identity, and promoting associations with prosocial peers (Landenberger and Lipsey, 2005). Treatment should also prepare individuals to understand the complexities of their parole or probation agreement and the restrictions and regulations by which they must abide.

The existence of ASPD among dually diagnosed individuals with schizophrenia and a substance use disorder further complicates how and what symptoms to target in treatment. Because ASPD may impact the probability of criminogenic thinking, it is important for treatments to target cognitive-based "reasoning" among those with ASPD and psychosis. Such interventions would be aimed at altering deeply entrenched maladaptive antisocial thought patterns and beliefs that could exacerbate delusions and desires to use substances. Research shows that individuals with schizophrenia display deficits in recognizing emotions, which may contribute to conduct problems and subsequent antisocial features (Blair et al., 2006), such as callousness and lack of empathy or regard for others. Thus, treatments targeted toward helping this subgroup of individuals may include developing awareness of other people's emotions, particularly sad and angry emotions, through skill-based practice and role playing (Penn et al., 2005). Ultimately, this may increase empathic responses and decrease aggressive, violent, or hostile tendencies toward others. Finally, recent investigations suggest that individuals with a dual disorder and co-occurring ASPD have strained interpersonal relationships with family members, suggesting family-based approaches to treating this group of individuals may be an especially effective and important component to treatment (Mueser et al., 2012). Later in this chapter, we discuss the possible benefits to clients with ASPD of providing integrated treatment for dual disorders on assertive community treatment (ACT) teams.

POINTS OF INTERVENTION IN THE CRIMINAL JUSTICE SETTING

In addition to the unique treatment needs of offenders with a dual diagnosis, there are several points of intervention for individuals to navigate as they move through the criminal justice setting, including in jail, prison, or the community. Individuals enter the first level of the criminal justice system through jail, often following a complaint, warrant, or arrest violation. They may be immediately incarcerated and booked or they may be released on bond or bail following an arraignment. Delivering treatment in a jail setting can be quite challenging for several reasons (Drake et al., 2006). First, the length of stay is often short and psychosocial interventions must be brief. For those who are severely dependent on alcohol, the process of withdrawal may begin during this time and could be highly dangerous if not medically monitored. Second, while medication may be prescribed for immediate symptom relief, longer-term skills for symptom management are rarely addressed. Finally, the type of treatment programs that are intensive enough to address both mental health and substance abuse problems can be difficult to implement in this time-limited setting. A variety of diversion programs have been developed, discussed below, to address some of these issues and to reduce the burden of mental health and substance use disorder treatment in the jail setting.

Once in prison, services may be available to address some of the needs of individuals with a dual diagnosis or they may be required as a stipulation of the sentence. These often include therapeutic communities (addressed in more detail below), 12-step recovery programs, cognitive-behavioral/motivational enhancement treatments, relapse prevention training, and family or group-based interventions. However, the prevailing view among researchers, stakeholders, and practitioners is that mental health treatment for incarcerated persons is generally inadequate to meet the multitude of needs of dually diagnosed individuals (Veysey et al., 1997; Wolff et al., 2002).

Finally, programs are offered that help individuals reintegrate into the community following release from jail or prison. In addition to stabilizing mental health symptoms and maintaining sobriety, substantive life areas for reintegration include employment, housing, family and social relationships, child care, and compliance with judicial entities. There are many different models for approaching reentry; primarily, these often include transitional housing, supported employment programs, and community supervision (Taxman, Yancey, and Bilanin, 2006). The goal of these programs is to provide dually diagnosed individuals with needed support services (e.g., housing, employment, counseling/treatment) that are intended to deter future criminal behavior, stabilize psychiatric functioning, and engage the individual in a supportive social/peer network.

PREDOMINANT CONCEPTUAL FRAMEWORKS FOR TREATMENT OFFENDERS WITH DUAL DIAGNOSIS

Two theoretical frameworks, the integrated dual diagnosis treatment (IDDT) model and the risk–needs–responsivity (RNR) model, have been used to guide treatment development and provision of services for individuals with a dual diagnosis who are involved in the criminal justice setting. In general, the consensus regarding the treatment and rehabilitation of offenders with a dual diagnosis is that the most effective approach is one that focuses on all the above listed areas of risks and problems (mental health needs, criminogenic needs, and recidivism/reoffending) in an integrated fashion (Drake et al., 2005; Morrissey, Meyer, and Cuddeback, 2007; Osher, 2008; Osher and Steadman, 2007).

IDDT Model

IDDT is one conceptual approach designed to address the multitude of needs and related services offered to individuals in the justice setting with co-occurring disorders (Davis et al., 2008. It is defined by the coordination of substance abuse and mental health treatments into one treatment program rather than a focus on one single disorder (Drake et al., 1998b; Mueser et al., 2003). Integrated treatment models are a program framework rather than an evidence-based treatment per se. In general, the research on the effectiveness of IDDT with psychiatric samples suggests that long-term programs that extend over several years are most beneficial (Drake et al., 2005; Flynn and Brown, 2008; Mueser et al., 2003).

The IDDT model has been applied primarily in community-based settings and has not been tested extensively in criminal justice settings (Peters, Sherman, and Osher, 2008). Research on IDDT in community settings has not fully taken into account the wide range of issues that uniquely affect individuals who are involved in the justice setting. These include focusing on structural/organizational issues that are particularly prevalent for justice-involved individuals postincarceration, such as legal supervision and judicial oversight, employment eligibility, homelessness, and coordinating care between judicial and mental health treatment programs.

In light of the increased need for integrated and evidence-based treatments for co-occurring disorders, the Substance Abuse Mental Health Services Administration (SAMHSA) initiated the Treatment Improvement Protocol No.42, which outlines three levels of treatment for persons with a dual diagnosis. The first level of treatment, *basic*, describes treatment that focuses on only one disorder while screening for the other. The second level, referred to as *intermediate*, focuses principally on one disorder while incorporating some basic treatment needs of another disorder. The third level of treatment, *advanced*, describes the type of treatment that integrates both substance abuse and mental health treatment needs into one program (Sacks and Ries, 2005). Preliminary research that has investigated the application of these three levels of treatment in justice-involved samples with dual diagnosis suggests that intermediate and advanced treatments are being offered to nearly 75% of offenders with a dual diagnosis (Melnick *et al.*, 2008). Further, advanced programs provide more in-depth assessment and screening services for dual disorders at an earlier time point (within the first month) than intermediate programs, are more likely to request medication management for clients in treatment plans, and are more likely to offer staff training related to treating mental disorders (Melnick *et al.*, 2008).

A major challenge for service planning of integrated treatment is actually providing access to the requisite services, both in prisons or jails as well as in the community. Several service strategies have been developed to help people with dual diagnosis involved in the justice setting access necessary services. Some of these strategies include postbooking jail diversion services (Broner *et al.*, 2004), reentry services (Draine, Wilson, and Pogorzelski, 2007; Osher, Steadman, and Barr, 2003), and drug courts and mental health courts (Boothroyd *et al.*, 2005; Cosden *et al.*, 2005). While there are differences in the structure and emphasis of each IDDT service model, access to community based mental health and substance abuse treatment, in collaboration with monitoring by judicial entities, is seen as playing a central role in each service.

RNR Model

The RNR model (Andrews, Bonta, and Hoge, 1990) of treatment and service provision extends the IDDT framework from community settings to criminal justice settings and aims to develop a clinical framework for integrating treatment on multiple levels while ensuring that the central needs/risks in each area are addressed. The RNR model includes factors that bring together (1) the offender's level of risk of reoffending; (2) criminogenic, as well as mental health/substance abuse needs; (3) and a degree of responsivity with which offenders are matched to a treatment that will maximize positive change (Andrews and Bonta, 2010; Andrews, Bonta, and Wormith, 2006; Bonta and Andrews, 2007). There are two core aspects of the responsivity principle: general and specific. *General responsivity* refers to the use of cognitive social learning methods to change behavior. Types of methods include prosocial modeling, reinforcement and reward incentives, and utilizing problem-solving techniques. *Specific responsivity* refers to the goal of adapting general approaches to the unique psychological, motivational, environmental, and personality needs of the individual. The general consensus among experts in the field is that interventions should place greater focus on individuals with a higher probability of recidivism through the delivery of intensive programs that target criminogenic and mental health needs rather than focus on individuals with lower risk (Skeem *et al.*, 2011).

PROMISING TREATMENTS FOR OFFENDERS WITH DUAL DIAGNOSIS

Assertive Community Treatment

ACT was first developed in the early 1970s, following a federal mandate to shift mental health care from the institutional setting to the community setting, and to address the problem of frequent relapses and hospitalizations in a subgroup of people with SMI who tended to not access services at local community mental health centers (Dixon, 2000; Stein and Santos, 1998; Stein and Test, 1980; Test and Stein, 1976). It is defined by a multidisciplinary approach to mental health treatment, wherein a team of treatment providers (social workers, psychiatric, nurse, case managers) coordinates and provides intensive services to clients primarily in natural community settings. ACT was partly designed to support the transition of care from the institutionalized setting for those with SMI, that is, those individuals who need concentrated assistance to deter homelessness and rehospitalization (Jennings, 2009; Lamberti, Weisman, and Faden, 2004; Phillips *et al.*, 2001; Stein and Santos, 1998). Among other community-based treatment models, ACT has demonstrated the strongest empirical support for persons with SMI. However, early trials of ACT have not reported improvements in criminal justice outcomes, although the rates of criminal involvement in this research were not high (Mueser *et al.*, 1998).

Several controlled studies have evaluated the benefits of delivering IDDT on ACT teams compared to usual case management teams, with mixed results. In a randomized controlled trial involving seven sites of clients with dual disorders, Drake *et al.* (1998a) showed that SMI clients with co-occurring substance abuse receiving IDDT on ACT teams had better alcohol use disorder outcomes, overall substance abuse outcomes, and quality of life improvements than those receiving IDDT from standard case management but did not differ in mental health outcomes. These effects were stronger at sites with the highest fidelity to the IDDT model (McHugo *et al.*, 1999). Similar controlled studies comparing IDDT delivered by ACT teams to IDDT provided by standard case management teams in more urban settings, including Hartford and Bridgeport, Connecticut (Essock *et al.*, 2006), and St. Louis (Calsyn *et al.*, 2005; Morse *et al.*, 2006), failed to show consistent differences favoring ACT. However, a secondary analysis of the Essock *et al.* (2006) study suggested that IDDT delivered on ACT teams may be an especially effective intervention for a subgroup of clients with dual disorders: individuals with ASPD benefited significantly more from ACT than standard case management in alcohol use outcomes and time spent in jail, whereas there were no differences between the treatment groups for dually diagnosed clients without ASPD, with clients in both ACT and standard case management improving on both outcomes (Frisman *et al.*, 2009). These promising findings suggest that those dually diagnosed individuals who have the greatest involvement in the criminal justice system and who tend to have the most severe substance use problems (i.e., dual disorder clients with ASPD) benefit the most from IDDT when it is provided more intensively and with closer monitoring by ACT teams.

Forensic modifications of ACT – forensic assertive community treatment (FACT) and forensic intensive case management (FICM) – evolved in response to the need to adapt ACT for justice-involved populations (Morrissey *et al.*, 2007). FACT programs were designed specifically for individuals with SMI and arrest or incarceration histories. The goal of FACT is to coordinate care between the community and the criminal justice system (Lamberti *et al.*, 2004). In general, evidence from the limited published literature on FACT shows that it may be effective at reducing the number of days in jail and the number of days in the hospital for treating mental health problems (Cimino and Jennings, 2002; Lamberti and Weisman, 2002; Lurigio, Fallon, and Dincin, 2000; Weisman, Lamberti, and Price, 2004). But the research does not show robust support for reductions in criminal behavior. For example, one small randomized study showed higher recidivism rates in the FACT group compared with a nontreatment control group immediately after treatment and at a 1-year follow-up (Solomon and Draine, 1995a,b), and no differences were found between FACT and two comparison groups on several social and clinical outcomes at the 1-year follow-up, suggesting, perhaps, that FACT is not beneficial for all groups of offenders. Equivocal findings regarding the effectiveness of FACT at improving criminal justice outcomes may also be partly attributable to a lack of methodological rigor and controlled, randomized trials that have been conducted (Cimino and Jennings, 2002; Jennings, 2009; Lamberti *et al.*, 2004). Further, studies have not parsed out the moderating or mediating influence of alcohol using subtypes versus drug-using subtypes on these outcomes, which may help clarify inconsistency in results.

FICM was designed to be less intensive than ACT by omitting full 24-hour support, as well as the dedicated interdisciplinary team that was originally formulated in the traditional ACT model. FICM has shown similarly mixed results, with some studies showing reductions in recidivism, but little to no improvement in mental health outcomes (Cosden *et al.*, 2003), while others have failed to show reductions in rearrest outcomes (Cosden *et al.*, 2003; Solomon and Draine, 1995a,b).

Mixed results for both FACT and FICM investigations may be explained, in part, by the fact that there was substantial heterogeneity in the samples being studied, particularly because of the presence of co-occurring disorders (Jennings, 2009). FACT and FICM may, in fact, perform better for individuals with a dual diagnosis, relative to those with a single mental disorder. For example, when one FACT program partitioned out the influence of dual disorders on their primary outcomes in an expanded follow-up, results showed that those with dual disorders had consistently positive changes in mental health outcomes, substance use abstinence, and stable housing (Cimino and Jennings, 2002; Smith, Jennings, and Cimino, 2009). This particular program was unique in that it included an additional IDDT component before the community treatment began. More research is needed to clarify whether FACT and FICM programs are most effective at reducing recidivism and other criminal outcomes for offenders with dual diagnosis, as opposed to those with a single mental disorder.

Diversion Programs and Specialty Courts

Diversion programs, including jail-based diversion, court-based diversion, and specialty courts (mental health and drug based), are a primary mechanism for diverting persons with SMI or substance use disorders out of the criminal justice system and into treatment and therefore reducing the burden of mental health treatment in the justice setting. Drug courts and mental health courts primarily focus on deterring criminal behavior by enhancing connections between treatment services provided to the defendant and the supervisory requests of the judicial system (Wenzel *et al.*, 2001; Naples, Morris, and Steadman, 2007). Underlying entry into drug courts is the assumption that drug or alcohol involvement is the primary determinant of the arrestee's criminal activity, whereas an SMI is presumed to underlie criminal activity for those entering a mental health court diversion program.

Diversion programs typically involve participation in treatment as an alternative to incarceration (prebooking) or as a way to reduce probation sentences (postbooking). Diversion that occurs at the level of prebooking is first enacted by the police, who are trained to assess and identify mental illness. Based on their assessment, and in collaboration with a mental health professional, the police determine whether the arrestee should not be charged with the offense and instead should be linked to appropriate treatment, or moved to the next step of criminal justice involvement. Diversion that occurs at the point of postbooking involves screening, assessment, and then negotiation with the court. A team of personnel from the criminal justice and mental health setting can make the decision to waive charges, reduce charges, or reduce time spent in jail provided that the arrestee engage in treatment and show improvement in symptoms (medication compliance, substance use abstinence).

A review of drug court and diversion programs suggests that drug use is much more common than alcohol use in offenders who participate in drug courts (Belenko, 2001), while alcohol problem severity is much lower and recent alcohol use is much less prevalent in offenders who are diverted to a specialty drug court compared with those who are not diverted (Broner *et al.*, 2004). This suggests that problem drinkers are much less likely to be diverted to a drug court, and alcohol may therefore not be a primary focus of the drug court. This may be reflected in the fact that there is a paucity of research on drug courts primarily for alcohol users. In recent years, however, driving under the influence (DUI) courts have been established as a way to funnel alcohol users into their own specialty court (Belenko, 2001). Results from these studies do not show promising effects for reducing DUI recidivism (Bouffard, Richardson, and Franklin, 2010).

Meta-analyses and empirical reviews show that diversion programs are more effective at reducing the risk of reoffending than improving mental health outcomes (Brown, 2010; Fulton Hora, 2002; Gordon, Barnes, and VanBenschoten, 2006; Grudzinskas *et al.*, 2005; Peters and Murrin, 2000; Sarteschi, Vaughn, and Kim, 2011; Steadman *et al.*, 2011; Trupin and Richards, 2003; Tyuse and Linhorst, 2005; Wilson, Mitchell, and MacKenzie, 2006). Despite this overall trend, there are differences in the findings across studies. Some studies suggest no relative improvement of criminal recidivism, days in jail, or arrests for new offenses across those in a specialty diversion program and those who are not (Cosden *et al.*, 2005), while others show the participation in a diversion program can significantly reduce the likelihood of new criminal charges and increase the amount of time between first arrest and recidivism (McNiel, 2007; Moore and Hiday, 2006). Broner *et al.* (2004) conducted a review of outcomes among persons with co-occurring disorders in eight different diversion programs across the country. In terms of mental health outcomes, results showed consistent effects of diversion on mental health service utilization in the areas of counseling, use of medication, as well as increased odds of hospitalization, use of emergency room services; however, statistically significant effects on improvements of mental health symptoms were not found. While alcohol and drug use were shown to decrease significantly across some studies in the short-term (3-month) period following baseline, the pooled effect across all sites showed no significant reductions in substance use in the long term.

Diversion programs have been criticized for several reasons. First, prerequisites for eligibility into a specialty drug court often exclude individuals with SMI or with a co-occurring disorder. Likewise, mental health courts often exclude individuals with serious substance abuse problems. Thus, diversion programs have often excluded people with dual disorders, despite their high level of involvement in the criminal justice system (Case *et al.*, 2009; DeMatteo *et al.*, 2009). Second, participation in a specialty court is of limited duration, and judicial entities may expect quick results. Critics of specialty courts argue that it is unrealistic to expect an individual to be symptom free in a matter of months, when most mental health and substance use disorders require several episodes of treatment in order to achieve remission (Grudzinskas *et al.*, 2005). Third, while effects on recidivism are consistent and robust across studies (Sarteschi *et al.*, 2011; Wilson *et al.*, 2006), the positive impact of diversion programs on mental health functioning is less clear. Fourth, variability in outcome effectiveness may be due to differences in study design, implementation, and sample composition (Redlich *et al.*, 2006; Wolff and Pogorzelski, 2005). Many studies lack random assignment, comparison groups, and have high drop-out rates (Wilson *et al.*, 2006), and there is a disproportionate representation of women and individuals with nonviolent and nonfelony offenses in jail diversion programs (Naples *et al.*, 2007). The decision not to accept individuals at greatest risk (males and those who were violent) may inappropriately funnel those who need targeted mental health and substance use treatment into the justice system, where in fact they may receive less intensive services (Veysey *et al.*, 1997).

Overall, the most immediate aim of diversion programs is to reduce criminal recidivism by diverting individuals with alcohol- or drug-related offenses and problems into treatment, and there appears to be some evidence supporting their success at this. However, it is less clear the extent to which diversion programs can affect improvement in mental health and substance use symptoms, and even less is known about the specific effectiveness of drug courts on alcohol-abusing subpopulations with a dual diagnosis. Improving SMI and substance abuse outcomes is an important goal for diversion programs to focus on in the future as they become more precise.

Therapeutic Community (TC)

The TC was originally developed for the treatment of disenfranchised, socially isolated people with a substance use disorder (including alcohol use disorders), and it has shown consistently positive effects on abstinence, employment, interpersonal functioning, and reduced criminal involvement in this specific group (De Leon, 1984; De Leon, Wexler, and Jainchill, 1982). The assumption of the TC is that, in order for treatment to be successful, rehabilitation must occur through an extended period of living in a 24-hour residential setting so that new life skills can be learned and integrated without the outside distractions (De Leon, 1984). Research on the TC approach in psychiatric samples has also shown it to be effective for people with co-occurring SMI and substance use disorder (Brunette, Mueser, and Drake, 2004).

Because of its effectiveness in treating dual disorders in nonoffender samples, the TC approach has been extended and modified to treat dually diagnosed populations in the justice system (De Leon, 2000; Sacks *et al.*, 2004; Van Stelle, Blumer, and Moberg, 2004; Zhang, Roberts, and McCollister, 2011). These modifications generally include segregation of the individual from the general prison population, group and community meetings, reinforcement/reward systems, using program graduates as aids for current enrollees, and incorporating a team treatment approach. TC delivered in the prison setting has ultimately been designed to shield prisoners with mental illness from the problems they experience as a result of prison life, such as victimization and social isolation. It has also been designed to lessen the impact of daily prison life on severe psychiatric symptoms, as well as employability and substance use abstinence upon release from prison. In addition to treatment during incarceration, modified TC programs have recently begun to incorporate a community after-care component that allows prisoners to reintegrate into society and to apply new skills into the community after being released. These programs have been primarily designed to treat drug offenders as alcohol use is less often reported as the primary drug of choice among dually diagnosed offenders enrolled in a TC program (Messina *et al.*, 2004).

Modified TC for dually diagnosed individuals in the prison setting generally has been shown to be effective at reducing recidivism (Sacks *et al.*, 2004, 2010, 2012); although it is less clear whether the effects of TC relative to other treatments are robust (Inciardi, Martin, and Butzin, 2004; Prendergast *et al.*, 2004), and no studies to our knowledge have directly examined the impact of TC on reductions in drinking behavior, alcohol use consequences, or alcohol-related arrests (over drug-related arrests). Recently, Messina *et al.* (2004) found that, in comparison with offenders without a co-occurring disorder who participated in a prison-based TC, those who were dually diagnosed were significantly more likely to be reincarcerated in the year following release from prison and showed a shorter time to incarceration. Further, Sullivan *et al.* (2007) showed no significant effect of a modified TC on certain mental health factors, such as depression and psychiatric symptom severity relative to a treatment control group in a sample of offenders with a dual diagnosis. Other studies show that a modified TC approach may be effective at treating dual diagnosis in prison settings but has generally weak retention rates when implemented in the community for justice-involved samples.

In sum, the TC approach has been shown to be effective for the treatment of substance abuse in offender populations. However, the extent to which TC may work for offenders with dual diagnosis remains unclear, and further research in this area is needed specifically as it relates to understanding more about the unique impact on alcohol use outcomes.

Cognitive-Behavioral Models and Motivational Enhancement Therapies

Cognitive-behavioral therapy (CBT), including motivational enhancement therapy (MET), has been praised as one of the more promising and effective interventions for offender populations (Friedmann, Taxman, and Henderson, 2007; Landenberger and Lipsey, 2005; Lipsey, Landenberger, and Wilson, 2007). In addition to providing skills training, an additional goal of CBT programs with offender samples is to alter maladaptive thinking styles that influence criminal and antisocial behavior, such as poor moral reasoning, deficient empathy and perspective-taking ability, strong need for dominance and superiority, sense of entitlement, and attributions of threat from others. Clients are taught to identify and modify distorted thinking styles through empathy training, to control their anger, and to prevent substance use relapse. Behavioral techniques include social skills training, contingency management strategies, self-monitoring, and use of token economies.

CBT programs, including those that use anger management techniques (if offenses are driven by anger or violence) and interpersonal problem solving, appear to be most effective at targeting criminal outcomes compared with behavioral-only interventions, with an average of 20–30% reduction in rates of recidivism (Landenberger and Lipsey, 2005; Lipsey and Landenberger, 2006; Lipsey, Chapman, and Landenberger, 2001; Lipsey *et al.*, 2007; McMurran *et al.*, 2008; Pearson *et al.*, 2002; Wilson, Bouffard, and Mackenzie, 2005). Although empirical support has been widely demonstrated for MET programs as a component of CBT for nonoffender populations at reducing substance use, there has been less systematic research with dually diagnosed offenders. The majority of MET studies with offenders have focused on substance-using populations without a dual diagnosis (Mann, Ginsburg, and Weekes, 2002; McMurran, 2009). MET appears to be useful in having a positive impact on treatment retention and engagement (McMurran and Ward, 2010). However, the evidence in support of MET's effectiveness for reducing substance use and for improving recidivism outcomes in offenders is mixed (McMurran, 2009), and with regard to offenders with a dual diagnosis, there appears to be scant published research.

Research has also examined specific CBT programs for drug and alcohol offenders, although relatively few have focused on dually diagnosed individuals. Specific alcohol-related CBT programs for offenders have been primarily targeted toward those who are court mandated as a result of a DUI or domestic violence incident in which alcohol was involved. These forms of treatment vary considerably as a function of individual state mandates, which can impact frequency, duration, and content of the intervention delivered (Dill and Wells-Parker, 2006). The components of the most effective treatments for DUI offenders often include MET, psychoeducation about the effects of alcohol, as well as brief advice and feedback about one's drinking (Dill and Wells-Parker, 2006). The presence of comorbid mental disorders among alcohol-involved DUI offenders is relatively high and, as a result, many individuals involved in DUI programs may be referred to additional treatment programs that will address the presence of these comorbid mental health problems in greater detail (Dill and Wells-Parker, 2006; Wells-Parker and Popkin, 1994). As yet, there is not an extensive program of research that has examined the effectiveness of alcohol-related cognitive-behavioral interventions for dually diagnosed offenders.

Not surprisingly, results of the effectiveness of CBT programs are complicated by heterogeneity among samples. Research suggests that high-risk individuals appear to benefit more from the highly structured and concrete behavioral monitoring aspects of CBT. This is consistent with the tenets of the RNR model in that treatment would be most effective by targeting individuals with the greatest risk and level of need. Specifically, as it relates to alcohol use behavior, this would mean focusing on the unique risks and consequences that stem from drinking, particularly among those dually diagnosed offenders whose primary drug of choice is alcohol. While there are many different types of CBT programs being offered to offenders, their relative efficacy on recidivism rates appear to be roughly equivalent (Lipsey *et al.*, 2007). These findings are encouraging in that they suggest that the application of any CBT program, if delivered well, will have positive impacts on recidivism outcomes. There remains a paucity of research examining the effectiveness of CBT programs for offenders with dual diagnoses; many of them focus on one disorder (Peters and Hills, 1997).

Transitional Housing and Supported Employment Services

The treatment needs of people with a dual diagnosis who are incarcerated in jails or prisons are often exacerbated at the point of release (Davis *et al.*, 2008). While not necessarily treatments per se, transitional housing and supported employment services are important programs for offenders who are reentering the community. Ideally, a reentry program should include prerelease planning that ensures that the individual can obtain secure, affordable, and stable housing; however, this is not always the case. The primary option for returning offenders is to live with a family member or a friend. However, if this is not available, other housing options include community-based correctional housing, transitional housing, federally subsidized housing, homeless assistance supported housing, and the private market.

A substantial group of individuals who are released from jail or prison may end up homeless, in a shelter, or without a stable housing situation. This has significant public health implications as homelessness is cited as one of the top risk factors for substance use relapse, mental health decomposition, and rearrest among former offenders (Metraux and Culhane, 2004; Rodriguez, Sentencing, and Program, 2003; Roman, 2004; Roman and Travis, 2006). Additionally, living in transitional housing can exacerbate psychiatric symptoms, increase the risk of substance use relapse (especially if the individual is staying with friends or family who abuses substances), and can have a major influence on rehospitalization or rearrest (Roman, 2004).

Supported employment is an evidence-based practice originally developed for use with individuals with SMI. The supported employment model focuses on helping clients obtain and maintain competitive employment as a means of improving quality of life and curtailing negative mental health outcomes. Supported employment programs are characterized by zero exclusion, rapid job search, provision of follow-along supports, respect for client preferences, integration with mental health treatment, benefits counseling, and provision of services in the community (Becker and Drake, 2003).

Among people with SMI, supported employment has the strongest empirical support for improving vocational outcomes, with multiple controlled trials demonstrating its superiority to other vocational models (Bond, Drake, and Becker, 2008). For justice-involved samples, supported employment has also been shown to help with the reintegration of offenders with SMI, but far less is known about its effectiveness on mental health and criminal outcomes with dually diagnosed offenders (Buck and Ventures, 2000; Freeman, 2003; Pager, 2006; Solomon *et al.*, 2004).

A number of barriers may stand in the way of dually diagnosed prisoners obtaining or receiving access to supported employment services. First, because of the massive insurgence of individuals into the prison population over the past 20 years, fewer resources have been allocated to these types of programs, and thus access to employment assistant services is severely limited (Frounfelker *et al.*, 2010; Roman, 2004). Obtaining employment for those with a criminal history is further complicated by laws that may prohibit anyone with a prior drug conviction from receiving food stamps, veteran's benefits, or Temporary Assistance for Needy Families (TANF), and it may take up to several weeks after release from prison to receive social security benefits. Access to jobs and competition for skill-appropriate jobs may be overwhelming for the dually diagnosed individual who is also trying to stay sober and attend daily treatment sessions, stay on an appropriate medication schedule, and manage family/social/health issues with little money. This may explain why access to supported employment services has been shown to take significantly longer for justice-involved individuals with a severe mental illness than for those who are not involved in the justice setting (Frounfelker *et al.*, 2010). Further, psychiatric symptoms, efforts to maintain abstinence, perceived stigma by others because of criminal justice involvement, social network influences, and lack of employment skills have all been cited as major barriers to obtaining work for dually diagnosed offenders (Frounfelker *et al.*, 2010; Laudet *et al.*, 2002). However, despite these barriers, controlled research has shown that people with a dual diagnosis demonstrate significantly better vocational outcomes in supported employment programs compared with those in other vocational rehabilitation programs (Mueser, Campbell, and Drake, 2011).

ORGANIZATIONAL/STRUCTURAL FACTORS THAT IMPACT TREATMENT

A variety of organizational and structural factors may also impact the effectiveness and implementation of treatments for offenders with dual diagnosis. First, workplace climate has an impact on treatment delivery. Characteristics of the climate include placing priority on offender change (rather than punishment techniques) and providing medication-assisted treatment services to eligible individuals, such as naltrexone or Vivitrol for alcohol-dependent clients. Additionally, holding opinions that favor reinforcement of goal attainment rather than punishment appears to distinguish more effective climates from less effective ones (Lipsey and Cullen, 2007).

Second, organizational and capacity needs, including staff resources, training, professional development, facilities, technology, program development, and community political support can influence the effectiveness of treatments for offenders with a dual diagnosis. Of note, in Melnick and colleagues' (2008) analysis of organizational characteristics related to delivery of intermediate and advanced IDDT for offenders, no differences were found between the two types of interventions on overall program resources, including funding, psychiatric staff, and reimbursement. This suggests that advanced programs may be able to deliver effective dual diagnosis treatments with few costs added to the implementation of intermediate-level programs.

The culture of the treatment facility and clinical staff is a third organizational factor that has been shown to be related to the delivery of dual diagnosis treatment for justice-involved populations (Melnick *et al.*, 2008). Integrated dual diagnosis programs appear to have high levels of staff involvement, clinical supervision of staff, and availability of discharge planning and transitional services for "graduating" patients, and rely strongly on evidence-based treatment practices (Melnick *et al.*, 2008).

Finally, implementation and dissemination issues are key factors that influence the effectiveness of any integrated program for offenders. These include implementing policies and practices to improve service delivery, developing/ maintaining relationships between mental health and correctional agencies, and providing access to evidence-based treatment for offenders. In fact, the degree of integration with community substance abuse treatment programs is a primary distinguishing organizational factor between advanced treatment programs that offer IDDT and intermediate programs (Melnick *et al.*, 2008). For treatments with dually diagnosed offenders to be successful, communication between mental health providers and judicial entities must be a primary element of the program. Further, assisting offenders in the transition from mental health treatment to the community and "real life" should also be emphasized.

CONCLUSIONS AND IMPLICATIONS

Among several offender typologies, overwhelming empirical evidence shows that the co-occurrence of a serious mental disorder with alcohol or substance use problems and the presence of an alcohol or substance use disorder are a robust predictor of violence and criminal offending. At this point, little has been reported on the unique effects of alcohol use disorder diagnosis on criminal recidivism, violence, mental health, and substance use outcomes among dually diagnosed offenders receiving treatment. More routine attention to alcohol use disorders as a category of inquiry separate from drug use disorders is needed if we are to answer important questions about "how" treatments work, and "for whom" they are most effective.

What can also be concluded from this chapter is that the assessment, targeting, and timing of the treatment of dually diagnosed offenders are important factors that appear to distinguish highly effective integrated programs from those that are less comprehensive. Perhaps targeting alcohol use separately from drug use in specific subpopulations could improve the efficacy of current treatments for offenders with a dual diagnosis. There is substantial heterogeneity among subtypes of dually diagnosed offenders, with the term referring to a broad set of combinations of diagnoses with various clinical presentations, which often do not take into account differences that exist between people who abuse alcohol and drugs. Data remain inconsistent as to whether, how, and which type of integrated program has a significant impact on future involvement in criminal justice settings as well as improvement in mental health and alcohol use symptoms for the vast majority of justice-involved persons who have an alcohol use disorder (Morrissey *et al.*, 2007; Osher and Steadman, 2007; Steadman and Naples, 2005). Inconclusive findings may be attributed, in part, to the varied symptom presentation among offenders with dual diagnosis (i.e., that alcohol and drug use disorders are often examined together rather than separately), background and temperamental characteristics of each individual, the point at which intervention is delivered in the justice setting, and organizational factors that influence service delivery.

Identifying different clusters of individuals with co-occurring disorders, based on their presenting diagnostic characteristics and functioning and their response to existing treatment, may be fruitful in clarifying subgroups of problem drinking offenders with different treatment needs. This could lead to a more focused research agenda on which to build future alcohol-related interventions for dually diagnosed offenders (Flynn and Brown, 2008). Overall, the development of effective treatment programs for dually diagnosed offenders and for those with co-occurring alcohol use and SMI, is still in its infancy. Further, interventions that focus specifically on treating alcohol consumption and related negative consequences are warranted. The unique risks and needs of dually diagnosed offenders invite policy makers, stakeholders, and evaluators to consider how these programs should deal with the ways justice-involved persons manage successful community reintegration that minimize mental illness problems and substance use relapse.

REFERENCES

Abram, K.M. and Teplin, L.A. (1991) Co-occurring disorders among mentally ill jail detainees: Implications for public policy. *The American Psychologist*, **46**(10), 1036.

Abram, K.M., Teplin, L.A., and McClelland, G.M. (2003) Comorbidity of severe psychiatric disorders and substance use disorders among women in jail. *The American Journal of Psychiatry*, **160**(5), 1007–1010.

Allebeck, P., Adamsson, C., Engström, A., and Rydberg, U. (1993) Cannabis and schizophrenia: A longitudinal study of cases treated in Stockholm County. *Acta Psychiatrica Scandinavica*, **88**, 21–24.

American Psychiatric Association (APA) (2000) *Diagnostic and Statistical Manual of Mental Disorders, Fourth Edition, Text Revision*. Arlington, VA: APA.

Andréasson, S., Allebeck, P., Engström, A., and Rydberg, U. (1987) Cannabis and schizophrenia: A longitudinal study of Swedish conscripts. *Lancet*, **26**, 1483–1486.

Andréasson, S., Allebeck, P., and Rydberg, U. (1989) Schizophrenia in users and nonusers of cannabis: A longitudinal study in Stockholm County. *Acta Psychiatrica Scandinavica*, **79**, 505–510.

Andrews, D.A. and Bonta, J. (2010) *The Psychology of Criminal Conduct*. Anderson.

Andrews, D.A., Bonta, J., and Hoge, R.D. (1990) Classification for effective rehabilitation: Rediscovering psychology. *Criminal Justice and Behavior*, **17**, 19–52.

Andrews, D.A., Bonta, J., and Wormith, J.S. (2006) The recent past and near future of risk and/or need assessment. *Crime and Delinquency*, **52**(1), 7.

Arseneault, L., Moffitt, T.E., Caspi, A. *et al.* (2000) Mental disorders and violence in a total birth cohort: Results from the Dunedin Study. *Archives of General Psychiatry*, **57**(10), 979.

Baillargeon, J., Hoge, S.K., and Penn, J.V. (2010a) Addressing the challenge of community reentry among released inmates with serious mental illness. *American Journal of Community Psychology*, **46**, 361–375.

Baillargeon, J., Penn, J.V., Knight, K. *et al.* (2010b) Risk of reincarceration among prisoners with co-occurring severe mental illness and substance use disorders. *Administration and Policy in Mental Health and Mental Health Services Research*, **37**(4), 367–374.

Baillargeon, J., Williams, B.A., Mellow, J. *et al.* (2009) Parole revocation among prison inmates with psychiatric and substance use disorders. *Psychiatric Services (Washington, DC)*, **60**(11), 1516.

Bean, G.J., Jr., Mierson, J., and Pinta, E. (1988) The prevalence of mental illness among inmates in the Ohio prison system. Final report to the Department of Mental Health and the Ohio Department of Rehabilitation and Correction Interdepartmental Planning and Oversight Committee for Psychiatric Services to Corrections. Columbus: Ohio State University.

Becker, D.R. and Drake, R.E. (2003) *A Working Life for People with Severe Mental Illness*. New York: Oxford Press.

Belenko, S. (2001) *Research on Drug Courts: A Critical Review*. New York: The National Center on Addiction and Substance Abuse (CASA) at Columbia University.

Bellack, A.S., Bennet, M.E., and Gearson, J.S. (2007) *Behavioral Treatment for Substance Abuse in People with Serious and Persistent Mental Illness: A Handbook for Mental Health Professionals*. New York: Taylor and Francis.

Blair, R.J.R., Peschardt, K., Budhani, S. *et al.* (2006) The development of psychopathy. *Journal of Child Psychology and Psychiatry*, **47**(34), 262–276.

Bond, G.R., Drake, R.E., and Becker, D.R. (2008) An update on randomized controlled trials of evidence-based supported employment. *Psychiatric Rehabilitation Journal*, **31**, 280–290.

Bonta, J. and Andrews, D. (2007) Risk-need-responsivity model for offender assessment and rehabilitation. *Rehabilitation*, 06.

Boothroyd, R.A., Mercado, C.C., Poythress, N.G. *et al.* (2005) Clinical outcomes of defendants in mental health court. *Psychiatric Services (Washington, DC)*, **56**(7), 829–834.

Bouffard, J.A., Richardson, K.A., and Franklin, T. (2010) Drug courts fo DWI offenders? The effectiveness of two hybrid drug courts on DWI offenders. *Journal of Criminal Justice*, **38**, 25–33.

Broner, N., Lattimore, P.K., Cowell, A.J., and Schlenger, W.E. (2004) Effects of diversion on adults with co-occurring mental illness and substance use: Outcomes from a national multi-site study. *Behavioral Sciences & the Law*, **22**(4), 519–541.

Brown, R. (2010) Associations with substance abuse treatment completion among drug court participants. *Substance Use & Misuse*, **45**(12), 1874–1891.

Brunette, M., Mueser, K., and Drake, R. (2004) A review of research on residential programs for people with severe mental illness and co-occurring substance use disorders. *Drug and Alcohol Review*, **23**(4), 471–481.

Buck, M.L. and Ventures, C.f.P.P. (2000) *Getting Back to Work: Employment Programs for Ex-offenders*: Philadelphia: Public/Private Ventures.

Calsyn, R.J., Yonker, R.D., Lemming, M.R. *et al.* (2005) Impact of assertive community treatment and client characteristics on criminal justice outcomes in dual disorder homeless individuals. *Criminal Behaviour and Mental Health*, **15**, 236–248.

Case, B., Steadman, H.J., Dupuis, S.A., and Morris, L.S. (2009) Who succeeds in jail diversion programs for persons with mental illness? A multi-site study. *Behavioral Sciences & the Law*, **27**(5), 661–674.

Castillo, E.D. and Fiftal Alarid, L. (2011) Factors associated with recidivism among offenders with mental illness. *International Journal of Offender Therapy and Comparative Criminology*, **55**(1), 98–117.

Chandler, R.K., Peters, R.H., Field, G., and Juliano-Bult, D. (2004) Challenges in implementing evidence-based treatment practices for co-occurring disorders in the criminal justice system. *Behavioral Sciences & the Law*, **22**(4), 431–448.

Chloe, J.Y., Teplin, L.A., and Abram, K.E. (2008) Perpetartion of violence, violent victimizaiton, and severe mental illness: Balancing public health concerns. *Psychiatric Services (Washington, DC)*, **59**, 153–164.

Cimino, T. and Jennings, J.L. (2002) Arkansas partnership program: An innovative continuum of care program for dually diagnosed forensic patients. *Psychiatric Rehabilitation Skills*, **6**(1), 104–114.

Collins, P.A., Cooper, J.A., Horn, B. *et al.* (2010) The cost of substance abuse: The use of administrative data to investigate treatment benefits in a rural mountain state. *Western Criminology Review*, **11**(3), 12–28.

Conner, K.R., Pinquart, M., and Gamble, S.A. (2009) Meta-analysis of depression and substance use among individuals with alcohol use disorders. *Journal of Substance Abuse Treatment*, **37**(2), 127–137.

Constantine, R., Andel, R., Petrila, J. *et al.* (2010a) Characteristics and experiences of adults with a serious mental illness who were involved in the criminal justice system. *Psychiatric Services (Washington, DC)*, **61**(5), 451–457.

Constantine, R.J., Petrila, J., Andel, R. *et al.* (2010b) Arrest trajectories of adult offenders with a serious mental illness. *Psychology, Public Policy, and Law*, **16**(4), 319–339.

Conway, K.P., Compton, W., Stinson, F.S., and Grant, B.F. (2006) Lifetime comorbidity of DSM-IV mood and anxiety disorders and specific drug use disorders: Results from the National Epidemiologic Survey on Alcohol and Related Conditions. *The Journal of Clinical Psychiatry*, **67**(2), 247–257.

Cosden, M., Ellens, J., Schnell, J., and Yaminiâ-Diouf, Y. (2005) Efficacy of a mental health treatment court with assertive community treatment. *Behavioral Sciences & the Law*, **23**(2), 199–214.

Cosden, M., Ellens, J.K., Schnell, J.L. *et al.* (2003) Evaluation of a mental health treatment court with assertive community treatment. *Behavioral Sciences & the Law*, **21**(4), 415–427.

Davis, K., Fallon, J., Vogel, S., and Teachout, A. (2008) Integrating into the mental health system from the criminal justice system: Jail aftercare services for persons with a severe mental illness. *Journal of Offender Rehabilitation*, **46**(3), 217–231.

De Leon, G. (1984) Program-based evaluation research in therapeutic communities. *Drug Abuse Treatment Evaluation: Strategies, Progress, and Prospects. National Institute on Drug Abuse Research Monograph*, **51**, 69–87.

De Leon, G. (2000) *The Therapeutic Community: Theory, Model, and Method*. Springer Publishing Company.

De Leon, G., Wexler, H.K., and Jainchill, N. (1982) The therapeutic community: Success and improvement rates 5 years after treatment. *Substance Use & Misuse*, **17**(4), 703–747.

DeMatteo, D., Marlowe, D.B., Festinger, D.S., and Arabia, P.L. (2009) Outcome trajectories in drug court. *Criminal Justice and Behavior*, **36**(4), 354–368.

Diamond, P.M., Wang, E.W., Holzer, C.E. *et al.* (2001) The prevalence of mental illness in prison. *Administration and Police in Mental Health*, **29**(1), 21–40.

Dill, P.L. and Wells-Parker, E. (2006) Court-mandated treatment for convicted drinking drivers. *Alcohol Research and Health*, **29**(1), 41–48.

Dixon, L. (2000) Assertive community treatment: Twenty-five years of gold. *Psychiatric Services (Washington, DC)*, **51**(6), 759–765.

Dixon, L.B., Dickerson, F., Bellack, A.S. *et al.* (2010) The 2009 PORT psychosocial treatment recommendations and summary statements. *Schizophrenia Bulletin*, **36**, 48–70.

Douglas, K.S., Guy, L.S., and Hart, S.D. (2009) Psychosis as a risk factor for violence to others: A meta-analysis. *Psychological Bulletin*, **135**(5), 679–706.

Draine, J., Wilson, A.B., and Pogorzelski, W. (2007) Limitations and potential in current research on services for people with mental illness in the criminal justice system. *Journal of Offender Rehabilitation*, **45**(3–4), 159–177.

Drake, R.E. and Brunette, M.F. (1998) Complications of severe mental illness related to alcohol and drug use disorders. *Recent Developments in Alcoholism*, **14**, 285–299.

Drake, R.E., McHugo, G.J., Clark, R.E. *et al.* (1998a) Assertive community treatment for patients with co-occurring severe mental illness and substance use disorder: A clinical trial. *The American Journal of Orthopsychiatry*, **68**, 201–215.

Drake, R.E., Mercer-McFadden, C., Mueser, K.T. *et al.* (1998b) Review of integrated mental health and substance abuse treatment for patients with dual disorders. *Schizophrenia Bulletin*, **24**(4), 589–608.

Drake, R.E., Morrissey, J.P., and Mueser, K.T. (2006) The challenge of treating forensic dual diagnosis clients: Comment on integrated treatment for jail recidivists with co-occurring psychiatric and substance use disorders. *Community Mental Health Journal*, **42**(4), 427–432.

Drake, R.E., O'Neal, E.L., and Wallach, M.A. (2008) A systematic review of psychosocial research on psychosocial interventions for people with co-occurring severe mental and substance use disorders. *Journal of Substance Abuse Treatment*, **34**(1), 123–138.

Drake, R.E., Wallach, M.A., and McGovern, M.P. (2005) Special section on relapse prevention: Future directions in preventing relapse to substance abuse among clients with severe mental illnesses. *Psychiatric Services (Washington, DC)*, **56**(10), 1297–1302.

Elbogen, E.B. and Johnson, S.C. (2009) The intricate link between violence and mental disorder: Results from the National Epidemiologic Survey on Alcohol and Related Conditions. *Archives of General Psychiatry*, **66**(2), 152–161.

Elbogen, E.B., Van Dorn, R.A., Swanson, J.W. *et al.* (2006) Treatment engagement and violence risk in mental disorders. *The British Journal Of Psychiatry*, **189**(4), 354–360.

Essock, S.M., Mueser, K.T., Drake, R.E. *et al.* (2006) Comparison of ACT and standard case management for delivering integrated treatment for co-occurring disorders. *Psychiatric Services (Washington, DC)*, **57**, 185–196.

Farkas, K. and Hrouda, D. (2007) Co-occurring disorders among female jail detainees: Implications for service delivery. *Journal of Social Work Practice in the Addiction*, **7**, 51–67.

Fazel, S., Bains, P., and Doll, H. (2005) Substance abuse and dependence in prisoners: A systematic review. *Addiction*, **101**, 181–191.

Fazel, S. and Danesh, J. (2002) Serious mental disorder in 23 000 prisoners: A systematic review of 62 surveys. *Lancet*, **359**(9306), 545–550.

Fazel, S., Langstrom, N., Hjern, A. *et al.* (2009) Schizophrenia, substance abuse, and violent crime. *Journal of the American Medical Association*, **301**(9), 2016–2023.

Felitti, V.J., Anda, R.F., Nordenberg, D. *et al.* (1998) Relationship of childhood abuse and household dysfunction to many of the leading causes of death in adults: The Adverse Childhood Experiences (ACE) Study. *American Journal of Preventive Medicine*, **14**(4), 245–258.

Fergusson, D.M., Boden, J.M., and Horwood, L.J. (2011) Structural models of the comorbidity of internalizing disorders and substance use disorders in a longitudinal birth cohort. *Social Psychiatry and Psychiatric Epidemiology*, **46**, 933–942.

Fernandez-Espejo, E., Viveros, M., Nunez, L. *et al.* (2008) Role of cannabis and endocannabinoids in the genesis of schizophrenia. *Psychopharmacology*, **206**, 531–549.

Fletcher, B.W., Lehman, W.E.K., Wexler, H.K., and Melnick, G. (2007) Who participates in the criminal justice drug abuse treatment studies (CJ-DATS)? *The Prison Journal*, **87**(1), 25–57.

Flynn, P.M. and Brown, B.S. (2008) Co-occurring disorders in substance abuse treatment: Issues and prospects. *Journal of Substance Abuse Treatment*, **34**(1), 36–47.

Freeman, R.B. (2003) Can we close the revolving door?: Recidivism vs. *employment of ex-offenders in the US*. Retrieved March 6, 2012, from http://www.urban.org/url.cfm?ID=410857

French, M.T., Popovici, I., and Tapsell, L. (2008) The economic costs of substance abuse treatment: Updated estimates and cost bands for program assessment and reimbursement. *Journal of Substance Abuse Treatment*, **35**(4), 462–469.

Friedmann, P.D., Melnick, G., Jiang, L., and Hamilton, Z. (2008) Violent and disruptive behavior among drug-involved prisoners: Relationship with psychiatric symptoms. *Behavioral Sciences and the Law*, **26**, 389–401.

Friedmann, P.D., Taxman, F.S., and Henderson, C.E. (2007) Evidence-based treatment practices for drug-involved adults in the criminal justice system. *Journal of Substance Abuse Treatment*, **32**(3), 267–277.

Friend, J., Langhinrichsen-Rohling, J., and Eichold, B.H. (2011) Same-day substance use in men and women charged with felony domstic violence offenses. *Criminal Justice and Behavior*, **38**, 619–633.

Frisman, L.K., Mueser, K.T., Covell, N.H. *et al.* (2009) Use of integrated dual disorder treatment via assertive community treatment versus clinical case management for persons with co-occurring disorders and antisocial personality disorder. *Journal of Nervous and Mental Disorders*, **197**, 822–828.

Frounfelker, R.L., Glover, C.M., Teachout, A. *et al.* (2010) Access to supported employment for consumers with criminal justice involvement. *Psychiatric Rehabilitation Journal*, **34**(1), 49–56.

Fulton Hora, H.P. (2002) A dozen years of drug treatment courts: Uncovering our theoretical foundation and the construction of a mainstream paradigm. *Substance Use & Misuse*, **37**(12–13), 1469–1488.

Gordon, J.A., Barnes, C.M., and VanBenschoten, S.W. (2006) Dual treatment track program: A descriptive assessment of a new in-house jail diversion program. *Federal Probation*, **70**(3), 9–18.

Grant, B., Dawson, D., Stinson, F. *et al.* (2004) The 12-month prevalence and trends in DSM-IV alcohol abuse and dependence: United States, 1991–1992 and 2001–2002. *Drug and Alcohol Dependence*, **74**(3), 223–234.

Grant, B.F. (1995) Comorbidity between DSM-IV drug use disorders and major depression: Results of a national survey of adults. *Journal of Substance Abuse*, **7**(4), 481–497.

Grant, B.F. and Hartford, T.C. (1995) Comorbidity between DSM-IV alcohol use disorders and major depression: Results of a national survey. *Drug and Alcohol Dependence*, **39**(3), 197–206.

Green, A.I., Noordsy, D.L., Brunette, M.F., and O'Keefe, C. (2008) Substance abuse and schizophrenia: Pharmacotherapeutic intervention. *Journal of Substance Abuse Treatment*, **34**(1), 61–71.

Green, A.I., Zimmet, S.V., Straus, R.D., and Schildkraut, J.J. (1999) Clozapine for comorbid substance use disorder and schizophrenia: Do patients with schizophrenia have a reward-deficiency syndrome that can be ameliorated by clozapine? *Harvard Review of Psychiatry*, **6**(6), 287–296.

Greenfield, S.F., Weiss, R.D., Muenz, L.R. *et al.* (1998) The effect of depression on return to drinking: A prospective study. *Archives of General Psychiatry*, **55**(3), 259–265.

Grudzinskas, A.J., Clayfield, J.C., Roy-Bujnowski, K. *et al.* (2005) Integrating the criminal justice system into mental health service delivery: The Worcester diversion experience. *Behavioral Sciences & the Law*, **23**(2), 277–293.

Gumpert, C.H., Winerdal, U., Grundtman, M. *et al.* (2010) The Relationship between substance abuse treatment and crime relapse among individuals with suspected mental disorder, substance abuse, and antisocial behavior: Findings from the MSAC study. *International Journal of Forensic Mental Health*, **9**(2), 82–92.

Hall, W. and Degenhardt, L. (2008) Cannabis use and the risk of developing a psychotic disorder. *World Psychiatry*, **7**, 68–71.

Hasin, D., Liu, X., Nunes, E. *et al.* (2002) Effects of major depression on remission and relapse of substance dependence. *Archives of General Psychiatry*, **59**(4), 375–380.

Hasin, D.S., Stinson, F.S., Ogburn, E., and Grant, B.F. (2007) Prevalence, correlates, disability, and comorbidity of DSM-IV alcohol abuse and dependence in the United States: Results from the National Epidemiologic Survey on Alcohol and Related Conditions. *Archives of General Psychiatry*, **64**(7), 830–842.

Hawthorne, W.B., Folsom, D.P., Sommerfeld, D.H. *et al.* (2012) Incarceration among adults who are in the public mental health system: Rates, risk factors, and short-term outcomes. *Psychiatric Services (Washington, DC)*, **63**, 26–32.

Hesselbrock, M.N. (1986) Childhood behavior problems and adult antisocial personality disorder in alcoholism. In R.E. Meyer (ed.), *Psychopathology and Addictive Disorders* (pp. 78–94). New York: Guildford Press.

Hesselbrock, V.M., Hesselbrock, M.N., and Stabenau, J.R. (1985) Alcoholism in men patients subtyped by family history and antisocial personality. *Journal of Studies on Alcohol*, **46**(1), 59–64.

Hodgins, S. (2008) Violent behavior among people with schizophrenia: A framework for investigations of causes, and effective treatment, and intervention. *Philosophical Transactions of The Royal Society*, **363**, 2505–2518.

Hodgins, S., Cree, A., Alderton, J., and Mak, T. (2008) From conduct disorder to severe mental illness: Associations with aggressive behaviour, crime, and victimization. *Psychological Medicine*, **38**, 975–987.

Hodgins, S., Tiihonen, J., and Ross, D. (2005) The consequences of conduct disorder for males who develop schizophrenia: Associations with criminality, aggressive behavior, substance use, and psychiatric services. *Schizophrenia Research*, **78**(2–3), 323–335.

Hodgins, S., Toupin, J., and Côté, G. (1996) Schizophrenia and antisocial personality disorder: A criminal combination. In L.B. Schlesinger (ed.), *Explorations in Criminal Psychopathology: Clinical Syndromes with Forensic Implications* (pp. 217–237). Springfield, IL: Charles C. Thomas.

Ilgen, M. and Moos, R. (2005) Deterioration following alcohol-use disorder treatment in project MATCH. *Journal of Studies on Alcohol*, **66**(4), 517–525.

Ilgen, M. and Moos, R. (2006) Special section: A memorial tribute: Exacerbation of psychiatric symptoms during substance use disorder treatment. *Psychiatric Services (Washington, DC)*, **57**(12), 1758–1764.

Inciardi, J.A., Martin, S.S., and Butzin, C.A. (2004) Five-year outcomes of therapeutic community treatment of drug-involved offenders after release from prison. *Crime & Delinquency*, **50**(1), 88–107.

Jennings, J.L. (2009) Does assertive community treatment work with forensic populations? review and recommendations. *Open Psychiatry Journal*, **3**, 13–19.

Kelly, J. (2009) Violence in schizophrenia rare in the absence of substance abuse. *Journal of the American Medical Association*, **301**, 2016–2023.

Kerridge, B.T. (2009) Sociological, social psychological, and psychopathological correlates of substance use disorders in the US jail population. *International Journal of Offender Therapy and Comparative Criminology*, **53**(2), 168–190.

Kessler, R.C., Berglund, P., Demler, O. *et al.* (2005) Lifetime prevalence and age-of-onset distributions of DSM-IV disorders in the National Comorbidity Survey Replication. *Archives of General Psychiatry*, **62**(6), 593–602.

Kessler, R.C., Nelson, C.B., McGonagle, K.A. *et al.* (1996a) The epidemiology of co-occurring addictive and mental disorders: Implications for prevention and service utilization. *The American Journal of Orthopsychiatry*, **66**(1), 17–31.

Kessler, R.C., Nelson, C.B., McGonagle, K.A. *et al.* (1996b). Comorbidity of DSM-III-R major depressive disorder in the general population: results from the US National Comorbidity Survey. *British Journal of Psychiatry* (Suppl 30), 17–30.

Khantzian, E.J. (1997) The self-medication hypothesis of substance use disorders: A reconsideration and recent applications. *Harvard Review of Psychiatry*, **4**(5), 231–244.

Koskinen, J., Löhönen, J., Koponen, H. *et al.* (2010) Rate of cannabis use disorders in clinical samples of patients with schizophrenia: A meta-analysis. *Schizophrenia Bulletin*, **36**(6), 1115–1130.

Kushner, M.G. and Mueser, K.T. (1993) Psychiatric co-morbidity with alcohol use disorders. Vol. NIH Pub. No. 94-3699, *Eighth Special Report to the U.S. Congress on Alcohol and Health* (pp. 37–59). Rockville, MD: US Department of Health and Human Services.

Lamb, H.R., Weinberger, L.E., and Gross, B.H. (2004) Mentally ill persons in the criminal justice system: Some perspectives. *The Psychiatric Quarterly*, **75**(2), 107–126.

Lamberti, J.S., Weisman, R., and Faden, D.I. (2004) Forensic assertive community treatment: Preventing incarceration of adults with severe mental illness. *Psychiatric Services (Washington, DC)*, **55**(11), 1285–1293.

Lamberti, J.S. and Weisman, R.L. (2002) *Preventing Incarceration of Adults with Severe Mental Illness: Project Link*. New York: Springer Press.

Landenberger, N.A. and Lipsey, M.W. (2005) The positive effects of cognitive-behavioral programs for offenders: A meta-analysis of factors associated with effective treatment. *Journal of Experimental Criminology*, **1**(4), 451–476.

Laudet, A.B., Magura, S., Vogel, H.S., and Knight, E.L. (2002) Interest in and obstacles to pursuing work among unemployed dually diagnosed individuals. *Substance Use & Misuse*, **37**(2), 145–170.

Linszen, D.H., Dingemans, P.M., and Lenior, M.E. (1994) Cannabis abuse and the course of recent-onset schizophrenic disorders. *Archives of General Psychiatry*, **51**(4), 273–279.

Lipsey, M. and Landenberger, N. (2006) Cognitive-behavioral interventions. In B.C. Walsh and D.P. Farrington (eds), *Preventing Crime: What Works for Children Offenders, Victims, and Places* (pp. 57–71). Great Britain: Spring.

Lipsey, M.W., Chapman, G.L., and Landenberger, N.A. (2001) Cognitive-behavioral programs for offenders. *The Annals of the American Academy of Political and Social Science*, **578**(1), 144–157.

Lipsey, M.W. and Cullen, F.T. (2007) The effectiveness of correctional rehabilitation: A review of systematic reviews. *Annual Review of Law and Social Science*, **3**, 297–320.

Lipsey, M.W., Landenberger, N.A., and Wilson, S.J. (2007) Effects of cognitive-behavioral programs for criminal offenders. Center for Evaluation Research and Methodology, Vanderbilt Institute for Public Policy Studies, Campbell Collaboration. *Campbell Systematic Reivews*, **6**, 1–27.

Lo, C. and Stephens, R.C. (2002) The role of drugs in crime: Insights from a group of incoming prisoners. *Substance Use & Misuse*, **37**(1), 121–131.

Lurigio, A.J., Fallon, J.R., and Dincin, J. (2000) Helping the mentally ill in jails adjust to community life: A description of a postrelease ACT program and its clients. *International Journal of Offender Therapy and Comparative Criminology*, **44**(5), 532–548.

Mallik-Kane, K., and Visher, C.A. (2008) *Health and Prisoner Reentry: How Physical, Mental, and Substance Abuse Conditions Shape the Process of Reintegration*. Washington, DC: Urban Institute Justice Policy Center.

Mann, R.E., Ginsburg, J.I.D., and Weekes, J.R. (2002) Motivational interviewing with offenders. In M. McMurran (ed.), *Motivating Offenders to Change: A Guide to Enhancing Engagement in Therapy* (pp. 87–102). John Wiley & Sons.

Mazza, M., Mandelli, L., Di Nicola, M. *et al.* (2009) Clinical features, response to treatment and functional outcome of bipolar disorder patients with and without co-occurring substance use disorder: 1-year follow-up. *Journal of Affective Disorders*, **115**(1–2), 27–35.

McCabe, P.J., Christopher, P.P., Druhn, N. *et al.* (2012) Arrest types and co-occurring disorders in persons with schizophrenia or related psychoses. *The Journal of Behavioral Health Services and Research*. DOI: 10.1007/s11414-011-9269-4.

McHugo, G.J., Drake, R.E., Teague, G.B., and Xie, H. (1999) Fidelity to assertive community treatment and client outcomes in the New Hampshire dual disorders study. *Psychiatric Services (Washington, DC)*, **50**, 818–824.

McMurran, M. (2009) Motivational interviewing with offenders: A systematic review. *Legal and Criminological Psychology*, **14**(1), 83–100.

McMurran, M., Theodosi, E., Sweeney, A., and Sellen, J. (2008) What do prisoners want? Current concerns of adult male prisoners. *Psychology, Crime & Law*, **14**(3), 267–274.

McMurran, M. and Ward, T. (2010) Treatment readiness, treatment engagement and behaviour change. *Criminal Behaviour and Mental Health*, **20**(2), 75–85.

McNiel, D. (2007) Effectiveness of a mental health court in reducing criminal recidivism and violence. *The American Journal of Psychiatry*, **164**(9), 1395–1403.

Melnick, G., Coen, C., Taxman, F.S. *et al.* (2008) Community-based co-occurring disorder (COD) intermediate and advanced treatment for offenders. *Behavioral Sciences & the Law*, **26**(4), 457–473.

Merricle, A.A. and Havassy, B.E. (2008) Characteristics of recent violence among entrants to acute mental health and substance abuse services. *Social Psychiatry and Psychiatric Empidemiology*, **43**, 392–402.

Messina, N., Burdon, W., Hagopian, G., and Prendergast, M. (2004) One year return to custody rates among co-disordered offenders. *Behavioral Sciences & the Law*, **22**(4), 503–518.

Metraux, S. and Culhane, D.P. (2004) Homeless shelter use and reincarceration following prison release: Assessing the risk. *Journal of Criminology & Public Policy*, **3**(2), 139–160.

Moffitt, T.E. (1993) Adolescence-limited and life-course-persistent antisocial behavior: A developmental taxonomy. *Psychological Review*, **100**(4), 674–701.

Moore, M.E. and Hiday, V.A. (2006) Mental health court outcomes: A comparison of re-arrest and re-arrest severity between mental health court and traditional court participants. *Law and Human Behavior*, **30**(6), 659–674.

Moran, P. and Hodgins, S. (2004) The correlates of comorbid antisocial personality disorder in schizophrenia. *Schizophrenia Bulletin*, **30**(4), 791–802.

Morrissey, J., Meyer, P., and Cuddeback, G. (2007) Extending assertive community treatment to criminal justice settings: Origins, current evidence, and future directions. *Community Mental Health Journal*, **43**(5), 527–544.

Morse, G.A., Calsyn, R.J., Klinkenberg, D.W. *et al.* (2006) Treating homeless clients with severe mental illness and substance use disorders: Costs and outcomes. *Community Mental Health Journal*, **42**, 377–404.

Motiuk, L.L. and Porporino, F.J. (1991) *The Prevalence, Nature and Severity of Mental Health Problems among Federal Male Inmates in Canadian Penitentiaries*. Ottawa: Correctional Services of Canada.

Mueser, K.T., Bellack, A.S., and Blanchard, J.J. (1992) Comorbidity of schizophrenia and substance abuse: Implications for treatment. *Journal of Consulting and Clinical Psychology*, **60**(6), 845–856.

Mueser, K.T., Bond, G.R., Drake, R.E., and Resnick, S.G. (1998) Models of community care for severe mental illness: A review of research on case management. *Schizophrenia Bulletin*, **24**, 37–74.

Mueser, K.T., Campbell, K., and Drake, R.E. (2011) The effectiveness of supported employment in people with dual disorders. *Journal of Dual Diagnosis*, **7**, 90–102.

Mueser, K.T., Crocker, A.G., Frisman, L.B. *et al.* (2006) Conduct disorder and antisocial personality disorder in persons with severe psychiatric and substance use disorders. *Schizophrenia Bulletin*, **32**(4), 626–636.

Mueser, K.T., Drake, R.E., Ackerson, T.H. *et al.* (1997) Antisocial personality disorder, conduct disorder, and substance abuse in schizophrenia. *Journal of Abnormal Psychology*, **106**(3), 473–477.

Mueser, K.T., Drake, R.E., and Wallach, M.A. (1998) Dual diagnosis: A review of etiological theories. *Addictive Behaviors*, **23**(6), 717–734.

Mueser, K.T., Gottlieb, J.D., Cather, C. *et al.* (2012) Antisocial personality disorder in people with co-occurring severe mental illness and substance use disorders: Clinical, functional, and family relationship correlates. *Psychosis*, **4**(1), 52–62.

Mueser, K.T., Noordsy, D.L., and Drake, R.E. (2003) *Integrated Treatment for Dual Disorders: A Guide to Effective Practice*. New York: Guilford Press.

Mueser, K.T., Rosenberg, S.D., Drake, R.E. *et al.* (1999) Conduct disorder, antisocial personality disorder, and substance use disorders in schizophrenia and major affective disorders. *Journal of Studies on Alcohol*, **60**, 278–284.

Mueser, K.T., Torrey, W.C., Lynde, D. *et al.* (2003) Implementing evidence-based practices for people with severe mental illness. *Behavior Modification*, **27**(3), 387–411.

Mueser, K.T., Yarnold, P., and Bellack, A. (1992) Diagnostic and demographic correlates of substance abuse in schizophrenia and major affective disorder. *Acta Psychiatrica Scandinavica*, **85**(1), 48–55.

Mueser, K.T., Yarnold, P.R., Levinson, D.F. *et al.* (1990) Prevalence of substance abuse in schizophrenia: Demographic and clinical correlates. *Schizophrenia Bulletin*, **16**(1), 31–56.

Naples, M., Morris, L.S., and Steadman, H.J. (2007) Factors in disproportionate representation among persons recommended by programs and accepted by courts for jail diversion. *Psychiatric Services (Washington, DC)*, **58**(8), 1095–1101.

Neighbors, H.W., Williams, D.H., Gunnings, T.S. *et al.* (1987) The prevalence of mental disorder in Michigan prisons. Final report submitted to the Michigan Department of Corrections. Lansing. Corrections: Michigan Department of Corrections.

Novick, D., Haro, J.M., Suarez, D. *et al.* (2010) Predictors and clinical consequences of nonadherence with antipsychotic medication in the outpatient treatment of schizophrenia. *Psychiatry Research*, **176**(2–3), 109–113.

Osher, F.C. (2008) Integrated mental health/substance abuse responses to justice Involved persons with co-occurring disorders. *Journal of Dual Diagnosis*, **4**(1), 3–33.

Osher, F.C. and Steadman, H.J. (2007) Adapting evidence-based practices for persons with mental illness involved with the criminal justice system. *Psychiatric Services (Washington, DC)*, **58**(11), 1472–1478.

Osher, F.C., Steadman, H.J., and Barr, H. (2003) A best practice approach to community reentry from jails for inmates with co-occurring disorders: The APIC model. *Crime & Delinquency*, **49**(1), 79–96.

Owen, R.R., Fischer, E.P., Booth, B.M., and Cuffel, B.J. (1996) Medication noncompliance and substance abuse among patients with schizophrenia. *Psychiatric Services (Washington, DC)*, **47**(8), 853–858.

Pager, D. (2006) Evidence-based pollicy for successful prisoner re-entry. *Criminology & Public Policy*, **5**(3), 505–514.

Pearson, F.S., Cleland, C.M., Chaple, M. *et al.* (2008) Substance use, mental health problems, and behavior at risk for HIV: Evidence from CJDATS. *Journal of Psychoactive Drugs*, **40**(4), 459–469.

Pearson, F.S., Lipton, D.S., Cleland, C.M., and Yee, D.S. (2002) The effects of behavioral/ cognitive-behavioral programs on recidivism. *Crime & Delinquency*, **48**(3), 476–496.

Pelissier, B., Jones, N., and Cadigan, T. (2007) Drug treatment aftercare in the criminal justice system: A systematic review. *Journal of Substance Abuse Treatment*, **32**(3), 311–320.

Penn, D.L., Roberts, L.J., Munt, E.D. *et al.* (2005) A pilot study of social cognition and interaction training (SCIT) for schizophrenia. *Schizophrenia Research*, **80**, 357–359.

Peters, R.H. (2008) Co-occurring disorders. *Quality Improvement For Drug Courts*.

Peters, R.H. and Hills, H.A. (1997) *Intervention Strategies for Offenders with Co-Occurring Disorders: What Works?* Delmar, NY: The GAINS Center.

Peters, R.H. and Murrin, M.R. (2000) Effectiveness of treatment-based drug courts in reducing criminal recidivism. *Criminal Justice and Behavior*, **27**(1), 72–96.

Peters, R.H., Sherman, P.B., and Osher, F.C. (2008) Treatment in jails and prisons. In K.T. Mueser and D.V. Jeste (eds), *Clinical Handbook of Schizophrenia* (pp. 354–364). New York: Guildford Press.

Phillips, S.D., Burns, B.J., Edgar, E.R. *et al.* (2001) Moving assertive community treatment into standard practice. *Psychiatric Services (Washington, DC)*, **52**(6), 771–779.

Prendergast, M.L., Hall, E.A., Wexler, H.K. *et al.* (2004) Amity prison based therapeutic community: 5 year outcomes. *The Prison Journal*, **84**, 36–60.

Redlich, A.D., Steadman, H.J., Monahan, J. *et al.* (2006) Patterns of practice in mental health courts: A national survey. *Law and Human Behavior*, **30**(3), 347–362.

Regier, D.A., Farmer, M.E., Rae, D.S. *et al.* (1990a) Comorbidity of mental disorders with alcohol and other drug abuse. *Journal of the American Medical Association*, **264**(19), 2511–2518.

Regier, D.A., Farmer, M.E., Rae, D.S. *et al.* (1990b) Results from the Epidemiologic Catchment Area (ECA) Study. *Journal of the American Medical Association*, **264**, 2511–2518.

Robins, L. and McEvoy, L. (1992) Conduct problems as predictors of substance abuse. In L.N. Robins and M. Rutter (eds), *Straight and Devious Pathways from Childhood to Adulthood* (pp. 182–204). New York: Cambridge University Press.

Robins, L.N. and Price, R.K. (1991) Adult disorders predicted by childhood conduct problems: Results from the NIMH Epidemiologic Catchment Area project. *Psychiatry: Interpersonal and Biological Processes*, **52**, 116–132.

Rodriguez, N., Sentencing, V.I.o.J.S., and Program, C. (2003) *Preventing homelessness among people leaving prison*: Vera Institute of Justice, State Sentencing and Corrections Program.

Roman, C.G. (2004) *Taking stock: Housing, homelessness, and prisoner reentry*. Retrieved March 6, 2012, from http://www.urban.org/url.cfm?ID=411096

Roman, C.G. and Travis, J. (2004) *Taking Stock: Housing, Homelessness, and Prisoner Reentry*. Washington, DC: Urban Institute Press.

Roman, C.G. and Travis, J. (2006) Where will I sleep tomorrow? Housing, homelessness, and the returning prisoner. *Housing Policy Debate*, **17**(2), 389–418.

Roth, R.M., Brunette, M.F., and Green, A.I. (2005) Treatment of substance use disorders in schizophrenia: A unifying neurobiological mechanism? *Current Psychiatry Reports*, **7**(4), 283–291.

Ruiz, M.A., Douglas, K.S., Edens, J.F. *et al.* (2012) Co-occurring mental health and substance use problems in offenders: Implications for risk assessment. *Psychological Assessment*, **24**, 77–87.

Sacks, J.Y. (2004) Women with co-occurring substance use and mental disorders (COD) in the criminal justice system: A research review. *Behavioral Sciences and the Law*, **22**, 449–466.

Sacks, S., Chaple, M., Sacks, J.A.Y. *et al.* (2012) Randomized trial of a reentry modified therapeutic community for offenders with co-occurring disorders: Crime outcomes. *Journal of Substance Abuse Treatment*, **42**(3), 247–259.

Sacks, S., McKendrick, K., Sacks, J.A.Y., and Cleland, C.M. (2010) Modified therapeutic community for co-occurring disorders: Single investigator meta analysis. *Substance Abuse*, **31**(3), 146–161.

Sacks, S. and Ries, R.K. (2005) Substance Abuse Treatment for Persons with Co-Occurring Disorders. Treatment Improvement Protocol (TIP) Series 42. *Substance Abuse and Mental Health Services Administration*, 590.

Sacks, S., Sacks, J.A.Y., McKendrick, K. *et al.* (2004) Modified TC for MICA offenders: Crime outcomes. *Behavioral Sciences & the Law*, **22**(4), 477–501.

Sarteschi, C.M., Vaughn, M.G., and Kim, K. (2011) Assessing the effectiveness of mental health courts: A quantitative review. *Journal of Criminal Justice*, **39**(1), 12–20.

Semple, D.M., McIntosh, A.M., and Lawrie, S.M. (2005) Cannabis as a risk factor for psychosis: Systematic review. *Journal of Psychopharmacology (Oxford, England)*, **19**, 187–194.

Skeem, J., Eno Louden, J., Manchak, S. *et al.* (2009) Social networks and social control of probationers with co-occurring mental and substance abuse problems. *Law and Human Behavior*, **33**(2), 122–135.

Skeem, J., Manchak, S., and Peterson, J.K. (2011) Correctional policy for offenders with mental illness: Creating a new paradigm for recidivism reduction. *Law and Human Behavior*, **35**(2), 110–126.

Smith, N., and Trimboli, L. (2010) Comorbid substance and non-substance mental health disorders and re-offending among NSW prisoners. *Crime and Justice Bulletin* (No. 140). Sydney: NSW Bureau of Crime Statistics and Research.

Smith, R.J., Jennings, J.L., and Cimino, A. (2009) Forensic continuum of care with assertive community treatment (ACT) for persons recovering from co-occurring disabilities: Long-term outcomes. *Psychiatric Rehabilitation Journal*, **33**(3), 207–218.

Solomon, A.L., Johnson, K.D., Travis, J., and McBride, E.C. (2004) *From Prison to Work: The Employment Dimensions of Prisoner Reentry*. Washington, DC: Urban Institute Justice Policy Center.

Solomon, P. and Draine, J. (1995a) Jail recidivism in a forensic case management program. *Health and Social Work*, **20**, 167–167.

Solomon, P. and Draine, J. (1995b) One-year outcomes of a randomized trial of case management with seriously mentally ill clients leaving jail. *Evaluation Review*, **19**(3), 256–273.

Soyka, M. (2000) Substance misuse, psychiatric disorder and violent and disturbed behaviour. *The British Journal Of Psychiatry*, **176**(4), 345–350.

Steadman, H., Osher, F., Robbins, P.C. *et al.* (2009) Prevalence of serious mental illness among jail inmates. *Psychiatric Services (Washington, DC)*, **60**(6), 761–765.

Steadman, H.J. and Naples, M. (2005) Assessing the effectiveness of jail diversion programs for persons with serious mental illness and co-occurring substance use disorders. *Behavioral Sciences & the Law*, **23**(2), 163–170.

Steadman, H.J., Redlich, A., Callahan, L. *et al.* (2011) Effect of mental health courts on arrests and jail days: A multisite study. *Archives of General Psychiatry*, **68**(2), 167–172.

Stein, L.I. and Santos, A.B. (1998) *Assertive Community Treatment of Persons with Severe Mental Illness*. New York: WW Norton & Co.

Stein, L.I. and Test, M.A. (1980) Alternative to mental hospital treatment: I. Conceptual model, treatment program, and clinical evaluation. *Archives of General Psychiatry*, **37**(4), 392–397.

Strakowski, S.M. and DelBello, M.P. (2000) The co-occurrence of bipolar and substance use disorders. *Clinical Psychology Review*, **20**(2), 191–206.

Strakowski, S.M., McElroy, S.L., Keck, P.E., and West, S.A. (1996) The effects of antecedent substance abuse on the development of first-episode psychotic mania. *Journal of Psychiatric Research*, **30**(1), 59–68.

Sullivan, C.J., Sacks, S., Mckendrick, K. *et al.* (2007) Modified therapeutic community treatment for offenders with co-occurring disorders: Mental health outcomes. *Journal of Offender Rehabilitation*, **45**(1–2), 227–247.

Swanson, J.W., Swartz, M.S., Van Dorn, R.A. *et al.* (2006) A national study of violent behavior in persons with schizophrenia. *Archives of General Psychiatry*, **63**(5), 490–499.

Swartz, M.S., Wagner, H.R., Swanson, J.W. *et al.* (2006) Substance use in persons with schizophrenia: Baseline prevalence and correlates from the NIMH CATIE study. *The Journal of Nervous and Mental Disease*, **194**(3), 164–172.

Taxman, F.S., Yancey, C., and Bilanin, J.E. (2006) *Proactive community supervision in Maryland: Changing offender outcomes*: Maryland Division of Parole and Probation.

Teplin, L.A. (1994) Psychiatric and substance abuse disorders among male urban jail detainees. *American Journal of Public Health*, **84**(2), 290–293.

Teplin, L.A., Abram, K.M., and McClelland, G.M. (1994) Does psychiatric disorder predict violent crime among released jail detainees? A six-year longitudinal study. *The American Psychologist*, **49**(4), 335–342.

Test, M.A. and Stein, L.I. (1976) Practical guidelines for the community treatment of markedly impaired patients. *Community Mental Health Journal*, **12**(1), 72–82.

Tiet, Q.Q. and Mausbach, B. (2007) Treatments for patients with dual diagnosis: A review. *Alcoholism: Clinical and Experimental Research*, **31**(4), 513–536.

Trupin, E. and Richards, H. (2003) Seattle's mental health courts: Early indicators of effectiveness. *International Journal of Law and Psychiatry*, **26**(1), 33–54.

Tyuse, S.W. and Linhorst, D.M. (2005) Drug courts and mental health courts: Implications for social work. *Health and Social Work*, **30**(3), 233–240.

Van Stelle, K.R., Blumer, C., and Moberg, D.P. (2004) Treatment retention of dually diagnosed offenders in an institutional therapeutic community. *Behavioral Sciences & the Law*, **22**(4), 585–597.

Veysey, B.M., Steadman, H.J., Morrissey, J.P., and Johnsen, M. (1997) In search of the missing linkages: Continuity of care in US jails. *Behavioral Sciences & the Law*, **15**(4), 383–397.

Volkow, N.D. and Skolnick, N. (2012) New medications for substance use disorders: Challenges and opportunities. *Neuropsychopharmacology*, **37**, 290–292.

Webb, R.T., Qin, P., Stevens, H. *et al.* (2011) National study of suicide in all people with a criminal justice history. *Archives of General Psychiatry*, **68**(9), 591–599.

Weisman, R., Lamberti, J., and Price, N. (2004) Integrating criminal justice, community healthcare, and support services for adults with severe mental disorders. *The Psychiatric Quarterly*, **75**(1), 71–85.

Weiss, R.D. and Connery, H.S. (2011) *Integrated Group Therapy for Bipolar Disorder and Substance Abuse*. New York: Guilford Press.

Wells-Parker, E. and Popkin, C. (1994) Deterrence and rehabilitation: Rehabilitation and screening – Research needs for the next decade. *Journal of Traffic Medicine*, **23**, 71–78.

Wenzel, S.L., Longshore, D., Turner, S., and Ridgely, M.S. (2001) Drug courts: A bridge between criminal justice and health services. *Journal of Criminal Justice*, **29**(3), 241–253.

Wilkins, J.N. (1997) Pharmacotherapy of schizophrenia patients with comorbid substance abuse. *Schizophrenia Bulletin*, **23**(2), 215–225.

Wilper, A.P., Woolhandler, S., Boyd, J. *et al.* (2009) The health and health care of US prisoners: Results of a nationwide survey. *American Journal of Public Health*, **99**(4), 666–672.

Wilson, D.B., Bouffard, L.A., and Mackenzie, D.L. (2005) A quantitative review of structured, group-oriented, cognitive-behavioral programs for offenders. *Criminal Justice and Behavior*, **32**(2), 172–204.

Wilson, D.B., Mitchell, O., and MacKenzie, D.L. (2006) A systematic review of drug court effects on recidivism. *Journal of Experimental Criminology*, **2**(4), 459–487.

Wolff, N., Plemmons, D., Veysey, B., and Brandli, A. (2002) Release planning for inmates with mental illness compared with those who have other chronic illnesses. *Psychiatric Services (Washington, DC)*, **53**(11), 1469–1471.

Wolff, N. and Pogorzelski, W. (2005) Measuring the effectiveness of mental health courts: Challenges and recommendations. *Psychology, Public Policy, and Law*, **11**(4), 539.

Wright, S., Gournay, K., Glorney, E., and Thornicroft, G. (2002) Mental illness, substance abuse, demographics and offending: Dual diagnosis in the suburbs. *Journal of Forensic Psychiatry*, **13**(1), 35–52.

Zhang, S.X., Roberts, R.E.L., and McCollister, K.E. (2011) Therapeutic community in a California prison: Treatment outcomes after 5 years. *Crime & Delinquency*, **57**(1), 82–101.

Chapter 14

ALCOHOL USE AND OFFENDING IN PEOPLE WITH INTELLECTUAL DISABILITY

WILLIAM R. LINDSAY
Castlebeck, Darlington, England; University of Abertay, Dundee, Scotland; Bangor University, Bangor, Wales; and Deakin University, Melbourne, Australia

SAMANTHA TINSLEY
Castlebeck, Darlington, England

MEDHAT EMARA
Castlebeck, Darlington, England

INTRODUCTION

Changes in society produce significant changes in individuals within that society. We begin with this statement as a caution to this chapter. In the last 15 years, the advent of the Internet has caused changes to individuals and to society that could hardly have been realised in the mid-1990s. The range of goods and services that are available from around the world has increased exponentially to individual users. Societal changes are not always positive. Some are mildly frustrating, such as the annoyance felt by most Internet users when their server is interrupted or when their favourite web site is unobtainable. Sometimes, the consequences are more serious, such as the far greater availability of child pornography through the Internet (Seto, Cantor, and Blanchard, 2006).

We make this caution and use this analogy because the changes experienced as a result of the onset of the World Wide Web probably have had less individual impact than the changes to life circumstances seen by people with intellectual disability (ID) over the last 25 years. For many, living in a large institution of between 500 and 1000 people was a stable way of life. This completely changed with the advent of deinstitutionalisation and, it has to be said, all of us working

Alcohol-Related Violence: Prevention and Treatment, First Edition. Edited by Mary McMurran.
© 2013 John Wiley & Sons, Ltd. Published 2013 by John Wiley & Sons, Ltd.

in the field are still coming to terms with these changes. This leads us to the specific caution in relation to this chapter. Information that has been gathered over the last 20–30 years concerning alcohol use and people with ID is likely to be out of date as each generation moves into the new circumstances of community access and community living. Lindsay *et al.* (1991) wrote about the way in which access to pubs was highly valued by some people with ID who had been relocated to the community. There was a feeling that ordinary people living in the community were in pubs frequently. Some of these individuals relocated to 'an ordinary life' in the community felt that they would now access pubs frequently. This would have had an impact on their use of alcohol and on the way in which some people with ID related to alcohol. As a new generation emerges, unfamiliar with institutional living, they will take access to pubs as a more ordinary event rather than an unusual privilege that had been previously rationed or denied. However, this new generation will also have different influences – those experienced by the general population, such as the social conventions portrayed in advertising and in television series. Therefore, it is likely that one of the most rapidly changing aspects in the lives of people with ID as a population is the way in which people develop their relationship with alcohol and drugs. Having made this caution, we will review our knowledge of the prevalence of alcohol use, the views of people with ID in relation to alcohol, the prevalence of alcohol use in offenders with ID, and the relationship between alcohol and offending in this population.

PREVALENCE OF ALCOHOL USE IN PEOPLE WITH INTELLECTUAL DISABILITIES

One of the difficulties in establishing the extent to which alcohol is abused in the population of individuals with ID is the fact that substance abuse and alcohol abuse are often conflated in reports. McGillicuddy (2006) makes this point in a review of substance use in people with ID while going on to suggest that, in general, studies on the prevalence of alcohol use in people with ID have found lower rates than in the general population. Rimmer, Braddock, and Marks (1995) surveyed 329 people with ID and found that less than 5% used alcohol. In their study, they also found that those who did drink did so only occasionally with no more than four drinks per week. They found that those individuals who had recently moved out of institutions into community homes drank significantly more alcohol than those who continued to live in institutions or those who lived in the family home, giving some support to the clinical impression of the effects of deinstitutionalisation reported earlier. Lawrenson, Lindsay, and Walker (1995) surveyed a population of people with ID and found that, while males drank more than females, only around 40% drank any alcohol at all, and those who did drank fewer units per week than their non-ID counterparts and below the recommended safe limits.

Edgerton (1986), in a review specifically on alcohol and drug use, reported that use by adults with ID was lower than that of their parents, siblings and friends without disability. Similarly, McGillicuddy and Blane (1999) reviewed a sample of 122 people with ID. They reported that a majority of the sample did not drink alcohol or use illicit drugs, but around 39% did use alcohol and 4% illegal drugs. This study was interesting in that they found that of those who did drink alcohol, around half were drinking at problematic levels.

When one looks at patterns of drinking, some studies have reported greater causes of concern than when one simply looks at prevalence. Krishef and DiNitto (1981) used large samples of individuals with ID to review drinking patterns and found them comparable with the general population. However, for those individuals who did drink alcohol, abuse was a significant problem with 13% experiencing family problems and aggression and 7% reporting drinking while at work. In a study that stands out because it reports higher levels of problematic drinking, Pack, Wallander, and Browne (1998) studied a community-based sample of 194 African American adolescents with mild ID and found that, compared with a similar sample without ID, they engaged in significantly more binge drinking. This piece of work has not been replicated and so should be treated with some caution.

Emerson and Turnbull (2005) reviewed information on 95 teenagers with ID aged 11–15 using the large 1999 Office of National Statistics survey on the mental health of children and adolescents in Great Britain (Meltzer et al., 2000). They compared drinking patterns of this subsample against the whole sample (4,069 adolescents). They found, as one might expect from earlier studies on adults, that fewer of these teenagers reported drinking alcohol when compared with teenagers without ID (12% vs. 23%). These authors also constructed a predictive model based on other information gathered in the survey and found that greater parental stress and less use of punishment-based child management practices predicted higher alcohol use. The former was an important issue since high levels of parental stress indicate the possibility of higher levels of family distress. This study excluded children living in various forms of residential provision, a group where one might assume there has been the highest level of family/parental distress. Therefore, the group in residential provision might be the group at most risk of higher alcohol consumption.

RISK FACTORS IN ALCOHOL CONSUMPTION FOR PEOPLE WITH INTELLECTUAL DISABILITIES

Although Emerson and Turnbull (2005) found lower rates of alcohol use in teenagers with ID when compared with teenagers without ID, they also found that parental distress was a risk factor. Many studies have found that parenting factors are related to substance misuse in their children (e.g., Merikangas et al., 1998). However, few of these studies separate genetic influences from environmental influences (Weinberg, 2001). There is also some evidence that the effects of alcohol and drug use may be more serious for individuals with ID. Westermeyer, Kemp, and Nugent (1996) compared 40 participants with ID who had alcohol and drug problems with control participants and found that, in the group with ID, less substance use precipitated an equivalent degree of health problems, interpersonal conflict and psychosocial difficulties. These difficulties were reported despite the group with ID showing less frequent alcohol use, a later age of first use, fewer reports of physiological dependency and fewer substances used across the life span.

A further risk is that already suggested in the study by McGillicuddy and Blane (1999) in which, of the minority who did drink alcohol, around half drank at problematic levels. In addition, Rimmer *et al.* (1995) found that those who had recently moved out of institutions drank significantly more. This reinforces the hypothesis that, for a significant minority of individuals with ID, drinking alcohol, and associated establishments or stimuli such as pubs or peers who use alcohol regularly, may be highly valued, leading to the risk of overuse.

Molina and Pelham (2001) reviewed risk factors for substance abuse in 109 children with attention deficit hyperactivity disorder (ADHD). One of the risk factors they investigated was IQ and they found that where there was an association, it was those who had higher IQs that were likely to have their first drink of alcohol at an earlier age. However, although some of the associations between IQ and substance use were significant, the effect sizes were very small. The largest, most significant relationship was a correlation of .2 between IQ and smoking cigarettes. Although this was significant, it is a small effect size and did not emerge as significant in a regression analysis. There was also a similar negative correlation between IQ and age at which the teenagers had their first drink: the higher the IQ, the earlier the age at which they had their first drink.

Moore and Polsgrove (1991) suggested a number of risk factors, including a tendency towards low self-esteem, impaired self-regulation in people with ID, susceptibility to peer pressure, a desire for social acceptability, medical issues such as a compromised tolerance to drugs, cognitive limitations such as illiteracy and memory deficits, and some frustration about having a disability in the first place. Despite all these potential risk factors, it remains the case that people with ID appear to have a lower prevalence of alcohol and alcohol misuse than the general population. All of these issues must be considered in the light of continued changes in society and its relationship with alcohol and drugs.

ALCOHOL USE IN OFFENDERS WITH ID

One of the first studies to review alcohol use in offenders with ID was reported by Hayes and Carmody (1990). Hayes has produced a series of studies on offenders with ID in New South Wales prisons and courts and always notes that there is a high indigenous population in her cohorts, suggesting that they may be somewhat atypical samples. Hayes and Carmody (1990) reported that 66% of the samples either were intoxicated at the time of their offence or were previous alcohol abusers. In a subsequent investigation, Hayes (1996) studied two cohorts of offenders with ID in New South Wales courts. Comparing individuals with and without ID, she found that 90% of both groups had consumed some alcohol on the day of the alleged offence. Therefore, in both of the Hayes studies, she found high rates of alcohol use associated with offending behaviour in offenders with ID.

Klimecki, Jenkinson, and Wilson (1994) conducted a large-scale study reviewing characteristics and reoffending rates of previous prison inmates with ID 2 years after they were released. In relation to a history of alcohol and substance abuse, 45.1% of first offenders, 71.4% of second offenders, 66.6% of third offenders and 87.5% of fourth offenders had a significant history. This is certainly consistent with the Hayes studies, suggesting that in these Australian populations there are very high rates of alcohol and substance abuse associated with offending.

In another study from Australia, McGillivray and Moore (2001) compared 30 young adult offenders with ID and 30 non-offenders with ID. Both samples consisted of 27 men and 3 women. In the offender sample, they reported that 33.3% had used alcohol, 6.6% had used drugs, and 20% had used both alcohol and drugs prior to their index offence. Consistent with previous Australian studies, this amounted to 60% of the total sample. They then compared alcohol and drug use by both groups on a range of quantity and frequency measures. Twenty-one of the 30 offenders reported drinking beer every day, while 18 of the 30 offenders reported drinking spirits every day. In the control group, 13 of the 30 non-offenders reported drinking beer every day and 8 reported drinking spirits every day. While this high frequency in the offender group is consistent with previous studies, the relatively high frequency in the non-offender group is unusual when compared to previous studies. In relation to marijuana use and inhalant (solvent) use, the figures for the offenders were that 7 of 30 used the former every day, while 3 of the 30 used the latter. As has been seen from other chapters in this book (e.g., Howard and McMurran, Chapter 5), this reporting of a high association between use of alcohol and offending is a common finding with mainstream offenders. It is of some passing interest that of the three women in the McGillivray and Moore (2001) offender sample, all were heavy drinkers and all three stated that they were highly intoxicated at the time of the offence. In the comparison group, none of the females reported ever using substances.

Several authors have recently published more comprehensive studies reviewing offending and historical factors. In a study of 143 randomly selected prisoners in Norway, Sondenaa et al. (2008) found a prevalence of ID at 10.7%. Of those individuals, 40% reported problems with substance use or addiction compared to 57% of those prisoners without ID. Raina and Lunsky (2010) compared 39 offenders with ID and 39 adults with ID who had mental health problems. Both groups had been discharged from psychiatric services in Toronto. One of the major differences between the two groups was a history of substance abuse. In the forensic group, 37% had such a history where only one of the controls abused substances. In another study, the same research group compared 74 offenders with ID and 282 mental health patients with ID (Lunsky et al., 2011). On this occasion, only 11% of the former and 5% of the latter had substance abuse problems, a difference that was not significant. On the other hand, they compared the offenders with ID to 506 offenders without ID and found a highly significant difference, with 28.3% of the mainstream offenders having a substance abuse-related diagnosis. This latter study is not directly comparable with other studies since the contrast between groups was done on substance abuse diagnosis rather than a history of substance abuse or intoxication at the time of the offence. However, it does suggest that substance abuse disorders may be lower in offenders with ID than in mainstream offenders. More recently, Plant et al. (2011) reported on 74 patients with ID (54 males and 20 females) admitted to a forensic ID service. In a careful review of alcohol and substance misuse history, they found that 41% reported a previous harmful use of alcohol, while 28% reported an addiction to cannabis.

In a series of studies, Lindsay and colleagues (2004a,b, 2010a) have followed up cohorts of male sex offenders, other types of male offenders and female offenders. In their most recent 20-year follow-up, they compared 156 male sex offenders, 126 men with other types of offences and 27 female offenders, all with ID. Their reporting of previous alcohol problems is more consistent with the Lunsky *et al.* (2011) study in that a previous alcohol problem was evident in 9.3% of the non-sexual offending male cohort, 3.6% of the sex offender cohort and 12.5% of the female offenders. This is low compared to mainstream offender studies. When reviewing the rate of alcohol-related offences, the male non-sexual offenders recorded 15.3% and the female offenders 4.5% of alcohol-related offences. In the sex offender group, only 4% had alcohol recorded in their index offence. Therefore, although violent offences were relatively high in this study (over 60% for the male non-sexual offenders and female offenders), alcohol featured only in around 15% of offences. This is in marked contrast to the reports from Hayes and Carmody (1990), Klimecki *et al.* (1994), and McGillivray and Moore (2001), in which they recorded much higher rates of alcohol-related offending. It is also somewhat lower than the recent report by Plant *et al.* (2011).

It could be argued that the Lindsay *et al.* (2004a,b, 2010a) studies follow up a group of treated offenders from one region of Britain who are, therefore, atypical in their representation of offenders with ID. In a much larger series of studies, sampling offenders with ID across 25 different services ranging from generic community services through specialist forensic ID services, inpatient services, low secure, medium secure and maximum secure provision, O'Brien *et al.* (2010) studied 477 individuals from four large geographical areas in the United Kingdom, representing a total catchment population of approximately 12 million people or 20% of the UK population. This study was conducted in one calendar year, and during that year, only 6% had an index offence involving substance abuse. In a more comprehensive account of this population, Lindsay *et al.* (2010b) noted that only 3.8% of the referrals to community generic services, 7.2% of referrals to specialist forensic ID services and 13.2% to low/medium secure services involved substance abuse. None of the referrals to maximum security had an index offence involving substance abuse, but all of these came from other high secure services, which would have artificially reduced the average prevalence recorded in the total cohort by an estimated maximum of around 3–4% (O'Brien *et al.*, 2010). In this study, substance abuse prior to involvement with the referring services would be a more realistic indication of the prevalence in this population. Records showed that 9.6% of the generic community group, 13.4% of the specialist forensic ID group, 49.5% of the low/medium secure and 36% of the high secure cohorts had previous substance abuse problems. Therefore, substance abuse was more closely associated with secure services when compared with community services, and there were significant differences between the secure groups and community groups.

Carson *et al.* (2010) went on to construct a prediction model from these data to determine the extent to which a range of variables predicted referral to community services and referral to secure services. There was a significant difference between the rates of alcohol abuse in the community and secure groups, with the latter showing the higher prevalence. However, this difference was not retained in the regression model, suggesting that it was not a predictor of referral to secure services. Wheeler *et al.* (2009) conducted an analysis of the generic community referrals in this study ($N = 237$) and noted that, although the rate of previous substance abuse was generally low (9%), it was somewhat higher in those referrals that had criminal justice involvement (14.3%), which, in turn, was similar to that recorded in referrals to forensic ID services (13.4%).

From this series of studies (Carson *et al.*, 2010; Lindsay *et al.*, 2004a,b, 2010a; O'Brien *et al.*, 2010; Wheeler *et al.*, 2009), even taking the referrals with criminal justice service involvement alone, the figures are still lower than those recorded by the Australian studies. Indeed, even the highest figures recorded in this series of reports (49.5% previous substance abuse in the referrals to low and medium secure services) are still lower than those recorded in the Australian studies (Hayes, 1996; Klimecki *et al.*, 1994; McGillivray and Moore, 2001). Since the reports by O'Brien and colleagues cover broad geographical areas and a large number of participants, they are likely to be representative of offenders with ID in the United Kingdom. There are clear discrepancies between studies from different parts of the world. The studies from Ontario, Canada, record rates of substance use disorder or a history of substance use at between 11% and 38%, depending on the information reported. Studies from the UK report rates of between 4% and 50% depending on the type of offender, nature of the service referred to and the level of security of the service, with sex offenders in the community recording the lowest levels and offenders in low/medium secure services recording the highest levels of substance use problems. Studies from Australia record substance use problems at between 45.1% and 90.0%, depending on the indicator, with 45% of first offenders reporting substance use problems (Klimecki *et al.*, 1994) and 90% reporting that alcohol had been consumed on the day of the alleged offence (Hayes, 1996). However, in most cases, rates of alcohol and substance abuse among ID offenders are significantly higher than rates recorded for people with ID in general and suggest that appropriate intervention would be indicated in many cases in order to address offence-related issues.

EXPERIENCES OF PEOPLE WITH ID WHO MISUSE ALCOHOL AND DRUGS

Taggart *et al.* (2006) conducted a survey of people with ID known to services in Northern Ireland. They found 67 individuals who had a history of alcohol abuse, which provided an estimate that .8% of the population with ID had alcohol problems. Taggart *et al.* (2007) conducted a qualitative study on 10 of these individuals, interviewing them about reasons for and the impact of substance abuse. Unusually in this sample, there were more women ($N = 7$) than men ($N = 3$), and the low number reflected the fact that only 10 of the 67 accepted an invitation into the study. Seven reported abusing alcohol only, while three women reported a combination of alcohol, illegal drugs and prescription medication. All participants had at least a 5-year history of alcohol misuse. Two main reasons for alcohol abuse emerged. The first was psychological trauma, such as the death of a partner or relative, previous sexual abuse or rape, and deteriorating mental health. The second principal reason was social isolation and a perceived lack of companionship. In relation to this theme, participants mentioned exploitation of money, possessions and accommodation in relation to their drinking. Some participants were aware of the exploitation but were content to sustain it because of the company.

All of the individuals had contact with community ID teams and described the positive support and beneficial advice they received. However, all noted that it did little to persuade them to halt their alcohol abuse. Seven of the participants had been referred to mainstream addiction services, and five of them found it ineffective and intrusive. Two of the seven were positive about their interaction with mainstream services. One of the themes to emerge from this report is that alcohol abuse did not present in isolation but was accompanied by a range of issues such as mental health problems, self-harm, domestic violence, bereavement, physical abuse and sexual abuse. As with mainstream services, motivation to change was identified as an acute issue hampering any effective intervention.

EDUCATION AND TREATMENT FOR ALCOHOL PROBLEMS

There is very little information on the treatment of alcohol problems in people with ID. Several authors (e.g., Alexander *et al.*, 2010; Lindsay *et al.*, 2010a) have written that they include alcohol awareness education and treatment as part of comprehensive programmes for offenders with ID and people with mental illness and ID. However, there are only a few case reports illustrating the methods outlining the processes of treatment. Slayter (2010) wrote that there was a consensus that a cognitive-behavioural therapy approach is not ideal for people with ID. She wrote, 'an expert consensus panel surveyed 93 MR (mental retardation) focused clinicians about the treatment of substance abuse among people with MR or developmental disabilities, and results suggested the importance of family education, the management of the environment for safety, the development of social and communication skills and use of applied behaviour analysis . . . An informal consensus exists regarding drawing on reinforcement and punishment approaches versus using cognitive-behavioural approaches, supportive counseling and psychotherapy' (p. 196). One suspects that these conclusions are significantly influenced by the theoretical orientation of the experts on the panel. It is similarly clear, from the case studies published in the United Kingdom, that educational and cognitive approaches may have as much to offer as reinforcement and punishment approaches. Neither has been tested using appropriate experimental methods. Chapters in the book *Substance Related Disorders in Persons with Mental Retardation*, by Sturmey *et al.* (2003), provide descriptions of programmes and approaches that have been designed for people with developmental disabilities, acquired brain injury, autistic spectrum disorders and ID. However, the programmes do not have an empirical underpinning and there remains lack of evidence-based clinical knowledge on the reduction of substance abuse.

ISSUES IN TREATMENT

Several writers (e.g., Barter, 2007; Cosden, 2001; Lindsay *et al.*, 1991) have outlined some of the issues involved in the treatment of alcohol problems in people with ID. Cosden (2001) emphasises the importance of dealing with issues of disability itself. Clients may be aware of social stigma and negative social comparison, leading to difficulties with self-esteem and interpersonal sensitivity. Alcohol may be a way of coping with difficult social situations and the perception of negative evaluation from others. These issues of negative social comparison had been well documented through various research studies and reviews (Dagnan and Jahoda, 2006; Dagnan and Waring, 2004). These should be addressed during discussions and may be dealt with specifically on an individual basis using cognitive-behaviour therapy aimed at dealing with problems with self-esteem and self-perception (Jahoda *et al.*, 2006).

Ambivalent motivation to change is a problem in helping people to reduce or stop their alcohol intake (McMurran, 2009), and this is compounded in people with ID. The first additional factor hindering motivation to engage is the already mentioned aspect that going into pubs and drinking alcohol is such a highly valued activity in people with ID. For some, it is perceived as one of the quintessential freedoms of community living. Given that it is so highly valued, there is a consequent motivation to engage in this behaviour. The second additional factor is general to people with ID engaging in psychological therapy. Several writers have noted that, when people with ID are referred for a specific problem related to offending (violence or sexual offending), they may have significant resentment that others are interfering with their life and are expecting them to engage in a treatment (e.g., Lindsay, 2009; Taylor and Novaco, 2005). Therefore, motivation is a constant consideration in any treatment for people with ID, including treatment for alcohol abuse. Lindsay (2009) has outlined a number of methods for dealing with clients' motivation to engage. In relation to alcohol awareness and treatment for alcohol problems, it is probably better to raise motivation in relation to the specific issue that has been referred. While alcohol may be involved in the referral, it is probably the consequences of the alcohol abuse that have been the problem. Therefore, it may be the violence or destructiveness that has precipitated the referral from court or other sources and this would be the focus for raising motivation. Exercises to increase motivation would involve discussions of the importance of avoiding police contact, avoiding future referral to court, reducing family conflict and, in some cases, compliance with the criminal justice system or maintaining tenancy. Reducing alcohol intake would be a way of achieving these goals.

Motivational interviewing (MI) is a well-established approach to the treatment of addictions, including alcohol addiction (Hettema, Steele, and Miller, 2005). It is a strategic approach that increases readiness to change by helping clients explore the difficulties in relation to their addiction and overcome ambivalence. Techniques of decision making are often used in association with MI, and these have been used in other psychotherapeutic fields working with people with ID. Investigating the pros and cons of continuing with behaviours that create a risk for offending has been outlined as one technique to be included in sex offender treatment (Lindsay, 2009). Reflecting on effective strategies that have been used in the past to deal with difficulties and employing aspirations for the future that may be dependent on change are common techniques employed in some anger treatments and in sex offender treatment (Lindsay, 2009; Taylor and Novaco, 2005). Reviewing the consistency between the client's current behaviour and future aspirations is a very clear and straightforward way of analysing current problems and reflecting on how these will interfere with future plans. Selecting optimal behaviour change strategies in a person-centred approach is highly applicable to people with ID. While MI has been shown to be effective with mainstream populations (Burke, Arkowitz, and Menchola, 2003; McMurran, 2009), there have been no evaluations of these techniques with offenders with ID or people with ID who have problems with addiction.

In treatment for offenders with ID, relapse prevention (RP) techniques have been used extensively. RP techniques review the problems with the previous lifestyle in contrast to the advantages of a future offence-free lifestyle. In this way, if alcohol has been consistently involved with offending, then it will automatically be incorporated into an RP programme. This will include interpersonal situations that may promote the abuse of alcohol, environments that might encourage the use of alcohol, personal feelings of anxiety, depression or anger that may motivate the individual to drink, or situations of loss and isolation that might encourage drinking. All of these will be incorporated into RP plans.

A treatment programme for offenders with ID will focus on the offence-related issues, and so almost everyone who is incorporated into an alcohol treatment programme will also be treated using an anger programme. The treatment of anger and violence in this population is the most widely validated evidence-based treatment (Lindsay and Michie, 2012). Although anger management treatment does not include a review of the effects and individual consequences of alcohol abuse (Taylor and Novaco, 2005), other violence programmes do refer to the use and abuse of alcohol and its relationship to violence (Lindsay, Tinsley and Emara 2012). Any alcohol programme for people with ID will include discussions about the effects of alcohol. Psychological effects include problems in relationships with friends, problems at work, problems in retaining tenancies, problems with neighbours and difficulties of staff. Clients will also discuss what to do in difficult situations involving alcohol. These will include situations such as how to deal with friends teasing you for asking for a soft drink or putting on pressure to go to the pub when the individual wants to resist.

Much of the emphasis in treatment is on practical demonstrations and engagement with problem-solving situations and role play. Because of the intellectual disabilities, didactic methods are less useful than they might be with other populations. It is always better to use methods that will engage clients in a much more active manner. As will be seen from the following programme, an emphasis on practical tasks, quizzes and problem-solving exercises maximises the amount of information that can be conveyed during the session. Role play can be particularly useful and powerful. Realism can be enhanced by the use of props and staging. For example, a makeshift bar can be constructed by simply putting one facilitator behind a table with a number of glasses and jugs of water and soft drinks. Group members may then be asked to approach the 'bar' and ask for a soft drink. Despite the obvious role-play characteristics of this situation, some individuals find it difficult to ask for a soft drink. In one of our sessions, one group member found it so difficult to ask for an orange juice that he began sweating and asked for an orange juice 'and a whisky'. This is illustrates how valuable role playing can be as a learning process.

To illustrate our approach to alcohol treatment with offenders with ID, we will describe our alcohol component in detail, present a case study and offer some evaluation information.

AN ALCOHOL MODULE FOR A VIOLENCE PROGRAMME

As has been mentioned, treatment for offenders with ID focus on offence-related issues and, in the case of violent offenders, will often include a component on understanding the effects of alcohol in general, the effects of alcohol abuse and the relationship of alcohol to an individual's offending. It needs to be remembered that, as the evidence suggests, violence in this client group is less often associated with alcohol and so, for some offenders, this module may be less relevant. The module is designed to increase participants' understanding of the effects of alcohol and the relationship between alcohol abuse and violence. An educational approach about the nature of alcohol and its effects is analogous with treatment for sex offenders with ID who, unlike mainstream sex offenders, may require some sessions on sex education. Therefore, some of the alcohol module conveys information, and other aspects address offence-related issues such as anger and violence. The module is designed specifically to engage individuals with ID through practical exercises, general role plays in alcohol-related situations and specific role-play exercises related to the individuals' risk situations.

The module is designed to be suitable for clients with mild ID and borderline intelligence (IQ around 50–75). It is suitable for both male and female offenders who have a risk of alcohol-related violence or have been previously involved with alcohol. It can also be used with clients who may have alcohol problems in the absence of violence. We have conducted treatment for alcohol-related violence in most settings in which offenders with ID are generally seen, such as community settings, residential homes and hospitals. Although we have not used these procedures in secure settings, we do have extensive experience of anger programmes in secure settings, and this module could be included in such a programme for offenders with ID. The module consists of eight weekly sessions of around 1 hour each and may be conducted with groups of up to six people.

Sessions 1 and 2: The programme begins with orientation, introductions and rules generated by the group members. Simple games and quizzes that advance knowledge are typical procedures. Some examples are as follows. The group leader says a word related to alcohol or drinking and invites participants to state an associated word. Associations are discussed, leading to a general discussion about what the group knows and thinks about alcohol. There is a team competition to name places and times when it is OK and not OK to consume alcohol, and to say why people might drink. Role play is introduced in an exercise where participants pick a card showing an effect of being drunk, for example, falling over, and act this out for the other group members to guess. This leads into a discussion on appropriate drinking and its effects, giving group members a chance to share their own experiences of being drunk or seeing others drunk. From Session 2 onwards, sessions begin with a recap of the previous session.

Sessions 3, 4 and 5: These sessions introduce the differences between alcoholic and non-alcoholic drinks, the effects that alcohol has on the body and the brain, how the body gets rid of alcohol and how long it takes for this process to occur. We discuss ways of sobering up before revealing that the process depends largely on the passage of time. A comparison of alcoholic and non-alcoholic drinks is made, and ideas are generated on how to tell them apart. The cost of alcohol compared with non-alcoholic drinks is compared, demonstrating that price is not a guide to the amount of alcohol in each drink. The relative strengths of different beverages are discussed, and this is related to the volume of a standard measure. Next, sensible and hazardous limits are presented for men and women. Quizzes and games are used instead of didactic methods. A quiz to determine if drinks are alcoholic or not can reveal significant knowledge gaps.

Sessions 6 and 7: These sessions review the risks of alcohol misuse with exercises and discussions on its relationship to violence, conflict, money problems and stress. The theme of sensible drinking is developed with further time spent reviewing safe limits, strategies for sensible drinking in bars and at home, where there are no regulated measures. Role plays of asking for a non-alcoholic drink or of refusing a drink are conducted. These may be recorded and used for debriefing discussions. Clear links are made between alcohol misuse and the anger programme, and RP sessions combine violence and alcohol relapse risks.

Residential versus Community Applications

In an inpatient or more controlled setting, there are few opportunities for group members to gain access to alcohol. However, in community settings, it is useful to ask participants to keep a diary of alcohol intake. An alcohol diary can be a very simple construction, with pictures or drawings of alcoholic drinks along the top and rows for recording consumption for each weekday. The alcohol diary can be customised for each individual with pictures of the drinks that they most commonly use.

In community settings, it may also be possible to visit bars so that group members can practise asking for non-alcoholic drinks in a genuine drinking setting. Here, they can also discuss the information that has been presented during sessions so that it becomes more immediate and relevant. This also gives individuals the chance to learn that they may experience the atmosphere of pubs without drinking.

Programme Evaluation

Lindsay *et al*. (2012) have evaluated the alcohol module using a waiting list control design. Twelve individuals with ID and alcohol abuse who were involved with forensic services were compared with 10 individuals who remained on a waiting list for an equivalent period of time. Comparisons were made on an alcohol knowledge questionnaire, designed for use with people with ID and updated from the instrument used by Lindsay and colleagues (1991). It is important to update alcohol knowledge questionnaires since fashion around drinking and habits for drinking alcohol change significantly with time. They found that there was no difference between the groups at baseline, but after 2 months, during which the treatment group received the intervention, there was a significant improvement in those who had participated in treatment. At 2 months' follow-up, these differences remained significant.

A CASE OF ALCOHOL-RELATED VIOLENCE

The following case study of Ms A illustrates the relevance of the alcohol intervention component as part of an intervention to address alcohol-related violence. Ms A was 28 years old with an IQ of 66 (WAIS III) and a long history of alcohol abuse and subsequent involvement with the police. Her case illustrates some of the difficulties experienced by people with ID. She had attended school for people with learning disabilities, and there were no reports of any behavioural difficulties. Both of her parents had alcohol problems and both could become very aggressive after drinking. Ms A was very worried about her mother's alcohol abuse. She stayed with her parents until her mid-20s, when she moved into her own tenancy. However, she began stealing money and abusing alcohol increasingly seriously. Within 4 years of leaving home, she had 20 court disposals, all of which were related to alcohol abuse. Typically, she would become intoxicated while in a public house and become argumentative with either the staff or the customers. When asked to leave by the door staff, she would become aggressive towards them, whereupon the police would be called. She also developed a problem with gambling, and it was said that she could spend all of her fortnightly social security allowance in a couple of hours drinking in pubs and playing the gaming machines. She had had a number of periods in prison, all of short duration. A number of agencies had tried to engage her, but she felt that everyone who had seen her disliked her and that they were trying to control her.

Ms A was included in an alcohol treatment module, as described above. The initial assessments included a questionnaire designed for people with ID and adapted from the health promotion material published by the National Health Service (NHS) Tayside (Lindsay *et al*., 1998). The assessment contains 40 items on the nature of alcohol use and abuse, the effects of alcohol, drink strengths, and the social acceptability and social consequences of alcohol use and abuse. A higher score on this questionnaire indicates greater understanding. At the initial

Table 14.1   Ms A's progress on the Dundee Provocation Inventory.

DPI Factor	Feb	May	Oct	Dec	Jan	Mar	May	Jul
Threat to self-esteem	18	18	15	12	8	8	8	8
External locus of control	4	4	4	1	0	0	0	0
Resentment	5	5	5	1	0	1	1	1
Frustration	7	8	7	2	2	1	1	2
Disappointment	12	12	8	4	4	3	3	1
Adaptive action score	14	13	26	30	10	34	32	34

pre-awareness group assessment, Ms A's score on the test was 24 out of a total score of 40. This was near the average of 24.7 for individuals referred to the service. Following the treatment group, her score rose to 36 and remained there at 2-month follow-up. She became much more aware of the effects that alcohol was having on her daily life. Although one might think it fairly obvious that drinking was related to her aggression and subsequent police involvement, it was only after attending group sessions that she appeared to fully understand that alcohol was a major factor in her repeated episodes with the police.

Because of her history of aggression and alcohol abuse, she was also included in an anger management treatment group. Table 14.1 shows her responses on the Dundee Provocation Inventory (DPI) across the period of anger management treatment. The DPI assesses an individual's self-reported responses to a range of provocation situations in the areas of threat to self-esteem, resentment, frustration and disappointment (Alder and Lindsay, 2007). The assessment taken in February was done prior to her appearing in court for another series of charges of Breach of the Peace. Treatment began in May and continued through to December. Ms A returned for assessment sessions and individual booster sessions in January, March, May and July the following year.

Ms A's responses on the DPI across the repeated measures demonstrate that she scored very highly on the factors of threat to self-esteem, frustration and disappointment. Within these factors, there were a number of items that she said would provoke her to anger, such as people staring at her, someone making jokes about her, breaking her iPod, arranging to meet people who did not turn up and losing money on her mobile phone. The adaptive action score reflects a response to the question 'What would you do?' The response is scored 2 if it is a socialised, adaptive response, 1 if it is verbal aggression and 0 if it is physical aggression. It can be seen that, through the course of treatment from May to December, her aggressive responding to provocation reduced considerably, while her adaptive responding increased. Her maladaptive responses were typified by going for a drink, getting drunk or attacking the person in the scenario.

Following improvements, Ms A began to have an increasing number of home visits with her family. Towards the end of her period of treatment in the hospital, she was having visits every weekend, during which she had open access to the community and to places where she could buy alcohol. In fact, she reported consuming alcohol with the family, but always in moderation. She has now left the hospital and has returned to her local area.

SUMMARY AND CONCLUSIONS

In this chapter, we have noted that studies on the prevalence of alcohol use in people with ID have generally found lower rates than in the general population. For offenders, studies from Australia have suggested high levels of alcohol intake associated with index offences and significant substance use histories (Hayes and Carmody, 1990; Klimecki et al., 1994; McGillivray and Moore, 2001). In studies from other jurisdictions (Canada and the United Kingdom), lower levels of alcohol use have been found in offenders with ID compared with mainstream offenders (Lindsay et al., 2010b; Lunsky et al., 2011). However, some authors have reported that, for those who do drink alcohol, a greater proportion have problems related to their alcohol consumption. In addition, there are some indications that smaller quantities of alcohol can have significant effects on people with ID.

One of the important aspects of treatment for alcohol-related violence is that we use an alcohol module in conjunction with anger management. Any treatment for violence should employ anger management, incorporating stress inoculation, which is the best validated treatment for offenders with ID (Lindsay and Michie, 2012). We have described an alcohol treatment module that can be added to a violence programme. One essential feature of both the alcohol and the violence programmes is that RP sessions are included. Sessions on understanding alcohol will prime the individual to consider the importance of including self-regulation procedures regarding alcohol use in their RP measures. Because these issues have been discussed during the alcohol module and then have been related to violence in the anger management group, it becomes much easier to combine them in an RP plan. The case illustration describes the way in which the alcohol module can be incorporated into treatment for individuals who have been in contact with a forensic service and for whom alcohol has featured as a significant problem in relation to violence.

It is often the case in the evaluation of offence-related programmes that the programme contains so many components that the effectiveness of each part is difficult to specify. For example, anger management includes arousal reduction, understanding emotion, discussions on the nature of anger, normalising anger as an emotion, developing an anger hierarchy and stress inoculation. However, the programme is normally evaluated as a single treatment (e.g., Lindsay et al., 2004a; Taylor et al., 2005), preventing any understanding of the effectiveness (or otherwise) of individual components. Adding the alcohol module complicates evaluation further. However, we have evaluated this aspect separately with participants who have had problems with alcohol misuse, demonstrating that participants have gained and maintained appropriate knowledge when compared to controls (Lindsay et al., 2012). We have not evaluated the effect separately on future violence. Future research may concentrate on testing the effects of these components on violence outcomes with offenders with ID who have committed alcohol-related violence.

REFERENCES

Alder, L. and Lindsay, W.R. (2007) Exploratory factor analysis and convergent validity of the Dundee Provocation Inventory. *Journal of Intellectual and Developmental Disabilities*, **32**, 179–188.

Alexander, R.T., Green, E.N., O'Mahony, B. *et al.* (2010) Personality disorders in offenders with intellectual disability: A comparison of clinical, forensic and outcome variables and implications for service provision. *Journal of Intellectual Disability Research*, **54**, 650–658.

Barter, G. (2007) Learning disability and co existing drug and alcohol problems. In A. Baker and R. Velleman (eds), *Clinical Handbook of Coexisting Mental Health and Drug and Alcohol Problems* (Chapter 17, pp. 329–350). New York: Routledge.

Burke, B., Arkowitz, H., and Menchola, M. (2003) The efficacy of motivational interviewing: A meta-analysis of controlled clinical trials. *Journal of Consulting and Clinical Psychology*, **71**, 843–861.

Carson, D., Lindsay, W.R., O'Brien, G. *et al.* (2010) Referrals into services for offenders with intellectual disabilities: Variables predicting community or secure provision. *Criminal Behaviour and Mental Health*, **20**, 39–50.

Cosden, M. (2001) Risk and resilience for substance abuse among adolescents and adults with learning disabilities. *Journal of Learning Disabilities*, **24**, 352–358.

Dagnan, D. and Jahoda, A. (2006) Cognitive behavioural interventions for people with intellectual disability and anxiety disorders. *Journal of Applied Research and Intellectual Disabilities*, **19**, 91–98.

Dagnan, D. and Waring, M. (2004) Linking stigma to psychological distress: Testing a social-cognitive model of the experience of people with intellectual disabilities. *Clinical Psychology and Psychotherapy*, **11**, 241–254.

Edgerton, R.B. (1986) Alcohol and drug use by mentally retarded adults. *American Journal of Mental Deficiency*, **90**, 602–609.

Emerson, E. and Turnbull, L. (2005) Self-reported smoking and alcohol use by adolescents with and without intellectual disabilities. *Journal of Intellectual Disabilities*, **9**, 58–69.

Hayes, S.C. (1996) *People with an Intellectual Disability and Criminal Justice System: Two Rural Courts*. Research report number 5. Sydney: New South Wales Law Reform Commission.

Hayes, S.C. and Carmody, J. (1990) Helping those imprisoned for alcohol related crimes. In J. Vernon (ed.), *Alcohol and Crime: Proceedings of a conference held 4–6 April 1989* (pp. 179–186). Canberra: Australian Institute of Criminology.

Hettema, J., Steele, J., and Miller, W. (2005) Motivational interviewing. *Annual Review of Clinical Psychology*, **1**, 91–111.

Jahoda, A., Dagnan, D., Jarvie, P., and Kerr, W. (2006) Depression, social context and cognitive behavioural therapy for people who have intellectual disabilities. *Journal of Applied Research in Intellectual Disabilities*, **19**, 81–89.

Klimecki, M.R., Jenkinson, J., and Wilson, L. (1994) A study of recidivism among offenders with intellectual disability. *Australia and New Zealand Journal of Developmental Disabilities (Journal of Intellectual and Developmental Disabilities)*, **19**, 209–219.

Krishef, C. and DiNitto, D. (1981) Alcohol use among mentally retarded individuals. *Mental Retardation*, **19**, 151–155.

Lawrenson, H., Lindsay, W.R., and Walker, P. (1995) The pattern of alcohol consumption within a sample of mentally handicapped people in Tayside. *Mental Handicap Research*, **8**, 54–59.

Lindsay, W.R. (2009) *The Treatment of Sex Offenders with Developmental Disabilities. A Practice Workbook*. Chichester: Wiley-Blackwell.

Lindsay, W.R., Allan, R., Parry, C. *et al.* (2004a) Anger and aggression in people with intellectual disabilities: Treatment and follow-up of consecutive referrals and a waiting list comparison. *Clinical Psychology & Psychotherapy*, **11**, 255–264.

Lindsay, W.R., Allen, R., Walker, P. *et al.* (1991) An alcohol education service for people with intellectual disabilities. *Mental Handicap (British Journal of Learning Disabilities)*, **19**, 101–104.

Lindsay, W.R., Holland, T., Wheeler, J.R. *et al.* (2010a) Pathways through services for offenders with intellectual disability: A one- and two-year follow-up study. *American Journal on Intellectual and Developmental Disabilities*, **115**, 250–262.

Lindsay, W.R., MacPherson, F., Mathewson, Z., and Kelman, L. (1998) *Health Promotion Resource for People with Learning Disabilities: 2 Alcohol.* Dundee: Dundee Healthcare.

Lindsay, W.R. and Michie, A.M. (2012) What works for offenders with intellectual disabilities. In L.A. Craig, L. Dixon, and T.A. Gannon (eds), *What Works in Offender Rehabilitation: An Evidence Based Approach to Assessment and Treatment (ch 15)* Chichester: Wiley-Blackwell.

Lindsay, W.R., O'Brien, G., Carson, D.R. *et al.* (2010b) Pathways into services for offenders with intellectual disabilities: Childhood experiences, diagnostic information and offence related variables. *Criminal Justice and Behaviour*, **37**, 678–694.

Lindsay, W.R., Smith, A.H.W., Law, J. *et al.* (2004b) Sexual and non-sexual offenders with intellectual and learning disabilities: A comparison of characteristics, referral patterns and outcome. *Journal of Interpersonal Violence*, **19**, 875–890.

Lindsay, W.R. Tinsley, S., and Emara, M. (2012) A controlled trial of an alcohol treatment for adults with intellectual disability who have offended, in preparation.

Lunsky, Y., Gracey, C., Koegl, C. *et al.* (2011) The clinical profile and service needs of psychiatric inpatients with intellectual disabilities and forensic involvement. *Psychology Crime and Law*, **17**, 9–25.

McGillicuddy, N.B. (2006) A review of substance use research among those with mental retardation. *Mental Retardation and Developmental Disabilities Research Reviews*, **12**, 41–47.

McGillicuddy, N.B. and Blane, H.T. (1999) Substance use in individuals with mental retardation. *Addictive Behaviors*, **24**, 869–878.

McGillivray, J.A. and Moore, M.R. (2001) Substance use by offenders with mild intellectual disability. *Journal of Intellectual and Developmental Disability*, **26**, 297–310.

McMurran, M. (2009) Motivational interviewing with offenders: A systematic review. *Legal and Criminological Psychology*, **14**, 83–100.

Meltzer, H., Gatward, R., Goodman, R., and Ford, T. (2000) *Mental Health of Children and Adolescents in Great Britain.* London: Stationery Office.

Merikangas, K., Stolar, M., Stevens, D. *et al.* (1998) Familial transmission of substance use disorders. *Archives of General Psychiatry*, **55**, 973–979.

Molina, B. and Pelham, W. (2001) Substance use, substance abuse, and LD among adolescents with childhood history of ADHD. *Journal of Learning Disabilities*, **34**, 333–342.

Moore, D. and Polsgrove, L. (1991) Disabilities, developmental handicaps and substance misuse: A review. *The International Journal of the Addictions*, **26**, 65–90.

O'Brien, G., Taylor, J.L., Lindsay, W.R. *et al.* (2010) A multi-centre study of adults with learning disabilities referred to services for antisocial or offending behaviour: Demographic, individual, offending and service characteristics. *Journal of Learning Disabilities and Offending Behaviour*, **1**, 5–15.

Pack, R., Wallander, J., and Browne, D. (1998) Health risk behaviours of African American adolescents with mild mental retardation: Prevalence depends on measurement method. *American Journal on Mental Retardation*, **102**, 409–420.

Plant, A., McDermott, E., Chester, V., and Alexander, R. (2011) Substance misuse among offenders in a forensic intellectual disability service. *Journal of Learning Disabilities and Offending Behaviour*, **2**, 187–195.

Raina, P. and Lunsky, Y. (2010) A comparison study of adults with intellectual disability and psychiatric disorder with and without forensic involvement. *Research in Developmental Disabilities*, **31**, 218–223.

Rimmer, J.H., Braddock, D., and Marks, B. (1995) Health characteristics and behaviour of adults with mental retardation residing in three living arrangements. *Research in Developmental Disabilities*, **16**, 489–499.

Seto, M.C., Cantor, J.M., and Blanchard, R. (2006) Child pornography offenses are a valid diagnostic indicator of pedophilia. *Journal of Abnormal Psychology*, **115**, 610–615.

Slayter, E.M. (2010) Not immune: Access to substance abuse treatment among Medicaid covered youth with mental retardation. *Journal of Disability Policy Studies*, **20**, 195–204.

Sondenaa, E., Rasmussen, K., Palmstierna, T., and Nottestad, J. (2008) The prevalence and nature of intellectual disability in Norwegian prisons. *Journal of Intellectual Disability Research*, **52**, 1129–1137.

Sturmey, P., Reyer, H., Lee, R., and Robeck, A. (2003) *Substance Related Disorders in Persons with Mental Retardation*. Kingston, NY: NADD Press.

Taggart, L., McLaughlin, D., Quinn, B., and McFarlane, C. (2007) Listening to people with intellectual disabilities who misuse alcohol and drugs. *Health and Social Care in the Community*, **15**, 160–368.

Taggart, L., McLaughlin, D., Quinn, B., and Milligan, C. (2006) An exploration of substance misuse in people with intellectual disabilities. *Journal of Intellectual Disability Research*, **50**, 588–597.

Taylor, J.L. and Novaco, R.W. (2005) *Anger Treatment for People with Developmental Disabilities: A Theory, Evidence and Manual Based Approach*. Chichester: John Wiley & Sons, Ltd.

Taylor, J.L., Novaco, R.W., Gillmer, B.T. *et al.* (2005) Individual cognitive behavioural anger treatment for people with mild-borderline intellectual disabilities and histories of aggression: A controlled trial. *The British Journal of Clinical Psychology*, **44**, 367–382.

Weinberg, N. (2001) Risk factors for adolescent substance abuse. *Journal of Learning Disabilities*, **34**, 343–351.

Westermeyer, J., Kemp, K., and Nugent, S. (1996) Substance disorder among persons with mild mental retardation: A comparative study. *The American Journal on Addictions*, **5**, 23–31.

Wheeler, J.R., Holland, A.J., Bambrick, M. *et al.* (2009) Community services and people with intellectual disabilities who engage in anti-social or offending behaviour: Referral rates, characteristics, and care pathways. *Journal of Forensic Psychiatry and Psychology*, **20**, 717–740.

Chapter 15

TREATMENTS FOR ALCOHOL-RELATED IMPAIRED DRIVING

THOMAS G. BROWN

Research Centre, Douglas Mental Health University Institute, Montreal; Department of Psychiatry, McGill University, Montreal; and Foster Addiction Rehabilitation Centre, Montreal, Quebec, Canada

MARIE CLAUDE OUIMET

Faculty of Medicine and Health Sciences, University of Sherbrooke, Longueuil, Quebec, Canada

INTRODUCTION

Driving while impaired (DWI) by alcohol and/or drugs is a persistent and growing global public health problem. While drivers convicted for a first offense are at greater risk for crash involvement and contributing to injury, death, and property damage compared to DWI-free drivers, reoffenders (i.e., recidivists) are significantly more dangerous. Hence, many jurisdictions have committed considerable resources to deploy both universal and selective prevention programs to reduce the probability that drivers convicted of a first DWI offense will transition to recidivist status. The main purpose of this chapter is to critically review common and emerging selective DWI prevention approaches to curtail alcohol-related DWI recidivism following a first conviction. In particular, focus is placed upon assessment techniques for informing risk appraisal and remediation planning, and psychosocial, pharmacological, and technology-assisted therapeutic strategies that target lasting DWI behavior change. Along with the influence of these measures on traditional downstream DWI outcomes (e.g., continued substance misuse, DWI reconviction and substance-related road traffic crash [RTC] rates), their impact on more proximal yet potentially crucial processes that mediate outcomes (e.g., engagement and retention) is also considered. The chapter also discusses intrapersonal factors (e.g., age, sex, readiness to change) that may

Alcohol-Related Violence: Prevention and Treatment, First Edition. Edited by Mary McMurran.
© 2013 John Wiley & Sons, Ltd. Published 2013 by John Wiley & Sons, Ltd.

moderate outcomes and help better understand the marked heterogeneity in the effectiveness of remedial programs.

The DWI Problem

In 2001, the World Health Organization (Peden *et al.*, 2004) proclaimed road traffic injuries as a preventable global health problem and a major target for change. RTCs represent the ninth leading cause of disability-adjusted life years lost globally and, if current trends continue unabated, they will represent the third leading cause by 2020 (Sleet and Branche, 2004; Sleet *et al.*, 2004). Canada, with a population of approximately 33 million, documented in 2009 2,209 individuals killed by RTCs and 172,883 injured, of which 11,451 were serious enough to cause long-standing disability (Transport Canada, 2011). Some groups are particularly vulnerable. Worldwide, RTCs are the leading cause of morbidity in young people aged 15–29 (Mathers and Loncar, 2006). Overall, the health, social and economic costs related to traffic crashes remain so intolerably high that the United Nations General Assembly (A/64/L.44/Rev.1) has proclaimed 2011–2020 as the "Decade of Action for Road Safety" to spur global efforts to reduce the carnage.

Human factors, including speeding, DWI, unbelted and distracted driving, together account for up to 90% of all fatal RTCs (Lum and Reagan, 1995). DWI is a major contributing factor to RTC morbidity, implicated in almost 40% of all RTC-related fatalities in the developed world (Traffic Injury Research Foundation [TIRF], 2010) and more than doubling the risk of a driver being involved in a fatal crash (Voas, 2010). Blood alcohol concentration (BAC) levels of greater than $0.01\,g/dL$ (i.e., 0.01%) are associated with a significant increase in overall injury risk compared to 0.00% BAC (Phillips and Brewer, 2011; Taylor *et al.*, 2010). Further, the impact of positive BAC on RTC risk surges monotonically, increasing RTC risk fourfold at 0.05% BAC and 10-fold at 0.07% BAC. In certain vulnerable groups, such as young and novice drivers and motorcyclists, crash risk is significantly higher at all BAC levels compared with that of the general driver population (Moskowitz *et al.*, 2000; National Highway Traffic Safety Administration [NHTSA], 2009). Currently, many jurisdictions have per se DWI laws that target drivers who operate a vehicle with a BAC ranging from 0.05% to 0.08%. In novice or young drivers, BAC below these levels (e.g., 0.0%, 0.02%) is in force in some jurisdictions during a probationary licensure period or until a certain age.

The role of drug use in traffic crashes is more complicated to appraise. Though alcohol remains the primary psychoactive substance identified in fatally injured drivers and in drivers tested at roadside, drugs are increasingly detected at rates that in some studies have rivalled those seen with alcohol (e.g., Beirness, Simpson, and Desmond, 2003; Dussault *et al.*, 2002; Sweedler *et al.*, 2004), with cannabis and benzodiazepines usually the most frequently detected (Christophersen and Morland, 2008). Available evidence suggests that cannabis alone approximately doubles RTC risk. At the same time, there are myriad classes of drugs, both licit and illicit, that can impair driving performance. For most substances, the levels required to increase RTC risk have yet to be unequivocally determined. Difficulties in quantifying concentrations of all drugs associated with increased crash risk when consumed illicitly, understanding the compounding effect when drugs are consumed with alcohol and/or other drugs, and determining whether driving is temporally coupled to drug use also remain unresolved. Nevertheless, the rapid emergence of DWI from drug misuse, often in combination with alcohol, has led some jurisdictions to adopt per se laws that hinge upon evidence or behavioral signs of any illicit drug use while driving. Given that the basis of an arrest and conviction for the vast majority of DWI events remains excessive alcohol consumption, as well as the relatively nascent stage of the drugged driving literature on selective prevention, this review focuses on alcohol-related DWI.

Who Are DWI Drivers?

Fundamentally, DWI involves an individual engaging in an episode of excessive alcohol or drug use, the availability of a vehicle, and his/her propensity to drive it. As a group, DWI offenders' risk for all-source mortality is significantly higher than nonoffenders (Skurtveit et al., 2002; Zador, Krawchuk, and Voas, 2000). Beyond these observations, however, DWI offenders make up a heterogeneous population in terms of risk of further offending and crash involvement as well as demographic, psychosocial and substance use characteristics (Nochajski and Stasiewicz, 2006). Descriptive research has consistently found DWI offender status to be correlated with the male sex; single marital status; hostility; sensation seeking; psychopathic deviance; poor psychosocial, socioeconomic, and psychiatric functioning; legal problems; disrespect for legal authorities and sanctions; family history of alcoholism; and engagement in other risky driving behaviors; and in the case of recidivism status, younger age, early onset of alcohol problems, alcoholism, and high BAC at the time of arrest (Begg and Langley, 2004; Dahlen et al., 2005; Fernandes, Hatfield, and Job, 2010; Franques et al., 2003; Hatfield and Fernandes, 2009; Hubicka, Laurell, and Bergman, 2008; Iversen and Rundmo, 2002; Lonczak, Neighbors, and Donovan, 2007; Oltedal and Rundmo, 2006; Romano, Kelley-Baker, and Voas, 2008; Schwebel et al., 2006; Smart and Vassalo, 2005; Steinberg, 2007; Ulleberg and Rundmo, 2003; Williams, Kyrychenko, and Retting, 2006).

In addition, DWI offenders harbor attitudes that challenge efforts to change their behavior, including the tendency to minimize personal concern for their DWI risk and to overestimate personal control over DWI risks (e.g., intoxication) (Brown et al., 2008, 2010; Donovan, Marlatt, and Salzberg, 1983). As antagonistic as these attitudes may be for changing DWI behavior, they are reinforced to some degree by reality: negative consequences associated with DWI (e.g., crashes, arrests and convictions) are unlikely events (Voas and Fisher, 2001). The next sections briefly highlight major prevention strategies and methodological challenges that vex both our understanding of DWI and our ability to mount evidence-informed approaches to DWI reduction.

Universal and Selective Prevention of DWI

Universal prevention involves initiatives that seek to deter DWI behavior from occurring. Its rationale is that it aims to reduce the risks in the large group of drivers responsible for the majority of DWI-related events, namely, those without a previous DWI conviction (Woodall *et al.*, 2004). Reductions of 25–50% in DWI morbidity documented in the developed countries in the 1990s are attributable at least in part to universal prevention programs (Schmukle, Chollet, and Daeppen, 2005; Sweedler *et al.*, 2004). More recently, decreases in DWI and alcohol-related crash rates have stalled (Fell, Tippetts, and Voas, 2009; Voas *et al.*, 2011). Most universal prevention strategies are multicomponent initiatives involving such elements as policy and legislation, law enforcement, and mass public information and education campaigns (Novoa, Perez, and Borrell, 2009). Although disentangling the relative effectiveness of specific program elements from these multicomponent programs is difficult (Shults *et al.*, 2009), several systematic reviews have identified a number of effective measures and the conditions under which their impact is optimized. These include DWI legislation when adequately enforced (e.g., lowering BAC limits, raising the minimum drinking age) (Fell and Voas, 2006; Morrison, Petticrew, and Thomson, 2003; Redelmeier, Tibshirani, and Evans, 2003; Shults *et al.*, 2001; Wagenaar and Toomey, 2002), random or selective breath testing/sobriety checkpoints when legally feasible and supported by the community (Elder *et al.*, 2002; Fell, Lacey, and Voas, 2004), and mass media campaigns if well planned, executed and implemented (Elder *et al.*, 2004). Unfortunately, despite these efforts, DWI behavior remains unacceptably high.

Selective prevention involves the identification of higher-risk drivers and exposing them to measures to reduce their risk (Health Canada, 2004). A first arrest and conviction for DWI is a significant opportunity for identifying higher-risk drivers. Although the punishing sanctions, fines and other negative consequences are sufficient to deter the majority of offenders from further DWI behavior (Redelmeier *et al.*, 2003), many persist. The recidivism risk of offenders with a previous conviction is 6–20 times greater compared with drivers with no previous violations depending on their age (Zador *et al.*, 2011). Compared to the estimated 2% conviction rate for non-DWI drivers over a 3-year period (Donovan, Umlauf, and Salzberg, 1990), the reconviction rate for DWI offenders is 30% within 5 years of their first conviction, which does not include the many offenders who continue to engage in DWI undetected (Impinen *et al.*, 2009; Lapham *et al.*, 2002; Portman *et al.*, 2010). Recidivism is especially significant as recidivists contribute disproportionately to RTC-related morbidity (Hingson and Winter, 2003). Moreover, as the number of previous DWI convictions increases, so, too, does the offender's risk of being involved in further DWI and fatal RTCs (Brewer *et al.*, 1994; Zador *et al.*, 2011). Thus, a first conviction for DWI is considered a prime opportunity for deploying selective prevention efforts.

Methodological Challenges in DWI Research

Our ability to prevent recidivism by developing more effective remedial measures is challenged by several methodological hurdles in conducting DWI research.

Several reviews have outlined these difficulties (e.g., Beirness, Mayhew, and Simpson, 1997; Brown et al., 2009; Chang, Gregory, and Lapham, 2002; Dill and Wells-Parker, 2006; Macdonald and Mann, 1996; Mann et al., 1983; Nochajski and Stasiewicz, 2006; Wells-Parker et al., 1995). The most vexing include the lack of clarity, insensitivity and validity of measures to track recidivism status and intervention outcomes (e.g., alcohol-related road crashes, DWI arrests or convictions), the validity of self-report during mandatory evaluation and treatment, sampling bias, overreliance on correlational methodologies that prevent causal inferences, and environmental, geographic, and jurisdictional discrepancies (e.g., local BAC limits, enforcement, and prosecution vigor) that influence who are designated as first-time offenders versus recidivists. These hurdles complicate comparison of findings between studies and jurisdictions. Certain approaches to assessment and remediation are less vulnerable to some of these shortcomings, however, and are discussed below.

ASSESSMENT OF DWI OFFENDERS

There are three main reasons for assessing first-time DWI offenders: (1) to appraise their risk for further DWI offending, (2) to justify the severity of sanctioning, and (3) to adjust the intensity and modality of remedial interventions to offender characteristics and needs (Anderson, Snow, and Wells-Parker, 2000). This section focuses on assessment of DWI offenders for informing risk appraisal and remediation planning. Assessment targets reviewed here include alcohol abuse (e.g., self-reported data and biological markers), other correlates of DWI, and multidimensional assessment.

Background

If first-time DWI offenders are submitted to uniform sanctions and interventions as prerequisites for relicensing, the need for assessment as a preliminary step in the remediation process is somewhat obviated. In jurisdictions that do attempt to inform and adjust remedial strategies (Mann et al., 2009), assessment offers several potential advantages. More judicious use of deterrence and punitive sanctions, such as longer license suspension periods, in those offenders classified as the riskiest can remove them, and the hazards they pose, from the road. In contrast, reducing overtreatment of low-risk drivers can improve system efficiency. Further, it may avoid unintended counter-therapeutic consequences. For example, sanctions that are injudiciously and unevenly applied to low-risk individuals can dilute their deterrent effect (Williams, McCartt, and Ferguson, 2007), while intensive intervention may desensitize them to interventions they might require in future (C'De Baca, Miller, and Lapham, 2001b). Alternatively, matching intervention strategies to individual needs, such as referral to specialized alcoholism treatment for those in need of such services, is considered a way to improve outcomes (Ball et al., 2000; Dill and Wells-Parker, 2006; Health Canada, 2004; Wells-Parker, Landrum, and Topping, 1990).

Alcohol Abuse

Given the sentinel role of alcohol misuse in DWI (Hingson and Winter, 2003), DWI assessment protocols frequently include brief alcohol abuse screening measures like the Michigan Alcohol Screening Test (MAST), the Alcohol Use Disorders Identification Test (AUDIT), and the Cut Down, Annoyed, Guilt and Eye-Opener (CAGE) (Chang *et al.*, 2002). Although efficient and validated in several settings, their performance in real-world DWI assessment has not been particularly good (Mann *et al.*, 1983). This is due in large part to the face validity of these screening instruments, which makes them easily falsifiable by offenders motivated to avoid severe sanctions and relicensing requirements (Anderson *et al.*, 2000; Cavaiola *et al.*, 2003; Del Boca and Darkes, 2003; Dill and Wells-Parker, 2006; Lapham *et al.*, 2000, 2002; Lapham and Skipper, 2010; Marowitz, 1998; Nochajski and Stasiewicz, 2006; Schell, Chan, and Morral, 2006; Voas, 2010; Wieczorek, Miller, and Nochajski, 1992).

The use of biomarkers of alcohol misuse has been explored as a way to overcome this shortcoming. Various indirect (e.g., carbohydrate-deficient transferrin [CDT] and gamma glutamyltransferase [GGT]) and direct biomarkers (e.g., phosphatidyl ethanol, ethyl glucuronide, ethyl sulfate, fatty acid ethyl esters) are capable of detecting either chronic or recent alcohol use, respectively. Their effectiveness in predicting recidivism among offenders participating in a DWI license reacquisition program has been mixed. For example, one prospective study (Marques *et al.*, 2010) found that higher levels on certain indirect and direct biomarkers were associated with more failed ignition attempts in drivers participating in an interlock program over a 1-year period. At the same time, a direct relationship between DWI behavior while an interlock device is installed and after the device has been removed has not been established (Elder *et al.*, 2011; see further discussion on interlock below). Another prospective study (Portman *et al.*, 2010) failed to find a relationship between indirect biomarkers and subsequent rearrests in offenders participating in a DWI remedial program over a 10-year period.

Epidemiological studies (Flowers *et al.*, 2008; Naimi, Nelson, and Brewer, 2009; Valencia-Martín, Galán, and Rodríguez-Artalejo, 2008; Voas *et al.*, 2006; Woodall *et al.*, 2004) have indicated that binge drinking (e.g., more than five standard drinks in one episode) is responsible for more DWI occurrences than alcohol dependence than previously thought, with estimates as high as 85% (Centers for Disease Control, 2011). In contrast, offenders who are alcohol dependent, though overrepresented among recidivists compared to the general population, represent a minority within the DWI recidivist population (Couture *et al.*, 2010; Dawson, 1999; Korzec *et al.*, 2001; Lapham, Skipper, and Simpson, 1997; Lapham *et al.*, 2011; Williams *et al.*, 2007; Woerle, Roeber, and Landen, 2007). Binge drinking is less amenable to detection by biomarkers sensitive to more chronic drinking patterns and, by its sporadic nature, may escape detection by direct biomarkers with a more limited detection horizon. Moreover, in certain subgroups such as young drivers and females, severe drinking patterns may not be as significant an explanatory factor in DWI as in other subgroups such as older males (Farrow and Brissing, 1990; Liang *et al.*, 1999; Shope, Waller, and Lang, 1996).

An alternative biomarker approach uses driver BAC at the time of arrest as a more proximal DWI risk factor. BAC in excess of 0.15% is frequently considered the signal of the high-risk driver deserving of more severe sanctioning and intense remediation. The results concerning relationships between higher arrest BAC, alcohol problems, recidivism, and crash risk in DWI offenders, however, have also produced complex or nonlinear relationships possibly moderated by factors such as offender sex (C'De Baca *et al.*, 2001b; Cavaiola *et al.*, 2003; Couture *et al.*, 2010; Impinen *et al.*, 2009; Lapham *et al.*, 1997; Marowitz, 1998; McCutcheon *et al.*, 2009; Portman *et al.*, 2010; Wieczorek *et al.*, 1992; Woodall *et al.*, 2004). More research is needed to better understand the clinical significance of arrest BAC as well as how it might interact with other factors to increase future DWI risk. At the moment, the most direct benefit of using alcohol biomarkers appears to be (1) identification of offenders who need and are likely to benefit from specialized intensive alcohol abuse treatment in the case of biomarkers of chronic abuse and (2) monitoring offenders' attainment of abstinence or reduced drinking objectives as a condition for relicensing.

Other Correlates of DWI

Along with alcohol misuse, research has consistently detected significant associations between recidivism status and certain sociodemographic (e.g., sex, low academic achievement, unemployment, marital status), psychosocial (e.g., criminality, previous offenses, drug misuse) and psychological factors (e.g., sensation seeking, impulsivity) (Cavaiola, Strohmetz, and Abreo, 2007; Hubicka *et al.*, 2008; Nochajski and Stasiewicz, 2006; Schell *et al.*, 2006). Their predictive value, alone or in combination, however, has been disappointing (Lapham and Skipper, 2010; Lapham *et al.*, 2000; Marowitz, 1998; Schell *et al.*, 2006; Wieczorek *et al.*, 1992). For example, research algorithms for prediction of DWI reconviction using different combinations of these variables have been estimated to yield prediction with 70% sensitivity and 50% specificity (e.g., C'De Baca *et al.*, 2001b; Chang *et al.*, 2002; Marowitz, 1998), performance that is not clinically viable.

The awareness that descriptive correlates of DWI status are inadequate for either accurate prediction or orchestration of evidence-informed remediation has motivated researchers to explore the web of dynamic factors that likely contribute more causally to DWI behavior, including change in substance use patterns, motivation to change, attitudes about DWI behaviors and laws, mood and risk-taking tendencies (Chang *et al.*, 2002; Constant *et al.*, 2011; Donovan *et al.*, 1983; Fernandes, Job, and Hatfield, 2007; Fynbo and Jarvinen, 2011; Greenberg, Morral, and Jain, 2004; Zylman, 1974). Some of the more promising assessment protocols that use single or multiple scales to tap into these dimensions are discussed below.

Multidimensional Assessment

The original MacAndrew subscale (MAC) of the Minnesota Multiphasic Personality Inventory (MMPI) (MacAndrew, 1965) and its revised version (MAC-R) were designed to be sensitive to substance abuse problems in individuals who may be motivated to avoid detection. Its interest for DWI assessment is its use of items that are both less vulnerable to manipulation as they are not obviously linked to substance abuse, and that tap into factors related to both substance abuse and DWI recidivism, such as reward-seeking personality features (e.g., risk taking and extroversion), cognitive impairment, and social maladjustment involving rule breaking, acting out, and interpersonal competence (Beerman, Smith, and Hall, 1988; Cavaiola *et al.*, 2003; Chang *et al.*, 2001, 2002; Harwood and Leonard, 1989; Impinen *et al.*, 2009; Jonah, 1997; Lapham *et al.*, 2001; LaPlante *et al.*, 2008; Macdonald and Mann, 1996; Michiels and La Harpe, 1996; Nochajski and Stasiewicz, 2006; Ouimet *et al.*, 2007; Portman *et al.*, 2010; Voas, 2008; Voas and Fisher, 2001; Wieczorek *et al.*, 1992; Zhang, Wieczorek, and Welte, 2011).

The MAC appears predictive of DWI recidivism. One study found the MAC-R to be the most predictive instrument compared with the MAST and the Alcohol Use Inventory over a 4-year period (Lapham *et al.*, 1997). Another study investigating the use of multiple measures simultaneously to predict outcome found that the MAC-R scale increased the accuracy of post-arrest prediction of recidivism over a 4-year period in addition to young age, low academic achievement, elevated BAC at arrest, and the receptive area scale score of the Alcohol Use Inventory (C'De Baca *et al.*, 2001b). Cross-sectional analysis of MAC-R scores discriminated between nonoffenders, first-time offenders, and recidivists (Cavaiola *et al.*, 2003), but a prospective study over a 12-year period with first-time offenders produced inconclusive results (Cavaiola *et al.*, 2007). Interestingly, two test-taking attitudinal scales on the MMPI, the L (lie) and K (defensiveness) scales, also significantly predicted recidivism. Offenders who responded to the MMPI in a way consistent with "faking good" and defensiveness were more likely to recidivate. At the same time, these scales were unable to discriminate between first-time and repeat offenders at intake, signaling that discriminative validity is not synonymous with predictive validity. In sum, there is support for the MAC scale's predictive validity for DWI risk assessment but more mitigated support for other MMPI scales. What is needed is clarification of whether administration of the MAC scale alone, without the entire MMPI questionnaire (with over 500 items), can provide valid data more feasibly for pragmatic DWI assessment.

In an attempt to improve DWI assessment technology, a number of DWI-specific multidimensional instruments have recently emerged. The Research Institute on Addictions Self-Inventory (RIASI) (Mann *et al.*, 2009; Shuggi *et al.*, 2006), for example, is a 52-item instrument designed for DWI assessment. It measures both distal (hostility/aggression, sensation seeking, depression, anxiety, interpersonal competence, childhood risk factors, social problems such as criminal history and health issues) and proximal factors (current drinking habits, preoccupation with alcohol, alcohol beliefs, use of alcohol to alleviate problems, and family history) associated with alcohol or drug problems. The Behaviors and Attitudes Drinking and Driving Scale (BADDS) (Jewell, Hupp, and Segrist, 2008) is a 31-item self-administered questionnaire comprising four scales that assess attitudes toward DWI behavior and actual DWI behavior: *rationalizations for drinking and driving, likelihood of drinking and driving, drinking and driving behaviors*, and *riding behaviors with a drinking driver*. The *positive expectancies for drinking and driving* addresses assessment in the distinct, high-risk group of young drivers (PEDD-Y) (McCarthy *et al.*, 2006). While these instruments have demonstrated coherent factor structure, adequate internal consistency, and discriminative and criterion validity, their predictive validity in identifying first-time offenders who will convert to recidivism status has yet to be established in published longitudinal studies.

Conclusions and Future Directions

Current initial DWI assessment procedures attempt to predict DWI recidivism risk in first-time offenders and to tailor remedial programs to offender characteristics. Research has revealed consistent relationships between DWI recidivism and several sociodemographic, psychosocial, psychological and substance use characteristics. Except in rare instances (e.g., Beerman *et al.*, 1988; Cavaiola *et al.*, 2003; Lapham *et al.*, 1997, 2000; Marowitz, 1998), these studies have not clearly distinguished between their correlational, causal or clinical significance (Macdonald and Mann, 1996). Not surprisingly, the correlational research has failed to yield clinically useful predictive assessment protocols (C'De Baca *et al.*, 2001b). Longer duration prospective evaluations of assessment protocols for prediction of recidivism are urgently needed.

Signal detection theory may provide a more germane conceptual approach to the problem of clinically useful DWI prediction, but it is seldom applied in this field. This approach and the analyses used to apply it can help better understand both DWI prediction efficiency (i.e., sensitivity and specificity) as well as decision error (i.e., false negatives and false positives) of specific variables. Analysis of the receiver operating characteristic curve of a measure or protocol can also help clarify not only test sensitivity but also implicit policy and examiner biases at play in setting cut-offs. This knowledge can guide adjustments to clinical cut-offs that optimally reconcile the often competing needs of society (e.g., optimizing public security) and of the offender (e.g., fair exercise of justice) (Leshowitz and Meyers, 1996).

A small number of recent studies have attempted to identify markers of more explanatory pathways to DWI recidivism in addition to substance dependence. For example, susceptibility to alcohol abuse as well as other risky behavior has been linked to neuropsychological factors that may be preexisting or may be a consequence of exposure to alcohol (Bechara, 2005; Guerri and Pascual, 2010; Llewellyn, 2008). Similarly, DWI behavior and recidivism in some offenders have been linked to dysfunction in autoregulatory and executive function (Brown *et al.*, 2008; Fillmore, Blackburn, and Harrison, 2008; Glass, Chan, and Rentz, 2000; Ouimet *et al.*, 2007), negative mood (Wells-Parker *et al.*, 2009), emotional information processing and decision making (Bouchard, Brown, and Nadeau, 2011; Kasar *et al.*, 2010; Lev, Hershkovitz, and Yechiam, 2008; Yechiam *et al.*, 2008), and neurobiological substrates of arousal, sensation seeking, and fearlessness (Brown *et al.*, 2009; Couture *et al.*, 2008; Eensoo *et al.*, 2005) that may be preexisting or a consequence of alcohol misuse. Inclusion of such markers in DWI assessment protocols is still speculative. Nevertheless, their assessment may strike more at the heart of why some individuals continue in their dangerous behavior despite the risks and help in the design of interventions to disrupt these explanatory pathways.

REMEDIAL PROGRAMS FOR DWI OFFENDERS

Psychosocial, pharmacological and technology-assisted remedial approaches have been deployed in the field to reduce DWI recidivism by targeting lasting behavioral change. This section reviews some of the more promising and empirically supported strategies.

Background

Remedial programs for DWI have traditionally targeted the reduction of problem drinking and decoupling drinking from driving using a combination of monitoring and provision of knowledge, supervision, skills and other strategies to effectively avoid future offending. There is evidence supporting the intuitive logic that reduction in alcohol or substance use through treatment reduces injury risk generally (Dinh-Zarr et al., 1999). Direct support for the aggregate effectiveness of remedial programs in reducing DWI risks, however, comes mainly from a small number of systematic reviews (Foon, 1988; Mann et al., 1983; Wells-Parker et al., 1995). In the most rigorous, Wells-Parker et al. (1995) compared exposure to remediation versus no remediation on recidivism, RTC rates and drinking indices. Remediation involved multiple components, including license sanctions, assessment followed by interventions such as psychotherapy/counseling, education, contact probation, self-help group participation (e.g., Alcoholics Anonymous [AA]), administration of disulfiram (i.e., Antabuse), and psychosocial alcohol/drug treatment. The "no remediation" condition, on the other hand, involved only license sanctions and some form of face-to-face assessment and follow-up. Their meta-analysis revealed that remediation produced a statistically significant but modest 7–9% improvement in outcome over no remediation. The analysis included studies suffering from important shortcomings, however. These included poor reporting practices, limited coverage of intervention modalities beyond education, narrow and insensitive outcome indices, and effect sizes that were inversely correlated to methodological quality. Moreover, not all interventions were effective. Court-mandated treatment and AA attendance produced detrimental effects, findings consistent with those reported elsewhere (Dill and Wells-Parker, 2006; MacDonald, Zanna, and Fong, 1995).

Curiously, with the exception of a number of narrative reviews and more local, naturalistic program evaluations with limited experimental control (e.g., Deyoung, 1997; Ferguson et al., 2001; Mills et al., 2008; Schmukle et al., 2005; Sleet and Dellinger, 2009; The Century Council, 2003; Voas et al., 2011; Wieczorek, 1995), a systematic review of the general DWI remediation area has not been published in the 15 years since the Wells-Parker et al. (1995) meta-analysis. Nevertheless, several more recent systematic reviews have addressed the benefits of specific remedial approaches such as Victim Impact Panels (VIPs), alcohol safety action programs, mandated AA or substance abuse treatment attendance, and driver improvement counseling and education. Many of these approaches were also among those considered in the Wells-Parker *et al.* meta-analysis. Overall, when only studies of acceptable methodological rigor were included, these reviews converged in concluding that no more than marginal support currently existed for either the effectiveness of the reviewed approaches or their continued use in the field (e.g., Anderson, Chisholm, and Fuhr, 2009; C'De Baca *et al.*, 2001a; Dill and Wells-Parker, 2006; Elder *et al.*, 2005; Timko *et al.*, 2011; Voas and Fisher, 2001; Wieczorek, 1995; Williams *et al.*, 2007). In light of these findings, exploration of alternative approaches for promoting further reductions in individual DWI behavior is critically needed.

The failure of mandated treatment to produce positive outcomes suggests that offender motivation may be a necessary component of intervention effectiveness. This hypothesis has been given preliminary support by qualitative studies of offenders' reaction to treatment. In one study, offenders frequently felt that they did not belong in mandated treatment especially when it was an AA-type intervention; they had negative perceptions of intervention as being confrontative and antagonistic, or they were not ready to alter their lifestyle (Lapham and England-Kennedy, 2012). Similarly, a study by our group found that offenders' reluctance to engage in DWI remedial measures was in part attributed to the gap between their personal objectives for change, which were discordant with the objectives of intervention (e.g., significant reduction in drinking) (Brown *et al.*, 2008). The possibility that mandated interventions that have a rigid agenda for change may not be the most beneficial with this population has led to interest in more flexible motivational approaches, which are discussed below.

Psychosocial Remediation Approaches

Cognitive-Behavioral Therapy (CBT)

CBT is an approach frequently utilized to reduce substance abuse. While there are many variations of CBT, one version, relapse prevention (RP), predominates in the addiction treatment field. RP (Marlatt and George, 1984) involves the identification of individual environmental, interpersonal and emotional situations associated with relapse, and the learning and mastery of new skills and coping strategies to deal with these triggers of relapse, typically delivered over 8–10 structured sessions. RP has the strongest support for the treatment of alcohol problems (Irvin *et al.*, 1999) and is considered an evidence-based treatment for substance abuse by the US Substance Abuse and Mental Health Services Administration (Hendershot *et al.*, 2011). Evidence of CBT's effectiveness in reducing recidivism in non-DWI criminal offenders (Landenberger and Lipsey, 2005) as well as in alcohol abuse individuals makes it an appealing remedial approach for reducing DWI recidivism.

While CBT is one of the most researched intervention approaches for substance abuse, studies of the effectiveness of CBT in reducing DWI recidivism are, in fact, rare. One early quasi-experimental study with DWI recidivists (Rosenberg and

Brian, 1986) compared CBT-based coping skills therapy, rational emotive therapy, and unstructured therapy delivered in a group format. The results failed to produce between-group differences on drinking or drink-driving outcomes or any reductions in drinking over the 6-month duration of the programs. Another study randomized recidivists to either an individualized self-control behavioral group treatment or a general behavioral group treatment involving alcohol education, relaxation, and guided reevaluation of situations associated with DWI arrests (Connors, Maisto, and Ersner-Hershfield, 1986). The results found no group differences over 3 years in DWI recidivism rates but some indications that both treatments increased latency to rearrest. A preliminary study combined RP with another therapeutic approach, motivational interviewing (MI), for treating DWI offenders, with indications that RP plus MI was preferred over treatment as usual and was superior at improving coping skills (Stein and Lebeau-Craven, 2002).

Overall, a significant mass of studies supports the effectiveness of different forms of CBT for reducing both alcohol abuse and criminal recidivism. Reductions in alcohol use will likely lessen alcohol-related injury risk. Nevertheless, few studies have directly and rigorously tested the effectiveness of CBT or its variants with DWI offenders in reducing either alcohol misuse or DWI behavior. Moreover, evaluations of CBT for DWI often have inferred its effectiveness, though it is embedded within a multimodal approach, hindering appraisal of RP's unique benefits. Finally, CBT is most suitable for patients who possess attributes that many offenders do not possess, namely, acknowledgement of a significant and disruptive problem, capability to identify concrete situations and environments associated with substance misuse and urges to use, and willingness to actively engage in problem solving and exercises.

Brief Interventions

Many offenders exhibit poor problem recognition regarding their substance misuse and DWI behavior and hence have little willingness to change. Engaging these offenders in a remedial process represents an important therapeutic challenge (Brown et al., 2008; Voas, Tippetts, and McKnight, 2010a). Interest is growing in brief and motivational interventions as an opportunistic way to enhance the offenders' reappraisal of their hazardous drinking, commitment to behavioral change, and engagement in remedial programs. The specific components of brief interventions vary considerably between studies, but common elements include significantly less clinician time than most other psychosocial alcohol abuse intervention approaches (i.e., several minutes to one or two sessions), screening for substance use problems, and provision of personalized feedback, information, advice, and options for change (Heather, 1989).

The brevity of these interventions makes them amenable to opportunistic application in hard-to-reach substance-abusing populations. For example, hazardous drinkers are overrepresented among patients seen in frontline medical, emergency and trauma settings. Hence, detecting drinkers at high risk for DWI in these settings and exposing them to a brief intervention seems feasible and advantageous. Detection and intervention in these settings may also represent a "teachable moment" when individuals who have just suffered a significant negative consequence of alcohol misuse may be more receptive to change (American College of Emergency Physicians, 2006; Blow *et al.*, 2006; Dill and Wells-Parker, 2004; D'Onofrio and Degutis, 2002; Kaner *et al.*, 2007; Moyer *et al.*, 2002; Nilsen *et al.*, 2008; Walton *et al.*, 2008). Other potential opportunistic settings include jails and DWI courtrooms.

Several studies investigating the impact of brief intervention on hazardous drinking and its negative consequences have indicated its benefit for reducing alcohol-related RTCs as well. For example, a randomized controlled trial was conducted in a routine medical care setting with patients screened with hazardous drinking (Fleming *et al.*, 2002). Results indicated significantly less medical care costs due to RTCs over a 12-month follow-up duration in patients who received a brief intervention consisting of two 15-minute physician encounters and two 5-minute nurse follow-up calls compared to those who received an information booklet alone. Another more recent study (Sommers *et al.*, 2006) randomized trauma center patients with an alcohol-related vehicle injury into one of three conditions: (1) two sessions of brief counseling based upon a combination of the FRAMES intervention model (Feedback, Responsibility, Advice to Change, Menu of Alternative Choices, Empathy, and Self-Efficacy) (Bien, Miller, and Tonigan, 1993) plus simple advice (i.e., five minutes of feedback, advice and discussion of different targets for changing alcohol use); (2) simple advice alone with a booster session; or (3) a standard care control condition involving the assessment alone. The results at 12-month follow-up revealed that while all groups improved on hazardous drinking and adverse driving outcomes (i.e., number of traffic infractions), no between-group differences were detected. While promising, the mechanisms by which these different conditions yielded comparable outcomes were not systematically explored.

MI (Miller, 1996) is a sophisticated variant of brief intervention lasting from one session of several minutes to four sessions. It incorporates a precise empathic communication style and an assortment of therapeutic tactics to (1) increase intrapersonal dissonance between clients' deeply held values and current problem behaviors, (2) resolve deep-seated ambivalence about change, (3) enhance willingness and autonomy to take action, and (4) reinforce self-efficacy. MI is effective in treating various tenacious problem behaviors in a variety of settings, among them substance use disorders, pathological gambling, high-risk sexual practices and problem behavior in different offender groups (Burke, Arkowitz, and Menchola, 2003; Carroll *et al.*, 2006; Dunn, Deroo, and Rivara, 2001; Field and Caetano, 2010; Hettema, Steele, and Miller, 2005; McCambridge, 2004; McMurran, 2009; Rubak *et al.*, 2005). There is also support for its effectiveness in reducing injuries in problem drinkers (Dinh-Zarr *et al.*, 1999). Given the reluctance of many offenders to acknowledge their problem drinking and to engage voluntarily in remedial programs, this approach seems well suited in dealing with the therapeutic challenges posed by DWI offenders as well.

Preliminary studies have evaluated MI specifically in DWI. For example, one quasi-experimental pilot study of mandated DWI offenders revealed that those who participated in a MI pretreatment group were more likely to complete treatment than those who did not (Lincourt, Kuettel, and Bombardier, 2002). Other studies demonstrated positive effects when MI was incorporated into existing

DWI intervention programs (Marques *et al.*, 1999; Stein and Lebeau-Craven, 2002), leaving uncertain MI's unique contribution to outcome.

Two more rigorously designed randomized controlled trials with DWI offenders have been published. One study examined the added effect of MI appended to incarceration versus incarceration alone in first-time DWI offenders ($N = 244$) (Woodall *et al.*, 2007). The investigators found that the addition of MI resulted in greater reduction in drinking from baseline levels but no effects on recidivism rates over a two year follow-up. However, the lack of blinding and a control condition that would mimic the impact of added experimenter attention weakened the appraisal of MI's impact on outcome. A randomized controlled trial conducted by our research group appraised MI's potential as a remedial strategy in a high-risk group of DWI offenders (Brown *et al.*, 2010). This double-blind study randomized a non-help-seeking sample of recidivists ($N = 184$) with active substance abuse problems, the majority of whom had a history of significant delay in seeking relicensure, into one of two 30-minute individual interventions, MI or a didactic information-feedback 'usual care' condition. The results indicated that while both interventions resulted in significant reductions in risky drinking, MI produced greater reduction (i.e., 25%) in risky drinking over a one year duration, a finding corroborated by biomarkers of alcohol use. While not addressing reductions in DWI behavior specifically, this study indicated that improvements in risky alcohol use could be expected with exposure to MI in the poorly motivated, non-help-seeking offenders.

Other intriguing but indirect support (i.e., through secondary analysis) for MI in DWI comes from two well-designed randomized controlled trials conducted in emergency and trauma settings. In emergency room patients with alcohol-related subcritical injuries, a two-session MI-based brief intervention was compared to standard care (Mello *et al.*, 2005). In a subgroup of RTC patients, two sessions of MI resulted in fewer alcohol-related injuries than standard care over a 12-month follow-up. Another study examined MI's benefits in the emergency room for reducing subsequent DWI arrests (Schermer *et al.*, 2006). Patients involved in RTCs (i.e., drivers or passengers) were randomized into either standard care involving a list of resources for alcohol treatment ($N = 64$) or a 30-minute MI session ($N = 62$). Using administrative driving records over three years following hospital discharge, 21.9% of the standard care patients had been arrested for DWI compared to 11.3% of MI patients. Though group differences did not reach statistical significance, the authors nevertheless interpreted the results as clinically important.

Overall, the findings indicate that brief interventions and MI are promising opportunistic interventions for reducing hazardous drinking and injury risk in individuals seen in a variety of settings. A number of issues in the literature on the application of MI for DWI complicate the full appraisal and deployment of MI in the field, however. Currently, MI, as other brief interventions, is applied in diverse ways in effectiveness studies. The format and content necessary for producing positive outcomes and the generalizability of findings from one study to the next are hard to discern (Moyer *et al.*, 2002; Vasilaki, Hosier, and Cox, 2006). Relatedly, effectiveness in MI appears contingent on the clinician attaining an adequate degree of mastery. It is a nondidactic approach with an exacting communication style and a sophisticated repertoire of tactics that appears to lose potency when manualized (Hettema *et al.*, 2005; Miller and Rollnick, 2009). As such, MI requires reasonably talented and highly motivated clinicians who are prepared to participate in prolonged supervision to achieve and sustain its practice integrity (Miller *et al.*, 2004). These preconditions for effectiveness may hamper adequate across-the-board implementation and sustainability of MI practice in a DWI service context. Finally, the available studies have targeted hazardous drinking rather than DWI behavior directly. An investigation of the feasibility and effectiveness of an adapted form of MI that seeks to alter DWI behavior is clearly needed.

Preventing Alcohol-Related Convictions (PARC) Program

PARC is a novel specialized approach to DWI recidivism (Rider *et al.*, 2006). This program focuses on the driving side of the DWI equation as opposed to the drinking side. Thus, PARC targets the decision-making process involved in controlling vehicle usage prior to drinking (i.e., when the offender is not intoxicated) instead of attempting to control drinking and/or driving after drinking has occurred when rational decision-making capacities and the ability to resist social and environmental triggers are likely impaired. A large-scale randomized trial found this approach to be superior to usual care in moving first-time offenders toward more readiness to change and in using a strategy of planning ahead to avoid driving to a drinking venue (Rider *et al.*, 2006). Investigation of whether participation in the PARC program provides benefits to DWI prevention is in progress.

The PARC program may strike at the core of why some DWI offenders persist in drink-driving even in the face of increasingly severe consequences. Recent neuroscience studies in problem behaviors such as alcohol abuse, gambling, and risky sexual practices reveal that individuals who persistently engage in these self-destructive behaviors are prone to dysregulation of the paralimbic system involved in emotion-based decision making (Bechara, 2003; Wardle *et al.*, 2010; Yechiam *et al.*, 2005). This style of decision making favors greater short-term gains (e.g., the convenience of driving to a drinking venue) even when accompanied by greater potential losses (e.g., crash risk or a DWI arrest) versus smaller gains (e.g., a safe ride home) accompanied by smaller potential losses (e.g., taking a taxi home). DWI recidivists are more prone to be impulsive, and emerging evidence indicates that many share the executive control and decision-making difficulties of other high-risk groups when not drinking as well (Bouchard *et al.*, 2011; Kasar *et al.*, 2010; Lev *et al.*, 2008). More research is needed to evaluate whether DWI remedial approaches like PARC can preferentially benefit those offenders who suffer from greater degrees of decision-making impairments.

Matching Psychosocial Intake Characteristics to Remediation

The heterogeneity common to many clinical populations has led to interest in the possibility of propitious matching of specific interventions to offenders most likely to benefit. In the alcoholism field, Project MATCH exemplifies this interest by hypothesizing that alcoholism patients possessing certain characteristics would selectively benefit from one of the three distinct interventions provided (Project MATCH Research Group, 1993). Despite the controversial impact Project MATCH and the other large-scale matching studies that followed have had for the substance abuse treatment field (Cutler and Fishbain, 2005; Glaser, 1999; UKATT, 2005), the possibility of matching continues to captivate the DWI research community (Mattson, 2002; Nochajski and Stasiewicz, 2006; Wells-Parker, Cosby, and Landrum, 1986; Wells-Parker et al., 1990).

DWI investigators have employed diverse approaches to solve the matching puzzle. For example, a statistical approach uses cluster analysis to derive subgroups of offenders who share characteristics that might be selectively amenable to certain intervention approaches (e.g., Donovan and Marlatt, 1982; Wells-Parker et al., 1986; Wieczorek and Miller, 1992). A variation of this strategy applies putative alcoholism and criminal subtypes to cluster DWI offenders (e.g., Ball et al., 2000; LaBrie et al., 2007). An empirical approach involves retrospectively examining the characteristics of offenders who most benefited from a given intervention (Wells-Parker et al., 1989) or, alternatively, to understand the impact of offender intake characteristics (e.g., sex, self-competence) on outcome from intervention (McMurran et al., 2011; Wells-Parker et al., 1991, 2000). A more conceptually coherent approach investigates the impact of interactions between specific offender characteristics linked to DWI recidivism risk (e.g., depression, readiness to change, antisocial personality features) and interventions that aim to address them (e.g., depression treatment, MI) (Brown et al., 2012; Wells-Parker et al., 2006; Woodall et al., 2007).

While individual studies have yielded suggestive results, the aggregate of this literature has, like in alcoholism, failed to make a compelling case for the viability of evidence-informed DWI offender–treatment matching. At the same time, on a practical level, it is questionable to what degree matching is possible in most DWI remedial contexts, as offering multiple distinct intervention approaches in one setting may be challenging. A more fundamental concern, however, is that a comprehensive model has failed to emerge that clarifies the diverse mechanisms and pathways to persistent DWI offending (possibly with the exception of alcoholism), and upon which specific interventions designed to interrupt them may be targeted. The addiction model of DWI (Nochajski and Stasiewicz, 2006), reflected in the omnipresent focus on detection and treatment of substance use disorders in contemporary DWI programs, is applicable to only a minority of dependent offenders whose DWI risk is plainly tied to frequent impairment from substances. The statistical and empirical methods for clustering offenders and for studying selective intervention effects described above have not resulted in significant headway to date.

In this regard, efforts to identify 'clinically meaningful subgroups' of DWI offenders, like research efforts with other clinical groups, promise to be a more fruitful approach to the challenge of matching in DWI as well (Brown et al., 2009; Hines et al., 2005). Here, subgroups are derived whose members share (1) an objective marker of an explanatory pathway to their problem, (2) distinct behavioral features, and (3) selective treatment responsiveness. Recent research into markers of disadvantageous autoregulatory executive function (e.g., Brown et al.,

2008; Fillmore *et al.*, 2008; Glass *et al.*, 2000; Ouimet *et al.*, 2007), negative mood (Wells-Parker *et al.*, 2009), emotional information processing and decision making (Bouchard *et al.*, 2011; Kasar *et al.*, 2010; Lev *et al.*, 2008; Yechiam *et al.*, 2008), and the neurobiological substrates of arousal, novelty seeking and fearlessness (Brown *et al.*, 2009; Couture *et al.*, 2008; Eensoo *et al.*, 2005) linked to persistent DWI behavior promise deeper insight into how both clinically meaningful subgroups may be derived and interventions with selective impact on putative explanatory processes may be designed and applied.

Pharmacological Remediation Approaches

Pharmacotherapy for reducing the symptoms of addiction and for producing more sustained abstinence is a developing research field. While medications have been developed that relieve symptoms and improve function, they have yet to produce lasting cures (O'Brien, 2008). Complications confronted in the field are that different compounds may act on mechanisms that are determined by a combination of alcohol's selective effects on neural structures and capacities in certain individuals (e.g., based upon sex or ethnic background) as well as by specific gene–environment interactions that may contribute to individual vulnerability (Haile, Kosten, and Kosten, 2008; Pettinati *et al.*, 2008). For those DWI offenders who have significant alcohol dependencies, however, effective psychosocial and pharmacological interventions that reduce their drinking problems promise to reduce drink-driving as well.

A recent pilot study has examined the impact of one alcohol medication, naltrexone, in treatment seeking recidivists ($N = 7$) participating in an interlock program (Lapham and McMillan, 2011). An injected extended-release naltrexone suspension (XR-NTX) was used because of poor compliance observed with oral formulations and the convenience and increased effectiveness of this formulation. This was accompanied by medical management therapy, a manualized intervention that involves a discussion of the adverse effects of the medication, and provision of patient education, emotional support, medication monitoring, and brief intervention to support recovery and medication adherence. The main DWI dependent variable in this investigation was frequency of attempted ignitions with BAC of more than 0.025%. BAC positive ignition attempts declined from baseline while the offenders were under treatment with XR-NTX and increased once treatment was terminated. While this study was clearly underpowered and lacked the control to infer the significant benefits of XR-NTX, it supports the potential role of pharmacotherapeutic interventions in the treatment of alcohol-dependent DWI offenders.

Technology-Assisted Remediation Approaches

There is growing interest in preventing DWI recidivism with technology that can be used to monitor offenders' attempts to operate a vehicle at elevated BAC as well as their drinking patterns (Voas, 2010). While technology may be used to help enforcement of curfews and court-ordered abstinence, attempts have also been made to use technology to effect long-lasting behavior change. Some of the more empirically supported approaches that target behavioral change are discussed below.

Interlock Programs

While interlock devices are often offered on a voluntary basis to offenders in order to shorten their license suspension periods, an increasing number of jurisdictions are enacting laws that make installation of an interlock device a prerequisite for relicensing (Beirness and Marques, 2004; Elder *et al.*, 2011). In some jurisdictions (e.g., Quebec, Canada), drivers with three prior convictions are required to submit to mandatory interlock installation for life to reacquire their license to drive. Once installed in the offenders' vehicle, offenders must blow into the device to start and continue operating their vehicles. Typically, readings over 0.02% result in ignition being interrupted. There is consistent evidence that interlock devices installed in the vehicles as part of a relicensing program significantly reduce DWI rates in the order of 40–90% during the time of installation (Elder *et al.*, 2011; Willis, Lybrand, and Bellamy, 2004) and are cost-effective particularly with first-time offenders (Roth, Voas, and Marques, 2007). Unfortunately, DWI rates return to preinstallation levels once the device is removed (Coben and Larkin, 1999; Willis *et al.*, 2004). The argument for the device's usefulness as an enduring behavioral change strategy remains weak. Hence, with the exception of preliminary evidence suggesting that adding MI with installation of an interlock device may prolong the latter's effectiveness (Bjerre, 2005; Marques *et al.*, 1999).

Despite the proven capability of interlock to curtail DWI, albeit over limited periods of time, deployment of interlock programs has been incremental (Voas and Marques, 2003). There are several possible reasons for this observation. Drivers can easily circumvent their instalment either by choosing not to participate in voluntary programs, driving unlicensed, or accessing another vehicle without the device (Beirness and Marques, 2004; Beirness *et al.*, 2003; Elder *et al.*, 2011; Voas and Marques, 2003; Voas *et al.*, 2010b). What's more, systemic factors may motivate high-risk drivers to do just that. The expense of installation and servicing of the device, which can run up to several thousand dollars depending on the duration of installation, is borne by the offender. Given the low socioeconomic status and willingness to drive unlicensed of many high-risk offenders, voluntary installation of these devices may be unattractive or unaffordable for the drivers who need them (Beirness and Marques, 2004; Beirness *et al.*, 2003).

Future investigations need to explore ways to both increase participation in interlock programs and prolong their effectiveness. For example, studies are needed concerning the impact of reducing their cost or the relative merit of providing drivers with positive incentives for device installation and program compliance (e.g., subsidies for those in need) versus negative consequences for device noninstallation and program noncompliance (e.g., more severe alternate sanctions) (Roth, Marques, and Voas, 2009; Task Force on Community Preventive Services, 2011; Voas and Marques, 2003). At the same time, some may perceive a strategy of providing reduced costs and other incentives for participation in interlock programs, or any other effective DWI remedial programs, as rewarding offenders for delinquent behavior. Results from preliminary studies have hinted that combining a psychosocial intervention, MI, with an interlock device may prolong the latter's effectiveness in preventing DWI (Bjerre, 2005; Marques *et al.*, 1999). Another investigation indicated that more regular monitoring of interlock data and sharing this information with offenders increased offender compliance and reduced ignition failures (Zador *et al.*, 2011). A more systematic study of how best to combine interlock and other remedial interventions is needed.

In addition to effectively preventing DWI offenders from operating their vehicles when designated BAC limits are surpassed, interlock devices can provide objective monitoring of driver behavior. The possibility that interlock as well as other forms of electronic monitoring can prevent recidivism in diverse criminal offender groups has been of interest for some time, in particular as an alternative to more restrictive sanctions. Information derived from monitoring not only allows data-informed sanctioning but also may provide opportunities for enhancing the effectiveness of remedial measures. Unfortunately, studies measuring the effectiveness of this approach have yielded mixed results (Rogers and Jolin, 1989).

Regarding DWI and interlock-based monitoring, the frequency of ignition interruption due to elevated BAC typically follows a regular descending pattern over time (Marques *et al.*, 1999). In some jurisdictions, too frequent or a sustained pattern of unsuccessful ignition attempts results in a prolongation of device installation or, conversely, the exclusion of the program (Voas, 2010). The effectiveness of these contrasting strategies is unknown. Moreover, implicit in this approach is the assumption that interlock data predict DWI recidivism. Support for the predictive potential of interlock data is limited, however, to three studies sharing the same source of data. Though large in absolute sample size, the core sample actually represents a self-selected and highly restricted subgroup of interlock program volunteers (Marques, Tippetts, and Voas, 2003a,b; Marques *et al.*, 1999).

For the moment, use of alcohol monitoring devices like interlock as well as its nonvehicular analogues (e.g., SCRAM™, Giner WrisTAS™, IN-HOM) appear most advantageous for those DWI offenders whose alcohol use is deemed a clear public safety risk (Marques and McKnight, 2009; Voas, 2010). Its therapeutic importance for encouraging alcohol abstinence is in need of further substantiation. At the same time, a more fundamental requirement for our ability to appraise the utility of these technologies is a comprehensive explanatory model of the relationship between alcohol misuse, interlock ignition failure and DWI recidivism risk.

CONCLUSIONS AND FUTURE DIRECTIONS

Some scepticism about the evidence base and usefulness of many of the components deployed in contemporary remedial programs to DWI risk seems warranted. Nevertheless, there is no argument that DWI recidivism is preventable. This review highlights our subjective perspective concerning some of the more promising selective therapeutic prevention approaches to DWI. Motivational approaches, emerging programs like PARC, and the use of interlock devices seem particularly promising.

Looking forward, research in a number of areas is urgently needed. Up-to-date, comprehensive and rigorous reviews of evidence in support of current DWI remedial approaches are required. In the laboratory, methodologically rigorous randomized controlled trials are needed to determine the efficacy of specific remedial elements as well as provide presumptive support for their hypothesized mechanisms of action (Longabaugh et al., 2005). Evaluation in real-world settings of the effectiveness of novel remedial approaches, refined and tested in the laboratory, represents a natural next step in the systematic development of an evidence-informed remedial approach. Both efficacy and effectiveness studies are also indispensable for comprehensively identifying new avenues for research, development and practice.

Laboratory studies of more theory-driven approaches to alter a broader range of behaviors contributing to DWI risk, beyond alcohol disorders, are also warranted. In this regard, studies looking at the motivational basis of DWI behavior, as a variant of risk-taking behavior, are promising. Several theoretical models have been proposed to understand high-risk driving, including DWI. Among the more popular are Jessor's problem behavior theory (Jessor, Chase, and Donovan, 1980) and Zuckerman's sensation-seeking model (Zuckerman and Kuhlman, 2000) that point to common and stable personality underpinnings of a generalized form of risk taking (Beirness, Simpson, and Desmond, 2002; Fillmore et al., 2008; Husted et al., 2006; Jonah, 1997). Paradoxically, and consistent with the heterogeneity of the DWI population, not all DWI offenders appear to engage in all forms of high-risk behavior as predicted by the problem behavior theory (Fernandes et al., 2007, 2010; Smart and Vassalo, 2005).

Alternatively, DWI may be viewed as one manifestation of high-risk behavior. Current thinking is pointing to the importance of dynamic processes involving both situational and cognitive contingencies (e.g., perceived benefits of committing infractions under certain circumstances; peer influence) and self-regulatory capacities (e.g., decision making) as crucial motivators of high-risk behavior and that are not adequately accounted for by previous theories (Bechara, 2005; Boyer, 2006; Dastrup et al., 2010; Domingues et al., 2009; Gardner and Steinberg, 2005; Hoyle, 2000; Llewellyn, 2008; Piquero and Tibbetts, 1996; Steinberg, 2007). Methodologically, this represents a shift away from reliance on self-report measures of broad personality characteristics and correlational analysis to tasks that can be manipulated to elicit the individual biochemical, cognitive, affective and social processes that appear to underlie risk taking (Bevins, 2001; Harrison et al., 2005; Skeel et al., 2007). In this regard, randomized controlled experiments and simulation (e.g., of driving and related risk-taking behaviors) are useful tools. They can provide causal inferences about explanatory pathways underlying risky driving behavior under very specific conditions, as well as an intervention's effectiveness (Ouimet et al., 2011; Schwebel et al., 2006; White, Lejuez, and de Wit, 2008). Overall, viewing DWI within a broader category of high-risk behavior and deploying methodologies that offer more explanatory information may help to renew the way in which the DWI field understands and solves the DWI problem.

REFERENCES

American College of Emergency Physicians (2006) *Alcohol Screening and Brief Intervention in the ED*. Washington, DC: American College of Emergency Physicians.

Anderson, B.J., Snow, R.W., and Wells-Parker, E. (2000) Comparing the predictive validity of DUI risk screening instruments: Development of validation standards. *Addiction*, **95**(6), 915–929.

Anderson, P., Chisholm, D., and Fuhr, D.C. (2009) Effectiveness and cost-effectiveness of policies and programmes to reduce the harm caused by alcohol. *The Lancet*, **373**(9682), 2234–2246.

Ball, S.A., Jaffe, A.J., Crouse-Artus, M.S. *et al.* (2000) Multidimensional subtypes and treatment outcome in first time DWI offenders. *Addictive Behaviors*, **25**(2), 167–181.

Bechara, A. (2003) Risky business: Emotion, decision-making, and addiction. *Journal of Gambling Studies*, **19**(1), 23–51.

Bechara, A. (2005) Decision making, impulse control and loss of willpower to resist drugs: A neurocognitive perspective. *Nature Neuroscience*, **8**(11), 1458–1463.

Beerman, K.A., Smith, M.M., and Hall, R.L. (1988) Predictors of recidivism in DUIIs. *Journal of Studies on Alcohol*, **49**(5), 443–449.

Begg, D.J. and Langley, J.D. (2004) Identifying predictors of persistent non-alcohol or drug-related risky driving behaviours among a cohort of young adults. *Accident Analysis and Prevention*, **36**(6), 1067–1071.

Beirness, D., Simpson, H.M., and Desmond, K. (2003) *The Road Safety Monitor 2002: Drugs and Driving*. Ottawa: Traffic Injury Research Foundation.

Beirness, D.J. and Marques, P.R. (2004) Alcohol ignition interlock programs. *Traffic Injury Prevention*, **5**(3), 299–308.

Beirness, D.J., Marques, P.R., Voas, R.B., and Tippetts, A.S. (2003) The impact of mandatory versus voluntary participation in the alberta ignition interlock program. *Traffic Injury Prevention*, **4**(3), 195–198.

Beirness, D.J., Mayhew, D.R., and Simpson, H.M. (1997) *DWI Repeat Offenders:A Review and Synthesis of the Literature*. (pp. 156–168). Ottawa: Health Canada.

Beirness, D.J., Simpson, H.M., and Desmond, K. (2002) Risky Driving. *The Road Safety Monitor 2002*, Traffic Injury Research Foundation.

Bevins, R.A. (2001) Novelty seeking and reward: Implications for the study of high-risk behaviors. *Current Directions in Psychological Science*, **10**(6), 189–193.

Bien, T.H., Miller, W.R., and Tonigan, J.S. (1993) Brief interventions for alcohol problems: A review. *Addiction*, **88**(3), 315–336.

Bjerre, B. (2005) Primary and secondary prevention of drinking and driving by the use of Alcolock device and program: The Swedish experience. In P.R. Marques (ed.), *Alcohol ignition Interlock Devices, Vol 2: Research, Policy, and Program Status 2005* (pp. 11–24). Oosterhout, The Netherlands: International Council on Alcohol, Drugs, and Traffic Safety [ICADTS].

Blow, F.C., Barry, K.L., Walton, M.A. *et al.* (2006) The efficacy of two brief intervention strategies among injured, at-risk drinkers in the emergency department: Impact of tailored messaging and brief advice. *Journal of Studies on Alcohol*, **67**(4), 568–578.

Bouchard, S.M., Brown, T.G., and Nadeau, L. (2011) Decision-making capacities and affective reward anticipation in DWI recidivists compared to non-offenders: A preliminary study. *Accident Analysis and Prevention*, **45**, 580–587.

Boyer, T.W. (2006) The development of risk-taking: A multi-perspective review. *Developmental Review*, **26**(3), 291–345.

Brewer, R.D., Morris, P.D., Cole, T.B. *et al.* (1994) The risk of dying in alcohol-related auto-mobile crashes among habitual drunk drivers. *New England Journal of Medicine*, **331**(8), 513–517.

Brown, T.G., Dongier, M., Ouimet, M.C. *et al.* (2012). The role of demographic characteris-tics and readiness to change in 12-month outcome from two distinct brief interventions for impaired drivers. *Journal of Substance Abuse Treatment*, **42**(4), 383–391.

Brown, T.G., Dongier, M., Ouimet, M.C. *et al.* (2010) Brief motivational interviewing for DWI recidivists who abuse alcohol and are not participating in DWI intervention: A randomized controlled trial. *Alcoholism-Clinical & Experimental Research*, **34**(2), 292–301.

Brown, T.G., Ouimet, M.C., Nadeau, L. *et al.* (2009) From the brain to bad behaviour and back again: Neurocognitive and psychobiological mechanisms of driving while impaired by alcohol. *Drug and Alcohol Review*, **28**(4), 406–418.

Brown, T.G., Ouimet, M.C., Nadeau, L. *et al.* (2008) DUI offenders who delay relicens-ing: A quantitative and qualitative investigation. *Traffic Injury Prevention*, **9**(2), 109–118.

Burke, B.L., Arkowitz, H., and Menchola, M. (2003) The efficacy of motivational interview-ing: A meta-analysis of controlled clinical trials. *Journal of Consulting and Clinical Psychol-ogy*, **71**(5), 843–861.

C'De Baca, J., Lapham, S.C., Liang, H.C., and Skipper, B.J. (2001a) Victim Impact Panels: Do they impact drunk drivers? A follow-up of female and male, first time and repeat offenders. *Journal of Studies on Alcohol*, **62**(5), 615–620.

C'De Baca, J., Miller, W.R., and Lapham, S. (2001b) A multiple risk factor approach for predicting DWI recidivism. *Journal of Substance Abuse Treatment*, **21**(4), 207–215.

Carroll, K.M., Ball, S.A., Nich, C. *et al.* (2006) Motivational interviewing to improve treat-ment engagement and outcome in individuals seeking treatment for substance abuse: A multisite effectiveness study. *Drug and Alcohol Dependence*, **81**(3), 301–312.

Cavaiola, A.A., Strohmetz, D.B., and Abreo, S.D. (2007) Characteristics of DUI recidivists: A 12-year follow-up study of first time DUI offenders. *Addictive Behaviors*, **32**(4), 855–861.

Cavaiola, A.A., Strohmetz, D.B., Wolf, J.M., and Lavender, N.J. (2003) Comparison of DWI offenders with non-DWI individuals on the MMPI-2 and the Michigan Alcoholism Screening Test. *Addictive Behaviors*, **28**(5), 971–977.

Centers for Disease Control (2011) Alcohol-impaired driving among adults – United States, 2010. *Morbidity and Mortality Weekly Report*, **60**, 1351–1356.

Chang, I., Gregory, C., and Lapham, S.C. (2002) *Review of Screening Instruments and Procedures for Evaluating DWI Offenders*. Washington, DC: AAA Foundation for Traffic Safety.

Chang, I., Lapham, S.C., C'De Baca, J., and Davis, J.W. (2001) Alcohol Use Inventory: Screening and assessment of first time driving-while-impaired offenders. II. Typology and predictive validity. *Alcohol and Alcoholism*, **36**(2), 122–130.

Christophersen, A.R.S. and Morland, J.R. (2008) Frequent detection of benzodiazepines in drugged drivers in norway. *Traffic Injury Prevention*, **9**(2), 98–104.

Coben, J.H. and Larkin, G.L. (1999) Effectiveness of ignition interlock devices in reducing drunk driving recidivism. *American Journal of Preventive Medicine*, **16**(1, Suppl. 1), 81–87.

Connors, G.J., Maisto, S.A., and Ersner-Hershfield, S.M. (1986) Behavioral treatment of drunk-driving recidivists: Short-term and long-term effects. *Behavioural and Cognitive Psychotherapy*, **14**(01), 34–45.

Constant, A., Encrenaz, G., Zins, M. *et al.* (2011) Why drivers start drinking and driving, a prospective study over a 6-year period in the GAZEL cohort. *Alcohol and Alcoholism*, **46**(6), 729–733.

Couture, S., Brown, T.G., Ouimet, M.C. *et al.* (2008) Hypothalamic-pituitary-adrenal axis response to stress in male DUI recidivists. *Accident Analysis and Prevention*, **40**(1), 246–253.

Couture, S., Brown, T.G., Tremblay, J. *et al.* (2010) Are biomarkers of chronic alcohol misuse useful in the assessment of DWI recidivism status? *Accident Analysis and Prevention*, **42**(1), 307–312.

Cutler, R.B. and Fishbain, D.A. (2005) Are alcoholism treatments effective? The Project MATCH data. *BMC Public Health*, **5**, 75.

Dahlen, E.R., Martin, R.C., Ragan, K., and Kuhlman, M.M. (2005) Driving anger, sensation seeking, impulsiveness, and boredom proneness in the prediction of unsafe driving. *Accident Analysis and Prevention*, **37**(2), 341–348.

Dastrup, E., Lees, M.N., Bechara, A. *et al.* (2010) Risky car following in abstinent users of MDMA. *Accident Analysis and Prevention*, **42**(3), 867–873.

Dawson, D.A. (1999) Alternative definitions of high risk for impaired driving: The overlap of high volume, frequent heavy drinking and alcohol dependence. *Drug and Alcohol Dependence*, **54**(3), 219–228.

Del Boca, F.K. and Darkes, J. (2003) The validity of self-reports of alcohol consumption: State of the science and challenges for research. *Addiction*, **98**, 1–12.

Deyoung, D.J. (1997) An evaluation of the effectiveness of alcohol treatment, driver license actions and jail terms in reducing drunk driving recidivism in California. *Addiction*, **92**(8), 989–997.

Dill, P.L. and Wells-Parker, E. (2004) The emergency care setting for screening and intervention for alcohol use problems among injured and high-risk drivers: A review. *Traffic Injury Prevention*, **5**, 278–291.

Dill, P.L. and Wells-Parker, E. (2006) Court-mandated treatment for convicted drinking drivers. *Alcohol Research and Health*, **29**(1), 41–48.

Dinh-Zarr, T., DiGuiseppi, C., Heitman, E., and Roberts, I. (1999) Preventing injuries through interventions for problem drinking: A systematic review of randomized controlled trials. *Alcohol and Alcoholism*, **34**(4), 609–621.

Domingues, S.C.A., Mendonça, J.B., Laranjeira, R., and Nakamura-Palacios, E.M. (2009) Drinking and driving: A decrease in executive frontal functions in young drivers with high blood alcohol concentration. *Alcohol*, **43**(8), 657–664.

D'Onofrio, G. and Degutis, L.C. (2002) Preventive care in the emergency department: Screening and brief intervention for alcohol problems in the emergency department: A systematic review. *Academic Emergency Medicine*, **9**(6), 627–638.

Donovan, D.M. and Marlatt, G.A. (1982) Personality subtypes among driving-while-intoxicated offenders: Relationship to drinking behavior and driving risk. *Journal of Consulting and Clinical Psychology*, **50**(2), 241–249.

Donovan, D.M., Marlatt, G.A., and Salzberg, P.M. (1983) Drinking behavior, personality factors and high-risk driving. A review and theoretical formulation. *Journal of Studies on Alcohol*, **44**(3), 395–428.

Donovan, D.M., Umlauf, R.L., and Salzberg, P.M. (1990) Bad drivers: Identification of a target group for alcohol-related prevention and early intervention. *Journal of Studies on Alcohol*, **51**(2), 136–141.

Dunn, C., Deroo, L., and Rivara, F.P. (2001) The use of brief interventions adapted from motivational interviewing across behavioral domains: A systematic review. *Addiction*, **96**(12), 1725–1742.

Dussault, C., Brault, M., Bouchard, J., and Lemire, A.M. (2002) Le rôle de l'alcool et des autres drogues dans les accidents mortels de la route au Québec – Résultats préliminaires.

Eensoo, D., Paaver, M., Harro, M., and Harro, J. (2005) Predicting drunk driving: Contribution of alcohol use and related problems, traffic behaviour, personality and platelet monoamine oxidase (MAO) activity. *Alcohol and Alcoholism*, **40**(2), 140–146.

Elder, R.W., Nichols, J.L., Shults, R.A. *et al.* (2005) Effectiveness of school-based programs for reducing drinking and driving and riding with drinking drivers: A systematic review. *American Journal of Preventive Medicine*, **28**(5, Suppl.), 288–304.

Elder, R.W., Shults, R.A., Sleet, D.A. *et al.* (2004) Effectiveness of mass media campaigns for reducing drinking and driving and alcohol-involved crashes: A systematic review. *American Journal of Preventive Medicine*, **27**(1), 57–65.

Elder, R.W., Shults, R.A., Sleet, D.A. *et al.* (2002) Effectiveness of sobriety checkpoints for reducing alcohol-involved crashes. *Traffic Injury and Prevention*, **3**(4), 266–274.

Elder, R.W., Voas, R., Beirness, D. *et al.* (2011) Effectiveness of ignition interlocks for preventing alcohol-impaired driving and alcohol-related crashes: A community guide systematic review. *American Journal of Preventive Medicine*, **40**(3), 362–376.

Farrow, J.A. and Brissing, P. (1990) Risk for DWI: A new look at gender differences in drinking and driving influences, experiences, and attitudes among new adolescent drivers. *Health Education Quarterly*, **17**, 213–221.

Fell, J.C., Lacey, J.H., and Voas, R.B. (2004) Sobriety checkpoints: Evidence of effectiveness is strong, but use is limited. *Traffic Injury Prevention*, **5**(3), 220–227.

Fell, J.C., Tippetts, A.S., and Voas, R.B. (2009) Fatal traffic crashes involving drinking drivers: What have we learned? *Annals of Advances in Automotive Medicine Scientific Conference*, **53**, 63–76.

Fell, J.C. and Voas, R.B. (2006) The effectiveness of reducing illegal blood alcohol concentration (BAC) limits for driving: Evidence for lowering the limit to .05 BAC. *Journal of Safety Research*, **37**(3), 233–243.

Ferguson, M., Schonfeld, C., Sheehan, M., and Siskind, V. (2001) *The Impact of the "Under the Limit" Drink Driving Rehabilitation Program on the Lifestyle and Behaviour of Offenders*. Queensland: Centre for Accident Research and Road Safety – Queensland, Queensland University of Technology.

Fernandes, R., Hatfield, J., and Job, R.F.S. (2010) A systematic investigation of the differential predictors for speeding, drink-driving, driving while fatigued, and not wearing a seat belt, among young drivers. *Transportation Research Part F: Traffic Psychology and Behaviour*, **13**(3), 179–196.

Fernandes, R., Job, R.F.S., and Hatfield, J. (2007) A challenge to the assumed generalizability of prediction and countermeasure for risky driving: Different factors predict different risky driving behaviors. *Journal of Safety Research*, **38**(1), 59–70.

Field, C.A. and Caetano, R. (2010) The effectiveness of brief intervention among injured patients with alcohol dependence: Who benefits from brief interventions? *Drug and Alcohol Dependence*, **111**(1–2), 13–20.

Fillmore, M.T., Blackburn, J.S., and Harrison, E.L. (2008) Acute disinhibiting effects of alcohol as a factor in risky driving behavior. *Drug and Alcohol Dependence*, **95**(1–2), 97–106.

Fleming, M.F., Mundt, M.P., French, M.T. *et al.* (2002) Brief physician advice for problem drinkers: Long-term efficacy and benefit-cost analysis. *Alcoholism-Clinical and Experimental Research*, **26**(1), 36–43.

Flowers, N.T., Naimi, T.S., Brewer, R.D. *et al.* (2008) Patterns of alcohol consumption and alcohol-impaired driving in the United States. *Alcoholism-Clinical and Experimental Research*, **32**(4), 639–644.

Foon, A.E. (1988) The dffectiveness of drinking-driving treatment programs: A critical review. *Substance Use and Misuse*, **23**(2), 151–174.

Franques, P., Auriacombe, M., Piquemal, E. *et al.* (2003) Sensation seeking as a common factor in opioid dependent subjects and high risk sport practicing subjects. A cross sectional study. *Drug and Alcohol Dependence*, **69**(2), 121–126.

Fynbo, L. and Jarvinen, M. (2011) The best drivers in the world: Drink-driving and risk assessment. *British Journal of Criminology*, **51**(5), 773–788.

Gardner, M. and Steinberg, L. (2005) Peer influence on risk taking, risk preference, and risky decision making in adolescence and adulthood: An experimental study. *Developmental Psychology*, **41**(4), 625–635.

Glaser, F.B. (1999) The unsinkable Project MATCH. *Addiction*, **94**(1), 34–36.

Glass, R.J., Chan, G., and Rentz, D. (2000) Cognitive impairment screening in second offense DUI programs. *Journal of Substance Abuse Treatment*, **19**(4), 369–373.

Greenberg, M.D., Morral, A.R., and Jain, A.K. (2004) How can repeat drunk drivers be influenced to change? Analysis of the association between drunk driving and DUI recidivists' attitudes and beliefs. *Journal of Studies on Alcohol*, **65**(4), 460–463.

Guerri, C. and Pascual, M. (2010) Mechanisms involved in the neurotoxic, cognitive, and neurobehavioral effects of alcohol consumption during adolescence. *Alcohol*, **44**(1), 15–26.

Haile, C.N., Kosten, T.A., and Kosten, T.R. (2008) Pharmacogenetic treatments for drug addiction: Alcohol and opiates. *The American Journal of Drug and Alcohol Abuse*, **34**(4), 355–381.

Harrison, J.D., Young, J.M., Butow, P. *et al.* (2005) Is it worth the risk? A systematic review of instruments that measure risk propensity for use in the health setting. *Social Science and Medicine*, **60**(6), 1385–1396.

Harwood, M.K. and Leonard, K.E. (1989) Family history of alcoholism, youthful antisocial behavior and problem drinking among DWI offenders. *Journal of Studies on Alcohol*, **50**(3), 210–216.

Hatfield, J. and Fernandes, R. (2009) The role of risk-propensity in the risky driving of younger drivers. *Accident Analysis and Prevention*, **41**(1), 25–35.

Health Canada (2004) *Best Practices: Treatment and Rehabilitation for Driving while Impaired Offenders*. Ottawa: Ministry of Public Works and Government Services.

Heather, N. (1989) Psychology and brief interventions. *British Journal of Addiction*, **84**(4), 357–370.

Hendershot, C.S., Witkiewitz, K., George, W.H., and Marlatt, G.A. (2011 epub) Relapse prevention for addictive behaviors. *Substance Abuse Treatment, Prevention, and Policy*, **6**, 17.

Hettema, J., Steele, J., and Miller, W.R. (2005) Motivational interviewing. *Annual Review of Clinical Psychology*, **1**, 91–111.

Hines, L.M., Ray, L., Hutchison, K., and Tabakoff, B. (2005) Alcoholism: The dissection for endophenotypes. *Dialogues in Clinical Neuroscience*, **7**(2), 153–163.

Hingson, R. and Winter, M. (2003) Epidemiology and consequences of drinking and driving. *Alcohol Research and Health*, **27**(1), 63–78.

Hoyle, R.H. (2000) Personality processes and problem behavior. *Journal of Personality*, **68**(6), 953–966.

Hubicka, B., Laurell, H., and Bergman, H. (2008) Criminal and alcohol problems among Swedish drunk drivers – predictors of DUI relapse. *International Journal of Law and Psychiatry*, **31**(6), 471–478.

Husted, D., Gold, M., Frost-Pineda, K. *et al.* (2006) Is speeding a form of gambling in adolescents? *Journal of Gambling Studies*, **22**(2), 209–219.

Impinen, A., Rahkonen, O., Karjalainen, K. *et al.* (2009) Substance use as a predictor of driving under the influence (DUI) rearrests. A 15-year retrospective study. *Traffic Injury Prevention*, **10**(3), 220–226.

Irvin, J.E., Bowers, C.A., Dunn, M.E., and Wang, M.C. (1999) Efficacy of relapse prevention: A meta-analytic review. *Journal of Consulting and Clinical Psychology*, **67**(4), 563–570.

Iversen, H. and Rundmo, T. (2002) Personality, risky driving and accident involvement among Norwegian drivers. *Personality and Individual Differences*, **33**(8), 1251–1263.

Jessor, R., Chase, J.A., and Donovan, J.E. (1980) Psychosocial correlates of marijuana use and problem drinking in a national sample of adolescents. *American Journal of Public Health*, **70**(6), 604–613.

Jewell, J.D., Hupp, S.D., and Segrist, D.J. (2008) Assessing DUI risk: Examination of the Behaviors & Attitudes Drinking & Driving Scale (BADDS). *Addictive Behaviors*, **33**(7), 853–865.

Jonah, B.A. (1997) Sensation seeking and risky driving: A review and synthesis of the literature. *Accidental Analysis and Prevention*, **29**(5), 651–665.

Kaner, E.F., Dickinson, H.O., Beyer, F.R. *et al.* (2007) Effectiveness of brief alcohol interventions in primary care populations. *Cochrane Database of Systematic Reviews*, (2), CD004148.

Kasar, M., Gleichgerrcht, E., Keskinkilic, C. *et al.* (2010) Decision-making in people who relapsed to driving under the influence of alcohol. *Alcoholism-Clinical and Experimental Research*, **34**(12), 2162–2168.

Korzec, A., Bar, M., Koeter, M.W., and de Kieviet, W. (2001) Diagnosing alcoholism in high-risk drinking drivers: Comparing different diagnostic procedures with estimated prevalence of hazardous alcohol use. *Alcohol Alcohol*, **36**(6), 594–602.

LaBrie, R.A., Kidman, R.C., Albanese, M. *et al.* (2007) Criminality and continued DUI offense: Criminal typologies and recidivism among repeat offenders. *Behavioral Sciences and the Law*, **25**(4), 603–614.

Landenberger, N. and Lipsey, M. (2005) The positive effects of cognitive-behavioral programs for offenders: A meta-analysis of factors associated with effective treatment. *Journal of Experimental Criminology*, **1**(4), 451–476.

Lapham, S. and England-Kennedy, E. (2012 epub) Convicted driving-while-impaired offenders' views on effectiveness of sanctions and treatment. *Qualitative Health Research.*, **22**, 17–30.

Lapham, S.C., C'De Baca, J., Chang, I. *et al.* (2002) Are drunk-driving offenders referred for screening accurately reporting their drug use? *Drug and Alcohol Dependence*, **66**(3), 243–253.

Lapham, S.C. and McMillan, G.P. (2011) Open-label pilot study of extended-release naltrexone to reduce drinking and driving among repeat offenders. *Journal of Addiction Medicine*, **5**(3), 163–169.

Lapham, S.C. and Skipper, B.J. (2010) Does screening classification predict long-term outcomes of DWI offenders. *American Journal of Health Behavior*, **34**(6), 737–749.

Lapham, S.C., Skipper, B.J., Hunt, W.C., and Chang, I. (2000) Do risk factors for re-arrest differ for female and male drunk-driving offenders? *Alcoholism-Clinical and Experimental Research*, **24**(11), 1647–1655.

Lapham, S.C., Skipper, B.J., and Simpson, G.L. (1997) A prospective study of the utility of standardized instruments in predicting recidivism among first DWI offenders. *Journal of Studies on Alcohol*, **58**(5), 524–530.

Lapham, S.C., Smith, E., C'De Baca, J. *et al.* (2001) Prevalence of psychiatric disorders among persons convicted of driving while impaired. *Archives of General Psychiatry*, **58**(10), 943–949.

Lapham, S.C., Stout, R., Laxton, G., and Skipper, B.J. (2011) Persistence of addictive disorders in a first-offender driving while impaired population. *Archives of General Psychiatry*, **68**(11), 1151–1157.

LaPlante, D.A., Nelson, S.E., Odegaard, S.S. *et al.* (2008) Substance and psychiatric disorders among men and women repeat driving under the influence offenders who accept a treatment-sentencing option. *Journal of Studies on Alcohol and Drugs*, **69**(2), 209–217.

Leshowitz, B. and Meyers, J.M. (1996) Application of decision theory to DUI assessment. *Alcoholism-Clinical and Experimental Research*, **20**(7), 1148–1152.

Lev, D., Hershkovitz, E., and Yechiam, E. (2008) Decision making and personality in traffic offenders: A study of Israeli drivers. *Accident Analysis and Prevention*, **40**(1), 223–230.

Liang, W., Shediac-Rizkallah, M.C., Celentano, D.D., and Rohde, C. (1999) A population-based study of age and gender differences in patterns of health-related behaviors. *American Journal Prevention Medicine*, **17**, 8–17.

Lincourt, P., Kuettel, T.J., and Bombardier, C.H. (2002) Motivational interviewing in a group setting with mandated clients: A pilot study. *Addictive Behaviors*, **27**(3), 381–391.

Llewellyn, D.J. (2008) The psychology of risk taking: Toward the integration of psychometric and neuropsychological paradigms. *The American Journal of Psychology*, **121**(3), 363–376.

Lonczak, H.S., Neighbors, C., and Donovan, D.M. (2007) Predicting risky and angry driving as a function of gender. *Accident Analysis and Prevention*, **39**(3), 536–545.

Longabaugh, R., Donovan, D.M., Karno, M.P. *et al.* (2005) Active ingredients: How and why evidence-based alcohol behavioral treatment interventions work. *Alcoholism, Clinical and Experimental Research*, **29**(2), 235–247.

Lum, H. and Reagan, J.A. (1995 Winter) Interactive highway safety design model: Accident predictive module. *Public Roads Magazine*.

MacAndrew, C. (1965) The differentiation of male alcoholic outpatients from nonalcoholic psychiatric outpatients by means of the MMPI. *Quarterly Journal of Studies on Alcohol*, **26**(2), 238–246.

Macdonald, S. and Mann, R.E. (1996) Distinguishing causes and correlates of drinking and driving. *Contemporary Drug Problems*, **23**(2), 259–290.

MacDonald, T.K., Zanna, M.P., and Fong, G.T. (1995) Decision making in altered states: Effects of alcohol on attitudes toward drinking and driving. *Journal of Personality and Social Psychology*, **68**(6), 973–985.

Mann, R.E., Leigh, G., Vingilis, E.R., and de Genova, K. (1983) A critical review on the effectiveness of drinking-driving rehabilitation programmes. *Accident Analysis and Prevention*, **15**(6), 441–461.

Mann, R.E., Stoduto, G., Zalcman, R.F. *et al.* (2009) Examining factors in the Research Institute on Addictions Self-Inventory (RIASI): Associations with alcohol use and problems at assessment and follow-up. *International Journal of Environmental Research and Public Health*, **6**(11), 2898–2918.

Marlatt, G.A. and George, W.H. (1984) Relapse prevention: Introduction and overview of the model. *British Journal of Addiction*, **79**(3), 261–273.

Marowitz, L.A. (1998) Predicting DUI recidivism: Blood alcohol concentration and driver record factors. *Accident Analysis and Prevention*, **30**(4), 545–554.

Marques, P., Tippetts, S., Allen, J. *et al.* (2010) Estimating driver risk using alcohol biomarkers, interlock blood alcohol concentration tests and psychometric assessments: Initial descriptives. *Addiction*, **105**(2), 226–239.

Marques, P.R. and McKnight, A.S. (2009) Field and laboratory alcohol detection with 2 types of transdermal devices. *Alcoholism-Clinical and Experimental Research*, **33**(4), 703–711.

Marques, P.R., Tippetts, A.S., and Voas, R.B. (2003a) Comparative and joint prediction of DUI recidivism from alcohol ignition interlock and driver records. *Journal of Studies on Alcohol*, **64**(1), 83–92.

Marques, P.R., Tippetts, A.S., and Voas, R.B. (2003b) The alcohol interlock: An underutilized resource for predicting and controlling drunk drivers. *Traffic Injury Prevention*, **4**(3), 188–194.

Marques, P.R., Voas, R.B., Tippetts, A.S., and Beirness, D.J. (1999) Behavioral monitoring of DUI offenders with the alcohol ignition interlock recorder. *Addiction*, **94**(12), 1861–1870.

Mathers, C.D. and Loncar, D. (2006) Projections of Global Mortality and Burden of Disease from 2002 to 2030. *PLoS Medicine*, **3**(11), e442.

Mattson, M.E. (2002) The search for a rational basis for treatment selection. *Recent Developments in Alcoholism*, **16**(3), 97–113.

McCambridge, J. (2004) Motivational interviewing is equivalent to more intensive treatment, superior to placebo, and will be tested more widely. *Evidence-Based Mental Health*, **7**(2), 843–861.

McCarthy, D.M., Pedersen, S.L., Thompsen, D.M., and Leuty, M.E. (2006) Development of a measure of drinking and driving expectancies for youth. *Psychological Assessment*, **18**(2), 155–164.

McCutcheon, V.V., Heath, A.C., Edenberg, H.J. *et al.* (2009) Alcohol criteria endorsement and psychiatric and drug use disorders among DUI offenders: Greater severity among women and multiple offenders. *Addictive Behaviors*, **34**(5), 432–439.

McMurran, M. (2009) Motivational interviewing with offenders: A systematic review. *Legal and Criminological Psychology*, **14**(1), 83–100.

McMurran, M., Riemsma, R., Manning, N. *et al.* (2011) Interventions for alcohol-related offending by women: A systematic review. *Clinical Psychology Review*, **31**(6), 909–922.

Mello, M.J., Nirenberg, T.D., Longabaugh, R. *et al.* (2005) Emergency department brief motivational interventions for alcohol with motor vehicle crash patients. *Annals of Emergency Medicine*, **45**(6), 620–625.

Michiels, W. and La Harpe, R. (1996) Drunkenness in traffic in Geneva: Occasional abuse or alcoholism. *Sozial- Und Praventivmedizin*, **41**(1), 28–35.

Miller, W.R. (1996) Motivational interviewing: Research, practice, and puzzles. *Addictive Behaviors*, **21**(6), 835–842.

Miller, W.R. and Rollnick, S. (2009) Ten things that motivational interviewing is not. *Behavioural and Cognitive Psychotherapy*, **37**(2), 129–140.

Miller, W.R., Yahne, C.E., Moyers, T.B. *et al.* (2004) A randomized trial of methods to help clinicians learn motivational interviewing. *Journal of Consulting and Clinical Psychology*, **72**(6), 1050–1062.

Mills, K.L., Hodge, W., Johansson, K., and Conigrave, K.M. (2008) An outcome evaluation of the New South Wales Sober Driver Programme: A remedial programme for recidivist drink drivers. *Drug and Alcohol Review*, **27**(1), 65–74.

Morrison, D.S., Petticrew, M., and Thomson, H. (2003) What are the most effective ways of improving population health through transport interventions? Evidence from systematic reviews. *Journal of Epidemiology and Community Health*, **57**(5), 327–333.

Moskowitz, H., Burns, M., Fiorentino, D. *et al.* (2000) *Driver Characteristics and Impairment at Various BACs*. Washington, DC: National Highway Traffic Safety Administration.

Moyer, A., Finney, J.W., Swearingen, C.E., and Vergun, P. (2002) Brief interventions for alcohol problems: A meta-analytic review of controlled investigations in treatment-seeking and non-treatment-seeking populations. *Addiction*, **97**(3), 279–292.

Naimi, T.S., Nelson, D.E., and Brewer, R.D. (2009) Driving after binge drinking. *American Journal of Preventive Medicine*, **37**(4), 314–320.

National Highway Traffic Safety Administration (NHTSA) (2009) Alcohol-impaired driving. *Traffic Safety Facts: 2009 Data*. Washington, DC.

Nilsen, P., Baird, J., Mello, M.J. *et al.* (2008) A systematic review of emergency care brief alcohol interventions for injury patients. *Journal of Substance Abuse Treatment*, **35**(2), 184–201.

Nochajski, T.H. and Stasiewicz, P.R. (2006) Relapse to driving under the influence (DUI): A review. *Clinical Psychology Review*, **26**(2), 179–195.

Novoa, A.M., Perez, K., and Borrell, C. (2009) Evidence-based effectiveness of road safety interventions: A literature review. *Gaceta Sanitaria*, **23**(6), 553.e1–553.e14.

O'Brien, C.P. (2008) Evidence-based treatments of addiction. *Philosophical Transactions of the Royal Society of London. Series B, Biological Sciences*, **363**(1507), 3277–3286.

Oltedal, S. and Rundmo, T. (2006) The effects of personality and gender on risky driving behaviour and accident involvement. *Safety Science*, **44**(7), 621–628.

Ouimet, M.C., Brown, T.G., Nadeau, L. *et al.* (2007) Neurocognitive characteristics of DUI recidivists. *Accident Analysis and Prevention*, **39**(4), 743–750.

Ouimet, M.C., Duffy, C., Simons-Morton, B. *et al.* (2011) Understanding and changing the young driver problem: A review of the randomized controlled trials conducted with driving simulation. In D.L. Fisher, M. Rizzo, J. Caird, and J.D. Lee (eds), *Handbook of Driving Simulation for Engineering, Medicine and Psychology*. CRC Press.

Peden, M. *et al.* (eds) (2004) *The World Report on Road Traffic Injury Prevention*. Geneva: World Health Organization.

Pettinati, H.M., Kampman, K.M., Lynch, K.G. *et al.* (2008) Gender differences with high-dose naltrexone in patients with co-occurring cocaine and alcohol dependence. *Journal of Substance Abuse Treatment*, **34**(4), 378–390.

Phillips, D.P. and Brewer, K.M. (2011) The relationship between serious injury and blood alcohol concentration (BAC) in fatal motor vehicle accidents: BAC = 0.01% is associated with significantly more dangerous accidents than BAC = 0.00%. *Addiction*, **106**(9), 1614–1622.

Piquero, A. and Tibbetts, S. (1996) Specifying the direct and indirect effects of low self-control and situational factors in offenders' decision making: Toward a more complete model of rational offending. *Justice Quarterly*, **13**(3), 481–510.

Portman, M., Penttila, A., Haukka, J. *et al.* (2010) Predicting DUI recidivism of male drunken driving: A prospective study of the impact of alcohol markers and previous drunken driving. *Drug and Alcohol Dependence*, **106**(2–3), 186–192.

Project MATCH Research Group (1993) Project MATCH (Matching Alcoholism Treatment to Client Heterogeneity): Rationale and methods for a multisite clinical trial matching patients to alcoholism treatment. *Alcoholism-Clinical and Experimental Research*, **17**(6), 1130–1145.

Redelmeier, D.A., Tibshirani, R.J., and Evans, L. (2003) Traffic-law enforcement and risk of death from motor-vehicle crashes: Case-crossover study. *The Lancet*, **361**(9376), 2177–2182.

Rider, R., Kelley-Baker, T., Voas, R.B. *et al.* (2006) The impact of a novel educational curriculum for first time DUI offenders on intermediate outcomes relevant to DUI recidivism. *Accident Analysis and Prevention*, **38**(3), 482–489.

Rogers, R. and Jolin, A. (1989) Electronic monitoring: A review of the empirical literature. *Journal of Contemporary Criminal Justice*, **5**(3), 141–152.

Romano, E., Kelley-Baker, T., and Voas, R.B. (2008) Female involvement in fatal crashes: Increasingly riskier or increasingly exposed? *Accident Analysis and Prevention*, **40**(5), 1781–1788.

Rosenberg, H. and Brian, T. (1986) Cognitive-behavioral group therapy for multiple-DUI offenders. *Alcoholism Treatment Quarterly*, **3**(2), 47–65.

Roth, R., Marques, P.R., and Voas, R.B. (2009) A note on the effectiveness of the house-arrest alternative for motivating DWI offenders to install ignition interlocks. *Journal of Safety Research*, **40**(6), 437–441.

Roth, R., Voas, R., and Marques, P. (2007) Interlocks for first offenders: Effective? *Traffic Injury Prevention*, **8**(4), 346–352.

Rubak, S., Sandbaek, A., Lauritzen, T., and Christensen, B. (2005) Motivational interviewing: A systematic review and meta-analysis. *The British Journal of General Practice*, **55**(513), 305–312.

Schell, T.L., Chan, K.S., and Morral, A.R. (2006) Predicting DUI recidivism: Personality, attitudinal, and behavioral risk factors. *Drug and Alcohol Dependence*, **82**(1), 33–40.

Schermer, C.R., Moyers, T.B., Miller, W.R., and Bloomfield, L.A. (2006) Trauma center brief interventions for alcohol disorders decrease subsequent driving under the influence arrests. *The Journal of Trauma*, **60**(1), 29–34.

Schmukle, V., Chollet, T., and Daeppen, J.B. (2005) Content and efficacy of remedial interventions with drink/drive offenders. *Revue Medicale Suisse*, **1**(26), 1717–1725.

Schwebel, D.C., Severson, J., Ball, K.K., and Rizzo, M. (2006) Individual difference factors in risky driving: The roles of anger/hostility, conscientiousness, and sensation-seeking. *Accident Analysis and Prevention*, **38**(4), 801–810.

Shope, J.T., Waller, P.F., and Lang, S.W. (1996) Alcohol-related predictors of adolescent driving: Gender differences in crashes and offenses. *Accident Analysis and Prevention*, **28**, 755–764.

Shuggi, R., Mann, R.E., Zalcman, R.F. *et al.* (2006) Predictive validity of the RIASI: Alcohol and drug use and problems six months following remedial program participation. *The American Journal of Drug and Alcohol Abuse*, **32**(1), 121–133.

Shults, R.A., Elder, R.W., Nichols, J.L. *et al.* (2009) Effectiveness of multicomponent programs with community mobilization for reducing alcohol-impaired driving. *American Journal of Preventive Medicine*, **37**(4), 360–371.

Shults, R.A., Elder, R.W., Sleet, D.A. *et al.* (2001) Reviews of evidence regarding interventions to reduce alcohol-impaired driving. *American Journal of Preventive Medicine*, **21**(4, Suppl. 1), 66–88.

Skeel, R.L., Neudecker, J., Pilarski, C., and Pytlak, K. (2007) The utility of personality variables and behaviorally-based measures in the prediction of risk-taking behavior. *Personality and Individual Differences*, **43**(1), 203–214.

Skurtveit, S., Christophersen, A.R.S., Grung, M., and Morland, J.R. (2002) Increased mortality among previously apprehended drunken and drugged drivers. *Drug and Alcohol Dependence*, **68**(2), 143–150.

Sleet, D.A. and Branche, C.M. (2004) Road safety is no accident. *Journal of Safety Research*, **35**(2), 173–174.

Sleet, D.A. and Dellinger, A. (2009) Preventing traffic injuries: Strategies that work. Paper presented at the Australasian College of Road Safety Conference, Road Safety 2020, Duxton Hotel Perth, Australia.

Sleet, D.A., Liller, K.D., White, D.D., and Hopkins, K. (2004) Injuries, injury prevention and public health. *American Journal of Health Behavior*, **28**(Suppl 1), S6–12.

Smart, D. and Vassalo, S. (2005) *In the Driver's Seat: Understanding Young Adults' Driving Behaviour. ATP Young Drivers Study*. Melbourne: Australian Institute of Family Studies, Royal Automobile Club of Victoria, Transport Accident Commission of Victoria.

Sommers, M.S., Dyehouse, J.M., Howe, S.R. *et al.* (2006) Effectiveness of brief interventions after alcohol-related vehicular injury: A randomized controlled trial. *The Journal of Trauma*, **61**(3), 523–533.

Stein, L.A.R. and Lebeau-Craven, R. (2002) Motivational interviewing and relapse prevention for DWI: A pilot study. *Journal of Drug Issues*, **32**(4), 1051–1069.

Steinberg, L. (2007) Risk taking in adolescence. *Current Directions in Psychological Science*, **16**(2), 55–59.

Sweedler, B.M., Biecheler, M.B., Laurell, H. *et al.* (2004) Worldwide trends in alcohol and drug impaired driving. *Traffic Injury Prevention*, **5**(3), 175–184.

Task Force on Community Preventive Services (2011) Recommendations on the effectiveness of ignition interlocks for preventing alcohol-impaired driving and alcohol-related crashes. *American Journal of Preventive Medicine*, **40**(3), 377.

Taylor, B., Irving, H.M., Kanteres, F. *et al.* (2010) The more you drink, the harder you fall: A systematic review and meta-analysis of how acute alcohol consumption and injury or collision risk increase together. *Drug and Alcohol Dependence*, **110**(1–2), 108–116.

The Century Council (2003) *Hardcore Drunk Driving: A Sourcebook of Promising Strategies, Laws & Programs*. Washington: Blakey & Agnew, LLC.

Timko, C., Desai, A., Blonigen, D.M. *et al.* (2011) Driving while intoxicated among individuals initially untreated for alcohol use disorders: One- and sixteen-year follow-ups. *Journal of Studies on Alcohol and Drugs*, **72**(2), 173–184.

Traffic Injury Research Foundation (TIRF) (2010) *Alcohol-Crash Problem in Canada: 2008 Canadian Council of Motor Transport Administrators*. Ottawa: Transport Canada.

Transport Canada (2011) *Canadian Motor Vehicle Traffic Collision Statistics: 2009*. Ottawa: Transport Canada.

UKATT (2005) Effectiveness of treatment for alcohol problems: Findings of the randomised UK alcohol treatment trial (UKATT). *BMJ (Clinical Research Ed.)*, **331**, 541.

Ulleberg, P. and Rundmo, T. (2003) Personality, attitudes and risk perception as predictors of risky driving behaviour among young drivers. *Safety Science*, **41**(5), 427–443.

Valencia-Martín, J.L., Galán, I., and Rodríguez-Artalejo, F. (2008) The joint association of average volume of alcohol and binge drinking with hazardous driving behaviour and traffic crashes. *Addiction*, **103**(5), 749–757.

Vasilaki, E.I., Hosier, S.G., and Cox, W.M. (2006) The efficacy of motivational interviewing as a brief intervention for excessive drinking: A meta-analytic review. *Alcohol and Alcoholism*, **41**(3), 328–335.

Voas, R.B. (2008) A new look at NHTSA's evaluation of the 1984 Charlottesville Sobriety Checkpoint Program: Implications for current checkpoint issues. *Traffic Injury and Prevention*, **9**(1), 22–30.

Voas, R.B. (2010) Monitoring drinking. *Transportation Research Record: Journal of the Transportation Research Board*, **2182**(-1), 1–7.

Voas, R.B., Dupont, R.L., Talpins, S.K., and Shea, C.L. (2011) Towards a national model for managing impaired driving offenders. *Addiction*, **106**(7), 1221–1227.

Voas, R.B. and Fisher, D.A. (2001) Court procedures for handling intoxicated drivers. *Alcohol Research and Health*, **25**(1), 32–42.

Voas, R.B. and Marques, P.R. (2003) Barriers to interlock implementation. *Traffic Injury and Prevention*, **4**(3), 183–187.

Voas, R.B., Romano, E., Tippetts, A.S., and Furr-Holden, C.D. (2006) Drinking status and fatal crashes: Which drinkers contribute most to the problem? *Journal of Studies on Alcohol*, **67**, 722–729.

Voas, R.B., Tippetts, A.S., and McKnight, A.S. (2010a) DUI offenders delay license reinstatement: A problem? *Alcoholism-Clinical and Experimental Research*, **34**(7), 1282–1290.

Voas, R.B., Tippetts, S.S., Fisher, D., and Grosz, M. (2010b) Requiring suspended drunk drivers to install alcohol interlocks to reinstate their licenses: Effective? *Addiction*, 105(8), 1422–1428.

Wagenaar, A.C. and Toomey, T.L. (2002) Effects of minimum drinking age laws: Review and analyses of the literature from 1960 to 2000. *Journal of Studies on Alcohol Supplement*, (Suppl 14), 206–225.

Walton, M.A., Goldstein, A.L., Chermack, S.T. *et al.* (2008) Brief alcohol intervention in the emergency department: Moderators of effectiveness. *Journal of Studies on Alcohol and Drugs*, 69(4), 550–560.

Wardle, M.C., Gonzalez, R., Bechara, A., and Martin-Thormeyer, E.M. (2010) Iowa Gambling Task performance and emotional distress interact to predict risky sexual behavior in individuals with dual substance and HIV diagnoses. *Journal of Clinical and Experimental Neuropsychology*, 32(10), 1110–1121.

Wells-Parker, E., Anderson, B.J., McMillen, D.L., and Landrum, J.W. (1989) Interactions among DUI offender characteristics and traditional intervention modalities: A long-term recidivism follow-up. *British Journal of Addiction*, 84(4), 381–390.

Wells-Parker, E., Bangert-Drowns, R., McMillen, R., and Williams, M. (1995) Final results from a meta-analysis of remedial interventions with drink/drive offenders. *Addiction*, 90(7), 907–926.

Wells-Parker, E., Cosby, P.J., and Landrum, J.W. (1986) A typology for drinking driving offenders: Methods for classification and policy implications. *Accidient Analysis and Prevention*, 18(6), 443–453.

Wells-Parker, E., Dill, P., Williams, M., and Stoduto, G. (2006) Are depressed drinking/driving offenders more receptive to brief intervention? *Addictive Behaviors*, 31(2), 339–350.

Wells-Parker, E., Kenne, D.R., Spratke, K.L., and Williams, M.T. (2000) Self-efficacy and motivation for controlling drinking and drinking/driving: An investigation of changes across a driving under the influence (DUI) intervention program and of recidivism prediction. *Addictive Behaviors*, 25(2), 229–238.

Wells-Parker, E., Landrum, J.W., and Topping, J.S. (1990) Matching the DWI offender to an effective intervention strategy: An emerging research agenda. In R.J. Wilson and R.E. Mann (eds), *Drinking and Driving: Advances in Research and Prevention* (pp. 267–289). New York: Guilford Press.

Wells-Parker, E., Mann, R.E., Dill, P.L. *et al.* (2009) Negative affect and drinking drivers: A review and conceptual model linking dissonance, efficacy and negative affect to risk and motivation for change. *Current Drug Abuse Reviews*, 2(2), 115–126.

Wells-Parker, E., Pang, M.G., Anderson, B.J. *et al.* (1991) Female DUI offenders: A comparison to male counterparts and an examination of the effects of intervention on women's recidivism rates. *Journal of Studies on Alcohol*, 52(2), 142–147.

White, T.L., Lejuez, C.W., and de Wit, H. (2008) Test-retest characteristics of the Balloon Analogue Risk Task (BART). *Experimental and Clinical Psychopharmacology*, 16(6), 565–570.

Wieczorek, W.F. (1995) The role of treatment in reducing alcohol-related accidents involving DWI offenders: Alcohol, cocaine, and accidents. In R.R. Watson (ed.), *Drug and Alcohol Reviews*, Vol. 7 (pp. 105–129). Humana Press.

Wieczorek, W.F. and Miller, B.A. (1992) Preliminary typology designed for treatment matching of driving-while-intoxicated offenders. *Journal of Consulting and Clinical Psychology*, 60(5), 757–765.

Wieczorek, W.F., Miller, B.A., and Nochajski, T.H. (1992) The limited utility of BAC for identifying alcohol-related problems among DWI offenders. *Journal of Studies on Alcohol*, 53(5), 415–419.

Williams, A.F., Kyrychenko, S.Y., and Retting, R.A. (2006) Characteristics of speeders. *Journal of Safety Research*, 37(3), 227–232.

Williams, A.F., McCartt, A.T., and Ferguson, S.A. (2007) Hardcore drinking drivers and other contributors to the alcohol-impaired driving problem: Need for a comprehensive approach. *Traffic Injury Prevention*, 8(1), 1–10.

Williams, S.B., Whitlock, E.P., Edgerton, E.A. *et al.* (2007) Counseling about proper use of motor vehicle occupant restraints and avoidance of alcohol use while driving: A systematic evidence review for the U.S. Preventive Services Task Force. *Annals of Internal Medicine*, **147**(3), 194–206.

Willis, C., Lybrand, S., and Bellamy, N. (2004) Alcohol ignition interlock programmes for reducing drink driving recidivism. *Cochrane Database of Systematic Reviews*, (4), CD004168.

Woerle, S., Roeber, J., and Landen, M.G. (2007) Prevalence of alcohol dependence among excessive drinkers in new Mexico. *Alcohol-Clinical and Experimental Research*, **31**(2), 293–298.

Woodall, W.G., Delaney, H.D., Kunitz, S.J. *et al.* (2007) A randomized trial of a DWI intervention program for first offenders: Intervention outcomes and interactions with antisocial personality disorder among a primarily American-Indian sample. *Alcoholism-Clinical and Experimental Research*, **31**(6), 974–987.

Woodall, W.G., Kunitz, S.J., Zhao, H. *et al.* (2004) The prevention paradox, traffic safety, and driving-while-intoxicated treatment. *American Journal of Preventive Medicine*, **27**(2), 106–111.

Yechiam, E., Busemeyer, J.R., Stout, J.C., and Bechara, A. (2005) Using cognitive models to map relations between neuropsychological disorders and human decision-making deficits. *Psychological Science*, **16**(12), 973–978.

Yechiam, E., Kanz, J.E., Bechara, A. *et al.* (2008) Neurocognitive deficits related to poor decision making in people behind bars. *Psychonomic Bulletin and Review*, **15**(1), 44–51.

Zador, P.L., Ahlin, E.M., Rauch, W.J. *et al.* (2011) The effects of closer monitoring on driver compliance with interlock restrictions. *Accident Analysis and Prevention*, **43**(6), 1960–1967.

Zador, P.L., Krawchuk, S.A., and Voas, R.B. (2000) Alcohol-related relative risk of driver fatalities and driver involvement in fatal crashes in relation to driver age and gender: An update using 1996 data. *Journal of Studies on Alcohol*, **61**(3), 387–395.

Zhang, L., Wieczorek, W.F., and Welte, J.W. (2011) Early onset of delinquency and the trajectory of alcohol-impaired driving among young males. *Addictive Behaviors*, **36**(12), 1154–1159.

Zuckerman, M. and Kuhlman, D.M. (2000) Personality and risk-taking: Common biosocial factors. *Journal of Personality*, **68**(6), 999–1029.

Zylman, R. (1974) A critical evaluation of the literature on alcohol involvement in highway deaths. *Accident Analysis and Prevention*, **6**(2), 163–204.

PART V

CONCLUSION

Chapter 16

ALCOHOL-RELATED VIOLENCE: AN ENDNOTE

MARY MCMURRAN

Institute of Mental Health, University of Nottingham, Nottingham, England

A report by the Cabinet Office (2004) Strategy Unit stated that the cost of alcohol-related harms in England, including health, crime, work and social costs, amounted to £20bn a year in 2001. Of this total burden, £1.7bn was borne by health services and £7.3bn related to crime and antisocial behavior. More recent government statistics have presented the annual cost of alcohol harm to the National Health Service (NHS) in England calculated at 2006/2007 prices; at £2.7bn, this shows an increase of over 50% since the previous calculation at 2001 prices (Health Improvement Analytical Team, 2008). A similar increase in crime-related costs would increase the burden to £11.5bn per year. Violence is the major crime associated with alcohol, and steps to reduce this are clearly important for the well-being of society. While the accountancy facts presented here refer to England, the problem of alcohol-related violence is of concern to other nations too.

Of course, the financial costs of alcohol-related harms represent individual suffering. Alcohol-related violence can have serious adverse physical and psychological effects on victims, families, witnesses and on perpetrators themselves. These adverse effects can be direct, such as injury and psychological trauma, or indirect, such as the consequences of criminal justice sanctions or family breakdown. The costs borne by society in efforts to prevent, control, punish and treat are intended to minimise these harms. Best that this money is spent wisely on strategies known to be effective.

The purpose of this book is to draw together sound information to enlighten policy makers, professionals, and researchers about the theory and evidence that should underpin prevention and treatment approaches. While general approaches to reducing a population's alcohol consumption may aim primarily to reduce health risks, they also have the power to reduce violent crime (Rossow and Bye, Chapter 1, this volume; Sheron *et al.*, 2012). Similarly, early crime prevention, such as pre-school programmes and family interventions, can have benefits in later life beyond just crime reduction, including reduced substance use and mental health problems, and improved educational attainment and employment prospects (Welsh and Farrington, 2011). Prevention is indeed better than cure, but strategies for prevention will never be totally successful; hence, there is also a place for specific approaches to tackling alcohol-related violence. These focus on drinking environments, families, couples and individuals who have offended.

There is much to be done to develop effective treatments for specific populations. What type of intervention works best for which client group and at what point in their contact with the criminal justice system? The evidence tells us that alcohol arrest referral schemes are not effective in reducing reoffending (Kennedy *et al.*, 2012; McCracken, 2012; McCracken and Sassi, Chapter 10, this volume). This may be due to what is delivered, namely, non-standard interventions that may drift away from what is known to be effective, or factors to do with the timing (e.g., when under arrest and possibly still intoxicated, hung-over or distressed) or location (e.g., in custody suites). However, standardised brief interventions that adhere to evidence of what works can be effective in reducing offending among convicted offenders on community orders (McGovern *et al.*, 2012). Additionally, there is new evidence of positive work with prisoners (Bowes *et al.*, 2012). So, interventions can work, but care must be taken about what is offered to whom, when it is offered and where it is offered.

This volume covers both prevention and treatment at a number of levels. The contributors are eminent researchers and professionals whose knowledge and experience are distilled into relatively few pages. Their evidence, along with their wisdom, has the potential to improve current policy and practice, and there is also the identification of directions for further experimental and applied research. Collating their work into this book has been an honour and a pleasure. I fervently hope that, by drawing together this body of theory and evidence, new audiences will be reached and the impact of their work will be enhanced.

REFERENCES

Bowes, N., McMurran, M., Williams, B. *et al.* (2012) Treating alcohol-related violence: Intermediate outcomes in a feasibility study for a randomised controlled trial in prisons. *Criminal Justice and Behavior*, **39**, 329–340.

Cabinet Office (2004) *Alcohol Harm Reduction Strategy for England.* London: Prime Minister's Strategy Unit. Retrieved February 22, 2012, from http://webarchive. nationalarchives.gov.uk/+/http://www.cabinetoffice.gov.uk/media/cabinetoffice/ strategy/assets/caboffce%20alcoholhar.pdf

Health Improvement Analytical Team (2008) *The Cost of Alcohol Harm to the NHS in England: An Update to the Cabinet Office (2003) Study.* London: Department of Health. Retrieved February 24, 2012, from http://www.parliament.uk/deposits/depositedpapers/2008/ DEP2008-2703.pdf

Kennedy, A., Dunbar, I., Boath, M. *et al.* (2012) *Evaluation of Alcohol Arrest Referral Pilot Schemes (Phase 1).* Occasional Report, No. 101. London: Home Office. Retrieved March

8, 2012, from http://www.homeoffice.gov.uk/publications/science-research-statistics/research-statistics/crime-research/occ101

McCracken, K. (2012) *Evaluation of Alcohol Arrest Referral Pilot Schemes (Phase 2)*. Occasional Report, No. 102. London: Home Office. Retrieved March 8, 2012, from http://www.homeoffice.gov.uk/publications/science-research-statistics/research-statistics/crime-research/occ102

McGovern, R., Newbury-Birch, D., Deluca, P., and Drummond, C. (2012) *Alcohol Screening and Brief Intervention in Probation*. London: Institute of Psychiatry. Retrieved March 8, 2012, from http://www.sips.iop.kcl.ac.uk/documents/factsheets/SIPS_factsheet_PHC.pdf

Sheron, N., Gilmore, I., Parsons, C., and Hawkey, C. (2012) Projections of alcohol-related deaths in England and Wales – Tragic toll or potential prize? *The Lancet*. DOI:10.1016/S0140-6736(12)60244-X.

Welsh, B.C. and Farrington, D.P. (2011) The benefits and costs of early prevention compared with imprisonment: Toward evidence-based policy. *The Prison Journal*, 91, 120S–137S.

INDEX